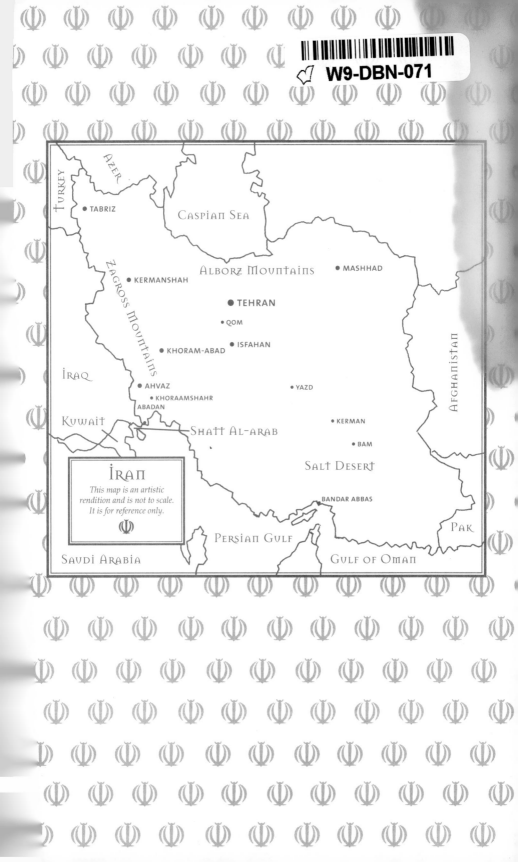

Living in Hell

A TRUE ODYSSEY OF A WOMAN'S STRUGGLE IN ISLAMIC IRAN AGAINST PERSONAL AND POLITICAL FORCES.

Ghazal Omid

Lost Soul

ISBN: 0-9759683-0-0

Library of Congress — Cataloguing in Publication Data
Omid, Ghazal 1970
Living in Hell... Islamic Iran/Ghazal Omid
ISBN: 0-9759683-0-0
1. Autobiography 2. History/Middle East/Iran 3. Political/Ideologies/Freedom
4. Religion/Islam 5. Social Science/Islam/Third World/Women's Rights
EAN: 9780975968307

www.livinginhell.com

10 9 8 7 6 5 4 3 2 1

Manufactured in the United States of America
Published in the United States of America by:
Park Avenue Publishers, Inc., PO Box 20010, Oklahoma City, Oklahoma, 73156
Parkavepub@sbcglobal.net

Acknowledgments appear on page 487

The author's photo, taken in March 2003, and the last photo in the photo section were taken by
two of my great photographer friends. Sadly, due to the controversial nature of the book, I am
obligated to conceal their identity and cannot give them the recognition they deserve.

Cover: The cover photo is from the authors passport issued specifically for her pilgrimage to
Mecca at age 14, a turning point in her life. The solemnity of her face reflects the inner despair
and hopelessness of her life to that point.

Font: The font chosen for the chapter headings is Mason. Although commonly perceived as a
European Christian style, it was selected because it reflects the relationship of cultures.
The architecture of Christian cathedrals of the 7th and 8th century was inspired by Islamic
mosque architecture, particularly Gothic arches and lattice work, which are of Arabic origin.
Also, it emphasizes that the book is deeper than just my life, exposing a culture that has reverted
to a medieval cult.

The title font, "LIving in Hell," speaks for itself.

Dedication

This book is dedicated to all people
who have endured pain and humiliation
in being abused physically,
emotionally and mentally.

It is to give the victims courage
to speak up against injustice,
to forgive and move on with their lives.

"Lost Soul" is a pen name... It was how I felt for so many years. I didn't know to whom I belonged or where to turn for help. Sadly, like millions of other women, I had vanished into the thin air, as if I was invisible in the eyes of everyone. I was, indeed, a lost soul.

Contents

FOREWORD

To the Western reader, this book offers a glimpse into the harshness of women's life in an Islamic country, a country scarred by dictatorship and revolution as well as by poverty and backwardness. Ghazal Omid's terrifying life story encapsulates all the extraordinary elements of growing up in the 'East', in far-away lands of which Westerners know very little. Unfortunately, this is not an extraordinary story. On the contrary, it is, sadly, a common tale of women's suffering in Muslim and non-Muslim countries. When I was a child, growing up in Italy, I remember listening to stories of Sicilian girls who were abducted by men whom they had refused as suitors. To avoid being shunned by society, these women were forced to marry their kidnappers — who often were their rapists — until, in the 1970s, one of them, Franca Viola, shocked the entire nation by refusing to comply with such an inhuman rule. Regardless of religion, life has always been easier for boys than for girls. Ghazal Omid's story is, therefore, universal and has to be read and appreciated as a global message to both men and women, in the West and in the East.

Beyond the courage of the girl, the adolescent and the woman, beyond her strength in fighting back, beyond her stubbornness, beyond her survival instinct, the great lesson of this book rests in the symbolism of the condition of women — a symbolism which encapsulates the history of entire nations in their struggle to achieve modernity through gender equality. Reading it, one cannot fail to sense that the primary victims of the political turmoil which marked the last 30 years of Iran were the women; those who suffered the most from the harshness of the Shah's feudal dictatorship, those who were initially manipulated by the Islamic revolution and then became its first victims; mothers, sisters, daughters of men who even failed 'to see them as human beings.' Veiled women constantly in the background of a society too poor and too ignorant even to notice them. Girls and women prisoners of fear, locked inside high psychological walls, mothers unable to help their own daughters, daughters too frightened to ask their own mothers for help.

As the story unfolds, chapter after chapter, the reader shares the author's deep sense of loneliness. Not only nations but also families are dangerous environments, full of perils, cruelty and dishonesty. This uncomfortable feeling permeates the entire book and at times fuels the reader's rage. Rage at the father who is unaware that he has been blessed with a remarkable daughter, at the brother who molests her, at the mother, herself victim of the same society, who is unable and unwilling to save her own daughter from a similar ordeal. Throughout the book, one continually hopes for Ghazal Omid's life to take a radical change, for something truly exceptional to occur which will make her sufferings worthwhile, anything that will 'brighten' the darkness of her life; even a 'prince charming on a white horse' would do, but at every page these hopes are frustrated. Ghazal Omid's life, even in the West, continues to be hard as, in Canada, she continues to battle against her brothers and father.

Although life in Canada is easier, less harsh than back in Iran—and Ghazal Omid is immensely thankful for that—life is still not safe. The entire book is a testimony of the fragility of a woman's life, of her dependency on the male members of her family, from Ghazal Omid's physical sicknesses to the sexual abuses, from the insecurity at school to the fear of the Mullahs in Tehran. Dreams, premonitions and intuitions constantly admonish the mother as well as the daughter about dark events ready to happen; they remind them of how insecure their existence really is. Even in Canada, far away from the ghosts of her previous life, Ghazal Omid is unable to escape this sense of uncertainty. Thus, 9/11 is for her a double blow. It ruthlessly brings her back to the cruelty of the revolution and it reminds her that nowhere is safe, not even the West.

This deeply disturbing feeling of insecurity is the final message of the book, a feeling shared by those who, like Ghazal Omid, have lived through major political upheaval and have fled their country and their past seeking shelter. It is through their eyes that we must revisit 9/11, because they saw in it something that many of us, born and raised in the West, have failed to understand: the danger of a life constantly threatened by terrorism, darkened by religious fundamentalism, scarred by poverty and ignorance. Their advice to us is to open up our eyes, to confront the enemy and find a solution as soon as possible. And to them we must today turn for advice and hope about our future.

Loretta Napoleoni
Modern Jihad

İRAΠ/POLİTİCAL/ΠULLAHS

The world has heard and seen the hordes of women swarming the streets of Iran, covered from head to toe in black chadors, shouting insults against the United States and the West. Westerners generally protest for a cause, not to blindly condemn a different culture. The world does not know these are paid protestors and assumes they represent the sentiment of the people of Iran. This rabble does not represent the majority. They have been selected and coerced to demonstrate. The Iranian government, not the people, approves and orchestrates the protests.

They are a fanatical, fatuous minority. Iranians call them 'Fatimeh Commando,' incorrigible women who patrol the city in SUVs looking for 'sinners'; a sinner being a woman with a few strands of hair peeking out of her scarf or wearing lipstick. These brainwashed, mostly illiterate women think of the leaders of this ruinous regime as the ultimate Messiah. They believe serving this Hell on Earth will land them in heaven and have been conditioned to kill, if they must, to show their loyalty to the regime. They have been taught that God sent Khomeini and his successors to guide the unscrupulous regime. These gullible individuals help the oppressive, tunnel-vision government keep a nation quiet. They torture and torment dissenters, tantalize minds and emotions with false promises, exploit people's ingrained beliefs and make false, scurrilous accusations about those who don't toe the party line.

Living in Hell will introduce the reader to some who dared criticize the ignominious medieval traditions and continuation of ancient courtship practices that rob women of their dignity in order to satisfy men. It will reveal the degrading treatment of women. It will expose chauvinistic behavior re-introduced into Iranian culture by mullahs educated only in religious studies, who have usurped the government of Iran. It relates long-standing indignities heaped on helpless women in the name of religion as interpreted by legally and morally corrupt mullahs.

A cruel Persian joke, after the 1977 revolution, is that the mullahs governing Iran are really kings wearing turbans instead crowns. Almost none of Iran's highest-ranking mullahs studied law, most did not even finish high school, but they declared themselves politicians and lawmakers with the authority to make and break rules at will. They have brought Persian civilization to the lowest point in its five thousand year history. An Iranian child with common sense could run the country better than the mullahs. They schemed to overthrow the Shah and seize his throne so they could restore the harems and corruption of the Qajar Dynasty, and so they did.

Iranian women do not want to be portrayed as weak harem whores. In Persia's glorious past, women were queens and governors. In the twenty-first century their lives resemble modern slavery, except that they are not openly sold. Instead they are married, frequently without their consent, to their master; a husband they may not have known before their wedding night.

Living in Hell will not by itself bring back the days of glory but it can alert the world to the inside horror stories. Stories about a culture so rich and so dark at the same time that only someone who lived it can know it. I don't expect to change a generation with one book or one voice. I am trying to scratch the conscience of men who believe they are superior to women. I want them to question their obsessive, barbaric behavior toward women. To change future generations we must reach one person at a time and hope the change spreads like a honeycomb.

I have used my life experiences to reveal what goes on inside Iran. I do not care if I am judged a rebel. I am not invincible, nor am I a hero. I am a woman who feels the pain of my sisters. What matters most to me is to positively affect the lives of women who have long lived hopelessly in abusive relationships with nothing to look forward to except a minimal subservient existence. *May God help us to set them free.*

İRAΠ/ΤERRORİSΠ/İSLAΠ

Living in Hell will interest a broad spectrum of post 9/11 readers worldwide in light of the current world unrest. It will help readers understand the circumstances of Iran after the Revolution and the conflict between certain Muslim nations and the rest of the world.

This book is for all ages and genders that are curious about life in pre and post revolutionary Iran. It is a captivating insider's account that illustrates the cultural differences through a real life odyssey. It will educate the Western world as to why so many Middle Eastern people hate the West, particularly the United States.

It will inform the reader about the lives of fellow human beings, trapped behind the closed doors and walls of a *radical Islamic cult* for over two decades, whose plea for freedom is stifled. It will echo lost pleas and voices from the *black hole* of the Islamic Republic of Iran that has consumed the bright future of Persian civilization. A black hole created by ignorant, ruthless mullahs who have corrupted the name of Islam as they ruinously plunder the country. Mullahs who manage a full and rewarding life for themselves as they abuse and kill innocent citizens, train, shelter and subsidize terrorists and export terror to other countries.

Living in Hell, explains the myths and filters fact from fiction about Islam in the format of a biographical account of one woman's travail in fleeing persecution and building a life in a new country. It will enlighten readers by explaining the traditions and deciphering cultural perceptions, that have been purposely and misleadingly presented as the truth, from the real rules of Islam. It explains why and how a perverted interpretation of Islam has been taught to a generation as their *only* path of life. These are the misguided individuals who become a *Shahid* or martyr in the belief they can earn their way to eternal happiness in Heaven by killing Westerners, in particular Americans.

Living in Hell reveals the blunders of the Islamic government and laments the flood of blood shed in the name of Islam. We have witnessed post 9/11 crimes against humanity by evil groups, such as Al Qaeda, which has nothing to do with any religion. The radical groups, who willfully massacre to preserve their ragged existence, try to justify killing innocent people; claiming they are following God's order of Jihad. God never needs sacrifices; otherwise He would have let Abraham sacrifice his own son.

Living in Hell is a book for the times about the political, social and physical torment of women in a repressive Muslim society. The author was nearly killed by authorities in an attempt to stop her from conveying her message. Her only crime was demanding to be treated as an equal to men and freedom to voice an opinion. The book evolves around women and their suffering but it is not narrowly about women or restricted to the women of her native country.

Living in Hell is the symbolic story of women who are not noticed because they have been relegated to the role of baby-makers with little active participation in society. It is about women in every culture who are treated without respect. It is an unfortunate fact that since the 1978 revolution Iran has experienced an increase in prejudice against women.

One person from a religion who causes great suffering for humankind is not a legitimate ambassador for that religion. Osama Bin Laden and his ilk are culturally ignorant individuals, who prey upon the equally ignorant, turning them into mindless robots doing their bidding. They are magicians who mislead their followers into believing they are Messiahs and manipulate them to blindly carry out the atrocities they prescribe.

It has been almost three decades since Al Qaeda started its work. They have taught the young virtually nothing except to parrot the Koran and how to shoot a gun, make bombs and terrorize civilized people. Bin Laden has been successful, at least for the time being. It will take another generation, or more, to undo the harm these groups and individuals have done.

In researching Bin Laden's Jihad orders encouraging people to kill Jews, Americans and others, Ghazal was puzzled that he, a rich Saudi business man who traveled extensively in Europe and the United States in his younger days, could be almost schizophrenic in his late life behavior. His hatred for the West is difficult to understand since his family fortune flourished because of western involvement in his native Saudi Arabia. In the eyes of his followers, he still remains a warrior who stood up to the Russians. Now, he issues and they follow the most odious secret orders in the Islamic world.

Recently, CBC Canada interviewed members of the Khadr family. Khadr, a Canadian, is a founding member of Al Qaeda. His son, who was incarcerated in Guantanamo prison and now lives in Toronto said in an interview that America must pay a price for its crimes but he did not condone the killing of women, children and innocent people in 911. His wife said they were happy with the result of 9/11 and thought people of the United States should feel the pain they have felt for so long. Even his own family is divided about his message. One thing seems clear; his rage toward the United States is an inexplicable personal revenge rather than any other grounds he might argue. It is not clear exactly what crimes the United States has committed against Islam or how he has been personally persecuted.

In his latest video, Bin Laden emphasizes that his hatred is of the US government and not of the people, 3,000 of whom he killed in the World Trade Center tragedy, and tries to influence the presidential election. He also made a crucial mistake in acknowledging that he was behind the 9/11 incident, destroying the claims of his apologists and revealing himself as an inhuman mass murderer.

In recent months, the man who was behind the bombing of a hotel in Indonesia raised a triumphant thumbs-up upon being sentenced to death. He rejoiced that he would land in heaven in the arms of promised virgins, not seeming to know that in the teachings of Islam, that he professes to love, indiscriminate killing and gloating over the death of blameless people makes his crime even more unforgivable in God's justice system. These brainwashed individuals have been promised Utopia, not recognizing that it was the face of Satan who appeared to them, not promises from the Angel Gabriel.

İRAП/CULTURE

L iving in Hell will introduce you to the deepest, darkest avenues and alleys of Iranian culture. You will meet women from diverse walks of life. As you read my story, you may be dismayed that anyone could endure such a life. I assure you, mine is not a unique, passé or even a significant case. It is representative of the living condition of virtually all women in my country.

If the construction of the Iranian family is compared to a house, the father is the floor, the mother is the ceiling, boys are the walls and girls are the dust sitting in the shadows on the wall. A breeze creates a dust hurricane and all that is left is their shadow on the walls. The breeze is the arrival of their husbands, wiping them away; leaving only a name in their family history to mark their existence. They will not be consulted on family affairs. That is the status of girls in Iranian families.

These voiceless women are trapped in a society where they cannot protest against domineering parents or brothers who deliver them into arranged loveless marriages; sentencing them to a lifetime of thankless servitude. It is an ancient form of slavery, preserved into modern times, to be literally sold to a husband on the wedding night. The bride and groom may not know each other and in fact may have never met before the wedding.

According to custom still followed in parts of Iran, the prospective groom pays his bride's mother a sum of money for permission to marry her daughter. Often, the bride is no more than a child or teenager. The young bride's family ostensibly uses the money to buy their daughter the basic furnishings for her new home. In reality, this money has bargained her out of her parents' home. He pays the market price as he would for a used car. Except, in this instance the merchandise is expected to be unused.

You can literally call it *blood money* because there is a degrading custom, inherited from the Qajar dynasty, linked to marriage. Immediately after the wedding, the parents and family of the bride linger while the groom and bride retire to the bridal chamber, eagerly anticipating a hymen-rupturing induced scream. This ghoulish vigil continues until the groom emerges and delivers a bloody pad or towel to the family as evidence of consummation of the marriage and the bride's virginity. For the next couple of days the bloody trophy is showcased for the entire family to confirm that the bride was a virgin. Although educated people are slowly moving away from the ignorant tradition, it is still widely practiced in rural areas, small towns and villages where everything about the past seems part of their world.

Virginity plays a great role in the Iranian and Muslim culture, symbolizing virtue and purity. Virginity is admirable but the double standard for women and men is sickening. Women must stay pure but no one questions the morals of non-virgin men who desire and demand such perfection. Purity is so greatly valued among Iranian families that if a bride is found not to be a virgin, she is at risk of taking a bath in her own blood. Even suspicion of non-virginity places her in jeopardy. If a woman reveals her non-virginity to her husband before marriage, he may still marry her out of pity but she can expect to be treated as a whore forever thereafter.

Another widely celebrated tradition in all Iranian cities is that the day after the wedding night is the ceremony called *Pa-Gosha*. It literally means '*Open Legs.*' Discovery, after the wedding, of a non-virgin bride can precipitate a physical fight between the two families. The bride will assuredly be deemed immediately divorced and, not infrequently, is killed.

These traditions were absorbed in Persian culture by the Qajar Dynasty that opened the door in the early 1900s for the mullah's influence in Iran. Traditions don't appear by themselves. Someone had to introduce an act into society and that someone had to be influential enough for others to follow in his footsteps. Unfortunately, most traditions have been a chain of ignorance tying up people's imagination in the wrong idea. The effect of traditions among nations deeply affects future generations.

The bride is often much younger than her birth certificate. Although she will be given away or sold as a putative woman, she is actually still a child. The purpose of this deception is to unburden the family of the girl as soon as possible. The practice was common countrywide until the late 1980s and still is in remote villages.

While a father will add years to a daughter's birth certificate in order to marry her off sooner, conversely, for boys, fathers would decrease their ages so they could avoid mandatory military service as long as possible.

Every morning, the Iranian woman, haggard from years of torment and from bearing and caring for multiple children, arises from a hard bed or pad on the floor in a room frequently shared with children. If a man has multiple wives and it happens to be the weekend or the day for her husband to share her bed and he is 'in the mood,' the presence of the children will not deter him from demanding his marital rights.

She feeds her children and husband and begins the daily battle, begging him for money to get through another day, knowing that no matter how carefully she shops and bargains, she will be berated for spending too much of his hard earned cash. She sends the kids off to school or to work. Since many modern conveniences are hard to come by and, even if available in shops, are very expensive for the average families, most women, still wash dishes and clothes in a small plastic or rubber tub. They sweep and clean the house manually and after doing their house chores shop for groceries. Because there is a shortage of virtually everything in Iran, she stands in lines for hours for milk, butter, bread and the rest of the family's necessities.

In the afternoon, the hungry children come home from school but must wait for the husband to arrive before they can have dinner. After dinner, children do their homework. If the wife has any education she is required to help the children with their homework. This is the life to which her parents sentenced her. The husband's responsibilities are to socialize with his own family and friends, watch TV and sleep.

A small number of women are fortunate to have attended university and, if lucky, find work. Some of these women may even have been blessed with parents who allowed them to choose their own husband. Having the choice of a husband, however, does not guarantee that they will have a better life. They too are still likely to become slaves to their husbands but at least they were allowed to choose their master.

Complaining is futile. If a woman complains, she is suspected to be having a relationship with another man. I have known innocent women accused of adultery by their husband. The gossip and accusation alone creates turmoil in families and causes constant harassment for the woman. If she is determined to escape the accusation, she will likely be divorced, separated from her children, cast out penniless and face the continued constant sarcasm of her own family. In divorce, the justice system grants supervision of a girl up to seven years of age and a boy up to two years old to the mother. After those prescribed ages, the child must live with the father.

An even smaller third group consists of intellectual, successful women who were often educated outside the country. They are generally from families that are, or were at one time, wealthy and influential. However, a place in the sun is by no means permanent from one regime to the next. These women generally have no trouble within their own families but if they dare to speak out in public for the less fortunate, they put themselves in danger. Many have been hanged and many more imprisoned on one pretext or another. Despite their relatively privileged position, they live under the constant terror of being arrested or killed. They are an inspiration and mentor to other women and I join them in urging future generations to rise up against the antiquated mentality of this male-dominated culture.

While not exactly fitting in this third category, I was on the verge of becoming a statistic when I escaped Iran. The example of such women as Ms. Kazemi and Ms. Shirin Ebadi encourages women to continue the struggle to make a difference in Iran. As a reflection of women like them, I am here to continue their mission to help and inform other people. Despite all their efforts, I have heard too much unwarranted criticism toward them. In their defense, I resent the nagging voices I hear complaining that these women didn't do enough. People who criticize others often reside in their own safe haven. These critics are a bunch of cowards; like spectators who watch a fight from a distance, yelling and urging the combatants on. I ask the critics; if you could do a better job, why don't you? It is time for the *brave voices* to come out of their closets and, instead of telling everyone else what to do, roll up their sleeves and get down and dirty. Talk is cheap, actions speak louder than words.

A Letter to My Readers

Over and over again, I have heard people wish that someone would write a book such as this. I am proud that I wrote it and I stand behind it one hundred percent. I didn't write it for a special group of people. I wrote it for everyone, men and women, young and old, mainstream and educated.

My story is distinctly my own. I chose my own life story to tell because I didn't know anyone else better. *Living in Hell*, however, is not solely about my life. I represent the majority of women from my culture. I am certainly not the only woman who has suffered. I am just one of the few who dares to tell it like it is.

This book is not about a noble woman standing up for the rights of a particular group or bemoaning the loss of status. I am not a noble woman and, as you are about to find out, nothing about my life was privileged; at least not in a material way.

Living in Hell is a story of surviving evil forces; a lesson for people struggling with life's problems, who may consider their lives insignificant, to learn and remember. It is an account by a participant of Iranian life at ground level who wants to break the silence about what is happening to the invisibles.

Living in Hell is a window of opportunity to observe the lives of millions of people. It was written with utmost respect for Islam and all other religions. Criticism in this book is not pointed at any religion but at the unlawful and unscrupulous governments and individuals who use a pure religion in their attempt to legitimize their corrupt ideas.

Being born into a faith does not guarantee that a person is a good Muslim, Christian or Jew. Faith can help only if the individual uses it the right way. It is what we do with our faith and belief that makes us outstanding in society. Our path makes us different, not our faith alone.

In recent volatile times, more than ever before in world history, Islam has been negatively and wrongly portrayed as a bloodthirsty religion. It is in reality a religion of brotherhood and peace. Those who study it will understand the true nature of Islam. The true message of Islam is; care for others as you care for yourself. Help others in need, love others as brothers and sisters and do unto others as you would be done unto. Mohammad's message is the same as Jesus', the same as Moses' and the same as Abrahams'. In short, it is the ubiquitous *Golden Rule* that pervades all religion.

This one-book journey is just the beginning for me. I repeat myself in stating that I don't expect a life-changing miracle. I am simply trying to stimulate the conscience of readers. I ask you to allow yourself to feel and reflect on the pain of the oppressed and pass on the messages of this book. I hope to create awareness in people around the world and bring us one step closer as nations, united with a common goal, ignoring the color of skin. I plead to the world for brotherhood among all religions and nations.

I am not a devil's advocate for or against anyone. I want to make this a better world for the disadvantaged. I have experienced first hand the dubious privilege of living in a repressive environment under barbaric rules and to have endured what women from disadvantaged, dysfunctional families go through. I know how it feels to exist in pain behind the door to freedom.

In the Middle East, freedom is a strange concept, a dangerous territory in which we cannot walk. We can only swallow our pride and dream about freedom but dare not talk about it. Alas, in Western cultures, many take freedom for granted. Only those who suffered and fought to find or keep it know its true value.

Let us pause to remember and salute the heroes in every culture who have died in battles, at home and abroad, so humankind can live safe and free and aspire to a better life. They died so that we can taste freedom with every sunrise, every sunset, every breath of fresh air and every beat of our hearts. We owe them our lives and the freedom we experience. *God Bless their souls.*

Some may see me as gifted; others may think of me as insane for jeopardizing my life to say what it is my right to say and hoping to help and to save lives. Admittedly, I have not had an immaculate life. I think of myself as a rebel with a cause. Frankly, it would often be easier to shut my mouth and close my eyes to injustice and live in peace. That would be my deepest desire in a perfect world. I cannot in good conscience stand to see others suffering. In my view, life is only worth living if I can be a possitive force; which I will try to do as long as I can raise a finger to help others. My mission is to salvage one life at a time.

I hope this book will help others overcome their unfortunate circumstances. I want to make a difference, but I cannot do it alone. How much, or how little, I achieve depends to a large degree on you, the reader.

As a Persian proverb says, 'The sun doesn't stay behind the clouds forever.' Meaning; truth will eventually win.

Together and united I believe, in my heart and soul that we can provoke and prevail and accomplish the mission impossible. The truth may take time but it will *always* win.

I suggest to my readers that they read the Afterword where I have elaborated on religious and historical events, for which a full explanation would interrupt the flow of the narrative.

Ghazal Omid

*The logo of Islamic Iran on the cover and title
pages is an artistic variation of the Arabic word
for God. Hailed by the regime as a symbol of
purity and virtue, for Iranians it has, in truth,
represented the end of freedom and humanity.*

Social and Cultural Legacy

I was born, prior to the Iran/Iraq war, in Abadan, Iran, a large industrial city located at the head of the Persian Gulf. My father, born to a lower class farm family, was raised in the near medieval core of Iran. Although illiterate, thanks to his innate cunning and vigilance he accumulated substantial wealth and in the 1950s was recognized as one of the leading businessmen of the city of Abadan. My mother, a Kurd, was born to a prominent family that had lost its wealth but still carried and cherished the family reputation. She is more than twenty years his junior and was the second of his two wives. I was the last of a dozen offspring my father created with his wives and the only daughter of the four children my mother bore him.

I must go back a generation to give you a better understanding of the culture into which I was born. Being born rich does not mean being happy. Being poor should not mean being miserable. I was given the privilege and curse of being both rich and poor at the same time. This dichotomy certainly affected my upbringing.

My father, Ali Senior, was named after the first Imam of Shiah but he himself was an agnostic. The only God he ever worshipped was the one who created money.

According to his birth certificate he was born in 1919 but his birth was not registered until he was ten years old. He lived an extremely harsh early life and perhaps the degradation of his childhood turned him into the dry, insensitive, 'Ebenezer Scrooge' soul that he was. His birthplace was a two-bedroom, raw brick hovel overlooking a small muddy back yard in Najaf-Abad, a rural suburb twelve miles from the large city of Isfahan.

The town, with a population of about five thousand, had two public bathrooms; one for men and one for women, one mosque, one Mullah and one graveyard. Only a few main streets were even sandblasted; the rough sand-gravel, pre-asphalt stage of road construction. The secondary roads were still dirt. At this time only the major cities had asphalt, handcrafted stone, or brick roads. With a harsh climate; dry desert weather in summer and freezing cold and snow in winter, life was not easy. Although the climate is harsh for living, it is suitable for fruits that require lots of sun and dry weather. The high-desert climate has abetted a thriving business exporting pomegranate, chestnut, walnut and other harsh climate fruits. Weavers use some of the natural fruits to create color dyes for the Persian carpets that are still the major source of income in most rural towns.

The town was comprised mainly of tiny, one level, dirt floored houses. Typically, the doors stand half open permitting a view of the interiors from the street. Every family had a yard full of children; usually dressed in dirty, muddy, ragged clothing that had not been changed for weeks. Work started young for the children, to get them accustomed to a life of hard work. Children helped with the house chores, worked as nannies to their younger brothers and sisters or labored on the surrounding farms, almost as soon as they were out of diapers. Older boys helped their dad on the family farm and took care of livestock. Pre-teen girls worked on their handmade Persian carpets as a source of income and to earn the dowry for their inevitable near-future marriage. Education for most villagers was little more than learning to read and write the alphabet and memorizing their daily Arabic prayers. Their only holidays were Muslim Holy days, New Years' day and the day of some close family member's funeral.

Old folks habitually gathered by a muddy wall on one of the cities' favorite corners, much like a corner café, napping in the sun, chit-chatting and rocking the little babies of the family in their arms. The women spin piles of wool for the family carpets as they talk about their new, ready-for-sale carpet or when their granddaughter is getting married. They pass their dotage gossiping, scratching their skin for ticks, fleas and flies or simply picking their nose.

In Najaf-Abad many still wear their old costumes. Men wear locally made wool hats, similar to a deep Japanese rice bowl, which most men used to drink water from the spring or carry fruits in their garden, long white shirt, over-sized black satin-shiny jersey pants, much like hip hop singers pants, with a black vest over the shirt. In the winter they wear a long, over sized black coat on top of the vest.

Women used to wear a locally tailored, multi-layered skirt, each layer made with different color fabric and more colors than the rainbow. Under the skirt were black jersey pajamas. The top was an oversized shirt and coat and on their heads they wore a large colorful scarf. The scarf was a much shorter version of the ever-popular black chador. Sometimes, it was knee length in printed, predominantly light colors. Elders wore ankle length chadors, mostly with a white background.

His father was a farmer, his mother a homemaker. He was the eldest of their six children who did not die at birth or in infancy and survived to be adults. Eight people plus their goats, sheep, cows, and pet chickens were sardined into a two thousand square foot mud house and courtyard. The entrance was at the end of a long, narrow, dark hallway. Next to the door you couldn't miss the distinctive odor coming from a tiny stall. A whiff of the over-whelming aroma was enough to induce instant queasiness in anyone not inured to the smell. Inside the stinky washroom was a toilet with no lavatory. The washbasin was inconveniently located in the open yard near a hose on a small fountain. Next to the fountain was the water well, the family's only source of water. Wastewater pooled beneath the toilet in a pit which typically was left untreated for months and pumped out when it was near overflowing.

In the winter, water in the hose froze. My father's family, like the other farmers, was accustomed to the smell and was generally oblivious to the lack of fresh water for hygiene. Hygiene was not the main topic of their nightly discussions. Not bathing for months wasn't important either. As customary for the time, in summer he bathed in the river once a week or every two weeks. In the winter, he only bathed once every three or four weeks, if at all.

Due to the rudimentary hygiene and spending too much time in too close quarters with the family animals, his entire town had lice infestation. One of the greatest accomplishments of the Shah was the introduction, in the late 1960s of mandatory lice inspections. Until the Shah introduced mandatory health care and checkups, particularly for children, fleas plagued most of the village's population.

The washroom odor wasn't the only distinctive odor. In the house, next to the washroom, there was a stable, next to that was the little pet chicken house. At night, as rats feasted on leftover pet waste, water cockroaches were having a party in the stable, sucking on the raw, untreated sores on the sheep, goats, and cows. During the day, flies celebrate a wedding over the animal feces in the house. His family lived with the animal by-products, even using their dung as fuel for cooking. That must have added the particular flavor and zesty taste about which he always reminisced and bragged.

During the long, harsh winter nights the entire family, including his parents, slept under one gigantic comforter. Under the comforter, made of cotton harvested from their own fields or wool from their own animals, a little fire was carefully placed inside a *Korsy*, a small wooden cube covered only on the top. In summer, he slept in the muddy yard on an uneven cotton pad laid on a small rug and barely thick enough to blunt the edges of the dirt clods. On summer nights, the entire insect population of the yard paraded over his body and sucked his blood, leaving him with bite marks, still visible to the naked eye later in life.

Just as the other kids from his village, he was put to work young. At age six, his father gave him the responsibility of caring for the domestic animals they kept in the little stable for milk. With no time for play, he barely had a childhood. When the rooster sang at dawn, he had to get up to take the animals to grassland. He returned home to have breakfast and drag himself five miles to school, walking barefooted in snow and rain. We children swallowed most of this malarkey but remained skeptical that it was uphill both ways. Coming home from school through dark alleys with no light must have been a frightening experience for a six year old. After arriving home from school, he had to bring the animals back home and milk the cows before doing his homework at dusk by the light of a small oil lantern. As a result of the sacrifices he made, he owned a cow at the young age of seven and in no time, picking up pennies here and there, he was making a dollar a year.

Earning money at a young age and failing at the same class twice, he never developed a strong desire for education. Influenced by his parents' preference for money over education, he quit school before he reached the second grade. His options were to continue working for his father or to get a job at the local construction company. He was an ambitious kid and decided to join the leading local bricklayer to learn how to build houses of raw-mud bricks. The man noticed his talent and took him under his wing. For the next few years he built raw-brick houses. He soon mastered the craft and always spoke of himself proudly, often mentioning a particular one-story, sun-dried brick house; the first he had built himself. As a child, I couldn't grasp the significance of that house. To me it was a raw, brick shed. To him, however, it was his dream house.

When he was twelve, his father passed away. Being the eldest of six children, he became overnight the responsible man of the house. He was very protective of his family and perhaps it was the burden of this responsibility that made him a callous husband. He unfailingly walked on everyone else to reach a hand to help his own brothers and sisters. I childishly thought, even as he ignored our family, that they were lucky to have him as their brother.

I never saw him crying for his father or showing remorse for anything or anyone, for that matter. In my culture it is offensive to wear white when attending a funeral. Yet, he refused to wear black for anyone's funeral, even though everyone was annoyed by his gesture of disrespect.

He seldom spoke of his father. It didn't seem he was much loved by his sire, perhaps because they had no relationship other than work. From what I understood, his father was a simple, honest, hard-working man who did not know how to show affection toward his kids. On the day his father died, he had been working from early morning on a summer day in the fruit garden they owned. When he did not return home at night, relatives searched and found him dead. He had passed away of a stroke while watering the garden at midday under the blazing sun. Neighbors said they last saw him sitting by the water alone, perhaps cooling off from a long days work. Or, maybe he knew this was his last day and was hoping and praying to get one more chance with his children. I never met my paternal grandfather. He died forty-five years before I was born but somehow the mental picture of his last day has stuck in my mind ever since I was a child.

After his father's death, my father's life didn't change much since he had already chosen his future path. At such a tender age, it perhaps became a little more complicated than he had anticipated. His mother couldn't afford even the humble lifestyle they had led and support all six children. She sold all the animals and the garden and all my father's siblings had to go to work. The three girls of the family were considered spinsters by ages nine, eleven and twelve. Since my father came from a poor family and had no dowry to give his sisters, no one would marry them. My eldest auntie was still at home at seventeen and was considered an old maid. Finally, in desperation, she was married to a cousin. Her youngest sister was still at home until age sixteen. Late marriages were uncommon. Families would give their children away to lighten the burden on their father's shoulders.

By age seventeen, my father had come a long way. He had enough money to build a large house for himself and his wife-to-be, the daughter of the man who taught him his craft. His future father-in-law fortuitously died rather suddenly and left my father a small fortune. With the skills he had mastered, my father quickly garnered a larger fortune and married his late benefactor's daughter. At age twenty-seven, he left his birthplace and first family and came south to seek greater opportunities in the city of Abadan.

With his charm and business savvy, he soon was building half the houses in the town. In the 1950s, Abadan flourished into one of the largest ports of Iran. He made himself into a very wealthy man. Considering that he started from a dollar per year he must have been ruthless. Money opened new doors of opportunity. Although he never attended school, when he saw a business opportunity he didn't waste any time in snatching it. One wonders if he had attended school if he might have become the Iranian Rockefeller.

With greed and hard work, he got what he had long wished for. He became the wealthiest man in the city of a half million people. However, as was eventually found out, he didn't leave his village merely for a better life; he was escaping from his past. My father wasn't all fatherly to his siblings. He had a dark secret that his family kept for many years. That is perhaps why he left his birthplace to distance himself from the rumors. His guilty secret and fear of exposure may explain why he was extremely generous to his paternal family, even as he neglected his own.

He had come to Abadan to start a new life. Definitely looking good, at least in his own mind, he was shopping for a second wife. At the time, the Shah had not yet banned polygamy. What better way to dismiss the rumors than a second marriage to a younger woman? To keep close to his business and not have to travel three hundred miles to Najaf-Abad to be with a woman, he searched for a wife in Abadan, pretending he was divorced and had no children. Destiny has a funny way of connecting people. At the time, my grandmother was also shopping for a husband for her divorced daughter. Separated by three hundred miles distance and more than twenty years of age difference, they were destined to be husband and wife.

My mother is called Shokooh, which, in Persian, means Honor and Victory. She is an ethnic Kurd, born in Kermanshahan province. Her Kurdish ancestry leads back to the first Aryan people to live in present day Iran.

Although I share some Kurdish ethnic features with my mother, her fair skin, hazel eyes, and thin curly dirty-blond hair are the opposite of mine. Her smile is sweeter than honey and I like to think I have inherited her attitude, her outspokenness, her caring and her generous heart.

Persian history has cultivated many heroes and meritorious rulers from this region; kings and queens who ruled an empire unlike any other. They stood up to enemies and fought bravely, shedding their last drop of blood before being captured or killed. The king, Darius, who fought Alexander the Great bravely, ruled the entire empire of Persia from Kermanshahan.

Kermanshahan is a beautiful, mystical province, located in northwest Iran in the heart of the Zagros Mountains, where for thousands of years, history has been painted all over its body. Loaded with history and culture, it was the capital of many of the ancient Persian kings. It was, in fact, the capital of one of the earliest human civilizations on earth. There are two theories about the origin of the Kurds. One is that Kurds are the descendents of the Aryan tribes of Europe who retreated before the advance of the last Ice Age some 15,000 years ago. The other is that their presence in modern day Iran predates the Ice Age and they are indigenous to the area. They revere their rich history. Over five thousand years of the history of the kingdom has been recorded but their story goes back beyond written history.

The city is a cult of its own and has kept much of its old charm. Logistically, it is difficult to reach the city, which may be the reason ancient kings, chose it as their hometown. Proud of their heritage, Kurds are very protective of the memory of their grandfathers. They still like to tell stories about the ancient kings who lived in this city. Although it is much more modern than it used to be, it has preserved the passage of history and carries reminders on every street corner. A mixture of ancient and modern has been wedded in this region.

Ancient stones cover the streets and alleys, carrying the scars and marks of generations; engravings of glorious times past and the friendly people of city of Kermanshah. Trees in the gardens still smell like the perfume of queens crossing the market in a royal carriage. The incredible works of art, plaster moldings and carved stone ornaments that cap the pillars supporting the balconies facing the yard, resemble ancient Greek architecture, standing strong and proud for decades and, in some cases, for centuries. Hand carved, decorative stone busts and mosaic patterns resembling large paintings are above the entrances of the larger old houses. These icons, were much like a welcome mat, creating an ambiance and relating a fairy tale about legendary heroes that are still popular bedtime stories for children. Either the spirits favor the city or the people like the spirits. Something about the city makes the spirits come back often. Their friendly reminders appear everywhere.

Kermanshah is the capital of Kermanshahan Province. With an altitude of 1,420 meters above sea level it has delightful, mild summers with waterfalls streaming over the rocks, providing fresh natural spring water.

A rare and remarkable legend has made this city one of the most talked about cities in Persian poetry, and culture. Kermanshahan, founded by the Sassanids Dynasty in the 4th century A.D., became the royal residence of the dynasty. The city was nearly destroyed when it was captured by the Arabs in the 7th century. It was again a frontier fortress against the Ottoman Turks, who occupied it 1915 through 1917. Its name has been the subject of many debates during the current regime. After the revolution, the regime tried to change the name, which means 'City of Kings' in the Persian language. The proud people of Kermanshah demanded the name be restored or they would protest all the way to Tehran. After several years of arguments in the Senate and protests in the streets by the people of Kermanshahan, the name was restored.

The city has many historical archeological sites dating back to the 6th century B.C. In the time of the Sassanids Dynasty, having a carving on the mountain was a symbol immortalizing their reign. There are a number of these sites around the province. The most important is the Darius the Great site at Bisotoun, scripted in 522 B.C. Another remarkably well preserved site is the Tag-e Bostan, located four miles north east of the city, dated back to 224-651 B.C.E. Although the site was never finished, the carving is a portrait of Shahpur III, who succeeded Ardishier II. Sassanids, didn't bury their dead in the ground but placed them in stone or ceramic caskets in a cave, many of which were excavated during the Pahlavi Dynasty. Building stone houses with three levels and stone roads for their horses and buggies seems to have been the IT-Tech job of the time. Cobblestone roads were built with such care and precisions that they have been preserved along with paved streets.

Modern cultivation has not changed the practices of some old folks on the local farms. Grass, flowers, vegetables, fruits and oil seeds are the main agricultural product of the province and are still cultivated the old fashioned organic way. Winters, although cold and with heavy snow, were tolerable with oil heating and electricity making light and warm water possible in most homes at the time my mother lived there. Some people even had private bathtubs in their homes, a practice taken for granted in the west but a luxury in much of Iran where public bathhouses are the norm, even in major cities. In the early 1900s, the city was considered to be more modern than the rest of the country. The people of Kermanshahan, at the time my grandfather lived there, were not all farmers. Some were merchants or worked at the local refinery. There were more educated adults and children than in the rest of the country combined. Children attended school and public health had always been the highest priority of the people. Having a proper sewage system, the city did not experience many of the deadly epidemics of diseases that devastated the population of many provinces.

The charm is in the affluent old neighborhoods; ancient heritage-protected stone houses with tapered native stone foundations, up to two meters thick, to compensate for the hilly terrain. These foundations enclosed basements used for cool storage of salt-dried or gourmet meat and for vinegar production. The multi-storied houses, customarily constructed of brick, are protected by hand crafted, stone walls, three to four meters high, lined on the interior side with brick, with massive old doors that have opened and closed to tens of generations for hundreds of years.

In more modest neighborhoods, the one and two story houses are made of mud and straw. From a distance, the old walls protecting these homes look like a map. For countless generations, millions of people have embedded their fingerprints and messages on the ancient walls. In the old neighborhood shops and in the Bazaar, merchants still use an abacus to sell their wares as they have for centuries.

People who live in nearby villages and towns still wear their beautiful costumes. Tall, handsome men, in great shape, freshen up in local public bathrooms. Closely shaved with a large, thick moustache covering their upper lips, thick joined eyebrows give them a determined look that can scare even the ghosts of the city. They gather in local tea cafés in the late afternoon to participate in hand wrestling or go to local sports club to practice traditional wrestling. Their costume is a pair of pants that look like Ali Baba's in the Sinbad stories but not quite as bulky or blousy. The pants are made from wool or cotton in solid colors and from afar look like a jump suit. An Ali Baba mini-vest is worn over a small collared white shirt that is neatly tucked under a large silk shawl used as a belt. A small turban completes the costume. Their turban is not like the Indians' or the Mullah's. It is a black and white, cotton or silk, printed scarf with little fringes dangling around it.

Their beautiful women are mostly tall, with baby soft skin, light hazel eyes, blond or brunette hair and stunning features. These women wear a full, long, multi-layered skirt, a small top, and an overcoat with gold coin decorations or modern beaded work along the edges. On their head, they wear a large, black silk scarf with local Kurdish design print, tightened up by tucking the edges behind their ears. They don't completely cover their head; in fact their long hair and neckline are visible. Children are often seen with couples, dressed in the same traditional clothes as their parents. Clean little girls and boys, shy at first, smile and hide behind their parents or climb dad's leg. From afar, without headbands, they look like little Barbie dolls in a Kurdish outfit. Their shiny hair waves in the wind and their little cheeks glow like two red apples.

Their costumes have been the subject of controversial debates in the Iranian Senate many times for over two decades. Although banned, they still wear what their fathers of fathers wore, regardless of what the mullah's say.

The Kurds of Kermanshahan and the surrounding area still speak the same dialect of the Aryan language that they did thousands of years ago. Citizens of Kermanshah in particular among other Kurds are known for their bravery, honesty, and hospitality that are still tangible, even in a modern era. They are known as some of the best people of Iran and have a long legacy to back it up. They will sacrifice their own child to save others. They still seal deals on a handshake and verbal agreements. It is a rare occasion that they break a promise because keeping their word is a sign of their Kurdish honor and the community would shun them if they abused the trust vested in them.

Legend has it that spirits haunt the city. The residents of Kermanshahan seem to be fine with the idea of living among the spirits, believing they are the protectors of the city and respecting their territory. Haunted houses are generally off limits but curious people who think they are up to the challenge of the strange events that often occur in these places, sometimes live there. Usually one night is adequate to satisfy their curiosity. Such observers are frequently short of words and unable to describe what they saw.

My grandfather, who feared nothing in this life, found the idea of living among the sprits in haunted houses fascinating and amusing. The friendly souls often appear to people who can overcome the fear. My grandfather was one of their old buddies. My grandmother had her own stories to tell, of drumming noises emanating from the closet and watching my grandfather shake hands with a genie or Jen, as we call them in the Persian language, who appeared to be twenty feet tall and disappeared from sight right in front of her eyes. Growing up, as skeptical as I always was toward my grandmother, I knew when I heard it from my grandfather that the story was true.

Granny was terrified watching him chat with the apparition as if they were just fellows. Grandfather's stepbrother couldn't bear to see him consort with so-called 'friendly souls' with whom he wasn't particularly interested in associating. He agitatedly described meeting the genies that apparently got too close to him for comfort. Till the last day of his life, he wasn't ashamed to express prejudice against the friendly ghosts, blaming them for forcing him to leave his birthplace. The city of ghosts and of people who appreciate the ghosts is where my mum enjoyed life as a child.

My maternal grandfather was the son of a Kurd chief from a prominent family. In the early 1900s, at age fourteen, he inherited millions of hectares of land and a large amount of money. His father passed away at the age of 101 upon hearing of the death of his three eldest sons in less than a week. All were educated men who died mysteriously. In later years, the family was told they might have had a rare form of blood cancer.

Great-grandpa was married three times but not to more than one wife at a time. At his death, he left behind my grandfather and, as testimony to the virility and fecundity of Kurdish mountain men, a six months old baby son. The baby boy was from his nineteen-year-old third wife who had been a family maid. My grandfather was from his second wife, who died giving birth to him. The elder boys were from his first wife, who died many years earlier.

My grandfather was left in the hands of his wealthy uncles in a small village on the outskirts of Kermanshahan. One of the uncles, Sardar-Khan, was a good man, not only an influential local celebrity and a chief but also a provincial ruler who owned the territories between Kermanshahan and Loerestan Province. His main residence was in Khoram-Abad. He had fought with and was in held in favor by Reza Shah.

Reza Shah, who ruled Iran from 1921 to 1941, considered it his duty to subdue the tribal leaders to bring unity to the country. As pre-planned strategy, after consolidating his power, in order for the central government to control the entire country, he had all the influential Khans arrested and killed. He invited Sardar-Khan, my grandfather's uncle, an influential provincial ruler, to his palace where he dined and was photographed shaking hands with the Shah. With a cashmere shawl on his shoulder, he sang, in the Kurdish language, this poem, 'Bring a chair for the chief to sit down, bring a chair for the chief to sit and take a picture of him.' His poetic gesture must not have favorably impressed the arrogant Reza Shah who, like previous kings, did not abide any threats.

Sardar-Khan, along with many of his children, was massacred in a sneak midnight attack on his residence. Most of his children were killed trying to escape. The survivors of his family, including my great aunties, were taken to Falak-ol-Aflak, the notorious prison in Khoram-Abad that is now a museum.

Left alone again, without a father figure, my grandfather was spoiled by his aunties. But, they couldn't teach him what he needed most. With no schooling and not knowing how to manage his money, he trusted his surviving step-uncles who had been chosen as his guardians by the elders of his village. Instead of keeping his money safe, they did not waste any time in devising means to get his wealth out of his hands. Desperate for their approval, he grew up too fast and at a very young age was introduced to opium, wine and gambling.

One day, when he was in his early twenties, while gossiping with friends, he met the man who later became his father-in-law entering the village. A young woman sat on his horse with her protective father walking at her side. Her hazel eyes, blond hair and fair skin must have been quite attractive in his eyes. Grandma often proudly pointed at my auntie stating that she was her copy. It must have been love at first sight for him. Never having been in love, he was sure she was the one. In talking to her father, he found out that the man had known my great grandfather. However, the man said to him, "I liked your father but I am not going to give my daughter to you." When my grandfather asked him why, he answered, "You drink, smoke opium and you don't pray. I don't want you as my son in law." Hopelessly romantic, he was crushed.

His uncles invited him to an immoral night of drinking and gambling. To overcome his disappointment and desperation and not knowing it was all planned, he drank and gambled till early morning. In one night, he gambled away all that was left of his inheritance.

The next morning, he woke up coatless and shoeless in the lee of a collapsing mud wall in a back alley near the edge of the village. Shamed, to avoid public humiliation, he dropped his head and ran like an ostrich with its head in the sand, to his auntie's house. The elders tried to get his inheritance back but it was too late. He had signed papers while he was drunk that left him penniless. He couldn't eat or talk for days.

Mortified, he resorted to desperate attempts to restore his dignity. While everyone was asleep, he made a small fire, brought some prods and left them on the fire until they glowed red. One by one, he seared his skin with the hot prods, marking the day he lost his wealth and promising God and himself to never touch alcohol or gamble again. He kept his promise for the rest of his life. Leaving his hometown village on foot, it took him five days and nights of walking to reach Kermanshahan province where he had a cousin who taught him to read and write and sent him to night school. My grandfather started working in the oil refinery at Kermanshah as a laborer. He learned to speak English, Arabic, and Hindi the necessary languages of the time due to the English importation of Indian laborers. The Iranians had to learn to communicate with their fellow workers. He was promoted to a good job as a security officer and eventually, due to his honesty and hard work, was promoted to chief special security officer for the oil refinery at Kermanshah.

Origin of a Dysfunctional Family

My grandfather, although well educated for his time, was deprived of a decent life for himself and his future generations. My grandmother, who was nothing like him, manipulated him unmercifully. She was the same girl on horseback he met in his village years ago. Through great coincidence, she was now living only a block away from him. Being the only educated man in the neighborhood, people brought their letters to him to read.

My grandmother was in touch through correspondence with her father, who was a merchant living in Iraq. She brought letters from her father to him to be read to her. This caused her suspicious husband to start a rumor and he took it as an excuse to beat her severely. Her father, a good man and a fair merchant with a mysterious past, had given her away at age twelve to a man more than twice her age. Shortly after their marriage, when she became pregnant, her husband tormented her over her cravings and made her beg for food to the point that she nearly died. She finally left him in fear of her life. She also had to leave behind her four children. My grandmother was divorced, at age twenty-six, after fourteen years of marriage.

Years after his first disappointment in love, being rejected by his intended's father, he had accepted the elderly chief's decision to hand him a female cousin in marriage. She was engaged to his name and he was about to travel to his village to be married.

On learning that his first love was again available, my grandfather, who by this time was 35 years old, broke his engagement to his cousin. This time, he didn't wait for her father's approval. He proposed to her at once and with the help of a family member celebrated their union with a small reception. Then, for the second time, he asked my grandmother's father for his blessing. Her father finally realized his daughter was loved and shortly before he passed away wished her the best.

Soon after the birth of their third child, my grandfather fell ill. When he heard of his wife's new pregnancy, he prayed that it would be a girl and vowed to keep her close to his heart. His prayer came true, it was a girl. My mother was born December 7, 1939 bringing abundant joy to her family. According to her father, her birth certificate was registered a year older than her real age.

She was born into a family of fourteen brothers and sisters, most of whom died in infancy. There was obviously a defective gene in the family. An older brother and sister were Down's syndrome babies and deaf. Both died at age nine. Her brother, Yadollah, one year her senior, despite all the odds was a reputed genius. Yadollah, my mum, three other boys and a girl survived. My auntie did not have Down's syndrome but carried the gene to her children. All four of her children were born with the defective gene. The youngest boy of my mum's family also was affected with Down's syndrome.

The entire neighborhood celebrated my mother's birth for a week and danced all night long at the expense of my grandfather who was glad he had finally met his angel. He made no secret that she was especially dear to his heart. He idolized her and enjoyed the rarity of spoiling a child, particularly a girl, during a time of depression.

In the 1930s, Reza Shah; made many moves to bring Persia into the twentieth century. In 1935, four years before my mother's birth, to distinguish himself from previous kings, he took the drastic measure of changing the name of our country from Persia to Iran. He took many positive steps toward the future of Iran. He wanted education for the people, especially women. That year he opened the first schools and modern European-style universities. Education became mandatory for every individual and every child had to go to school. Previously, only those studying to become a cleric learned to read and write. He stressed equality for women and in 1936 ordered women to remove their veils and promised that they could walk the streets in European dress under his protection and without fear. He kept his promise.

Unlike the kings of the Qajar and Safavids dynasties, he excluded the influential mullahs from politics. He created a secular government and decreed the separation of religion from state. Although Reza Shah had a noble idea and desire to elevate women's status and liberate them, he was often compared to Ata Turk. Both eventually became fathers of liberation but were also known as dictators. Reza Shah was a brutally ruthless man who enforced his ideas with zero tolerance and maximum force.

The cultural changes must have been traumatic for many elderly women who had to take off their headbands and chadors. Even my grandmother, a young woman at the time, was slow to comply. She used to tell me a story. My grandfather had purchased her two European hats but, reluctant to change a lifetime dress habit, she stepped out into the street with her hair covered by the traditional scarf. A police officer or gendarme, adopted from the French language, on seeing her covered hair, without warning struck my grandma with his baton, bloodying her face. My grandfather, a powerful man, beat the policeman severely. If the local people, who saw the gendarme insult my grandma, had not come to his defense he could have be jailed

Obviously, liberating women from their outdated outfits was not everyone's idealistic way to freedom. However, for a few women in Tehran, including Persia's first famous female singer, Ms. Ghamar Moluke Vaziry, it became a turning point. She was an orphan who rose to fame singing religious songs and stormed the Persian orchestra with her great voice.

My grandmother was a stay-at-home mum and very pregnant again. She breastfed my mother for only a few months before her milk dried up as the result of her new pregnancy with my uncle Azam. Grandpa hired a nanny. My mother was breastfed by another woman who liked her and treated her as her own child. Unlike my grandfather, who spoiled my mother in every possible way, my grandmother never missed an opportunity to tell her that she meant nothing and abused her in any way possible. Although mum was her own biological child, she treated her as if she were a despised stepchild. Grandma was jealous that my grandpa treated his daughter with love. She beat my mum at every opportunity and at four years old made her take care of her newborn brother, washing his cotton diapers in the midst of a cold winter in the yard's fountain. To spare herself any discomfort, she went so far as to have her suck her breast and spit the extra milk out.

On my mother's first birthday, in 1940, there was tragedy for her father. In coordinated 'accidents' against the English, who were occupying Iran at the time, there was a fire at the Kermanshah refinery. The English chief engineer spotted a problem with one of the main oil and gas pumps, which had been tampered with previously. The occupying forces were located in key positions and the local opposition and insurgents didn't hesitate when given any opportunity to attack them; even if it meant destroying the whole city and killing their own people. Before the chief engineer was able to call for back up, the pump burst into flames. In an effort to save the petroleum and the city, the Englishman ran to the fire to close the main valve. Unprotected, he caught on fire. My grandfather, over six feet tall and known for his physical strength ran to the man's rescue. My grandfather was able to close the valve and save the Englishman's life by carrying him out of the fire. Both were badly burned. The English man was sent to England for recovery. My grand father was sent to a local hospital. He had second and third degree burns all over his body but his hands, burned while closing the valve, were the worst.

He was in a hospital bed for more than three months. If he had not closed the valve, the entire refinery could have become an inferno. The city would have been in danger and thousands of lives could have been lost. After partially recovering from the accident that almost cost him his life, he lost his job. Because someone had misinformed his superiors, instead of getting a bonus and a Heroes Medal, he got the boot.

Unable to work for two years, he was paid a small early retirement package and let go. Bedridden for a year and facing a money shortage for the first time in his life, it preyed hard on his self-esteem. Having lost his fortune, his life savings, his job, his health, his retirement and almost losing his life, he faced a bleak future. Grandfather had never saved a penny of his large paychecks. In fact, he had lived on a monthly allowance doled out by his wife from his paychecks that he turned over to her, a rare scenario given the male mentality of the early 1940s. She, of course, knew nothing about investment or saving and always blew the money as fast as it came in. While it lasted, they lived lavishly in three very large rented rooms on the third floor of an opulent home and believed God would always save them. Even God, it seems, has his limits.

Out of money, he had to sell everything they owned, including my mother's lambskin coat, her new handmade boots and her gold jewelry. She had to live without her nanny who had taken care of her for four years. His solution was to move his five children away from the pain of seeing their belongings worn by the neighbors. Nearly fifty years old, disabled by his burns, my grandfather had to start all over again. He decided to move his family to Abadan where, six years later, Uncle Akbar was born.

At this time, the British decided to remove Reza Shah from power. At his own request, on September 16, 1941, his son Mohammad Reza Shah Pahlavi ascended to the throne. Reza Shah was deported and died in Johannesburg on July 26, 1944.

The city of Abadan is located at the head of the Persian Gulf in Khuzestan Province, also known as the black gold province, an oil-producing region in the southwest corner of Iran. The city lies on an island of the same name along the eastern bank of the Shatt Al-Arab River that divides Iran from Iraq. The island is 33 miles (53 km) from the Persian Gulf and is 42 miles (68 km) long and from 2 to 12 miles (3 to 19 km) wide.

The history of Abadan is not crystal clear but its legend, passed through generations by bedtime stories, is that it was founded by a holy man named 'Abbad in the 8th century.

For centuries, before the discovery of oil, it was known for little more than its hot climate, fishing, salt and woven mats. When visited by the Arab geographer Battutah in the 14th century, the town was described as a large, hot and humid village on a flat, salty plain. As centuries passed, the extension of the delta by Shatt Al-Arab silt deposition caused the coast of the Persian Gulf to gradually recede from Abadan. The retreat of the Gulf apparently had a positive impact on this island. When Marco Polo visited Abadan, he described it as the Jewel of the Persian Gulf. After years of tension and many wars with the neighboring Ottoman Empire over whom Abadan belonged to, the Persian Empire finally acquired it in 1847.

Still, the island of Abadan was nothing but a flat village that remained unpopular and unchanged until the early 20th century when the Anglo-Persian Oil Company discovered rich oilfields in Khuzestan province in 1909. Through the efforts of the beloved Prime Minster, Mosadegh, its Iranian properties were nationalized in 1951 as the National Iranian Oil Company and turned to the people. The company established its pipeline terminus refinery at Abadan. The refinery began operating in 1913 and by 1956 Abadan had become a city of more than 220,000 inhabitants, with an economy almost entirely based on petroleum refining and shipping.

By the late 1970s, the city had become extremely prosperous and the oil refinery was among the largest in the world.

In the 1950s, British forces still occupied Abadan and oil pumps were sprouting up daily. Prior to the oil discoveries in Khuzestan province, Kermanshah was the oil capital of Iran but Abadan was now the hot spot, suggestive of the mad California Gold Rush in the 1850s. Everyone wanted a piece of the petroleum pie.

My mum was four years old at the time and still not able to speak Farsi. Her language was the Kurdish dialect she had learned in her home town. It was painful for her to leave her childhood friends and memories of her beloved city behind. Missing her friends, for months she climbed up to the roof of her new, little, two-bedroom home, comparing it to the multi level, one and half acre home they left behind. Sobbing and hollering, "Kermanshah, can you hear me?" in the Kurdish language. She often cried till she fell asleep on the roof. At night, her father climbed up to carry her down to her bed.

Unlike Kermanshah, Abadan, in 1944, didn't have tap water or a sewage system. The family had to squeeze into two small over crowded bedrooms with no fan or air conditioning. The new living conditions and leaving the comparative luxury they once had enjoyed was extremely depressing. The experience made my mother vulnerable. Shortly after the move, she came down with malaria.

She was left at home to get well or die. When she saw other kids going to school, she pleaded with her father to let her go to school. Except for the top executives and people who had benefits from work, schools were private. Parents had to pay money for their children to attend school. My grandfather didn't think girls needed education and had no plans for his daughters to attend school. Finally, due to her intense desire to attend school, fearing she would die if not permitted to do so, he relented and made temporary arrangements for her to attend a nearby school for one season. She finally got her wish and entered school at age five. Bright and vibrant, she learned to speak Farsi rapidly, got well, made new friends and had an excellent track record. In no time she was on the school honor list.

Days in Abadan were unbearably hot, and long. My grandfather was an old man and had very little going for his future and his small kids.By a stroke of luck, one day on his way to the office where he worked for start up wages like anyone else, he met the Englishman whose life he had saved. After years of being away, my grandfather, didn't recognize the man but the Englishman, now a top executive had not forgotten the face and hands that carried him out of the fire. The excited Englishman hugged him, asking, "My gosh, is it really you?" He told my grandfather that after returning to Iran from England, he had looked for him everywhere but no one knew where to find him. My grandfather listened hopelessly to the man, nodding his head and saying, "Well, that is great but if you will excuse me I must go now. My shift is starting in a few minutes. I don't want to be late. My supervisor won't be happy seeing me talking to you."

The Englishman, confused, sputtered, "Your superior! Didn't you get a promotion?" With tears in his eyes grandfather whispered, "I got the promotion alright. I was given the option of accepting retirement or getting fired." The angry Englishman stormed into my grandfathers' superior, yelling, "Do you know who is this man is? He is a hero. He saved my life and you imbeciles hired him as a simple worker with no rank."

My grandfather, impressed with the man, smiled and watched in anguish, scratching his baldhead and thinking, "I hope something good comes from this." Indeed, it did. My grandfather didn't know that the Englishman had become the top executive of the refinery at Abadan. He was promoted instantly from a simple security guard with no privileges to a manager with full benefits; free school for his kids, access to top colleges and university, 100 percent medical insurance and a free, large four bedroom house. His retirement package was restored and he was paid for all the damages and unpaid wages for the time he had been bedridden.

During the short course of their reunion the Englishman and my grandfather became close friends. One day he called my grandfather to his office and said to him, "Reza, I am leaving Iran. Join me in England. Your children would have a better future in Europe." My grandfather was never much of a dreamer. He had no particular desire to leave his hometown, much less his country. He thanked the Englishman and wished him the best. They never met again.

Due to grandfather's hard work, sacrifices and the bravery he showed in saving the Englishman's life, his promotion dated back to the time he was a security chief in Kermanshah. Now, he once again worked at the same job in Iran's largest oil refinery. Before his retirement he received one more promotion that took him to a much higher position than he could ever have hoped to achieve with his minimal education. Soon after this, two of his Down's syndrome children died. He took them back to Kermanshah for a small burial. It seemed he also left his spirit there. After returning to Abadan, he was never quite the same again. My mother described him as a sad father, like a giant elephant brought to his knees by the loss of his babies and wailing in pain for their absence.

After earning the big promotion, he took the entire family for a visit to his hometown. At the end of World War II the economy was in a slump but he had regained some of his prosperity and was feeling pretty good about himself. He brought a considerable amount of money with him and was able to buy back some of his lost lands. My mum, six years old at the time, had a blast in the country riding horses, eating fresh fruits and cheese, playing in the garden with other children and observing the quaint customs of her father's village. Her pleasant experience was jolted one day when she overheard some elderly men chatting with her father, talking about her. She heard them say, "Leave your daughter with us and we will give your entire lands back to you at no cost." Frightened, she thought her father was giving her away and leaving her behind among his distant family. She ran away to her father's auntie's house. Hungry and sad, she fell asleep behind a large bolster in a corner room. After hours of searching the entire village, my grandfather found her. He asked her why she was hiding. She answered, "I heard you are considering leaving me behind." He assured her, not in a million years. That, obviously, was an affectionate answer. If my grandfather had not wanted to keep her, my grandmother would gladly have left her behind. Years ago, female children were commonly given away to families of the intended groom. The two children grow up in the groom's family and were married at the age the groom's family considered proper.

Child Bride

Four years went by after that incident in the village. It seemed only yesterday that mum's family had moved to Abadan. When my mum was ten years old, her mother gave birth to her youngest brother, Akbar. Unfortunately the Down's syndrome resurfaced.

Mum and her older brother were irritated with their parent's treatment of their children, particularly with grandma, who thought of a child as just a toy. She didn't take good care of the baby. When he got sick, she didn't take him to the hospital. She relied instead on home remedies that sounded like a lot of hocus-pocus from Harry Potter stories. The grandparents bathed the baby in sheep's blood and cow's urine, dunked him in a bath of pure ice and then put him under thick heavy wool blankets in the 104° F temperature of Abadan.

My mother and her brother, Yadollah, tried to get help of any kind for the baby but they were children themselves and didn't know how. Granny had my grandfather's leash in her hand and even persuaded him to live his life according to the deceptive stories of a fortuneteller who, if he knew anything valuable about the future, could have used it for his own benefit. Watching their life going to waste, listening to a bunch of mumbo jumbo, mum was furious at her mother. Her innocent sarcasms, which came across as rudeness, caused her mother to see her, not as her child, but as an enemy. My grandmother was determined to get rid of my mother at the first opportunity.

One day, when my mother was ten years old, a friend of the family, a young man in his early twenties, and his mother visited them. It was a hot summer day and my mother was playing with her brother and sister in the back yard. She heard them call my grandfather 'uncle.' The good-looking young man was a distant cousin of my grandfather and had traveled with his mother from Kermanshah to visit them. In the smaller cities of Iran, it is customary that every distant cousin knows the head of the family as uncle and as respect they call his wife auntie. My mum didn't know the man who was socializing with her old brother and had only seen him once from a distance but he could have become her future husband. She was still very much a child. She overheard her father saying, "Come back when she is older." Wary, she ran to her father, hugging him, asking "Are you giving me away?" Her father reassured her, saying, "No, relax. I am not giving you away."

Little did she know what was to be. One day, in the summer of her fourteenth year, she came home from high school and was met by several women, complete strangers, from her future husband's family. Without even asking or considering whether she wanted to get married, they bathed her and dressed her as a bride. My mother hardly knew what to make of this but she was old enough to have heard the stories of this happening to other young women. She was taken to the grooms' house. For the first time they met eye to eye. The same boy, now a twenty-five year-old man, had come back to claim her. Shaken, but obedient to her heritage, in fact having no choice in the matter, she reluctantly married this stranger.

He must have wanted her very badly. He had finished university since his first visit to her house and was working at the refinery as an engineer where he earned a relatively good salary. He gave 3,000 Toman, approximately US $4,000 in 1946, to my grandparents for his new bride's dowry. Instead, my grandmother used the money from my mother's marriage and went on a tour of Iran for her own honeymoon. This didn't sit very well with the groom's family, causing constant criticism.

The morning after the wedding night, her husband complained bitterly to his relatives about my mother's ignorance of her marital duties, saying that any village girl could have performed better. He immediately abandoned her. For a year, my mother knew nothing of his whereabouts until he returned from Tehran, addicted to heroin and accompanied by a mistress/madam. He demanded that my mother resume the marriage. She did not even recognize him and refused to suffer further indignities at his hand.

There was not a single moment of happiness in this overnight marriage. Despite opposition from her family; after all, my grandmother had been paid for her daughter's hand and body, she succeeded in divorcing him. But not without being physically assaulted by the woman he had brought back as a reminder of his Tehran life style, who, by all accounts, was a Tehran madam with ideas of adding mum to her brothel.

After a year of battling her husband in divorce court, the judge finally ruled in her favor and my mum, only sixteen years old, was divorced in the prime of her life. She was literally a child bride when she married her husband for one night. After being away from her abusive mother, she had blossomed, at sixteen, into a beautiful young woman. Despite the fact that my grandmother had also divorced in her younger years, divorce was a taboo subject in their family and, indeed, in most families. It was almost unheard of when my mum asked for one. Her parents treated her as an outcast; they would rather have seen her dead than divorced.

Within two months, my grandmother was ready to sell her again. She told everyone within earshot that my mother was eligible and available. This time, mum made sure everyone in her family knew that she was not interested in marriage. She was determined to choose her own husband if she ever remarried. She had a good outlook of her future plans. My grandmother, however, had her own plans for her. She acted as the publicist to promote her goods. She announced to all the neighbors that her daughter was again eligible for marriage. When neighbors asked if my mother wished to remarry, my grandmother's answer was 'yes.' My mother's answer was 'no.'

A Second Forced Marriage

The interval between her marriages was a bitter time for my mother. She attended night school, showing the tenacity to finish high school. She was determined to enter medical school and become a nurse. In those years, some doctors used their stature to have an affair, outside of their marriage, with their nurses, some of whom welcomed the flirtatious attention. My mum was never flirtatious and had no desire to become anyone's mistress. She had a bad experience with the only man she ever knew and did not let any man misinterpret her poised attitude. That didn't change her father's opinion of doctors and nurses nor stop him from ranting his ideology at her. Her beloved father had changed, no longer looking at her as his angel. He told her she could not be a nurse because he assumed all the doctors slept with the nurses. He accused her of wanting to ruin their family reputation by becoming the doctor's whore and said only a bad girl would think that such a place was for her. He gave her an ultimatum that she had to get out of his home if she became a nurse.

Mum didn't have much money to buy clothing so she got herself an apprenticeship in a tailor shop/school. She sewed clothing for her friends and neighbors and made a dollar, here and there. The job served a dual purpose of learning to sew and saving money by not paying for the tutoring and lessons she received from her instructor. She was away most of day but was always wary of my grandmother's desire to get rid of her. Mum even heard her mother whispering to her father that she was becoming old goods, meaning she was getting too old to marry off.

One summer afternoon, as she came home from her work, she had an ominous feeling that an unpleasant event was about to happen. Her apprehension grew when she saw the man who would become my father. He and some of his friends were waiting at my grandmother's house to see her. Her mother asked her to bring some tea for the guests. Girls who have grown up behind closed curtains and locked rooms know that when parents order her to bring tea to a strange guest, this is an indication that the guest is a suitor. My mother immediately rebelled, knowing that taking tea to guests is the sign that her parents or elders of the family had already accepted a proposal. Her mother would not be deterred, slapping my mother repeatedly. In general, the tea ceremony is a chance for the girl to meet the suitor and his family. Most of the less strict parents allow their daughter to say if she liked the man's looks but for the strict parents, this is the chance to show their goods and seal the deal.

She finally surrendered and did as told, she entered the room and looked at her prospective husband, a thirty-four year old, rough-looking, overweight, bald man. My mother immediately fled the room, rejecting the marriage proposal but my grandmother called on her eldest son, Yadollah, to stop her.

Uncle Yadollah, who, to his credit, later apologized to my mum a thousand times, stopped my mother. She fought him but he slapped her forcefully and grabbed her arms, forcing her to stay. Her father was aware of his daughter's affection for him and knew if he called her name she would respond. In the midst of their argument, he called my mother from the next room. She thought her father needed to speak with her and replied, "Yes?" My grandmother and father had called the registrar from the marriage registration bureau, Aghd Mahzari, who was present in the same room from which my grandfather was calling. When he heard the word Yes, the official immediately and illegally announced my mum and the stranger were husband and wife. Yes, in the Farsi language is used in the matrimonial ceremony as, "Yes, I do." That stranger became my biological father. My grandfather was a kind man but he was a weak, obedient child in my grandmother's hand. So much so, that he tricked his beloved daughter to please his wife. Although, he himself married out of love, it never occurred to him that his children should have the same opportunity.

The minute that she said, "Yes," in answering her father's call, he had unknowingly forced his beloved daughter into polygamy. Although polygamy has been practiced in Iran since the Khajar's dynasty, it has never been a favorable situation for a young woman or a common practice, particularly among Kurds. He fantasized that his daughter would be able to enjoy cars, a large home, telephone, servants and all the comfort and luxury he had never been able to provide. My grandpa took my father at his word and shook hands with him. He surmised that this man would provide a life of luxury for my mother and lavish her with gifts that he or other men of his own rank were not able to give her.

My father promised my grandfather that he would give my mother the sun and the moon, lavish her with utmost luxury and everything he had would be at her finger tips. He thought he made a smart move in marrying off his divorced daughter before she ran away, not knowing my father was simply a wolf dressed as a lamb. My father charmed him with his smooth behavior. His colorful promises all turned out to be big empty lies.

Grandfather later regretted his part in the deception. He was blind for the last ten years of his life and believed his blindness was retribution for what he did to his daughter. In order to marry my mother, my father lied to my grandparents about his other wife, or at least to my grandfather. My father always said he had told my grandmother he was married but she always swore that she never knew. Whatever the truth, the two remained close friends even when mum wanted nothing to do with my father. Mum always said her mother's deepest desire was to get rid of her. She considered my mother not just her child but also her competitor who criticized her irrational behavior. My father paid my grandmother 1,000 Toman, a large sum of money at the time, supposedly to buy my mother a dowry. This second time around, she was slightly more generous and bought my mother a couple of small rugs before spending the rest on new clothing for my uncles, a heavy gold bracelet for herself and a change to a different hospital for my chronically-ill Uncle Akbar

Although my father was quite wealthy, he didn't make any effort to celebrate his union with my mother; which was just as well because she wasn't enthusiastic about having a wedding ceremony either. At the door, as she was shoveled out of the house, grandpa lectured her with a metaphoric slogan, "I give you away wearing white (wedding gown.) I expect you to come out of this marriage wearing white (a shroud)." Muslims are wrapped in a shroud after departure from this life and it is scripted in the Koran that will be what that person will wear when resurrected for her questioning. He meant that no matter how hard this marriage might be, you have to stay in it till you take your last breath. She replied to him, "I am not wearing a white gown and I will divorce this man even if I only have one day left to live."

Hearing this, my father shoved her to his car like livestock. Watching him taking her away, it didn't bother their conscience in the least that although he may fraudulently be her legal husband; in truth he was a complete stranger that they knew nothing about. Whether the charade was planned beforehand or just happened, for my mother it was a shock akin to an uprooted plant adjusting to new a habitat.

She stopped talking to her parents until one day when her mother stopped by her house. She didn't want to open the door for her but my father ordered her to treat my grandma with respect. He had managed to maintain a somewhat cordial relationship with his in-laws. Although he never spared them a penny, they worshipped him because he was wealthy. It was irrelevant to them that he was not kind to my mother.

My grandma came back into my mother's life and interfered again and again. She constantly visited her, not because she missed her, but to extort her, asking for food, clothing, household items or anything my mother could spare. My grandpa's family, although, by all accounts not wealthy, was not poor either. That didn't stop the greed of my grandma from using her daughter as a source of barter. At first, my mother wasn't sure if she could give her what she asked but my grandma kept telling the seventeen year old girl horrific stories of her father's sickness and how her brothers and sister were starving and needed food and how much it meant to everyone if she could help them. In the end, the greedy granny nailed it when she told my mother it was her responsibility as the family's second eldest child to help her family.

Thinking she was saving her family, she bought into the idea for a while before her conscience bothered her enough to show up one day at her brother's high school, asking him whether the family was indeed starving. When she found out everything her mother told her was a lie and she was making money selling the items mum gave her, nearly daily, she was devastated. Grandma was earning money off her. Manipulated by her mother one more time, mum found the courage to tell her she was not welcome to visit her if she was coming to extort her. For almost three years after her marriage her wounds were still fresh. Neither grandma's annoying visits nor her demands and orders could influence her to start talking to her father. She finally forgave him when she found out he actually had suffered a fall and aneurysm that nearly ended his life.

My father, had managed to accumulate enough wealth to fulfill his dream of becoming one of the richest men in the city of Abadan. He owned a large house, new cars that he changed often to display his wealth to outsiders, more than 1,000,000 hectares (2,500,000 acres, 3,858 m^2) of land, industrial machines, and a factory next to his house.

Not that it mattered; he also had another family that my unsuspecting mother knew nothing about until she was seven months pregnant with her first child.

His first wife, coincidentally also seven months pregnant, on hearing her husband had married another woman, was equally surprised and lost the baby, either through miscarriage or stillbirth. Family legend has it that when she gave birth she refused to feed the baby and it starved to death. Understandably, that woman was determined that she would have no more children with my father.

Hearing about his other baby, he rushed to visit his first wife. He returned to my mother's quarters with two of his children, filthy teenagers, a boy and a girl. He had managed to maintain them in the remote town of Najaf-Abad, in the house he himself built. He visited them at every opportunity on his frequent 'business trips.' At twelve and fourteen, these children were nearly as old as my mother.

Since he often hired young girls and boys as servants, mum thought they were new servants come to help her with the house chores. She told my father that they were not strong enough to be much help around the house and he should let them go. He harshly answered that these were his kids, not her servants.

Floored by this revelation and unable to absorb the shock of this horrendous news, she developed false labor pains and from that point on, her pregnancy became complicated. My father, in typical fashion, reacted by leaving her to live full time with his other family until mum either gave birth or died in child labor. He didn't like to be around his pregnant women. My mother was left alone. As days passed she became intensely weak to the point she could no longer carry the weight of the baby.

My Uncle Yadollah, a repentant, unwitting party to the sham marriage had just graduated from high school. Not having a job, he welcomed my father's offer to run the office in his absence. It was a chance to see his sister. He didn't know my mother had a difficult pregnancy till he saw her alone and in pain. He was so alarmed he took her to a doctor immediately. The doctor mistakenly thought he was the neglectful man and told him that she was in such bad shape that he must pray hard because it was too late and there was very little he could do for her. My uncle explained that she was his sister and begged the doctor to do whatever he could to save her life while he was praying

While my father attended to his other family, my uncle went to work, visited his sister every day, helped her to bathe and even took her to the bathroom. Mum said he had tears in his eyes, and cried for forcing her into this marriage. With the sacrifices of my uncle, the eldest boy of the family was born two months early. He weighed barely four pounds but nevertheless was a healthy child. He was the joy of her life for a short time. My mother named him Khosro after one of the Sassanian kings. My father didn't show up until his son was two months old. After his return, he never apologized to my mother or her brother for his absence.

He was glad that he had another son to add to the crowd of children to carry his name. Even in present day Iran, much like the medieval era, everyone assumes a son is the result of a woman's desire and ability to produce a male heir, although modern technology has proven it is the man's sperm that determines the sex of the child. Many women are still being ostracized for giving a man or his family a baby girl instead of the boy everyone so eagerly anticipates at the end of her nine-month journey and painful labor. Happy for having a baby boy, he simply continued his life and business as usual. He and Yadollah got into an argument. My uncle challenged him about his cruel behavior toward his sister. My father dismissed his concern, insultingly saying, "She is still alive, isn't she?" Uncle Yadollah left his house, telling mum he would get her out of her marriage.

Regrettably, Yadollah never came back. That was the last time mum saw her brother healthy. The two met a few years later when he was on his deathbed, dying from leukemia and remorseful for what he had done to her. Even on his deathbed, he tried to introduce my mother to his senior partner at work so she could have a job after he was gone and be able to provide for herself and her children.

Shortly after this argument, my grandfather, who was retired, relocated his family from Abadan to Khoram-Abad without even saying goodbye to his own daughter, leaving her alone to my father's tender mercies.

When my father came back from his 'business trip,' my mother was still bedridden. He callously took the opportunity to tell her he did not want any more children with her and that she should consider a hysterectomy. My mother refused. She was very young and didn't want the surgery in case she divorced my father and remarried. In addition to her youth and concerns, surgery, in those days, wasn't all that safe either.

She told him, he should consider the surgery himself and reminded him it takes two to tango. He never planned to have children but didn't make any particular effort to stop making them either. He assumed it was the woman's responsibility to take care of the prevention. Miraculously, my mum recovered and two years later she was pregnant again.

My mother, still in her early twenties, was young, alluring, charismatic very inexperienced, and delighted to be having another baby. She had a good feeling about this baby, whose heart she could hear beating inside her. In fact, prior to becoming pregnant, she had a dream that angels delivered her with a baby boy from heaven. My father again left her alone near the end of her pregnancy. This time she didn't waste any time. She registered at the local hospital and checked in when she was due to give birth. None of her family members were around but she took care of herself and made my father pay for her hospital expenses and private room.

Prisoner of Thought

The second baby was another boy. She called him Siavash, after the ancient Persian hero who died for love. She came home from the hospital to chaos.

My father was in trouble. His business was in jeopardy. He was at the end of his financial rope. In an attempt to hide his desperation, he lavished his family and network of friends with parties and gifts to make them believe he was still wealthy. He had a non-stop parade of guests at the house, creating a load of household chores for a woman who just had given birth. She had no time to rest and no support help. Her days seemed endless.

She was also burdened by the jealousy and resentment of my father's other family. The constant sarcasms and negative comments from my father's brother and eldest sister seemed to eat into her soul. My father ordered her about and used her, more or less, as a servant. Mum felt lost and lonely. My father banned her from communication with anyone outside of his approved circle of friends and family. She was prohibited from walking by herself, doing her own grocery shopping or having her friends for tea. Just as many wealthy men still do in present day Iran, he did what he knew best to claim his supposed rights as a man and a husband to his new wife. My overly possessive father set a rule that my mother always must be accompanied by a trusted person from my father's family or his network of close friends or workers, mostly women of her family. Overwhelmed by her circumstances, my mother, who had no friends or family members of her own, became severely depressed and required immediate psychiatric help. She was 21 years old.

She had a severe lapse from reality. One day while breastfeeding her baby, her arms went numb and the baby fell to the floor. Although her eyes were open she was unable to wake up and feel or hear anything. She slipped into a vegetative state. She had no sense of who she was. My father rushed her to their family doctor who warned him, "She is not ill physiologically, but is extremely depressed." The doctor told him to let her speak her opinion freely and if she broke or tore something not to stop her. He added, "If you stop her she will either end up in a psychiatric hospital, or in the grave yard."

It was hard for him to comprehend and accept her condition since he wanted to be the center of everyone's attention. Reluctantly, he agreed to follow the doctor's orders. It was several weeks before mum responded to treatment but some months later she was in better spirits although her breast milk dried up and she had to bottle feed her son powdered milk. After a year of counseling and medication, my mother was better emotionally and physically but still not completely cured.

One afternoon, she was busy cooking a simple dinner for herself and another dish for my father when he arrived, telling her his oldest sister would come for dinner. Although not yet fully recovered, she was still expected to be Mrs. Perfect in serving her husband and putting up with his demands. She told him, "I am not prepared. I only cooked for you and me." He told her it was ok; they would share whatever they had and add some snacks. Thinking it was a good idea, she welcomed her sister-in-law. That night, my father's sister abused her more than ever. She insulted mum and her family; saying she was an opportunist who had married my father for his wealth. She said mum was just a prostitute, trying to find a new home. Auntie endlessly insulted mum as my father sat silent. Increasingly uncomfortable, my mum was at the end of her rope. Humiliated, she silently wiped the tears from her eyes. Mum tried to remain calm, but auntie kept bullying, made no apologies for the insults and paid no attention to the warning signs or my father's gentle admonitions of "Sis, keep quiet." As the accusing comments progressed, her tears turned into anger, anger turned to hate, and hate to rage.

My mother lost it for the first time in her life. My father's sister would probably have been killed if her brother had not rescued her. Mum expressed her anger physically for the first time. She wasn't just angry with my father for taking advantage of her. She was angry with everyone who tried to take charge of her life and for all the insults and gossip she had endured.

When her anger exploded, she tore her dress, broke most of the antique china my father owned and in retaliation even slapped his face as he so frequently slapped her. She has always maintained the she does not remember much of that night except that she felt like an unstoppable hulk and never felt greater in her life. After that night, believing the rage of emotions was her cure, she didn't touch the depression medications anymore.

The next day, she decided to change. For years, my father had instructed her in how to dress, how to talk and how to live. Now she was determined to live for herself. She sported a long ponytail and wore over sized shirts, long skirts with a pair of cotton pajamas beneath her skirt, in case her skirt was blown up by wind and socks pulled over her pajamas. From her pictures, she looked like an Amish woman in a Muslim country. My father wanted her to look ugly so she would have no self-esteem and would not leave him. In his mind, if she looked good, she would marry a younger man. He often teased her, "If I die, I know you are going to marry a younger man."

Mum Comes Out of the Shadows

The next time my father brought a guest to his home office, he sent one of his workers to tell mum to make some tea. She dismissed the worker, telling him she would bring the tea when it was ready. She made the tea and dressed up in a sleeveless, décolleté silk mini-dress she had sewn. After that pivotal night, she wore it with no pantyhose. She put on heavy evening make up and let her beautiful long, curly, blond hair fall down her back in a sexual way, swinging it on her shoulders as she walked into the room. She left the tea on his desk in the office and slammed the door behind her. The guest was appropriately shocked.

My father ran home from his next-door office saying, "What were you thinking?" She answered, "If you don't like what you see, we can get a divorce. I will run my life my way, not yours, or we don't have to live together." Knowing she had changed, he reluctantly agreed but told her not to wear that dress anymore. He belatedly enjoyed her culinary skills, her fresh new look and the way she carried herself among other woman. Seeing how much everyone praised her, my father started looking my mother's way again. She carried herself well and looked like a true lady. My father liked to take her around to show her off.

Shortly after she began feeling better, her womanly intuition warned her something was wrong. On a hot summer day, she awoke from an afternoon nap and noticed her youngest son, Siavash, now nine months old and his older brother, Khosro, almost three, were missing. In a panic, she ran to the factory, asking the workers if they have seen the children. They had not. She searched every corner and found her stepson, Ali Junior, who was now 17 years old, in his usual hide out, a back room in the factory. He was half naked, his pants down around his knees. Siavash was on the floor, his diapers' open, and Ali was trying to rape him. In his mind, this was a quest for justice and revenge on our father for marrying my mother and on her for replacing his own mother. My mother screamed, threw him off, picked up the baby, grabbed Khosro and took them away. She asked Khosro, a smart three year old, if he had seen Ali doing this before. Khosro answered, "He always did this to me. It hurts, kill him."

My mother, seeing her son being abused, felt the anger that only a mother can feel. Without saying anything to anyone, she asked one of the neighbors to take care of the children for the night. She went after Ali Junior, who had run away. My mum waited for nightfall. She knew he would be back. She had a thick wooden club hidden. Hiding away all the long night, he finally came home, thinking my mum must be asleep. Mum had closed the entrance between the factory and home and locked the home door from inside with a large lock. Ali Junior didn't yet appreciate that, as we say in the Persian language, an angry lioness is equally as dangerous as the lion, if not more so. She called him outside into the yard, like a gladiator looking for blood and told him to pick up something to defend himself. He thought my mother was joking and started laughing, boasting that he was much stronger than she. Then he picked up a knife. She rushed him, grabbed his arm and twisted it, breaking it in two places. She kicked and beat him nearly to death, broke his nose and made him cry like a kitten. She swore that if he came near her children again she would kill him. She told him: "If you touch my kids one more time, I will send your pieces to your mother." She threw him out on the street, like yesterday's trash.

The next morning, an army of my father's family, in the company of my eldest uncle who we barely knew, appeared. He ranted and swore at my mother like a warrior, threatening to sue her. She went outside with the same club in hand and asked him, "Why are you swearing at me?" He said, "You beat this child," my mum said, "did this child tell you what he did? Did he tell you the whole story?" He said, "No, but I am sure he didn't do anything to deserve this punishment." My mum approached him and said, "If you don't get your army off my pavement in five minutes, I will make sure the police arrests you and your entire family for conspiracy and crimes against a minor, for molesting my minor boys." He said: "What?" She said: "You heard me, he hurt my children, he was about to rape my baby, I pulled him off the baby." The entire crowd dropped their head in shame and disappeared.

The family never spoke again about this incident. My father, who knew his own son, and had his own secret, never mentioned the incident to my mum. Soon after this altercation, he sent Ali Junior to the United States where he still lives quietly.

Some years previously, before the end of her last year of life, my father's mother confessed to my mother the deep, dark secret that my father had hidden all his adult life. Although my grandmother adored her son, one day she started crying for no apparent reason. My mother asked her why was she was crying. She said, "I need to tell someone this story before I die. Even though I didn't know how to protect my daughter and tried to forgive myself for what happened to her, I am afraid God will not forgive me if I remain silent." Then in great anguish she said, "I want someone to know, Ali Senior raped my oldest daughter, who was never married. The shock effect of the rape was too much for her to bear; she hemorrhaged and died a few days after her seventeenth birthday." This was the scandal he had come to Abadan to escape.

My father had always flaunted his presumed wealth but mum was the last person to know about his business. In a rare incident, either wanting to show his trust in her or as part of a scheme, he showed her some contracts, checks and other business documents and asked her to do some accounting for him. Although my mother was hardly an accountant, she could tell with a glance at the books that the amount of money going out of their accounts was much greater than the amount coming in. It was clearly a warning sign. She quickly realized that they were very much in debt and could not afford the lifestyle they were living. Determined to help him, she questioned my father about the personal expenses. His trust vanished instantly when she criticized him, saying that they could not afford the life style he portrayed to others. He snapped, "It is not your business. I shouldn't have shown you these." That was the end of her involvement in his business. In the meantime, mum had problems of her own to worry about.

DR. MOSSADEGH,
1951 MAN OF THE YEAR

During his reign, Mohammad Reza Shah campaigned for women's education and the development of new economic programs as his father did. One program was land reform, termed the White Revolution because it was relatively bloodless. The Shah took land from the rich and gave it to the poor. This project did not fare well in stimulating Iran's economy, primarily because the allotted lands were insufficient to be viable for agricultural purposes. Many people lost their redistributed lands. During this period, in the 1960s, my grandfather lost all of his land through a subsidized irrigation project. In the years 1948 to 1978, the development plan went through five stages of varying lengths of time. The sixth stage, commenced in 1978, was not completed because of the 1979 revolution which overthrew the Shah. During the course of this economic disaster, there were other obstacles in the path of many self-made millionaires.

Mohammad Mossadegh, born May 19, 1882, emerged as a national leader. His father had worked for Naser din Shah. His mother was a granddaughter of Prince Abass Mirza. Mossadegh left Iran in 1909 to study law in Paris and Switzerland, received his doctorate in 1913 and returned to Persia (Iran) in 1914 to practice law. In 1935, Mossadegh was arrested and imprisoned until 1944 when Reza Shah went into exile. He returned to politics and the Shah soon died in exile.

In 1951, Mossadegh became Prime Minister. His first act was to enforce the Oil Nationalization Bill, declaring Iran's oil to be the rightful property of Iran, nullifying the development contracts under which Britain had developed the oil industry. He held that Iran's main natural resource was being unfairly depleted. Dr. Mossadegh defended the rights of Iran in a lawsuit brought against Britain in the United Nations Security Council. Mossadegh resigned when the Shah refused to transfer the War Ministry to his cabinet. Parliament chose another Prime Minster. The people, who loved Mossadegh, angered by his dismissal, protested against the new government and the Shah. After four days of bloody protest, the Shah and his army were defeated and Mossadegh was named Prime Minister.

Once in control of the Defense Ministry, Mossadegh cleaned out the corrupt officers, angering his opposition in the royal court. In 1953, these officers, aided by the clergy, conspired against him in circulating a story that he was en route to the Royal Palace to ask the Shah to leave the country, planning to use this as an excuse to murder him but he escaped the ambush.

Mossadegh announced a referendum to elect a new cabinet in August 1953. On August 16, 1953, the Shah sent a dismissal notice by Royal Guard to Dr. Mossadegh. His guards arrested the Royal Guard instead. On hearing this, Shah escaped the country for Italy. People showed incredible support for Mossadegh with massive protests for two days.

Mossadegh, in an effort to avoid bloodshed, surrendered a few days later to the new Prime Minster, General Zahedi. The Shah returned from Italy and Dr. Mossadegh was given a military trial. He went to prison for three years and remained under house arrest until he died of cancer in 1964 at age 84. He was chosen 'Man of the Year' by Time magazine in 1951.

The people of Iran never forgot his sacrifices. His idea for taking on the Shah remains in the heart and soul of the people, even though he died many years before my generation was born. Unfortunately, many years later, his memory is taken for granted. The light he shed on the path to freedom for future Iranian generations was stolen and used against his beliefs to remove the Shah from power and replace him with yet another dictatorship.

My Guardian Angel

Uncle Yadollah was barely out of college when he got his first job. By the time he had been at his job for five months, his bosses were amazed and impressed. He taught himself English and won first prize in the national academic competition. He raced up the corporate ladder at his new job. In less than two years he became Vice President of a government company. He seemed destined to be the pride and savior of the family.

He was a political observer, participated in meetings of many groups and wanted to know about the future of Iran. Moving to Tehran for a chance of finding a better job, he was disappointed by what he saw in the capital. He actively participated in protests in defense of Dr. Mossadegh and like many others was chased by the Shah's soldiers. He narrowly escaped death when soldiers shot his friends. Soon after these incidents, he fell very ill.

Unfortunately, soon after his promotion to Vice-President, he was diagnosed with leukemia. Mum visited him in the hospital but he didn't tell her how serious his illness was. His company paid for ten months of surgeries, experimental drugs and all medical bills. Despite the efforts of great doctors, multiple operations and voluminous blood transfusions, nothing seemed to work. In addition to worrying about her brother, mum had started to worry about her own financial situation from the day her husband showed her the business documents. She knew that, sooner or later, his sand castle would crumble and she and her children would go down with it.

Despite her warnings, my father kept spending the way he always had, buying expensive gifts for his entire family and still more land. He saw himself as the head of the family and the envy of his siblings. To maintain his reputation as a 'millionaire,' he bought cars and more equipment that he didn't need. He bought land on speculation, borrowing at high interest rates. In the depression that followed the white, or 'bloodless,' revolution, he could not find buyers and lost millions of hectares to foreclosure.

Ever since mum's first baby, Yadollah had promised her that he would return in the spring and save her and her children from this marriage. That promise was never fulfilled. On December 1, 1963 he died of leukemia. He was twenty-five years old. Four hundred and fifty employees and colleagues took part in his funeral. He had promised, if he got up from his deathbed, to marry the nurse who cared for him for six months and fell in love with him. He asked my mother's opinion of the girl, saying he wanted mum to be close to her and their children but he would not marry the nurse unless she gave her blessing. He expressed his wish to have a child but that wish went to the grave with him. My mother was content that he didn't leave a child because she feared she could not look at the child and explain what happened to her or his daddy. His coffin was transferred from Tehran to the holy city of Qom for burial. The nurse ended her own life the day after he died.

Traditionally, Iranians prefer to be buried near holy places rather than their own birthplace. It is scripted in the Muslim religion, Shiah in particular, that the holy 'saints' will save the spirit from any minor punishment or the loneliness and the fear of the afterlife that is taught in our religion. Qom is Imam Reza's sister's burial place and considered quite holy by Shiah.

While he was in the hospital seriously ill, he said that he had never forgiven himself for forcing his sister to marry someone inappropriate. To help her, he asked his bosses to hire my mother in the company where he was working. To honor his request, after his death, the company made many inquires about my mother, trying to hire her, but grandma made sure the executives were never able to contact my mother.

On his deathbed, his last testament was, "If I ever have a niece from Shokooh call her Ghazal." Seven years later, I was born in the spring. I believe that he has been watching over me ever since my birth.

My mother, who was pregnant for the third time during his treatment, had no clue he had passed away. Her parents didn't call her for his burial; her mother believing the newborn was a death wish. In his last letter to mum, he had written that he would come for a visit but he never showed up. A few days after his death, she gave birth to her youngest son, whom she named Manoocheher after one of the first kings in Persian history. Yadollah's death remained the family's secret for almost two months until one day when my mother's younger brother, Asgar, phoned her and said he needed to see her, right away. Before she could ask why, he hung up. Panicked by the mysterious call, she rushed to Khoram-Abad. She arrived at midnight but wasn't allowed to enter her parents' house for more than forty-five minutes while everyone inside changed from black mourning clothes, hoping, through some convoluted reasoning, to spare her the shock of walking into an obvious wake.

Knowing how close the two brothers and sisters were, my grandfather did not immediately allow her to enter the house that my grandmother had converted into a virtual shrine to the deceased, displaying his possessions and arranging his clothes on his bed. She and her brother had grown closer than ever after he saved her life. He had already been buried for over forty days, denying her the opportunity to say farewell. The day after her arrival, she phoned my father, who had already been notified of my uncle's death but didn't tell her, uncharacteristically sharing my grandparents concern over her reaction. She asked him to join her for a memorial service for her brother. My father refused, sending instead their eldest son, a five-year-old child.

When my mother returned, after a week of mourning, from the memorial service she had organized to say her own farewell, my father would not let her into the house. He told her that nothing belonged to her and began swearing at her in front of her children and the entire neighborhood. With the help of some of my father's factory workers who lived next door, she got inside the house to find that his first wife had moved in. The humiliation had only begun.

Six months after Yadollah's death, my grandmother and her youngest daughter, my auntie Mollook, came to visit my mother. One afternoon my mother left her son, Manoocheher, with them to do some grocery shopping. At her return she was furious at what she saw. Her mother and sister had punished her six months old baby. She asked them why they did that. My grandma answered, "Your baby brought death to my son; it is your son's fault that my son died. I want to kill him." My mum tried, unsuccessfully, to be calm and reminded her that it was she that drove my uncle to the edge. So much so, that he often played alone in the fields that were covered by high voltage wires that research shows can cause blood cancer in human and animals. Granny didn't blame herself for driving him and everyone else nuts by her backward notions and stubbornness. She saw herself as the owner of her children instead of their parents. My mother realized that she could never convince her mother that her superstitions were groundless and asked her to leave her home

Father Bankrupt

Shokooh was only twenty-four and had three small children. Her brother, her rock, her supporter and best friend in the whole world was dead and, now, her husband wanted to divorce her. She was crushed. Even though she had wanted out of the marriage from the moment she was tricked into it; now that he humiliated her she would not go easily. Not respecting my mother, he didn't honor the death of her brother and had set up his daughter's wedding while she was still mourning.

He knew his downfall was imminent and unavoidable and privately had decided to celebrate his daughter's union to her cousin, before his bankruptcy. He knew this was his last party before he packed his bags to spend some time in jail. That night, my mother asked my father to give the children some money and land and told him she would be gone by sunrise. He refused and said, "Tonight is my daughter's wedding night. I want you to serve her and assist her with her every need."

There was little my mother could do. As angry as she was with my father, she wished no ill will or harm to her stepdaughter. To demonstrate how little he cared for my mother, he gave his daughter my mother's Victorian 24K gold coin, and her fur jacket that he had bought her as a gift for the birth of their first son.

She prayed for strength and, perhaps, revenge. For the next two months, everything seemed relatively quiet. My father was a smooth man and apparently had a few new business deals. Mum continued to wear mourning clothes and waited for the next shoe to drop.

One evening, while she was cooking dinner, my father arrived in an obvious rush. Normally he was cool, calm and collected and very charming but that day, his face was pale, he was unusually nervous and was shaking. She asked him if he was sick. He said he was in a rush and asked if there was anything ready to eat. A few minutes later there was a knock at the door. Before he could move, five year old Khosro ran and opened the door. A squad of policemen entered with guns drawn and arrested him. The police had been watching the house all day; knowing that he would come home. He had not cared enough to tell her the truth before the police arrived; not even a hint to prepare her to cope with the shock of his arrest. She instantly inherited the broken business stigma and felt the pressure on her shoulders. She could not go back to her parents and had no support. She sobbed and prayed simultaneously for hours before deciding to find a way.

His lavish spending on his friends and family finally brought him down. None of his so-called 'friends' helped him or posted bond for his release from jail. His own family, the benefactors of much of his largess, considered him a disgrace and would not mention his name in public.

My mother was left alone that night with one Toman, worth about a dollar at the time, in my father's office safe. Helpless, with three children to feed and no one to turn to, she was stuck. She went to see my father in jail, and asked him what she could do. He asked her to get a lawyer. Not knowing how to hire a lawyer or where to go to find one, she felt overwhelmed by the task. She hoped and prayed for a miracle.

My father was a well-known man in Abadan. Rumors of his arrest became the talk of the town. A few days after my father's arrest, her miracle appeared in the person of an influential judge who had been sitting on the bench of the Supreme Court in Tehran for more than forty years. A competent jurist, he lost his position due to his addiction to opium. The judge surfaced in Abadan; seeking a hideout to escape his demons.

In the early 1960s, the Shah was under pressure from his western allies to clean up the corruption and drug trafficking that was becoming a part of organized crime in Iran. The Shah himself planned and orchestrated the 'bloodless' revolution to centralize power, put money in the hands of ordinary people and create a balance between the very rich and very poor in Iran's society.

The Safaivds and Qajar dynasty introduced opium into Iran in the late 1800s. Many people were using one form or another of opium, which is harvested much like a field of cottonseeds. The easy growing poppies brought great fortunes to many people but a great deal of misery to a great many more. Iran needed drug control before the country became the next drug cartel. In desperation, the Shah ordered a ban on all production and use of the drug, except for medicinal use. The drugs were once sold by the kilogram at local corner stores and cafes but now the use or sale of any amount was sufficient to receive severe punishment, presumably regardless of rank or social status. The Shah and his family were, of course, above the law and years later some of the Shah's own siblings died from overdoses of cocaine or other drugs.

The rules were very strict about drug use and there were thousands of arrests. Capital punishment is still very much in practice in Iran. Many big dealers and repeat offenders received the death sentence if they did not become sober. Others died when they couldn't buy the drugs on which their lives had become dependent.

Not even a Supreme Court judge was exempt. The judge needed a place to hide and a way to feed himself. His search for a fresh start had brought him to my mother's door in Abadan. He had heard about my fathers' arrest through conversation and sought out my mother. He told her he had heard about her situation and could help get her husband out of prison. He gave her his business card and asked her to call him if she was interested in hiring him. She told him she could only pay him when her husband got out of jail. He accepted her offer and was hired on a contingency basis.

The judge had the experience but since he had retired himself to get away, he couldn't attend court sessions. Mum had to do it herself. He explained the law to my mother and wrote down the arguments. She worked as his legal secretary and mouthpiece for ten long years. Three months later, with a lot of hard work, my father got out of prison. For two years after he went bankrupt, my father hid from his creditors who wanted him dead.

The only assets mum had left were the household items and some Persian carpets. Afraid his creditors would take everything away the next day, she decided to auction off all the Persian carpets, fancy dishes and anything else in the house that could be liquidated into cash. That would enable her and her children to survive for a couple of months.

My father had borrowed money, not from wealthy people who could afford lawyers, but from the very poor. Very much like the executives involved in the Enron fiasco, he made himself a fortune and lived a lavish life style with dirt-poor people's money. The crowd of three hundred creditors included retirees who had given him their life savings, single mothers and grandmas who took care of orphan children. My mother's heart went out to them. Some of these people had lost everything and were so poor they would have to become panhandlers if mum decided to take the high road and find a way not to pay them their money. Mum cried on their shoulders and cried for their pain.

My mother worked as an unpaid assistant to the lawyer for ten years to recover some land and money before the household was solvent again. On the day of her first court hearing, mum, unwittingly, wore a beautiful suit. A woman, from whom my father had borrowed money, approached my mother and told her, "The way you dress and present yourself is the reason your husband gets away with the fraud he commits against poor people." To change her image, she burnt all her fancy clothes that very day, leaving her with two washed out dresses. She now looked like the poor people she had to face in the courtroom, as indeed she was. She didn't want people see her as the rich man's wife. She was trying to salvage what was left to save her children.

Mum's Life in Danger

In the mean time, she was facing another challenge. A life threatening tumor and the loss of a baby boy were among the stream of events she was to face.

On two different occasions, the growth of a tumor around her spinal cord paralyzed her from the neck down, compelling her to stay in bed for hours, unable to move her arms or legs. Devastated and aggravated by the pain, she was forced to visit her doctor. Her physician told her that a tumor had developed among her right shoulder nerves, close to the spinal cord, causing the numbness in her right arm and fingers. She had to bear the pain until she could find a way to come up with the money for the surgery. Her doctor warned her that if the tumor was not taken out right away it could permanently paralyze her. The rare operation had never been done in Iran. The doctors gave her a fifty percent chance to survive the surgery.

Weighing the money versus a fifty-fifty life or death chance of survival, she decided to take a chance. Money, however, proved to be the nastier of the two devils. After a delay of a couple of months, she finally decided to ask her parents for help. They reluctantly lent her the money for her operation. She said her goodbyes. Yadollah appeared to her in a dream, telling her she was going to be ok. Confident that he was watching over her and her children, she took the risk and faced the brutal, ten-hour surgery. After regaining consciousness, she was in severe pain for four months.

Dr. Javady, the renowned surgeon, who saved her life, received national recognition. Sadly, he was killed in revenge a year later in a car accident set up by an obsessive stalker, the husband of one his patients, who thought the surgeon had killed his wife. The lady had not made it out alive from one of his difficult surgeries. Dr. Javady bled to death on a remote side road. When he was transferred to the hospital named after him, no one was able to save his life.

After her surgery, mum also had to face the loss of an unborn baby boy. The health of the baby was a great concern to the surgeon because of the large dosage of morphine and an array of other painkillers she had been given for three months after the surgery. Her doctor recommended an abortion. It was necessary but it wasn't an easy decision. Her decision was a reflection of my father's cold-heartedness. Recently, she confessed to me that my father told her it was his money, his baby and ordered her to have the abortion. She said that he gave her the same lecture when she was pregnant with me but she didn't have the heart to kill me.

Those were not easy years. She had to face ludicrous accusations and a false arrest, orchestrated by my father's creditors. He had been in hiding for almost two years. My mother had no idea of his whereabouts. In an attempt to locate him, his creditors arranged to have my mother publicly arrested for helping a fugitive. At the meat market, while shopping for groceries for her children's lunch, she was arrested in front of her friends and neighbors. With her faded black veil falling down, she was dragged to jail where she fasted and refused to eat or drink for twenty-four hours as she proclaimed her innocence. Ultimately, my mother was exonerated and the conspirators were jailed for their duplicity.

In those years, mum frequently visited her brother's grave and often dreamed about him. In her dreams he showed her his life and his companions. He told her that he knew she was in a great deal of pain and begged her to stop wearing the black mourning clothes that she still wore five years after his death. He told her he was happy where he was and by wearing mourning clothes she constantly reminded him of the life he could never have and he didn't want to be reminded any more. He told her that he had moved on and so should she.

He also warned her that a member of her family was in great danger; frightened, she woke up. She didn't have the courage to face another death in her family. She thought it would be her father, who suffered a great deal after losing his son, but things were closer to her than she imagined. Nervous, at her deceased brother's posthumous request, she went shopping for clothes and celebrated a traditional New Year 1967. Wearing pink for the first time in years, she visited her close friends for a few hours.

Coming home, she felt a great sadness. Soon, she noticed her youngest son's face was completely pale. Scared, she took him to the hospital but the doctors couldn't find anything wrong. A few hours later, he became nauseous. She knocked on the neighborhood doctor's door. The doctor looked at him and told her to take him to the hospital right away. When she arrived at the hospital, a nurse took Manoocheher away and immediately rushed to the operating room to tap his spinal fluid. He had come down with a case of meningitis. That was a year of a meningitis epidemic in Abadan. There was no vaccine available in Iran. Ninety percent of the patients were children under twelve. Only a few survived.

Unexpected Addition to the Family

Until my 29th birthday, I had never blown out candles on a birthday cake. I had never received a birthday present from anyone, other than my mother. It is not about cake or candles; it is about being remembered. I didn't choose to come into this world. I didn't want to come into the family in which I was born. I don't want them to remember me in my death; I wish they cared to remember me in my life. I am not unique; millions of women like me faced a destiny they didn't choose. It is not fun to come into this world unwanted and unloved.

In the early 1970s, eight years had passed since the night my father had gone to debtor's prison. For nearly a decade, my mother had gone to extreme lengths to make sure her family had a roof over their head and food on their table. She helped the boys with their school and tried to manage and balance her work and fulfill her duties as a loving, caring mother. To save my father, she had sold everything and for years she had existed near starvation because she didn't have any money to feed her boys. She even washed off bread that has been exposed to rat droppings and was intended only to feed family pets. She lived on a threadbare, pileless carpet, with no refrigerator, drinking near-boiling water, and trying to rest in non air-conditioned, humid, moldy rooms, sweating in Abadan's 140° F degree summer temperatures. By this time, my mother had paid most of my father's debts and he was home again. Things were finally getting back to normal.

My mother had been taking birth control pills but was having bad side effects. Her doctor suggested that she should stop taking them, predicting the chance of her getting pregnant was very slim. My mother decided that she didn't want more children and asked her doctor to tie her tubes. Her doctor said she needed her husband's permission. Mum decided to take her chances off the pill.

When she discovered she was pregnant with me, she remembered that she had always wanted a girl and when I was born she was happier than she had ever been. Eight years had passed since she had held a baby of her own in her arms. She didn't think that would ever happen again but about nine months, two days, seven hours, and fifteen minutes later, at twelve noon on a beautiful spring Wednesday, I came along. Khosro was the happiest boy of the family. When he heard that there was a new baby girl added to the family, he danced on the street and told everyone in the neighborhood.

However, the momentary happiness didn't last long. The reality of our financial situation required her to leave me with others and work very hard outside of our home. Customarily, a grandmother tends to a baby for the first forty days. In my case, my grandmother, the only family member who could help, claimed, after a week, to be ill. That, of course, proved to be a lie. The real reason was, she wanted to go back to her life. As years passed, she finally told my mother that she left because she felt insecure around my father.

Apparently my father had tried to take advantage of my mother's absence. He had cornered her younger sister, a 20 year old married woman, and hugged and kissed her sexually. And, he had tried to touch her mother while she was asleep. My dad, who was a free man now, was rarely around and was no help when he was. He brought only agony, ordered people around and seemed unable to do anything right. Friends could only do so much. Mum had no choice but to leave me with her sons, who ranged in age from eight to thirteen, and saw me as a toy as much as a little baby girl. She left the boys with careful instructions on how to take care of me, but there were still mishaps—a swallowed curtain hook that nearly choked me to death, electric shocks from an old iron, pneumonia, a three month period of bloody diarrhea caused by feeding me the wrong food that nearly killed me, to name a few.

When I was a child, I heard everyone declaring over and over again that my birth was an omen of our family revival; that I brought prosperity back to the family. I never felt deserving of such a credit. My birth perhaps brought joy and unity to the family but it is hardly realistic for me to get credit for something I really had nothing to do with. It was my mother's ten years of sacrifice and effort that paid off. I simply happened to come along at the right time. Whatever the reason, perhaps for the first time ever, there was a sense of freshness in our home. After years of struggle, as Persians put it in a metaphoric wording; there was, at long last, *a light at the end of the tunnel*.

After a decade of her hard work we had a working air conditioner, a few new carpets and a refrigerator to make the daily struggle a little more bearable.

The earliest memory of my childhood goes back to the time my mum left me with my eldest step-sister at her house in Khoram-Shahr while she helped my dad with the transfer of a piece of land she had just won from the court. I was in the hallway when mum arrived, I ran to her arms, crying that I was hungry. She found out that the stepsister had not fed me because I had not been quiet. Mum later told me I was only one year old and wondered how I could remember anything from that young an age.

By the time I was three years old, things were looking up in our house. Our finances had improved a little but not enough to enable us to hire a nanny. Despite the emergence from poverty, my father was extremely unhappy. The bankruptcy had humiliated him and deprived him of his former position. As we say in Persian, 'A man is the king of his own palace.' He saw himself as a king without a kingdom. It was hard for him to face his ego. He only knew himself through what he had accomplished and when he lost his money, he was lost. He saw himself as a self-reliant man. Pleading to my mother to save him wasn't quite his style, but he took full advantage of my mother by shedding crocodile tears and she believed him. Now that everything was coming along and his bankruptcy was under control, he had forgotten the night he went to jail, crying like a kitten for my mum to get him out. Now he was telling her that he didn't need her to free him, everything would have worked out and been resolved just fine.

No one would trust him or lend him money any more. It must have been agonizing for him to see the same crowd, who once thought him wealthy, showing my mother more respect for having saved her failed husband. In 1973, unable to cope with his diminished stature in the business community, he secretly decided to sell the house and factory, and move us to Isfahan province, where he was born. Although mum had worked diligently to get him out of jail and saved his life, he didn't bother to ask her if she was willing to move. Not to mention, he didn't even bother thanking her.

ABADAN BEFORE THE WAR

Before the revolution, Abadan was a clean, industrial city with good living conditions and clean beaches. The city, which was built for the newcomers of the 1940s and 1950s after new sources of oil and gas were discovered, had turned into an industrial/tourist destination.

The climate is tropical. During the hot and humid summers, the temperature rises as high as high as 65° C (140° F).

The sparkling turquoise blue waters of the Persian Gulf teem with gigantic shrimp. Clean, well kept sandy beaches shine in the blazing sun. The abundant date trees remind one of beautiful pregnant women carrying a baby in their belly. As they sway from side to side, their long stems and branches wave in the warm breeze of fresh sea air like long hair on an exotic woman. The date trees cast cool, long shadows. Everywhere, crabs scuttle along or rest from the daily heat. Sunsets are breathtaking when the sun seems to stick his golden face in the water far onto the horizon. As it goes down, ships are sailing home and sea eagles are flying, calling noisily to each other, perhaps saying 'good night.' At dusk, waves wash the warm sands of the shore line. Heat from the land and cool breezes from the Persian gulf create a harmonious, tranquil atmosphere; touched by the gentle motion of date tree leaves, gracefully swimming in the air like a bald eagle.

The moonlight is even more breathtaking than the sunset. When the moon reaches its zenith, it illuminates the sea like a dazzling black pearl around a princess' neck. The music of the sea, the seamen and the fishermen singing their folklore melodies, the cooling breeze, the waving leaves of the date trees and, sometimes, the sounds of the local's weddings create an unparalleled mood for relaxation. Before the revolution, the unexpected hospitality brought westerners closer to Iranians.

Persian music and the dancing of a happy crowd around a fire on the beach, enjoying an array of ethnic southern cuisine; seafood dishes, mixed flavors of old Persian cuisine and recipes from Middle Eastern countries. Westerners left the New World behind as they shared the potluck feast. These were the simple pleasures people cherished and did not take for granted. Even the face of the moon seemed to light up with a smile.

At the peak of Abadan's prosperity, westerners were so mesmerized by the natural beauty, the sunny days and the warm welcome by the people of Abadan that they couldn't refuse the invitation. They came by the thousands and many stayed as long as they could. They brought oil and petroleum workmanship and instructed locals on housing, city engineering, industrial fishing, cultivating agricultural crops, medicine and the technology for every aspect of daily life. The marriage of two very different cultures, Persian and Western, turned Abadan into a paradise for tourists.

The city didn't have high rises. The few tall buildings housed government headquarters. The paucity of tall buildings was due to its zero altitude that allowed seawater to burst into basements. Technology had not yet been developed for building high-rises in the long, narrow city that grew along the beach line. Houses were of simple construction with two, three and four bedrooms, one or two baths and showers, low ceilings and large back yards, mostly designed by the English engineers.

Beautiful boulevards, with tropical decorative palm trees and Amazon forest foliage were seeded to give them an authentic, exotic look. The clean, newly asphalted streets and lanes were favorite places for children to play before bedtime, after the hot midday summer subsided. The city resembled the British colony but no one really cared how the housing looked. People lived in those homes in happy comfort with their families; most with five to seven children. Boys and girls went to the same schools. The oil and gas industry founded the famous, public University of Abadan. One in every five graduates of this university worked as the second generation at the refinery or some sector of this industry their fathers had pioneered.

Their exotic features, sun-kissed olive skin, dark hair and sense of humor easily distinguish the people from the tropical areas of Iran. Most Abadanians came from different parts of Iran and some even from different countries but most people speak Arabic, have Arab relatives and friends or they are the second or third generations of Arabs whose ancestors migrated to Abadan centuries ago. In most families, Arabic is spoken as their second language.

People get along extremely well. Color is not an issue, although people from Kurdish families are considered white. The people of the Arab tribes have extremely dark pigmented skin; having been brought to Persia and neighboring countries during the time of slavery and left behind when Europeans left. Abadanians are not the most eloquently spoken people in the world. There is no prejudice toward anyone. Fars means 'the Persian' in Farsi, which is the Persian language. Their accent ends every word, with a nasal 'm.' Abadan's dialect is a mixture of Farsi, Arabic and Semitic languages and English words used and adopted as a reminder of the English dominance for more than 50 years. Semitic languages are Hebrew and Assyrian. As much as some Arabs and some Jews might hate each other, it is clear that the Arabic language and Hebrew have common roots.

There are a few bad apples in every culture and the diverse society of Abadan wasn't immune from characters such as my greedy grandmother, my charlatan father and many more snakes that covered themselves in different hats. However, generally speaking, most of the Abadan population were honest, sincere, caring, warm hearted and charming. Society tried to shun the bullies and love one another. Nobody really cared who came from where. They referred to each other as Bro, which means' brother.' Men refer to older women as mother, to younger women as sister, and to married women as *Om*, which in Arabic means, mother, adding the name of her first born, as is customary in Arab countries, as a sign of respect.

People of Abadan have a unique bond, which has attracted not only people of different color but also people of different religions. Before the Shah left power, Abadan had a large community of non-Muslims who enjoyed living in peace and freedom alongside their Muslim friends. My mother had plenty of non-Muslim friends growing up. They all love to laugh, sing and dance all night long, regardless of who is who.

The new generation was the dream of the future for the country; beautiful girls, poised, modern, talented and motherly skillful were becoming the mothers of an even better, predominately cosmopolitan generation. Handsome boys, cool, hip, educated, mainly cultured and extremely respectful toward women, were the fathers of the new generation. The male population of Abadan, and southwest Iran, had learned to treat women not as slaves but as their queen bee. The respect toward women is quite apparent in their manners toward their sisters, mothers, and even toward strangers. People of Khuzestan, though culturally different from Kermanshahanians, have in common the same respect toward women.

The older generation of Abadan couldn't have been happier to see the seeds they had planted blossom into a great generation that would take Iran to an even higher place on the platform of history. The early 1970s were pivotal years for Iran and in particular for Abadan. The city was filled with mostly solid citizens and a well-educated young generation, healthy children, that were the starlight of Iran's future.

Arriving in Isfahan

M y father told mum he wanted to take us on a summer trip. I was nearly four years old. Excited, my family traveled in the car, from Abadan to Isfahan, 300 miles inland, in central Iran. It was quite a treat. We packed light and spent three weeks sight seeing, stopping at cities on our way. Life wasn't bad until we reached Isfahan. Our first impression of Isfahan was that it was a dirty, unfriendly old city, much smaller, at that time, than Abadan.

It has been said that Isfahan is located in the center of all the world's deserts. Mystical and unique in its own way; Isfahan was the capital of the Safavids dynasty for more than 200 years.

The beauty of the artwork and the prosperity of this city amazed many archeologists and well-known travelers of ancient times. When Marco Polo traveled through the city he was mesmerized by the enameling artwork and the azure blue mosaic tiles and artwork on the domes of the immense mosques of Nagshe'-Jahan square, where Isfahan's famous Bazaar is located. The artists sit in their private workshops, occupied with creating new artifacts from metals; sometimes precious, such as gold or silver, other times, of materials such as copper, marble or wood or laboriously weaving their famous Isfahan carpets thread by thread.

The Ziandeh River divides the city into north and south divisions. Along its shore, farmers still cultivate their famous local Lengan rice. Astride the river there now lies a city of more than three million. Most people still earn their way working as art gallery owners and manufacturers of the motifs artifacts, miniature statuettes, still produced the old way their fathers did. Gas, oil and various other minerals enrich the province.

The palace of Hasht Behesht, or Chehel-Sotun Palace, is a marvelous, remarkably well preserved 17th century building from the Safavids dynasty era. The pavilion, completed in 1669, was built amidst a vast garden covering an area of 67,000 m² It was part of the Shah Abass' quarters; used mainly as a guest house. The building has a veranda with 18 pillars and a large pool facing the building. The building name was derived from Persian/ Islamic lore but it is nicknamed, 'The 40 Pillars.' In Persian culture, some numbers, including the number 40, are considered lucky or blessed. The second reason for the building's nickname was because the 18 pillars reflected in the pool facing the palace, create a beautiful impression of almost 40 pillars.

Also, in Isfahan, there is a Christian community of Jolfa, where a number of churches are still widely visited and used, including the most important historical church in Iran, the old cathedral commonly known as the Vank.

Isfahan has a rich history, bigger than life itself. Scientists, engineers and architects in ancient times, created amazing, enduring masterpieces with their limited material and equipment. It is hard to grasp how these people brought their brilliant ideas to life with only primitive tools and lantern light. How was it possible to measure everything so accurately that even today, after centuries, scientists and tourists visit the remains of these places in awe? Legend has it, that Sheikh Bah, the man who helped with the design of the subterranean canals, wrote in his book, "Isfahan will never see an earthquake." Although it has been shaken gently, it has not yet faced a disastrous earthquake.

The mesmerizing arch shaped bridges of SiosehPoll and Khajoo, designed by Sheikh Bah and constructed of raw mud, egg shells and brick have been resisting erosion by water for centuries while joining the two parts of the city, carrying millions of feet across their backs. The blue turquoise of the mosaic and the amazing tile work has inspired visitors, including architects from all over the globe. They are even reflected in some of the European cathedrals built in the 1700s. It is hard to grasp the immensity of the mosque domes from below. From above, the mosaics tell stories of the ancient past. The inside of the Shah's Mosque leaves people in awe. If someone stands on the stone marking the center of the dome, he will hear a perfect echo of his own voice, as if he were standing on top of a mountain.

The magnificent, multi-level Safavids Alligapoo palace, built in the early 1700s by Shah Abass from the Safavids Dynasty for his guests' entertainment, has an intricate, unique music room that, although small, makes a perfect sound of every instrument as if it were being recorded in a modern studio. A rooftop swimming pool on the third deck makes every architect wonder, how it was possible to make such a magnificent palace from raw mud in the early 1700s. Standing proud, six stories high on one side, it appears to be a two story building from the garden view.

The Monar-Jonban is yet another unique composite monument and a remarkable engineering feat. The two handcrafted towers still astonish most modern, architects. The monument was built in the early 1200s and contains shaking twin towers, approximately six feet in diameter and sixty feet tall. When someone enters one of the towers, the other starts shaking on its own. Also, tourists can shake the one they are standing within. It is a lifetime experience. A mystery surrounds the towers. The mathematician who designed the towers is buried in the yard of the monument. Engraved on his stone is his desire to leave a legacy behind. Some people believe his masterpiece has something to do with the gravity of the earth under the towers.

Isfahan has been declared the seventh most historical city in the world.

The desert climate, dry winters and year round sunshine has been an element in preserving these national treasures.

People of Isfahan delicately craft art and are dexterous and talented in most avenues of craftsmanship. They are hard working, dedicated artists. The history of Persia records Isfahan evolving as centuries pass.

But the cruelty of its people's hearts has managed to stay stable throughout the times. They can be as hard as the metal from which they are creating an artifact or as warm as the number sign on the dollar bill.

The people of Isfahan are a living paradox. Their kindness fluctuates; depending on the size of the visitor's wallet and how deeply they can dig into it. My culture is not color driven. We don't have racial issues but one color does dominate society; the color green of money. Show them the money and they are kind, otherwise be prepared to see a very different, ugly side of these people.

To assist westerners in comprehending the true nature of the people of Isfahan, I offer a metaphoric explanation.

The attitude of the people of Isfahan is rather like the classic redneck attitude. You can either love them or hate them. The cold behavior of Isfahanians resembles the attitude of the snobbish aristocrats of English nobles in the early 1800s that treated everyone else in the world as commoners. Their funny accent resembles the Germans when they try to speak English and end every word with an 's.' The funny Germans, however, proved to be not so funny after all. They too, thinking they were superior humans and better than the rest of Europe in early and mid 1900s, ignited two World Wars. This sickening, show-off attitude of the wealthy individuals persists to this day.

They have adopted the attitude of the barbaric Saudi Arab rulers and their treatment of women that puts men in a superior position. One slight improvement in the status of women in Iran is that they are permitted to drive a vehicle; whereas women in Saudi, no matter what their rank, still agonize on not having that right. They also have adopted the disloyalty of the French government, toward its allies, which seems to have forgotten it was the Americans, British and Canadians who died on the beaches of Normandy sixty years ago to deliver them from occupation by Nazi Germany. Such disloyalty resembles the characteristic of the people of Isfahan. When they need someone, they unabashedly pretend to be his brother. When they are done, they are done with that person.

Having said all that, not everyone is the same, but fear of being ostracized sometimes forces even good people to pretend they are the same as the rest of crowd. As a Persian proverb says, 'If you want to be safe living in a rough neighborhood among a tough crowd, dress rough, and pretend that you are one of them.'

In Isfahan it is difficult to tell who is genuine and who is not. When it comes to money, everything is for sale. Their integrity, pride, mother, father's grave, heaven, even religion and God are for sale. Nothing is off limits. They are great business people but they are ruthless. In order to earn their way, they have no qualms about lying to the bone. Their only loyalty is to money. The older generation of Isfahan was famous for living a lifetime of misery, hoarding every penny and leaving behind uncounted stacks of cash in hidden places. The new generation might go to bed hungry but must have silver and gold dishes and jewelry to show off at the next party. Fathers suck everyone's blood to give their own children a good start, giving their daughters an impressive dowry that includes everything to fill a four-bedroom house.

People of Isfahan are among the richest in Iran, if not in the world. They are calculating and penny pinching. When their children can barely count their fingers, parents teach them to start earning and saving money. They also teach them that if they can't have what they want, it is ok to use the other kid's. They learn early on and grow up ruthless.

There is a joke about the people of Isfahan saying they will go to heaven's gate but they can't enter because they forgot something in this earthly life. There is another sad joke about a man from Isfahan who cried for a long time to see Mahdy, the Messiah of Muslims, in heaven. His wish was finally granted. On the way to see the Mahdy, the Angel Gabriel gave the man a ride on his wings. It started raining. The man who had been ecstatically happy, suddenly become sad. Gabriel noticed the man's change of mood and asked him why he was sad? In his funny accent, he answered, "I left my soap at the pond. By the time I go back, the rain will wash it away. Then I will be forced to spend another dollar to get a new one. Can you make the rain go away?" Angel Gabriel shook his head, telling the man, "We don't make deals in heaven." and sent the man back to his earthly life.

We excitedly arrived in Isfahan, expecting to stay for a few days, only to discover that my father had tricked us. The summer retreat turned into a lifetime of nightmares. He moved us into one pre-rented room in a two-bedroom house. We shared the 1500 ft² house with the landlord, his wife and their six kids. There was a small kitchen, to which we didn't have access, and one small washroom for fourteen people.

He promised to relocate all our furniture and household goods to a new house in Isfahan. That promise was not doable. He left us behind in Isfahan and flew to Abadan. He came back carrying only his own suitcase. He had auctioned off everything we owned. Even the boy's bicycles and souvenirs and momentums that mum had gathered and kept during her years of hardship. My mother was furious. She did not know the trouble had just begun.

There is a sarcastic Persian proverb referring to people who turn on the charm when they need help and turn it off when they are done. It says, 'His donkey had crossed the bridge.' It means he has succeeded with his plans and is done with whomever he is dealing with. My father's donkey had again crossed the bridge and he was done with my mother.

It was his turn to rule. He had received the money mum earned, bought new cars and restored his business name again. The house that mum worked so hard to keep from foreclosure was sold and he took all the money, not giving her a red cent. The day he sold the house in Abadan, he said not a simple 'Thank you' to her. Instead, he told her it was her duty to help him. If she didn't like it, she could go back to her father. At this point mum had been married for more than 17 years. Her family had made it clear long ago that they didn't want her back. It seemed she had wasted ten of her younger years to save a cynical, thankless man.

They say the first impressions are critical. I recall that at four, he had not left me with a good impression of himself. I remember having my first strong resentment toward him. I thought he must be crazy if he can't see that six of us can't fit into such a small place, particularly since we had grown up in a ten thousand square foot house and factory. Or, I thought, he must have intentions to get rid of us. It was sickening to look at him. The rest of us were miserable. He, on the other hand, was carefree and having a ball.

One of my earliest memories of my father occurred in the first rented house. I prevented the landlord's daughter from injuring our beloved canary. My father arrived home only to see the landlords' daughter burst into tears. I was four years old barely 30 pounds, he was 51 years old, 270 pounds, 6 feet tall. Without waiting for any explanation, he slapped me so hard that it left his handprint on my face. I passed out from fear and pain. To show off, he lied that he had only tried to save the kid from me and pretended he was a good dad and wasn't letting his child abuse anyone. The incident left an unmistakable imprint on my face. The handprint gradually disappeared in a few days but his rash, unpredictable judgment left me with a permanent scar. I forever marked him in my child's mind and heart as a cold-hearted menace and as an untrustworthy, opportunist chauvinist. He has never proven me wrong. I never thought of having a relationship with him.

Whether or not he was living in our home, he constantly blamed my mother for my attitude toward him, accusing her of influencing me. She had nothing to do with my feelings toward him. That was something he had done without any help from anyone. I was a blank canvas. His sarcasm, poisonous words and negative actions painted heinous feelings on my consciousness. He discarded and abandoned me into an environment that left me with no choice but to hate him.

My mother was a tough cookie. She was the positive alternative and role model in my life. She was trying to undo the damage my father inflicted on my spirit, fearing that in the future I would behave as a discarded person with lack of self-worth. Unlike the emotional scars, the physical effects were visible. Outraged by the harsh punishment, when she saw my face, she told him not to touch me again or she would burn everything he owned. He was never to touch me again; in anger or love.

Two months later, he moved us to a different but no more comfortable place. The only thing I really remember from the second place was that my mother cried all the time. Every time she prayed, I would go to her, kiss her face and ask her why she was crying. She would say, "I am crying for my brother." I would kiss her until she smiled. In that year we moved four times, the third time wasn't any better than the other two. Finally, we rented the second floor of an old house from a Jewish family that mum found.

†HE KɪɴD ʝEWɪSH FAᴍɪLY

It is not common in Iran, or any other Muslim country, for Muslims to live in non-Muslim houses but since mum grew up in Abadan with friends of different religions, she decided it was permissible for us to live there. It was a great neighborhood. The house belonged to a super-nice Jewish family. Mullahs, in general, do not speak favorably about Jews but this family and ours developed a strong friendship and bonded for many years to come. Mum would not allow us to live with people with nasty behavior and habits. And she did not want to put up with men landlords who turned on their cheap flattery to try to get to her. Also, she did not want to cause the unwarranted jealousy this behavior provoked in their wives. My mum, although, burdened with all the pain of living with my father, was still beautiful when she dressed up.

The owner and his wife both were born and raised in Isfahan. They were from prominent families. Mr. Sassoness was quite a well-known individual in Isfahan's Bazaar. He was a rabbi in his synagogue and was a trusted middleman for a lot of merchants and business people.

Trust is a rarity among the people of the province of Isfahan. Mr. Sassoness was the exception. In my childhood imagination he set an example of trustworthiness. His ancestors had come to Iran at the time of King Darius the Great. The family loved Iran as their own country, which, in deed, it had been for many centuries. They celebrated Norooz and had given to society succeeding generations of doctors and engineers. They spoke an accented dialogue of Isfahan Farsi, mixed with Hebrew; otherwise, nothing they did was similar to other people. They were a minority in the country, sympathized with our family and understood our problems perfectly.

After a short while our commonalities grew stronger. Their youngest daughter, Shahin, looked like a goddess of Venus. She was about 5'11"and her long flat blond hair hung to her waist. Her external beauty and internal kind heart made her an incredibly attractive and desirable person. Her family was so afraid for her safety that she was not allowed to walk alone. After finishing post secondary school she still couldn't find a job. During the day, when mum took me out, she asked to come with us. Mum took care of her as if she was my sister. Shahin held my hand like an older sister taking care of her younger. I can never forget those days.

I wasn't the only one admiring her beauty and kind heart. Khosro had become quite fond of her and apparently worked up the courage to talk to her. Mum noticed the attraction and brought it to her parent's attention, asking her father's blessing if Khosro should marry Shahin. The whole family loved us very much but said if they gave their daughter to a Muslim boy, their community would shun them. Mum never wanted that to happen. In years to come, Shahin was given to a man who took her to California. From the reports we heard, she didn't end up living a fairy tale but had a difficult life. Although I was a child, I knew they were meant for each other. Years later, Khosro married a Muslim girl that mum did not approve and she shunned him as well.

Friendship aside, we had some troubles with their house. It was very old and near collapse. In 1975, when we moved in, it was already well past its prime and should have been registered as a heritage building. It had observed more than a half-century of history. There was no air-conditioning for the hot summers and no heating system for the winter and, like the rest of the city, it had no sewage system. It could be brutal, winter and summer, in the high, arid climate of Isfahan and the smell from the sewage wells was disgusting. Unlike Abadan, where the sewage system was mandatory, in Isfahan, people had to voluntarily apply for sewage service and pay for the installation. Of course, almost no one cared to pay the fees. So, the yucky smell of the family wastewater and the marching of the entire fly population over our food had become part of our lifestyle.

While the flies amused people with their dances over the food, they also infected them with the newest bacteria and delivered new diseases. The infectious bite marks were obviously the cause of most of the past epidemics that wiped out quite a lot of people. Even after medicine became widely available, some still had bite marks on their skin that, without the medical technology, could have been deadly. The flies dancing did not amuse me nor was I looking forward to a scarred skin and health hazards. It was a nightmare for me. Due to my age and health problems, I was the most vulnerable. I was picking up all the new diseases as fast as a fly could pass them on.

In our first winter, I came down with the second case of pneumonia of my life. This time, it was pretty severe. At five years old I didn't know what was happening to me but I recall one night my mum woke my father up and he carried me, for the first and the last time in my life, to the nearby hospital. I was in the hospital for a few hours and in the early morning I was sent home. In the early morning when we were sent home, my father sent Siavash to get my prescription from the nearby pharmacy. My prescription came to nearly $400. My father was reluctant to pay it but my mum finally convinced him it was cheaper than a funeral. This is probably the most money my father spent on me in my entire life.

We didn't have any recreation and mum didn't like for any of us to play in the yard or in the lane. When we ran on the second floor, the roof over our landlord shook like a weeping willow in the fall wind. I didn't know how bad it was, until one day I saw it myself. I was ready to run out of the door, thinking it was an earthquake. Our landlord smiled and kindly requested of my mother, "Please tell your sons not to run."

Shortly after I recovered from my latest near death experience, I started kindergarten. One day, early on, I came home and told my mother that I wouldn't be going back to school any more. Mum asked me why. I told her about two boys who were touching me from behind. Back in Iran, many men take great pleasure in disrespecting women by groping them in public or directing degrading salutatory insults toward them. These boys were old enough to copy the behavior from someone in their life. My mother went to school and talked to the principal but since the father of these two boys was an influential man, the principal refused to address the issue.

In the Iranian culture, boys are regarded as superior. A numbskull boy is favored over a Mensa-eligible girl simply because he is a boy. I expected her to go into a rage against the boys' father and do something about it but she was simply too busy with her own boys. She came home and told me she had been informed that it was my responsibility to prevent these boys from touching me. I refused to go back to school and for the remainder of the year I relied on help from my brothers and mum; not a satisfying educational experience.

The boys and I, like any other kids, used to fight all the time. When they were angry with me they would slap me on the back of my head, which was both painful and humiliating. I complained to mum a dozen times but she didn't take me seriously. I hated hearing the dismissive cliché, 'they are boys.' "So what?", I thought. She never punished them so I decided to do it for her. I pondered for days, trying to come up with a plan to stop them from pestering me. I was, after all, only five years old and my alternatives were limited.

A few days later, at about 11:00 p.m., I let them slap my head one last time. I asked my mother to do something about it. She said, ever so gently, in a very loving way, "Don't slap my daughter." I was angry. Even I wouldn't have stopped doing it if she said it to me that softly. As if I wasn't humiliated enough she went on to say, "You will make her go blind and what am I supposed to do with a blind girl?" She didn't mean it literally but it really ticked me off. I was thinking, "Damn, am I worth so little?" Suddenly I had an epiphany. I thought to myself, "Boys you asked for it, you got it."

I waited until everyone went to bed. About an hour later I woke my mother and told her there was something in my eye and I couldn't see. She was very tired and sleepy but turned on the light and looked in my eye. She said she couldn't see anything that might be bothering me. I said I couldn't see anything either. She was so tired she didn't get it at first. She told me to turn the light off and get some sleep. I said I could not because I can't see the light switch. Then I said, "Good night."

Suddenly, she realized what I had said and repeated, "What did you just say? You can't see anything?" I told her that is what I said and told her good night. She grabbed me and looked into my eyes, put her hand right in front of my eyes and yelled, "How many fingers do you see?" I was scared but I said I didn't know, I couldn't see. I thought I had a good plan until I saw my mother raging. She looked dangerous. I almost regretted my actions and wanted to tell her I was sorry. Then, realizing I had come that far and most probably was going to be punished, I decided to forge ahead and take my bratty brothers with me.

Mum screamed at the boys who jumped up from sleep. She was roaring. Scared and quiet, fear was apparent on Siavash's pale, chunky face, he looked like Mr. Scrooge upon seeing the ghost of Christmas past. For the first time, he was apologetic. I almost felt sorry for him but it was my only chance for revenge. I had to finish what I had started. Mum thought I had developed visual agnosia or propagnosia, due to damage to the inferotemporal cortex, which, while uncommon, can happen. Not likely overnight but, luckily, she didn't know that.

At this point, a little excited and a little scared, I couldn't contain myself and needed to go to the washroom. Continuing my inspired performance, I asked my mother to help me to the washroom. I held mum's hand and walked step by step as if I had gone blind. My Oscar-worthy performance was so authentic that my poor mother actually believed me, which in a way was a relief. I had seen her provoked a few times and she was ultra-formidable when she was in her rage mode. If she had found out that it was all a setup, the biggest piece left of me would have been my ears.

The only washroom was located at the end of a long hallway, a long narrow path that connected the balcony without any doors or windows. It acted as a natural fan in summer but it didn't quite work for freezing winter weather. Water inside the bathroom was often frozen in the pipes and by standing in the path of the breeze I could have caught a cold. At the other end of the hallway, was a small kitchen; between the kitchen and bath was a small shower.

Mum asked me to wait outside the washroom for her to bring me back. The whole area was unheated and, as I was getting very cold, I ran back to the room. Manoocheher, who always was the naughty one and got all the attention said, "Liar, if you are blind, how could you run so quickly?" He was right but I was ready for this question and said, "Before I was blinded by you two, I ran through these hallways all the time. I have a perfect picture of this apartment in my mind." He wasn't sure what to say about my brilliant explanation, so, like a bully kid, he just mocked me. As mum entered, he didn't hesitate to try to persuade her that I was lying. I suspect that she too had her doubts but thankfully dismissed it, saying that I needed to get some sleep. What a relief. By late morning the following day, I said I was better, and by afternoon my vision had been miraculously restored to normal. When it was all over, I told my mum the whole story. She laughed very hard but made me promise not to lie to her again or she would punish me. I reluctantly agreed. As for the boys, they have never slapped me on the back of my head again. The boys and my parents never forgot the unique punishment but it didn't necessarily start a revolution for them to respect me. These were the best of the rare good times.

As time passed I learned more and more about my father. I was just a girl he didn't care to have and meant nothing to him. He showed his true feelings when he returned from his business trips; bringing a pellet gun for his favorite son Manoocheher, modest gifts for the other boys and nothing for me. Although mum loved me, to her, I was just a child, incapable of understanding the family situation and comprehending our dilemma. She was incredibly busy with everyone else and consumed with life's difficulties. She didn't have any spare time to spend with me. To the boys, I was merely a little toy; they manipulated me and enjoyed my frustrations and embarrassments. Despite everyone's assumption that I was only a child and knew nothing, I knew.

I have a vivid memory of those days and events, particularly when major incidents impacted the whole family. Sometimes, I was suffering from malnourishment. Other times, I was running a gamut of emotions. I felt as if I were an adult living in a child's body. On a couple of occasions when I precociously gave my father advice, he yelled at me, "You are only five years old. Stop giving me advice and acting like an adult."

Little by little, due to the sarcasms of the family, I lost the poise and vibrancy of the funny little girl I once was. I often felt lost and alone, as if I were an orphan child.

I became sick more often and was frequently bedridden. One day, on a visit to my doctor, I saw a beautiful doll in a shop window. In my childish imagination, she was blinking at me from the window of the doll shop. My mother said, "I don't have enough money for both your prescription and the doll. Which one should I get you first?" With innocent wisdom, I replied, "Get me the doll and I will feel better." Which is what she did and so did I. I had that doll until I was thirteen years old; the only doll I ever owned. That night my father berated my mother for spoiling me by spending $12 on a doll. I spent many hours talking to that doll that I never named. She was often the only friend I had and listened to me silently.

The only other exciting event of that period was when mum took me to her sewing classes. Continuing where she had left off, my mum convinced my father that it would be good for her and the children if she had a diploma in a useful trade in which she could earn money. Motivated by money, my father welcomed the idea and even paid for her class and bought her a sewing machine; the only gift he ever purchased her.

I was five years old and although her teacher didn't like to have a child in her class, mum made her a promise that I would not fuss. I started picking up patterns and playing with fabrics. The childhood practice played a great role in my imagination as I grew older.

Unlike in North America, where the latest fashions start with the outfits on the manikins in the windows of large boutiques and are available in large stores, many women of Iran still like the idea of tailor made and specialty clothing. My mother had an eye for design and an expertise in sewing that I have rarely seen; only among the great designer am I sure there is such expertise.

She never used the usual do-it-yourself patterns to create an outfit but did her cuts directly on the fabric and from her imagination. Also, she could touch a fabric and identify the fiber. This made me very interested in fashion in my early years of life. So much so, that by age seven I had a complete collection of doll clothing. I didn't follow in my mother's footsteps and earn academic achievement but she was stubborn enough to teach me that, although I am a modern woman, I needed to know how to sew my own clothing if I must. I owe her the common sense knowledge and independence in many facets of my life.

My mother took the classes in hope that when she moved to a larger home she could have her own shop and school. Unfortunately, she was never to do that as, in the years to come, the economy and our lives changed drastically.

After living in the home of the kind Jewish family for two years, my mum had enough of my father's neglect. Desperate, living on the second floor of an old house that might collapse at any time with three teenage boys who loved to play soccer, she was determined to move. My father wasn't concerned that we couldn't run, couldn't wrestle and couldn't play. The Jewish family was very nice but it was hard for my mum to keep the boys and me quiet all the time. It was a constant battle of heated arguments and anguish for my mother but my father ignored her pleas and seemed completely unaffected by her concerns about us.

What mattered to him was getting his factories going and buying land again. He was determined to regain the stature he had before his bankruptcy and would do whatever it took to attain it. To get to his next deal, on one occasion he almost gave away his favorite son, Manoocheher, for adoption. While neglecting our family for years, my father had managed to re-accumulate a considerable fortune. There is a proverb in Persian that says 'If you want to be rich, don't spend any money.' This was my father's mantra and he followed it religiously. He spent almost nothing on groceries, clothing, and education for us. He destroyed my childhood fantasies by repeatedly making false promises to me that he never meant to keep. He often promised he would buy me a bicycle for my birthday. I used to ride my friends' bike but when I found out that he had bought a bike for my stepsister's boy and not for me, I was so disappointed that I quit riding bikes. Recently, I bought myself a bike only to discover that it is not true that riding a bike is a skill you never forget. I cannot undo what he has done to my subconscious. Now, I cannot ride a bike; not even if my life depended on it.

Not all businessmen and colleagues trusted him. One of our neighbors was among the businessmen who had been wary of my father's business solicitations all along. My father was trying to get the man to trust him but all his efforts had failed. In a final attempt, he almost managed to pull off one last despicable trick in order to have a successful business relationship with the man. He found the man's weak spot. He had no children and wanted a son. With utter disregard for my mother's feelings and without asking her opinion, he had promised Manoocheher to the man and was ready to sacrifice his son. Mum, didn't quite know what was going on but had noticed the man and his wife's affection toward Manoochehr. When she found out the plan, she was outraged. My father had already signed the adoption papers. If she had not interfered in time, telling the neighbor to back off, he would have given his son to a total stranger because it could have had a positive impact on his business.

Our living conditions were nearly intolerable but the rent was so low that my father had no incentive to move elsewhere. Mum talked to our landlord about the problem and asked him to help make her wish to buy a house for us come true. The landlord and his family had become our close friends and, although we knew we would miss each other a great deal, he agreed to help us. When our lease came up for renewal, the landlord doubled the rent. My father, predictably, wasn't happy about the increased rent. In fact, he panicked.

Mum wanted to buy a house with the money she had received from the sale of lands she recovered in winning the multiple lawsuits. As previously related, when my father went to debtor's prison, my mother, through grit and innate wisdom, gained his release and, to some degree, restored our family fortune by her persistence in suing my father's creditors for fraudulently double collecting money he owed and foreclosing on the land he had pledged as collateral.

When she received the money, my father jumped in, trying to take over her funds. He was considerably agitated and frustrated when she wisely declined his assistance. Little by little, from sales of her own lands, mum finally accumulated the money she needed to buy a house. She was determined to buy a house in her name only but, unlike Abadan, in Isfahan a woman could not go to an agent alone. The people of Isfahan were not accustomed to the independent class of woman and would have start gossiping about her, regarding her as a loose woman.

Reluctantly, she agreed to bring my father along for the transaction. My father had planned a trap to get as much money as he could out of her. Mum had not yet received her money from the land sale, so my father reluctantly wrote a check for the earnest money, getting a promissory note from my mother. He did not expect her to be able to pay on time, in which case he would foreclose. Fortunately, as it turned out, his plan failed.

He didn't want to buy us a home. He wanted to buy a piece of valuable land with a shell of a house on it that he planned to tear down but, in the meantime, he expected us to live in it. At my father's insistence, mum paid nearly $500,000 for the house from the proceeds of ten years of slaving to recover what my father lost in his bankruptcy. She bought the house in her name because of my father's history of neglect and domineering greed. He wrongly assumed he would still be able to control her assets. The battles between my parents resumed. Before we even moved into the new house, he had found a buyer for the property and was negotiating a deal. Mum wanted to keep the house for us and resisted him. Heated arguments began. Knowing that my mother depended on his limited support, my father repeatedly threatened to leave.

In October 1976, after three months delay, we finally moved to our first family-owned house in Isfahan. For a short time, it was a happy middle ground between the two warring factions.

†HE MASTER

The house we called home for the next seventeen long years was a fairly large, flat roofed, two-story house, about 5,000 ft² in size, with seven bedrooms and one bathroom. It was considered modern in its time, mainly because most previous houses were built as private and public quarters, called Andaroon and Biroon. The private quarters included the kitchen and one or two large bedrooms with a private back yard to seclude and protect the women. It was considered the main residency for wives, children and other females who stayed at the house. To access the public quarters, it was connected through a long, narrow hallway with a door. The public area was an open space; a large two or three-bedroom compound; sort of a large guesthouse overlooking the courtyard garden or pool.

The master of the house usually shared his room with his favorite wife once or twice per week, depending on how many wives he had. Most of the time, he spent his days entertaining male guests, resting or spending time with his sons in his quarters. Girls rarely spent any time with their aloof father and called him Agha, in Farsi, which translates to Master in English. The citizens of Isfahan, in particular the older generation considered themselves religious people and the true followers of Islam.

People are most often mislead when they have only been told to follow instead of questioning. So much so, that the showing of affection by a father to girls of nine years or older is discouraged in many religious families and is even taken as a sign of incestuous weakness and a sin.

Mullahs who see themselves as the true ambassador of Prophet Mohammad's legacy have written too many books. And, too many of them have managed to deceive people to the extent they have accepted a wrong perception and interpretation of Islam. They think a man watching his daughter becoming a young woman is a great sin; as if abusive men needed any more assistance to enslave women. These ignorant mullahs have given them the thumbs up to go ahead with even more malicious behavior and blessed it as the heavenly, reward of God. As in the medieval era, the perception about a woman's body is that as soon as a daughter reaches puberty it is a blessing for the father and the family to get her out of the household.

Religious families are frequently blindsided into believing what purposely absent-minded mullahs preach; to the degree that fathers will give away their daughters, believing they are buying themselves a place in heaven. The preachers have managed to mutilate true Islam. They spread the illogical propaganda that it is a sin for a girl to reach puberty in her father's house and is a blessing if she has her first period in her husband's house. This misguided theory is supposedly o protect girls and young women from incest. This meant if she reached puberty by ten years of age, she should be married off by that age. It also means the child bride had no choice of her own. Her parents choose someone they think is suitable.

This vicious cycle of modern slavery has continued throughout generations; ever since the mullahs have been able to influence people's judgment. Since the times of the Safavids and the Gajar, two of Iran's latest dynasties, the most devastating acts have been practiced to keep the population busy with man-made problems to distract them from more important issues. Before these two dynasties and prior to the invasion by Arabs that captured and ruled the empire for centuries, Persia had a different marriage system. After the Arab invasion, the captured Persian emperor's daughter was given a choice by Hossain and the Prophet's family to marry anyone she chose. She chose to marry Hossain, the third Imam of Shiah. Ever since her marriage, the Iranian nation has a great deal of respect for the religion and for the Prophet's family. The preachers try to say that the customs represent Islam but in truth there is no excuse for the lies and tricks they pull to make people follow them.

The Prophet would have never agreed, no matter who the preacher or writer of these rules. It does not exonerate those who deliberately manipulate any religion. God doesn't give a damn about the stature of the manipulator.

Worshipers Beware!

People, who often fall into the trap of ignorance, assume that those who teach the rules are Saints sent by God and therefore, what they say is what God would want them to say. God himself wrote the Ten Commandments in stone. Yet, they are not willing to admit that he never approves such cruelty toward women. People, who have rebounded to a normal life, often leave organized religion forever and despise religion for the rest of their lives. And, in the case of Islam, frequently blaming it for their problems; blaming God and Holy people for the difficulties they have experienced at the hand of organized religion advocates. Surprisingly, almost no one pauses to ask, "Can a thief be a mullah or a priest? Can a priest or a mullah become a thief or, as in many recent cases, child molesters?"

The preachers are ordinary people who wear a pile of linen on their head and can be just as greedy as anyone else. They are human, and therefore fallible. Those who fall into their spider webs of false admonitions find themselves numb and almost never ask questions; they only follow. People need to start taking responsibility for their own actions and do research to make sure they don't believe wolves attired as sheep. The sarcasm and negative criticism should put a stop to blaming God or religion for the problems caused by religious advocates. Because God is pure, religion is pure, and was sent us for our own good. No matter what religion we believe, people who have their own personal interest and agendas in their heart have seduced us all. It is not religion that should take the blame, but the people who manage to destroy it, and those who, as we say in Persian literature, follow like a blindfolded camel with a halter on his neck, going round and round on the same path everyday, not once questioning or resenting the leader. God himself says in the Koran that a true follower is the one who asks questions.

Of course, that doesn't mean having an argument simply for the sake of having an argument. Islam is certainly not the only religion that has been used and abused.

As a Muslim, I have been curious about Christianity and, having mostly Christian friends, I like to know what they think of their religion. A long time ago, I spent hours talking and discussing religion with a male friend who later resigned from his engineering job to become a Catholic priest. He even took me to attend four church ceremonies in one day. By the end of the day, I couldn't take it any more. I asked him why he wanted to become a priest. He replied that was his calling. I knew him well enough to ask him more personal questions. I asked him what would become of his dream of having a family. He said that if he became a Catholic priest that would only be possible if he moved to Lebanon where the Catholic Church has a different ruling.

I asked him, Aren't you guys following the same God and believing in the same Jesus or do they have a different one in Lebanon? I was pulling his leg. He laughed and said, No we believe in the same Guy. I then asked him what effect it would have on him when, sitting in his closet as a priest, a beautiful women comes to him to confess her carnal sins. He replied that if she were ugly, nothing, but, if she were beautiful, he would keep thinking, Gosh, I wonder how she looks naked and how could I get her into bed. I was shocked when he said that and told him that he needed to consider that in his decision. In my opinion, if he felt this way, it would be a great sin, to try to suppress his real feelings. He should instead look forward to getting married and perhaps do something else with his calling.

He didn't listen, and moved forward with his plans. In later years, when the stories about Catholic priests molesting alter boys and girls made headlines, my concern was renewed. I kept in touch with him and at every opportunity tried to wake him up from his dream of becoming pure by taking vows of celibacy. According to virtually all other religions, marriage is a great blessing; a rewarding element in our deed book and God's eye. I couldn't understand why celibacy for a priest would be a blessing. Recently, there was a documentary on the CBC about individuals in the Catholic church who abuse their power and misguide other's, who truly want to be guided by God, but end up in the gates of hell. I have read studies about sexually active priests who pretend to be inactive. They state that they were commonly told that having unmarried sex, sex with a person of the same gender or even sex with a minor is not as great a sin as getting married.

I favor equality of all people, regardless of gender issues, and allowing them to have the same place, respect and benefit in the eyes of law and society as the rest of us but I cannot comprehend how we can interpret pure religion to be what works for us. Finally, and the most severe question of all, how can the church justify protecting priests and bishops who molest boys and only offer an apology for their sins and behavior? The victims are told that these criminals are forgiven and in the eyes of the church they are still priests because Jesus is going to save them.

I am a Muslim, not a Christian, yet, I am curious to know how it is possible to forgive sins committed thousands of years ago. I hope Christians would forgive me but I thought that sins are personal affairs and only the sinner can ask for forgiveness. If it is possible for just anyone to ask forgiveness for someone else's sins, will Bin Laden, Khomeini and Sadam end up in their private heavenly quarters having paid someone to forgive them? I am just curious, are these people going to go the same heaven as the rest of us? Because the heaven promised to Muslims doesn't cut such deals for anyone.

The reason people fall for their tricks and trust the criminals who dress as a priest or a mullah is because they look trustworthy and they have been assured these saintly people will never abuse the trust. That is not so. If a priest wearing an Armani suit and Cartier loafers, flashing a diamond studded Rolex and puffing on a Cuban cigar disembarks from his private yacht and alights from his chauffer driven Rolls Royce limo looking like the Godfather, talking like the late Marlon Brando and telling you, "Between you and me, I am going to make a deal with you and Jesus that you can't refuse." Any good Christian would probably have bolted out the door of the church.

Unfortunately, the charlatans who dress as a priest or a mullah don't wear a 'Worshiper Beware, I Am A Criminal' stamp on his forehead. They do it smoothly. The reason Bin Laden hasn't been caught yet is because he is believable. He sits down on the same dirt floor as the rest of his gang, eats the same crappy food with his hands from the same tray as his men. He is a millionaire dressed in rags to make his followers believe he cares about them, even if he doesn't. That is why people follow him. His tactics are not new. All his predecessors who have made themselves a reputation for claiming they want to help people have used the same strategy but he does it really well. He portrays himself as the Messiah, promising heaven to those who kill a westerner or anyone who tells the truth. In order for people to know who tells the truth and who lies, they need to ask questions and look deeper than someone's modest outfit. And that is what becoming a vigilant Good Muslim, Good Jew or Good Christian is about.

Our Sanctuary

Our old house had been built for the first City Councilor in the 1930s and stood proudly in the old part of town. The house had three large bedrooms on the south side, two on the east and another two on the west on the second floor. Seven bedrooms, in total, but there was only one bathroom and it was at the far end of the courtyard. The house was made of sun-dried bricks, the usual material for the time. It had a large courtyard, enclosing several outbuildings. There were four external attached commercial shops. These shops were rented long before we bought the house, the tenants paid little or no rent and it was practically impossible to evict them, which was part of my father's plan to force my mum to sell the house.

The first time it rained when I was in the yard, in my imagination, the rain washed the dirt from its old face. The fragrance of rain and the smell of washed raw bricks were wonderfully strange; a delicacy to my olfactory system. The scent almost helped me to relax. I fell in love with the old house, like the meeting of two passionate lovers who embrace each other in a permanent sanctuary. I had finally found a place to call home. The reason for the love toward the house perhaps was the freedom I experienced; I could run freely without being stopped, could hear the birds singing in the early morning and inhale the fresh flowers fragrance from our little garden. It was unlike any experience I had ever had in the earlier years of my childhood.

Annoying Guests

A lthough my initial love for our new home increased daily, it did have its peculiarities and inhabitants that were not particularly a turn on. The solitary washroom was outside, accessible by a covered walk running parallel to our small garden. Our little Garden of Eden, although it helped moderate the hot, humid summer nights, was more like a miniature, creepy, crawly Serengeti wilderness.

Not to mention, we had a growth of few suspicious trees and bushes. Opium poppies sprang up by the dozens the following spring. The poppy seeds are edible, taste similar to sesame and mixed with sugar are a popular regional snack, being neither poisonous nor causing addiction. The liquid juice extracted from the petals of the poppy, however, is used to manufacture severely addictive opium. We also had marijuana plants that had grown into virtual trees blooming in our garden. We didn't know what they were until Uncle Azam enlightened us.

It is doubtful the seeds could have been transported by strong winds. Someone must have dropped or planted them in our garden in previous years. Mum was afraid the boys would indulge themselves on the leaves and poppies and burned and destroyed the tall marijuana plants and opium bushes as soon as she found out what they were. I am not sure how the rest of the neighborhood was affected; perhaps they got a high but when she burned them my nose hated the smell of marijuana. The disgusting smell which made me nauseous, coincidently, was similar to the smell of a pesticide that mum used for our pomegranate trees.

When we had to visit the washroom at night there was usually no light, thanks to the wartime blackout. Spiders the size of a man's hand would jump on us. And, there were lizards, lizards, lizards everywhere. Lizards had been declared an endangered species and could not be hunted but nothing in the law prevented them from hunting us, which they did in droves. So, despite the ban, we hunted them back with no discernable effect on the lizard population.

Even more pervasive was a profusion of cockroaches of all sizes. Iran must be the cockroach capital of the world. The smallest were the size of a dime. The largest, the water cockroach, was as big as a cucumber pickle. Termites flaunted all over the place. There must have been thousands of other kinds of insects I didn't recognize. A person could have earned an Entomology PhD without leaving our garden. Maybe they had been feasting on the bodies in the old graveyard under our house all these years. Whatever the reason for their fecundity, running the gauntlet of creepy crawly critters at night to reach the washroom remained an adventure for the next seventeen years.

Soon after we moved into our new home in late October 1977, I tasted my first night of fear and loneliness. I still have a chilling memory of that night. Khosro was supposed to pick me up after school but forgot about me. School let out at 3:00 p.m. I was left all alone until 9:00 p.m. in an unlighted, five-acre schoolyard. I was so frightened that I wouldn't even go into the warm room of the school's night shift caretaker. When I got home, I was hysterical and shouted at my mother. How could she not notice that I was missing? She had not thought to come pick me up or phone the school. It wasn't until Khosro came home from his English class at 8:30 p.m. only then, my mother asked about me and sent him to pick me up or perhaps to find me. She explained she was busy praying, cooking and entertaining guests and just forgot. I am sure she didn't mean it to happen. But I wasn't satisfied. I asked how she could forget about me and not the boys if they had been that late.

For many years, I was terrified of darkness and until my twenty-second birthday had a phobia of being alone. I forced myself to face my demons. I hypnotized myself and saw me walking all alone in pitch dark. When I came back to my normal self, I was drenched in sweat but the fear was finally replaced by confidence and I had laid the demons to rest for good.

As time passed, we started hearing rumors from neighbors that our house was haunted. At first, we thought they were simply saying such things to scare us because we had the largest property in the neighborhood but strange things started to occur. Finally, mum confronted the neighbors about their strange behavior and the rumors we were hearing. They assured her it was not a rumor; the house really was possessed. We paid little attention and chose to dismiss the little signs we started to see. In the beginning, we began to wake up to noises for which we could not find a source. In the morning we would find things that belonged in the kitchen in the middle of the yard although there was no evidence that anyone had broken in.

All the rumors and noises I heard and inexplicable happenings eventually sank in and changed my attitude toward the old house. The house had a mysterious past and as time passed, fear replaced the optimism I once had. We learned that our home had a dark legend; no previous owner had left this building alive. Supposedly, it had never been sold without first taking the life of the owner. Long before we bought the house, the city councilor had dived from the second floor and committed suicide. His wife sold the house to escape. Coincidence or not, she died shortly afterwards. Before we bought it, it had belonged to another family who vanished mysteriously. It seemed every owner of this house had died in the house or disappeared. It was impossible to sell and intolerable to live in. By the time we found out about all these stories, it was a bit too late.

Soon after we moved, I woke up one morning to find mum gone. The boys tried to keep me busy all day. In late afternoon she came home, looking pale and seemed very ill. I wasn't sure what to make of it. I wasn't told the truth as to why she didn't feel good until I was a teenager when I found out she had lost a baby boy. It seemed our mysterious house had taken its first sacrifice from our family.

Losing the baby and all the rumors had turned our old home, our sanctuary, and our paradise into anything but a safe haven. I could hardly bear living in it; The high walls, the smell of mud when it rained, the mold beneath the rugs, the invincible, million mice population, all became unbearable. I wasn't sure which I should be most terrified of; the large poisonous millipedes running around in our kitchen sink, the sounds coming from the kitchen next to the room where I studied at night, the small creatures and spiders crawling around everywhere, the cracked walls that could collapse any moment, the broken doors and windows, the whistling wind sounding like a ghosts howling for a lost love, the pale, washed-out bare walls amidst whose holes you could see the strangest faces.

The very musty, rotten smell coming from the creepy basement that was cooler than usual, even in the midst of summer heat, was a factor in our growing suspicious that the haunted rumors were true. I know now that the cool and mysterious basement was in fact nearly six feet under and it was dug into graves. I recall one time I was in the basement when the light went off. I had such a fear. I ran toward the door and nearly fainted. The noise, smell and array of strange coincidences kept me awake at night. It sounds like a scene from a Harry Potter movie except this wasn't a movie and we were cursed to live in it; not for an episode but for a whole series. I was sure we were indeed living in a haunted house and would never survive.

Haunted or not, life must goes on. We had nowhere else to go. After we had lived there for two months, we discovered the house didn't have a working sewage system and would have to be connected to the city's system. Due to the fact the house was located in a heritage part of town, City Hall would not issue a permit because it had to come from the Mayor himself and he wasn't available to comment.

For three months, mum went to City Hall every day. Frustrated and fed up with the man's eternal absence, she started to make a scene. Finally, her perseverance paid off. She was not able to meet with the mystery mayor himself but, to avoid further embarrassment, City Hall assigned a top executive who could make a decision in her case. When her case was over, mum asked the people in the mayor's office why someone was getting paid for a job he never attended. One of the employees quietly and privately whispered to her that the mayor is a Freemason. We had no idea what a Freemason was and quite frankly didn't care, until much later when it became public during the revolution.

After a long delay and interminable arguments, the city council was finally satisfied that heritage or not, we needed a working sewage system. The city sent a crew to hook us up to the city sewage system. When the workers started digging, they found scores of completely intact human bodies and skeletons. We hadn't been told that forty years earlier the entire ten block square neighborhood had been a graveyard. For some reason, none of the other houses seemed as mysterious as ours. We were walking on their bones; no wonder the ghosts made our lives increasingly hard.

Inside the walls, we prayed that God would save us from nasty creatures and spirits and a possible collapse that could cave the house on top of us. Outside, our neighbors and the renters became our number one enemies and prayed for the day we died. They did not like the rundown condition of the house and wanted us out, figuring that a new owner could bring it up to the standard of the neighborhood. Against all odds, we lived in that haunted house for nearly seventeen long years. In my mind, it was the turnover of the century when we finally managed to close a deal on the old mausoleum.

Chilling Memories

My childhood was certainly nothing ordinary. I can vividly recall days that I was glued to the TV watching Les Miserable, tears flowing down my face. I knew the story was fiction, I wasn't crying for the characters but for me, the way my life seemed so tragically similar to the character of the story. My father's behavior resembled that of the man enslaving the little girl in the Les Miserable story.

I remember the resentment I felt toward my father. I despised him early on for making my mother suffer. At age seven, I often questioned my mother, asking her why she brought me into this world when she knew she could not give me a father and why she continued to live and suffer with a person who doesn't love her. These were big questions and big words for a child to ask. Mum knew that I was sick so much because I didn't have winter clothing to keep me warm. She told me to ask my father to buy me a coat. I shouldn't have bothered. I knew what he was going to say; he didn't have any money to buy me a coat. He had money for his new investments; buildings, factories, land and commercial equipment but not enough money to buy his six-year-old daughter a winter coat.

Hoping not to repeat the fearful experience of the night when I was left in the schoolyard, mum decided to register me in the elementary school next door to our house. I didn't enjoy my school years because I was constantly bullied by students and punished by teachers for my outgoing personality. After being bedridden for a week, I was not ready for a math test. My first grade teacher punished me severely because she wanted to make a point to other students that laziness was not permitted. I was never a lazy child but I was a very sick one.

The neighborhood where we had formerly lived in the Jewish family home was a rich residential area and much cleaner than the one to which we had moved. Our new home was in a market area in a busy part of town. We were close to a clinic that served a poor neighborhood and there was a great deal of bacteria from different sicknesses in the air. I was seriously ill much of the first year and barely finished the first grade. At school every morning before classes began, we had to stand in a lineup in rain and snow to listen to the principal's political speeches. The Shah thought children needed to know what a great man he was. The principal rambled on about the Shah and what a wonderful father he had been to all of us. With all honesty, I admit he was a great man for the country, at least, in comparison to the current government, but standing in snow and cold didn't particularly make me like him more.

Most teachers in Iran have training only in the subject they teach. There is no such thing for teachers as child psychology. The first grade teacher slapped me on the hands with a wooden ruler so many times that my hands became completely numb. When I would not cry, she became even more determined to break me and slapped me some more. After half an hour of beating my small hands with the ruler, even though she wasn't satisfied, she finally let me go. I was hurt; but as a child I had such pride that I would never cry in public. In my childish rationale, babies cried because they couldn't speak. I was a big girl, and could say what was on my mind. After coming home it was hours before I could feel my fingers. That early experience changed my attitude toward authorities and my mother. I told mum that I hated school and I was not going to go back again. I did, of course.

My mother, instead of confronting the teacher who took her anger out on me, presented her with a bouquet of flowers. I was furious when she told me about it. I asked her why she gave my tormentor flowers. Mum answered, Your teacher was trying to help you. I answered back, Helping me! How? By punishing me for being sick? You rewarded her with flowers to prove a point? If my teacher were that smart, she wouldn't have punished me in the first place; she would have asked me why I was not prepared. I don't think she is getting what you are trying to tell her. If you are as smart as you claim, you would not have wasted the money. It was rude of me to question mum in such a manner but my pride was hurt. I was devastated and felt as if I had been punished all over again.

I guess my childish advice sank in. I vividly recall, on a pouring rain evening in October 1977, mum took me shopping and bought me a lamb coat and matching hat and a pair of leather boots. After years of shivering in the cold weather, she had planned to use that money to buy a coat for herself but she spent it on me. When we returned home, my father saw the coat and asked her where she got the money. Mum tried to explain that she had been saving the money for a long time. He told her she was spoiling me. His words were as sharp as knives going through me. To this day, in early October of every year when the lights go on and rain falls I have a nostalgic flashback about my mother's loving sacrifice.

CHILDHOOD YEARS

Growing up, I didn't have any close friends, because I felt that I couldn't trust anyone. Inside the high walls of our home, my family didn't show me much affection. My best childhood friends were chickens, roosters, ducks, and my beloved nightingale. Gossiping, a way of life for many and popular in every society, is particularly virulent among the people of Isfahan. It is pastime talk. Kids learn to gossip from older family members and the whole family takes part in sharing talk about others and having fun at their expense. Although girls and boys had separate schools in this part of the town, their bad habits were equally as shocking as what I had experienced in the previous year. At a young age, girls were taught to behave submissively toward men. Some of our classes about religion even encouraged second graders to promote good behavior and how we should be poised and polite. The schoolgirls, however, had already learned within the family unit at a much earlier age to bully to get what they want. I did not like the girls' attitude and didn't belong to any group at school. I had a few friends in the old school but in the new school I felt lost and completely overwhelmed. Even when I found friends, mum wouldn't allow me to go play with them. She didn't want me to pick up their bad habits and jokes. Also, mum didn't want me to go to other girls' houses because she feared they might have a bad male relative who would rape me. After what eventually happened I couldn't blame her.

One day, one of my teachers jokingly called me a name that I didn't understand. I said, "Hello," and she answered, "Hello to you too, Nashossteh." It loosely translates as an unwashed face. It is a slang word used only in the region of Isfahan for a woman having sex with her husband, or, more precisely, someone other than her husband. The remark is a sarcastic comment that she is impure and dirty; hardly an appropriate greeting for a school girl.

I did not know that the people of Isfahan used sexual remarks toward each other. Just about everyone I met in those years used it in such a casual manner that I never thought it was something so graphic. This word was a euphemism for slut. I thought it was a funny word and didn't know what it meant; at least not before I paid a price.

I buzzed the doorbell at home and greeted mum, "Hi, Nashossteh," when she opened the door for me. Mum didn't wait to hear where I had learned the word or ask for an explanation. She slapped my face very hard. I screamed in pain and burst into tears. Most of all, I was embarrassed that, as our doorway was directly on the main route, I was hit in front of strangers passing by on the streets. I cried, "Why are you slapping me?"

She belatedly realized this must be something I didn't know; otherwise I wouldn't have questioned her. She then asked me where I learned the word. I said my teacher called me that. When I told her where I learned the word, she went after the teacher.

My childhood was extremely lonely. I had a couple of friends during the school year but I wasn't allowed to get in touch with them in the summer time. My cold-hearted behavior seemed strange in their eyes and I agreed with them but that is the way it was and I had to comply. Through hearsay conversations, mum had heard of cases of rape when young girls were invited to their friend's home, only to find themselves in a trap of family child molesters. She was trying to protect me from danger and did not let me go to anyone's home alone, not even years later when I was in my early twenties.

During the winter, due to sickness I had too many absences from class but I was bright, mature for my age and taller than most other students in my class. So much so, that one day when mum took me to the park to play, two men, who were watching their own children, made a remark about me being a giant, tall woman, who thinks she is a baby, playing around. I heard them and told my mum; she said not to bother. But, it did hurt me that she didn't answer them on my behalf.

In retrospect, I wasn't an angelic child and was, in some cases, even nutty. I always kept my guard up and made sure I knew something about the boys that I could use against them if I had to. It may sound like any brothers and sister, but ours wasn't.

I used to analyze people who were in my path and find their threshold. Mum took me to a neighbor's house for the Persian New Year. The elderly lady host, who seemed rich and wore a lot of gold, brought a small plate of nuts for us to enjoy, or perhaps just for looks. I liked almonds and pistachios and kept eating. As soon as the lady left, mum scolded me, "Why are you finishing the nuts plate?" I answered, "Because she said to." Mum said, "That is a gesture. This woman perhaps doesn't have a lot of money; she wanted to be kind but you have to watch yourself and you can't finish what you have in front of you." I asked, "Then why is she putting it in front of me and keeps saying to eat, if she doesn't mean it? She simply should say so." Mum, who had it with my growing questioning, said that is just how people are. In Farsi, we call the gesture *taroof*. It could be either real or fake, depending on the person and circumstance; a tough call for a child.

I was puzzled as to when should I take something for real and when to disregard it. In years to come, I decided to disregard the idiotic, adult traditions and cultural rules. My rules were simple and straight forward; if someone wanted something from me, they should ask and, if they give me something, they should mean it. Otherwise, I made myself a promise to not waste any time speculating what is real and what is not.

I wasn't taught to understand what was right in a correct way. As long as I didn't steal or physically hurt anyone, I thought that was enough. But, I didn't have mercy on others when they did. My school principals wrote to my mother that I was kind to the other kids but I recall that when a girl name Sara stole my art notebook, I was so mad at her, I publicly defamed her and didn't stop until I saw her in tears in front of other classmates. I made her confess to stealing but when she said that she didn't have a mother and her step-mother would not buy her school supplies, I felt great remorse and couldn't stop beating up on myself.

By the time the agonizing first school year was over, I could read the newspaper and had become a precocious chess and poker player; playing along with the boys, their friends and Uncle Asgar. I learned target practice with Manoocheher's small pellet gun. Uncle Azam, a radiologist, taught me how to use a syringe and I practiced injections on my doll. I developed an interest in photography, writing and music. I was curious about everything, including politics, which came naturally, of course, because we lived and breathed in the crucible of a festering revolution.

Those years, my creative and artistic side didn't get a chance to develop enough to become my future path because I was discouraged from following my talent and dreams. When I was very young, I wanted to be a doctor because I was always told that I should be a doctor and, for years, that was what I was led to believe was the right thing for me to pursue. Only when I realized that my dreams had to be mine alone, was I able to change my life's path for good.

I was stubbornly opinionated and perhaps a little eccentric. By the time I was seven years old I had planned my whole life. I would be a doctor. I would write a tell-all book about my mother's painful life. And, I would, of course, marry my prince. In my world and in my childish logic, my knight in shining armor, a boy of my age, was waiting for me somewhere in the world.

That was the reason I woke my mother up at six a.m. one October morning in 1977, asking her to take a picture of me. She asked why I needed a picture so early in the morning. I said someday I would have kids and I wanted to share this picture with them and show them that I was once a kid too. Mum laughed and ran after me but I persisted until she took the picture. I was animated and funny and acted out a role when I had the opportunity but mostly I was desperately trying to fit in the adult world.

So much so, that on the first day of second grade, I innocently got off on the wrong foot with my teacher. After giving us a warm welcome, my second grade teacher warned us that if we did not study as hard as she wanted us to, we would face punishment. I raised my hand and using my charm to dissuade her. I said, I don't think you need to do that; the first grade teacher has filled that position and punished us plenty already. All the kids laughed. At first, she thought I was being obnoxious but later when she saw my writing she became fond of me.

On one occasion, I wasn't sure whether she was trying to show me off or show me up. I had forgotten my composition notebook and told my fellow classmate, I hope she doesn't call on me again today. I had always heard teachers have students spy on each other. I never believed it until that day. Suddenly, she called my name to come up and read my composition in front of the class. This was the second time I had been called on in one week, an unusual coincidence in a class of forty students. I couldn't tell her I had forgotten mine, so I picked up a notebook and recited the entire composition by heart. She seemed to be pleased, gave me a great mark and encouraged every one to be a little more like me.

Years later, when I was in high school, I visited her and came clean about that incident. She said, I knew you did that. I am sorry; I wanted to punish you for answering me back. I was told by other students that you had forgotten your notebook but you did very well. I am proud of you and I predict someday you are going to be a writer.

The revolution in Iran started before my second year of school finished, giving me an unprecedented opportunity to socialize with mum's adult friends. They seemed to enjoy my outspoken personality but mum didn't; she thought I was too talkative. Mum's friends hugged me, and lavished me with gifts. I couldn't understand. She wasn't letting me be a child and play with other kids but now that I had given up on the idea of being a child, she didn't want me to hang out with adults either. It was confusing. I guess what she wanted was a little girl who behaved like a little doll, sitting in a toy cabinet and only coming out on command. Although she was in constant conflict with her own mother who tried to run her life and make her into something she was not, mum, unconsciously, was doing the same thing to me.

Even in today's Persian culture, most people think good girls are supposed to be neither seen nor heard. Particularly in religious families, girls are expected to stay in their rooms while guests are in the house. They are supposed to say hello to friends and family and then leave. That is how they are taught to be submissive to their future husband, inside and outside the family, and to silently suffer the abuse they receive. I had trouble conforming.

Mum initially welcomed my self-confidence and outgoing personality and admired the trait that I strived to be as stubborn as she was in her childhood. Everything she told me about her childhood I defined it my way and mimicked it as authentically as any actor playing a role. Mum told me a story about her mother buying her a pair of shoes that she didn't like and never wore. One day, mum bought me a pair of shoes I didn't like. I gave her the exact answer she had given her mother. As time swept by, she found herself in a paradox. In her eyes, I must have looked like her younger image in a mirror.

As time passed she found it difficult to deal with me and was alarmed by my personality development and independence. I now know that she was trying to protect me from the dangers of life and people who prey on a naïve child but her protection became intolerable to me. She was obsessed with controlling me to the point that it triggered lengthy arguments. She thought I was a rebellious child and started to resent me. She was afraid that I might never be able to marry or live in society if I continued to conduct myself in such an independent manner.

In retrospect, mum was afraid of people's opinion. She especially feared being judged as a lousy mother. She didn't want her children to be just another person. She wanted each of us to grow to our full potential. She wanted us to have what she never had in her life. She wanted her children to be outstanding citizens and role models for society. Although her ideas were admirable, she simply had no plan and didn't know how to achieve her noble objective. Mum always assumed she didn't have a good life because she wasn't able to please my father, not recognizing that my father wasn't capable of loving and showing affection. He had never been loved and therefore never learned to express his feelings. The only thing he loved was showing off a family he didn't care enough about to protect. She was afraid I had picked up on her.

Unlike her, I always tended to live for the day. I don't change my life to please anyone, regardless of what others think of my behavior. Having said all that, she was right about Iran's culture and the male dominated society, which doesn't agree with me and sees me as a rebel. Even women who share my opinion hesitate to accept or join in my liberating battle. They may feel in their hearts that I am right but hesitate, usually because they are attached to a man. Women are expected to conduct themselves according to what pleases their men. The submission instilled in girls by their families achieves its intended purpose to make women a mindless man pleaser.

All she knew to do was to impose smothering control on her children, hoping we would not try drugs or fall into traps before we became adults and could understand what she was trying to do for us. That is why she was so strict about what we were allowed to do, who we talked to and where we went. What she didn't understand was that under too much pressure, instead of blossoming into achievers, our talent was being suppressed and destroyed. She unknowingly created a prison and caused resentment toward her for the way she tried to achieve her dreams. In the end, it all collapsed when the boys didn't do what she wanted and I chose or, more correctly, had my own life's path chosen by circumstances.

Father Abandons Us

The year I went to second grade, my father and mother started fighting fiercely again. After my mother's years of struggling for my father's freedom and helping to restore his fortune, he again had her where he wanted her; at his non-existent mercy. He constantly threatened to leave if she didn't sell the house. He treated all of us, particularly me, like a sack of dirt. My mother said that the house was our only asset and she knew my father wouldn't provide for us if she sold it. One night, in the winter of 1978, true to his word, in the middle of night, he packed his bag and left us. As usual we were left with no money. An enormous silence prevailed in the house. The only sound was my mother's crying and praying at the same time, begging God to help her to feed us. She had three boys aged eighteen, seventeen and fifteen and me at eight years old. Nobody was working.

She also had Khosro's education to worry about. He was at a pivotal time of his life. He had to choose his life path and needed the most attention. He had the opportunity to become a navy pilot, a ship's captain or an engineer. He debated his choices for a long time before deciding to become a ship's captain. Mum was proud of him; even my father was willing to help him. Everyone in the family looked up to Khosro as a role model. I was only a child but I envied his chance to leave all the misery behind while I still had to witness and live it every day. I often told him I wished I were in his shoes. He had the opportunities the rest of us could only dream about.

Khosro left for the British naval university in Chahbahar. I missed him so much that I decided to write him a letter. In my first letter, I wasn't sure how to spell his name. In Farsi, the word for rooster, khoroos, is spelled similar to Khosro. I innocently misspelled his name. I thought I had written, My dear Khosro since you have gone, I missed you so. In the English translation, that is what I had intended to write. In Farsi, I had written, My dear rooster, I missed you so. He got a kick out of this and told everyone about it. It became the joke of our family, while it lasted. At first, I detested the laughs and was embarrassed. I took it personal that my family had a laugh at my lack of literacy. But, after a while I loosened up and soon even I had a little fun at my own expense.

I missed Khosro, because he was the only one who stuck up for me when the other two boys were mean to me. He even stood up to my mum to stop her from punishing me and was the only one who hugged and kissed me every day before he left for his university. He was the only family member who came to pick me up from school after he finished his own. Maybe it was because I was very much dependent on his affection that after he went off to Chahbahar, I became seriously ill. I had recurring problems with my stomach and was constantly forced to deal with poor health.

Also, Uncle Azam brought the boys some pigeons to entertain them since they didn't have school during the revolution. In no time, the pigeons multiplied and were plentiful. The boys were up on the roof flying the pigeons high. Mum hated that her brother introduced her boys to pigeon wrangling. His actions seemed very innocent and even entertained me. He was quite a character. Not having a boy of his own at that time, he kept giving the boys extra pocket money that was used for the wrong purposes. This encouraged the boys, particularly Manoocheher to hang out with a crowd that was not exactly harmless and the extra cash allowed him to go places he had no business being. Mum was furious with her brother; she had her reasons and some were quite valid. She didn't want to spoil the boys or have them get into drugs or other substances but uncle Azam wanted a father-son relationship with a boy and particularly adored Manoocheher. In addition, she was afraid that I would either fall off the ladder while climbing up to feed the pigeons or get infected with meningitis, which is found in pigeon droppings.

She asked him to stop giving her sons money and gifts. Mum and Uncle Azam had an argument and she stopped talking to him for a long time.

Unlike the rest of my family I was a sucker for affection and love, and I was very depressed that we couldn't associate with my uncle, the only family member we had in Isfahan. My father's family didn't consider us family and wanted nothing to do with us, in particular my mum and me.

We visited a platoon of doctors who dismissed the emotional effect of our poisonous family environment. They couldn't figure out anything wrong with me. They blamed me; stating that I was a spoiled child acting out. I was sure I wasn't acting, nor was I spoiled. My family didn't exactly treat me like a child star or a VIP. I was in constant pain and lost a lot of weight. Incompetent doctors stated I would feel better when I turned fourteen. I was afraid I might never see my fourteenth birthday if I did not receive proper treatment.

My deepest sympathy was toward my mother. She couldn't buy herself anything because whatever money we had was spent on doctors and medicine for me. It bothered me a great deal that I was sick all the time, I begged her to stop taking me to doctors and told her not to get the prescription filled. And, I often told her to let me go. But, she was a mother and couldn't let me die. For years, she ate the smallest piece of food and never touched the chicken legs, because she wanted us to get much needed protein. She said: You guys are in the growth stage, you must eat. As evidence, as I grew up, mum kept copies of the prescriptions she purchased for me. The file was one foot thick.

My health was so poor that even my deceased Uncle Yadollah seemed to be concerned about my welfare. I saw him in my dream for the first time. He was dressed as a doctor. My mother was holding me in her arms. She didn't know how else to help me. She was crying and her tears poured on my face. In fear that I might slip into a coma, she asked me what was happening and I remember telling her, "He is here." Suddenly, I jumped up, asking her why she was crying. Somehow my uncle was trying to communicate with the mortal world. He showed me affection and worries. At this time, he was dead more than sixteen years.

Early one morning, a few days later, I saw Uncle Azam by my bedside. He and my mum had not been on speaking terms for more than six months. "What brought you to my bedside this early in the morning?" I asked. He answered, Your Uncle Yadollah came to visit me in my dreams asked me if I had visited you lately. I told him I hadn't and then he said that he was praying for you every day and sitting on the roof, watching over you. According to Muslim belief, spirits who have been appointed to their afterlife rewards are able to visit their relatives in this life in the body of a bird.

From the window of the room where I was bedridden, I often saw a tiny ringdove, bending over and looking inside the window, I often wondered why that bird would do that. Was it really my uncle trying to tell me he was watching?

A few days later, mum found a doctor who diagnosed me with severe small intestine inflammation and put me on a strict diet. I wasn't permitted to eat anything except, plain rice without oil, non-fat yogurt, and barbecued lamb without spices or onion. After three months of this brutal diet, I was introduced to some other food but wasn't allowed to take milk or fruits, and vegetables for more than a year. I survived and lived through the most deadly of diseases with minor scars left on my body to remind me of those dark days. Uncle Azam's visitation from my deceased Uncle Yadollah seemed a little too mystical. Let me say that Uncle Azam was not a saint or a channeler to the spirits and I do not believe he would make up a bogus story as an excuse to see me. He was very fond of his deceased brother. Since his death, Yadollah has been accepted as my mother's family guardian angel. They swear by his grave and he has appeared to all of my mother's family members in their dreams with timely advice and counsel.

Surviving the Islamic Revolution

Khosro was away and studying for almost eight months now. In his second semester he lost one of his friends in a shark attack during a swimming practice session in the ocean. Reportedly, a great white attacked him. His body was never recovered.

The incident caused Khosro to panic and alter his career plans. He decided he no longer wanted to be a ship's captain. Swimming and scuba diving were a mandatory part of his training and he was terrified that he could be the next shark bait. Although he had a scholarship and was also being helped financially by both mum and my dad, he didn't study hard enough to keep his scholarship.

One of our neighbors, who happened to be passing through the city where Khosro was studying, saw him drunk with his friends and a group of girls. Perhaps this was an isolated incident but the truth is, Khosro, at an early age had demonstrated a destructive behavioral pattern; lying, stealing at age four, manipulating other kids, deception, smoking, drinking and gambling at age twelve. When he was eighteen years old, he stole my only gold necklace and blamed our friend's kids. He brought home books on sexuality when he was only fifteen years old. Obviously, he was entertaining the idea of having sex. I can't deny the reading perhaps was a good thing for him. But, if it were not for my mother's strict rules, he would never have finished his high school diploma and could have very well ended up in jail for the rest of his life. I detest sounding hypocritical or judgmental but, for some people, strict rules are the guarantors of success and a bright future and he was one of them. His behavior was never rational; he was driven by his compulsiveness. He had no sense of how to spend his money or who his true friends were.

Khosro was a financial burden for my mother and she felt compelled to tell him to return home. However, by November 1979, a full-fledged revolution was on the way. There were protests every day and since our house was next to a major street, we were in a danger zone. Mum had second thoughts about demanding that Khosro come home.

Soon, schools were forced to close. No one went to school or work, no one had a normal schedule and the economy was paralyzed. Thousands marched the streets in rain and snow, screaming insults to the Shah and his family. The Shah was trying his best to keep his cool. The Shah decided to take the high road His soldiers had orders not to shoot into the crowd of demonstrators but to crack down on the protesters by shooting bullets into the air. He tracked the protestors down and arrested them one by one. The jails were filled with protesters. Depending on the severity of their offense and how involved in the protests, they were incarcerated for periods of from 48 hours to near the end of the revolution when the people freed the prisoners.

Gangs of young kids, including Manoocheher and Siavash, forced businesses to close. They talked to the owner of the business and asked him to close his doors. If he said no, they would threaten him. If he still refused and if beatings did not persuade him to close, they burned his business to ashes. In the face of everything that was going on in Iran, my mother lived in fear that her sons were going to get themselves killed. Everything seemed to happen so fast. It was hard to predict what was going to happen next. Life had turned into non-stop chaos. Citizens and university and high school students tried to force the Bazaar, the Iranian equivalent of a mall or shopping center, to shut down but the Shah insisted it remain open. Had they managed to close the Bazaar, it would have been a direct indication that he was powerless. The Shah could not let that happen. Simple human concerns were crushed under the weight of politics.

At night we heard shooting, yelling and screaming from the streets and alleys. Bullets flew over our yard and some landed in our garden. At a young age, I had a bad feeling about the future of our country. I predicted that we were going to pay a heavy price for our naivety. People who were tired of the Shah and his lavish spending on himself and his family were eager to rush into the arms of the next person who proclaimed himself to be the Messiah. They were searching for a savior and Khomeini represented himself as the best choice. As a Persian proverb says, 'When a wolf takes a bait from being eaten by another, it doesn't guarantee that he wants to save her.'

My family spent many hours and sleepless nights on our roof watching the protestors and events with agony and nervousness as it unfolded right beneath our eyes; stunned, we didn't know what to make of all the chaos but hoped and prayed for the best.

I knew this revolution was a milestone in our country's history and I wasn't going to let it pass without observing every second of this historical event. Realistically and hopefully, it would only happen once in my lifetime. I wanted to see and believe it with my own eyes. Obviously, it was dangerous for a child to be on the roof until the wee hours every morning in the midst of a revolution and anything could happen. But, as much as mum resisted and tried to stop me from going onto the rooftop with the boys, I sneaked along anyway.

The revolution had given me a free pass to an apprenticeship program to observe an historical event. My bedtime stories were the daily news I was reading and questioning, eager to know what had happed during the previous decades. I kept questioning mum about the historical events she had witnessed during the Mossadegh Prime Ministry. I was curious about that revolution. I had never studied or known what happened in the past. The Shah had lead the younger generation to a dreamland hoping they would forget about the previous decades. Seemingly, it worked for a while but now everyone was curious to know more about the conflict the Shah had with the people during the protests of the 1940s and1950s. Revival of those memories and the terrible things he had done in the past made people bitter toward the Shah and his family.

It was exciting for me to learn more. Mum tried to stop me from thinking about the daily events and kept urging me, Don't you want to play? You are too young to understand. She soon discovered her efforts to distract me were futile and reluctantly started answering my questions. We had political discussions and debates every night. As she gave me the details about what happened during those years, it answered my questions as to why people were angry with the Shah when, apparently, he had provided them with everything.

With every new layer of detail, it appeared this revolution was meant to happen years ago. It only surfaced now because the Shah was weakened and preoccupied by health concerns. The resentment that unfolded as chants on the streets was the icing on the cake. The smoldering fire beneath the ashes of the protests twenty years ago burst into flames. The Shah had failed in his effort to extinguish this fire when Khomeini was arrested and exiled to Iraq and subsequently to France.

Looking back at previous decades, the Shah seemed callous and self-centered. But, seeing what he had done for the country it was hard to imagine the same man was capable of all the crimes of which he was being accused. For what it is worth, it is clear to me that politicians in the third world and in the Middle East in particular, don't care about the people as much as they do about their own agendas.

By the time mum finished her explanation, the pretty picture in my child's mind of the Shah as our father, who held our best interests in his heart, had been dissolved. But, I wasn't sure the revolution was the answer to our plight either. I wondered out loud where all the chaos was leading our country. My worries were valid but no one really cared about the questions and opinions of a nine-year-old girl. Often, when people rush from one choice to the next, they make terrible mistakes and incur consequences that take a long time to overcome. The new Islamic regime was the consequence and the Iranian nation is still paying for its mistake.

Back in our family, Khosro was stuck in Chahbahar for the next few months. A couple of weeks after the chaos started, mum changed her mind about his returning home because she thought the situation in Isfahan was too volatile. The Shah had quickly imposed curfew during the nights and when the protests increased he extended it to daytime as well. The situation was unavoidably progressing on a dangerous and intense path, particularly for us, because our home was located on a major road. In peacetime, the location was convenient and safe but it was at the edge of the war zone and in such turbulent times it was not a safe shelter.

Mum used to say her farewells every time she went to buy bread and other life necessities. Women wearing black chadors were being stopped and questioned by soldiers due to incidents on the streets of Tehran. Women belonging to a militia group called Mojahedin, initially founded by Khomeini in the early 1970s, dressed in black chadors and carried concealed automatic weapons with which they ambushed and killed soldiers. Mum changed her black chador to a colored one but even then she was stopped by soldiers and questioned.

My father abandoned us in the heat of the revolution. To get himself out of harm's way, he left Iran to visit Ali Junior in the United States where he remained for the duration of the revolution. I should not have been surprised that when we needed my father the most, he wasn't around to take care of us.

In the middle of all our troubles, my grandparents decided to pay us a sudden visit. We were the first stop for their yearly vacation. My mum had all of us to feed and we hardly had any money for food. She decided to sell some gold jewelry, including mine, and a very valuable Persian carpet for a lot less than it was worth. Gold, jewelry, Persian carpets and fine china are common investments in Iran and a source of emergency cash or barter.

As the protests became routine, the Shah's army started enforcing the curfew, night and day, to the degree that grocery shopping was nearly impossible and increasingly dangerous. Mum had stored some flour, Armenian cracked bread, beans, rice, potatoes, onions and cooking oil. We had hard times aplenty ahead of us.

People were all pumped up and eager to take their frustration out on the Shah. Rumors, true and false, about the Shah and his family emerged. Khomeini was lecturing from Paris and called upon everyone to set aside his or her own agenda and rise up united against the Shah. That included the Mojahedin that had now taken a different direction from their early days. The communists, who denied God, the Kurds, who wanted an independent country, the right and the left all came together with a common goal; to de-throne the Shah.

Khomeini made many empty promises; including one that when his government came to power, he would give each family their share of the nation's oil and virtually everything would be free. People looked to him as the Messiah. To expedite his devious plans, his speeches were printed and spread among the people every night. In an effort to make the Shah look like a monster, Khomeini's henchmen killed innocent people and blamed the Shah. Oil production workers were the first people to go on a long strike. Shortly after the chaos started, soldiers started to shoot people at the order of their superiors. From the rooftop, I saw bodies on the streets. People armed with shotguns and handguns roamed the streets. I watched with trepidation as the boys of the neighborhood came to our house and made street bombs.

It is unlikely the revolution would have happened except for the great promises of national integrity through self reliance which Khomeini and other leaders of the revolution made to millions of Iranians. The promised share of oil revenue and free electricity for everyone never came through. And, not so surprisingly, even though the revolutionaries had cursed the Shah for selling Iranian oil to the West, after coming to power the revolutionary government, even though denying it publicly, continued to do so in order to sustain its economy. The government of Iran continued to make hollow claims that the people could see did not have genuine merit. The first few months after the Iran revolution, many individuals rose to the challenge and stood up bravely against the regime. Kurds, Turks and Baloochs eventually rebelled. The reason they didn't succeed was because the government took strong measures, terrorized their families, killed thousands and arrested the remaining members of the opposition cells.

It is chilling to remember but during the Iranian revolution, people's senses and morals seemed to be altered. They failed the test of humanity. The picture of a kind, poised and cultured people seemed a distant dream. Crime seemed to be people's joy and pleasure. I witnessed protestors robbing shops and banks. I watched as one bank burned to ashes with charred money flying everywhere. Instead of playing with dolls and my playmates, at eight years old I was taken to the first of the many funerals, prayers, and burial ceremonies that I was to attend. It became a way of life and it was just the beginning of the miserable decade ahead. Life was chaotic and seemed pointless. Beyond the confines of the family, there was much to fear.

The Shah was trying to revive the corpse of his monarchy but by late October 1977, when he returned from his cancer treatment in the United States, people knew he had lost his US allies. President Carter wanted the Shah to stop ordering the torture of prisoners. The relationship between Iran and the United States was put on hold until the Shah met the demands of the UN International Human Rights advocates and the opposition groups active in Iran.

Khomeini in particular, among all the opposition, took advantage of the weakened relationship between the Shah and West. The Shah felt betrayed. The price of oil hit the apex for that decade. Khomeini knew it was time to stab the Shah once and for all. He was determined to take him out of power. In the eyes of Khomeini's followers, the Shah wasn't competent to run the country. Also, he was sick; constantly seeking new treatments for his cancer in the West, leaving the country in the hands of his trusted Prime Minister, his generals, close family members and friends. Some were members of the Senate or Majilis; all were members of the Shah's private elite club of Freemason that virtually no one knew about. The members of this club were his trustees and sworn members who would not have spoken about the Shah, no matter the circumstances.

Other rumors had surfaced, along with alleged pictures of tortured prisoners and inhuman behavior by SAVAK, the Shah's horrifying Intelligence center and Secret Service. Allegations against them were serious and quite graphic and, if in fact true, the Shah did not deserve to be our king. It was alleged that he watched as prisoners were tormented and killed by his officers in order to decimate the opposition and make him feel safer. Other allegations were about his boudoir habits, his lust for women, his countless mistresses and, more damning, the misuse of public funds for personal agendas. On top of it all, the extravagant 2,500[th] anniversary celebration of the Persian Kingdom at the ancient site of Persepolis in Shiraz, together with his attempt to abandon the lunar calendar in favor of a calendar based on Persian history caused people to conclude he didn't know what he was doing with the country.

In a desperate attempt to save his crown, he made drastic changes and fatal mistakes. In January 1978, Ettalaat newspaper, in an attempt to destroy Khomeini's reputation, printed a deadly article claiming he was a British agent. The article, intended to create a scandal, was false and backfired. It not only didn't help; it gave Khomeini's followers the opportunity they had been waiting for. The lies made people more furious than ever. First, the bold and then a flood of people violated the curfew the generals had set up. The Shah's top generals compounded the mistake when they tried to end the protest by opening fire on the crowd. Live pictures of September 4, 1978, at the end of Ramadan, showed more than 100,000 people pouring into the streets of Tehran to demonstrate against the Shah. Tanks surrounded by armed soldiers were moving toward the protestors. The demonstration started with chants but soon got out of hand and became a riot. Thousands of people were killed in an unequal battle of machines against human shields on that day which came to be called Black Friday.

TV stations were shut down. We were no longer able to hear or watch what was happening in different parts of our country. The Shah was able to control the media but could not undermine the power of the people. News travels with people. As in the past, they phoned each other. Those who did not have access to a telephone traveled from one city to the next, relaying the news to families and friends along with pictures of Khomeini and fliers of his latest speech.

The following day, a pale and disturbed man, a far cry from the confident commander that the Shah always portrayed himself as, appeared on national TV and told the outraged people that he had no idea what was happening until it was too late. Whether he knew or not, his name is forever smirched as the killer of thousands of his own people; comparable to Pinochet, the Chilean dictator.

To protect his crown, the Shah, unquestionably, did many dishonorable things of which he could not have been proud. He killed his opponents but, to damn him with faint praise, he was never known to permit anyone to kill the innocent. The Shah was furious about the incredibly stupid actions of his generals and even though he apologized immediately and fired or jailed those who ordered the massacre, the apology came too late. People remembered his actions against Mossadegh and other nationalists and this time they didn't forgive him. Now, more determined than ever, they wanted him to step down from power and many even wished him dead. This was a new beginning for people who had forever believed that Shahs were God sent.

In an attempt to repair his damaged image, Shah fired his long time friend, Prime Minster Manoocheher Hovaida, who became the designated scapegoat to take the blame for all the corruption, the disruption of the country and mismanaged money scandals. Hovaida occupied the post of Prime Minster longer by far than any of his predecessors. He was also a high-ranking politician with close ties to the English. Groundless rumors floated that he was secretly working for Her Majesty, the Queen of England, while he was Iran's Prime Minster. He was also correctly believed to be an influential member of the elite society of Freemason.

The Freemasons originated and played a great role during the Qajar dynasty. It was an important achievement in contrast to the backward Qajar's other failures. The highly secretive club was started by the first group of expatriate Iranian students, who were regarded as important as the ambassadors of Iran in Europe. The leader of this club, Asgar Khan AfsharRoomi, was among the first policy makers who had studied abroad. He created a more receptive diplomatic arena for Napoleon in Persia, as opposed to the hated British who remained neutral during the Iran-Russia War. After Napoleon's defeat, however, he was hunted by both the French and the British. To protect himself and other student activists, he started the Freemasons club. Students, including the Shah, who had studied in France or England, became familiar with the club. As the flow of students to Europe continued, club members became influential politicians, doctors, authors and economists. The idea was similar to Skull and Bones of Yale University. Although the club disappeared from the public eye, they were the first socially influential class of Iran and entered into a private political arena of their own. In time, the original slogan 'All for one and one for all,' was corrupted into 'All for the Shah,' who was the leader of the society. Freemasonry grew in Iran for more than 200 years before Iranians spoke or even knew about the society. Originally, nearly every member was located in a different city and held a sensitive government position. Membership is still secretive, elite and widely dispersed.

The Shah jailed him to show the people he had listened to their pleas. When Hovaida was arrested in his home, it was as if he knew this would happen. He was calm and didn't seem to be bothered by the fact he was being sent to jail. He was shown on TV in his jail cell that more resembled a large office with bars instead of windows. He thought, or perhaps was told, that his arrest was part of an act, a temporary gesture to calm the people down.

If it was an act, it went terribly, terribly wrong. Along with Hovaida, General Nagi, the man who gave the order to open fire on the crowd, was also arrested. The general, with good reason, wasn't as calm and seemed nervous and shaking. During his post-arrest TV publicity and interview, his mouth was foaming.

In January 1979, the Shah chose a new Prime Minster, Dr. Bakhtiar, who had belonged for more than thirty years to the Nationalist group, a well-known critic of the Shah and his policies. He had also been a deputy minister in the government of Dr. Mossadegh, the renowned Prime Minster who fought for years to nationalize Iran's oil. Reza Shah had killed his father. He spent six years in jail and was banned from the country for more than ten years. He was a colleague of Mr. Bazargan and his allegiance was to that party before Bazargan changed direction and joined Khomeini.

After the revolution settled down, Mehdi Bazargan, the next in line to succeed Dr. Bakhtiar, became the National Front leader and the first Prime Minster. The National Front expelled Bakhtiar from its membership claiming he wasn't a true opposition and had sided with a long time enemy, the Shah. Dr. Bakhtiar, in his own defense, called himself The Tornado Bird. Metaphorically, he analyzed revolution as a tornado and expressed through his poetic gestures that he was not scared and would be able to manage despite all the pressure. He had fought his entire life for the rights of the people and now that he had the chance of his lifetime, the people he wanted to serve had changed. Khomeini and his followers took every measure to show him as a weak, incompetent worshipper of the Monarchy. Khomeini became an over night celebrity when his picture appeared on the cover of Time Magazine as one of the 21st century's influential men; as indeed, he was.

Khomeini's followers even took measures far beyond the rational. It was maddening to see people fall for the tricks. I believe dressing a monkey as a wise man does not make him one. Khomeini's followers resorted to any deception and turned politics into a circus de soleil. On one occasion, only days before the Shah left Iran, Khomeini's minions made the shocking statement that Khomeini's image was on the moon. We all gathered on the roof. I was a child, uninfluenced by the hysteria of politics, and kept asking. Where is the image? Adults from all walks of life gazed at the moon's pockmarked face and everyone started saying, "Yes, there he is. He is on the moon, can you see him?" pointing at the same pimples on the moon's face that have been there for over four billion years. Some even shed tears of joy and bowed and prayed, declaring that God himself sent Khomeini and that is why his image appeared on the moon.

My dear God! It was sickening to watch adult people fall for the Las Vegas magic tricks. Khomeini was trying to find people's lowest threshold of gullibility and determine how much he was able to squeeze them. People were so naïve, thinking that because he wore the same outfit as the Prophet, he would never betray their trust and would lead them to a greater life.

Changes in the Shah's governing method had come along at a very rocky juncture and timing for the new Prime Minister couldn't have been worse. He took his shaky seat shortly after the Shah fled the country on January 16, 1979 for a vacation, leaving him in political limbo.

Dr. Bakhtiar was determined to prove he meant business but inadvisably conveyed his plans in lines of poetry; not realizing people were not into political poetry and did not necessarily find him charming. His softer side inspired many humiliating chants by angry protestors. To appease his opposition, Dr. Bakhtiar decided to free many of the Mojahedin prisoners. He lifted sanctions imposed on the media by the Shah and SAVAK and televised protests. His ideas were noble and could have lead Iran to a democratic state had he been given the chance. He held no grudge against people who mocked him and stopped censoring the national news. Of course, that didn't have any effect on the people who had already made up their mind and had seen their messiah on the moon. He even agreed to have an open-mike night with the leader of his opposition on national TV. He promised free referendum, free speech and to dissolve SAVAK. He cancelled a seven billion dollar army purchase contract with the US. To please Khomeini and to blunt their campaign against him on the issue, he announced that Iran would no longer sell its oil to the United States, Israel or South Africa, which was lead by an apartheid regime.

Had he come to power a few years earlier, it might have been possible to avoid or dissuade the rioting crowds and resulting mob madness. People could have achieved their dreams through a free democratic Iran. Although his actions were noble, they were not enough to stop the fevered, angry protestors who chose to close their eyes and ears and parrot their programmed mantras. People let their religious obligations be taken for granted by the radicals. Khomeini and his followers manipulated the nation by false promises and phony religious reasoning. Bakhtiar, who was in favor of modernism and separation of religion and politics, didn't survive the political maelstrom long enough to make any progressive differences.

He was left alone in charge of a chaotic country. The petroleum workers went on strike, hydro workers stopped working and followers of Khomeini sabotaged the numbers on hydro and water bills. Angry people received bills much higher than the actual amount due. In our home, our bill was ten times higher than usual. The inflated bills caused people's blood to boil, fueling the anger destined to force the Monarchy out of Iran's history for good.

Army and Navy loyalists, sworn to the Shah, encouraged and welcomed by Khomeini's camp were changing sides and joining the militia. The Shah's supporters were disappearing overnight. To save themselves from the militia's anger, even some SAVAK members betrayed the generals by revealing their plans and the time and place of secret rendezvous. One of the SAVAK members, who had long served the Shah, was the son of a distant friend of our family. As the new regime took power, his brothers also joined it. He helped them by giving them information. To save his own life, he changed sides and became a Khomeini supporter. He reported on people using our home phone.

In the last days of his presidency, Bakhtiar, in a desperate attempt to survive, sent a delegation to Paris to open a dialogue with Khomeini ministers. He thought Khomeini wanted a democratic country; unaware Khomeini didn't care about the country. Khomeini refused to meet with the messengers because he saw himself above the law. Although he hated the Shah, they had this arrogance in common. Khomeini's plan for the future of Iran was not to build a modern paradise but to force the country backward into a metaphoric cult similar to the Qajar dynasty, with women wearing covered outfits similar to Afghani's and children memorizing the Koran as the rode their donkeys on the way home.

Dr. Bakhtiar tried to buy time to calm the populace. He asked Khomeini to delay his arrival and tried to reason with him to come at a later time. The Prime Minister vowed he would not allow Khomeini's airplane to land and closed Tehran's airport. The Air Force countered that they would not follow the Prime Minister's orders and the airport patrol and personnel announced they would assist Khomeini's airplane.

On January 29, 1979, Khomeini exhorted the nation to come to the streets if they favored the end to the monarchy. That day was called 'Street Referendum.' People from all walks of life turned out on the streets. I was hesitant about going along but, since I was the only person in the entire neighborhood that wanted to stay at home, mum was afraid a stranger might take advantage of the situation and come to our home and hurt me, so she took me with her. Although Dr. Bakhtiar wasn't loved, the people didn't hate him either but, by this referendum, Khomeini's put the end to his ministry.

Two more protests on the scale of Black Friday followed. Khomeini arrived from France on February 1, 1979 and received a warm welcome from people who had risked their lives in the street to force his return. On the charter Air France Airbus flight to Mehr-Abad airport in Tehran, a journalist asked him what he felt, coming back victoriously after being away from his country for so many years. He coldly answered, "Nothing." I, along with my family, was watching him live on TV. I remember I was shocked and puzzled on seeing his cold, calculating face and emotionless behavior. This answer struck many of us as ominous but, regrettably, it was a little too late for regret. Upon his arrival, he made a trip to Tehran's famous graveyard where he made a speech containing many allegations, now censored, which his own regime forbids anyone to publicly repeat.

On the day of Khomeini's arrival in February of 1979, the Prime Minister fled the country under a death sentence by Khomeini's direct order that all elements of the Shah's regime were to be put to death. Nearly 11 years later, in 1991 at age 76, he was assassinated in his home in France. Despite the end result of the revolution, people's motives were honorable. They wanted a better government for the country, a better life for future generations. They had yet to learn that the mullah's were not quite so honest with their motives and robbed people of their dreams. Everything about the revolution was pre-planned. The people of Iran were kept misinformed and in the dark.

Even the Cinema Rex 'accident' that took more than 400 lives in Abadan in the summer of 1978 was pre-planned. Opposition sources believed the mullahs orchestrated the monumental tragedy in an attempt to portray the Shah as a monster. Although SAVAK wanted to destroy the opposition, it had no use for killing ordinary people. At the site of the incident, a large gasoline tank truck was parked outside and the unfortunates locked inside were burned and barbecued alive in an arson set fire. As insurgencies around the world proliferate, it shows how the hardcore fundamentalists of Shiah and other Muslims, take pride in paving their path to Hell with pools of blood of the innocent. The tragedy is now a reminder of how brutal the fundamentalists can be. In any effort to discredit the Shah, so far as the mullahs were concerned, the victims were expendable. Years later, the truth surfaced. Hashemi, the man behind the student takeover of the US embassy, confessed to taking part in many horrendous crimes. More evidence has surfaced that proves some of the higher mullahs had a hand directly or indirectly, through their followers, who were responsible for the emolument of hundreds of innocents. This incident proved they have no shame or reluctance to sacrifice others for their own agenda. Whether Khomeini approved this specific event doesn't matter. He had authorized his followers to kill for his benefit and therefore the blood is on his hands as well as the hands of the organizers and perpetrators of this atrocity.

THE AMERICAN HOSTAGES

While Khomeini was still in exile, he made sure his followers used every possible lead and bit of information to negatively portray the Shah. He then took it a step further from his usual anti-Shah monologue to being anti-American and added the United States to the Shah's picture. Iranians never had animosity toward the people of the United States and, in fact, had a good relationship with them ever since the two countries started having a political dialogue many years prior to the revolution. Their resentment was dictated and not earned.

The revolution was about Iran and its future, not about disconnecting the country from the rest of the world. The people's idea of the revolution was to get themselves out of the maze they had been forced to run for centuries. Khomeini's greed and his hidden agenda to influence other countries were buried in his original message and disguised his real goal.

Khomeini chastised the Shah for his lavish life and blamed the United States for allowing him to live it. That was the instigation and focus of the anti-American slogans chanted in Iran ever since. Khomeini blamed the West for women uncovering their hair in public, for the clothing they wore, for their independence, for letting the Shah stay in power and for every reason he offered and more that only he knew. Whatever point he was trying to prove, it appeared his grouch was more personal than religious or political.

It was never a secret from most of the informed people of Iran that the CIA and England had a hand in the Shah's decisions on running the country. What was surprising was that they left him isolated when he needed his allies the most. Despite all the tension in the country, people never had any desire to be anti-West. The people of Iran had good relations with Westerners and particularly the Americans who spent more tourist dollars in Iran than any other country. Many Iranian students were studying abroad in the United States, had married Americans and had families in the United States.

Iranians were always advocates for culture and dignity and stood proudly, with head on straight above everyone else in the Middle East. This was part of our heritage and pride of being one of the most peaceful nations among other volatile nations in the sensitive Middle East. We were an extremely proud nation and liked to boast that we would never take a life for political reasons or money. We were not accustomed to the concept of human shields or mixed rules of engagement with personal agendas. To us, honor was more important than anything else. Until the Islamic revolution, we had managed to set an enviable example for many Europeans and Americans to show how hospitable we were.

Khomeini changed all that. He taught the older generation and many of my generation to forget about rules and morals. He taught new rules of engagement and cultivated the seeds of hatred he had sown. During Khomeini's exile in Iraq, he said, "My soldiers are still in diapers," meaning his followers would come from the next generation. Khomeini pumped up the militia's blood by his constant warped message of his version of theoretical Islam. The true Islam would never have approved his actions. He proclaimed that whatever he did, he did for the country and for God.

His followers decided to take over the United States embassy on November 4, 1979 in an attempt to force the Shah to let Khomeini return to Iran. It was supposed to be a few days deal but it turned into 444 days of captivity for 52 Americans. Terrorizing the US citizens not only didn't help the revolution; it lessened the ability to open a meaningful dialogue for negotiation and future diplomatic relationship to achieve what the revolutionaries wanted to discover about the Shah. Revolutionaries claimed they wanted information about the Shah but, by the time they finally broke down the doors and entered the embassy, employees had managed to shred all the information. In retrospect, one suspects that all they needed to do was ask. Oil was far more important to the US than the Shah's old harem secrets.

The occupation of the embassy was a big set back for the new government and blocked communication between the US and Iran. The United States retaliated by blocking Iranian assets in US banks. Diplomatic efforts failed to resolve the standoff. To make matters worse, in April of 1980, a clandestine US mission to rescue the hostages went horribly wrong. The United States attempted to rescue the hostages by landing aircraft and troops in Tabas, a desert area east of Tehran. The operation turned into a disaster when a C-130 and a helicopter collided in a sandstorm, killing eight American crewmembers.

The lunatic government of Iran took advantage of the situation to further brainwash the naive people and disseminated propaganda that God wanted the Americans dead. Rumors had it that in a collaborated effort with the previous Russian government, the Kremlin had a hand in shooting down the helicopters. The mission was aborted. The Ayatollah Khomeini was a leader who did not oppose his followers chanting his name and calling him the successor of Mahdy and Imam Khomeini.

According to the rules of Shiah, as distinguished from Sunni, a person must be sinless to be an Imam. Only the twelve Imam who belonged to the prophet's family, or their direct descendants, can carry such a title. Khomeini held himself out to be, and made many believe, he was an Imam without sin. That, of course, in itself is a sin. Khomeini compared himself with the Prophet Mohammad and I heard him say in his own words, "The Prophet didn't finish his job, I have finished it." As the pressure directed at him increased, Khomeini shifted responsibility for the hostage debacle to others; surmising that if the outcome were deadly, the Senate would take the blame, not him. He loudly proclaimed to Bani-Sadr, the first President elected after the revolution, that only the Senate could free the hostages. Khomeini occupied the highest office in Iran yet dodged the responsibility of saving the American lives. It wasn't about politics, religion or the future of the country. Khomeini wasn't satisfied to let the Americans go; he didn't want anything from them but to humiliate them. His hatred was clearly personal.

In recent years I interviewed many of his followers. A number of them continue to maintain that Khomeini never approved hostage situations; but he never denied nor condemned the practice either. In fact, when the 3,000 students climbed the walls of the embassy, he praised them. He had their leash in his hand and directed them wherever he desired.

Finally, after 444 days in captivity, on January 20, 1981 with continued vigilance from the impeached president, Mr. Bani-Sadr, the Americans were sent home unharmed. There can be little doubt that the hostage fiasco was instrumental in President Jimmy Carter's loss to Ronald Reagan in his bid for re-election. The real losers of the hostage situation were the people of Iran who were and, to some extent still are, hated by Americans. Even today, many Americans look upon Iranians as terrorists.

Khomeini in
Behesht-Zahra Graveyard

On January 16, 1979, Khomeini arrived from France and went directly to Tehran's famous graveyard for a national broadcast from a podium set up among the gravestones. His choice of site for the address was strange but it was his statements that are recorded in history that brought years of misery.

The day Khomeini returned to Tehran was a sad day for the country. With his arrival, the evil spirits of demons buried by the heroes of Persian civilization were released from their coffins. After thousands of years of history, the future was gloomier than ever. To eliminate the 'remnants of the Shah,' as the new regime called them, Khomeini took every possible measure, some not quite legal, others blatantly illegal. Hundreds of people a day had hearings and by dawn of the next day their death sentences were carried out.

On the podium, Khomeini made what seemed to be an unrehearsed and shocking statement; an accusation motivated by anger. He said, "Shah has ruined our cities and built graveyards. We will change that." He certainly did but not for the better. Khomeini's murderous skills were far superior to the Shah's. If he and the Shah had entered into a graveyard contest, Khomeini would have had no trouble winning the people killing competition. For many years, even when he was alive, his statement was heavily censored. To this day, no one dares mention his words in public.

Quite the opposite of Khomeini's statement, it was his regime that ruined people's lives and his graveyards proliferated as a result of his brutality. Since the revolution, seventy percent of all villages have been destroyed or abandoned. Tehran's population has pushed the city to the verge of explosion. The graveyard, one of the largest in the world, has become a city unto itself. Since the Shah left, the famous Tehran graveyard has become the prime example of Khomeini's speech and the devastation his regime brought to Iranian's lives. Perhaps we could call it the silent Tehran. When it was built, over fifty years ago, it was a village compared to what it is now; a deluxe city within overcrowded Tehran. Behesht-Zahra, which means Zahra's Paradise, is unlike any other graveyard tourists have ever seen and has become a tourist attraction.

I am not sure why tourists want to visit a graveyard in the first place. I guess it must be the fascination and the excitement of this huge silent city that makes it an attraction. Where else on earth do people have to take a tour bus to find someone's grave? Graves are not just graves. There are high-rises and condos within the graveyard. People are sardined into the graveyard, much as the graves are. This method of graveyard development was new in the history of our country. Since the mullah's have no expertise in international law, politics or how to run a country, perhaps we should have shared some of the mullah's graveyard building expertise and knowledge with other nations.

Another famous and deadly declaration that Khomeini made was, "Iran will export its revolution to the neighboring countries." This was a direct threat to the Arab world and to kings who didn't want to repeat the same journey as the Shah. The Arab world was fed up and alarmed by Khomeini's arrogance and in the months to come there was a plan for Iran. The fire he started wasn't going to be put out for the next eight years.

Khomeini showed no affection toward people who later sacrificed their lives for his revolution. When people who had been injured in the war visited him, he would not touch them and wore latex gloves to bless them.

He also said, "Dealing with Western society, especially the United States, brought Iran nothing but misery." The regime came to power in a country that needed help from international organizations to stand on its own feet. To overcome the problem, they took land and money from every wealthy family, including the Shah's. Some was given to the masses; some disappeared into the coffers of the privileged. Most of the wealth in Iran comes from land, houses and Persian carpets. These were taken from wealthy families and now belong to the mullahs and their families.

During the time of the Shah, sixty percent of Iranian women were working; the highest employment rate for women in the history of the country. Women's education and the workforce went hand in hand and both were praised. After the revolution, most women were fired. A new dress code was declared for all women of Iran, requiring them to be covered in public except for their faces. Most women who held a civil service position had to take mandatory Islamic classes in order to stay in their positions. After the revolution, the workforce was severely restricted for professional women. The government opposed having women work any job that enabled them to supervise a male.

Little by little, aware Iranians became wary of Khomeini's motives. Every time he opened his mouth to give a new speech, he stated something against someone in some part of the world. His statements and actions brought irreversible consequences, misery and harsh times for the Iranian nation and turned our lives harder every day. The destruction of our country wasn't part of his promises when he landed, but it was what he carried forward without hesitation or any concerns for our welfare.

Soon after his speech, an organization called Liberation Movement Office started to work on liberating the neighboring countries. Understandably, criticism from the neighbors was harsh. Khomeini was not a politician and did not bother to consult or hire experts in that field. He apparently did not know what sovereignty meant or if his words were against the UN mandates. I have a feeling he did not even know what the UN was.

One of the members of this Liberation Movement was Mahdy Hashemi, a mullah who was arrested years later in 1987 and confessed to a series of gruesome murders. Among his victims was the innocent Ayatollah Shamsabadi, a *fagih* from Isfahan who, in the early months of the revolution, expressed strong opposition to the idea of the de-crowning the Shah and told the revolutionaries he would not support their ideas. Hashemi confessed and explained how he spent the afternoon in this man's home and by late afternoon when he fell asleep, used his turban to strangle him.

I was a child when he was killed. I vividly recall the day I heard this news. We still lived in the Jewish family's house. The Shah had come to Isfahan for a short visit. Mum and I went for a walk and I sat down outside on the stairs of a large bank. The automatic door kept opening and closing. Finally, the bank manager approached us and asked mum to remove me from where I enjoyed the view and to take me nearer the crowd to clap for the Shah.

I knew he was trying to get rid of me but I didn't feel any obligation to leave my perch to clap for a king. Mum and I resumed our walk. While passing across the street from an old house, we saw a large crowd of obvious mourners. Mum, who had my hand in hers, approached the women and asked them why they were crying. With tears in their eyes, they replied that the Ayatollah Shamsabadi had been killed. "He was the sponsor of many poor people," these women said. "Because he is gone, our children are going to die." Shocked and sad, mum asked who would kill an old man. She too started crying.

To secure its power, on March 31, 1979, the regime announced it would hold a free referendum and people would have the right to choose their government. Every individual, sixteen years old or above, was encouraged to vote. Millions turned out.

Manoocheher, after reading his ballot, did not cast his vote and brought his ballot home.

On the ballot, the choices were:

The Republic of Islam: Yes

The Monarchy: No.

I gather the regime, perhaps correctly, perceived people as totally ignorant and assumed no one would notice that both of the choices meant this regime is going to stay.

Aftershocks of the Revolution

For the first few weeks after Khomeini's arrival everyone was happy and celebrating. But, it didn't take long for people to say, "Now what? Can we go back to our lives?" They expected the new regime to bring progress and prosperity. Instead, they received disappointments and more bad news. During the revolution, Khomeini kept people going with false promises. As soon as he took power, he seemed to forget his promises. Some of the new government promises included a share of the public wealth; everyone would receive some money from the sale of oil. People were promised they would no longer have to pay for electricity and water and mothers would receive assistance money for every child. As usual, promises are easier made than kept.

In dreamland, this all looked very colorful but all the experts agreed the promises that the new government had made were simply impossible to fulfill. They were, in other words, bogus. Of course, that wasn't much of a concern for a government that didn't really care if it disappointed anyone. A job had been done, a mission accomplished and they were done with people.

The Iranian nation had been spoiled by modest prices and low inflation. The wonderful life that we now fondly remembered had been possible because of subsidized prices. The Shah's government picked up most of the tab. The least expectation was to keep the flow of the economy as it was for many years. However, within a month, people started observing increases in prices and six months after the Shah's demise, prices had risen drastically. The poor were getting poorer while the rich were getting richer. This was exactly the anti-Shah accusation that we used to hear from Khomeini; now we saw it in action.

After dissolving SAVAK, Khomeini took all measures to strengthen his new government. He arrested many of its high-ranking officers. Due to new residents, partially from the Mojahedin, who had not yet received a piece of the pie they were waiting for, tensions were rising again.

In December 1985, SAVAK was reinstated; this time under the name, SAVAMA, a much softer, more pleasant name for the horrendous organization that did the dirty work for the Shah. Now, a rose by another name but with the same smell was doing it for the new regime. Mr. Hashemi Rafsanjani, Senate speaker at the time, personally persisted in recalling some former employees of SAVAK who were expert in torturing prisoners and gathering information.

The regime took every step to protect itself. To this end, on March 5th 1979, Khomeini ordered the creation of a special private army. It was called Sepah Pasdaran and included both professional and newly trained soldiers. These people were the veterans of the revolution; they had no empathy for anyone and no remorse for their despicable actions. The Basige, the military Army, was an untrained, unprofessional gaggle that loved the new regime and was ready to sacrifice their lives to keep them in power. While the Basige was limited to as few as practical, it wasn't dissolved completely. It was kept as a back up in case the regime needed professional units quickly. Since they were not trusted, they had to put up with the new changes. The regime kept a watchful eye on them.

The people of Iran, seeing an opportunity to make a difference in their destiny, thought the leader of the 1979 revolution was another Mossadegh, a Messiah. Unfortunately, that wasn't true. The blood of young men and women who were killed in protests painted the streets and walls and lives were shattered. It all went to waste. The revolution was swept aside from its roots and would not have happened had not too many positions been filled by the wrong people. Many of Khomeini's new loyalists were the same people who once had sworn to save the Shah but, to protect their own position, turned their back on him and sold him out.

Many were hanged and death squadrons killed many more. The number of murdered in the first year rose to an alarming 12,000. This was the reported number. The actual number was much higher. Everyone who had a grouch against anybody, particularly if that person happened to be famous reported on him or her. Among the people who were reported were established patriots such as Ms. Farman Farman, a princess and a direct descendent to the Qajar Dynasty; the first Iranian woman who stepped on US soil in the midst of World War I. She was a cousin of Dr. Mossadegh, the beloved Prime Minster who was imprisoned by the Shah and died in his own home.

In her youth, her journey from Iran brought her to the United States where she was educated at the University of Southern California. She returned to Iran to establish a long legacy of helping ordinary people. She opened the first social service school and for years sacrificed her personal life to give women and men a better life. As she personally related to me, she was nearly killed by ignorant students who pointed a gun at her while arresting her on spurious charges; the main one being that she had attended a government approved social service convention in Israel some twenty years before. She was taken to Jamaran, Khomeini's residence after he came to power. She spent a day and a night in near freezing temperatures in the back courtyard of Jamaran, listening to the execution of other unfortunates.

Thankfully, she was lucky enough to be interrogated by Ayatollah Talegani who knew of her work and realized the absurdity of the charges against her. He quietly arranged for her to be left alone in the unlocked yard with an implied invitation to walk away. Talegani also provided refuge in his home for Mojahedin when the Pasdarn was arresting them for anti-regime actions in the post-revolution period. He supported their efforts to voice demands for reforms to benefit the majority of the people. His concern was not money or position; he wanted to protect people from the pretenders dressed in the Prophets garb. Talegani himself became a victim of this evil government after he voiced great concerns about the massive killing and dispossession of Khomeini's real and imagined enemies.

Many who had been thwarted in their wishes and ambition took power into their own hands and killed others, rationalizing their crime as revolutionary justice. The innocent paid a heavy price.

The generals, officers and anyone who had ever had any influence in the Shah's government were in danger of being reported to the new military, the Sepah Pasdaran. They were immediately arrested and sentenced in a matter of minutes. Hundreds were summarily executed. Among those killed was the former Prime Minster, Mr. Hovaida, who was imprisoned when the Shah fled the country. For once, he seemed distracted. He was sentenced the day following his first court hearing and was not given a trial or a chance to defend himself.

A Turban Replaced a Crown

These days, few, if any, of the Iranians who formerly chanted against the Shah, doubt that, despite his excesses, he provided a much better government for the country than his successors; even though, by all accounts, he was not a saint but a true dictator, by whose direct orders many men were brutally tortured, kidnapped and killed.

Khomeini, on the other hand, was supposedly a man of God and presumably opposed to such horrible actions. Yet, once he had the power, he was even more brutal than the Shah, with no compassion for the innocent. The consequences for the nation did not matter to him as long as he stayed in control. This was yet another blow to our face. Our trust was abused and our hopes and dreams for the future were mutilated. The white pigeon of freedom that was flying high after the revolution was captured and slaughtered one more time.

To confirm Khomeini's power, after the new members of the senate, mostly mullahs, were selected and began working, they promoted him to the same title as the Shah. He became the Commander in Chief; a commander who never stepped out of his own house.

His followers claim he was a scholar. He may have been a scholar in their minds but his only known academic credential was primary school before he was sent to the religious schools. The mind boggles at the absurdity. With no political education, no military experience, no grasp of economics or business. I cannot understand why anyone in their right mind would pick, as the leader of a country, a person who does not have the qualifications for any job at all.

It is not certain whether Khomeini was interested in power from the beginning or was manipulated by his disciples to accept the post. Either way, once he held the club, he relished the title, the power and the flattery he received. I wonder if it ever crossed his mind to ponder, What kind of commander am I, that doesn't even know the meaning of the word *logistic* without having it explained?

Ultimately, Khomeini, the Commander In Chief, controlled everything. According to Article Five of Iran's current constitution, his duties include: to book the names of the council guardians, the chief judges in the judicial system, the Chief of Staff for the armed forces, the Commanders for the Pasdar Army and the regular Army, Air Force, Navy, Supreme Defense Counsel and he had the direct vote and veto on who will be the President and who will not.

He was also in charge of who lives and who dies. He was a brutal dictator, a hundred times worse than his predecessors. Most of Khomeini's admirers that I interviewed defended him claiming he had nothing to do with the manipulation and atrocities. In dreamland, we would all be responsible only for what we wish in our heart. In the real world, it doesn't matter what people think, wish or desire. Whether Khomeini was a nice person and kind to his children or not is irrelevant. The world has endless proof that he wasn't a nice guy. Even if he was, when someone chooses an action, he must face the consequences. Whether or not he intended to destroy Persian civilization, he did not intervene to prevent his follower's from doing so. He did not make peace with the world. He is responsible, even though deep down in his heart, he might not have wished his followers to take us to the depth of darkness.

When he landed at Tehran's airport, it is probable that few people, except me, saw him as anything but a man of God, dropping from the sky to bring prosperity to our country and peace to the tinderbox of the Muslim world. The multitude thought it would be a great blessing for our nation.

It is a very sad life when a nine-year-old child, looking ahead to her future, can only see dark clouds and a gloomy life. I wasn't the only one facing that future. I was only one of millions of women but one of the few to realize our pending fate and question the inevitability of it.

Khomeini's descent on Iran turned out to be the mistake of our history. He became the king wearing a turban. Even, if he wasn't behind all the policies his followers carried out, his quest to influence other countries and his greed was apparent from his unrehearsed speeches. He didn't take orders from anyone and he did not question his close follower's actions; allowing them to burn, kill, and rob at will. The new regime took great pleasure in destroying the Shah's palaces, robbing museums and burning books. They even changed the names of the heroes of the past and the words of our poets to something more suitable to the regime's style. As the ultimate absurdity, the regime changed the names of cities that had *shah* in the historical name. Khomeini's ghouls didn't even have mercy or respect for the dead and opened the graves of our ancient kings.

I nearly became the victim of his Fatwa, or order, 'For the blessing, spy against your neighbor.' The order was carried out to the extent that neighbors went so far as to try to see if others listened to pop music or read books that the regime didn't approve. Khomeini promised paradise for people who reported on others. Obviously, there are evil and evil-spirited citizens among the population of any nations.

While sitting in the shade in our yard one day, hiding from the blazing hot sun and feeding my pet chicks, I was whistling a song that was indeed quite anti-regime. I saw two shadows of people running by on the roof. The neighbor had sent her daughters onto our roof to listen to a pop song I was quietly whistling, obviously waiting for me to defame our rulers. I was worried for a while but apparently I did not whistle off key because nothing came of it. The regime, which didn't approve of much besides the

Koran and religious chants, considered music a sin. As long as Khomeini was alive, women were not permitted to sing anything.

These opportunists jumped at any excuse, valid or not, to be rewarded for settling old scores. Many innocents fell victim to this order, ending up paying fines, scarred by the lash, in prison or in the ground.

Bazargan—Powerless Prime Minister, Paralyzed Economy

Contrary to what most young people fantasize about revolution, it is not a cool thing. The day after the revolution entered the history book and Khomeini sat on the throne, the short-lived celebration came to a halt. The massive recovery was a lot like the clean up job after a particularly raucous night of a rock and roll concert. Everyone is gone, the food is gone, the music and laughter is gone and a bunch of grumpy folks are left to clean up the mess. To much anticipation, the big elephant had finally landed. The revolutionaries had taken power, paralyzing Iran's economy. The Shah had left Iran for good this time and so had prosperity. It was the beginning of even greater misery for the Iranian people, most of whom had no idea they had jumped from the frying pan into the fire.

The clean up of the 1978 revolution was left for the people of Iran, most of whom by late March 1979, were out of jobs. Millions were laid off or fired. The irrational explanation by the government was that women were working in men's positions. To reduce the number of jobless men, women were fired in large numbers, without pension or explanation, from government positions in which they had worked for years. They were the first group to taste their revolutionary freedom. Instead of protesting the firings, women in bands of hundreds meekly walked the streets, with tears in their eyes, toward their homes. These were the same women who had chanted against the shah and protested against inequality under the Shah.

Most of these women had no job to go back to because their jobs had dissolved. The new Islamic republic didn't permit women in the Army so the jobs of women who worked in the military were given to men. Women who worked in mixed sectors along with men, such as factories, engineering, industrial farming or anything that required the presence of a male colleague were also sent home. All the companies that hired seasonal workers had vanished. No one was trying to start a new project. Villagers, who had prayed for the revolution to bring prosperity, and perhaps even rain, got neither.

After the revolution, many villagers, frustrated by living without running water and basic life necessities abandoned their villages for Tehran where they found themselves working at manual labor, daily work contracts and low paying jobs. It is estimated that seventy percent of the villages in Iran have been destroyed or abandoned. The capital population has exceeded a whopping thirteen million permanent residents plus seven million transients who travel in and out of the city every day. The crush of people has pushed the city to the verge of explosion.

Disillusioned people who lost their jobs and received unexpected bills for services they were promised would be free, faced a harsh reality. Little by little, people started talking and questioning the mullah's motives. Just as quickly as people realized they had made a mistake, the government moved to stifle dissent. The new government decreed that no one had the right to speak against the regime; not even in his own home.

In the revolutionary period between December 1978 and February 1979, lack of leadership at the General Staff level and below dulled the effectiveness of the military. At the same time, the regime, which was frightened of all ministers and generals who had ever sworn allegiance to the Shah, started executing anyone who they thought might by a threat. They called it 'revolutionary justice,' and the killings numbered in the hundreds every day. Amnesty International warned Iran about the international effect of the mass executions. Iran reported only 2,946 executions in twelve months, a fraction of the actual number.

Khomeini declared that anyone who spoke against the regime, who criticized the brutal murders and the robbing of the Shah's palaces, who opposed the confiscation of wealth or were suspected of ever having had anything to do with the Shah, were followers of the monarchy and foreign spies for the USA and the West. He granted himself the right to order everyone to immediately report anyone or anything they heard from their neighbors criticizing the regime. Khomeini gave the order that anyone who committed these perceived crimes should be arrested. One would think that anyone in his or her right mind would conclude he was looking out for his own government's interest and not for Islam. Still the majority of the people was fooled by his orders and went along with the edict.

In true Islam, gossiping, spying, eavesdropping, any action that violates the privacy or personal freedom of an individual, accusing anyone unfairly, diminishing anyone's dignity or jeopardizing his or her life, is considered a grave and unforgivable sin.

The old man was clearly out of his league, not to mention out his mind. Khomeini, who was neither a true politician nor a true Ayatollah, was making up political and religious rules as he went along. The order to spy against each other was the first step to divide us against each other so we would not unite against the regime.

Mahdy Bazargan, a prominent opponent of the Shah, and member of the Nationalist Front was appointed Prime Minister by Khomeini's direct order before an election was held. He started working in the office in February 1979, shortly after the revolution. Mr. Bazargan's government soon found itself in conflict with the fanatics and himself subject to Khomeini's direct order and control. Khomeini, however, didn't see himself as required to answer to any government. He was the Prime Minster's boss and if he didn't approve of the situation or whatever it was that Bazargan wanted, it had to be altered and come back with a new proposal. Khomeini saw himself as the ultimate wise man who knew what was best for the country. He had advisors, unqualified as they might be, but his was the only opinion that counted. In the Islamic republic, everyone who had long facial hair became an expert on the subject at hand.

Bazargan soon realized that his government was merely a sham and a phase of the mullah's dictatorship that was shifting power and brain washing people in the process.

If the regime had taken control straight from the Shah to Khomeini, most people would have probably understood the message. Had it been done delicately, using the Shah's distinguished opposition members who were also Nationalists to manipulate them, most people would not have hesitated to follow the regime. In Bazargan's era, Iran was chaotic. Everyone was in charge. In January 1979, Khomeini established his own party called the Revolutionary Council.

Ayatollah Mohammad Beheshti, a businessman who had been living in Germany with his family for many years selling Persian carpets, joined Khomeini in Paris and established the Islamic Republic Party (IRP). He, of course, wanted a piece of the Iranian pie. He moved to Iran to serve Khomeini and, after becoming the leader of his own party in 1979, became the number one enemy of our first President, Dr. Bani-Sadr. Beheshti made a great effort to impeach Bani-Sadr, who took his wish to be president to his grave and was ultimately assassinated by the Mojahedin.

Another political party was established by Ayatollah Shariatmadari who had a colony of followers in Tabriz, in Azerbaijan Province near the Turkish border. Ayatollah Shariatmadari later became a notorious opponent of Khomeini. Although he needed medical attention, he was denied permission to travel abroad to seek medical help and died without significant effect on the political process. Bazargan found himself in an odd position as Prime Minister. He had to share power with Khomeini and his hand-picked council of trusted clergymen, with a mix of secular political leaders such as Bani-Sadr and Qotbzadeh who were both Khomeini protégés. He also had to put up with the presence of two members representing the armed forces, who were also chosen directly by Khomeini. This was surely one of the most non-practical governments in history with too many bosses to answer to. Bazargan resigned a year later, bitterly complaining that the radical clerics undermined his effort to build a better Iran. He remained in Iran, serving as the not-so-beloved opposition of the radicals and was harassed until the last day of his life.

Sick and much in need of medical attention, he too was denied permission to leave Iran to seek health care. The government feared people of his stature and would rather see him silent in his grave than become a voice abroad. He died in early 1995, publicly regretting his help to the regime. Pitifully, regrets, as they say, are pitiful. Today Mr. Bazargan is remembered as a beloved Prime Minister and a man in search of democracy for his country. We all know he didn't intend for Iran to take the direction it did but his early day support of Khomeini inarguably built the regime's foundation.

BACK TO SCHOOL

After a long delay, in late March 1979, students were ordered back to school to wrap up the school year we had missed. Since students in the universities started the revolution, the regime imposed stricter rules for universities and did not immediately reopen them, calling for more time to *deterge* our university system from the Shah's influence. That meant firing the professors and hiring new ones to spout the government line.

They also used the extra time to wipe our history from the books in the libraries. There were book burnings in massive quantities. We have many books in Persian history that contain prophecies. The regime attempted to destroy any book that predicted either the rise or fall of their dynasty. This included a very special book of prophecy called Shah Nematollah Prophecies that explained Persian history. They changed the names, numbers and dates of history, poetry or anything that suggested the regime might fail. The new people hired for the teaching jobs didn't have to be qualified, just as long as they were loyal to Khomeini and said they had some university education. It didn't matter when, where or how much; they were hired.

University students, especially, were not ready for the major changes and the regime took its time to reopen the schools. Re-opening was postponed indefinitely but, bowing to the people's pressure, the universities finally reopened in October 1979.

The new regime knew young adults were not ready to accept the strict formalities and restrictions of the new government and the destruction of their future in the name of Islam. When the universities reopened, the government started a new unit to watch over student activities. The unit, called Irshad Islamic, was a venture by the followers of Imam, referring to Khomeini.

On April 1, 1979, the regime announced to the world that the result of the referendum was overwhelmingly 98 percent in favor of an Islamic Republic of Iran. They did not explain how two percent managed to vote otherwise when the only choices on the ballot were, in effect, a vote for the Islamic Republic. The government convened their new assembly and drafted a new constitution that also was approved by 98 percent of voters.

Return of the Estranged Father

My father returned from his 'vacation' in the USA in the summer of 1979. He knew Khosro was in a vulnerable situation because of both the revolution and the way he had blown his education opportunity. Khosro was at the university in Chahbahar, hanging out until it was safe to return to Isfahan. Now he planned to use a willing Khosro to weasel back into our lives again.

When the revolution started, the instructors at the school, who were all English, left Iran for good. The university dissolved. University authorities offered the students an opportunity to continue their education in England but we didn't have the funds to send him. Although, most universities in Europe were publicly funded, as a foreign student, he had to pay his own tuition. The University would have facilitated his student visa and accommodations and he would have lived in a dorm.

He came home; hoping mum would sell her house. Mum gave him the straight answer that he was not the only child and the house was for all our futures. She told him she had no objection to him continuing his education abroad but she could not help him. His father, however, had the means to help him if he chose. My father, who had no cash problem himself, had told him he would have to ask mum to sell the house. The reality was; even if mum wanted to sell, nobody would buy such a property in such chaotic times.

Khosro had proven time and again that he wasn't a man of commitment. I applauded my mother for not risking her life savings for him or any of us because there was no guarantee what might happen next. In my opinion, he had no right to expect that sort of sacrifice. Mum tried to make him understand but Khosro took it personal and whined that mum didn't care about his future.

Khosro was on a long waiting list for admission but mum talked to the University of Isfahan's President and miraculously convinced him to let Khosro enroll without making him study for the entrance exam. She accomplished the nearly impossible because everyone who wanted to change universities had to start from square one. But with mum's effort he was able to get in without much trouble. Ungrateful and unhappy, he was back in school.

About a year previously, my father had again abandoned us for his other family and had spent much of his money on them. Now, they had used him enough and he was persona non gratis due to personal conflicts, including accusing his son-in-law of sleeping with his wife's sister. He had tried to play the detective, climbing up to their windows in the middle of the night. He was caught, beaten and evicted from their lives. They called him crazy and reportedly threatened to kill him. Once again without a home and desperate for someone to call a family, he wanted to return to our family that he had repeatedly abandoned and did not support when he was present.

He was trying to find a way to squirm his way back in. He sent his sisters to our home to try to convince us to take him back. I didn't want him back because he was a cold stranger to me. Siavash didn't want him back because my father had nearly killed him twice. Manoocheher didn't care one way or the other but Khosro wanted him back because he thought he could help him continue his education abroad. My mother grudgingly capitulated.

One night, around 9:00 p.m., while we were getting ready to sleep outside in the yard, as we often did in the summer, there was a knock on the door. Khosro had been taking money from both my mother and father. In a collaborated plan, Khosro, who knew it was my father at the door, went to answer it and there stood my father on the steps to our yard. Just like that, my father was back in our lives.

Siavash immediately started an argument with my father while my mum was praying. She finished her prayer and told Siavash to watch his mouth. Despite the fact that he wasn't a good father, we were never allowed to show him disrespect.

Seeing mum crying on her prayer mat, I felt really sorry for her. Like countless women in Iran and around the world who have no one to help, she was stuck with a man she did not choose and did not want to live with. She didn't like to be treated like a second-class person, even though it is the norm for women in Iran. My father was using mum as a revolving door. He exited when he desired and entered when he wished, with no regards and respect to my mother's feelings.

Unhappy, and desperate, mum was smart enough to know he was using Khosro as an excuse to get back in. He entered into our lives, not to save us or help Khosro, but to save himself from his other family that wanted him dead. He used us as his protective shield.

Once again, he was in need; like the time when I was six years old and he took the whole family to confront the investors in one of his deals gone bad. The entire group of people who had lost their money swore to kill him but when they saw me, a six-year-old child innocently playing around, they relented. He used us to dodge another bullet.

For mum, it was a matter of need. She had four dependent children and none were working. It was hard for any mother to watch them starve. Mum was desperate for money. There is a Persian proverb; 'If she must, to save her child from hunger, a mother will kiss a donkey's ass.' And that was what she did. My father was no better than a donkey.

Shortly after his return, I made an attempt at establishing a father-daughter relationship. One day, while talking to him, I called him by his first name, Ali. He didn't like it. Then I called him dad. He said I was impolite to call him dad. Many times after that he complained to my mother that I was spoiled and impolite and not respectful enough to him to call him Father. To annoy him, I told him, dad is a friendly word; father is a title that he had not earned. If he wanted to be called father, he had to earn it. He was forever mad at me and showed that he did not like me. He always said, I was just like my mother, meaning I was not any good.

The new regime was cracking down on anyone suspected of being sympathetic to the former government or the deposed Shah. My mother had preserved several valuable hand painted pictures of Mohamed Reza Shah, Farah Pahlavi, Reza Shah and Mossadegh. One afternoon, I watched Siavash and my father destroy these paintings for fear someone might report them. The paintings could have been sold at auction in London for thousands of dollars. Had they belonged to my father, that might have been arranged but, since they were my mother's, he seemed to take a perverse pleasure in ripping them to shreds.

Our home turned into a reasonably tranquil environment for the first time in my memory. We started to enjoy our lives. Like other normal families we had family dinners, family picnics, real family talks and made plans for our future. It would have been wonderful had it lasted but, alas, it was a temporary acting job for my father who later said to my mother, I was just trying to get you to believe me.

He had come back with the intention of revenge and to try to seize mum's only asset, our home. Just as the last time, when mum had rescued him from bankruptcy, my father returned making empty promises. I don't think my mother believed him for a second but for our sake she decided to give him another chance to be a father to us.

For a change, everything seemed to be normal, whatever that means. To prove to my mother that he really meant what he said, he even purchased a VW bug for Khosro which, at mum s insistence, was soon traded for a sedan. His next purchases were a color TV, a few electronic items and a couple of Persian carpets. He even bought some plaster molding and for a couple of afternoons pretended that he wanted to repair our home. He was convincing enough to trick mum into registering two of the shops in two of the boy's names. This mistake caused a major delay in later years for the sale of the house. But, to my regret, he took one of his promises seriously; a trip to Mashhad.

A Trip to Remember

Mashhad, in far northeastern Iran, one of the holiest places in Islam is the site of shrines for eight Shiah Imam. To my regret, he kept this particular promise to visit Mashhad because he knew mum was quite religious. In order to touch her heart and earn her trust, he just had to pretend to respect her religious beliefs. As for my father, he only prays when he has a deal to make.

Inexplicably, he insisted on bringing his sister and three of her children along on this pilgrimage. There were already five of us. We sardined nine people and 300 pounds of luggage into an old, diesel Mercedes-Benz. Since I was the youngest, smallest and a girl to boot, there was no seat for me. I kept wondering why my mother agreed to take us on such a long, nuisance trip.

Mum is a great mother and a compassionate human being who has often been blindsided by religious obligation that she forces upon herself and all of us. To her, going on that trip was more important than our safety and welfare. I believe that she, like other obsessively religious persons, believed that the more suffering she endured, the bigger her reward in the afterlife. There is a famous Persian proverb; 'He has one foot over the grave,' which describes people who are getting close to the end of their life, fear their afterlife and become extremely, obsessively religious.

Although mum had good intentions in her heart, to prove their servitude to God, religious people often make choices and take drastic measures that can impact a generation or even future generations. Mum was too young to feel the way she did but she was very depressed and obsessed with prayers. Unfortunately, she was not the only one who experienced these feelings. It is because of religious people like her, that the government of Iran was able to brainwash the entire nation and is enjoying the carriage ride of their life on the back of poor people.

What was supposed to be an enjoyable family retreat turned into a circus. Mum made no objection to the extra passengers, thinking it would be the human thing to do because her sister-in-law had never been on such a trip. But, she put all of us in an uncomfortable, even dangerous position. Particularly me, who had no place to sit for the entire fifteen days, If we had an accident, I would have been the first one to be thrown out of the window.

It is about 500 miles as the crow flies from Isfahan to Mashhad. It is nearly twice that far if the crow is driving a sweltering, un-airconditioned, diesel-belching Mercedes crammed with nine people. We were sardined in like corn on the cob. In the summer heat of the desert areas we were traveling, the temperature inside the car was nearly 40° C or 100° F.

As we prepared to start our journey, my father's sister, her son and two daughters joined us. They brought nearly 200 pounds of luggage, blankets, and food. Mum had to leave some of our stuff behind. She crammed all she could in the trunk and the rest was strapped on the roof. When all of us tried to squeeze ourselves in the car, people gathered around to stare. It was funny because we must have looked like a family trying to break the Guiness world record for Mercedes stuffing and earn a place in Ripley's Believe it or Not.

With so much luggage and blankets, the onlookers must have thought we were going to have a wonderful, sightseeing, picnic style trip. When we were carefully shoehorned on top of each other, the car was sitting 15 centimeters above the asphalt. The weight was almost more than the old car could bear. Our cumulative passenger weight was over 1,000 pounds plus the 300 pounds of luggage and food.

Finally, the old car was ready to set out on our adventure. From afar, with all languages on deck and ropes crisscrossing the white bedding and sheets, we faintly resembled a tall ship that had unfurled its mainsail. Except, it was less majestic and we were nearly sinking into the asphalt. With much apprehension, we set sail for Mashhad.

The trip was not without mechanical incident. The carburetor croaked, the completely compressed shock absorbers had to be replaced, the broken exhaust pipe and muffler were dragging, the drive shaft broke, the transmission and oil pan were puddling on the road and the squealing brakes were completely ineffective. On the return trip, the radiator kept boiling over and we had to stop every five minutes. With unsynchronized rest stop requirements for nine people of both genders and a range of ages, it is a miracle we made it home in this lifetime.

To avoid the mountains, save time and take mercy on our old car, my father drove east from Isfahan to the edge of the Dasht-e-Kavier, or Salt Desert, where he turned north toward Tehran. The car was an unstructured intervention. My father was happy to have his sister and nieces and nephew along. He and Mum were not speaking during the trip. Neither was I, because when I said something everyone laughed at me. I kept myself quiet.

Crossing the desert, sitting on mum's legs, I crossed my arms beneath my chin and stared out the window at the passing scenery. The desert was barren. The dry trees were lashed relentlessly by the hot desert wind. Their hardened branches were spread wide open from side to side. Some resembled the faces of African women with outstretched arms, dying of Aids. Other trees resembled the skeletons of crucified individuals left behind on the crosses of the trees for generations to fear. They were thirsty but there was no reserve water beneath the dry soil. Although rich in minerals, the land was harshly empty. The only live plants were the native desert bristle bushes that sustained lonely feeding camels. Sometimes a small tornado picked them up and threw them from side to side. In the heat waves of the blazing sun, on the nearly melting asphalt, the only pretty scene was the waterscape mirage that seemed to be dazzling on the road ahead.

My head was still resting on my arms, looking at the desert. The sad, mystical scenery reminded me of a crystal ball. I couldn't get my eyes off of it. I was getting a feeling that I had a sad future ahead of me. From time to time, I choked and sometimes quietly burst to tears. Mum noticed I was tearing and asked me why I was crying. I replied that I wasn't crying; dust bothers my eyes. As a child, I was an expert of masking my emotions, and feelings. I believed babies cried. I was not a baby and under no circumstances did I want to cry in front of others.

When I got very tired, mum laid me on her shoulder. In the roasting temperature inside the car, our bodies were sweating profusely. I decided to give mum a rest from my 50 pound weight and lay down on the front floorboard. The other option was for the rest of the family to hold me on their knees; not a chance. I lay there until I finally fell asleep.

A Persian proverb says that if you want to know someone's true nature, the quickest way is to travel with him or her. I learned many things about my family. On the way, I was pushed around. If I followed mum, she told me to go with my father. If I followed him, he said follow mum. I received the same treatment from the cousins and the boys.

In my child's mind, I questioned this trip and its purpose over and over. I knew we were going to visit a holy shrine but I couldn't understand why this over-crowded pilgrimage had to be such a nightmare. If I had traveled with a convoy of US army military units across Iraq I would have had a more pleasant experience than this so called vacation.

On the way, we made a couple of rest stops but our first sleep stop was Tehran where we finally arrived in early morning. We slept in the car and ate a modest breakfast of bread and cheese, sitting before a shop door. I don't know why I thought it was funny but an old woman passing by asked me if I was in line for anything. I said. Yes, we are sitting here waiting for the shop to open and get our chicks. She believed me. Mum and everyone else laughed but suddenly I realized I had no right to be funny and make fun of her. I told her the truth; that we were just passing through and I was just joking and had no idea what this shop may have. She was pleased that I told her the truth and told us this actually was a meat shop and she knew that today was the chicken coupon day.

Around 8:00 a.m., we continued our journey through the dirty, crowded, smoky streets of Tehran. I didn't much like the city, and was grateful we didn't live there. My father drove by day and the boys, who didn't have driver's licenses, drove at night when the roads were quiet. The next morning we were in Challoss, ascending the extremely narrow and dangerous spiral road to the heart of the Alborz Mountains, similar to highways climbing the Rocky Mountains. For regular cars, without all the weight we carried, this road is a nightmare to drive. For us, mum could not rest from praying, her lips kept moving every minute to make sure we were not falling to the bottom of the gigantic canyons.

In his mind, my father was doing us a favor in taking us to Mashhad by way of the Caspian Sea, in Mazandaran province. Before reaching the sea, we stopped in a valley by one of the smaller rivers. The humidity was unbearable and there were waves of mosquitoes. Instead of taking us to a restaurant, he made mum cook some omelets. A swarm of mosquitoes engulfed mum, flying over the food she was cooking. I don't want to know how much mosquito protein we digested. Manoocheher had food poisoning that the local hospital emergency said could be from the mosquitoes. We went for a boat ride on the Caspian but my dad didn't join us. He didn't admit he was terrified of water but I knew he was. After one more day of torment we finally made it to Mashhad. Our journey was half completed. It took us five days to travel north from Isfahan to Tehran, cross the Alborz Mountains, descend to the Caspian Sea and turn east to Mashhad. It seemed like five eternities; long eternities.

When we finally arrived at the city of Mashhad, the first distinctive sight was the magnificent golden dome dazzling in the sun, soaring into the blue sky. The rosemary water was the first scent I smelled; infinitely better than a week of smelling each other's sweat.

City of Mashhad

The city of Mashhad is located 850 kilometers northeast of Tehran in the heart of Khorasan province. Mongols destroyed most of the city and massacred the people nearly seven hundred years ago. The city was reconstructed by the Safavids dynasty and its layout is similar to the old part of Tehran. A large Bazaar where merchandise is bought and sold and small homes are the indicators of a large city life style.

Today, Mashhad, is relatively more modern than other cities because the Shrine of Imam Reza has brought prosperity that most other cities lack. The population has increased many times over and is estimated at five million. This number triples in the summer as hordes of pilgrims visit the city. It is recognized as the first nation of Iran. Most of its original populations is indigenous; analogous to the Native Americans of North America.

The city has many food processing factories, pomegranate gardens and chestnuts. Mashhad Persian carpets are known worldwide. The famous Persian Saffron is also harvested in this province. Breeding Turkmen horses is a vital income factor among the Turkmen tribes. Khamani, who placed himself in the same position Khomeini once held, comes from this province and claims that his ancestors were Turkmen. The Turkmen are indigenous people and trace their ancestry and that of their horses back to Genghis Khan and Kubla Khan.

Other souvenirs, such as the handmade carpets and coarse, napped carpets woven by the Turkmen women are in much demand alongside tourism; the number one income source of the province. A variety of other merchandise is exported and it is a vital market for marble souvenirs.

Mashhad is one of the holiest cities in Iran. The eight Imams of Shiah, the Imam Reza, direct descendants of Ali, Fatimeh and the Prophet Mohammad, are resting in this city. According to Arabic calendar in 201 A.H., nearly 1,200 centuries ago, Ma'moon, Abasid Khalifeh, the Arab ruler, saw Imam Reza as a threat to his kingdom and forced him to come to Persia by sending him an obligatory trick invitation, made to look like he was coming on his own as successor to the throne. Imam Reza left his Medina home on his way to Kufa but was stopped and sent to Basrah, Ahwas, Fars and then Mashhad, where the Ma'moon Abassy ruled. When the Khalifeh felt that he could no longer contain Imam under his power, he gave him poisoned grapes, causing him to bleed to death. During his short life in Mashhad, he performed many miracles and restored life for the poor.

To portray the Imam as genuine and innocent after the incumbent Shah murdered him, he was buried, not as a saint, but as the respected successor to the king of Abassy, the benefactor to the Arab influenced government running the country. Soon thereafter, the people destroyed the Abassy government and his shrine has become a holy place for Shiah devotees. They come to visit the spectacular shrine, which sparkles in pure gold beneath azure skies, and to receive miracles from the sainted Imam. The spectacular Imam Reza's shrine was built and monitored personally by Shah Abass the First, the great and only influential king of the Safavids dynasty.

Mashhad is regarded as similar to the Vatican. Since Imam's death, his shrine has become the virtual Vatican of the Shiah world and has earned the respect of many other Muslims. The shrine has its own rules and regulations. People cannot buy the land on which they live; they can only rent from the Shrine. The Shrine collects millions of dollars per year income. Money is gathered during a clean up ceremony of the shrine that looks like someone emptied a giant piggy bank. The Imam is buried under this load of money that people have thrown into his holiness's shrine in hope of him returning a favor or a miracle, which he generously performs every year.

At the end of the year, when the clean up takes place, trusted mullahs clean the shrine and collect the accumulated money that has been thrown into it. The collection is not in small bags, but in four hundred pound bags that are taken to banks to be counted. His Holiness's shrine is then cleaned with the purest rosemary water; the same that is used in Saudi Arabia to clean the 'Kaba,' This rosemary water is produced in the rose valleys of Kerman, another ancient city located near the edge of large deserts between Isfahan and Tehran.

Pilgrims from all walks of life come in hope of a miracle and to unload their heart. Many elders come to ask the Imam for his intervention as the time nears for their departure from this life. People call the Imam Reza's shrine the 'Mecca for the Poor,' as it is less expensive to visit his shrine than to make a pilgrimage to Saudi Arabia. Also, his restaurant distributes free food among millions of pilgrims every day.

The city is visited not only because of the holy shrine but also for its museums and monuments. It is the resting place of Nadershah-Afshar, a vigilant and true hero from the Safavids dynasty, who saved Iran after the Afghans invasion of 1718 and restored our dignity and freedom.

Another much visited shrine is located in the city of Tous, a suburb of Mashhad, where one of the greatest Persians poets and the savior of our civilization, is laid in peace. Hakim Abol Qasem Ferdowsi was not only a great storyteller. He revived the Persian culture and language in a time of Arab influence when the official language in Iran was not Farsi but Arabic.

Ferdowsi lived and died in Tous, 940-1020 A.D., nearly a thousand years ago. Scholars from around the world visit the Ferdowsi Park and museum, his residence and burial chamber. The famous Persian poet wrote his testimonies in the form of poetry. He named his book Shahnameh of Ferdowsi, which in loose translation means a 'book of contributions for the king.' He was a sarcastic critic of the king and his lavish life style. Although, he wasn't paid for his life work, he saved Persian culture. Today he is not only a Persian cultural icon but also a world-renowned poet.

When we arrived in Mashhad, mum wanted decent accommodations but my father didn't care where he took us. We found two fairly decent rooms in a newly renovated motel. My father grumbled the entire time about the exorbitant cost of $15 per night for both rooms. Mum asked my dad to give her some money or to accompany her so that she could do some shopping for us. My father refused to do either. In retaliation, mum took me to the shrine and we disappeared for a couple of days, sleeping in the mosque.

I hurt for my mum for being stuck with my father who did not love her. She had no authority and the return of my dad only brought an additional burden, never ending, nerve wracking arguments and anguish to the family. To outsiders, he boasted and pretended that he took care of us but in reality it was mum who was burning herself like a candle.

After a couple of days, the rest of the family found us. My dad wasn't worried, just hungry. We rested for a day before we went back for another visit to the mosque and other places on the pilgrimage. I was tired of being dragged from one place to another. This was not exactly Disneyland. My eight-year-old interest span in visiting shrines was challenged. Although extremely holy, they were quite boring in a child's mind. I had to sit quietly beside mum for her prayers that seemed to go on for hours at a time, watching people crying and begging for forgiveness.

Although I love and respect the Imam, I was being stretched to the limit. I tried to go with the flow but, inevitably, I started fussing. I nagged and begged off from further excursions any time I could. My innocent behavior caused mum to go into a rage and she started beating me and pulling my ears and pinching me in front of my cousins. A few days after that, my cousins and I were playing with a scarf; shuffling it around like a volleyball, when Manoocheher interrupted our play and started flirting with my cousins. Although he was already an adult, he always rubbed his nose in my business. He took the scarf from me and gave it to my cousins. Everyone started laughing at me. I was angry and asked him why he did that. He said, "Because I wanted to and I can."

Well, maybe. It depends on one on one experience. I believe that sometimes the only way to make someone understand the effect of their vindictive behavior is to speak to them in their own language. My eyes turned red in anger. I grabbed his moustache and pulled a handful out by the roots. I started laughing, mocking him. It wasn't necessarily funny but I wanted to teach him a lesson. Mum arrived as I was laughing at him. She had not seen the whole episode. Manoocheher gave her his version and blamed me. Mum got angry again. I would have been punished that day if not for the intercession of my aunt and cousins defending me. This was just another incident in the boys-come-first saga of my life that has affected me deeply.

I had it up to my neck with everyone in the family. At eight, I was already worried about my future I wondered why was I born to a father who didn't care about me and a mother who used me as a small step-ladder and tension reducer, who punished me for no reason and expected me to be unthinkingly obedient like a pet instead of a child. She even joked with me that I was her pet. I didn't think she was choosing the best way to demonstrate her affection. When mum was shattered, she came undone on me. She was trapped in a verbally abusive relationship with my father who was the classic wife abuser, who seemed to enjoy hurting her and wouldn't rest his sarcasm until he saw her or me in tears.

In my heart, I knew she wasn't as monstrous as she sounded most of the time but she didn't behave angelically toward me either. Although I am sure she loved me deeply, the way she loved me was rough. Living with mum was like living in a boot camp with mum as the drill sergeant. I constantly had to be on my best behavior. My mother, although, not really abusive, unknowingly mirrored the nasty behavior of my father back to me in the form of strict rules. In her mind, she wanted a perfectly behaved daughter that everyone admired. I just wanted to be a child, just to be me.

Pilgrimed to exhaustion, we returned to Isfahan by the same route, arriving home after a dreadful fifteen-day ordeal. Thankfully, it was over. The ordeal was the trip of my life that I will never forget. I was never happier than when the old car limped back to our shady home from the trip to Mashhad.

After we returned home from Mashhad, mum, tired of my father's behavior, packed our bags and took me to visit my grandparents in Khoram-Abad.

Grandfather's Departure

My grandfather, after loosing his son and eyesight, had become a gentle giant and very much the only father figure I really knew. Although, in his late eighties, he had not lost much of his height and when he passed away the family had a hard time finding him a sizeable coffin.

He had been blind for ten years. He was very ill with pneumonia but, sadly, my grandmother did not coddle him. Grandma waited with eager anticipation for him to take his last breath so she would have access to all his retirement benefits and the house and lands he still owned. She fed him deep fried food to make him sicker, counted his days and tormented the poor man, telling him she could not wait for him to die.

I could tell that he still loved her deeply, despite her attitude. He kept telling her that she didn't really mean what she said because the day he died, people would stop coming to see her and she would be alone. She, on the other hand, kept telling him that she really hated him and it would be a joyful day for her when he kicked off. Obviously, it wasn't true; she cried for years after his death but at the time, her words were painful to hear.

He had become quite a spiritual man and regretted the pain that he and my grandmother had caused my mother by forcing her into marriage to my father. To show mum respect and how much he loved and cared about her, he had, years ago, given mum power of attorney to sell the house. I suspect he also favored me over his other grandchildren. Perhaps it was guilt over the pain he caused my mother. Perhaps he saw some of her personality in me.

Years ago, when we purchased the old house, he came for a visit and stayed for three and half months. Every day, three times a day, he asked me to lay his prayer mat, which I did. I finally got tired of it and asked him, Grandpa, in all your years, haven't you learned which direction you are supposed to pray? For years he told everyone in earshot how funny and vigilant his grandchild was. He was the only father figure I knew. He was kind and gave me the attention I craved.

Back in Khoram-Abad, in his last days, in the early hours one morning, I overheard him speaking very quietly, almost whispering, to mum, I don't want you to give me back the power of attorney, I want you to have this house, this is the least I can do for you. Mum didn't feel right taking over a house that belonged to all the siblings and wanted to give it back. Grandpa insisted he wanted to compensate her for having given her nothing but misery all her life.

Apparently, I wasn't the only one who overheard this conversation. Either grandma was listening or the mentally ill Uncle Akbar, who was more of a parrot pet than a son to my grandmother, might have reported it to her. The next morning, grandma was furious and told mum to get out; she was not welcome any more. Mum refused, saying she was there to care for her sick father. We stayed a few more days until it was impossible to bear my grandmother's grumpiness. It was hard to see Grandpa in tears but we returned home.

Almost immediately after our return to Isfahan, Uncle Asgar phoned to report that grandpa was worse and in the hospital. We rushed back to Khoram-Abad, to find my grandfather on oxygen support where he had lingered for three days before my grandma and uncles were forced to call us. The doctor told them that he was waiting for someone and would not pass away until he met them. He had been calling mum's and my name while unconscious. When we entered his room, he appeared to be in a coma, whispering our names. When I kissed him, he awakened, and said, "Is it you, Ghazal?" I said: "Yes, Grandpa, I am here." He said, "I have been waiting for you." His facial expression was a happy one. My grandma sent me home to pray and wait for good news. He revived one last time just before he exited from this life, telling mum, who held his hand at his bedside, that there would be a war soon and he would die in peace if all his children survived. At midnight, on Sep 13, 1980, he exhaled and departed in peace.

Mum called us from the hospital. I was wakened and became hysterical at the bad news. Everyone left for the morgue and despite mum's strong objections; her auntie took me along anyway. Mum was furious to see a nine-year-old child in a morgue. I was appalled to see a dead body wrapped in hospital sheets from head and toe, lying alone and lifeless like a chocolate toffee on a stretcher. What scared me most wasn't grandpa's body. It was when I saw a man, who I mistakenly thought was dead, moving. I was enormously frightened to a point I was shivering and crawled up beneath mum's chador. She assured me the man wasn't dead but was a hospital crewmember resting on a stretcher. When I finally realized that I was mistaken and got a grip of myself, grandpa's body wasn't frightening at all. He seemed to be in peace, smiling from above. My grandfather's wish was to be buried near Uncle Yadollah in the holy city of Qom. I wasn't allowed to go to the funeral but my heart was with him. I was saddened by his departure, but happy that he had left behind the agonizing life he had been living day in and day out. I constantly felt his presence around me, perhaps because I was the grandchild closest to him. Anytime he came to Isfahan or I was in Khoram-Abad, the only place for me to sit was on his lap. He constantly talked about me. We had a great bond and he was pretty much the only kind man in my growing up years. I missed him enormously. A few days after his memorial, we said our farewells and returned home. On the tenth day after his death, I dreamt about him. He arrived at our home as he used to when he was alive but looking much younger; maybe in his fifties. I noticed his eyes. His green eyes were wide open and bright for the first time in my memory. He sat me on his lap. I asked him what happened to him when he was buried. He answered that his eyesight was the first thing given back to him. I noticed the bridges of his fingers and knuckles were bare and skinless. At this point he was dead for ten days and his corpse must have deteriorated. It was the last time I saw him or sat on his lap.

DR. BANI-SADR—FIRST PRESIDENT, FIRST IMPEACHED

In January 1980, Dr. Bani-Sadr, himself the son of a mullah, was a close follower and protégé of Khomeini. Against the wishes of the radical members of the IRP, led by Beheshti, Khomeini picked him for President. Following their leader, the radicals took a liking to Bani-Sadr, who turned out to be a decent human being and was inaugurated as the first President in Iran's history.

In March 1980, Khomeini announced to the world that it would be a year of order. He was elected amidst much chaos and was expected to clean up the revolution's mess. Much like the previous Prime Minister, Mr. Bazargan, he found himself in a battle with various alliances. Although he was an economist and had the expertise to do the job, his job came with territories he wasn't prepared to explore. Just because he was the President, didn't mean he had all the power. He had to contend with the resentment of his powerful enemies, such as Beheshti, Rafsanjani and Khamenei, who were lined up for the post. They were the lions waiting for him to make a mistake and tear him apart.

In June 1980, Bani-Sadr failed in an attempt to save the lives of over 300 Army officers who were convicted of planning a coup d'etat to overcome the Islamic regime. The death of the 300 generals and army officers played a great role in Iran being in a disadvantaged position in the war with Iraq.

He knew his job wasn't an easy one. Daily fights with the members of the assembly made it even harder. At election time, people from poor families always cite the example of how great America is. Americans are told that only in America, the land of success and dreams, are the possibilities endless. That is not exactly true. What is true is: wherever you are located, it is whom you know not what you know that matters. Talk about dreams coming true; in the election of 1980, Mr. Rajai, a former teacher and street panhandler and a protégé of Beheshti became Prime Minister. He was forced on Dr. Bani-Sadr, to whom he took a dislike, and continually undermined his efforts.

Despite all the internal problems, Dr. Bani-Sadr faced them head on but he must have had a premonition. During the course of his presidency, he repeated over and over, "It is not a glorious job. I am here to help people."

Qotbzadeh, an educated liberal democrat and a moderate politician, who entered Iran on the same flight as Khomeini, was first given the post of Minster of Radio and Television. He was later accused of being a critic of the excesses of the post-revolution era and was executed for allegedly plotting against the Islamic Republic. The only man among the Ayatollahs who appeared to have the nation's welfare at heart was the unique and beloved Ayatollah Talegani. Among the crowd of pretenders, he was a true wise man who tried to warn people of the danger ahead. He was widely appreciated by many of the opposition, particularly by the Mojahedin.

The Mojahedin were not the only ones he protected. He intervened to save the lives of young men and women who had rashly voiced criticism of the government. Shortly before his sudden death, he and Hashemi Rafsanjani, speaker of the Majlis, or Senate, were addressing the Senate on public television. Talegani told the members and observers that they were not supposed to emulate the Shah but to restore freedom and unity. He said it was not proper for them to occupy their positions of privilege on the same luxury level as the previous government; they should live simply and modestly if they profess to be true followers of Prophet Mohammad. Rafsanjani replied, "We are building a new Senate." More than two decades have passed since the revolution but nothing has changed. The mullahs governing Iran still sit in the same seats as the Shah and cabinet members still live in their confiscated homes.

Tragically, the presumably robust and healthy Talegani died suddenly of a heart attack without any previous hint of health concern. An autopsy was never revealed and most likely never took place. As the years went by, the heart attack epidemic seemed to be virulent among those who voiced concerns about the government. After his death, the Mojahedin, who called him their father, had no shield and protection against the government.

With more than 25,000 members in 1979, Mojahedin had a huge impact in dethroning the Shah and made the biggest sacrifices for the revolution. Their leaders had expected seats in the assembly and high power positions. Instead, the regime told the leaders to take a hike. This did not set well with the Mojahedin. In the early days of the revolution, we witnessed protests and gunfire on the streets. Soon the government started to jail Mojahedin members. In the years after the revolution, Mojahedin who once took the side of Khomeini became his number one enemy. They terrorized and killed many of the key high members, including Prime Ministers and Presidents.

In January 1981, Iran launched a counteroffensive against Iraq with regular army and volunteers, eager to fight and regain the honor and the prestige of the country. This attack was a disaster for Iran. Bani-Sadr, as President, was blamed and impeached within a month. Rajai, replaced him August 5, 1981. Bani-Sadr went into exile, escaping by posing as an airline pilot on a flight to Paris where he lives today, still active among other exiled Iranian politicians. Rajai, his prime minister, ten cabinet ministers and two hundred officials were ultimately killed by a bomb blast in his office. Mojahedin, who helped the mullah's come to power, claimed responsibility for a series of attack against them. Mojahedin killed a large number of officials before being captured, tortured and hanged by Padars after televised trials, devoid of defense lawyers, designed to create fear.

†he War Begins

Two weeks after grandfather's death, true to his prophecy, on September 22, 1980, the world watched as Sadam Hussein, the Iraqi dictator, marched into Iran's territory from the west and south front.

The Iraqi airplanes attacked ten air bases in Iran in an attempt to destroy the Iranian air power on the ground; a lesson learned from Israel in the 1967 War. In a surprise attack, six Iraqi armies entered Iran on three fronts without being challenged.

By this time, Iran had purged more than eight thousand generals and high-ranking military experts. There were no generals left in Iran to create a battle plan and map out a defense or counter attack. Many had been killed and many were in hiding or had fled the country. Iran was in its most vulnerable position in history for a war. Iraq and the neighboring Gulf states recognized this weakness in Iran's army. Sadam Hussein took advantage of the situation and forged to the borders of Iran.

Khomeini was talking about exporting the revolution to the Persian Gulf countries. The Arab princes of the Gulf States saw Iran as a threat to their existence and used Iraq as a proxy to divert Iran from their own countries.

Prior to the war, Prime Minister Barzagan had visited Iraq hoping to improve on the volatile relationship between Iran and Iraq. His visits didn't prevent the conflict because, while he was promising that Iran would not do or say anything to aggravate the situation in Persian Gulf, Khomeini had set his own mind and no one was able to tell him what to say or not to say in his speeches. The contradiction between Iran's promises while trying to keep the peace and Khomeini's reaction to other governments in the Persian Gulf region gave the Iraqi leader and the rest of the Arab world excuses to defend their sovereignty.

Khomeini saw himself as the advocate chosen by Imam Mahdy for broadcasting Islam to other countries. The only thing he brought to our nation and Islam was the hatred of other countries.

November 3, 1980, Iraqi forces reached Abadan, the largest export and import center for Iran before the war. November 10, 1980, Khoram-Shahr, a city of half a million and one of the principal industrial cities of Iran lost its battle and was captured.

As Iraqi forces advanced, a special task force raped captured women. A friend of ours from Khoram-Shahr came to see us. He was wearing mourning clothes. When we asked him who had died, he said Iraqis had captured all the women of their families. To save them from slow torture and rape, as the Iraqi boat carrying the women and their captors pulled away onto the Shat-al-Arab, the river between Iran and Iraq, their brothers had thrown and shot grenades into the boats, sinking them and killing all on board.

People in favor of the regime were given the option of joining the Sepah or the Baseij. Those who wanted an official document, but were leery of the militia, joined the formal army. War was getting worse by the day. The government called all men age 18 to 38 to register and join the army. Many feared for their lives and refused to join. Joining, in any form was a great risk. Many young men fled the country to avoid the registry. In fear of losing essential potential soldiers, the Pasdaran set up camps on every street corner to screen men on the street. They were drafting men, checking birth certificates and service verification cards to catch deserters from the military. Anyone without a military service card was forced to join either the private or public army and fined for failure to register. If he refused, he was imprisoned and sent directly to the front lines as punishment.

The battle between Iraqi and Iranian soldiers was fierce. The ill prepared Iranian soldiers fought bravely trying to stop the Iraqis from entering the city, then fought house by house until the city was completely captured by the enemy. Iran quickly mustered an army that Khomeini called the 'Army of Twenty Million.' It was comprised of Pasdaran, pilots, new volunteers and some of the old regime's veterans, many trained in the United States, who were eager to use their expertise. The Baseij or People's Militia sent 100,000 to 200,000 soldiers to the borders. Most never came back.

Pasdaran picked up many of the Baseij solders from the schools. Children as young as 12 years were encouraged to join without the consent of their parents. One particular *shahid* made an influence on Khomeini. Mohamed Hossain Fahmideh, a twelve year old boy, committed suicide by running under a tank during the battle to save Khoram-Shahr, becoming an instant martyr and the subject of many Khomeini speeches encouraging young soldiers to emulate him. During the battle of Khoram-Shahr, Iraqi soldiers were instructed to kill everyone. Soldiers fought to their last drop of blood to not lose the city to the enemy and even a twelve year old boy made his mark on the pages of history. He didn't grow up to see the country for which he made the supreme sacrifice become a nesting ground for a monster who has made a mockery of Islam.

I was appalled by Khomeini's admiration for the scenario of a child committing suicide to get a pass to heaven. Did no one notice that none of the suicide advocates, who were issuing one-way tickets to heaven, were jumping into the vanguard of martyrs?

Khomeini shed tears for the kid but never stepped outside of his own villa. This hypocrisy is not uniquely Islamic. In most religions, those who claim leadership usually find themselves drowned in comfort. They claim that they work but getting paid for doing prayers it is not exactly hard labor. All the Prophets and the Shiah Twelvers all earned their living through hard work, often, physical labor. I am not suggesting that men of God carry a shovel on their shoulder and work on a farm but earning money through deception smacks too much of the Enron scandal. If heaven is earned through suicide, why do we never see a mullah throw himself in front of a tank? In the entire eight years of war, mullahs encouraged people from behind the front line but never saw one. Khomeini never stepped out onto the streets of Tehran, let alone travel to the front line.

Perhaps the most important reason for the war lies in the Iran/US relationship. Iran was holding US hostages and no better way than a war to pressure Iran to free the US citizens. Iraq was acquiring the latest military equipment from the United States and the allies; even the Communist countries were benefiting from the war. I am still not clear on how the war benefited Iran. Our people were killed and became refugees, millions of dollars was blown away in a futile effort to win a no-win war against modern military equipment. Khomeini, however, kept encouraging people and proclaiming the war a blessing. Petroleum has been the main industry in Iran since the 1920s. While at war, Iran, couldn't export most of its oil and people felt the crunch.

Khomeini often spoke in a dialect of the Persian language mixed with Arabic words. Many times, most of his cheering audience had no idea what he was talking about. They were encouraged to cheer and clap, as if they were sitting in a game show, by the Pasdars, who were always present at his speeches at the Jamaran. The crowd ultimately brought themselves and the rest of the nation the death sentence.

Family Divided

While we were away at my grandfather's funeral, Khosro did something incredibly stupid. Cruising around the campus in the car that mum had gone to the ends of earth to convince my father to buy him, he decided to take the fun to the next level and add some female flair to the beautiful ride. Like the Three Musketeers, gallantly, if foolishly, trying to help the helpless, he and two of his buddies squeezed in front and gave a ride to three girls from the university. That innocent car ride turned out to be a grievous mistake for Khosro and his friends and forever changed their destiny.

Their only 'sin' was to give a ride to three unrelated females. Under the new Islamic laws, imposed on students after the revolution, it was and still is, forbidden for men to give rides to fellow female students. After being interrogated for hours, the young men faced a critical multiple choice. They had three choices. Each of them either had to face dismissal from the university, receive 25 lashes with a whip and several months in jail or choose a partner and marry one of the girls, whom they had never met before the incident. One of the boys was an only son. His mother reluctantly accepted one girl as her daughter in law and celebrated her son's wedding. Khosro and the other boy were not as lucky.

He didn't challenge the ruling. He could have objected to the marriage, pleaded that it was a misunderstanding, a mistake that wouldn't happen again, that his parents were at his grandfather's funeral or send mum to see the President again. Instead of trying to extricate himself from his self-made mess, he pushed full steam ahead and chose to marry a girl whose name he did not even know before he volunteered his taxi service.

According to Persian custom, a person who loses a close family member and is in mourning must wait 40 days and obtain permission from the head of his family and ask for his blessing before getting married. Khosro set the formal wedding day for sometime in the near future while introducing his wife as his friend.

Perhaps the real reason was he was looking for a way out of our dysfunctional family and couldn't have found a more convincing excuse than being forced to marry. I didn't blame him for wanting out. Our family life was certainly contentious and getting out was my dream as well but Khosro was not mature enough to understand that marriage is not an easy way out. It is an enormous responsibility; a lifetime commitment that requires knowledge and personal sacrifices. I knew that better than anyone else because, after all, I was the accidental weakest link of the family chain.

After we retuned from the funeral, Khosro had a long conversation with mum in which he broached his interest in marrying this girl. Mum strongly rejected the idea of his marrying at age twenty-two. She reluctantly agreed to meet the girl, perhaps trying to negotiate with them to hold off the wedding while they learned more about life and each other.

When I came home from school one day, there was a young woman I'd never met before in our home. Mum told me to go and say 'hi' to her. I was curious about her affection toward me. Surprisingly, she knew more about me than I knew about her, which was nothing. I went to mum and asked her if she was Khosro's friend they had been talking about. Mum said, "Yes, how did you know?" Mum and Khosro kept their conversation pretty hushed. I wasn't invited for the discussions but I always was an observant person.

Khosro wasn't quite honest with mum. He told her that he and his wife were just friends, whereas they had already been legally married in a religious reception. They were anticipating a wedding celebration with family and friends, hoping to get mum's approval and possibly a contribution and an invitation for the newlyweds to come and live with us. I was present when mum asked my now sister in-law how good friends they were. She answered, "We are more than friends." Mum asked her again how much more and she replied, "A lot more." Mum may have thought she understood what her future daughter in-law meant but I don't think, even then, that she really grasped the whole truth; maybe because she loved Khosro deeply and wanted to stay in a state of denial to hang on to him a bit longer.

Mum was an authoritive woman and, right or wrong, she was overly protective toward Khosro. He was twenty-two years old and the role model for his brothers. After he left his education, Siavash and Manoocheher followed in his footsteps of not having any interest in school. She was devastated by the bad example he was setting and blamed the girl who had robbed her son away. She didn't much like this woman. She considered her an opportunist who had been looking for a husband and one had fallen into her lap, or vice versa.

Mum tried to reason with them and convince Khosro to wait until both of them finished their school and got jobs before starting a family. Desperate to stop him, mum suggested they become engaged. Khosro never admitted to mum that it was a little too late for that. He tried to convince mum that he really loved the girl and she should accept her as her daughter-in-law. Mum saw her as a dream destroyer and has never accepted her. Mum was right about asking them to wait and finish their education but Khosro was thinking that his father had no education and made himself a wealthy man. Why couldn't he do that?

Mum was hurt that Khosro, her four-pound premature first born, the child that shaped her decision to stay in her marriage with my father in order to give him a home, never asked her opinion or gave her a chance to be part of his happiness. It is still hard for her to let this go because after years of hard work, taking care of the kids and being a super mum to her children, she expected more respect. She told Khosro that if he wanted to get married he would have to leave her house and do it at his own expense.

He promised he would think about what she said but his father-in-law was pressuring him, constantly telling him his mother was only a woman who didn't know anything about a man's world and she shouldn't be running his life. Mum wasn't trying to run his life. She just pointed out that he had no job, had not finished his education and had no way to support himself and a wife. Mum was concerned about him and his future. But for him, as a man, his pride was injured; it was being the superior man and making his own decisions that mattered most. He envisioned an unlikely rosy future and was willing to pay a heavy price, even the relationship with his mother. He looked at mum as his competition and was trying to prove her wrong.

On a Friday, a couple of weeks later, Khosro was preparing to go out and seemed unusually concerned about his appearance. I asked him if there was something special about this Friday. He said he was going to a friend's wedding. I wondered why he had to look so meticulous about every detail for someone else's wedding. Unaware that it was his big day, with a surprised look, I asked him, "What would you do if it was your own wedding?" He laughed and didn't answer my question. He and the other two boys and the girls had a joint wedding. Only one of the other boy's mother and father attended. My father, Manoocheher and my aunties also attended. Both of his brothers were invited but he didn't bother to invite me to his wedding.

Manoocheher, who had a good relationship with him, went to the wedding but Siavash who was always controlled by Khosro didn't care to attend. A few days later, Khosro gathered his belongings and moved into his father-in-law's house. I was the only person who hugged him as he left. I knew I wouldn't see him again any time soon, or ever. The real Khosro who loved me deeply never came back. The new Khosro barely remembered my name.

Khosro's leaving was a big blow to my mum. She loved her first born. She was only 18 years old when she gave birth to him. She adored him and was immensely proud of him. Losing him seemed to age her. She mourned his marriage as if she had lost him forever.

Somehow, I was the one to bear the brunt of her unhappiness. One Friday, the Muslim holy day and the day of the week for Middle Eastern family gatherings as Sunday is in most Christian countries, mum, the two other boys and I were having a home cooked meal of chicken and rice. I was playfully arguing with Manoocheher over a chicken leg. I wasn't nasty, just playful. I thought it would be good to change the mood from constant talk about Khosro. With him gone from our lives, I craved affection and tried to re-focus family attention on me.

I pretended to be angry and left the table, saying I wouldn't eat my lunch if I couldn't have the leg. It was all in fun but my mother suddenly became very angry. She let everyone finish their food then harshly ordered me to go back to the table and clean up my plate. She watched me putting the last bite in my mouth when she suddenly flew into a rage. She grabbed me by my hair and while holding my hair in her left hand slapped me repeatedly on the face with her right. I was trying to swallow what I had been chewing and breathe at the same time. I wasn't crying, I couldn't even scream. I don't remember what was she yelling and swearing at me but I still heard her voice. I started to choke and don't know how much time passed. Manoocheher, who often enjoyed seeing me punished, was alarmed enough to run to the room and I heard him scream, "Mum, stop it, you'll kill her." At this stage, mum was emotionally bankrupt. She was beyond exhausted. She needed to empty her rage. I happened to be in the wrong place at the wrong time.

This wasn't the first or last time my mother punished me this harshly. On another occasion when I was nine, I innocently climbed on pathetic Uncle Asgar's back while he was taking a nap. He woke up and yelled at me to get off and get out. We had always wrestled and played. I was puzzled by his reaction. Later, I heard his allegation that I had demonstrated indications of sexual behavior in a back position. At nine, I was very small. I had no concept of the ludicrous sexual implications the adults read into the incident and could not guess at the reason for such cruel punishment, undeserved as it was.

Mum, who I assume found punishing me a way of de-stressing herself, tracked me down in the washroom to satisfy her brother's demand that I be punished. She flew into me with a fury, slapping my face and head until I passed out. When I woke up the family was at dinner. Mum had a ridiculous, humiliating ritual that after such punishment the offender had to kiss everyone's face and ask for forgiveness. That night, as I performed this ritual, I asked myself what I was apologizing for. What had I done wrong? Even then, I must have understood I was being made to pay for Khosro's transgressions.

Shortly after this ominous incident, Manoocheher made the first tentative move toward molesting me. He invited me to his room and we were joking around and laughing. He was tickling me, playing innocently when he suddenly slid his hand down inside my pants and touched my lower abdomen near my private parts. Just as quickly, he took his hand away and told me to leave. I had no idea what had just happened and why he asked me to leave, I was told the boys had taken care of me when I was a baby and I had no sense of fear and made no distinction that my mother's touch would be different than the family boys because I had never learned they were different. The boys and I never had any sexual inclinations toward each other and if there were any, I didn't have the

132

knowledge to recognize a sexual touch. I found his behavior puzzling and asked what I did wrong but he just yelled at me to get out.

I had no inkling of what had just happened and no premonition of what was to come. With Khosro, the eldest, out of our lives, mom was constantly praying and battling my father who admitted that he did not return to take care of us but to get the only home we had into his name and sell it.

After Khosro left, mum was alone and devastated. Her love for Manoocheher and Siavash's blinded her conscience. To avoid another son running off, she was determined to keep the boys under her wing until they became men. Considering my age and frail physical body, Manoocheher was in an advantageous position over me. He was the adored boy and with mum continually punishing me for no reason and being ill, physically weak and emotionally troubled, there was no way on earth I could find the courage to go to her and tell her what happened. I had no choice but to force myself to forget about this incident and never spoke of it. I am sure I am not the only girl that ever faced this terrible dilemma and destiny.

Meanwhile, on the national front, the war was getting worse. People back in Abadan, who had helped my father stay in hiding from his creditors, had heard of his new life. They called in their markers and took refuge in our home in Isfahan to escape the battleground in Abadan. We had no money to give them, but had enough space to shelter a few families. My father, who never followed through on any of his promises to anyone, had no compassion for the refugees and no intention of helping them. He opposed mum's good-hearted generosity. They had a terrific row. Mum finally told my father, This is my house and I run it my way. If you don't want to stay, move out.

After invading Iran and capturing most of Iran's border cities, Sadam announced numerous times that he wanted peace. Either it was a desperate attempt to portray himself as a passionate human being, which we all know was not possible, even if he washed himself in holy spring water in Mecca, or it was to seek more time. Either way, Khomeini didn't waste time considering that there might be merit to seeking peace. His arrogance didn't allow him to even consider meeting with his Iraqi fellow dictator, just in case if they were able to save lives for both countries.

After eight days of war, Sadam proposed to withdraw his troops. Arab countries, including Saudi Arabia, did not want a fundamentalist Islamic republic threatening to export revolution on their doorstep. They sent emissaries to Iran for mediation. Sadam requested a face-to-face meeting with Khomeini. Khomeini said under no circumstances would he meet with Sadam. Knowing the war might be a long fight for their Iraqi brother, as they used to call him, and that he could expect to expend enormous funds by the time the war ended, they proposed to give Iran millions of dollars to accept Iraq's proposal. Khomeini encouraged people to not listen, saying they were bluffing.

During the eight year war, the bodies of 500,000 Iranian men, an average of 171 per day, 62,500 per year, were sent back to their families, not counting the injured soldiers who died later or the missing prisoners who were killed by Iraq and buried in the battlefield. In exchange for such a great price Iran had extremely marginal victories.

Of all the presidents Iran has had since the revolution, during his short term presidency, Mr. Bani-Sadr was the only one who jeopardized his life by going to the front lines and directly observing the fighting. That was the secret of his popularity with people and the troops. His honest sincerity and the care he showed toward men in uniform saved his life during the volatile times ahead.

I was eleven years old when Siavash obstinately enlisted in the military. Mum did not want Siavash to enlist but, thank God, he refused to listen. He wanted to be able to leave the country if he survived the war and needed his military service record card to obtain a passport. He certainly needed to get away from mum's constant smothering to learn how to be a man. Unlike my relationship with Khosro, ours was not good. He seemed to go out of his way to treat me cruelly. When mum infrequently asked him to help with my homework, he kept slapping my face if I didn't understand what he explained. He called me degrading names and tormented me for my mistakes. He seemed to take great pleasure of seeing me suffer, bringing me to tears. I was happy that he was leaving for a couple of years to learn to at least act like a man.

An example of typical Siavash behavior; just before he left for the service he bought a very nice pen and pencil set in a beautiful box. He was not going to take it with him so I asked if I could have it. He mocked me. I asked if I could have the box. He said he would rather break it than give it to me and that is what he did. He snapped it and threw it in the garbage. When I told mum what happened, she didn't even bother to ask him why he was cruel toward me.

Mum always said she treated the boys and me with the same love and respect. That sounds nice but I could tell that I didn't mean much to her in comparison with them. I had seen her in action and what she said wasn't the way she acted toward me. She always gave in to them and went beyond her capacity to help them. With me, it was make do, take it or leave it. Even so, the boys always saw me as their competitor and the spoiled girl who got the best of everything.

In the time of Bani-Sadr, one of Siavash's friend s father was a general. My ever-resourceful mother, clothed in full chador and pious mien, called on the general who, impressed by my mother's demeanor and familial concern, used his influence to get Siavash into the Air Force. This assignment allowed him to be stationed in Tabriz, capital of the province of Azerbaijan and far from the war.

Tabriz

Tabriz, located in the northwest part of Iran, close to the Turkey and Azerbaijan borders was about as far from the war as a soldier could get and still serve his country. It is another ancient Iranian city that has long been a major merchant center in the north, much like Isfahan and Shiraz in central and south Iran. The people of Tabriz are mostly ethnic Turk. They still speak their own traditional dialect, called Turkish, which is similar in phonics to Turkish spoken in Azerbaijan and Turkey but the Turkish in Turkey was invented after Ata Turk came to power in that country. The Turkish speaking nations of Persia, Azerbaijan and Turkey, prior to Ata Turk, have been closely related since the time of the Ottoman Empire. Azerbaijan was part of Iran until the time of the Qajar Dynasty when it was lost to Russia but relationship between the people has continued.

Tabrizians are physically easily distinguished from most people of Iran; men are buffed, tall, with fair skin mostly blond with blue eyes and women look more European than Persian. Their colder climate is similar to most of Europe. They have been considered a fairly hospitable, brave, honest and kind people throughout history. They are not as religious as the people of other cities, and perhaps are not as liberated as southerners. They have kept their own traditions and values and have been a constant anguish for the government of Iran.

Constantly looking for a way to find their own independence, communist groups used to have major influence on the political thought of these people prior to the revolution. Khomeini's regime was able to destroy their operating cells to the point of extinction.

Siavash was drafted into the military and sent to Tabriz in the early spring of 1982, a time when fresh grass and wild tulips cover the fields. It was a safe place but his military training camp was located miles from Tabriz in the heart of the mountains and even in spring it was bitter cold. For someone from a warm climate, night shifts in the mountains were an artic ordeal. The temperature could be near or below zero centigrade. The Iranian armed forces do not lavish the troops with clothing and the latest equipment. In fact, most of the soldiers buy their own clothing. Siavash asked mum to buy him some winter clothes. It was nearly April and almost impossible to find winter clothing but she did her best. With the help of some of the Bazaar merchants who, just to share the honor of helping a soldier, retrieved some of their winter merchandises from the warehouse, she was able to send him some warm clothes. My mum and dad were in a tug of war. My father, of course, said he did not have any money, not even for his son. My father didn't like Siavash very much because he was on mum's side and whoever was on mum's side was his enemy. I guess that explains why he hated me so much.

Ghazal Omid

The Invisible Me

After finishing Primary school, I entered the first year of a three-year Middle school before entering High school. Our educational system, a program of five elementary, three middle school and four high school years, was adapted from the French school system. In recent years, there has been discussion of changing to a more efficient two cycle system resembling the North American education system but not much has actually changed since I was a student.

I had a very hard time adjusting. Suddenly, I had to study English, Arabic, Physics and Biology and had no one to help me. Mum had registered me at one of the worst schools in town. In her opinion, as long as I was close to home and she could check on me, it was sufficient. Mum was busy with her own mission to save others. One day I came home to find more than thirty people living in our house. I had no objections to helping; as a matter of fact, I was in favor of assisting people but only so long as she didn't forget that her priorities were to us, not the strangers.

Maybe I expected too much but I felt I should have been her priority. I had a completely lost feeling with no one to turn to for help. Unfortunately, taking care of me and my emotional needs wasn't much of a priority. It was as if I was completely invisible. I did not criticize her because every time I tried to say something she ended up hating me even more.

I spent my free time with my pet chickens. On one occasion, I caused them harm that made me hate myself even more. Our house was infested with of all sorts of insects and apparently they were feeding on our pets; the smaller chicks had fleas. Mum had purchased a series of chemicals that had a label warning against use by children and a skull to alert adults to use with caution. Although, the powders and sprays have been banned, due to the dangerous side effects, chemical companies inside Iran still produce them. I thought if it was effective for our pests, it could be effective for our pet's problem too.

I used the chemicals while she was asleep without her permission, thinking I was doing the pets a favor. I grabbed my chicks, one by one, and spread the chemical on their fragile wings and legs. In a matter of a few seconds I watch them dropping dead. I had no clue what I had done, I was fearful and started crying and screaming for help. When mum got up from her Ramadan nap and saw what I had done, she tried to revive them by giving them fresh water, washing them and giving them yogurt to perhaps help them to fight the poison but it didn't work. I killed nine of the innocent creatures. While burying them in the garden, I cried as if I lost my best friend. In a sense, I had killed my best friends.

†HE BARBARIC PUNISHMEN†
OF †HE ARAB GIRL

As the war intensified, there was a stream of refugees from the south heading for safer areas. A few days later, three brothers of Arab descent from Abadan, who had worked for my father came to us for help. One of them moved on to Shiraz while the other two stayed with us. The two brothers, with wives and children, were altogether 12 people.

Mum was determined to help them. Nearly every day, she left at dawn to go with the families to various government agencies, trying to locate funds to help these families. Her efforts paid off and she was able to get much badly needed help.

A few days later, I came home from school to find another Arab family, complete strangers, in our home, increasing the number of people living with us by nineteen.

Most residents of the southern province of Khuzestan are Arabs that have been living in Iran for centuries. They still speak Arabic at home and Farsi with outsiders. Persians never treated them as anything but part of the big Persian family. To us, it didn't matter what tribe they descended from; they contributed to our country and considered it their home.

The new family mum had allowed into our home had a unique situation. Mum had met the girl, named Zahra, at the bakery store, where mum frequently stopped. Zahra overheard her talking to one of her friends about her efforts to help people and begged mum to help her family as well. Reluctantly, Mum told her she would do what she could. Zahra took mum to the place where she, her pregnant stepmother and her stepbrothers and sisters were living. The place was little more than a hole in the ground with no facilities and no glass on the windows. The family was facing the cold winds of winter. Mum had no heart to watch others in hard times and didn't hesitate to help them pack their bags and bring them to our home.

Zahra had not told mum the whole story. A day after their arrival, we found out, her dad and three older brothers were also coming to live with us. Mum didn't want to help people who could afford to rent a home and just wanted to use her home as a rent-free motel. Zahra had tricked her to do exactly that. Mum was stuck with a promise she didn't have the heart to break. It was an uncomfortable situation for all of us. Mum had made a commitment and wanted to stand by it until they could find their way around town.

A couple of months passed. We started hearing rumors about Zahra. Apparently, being away from her native city of Ahvaz had given her the unprecedented opportunity and freedom to socialize and mingle. She was young, about nineteen years old, and her pregnant stepmother had given her every freedom and treated her like her own. She was responsible for all the grocery shopping. With her brothers coming and going to town, she had found a man. Apparently, the two of them were quite fond of each other. The man was a police officer. When his mother heard of the affair, she confronted my mother, telling her to stop your daughter from following my son. Mum, who knew I wasn't allowed to go anywhere except to my school, told the woman that Zahra wasn't her daughter but someone who lives at her house. When her brothers arrived, mum went to talk to them while Zahra was out shopping. Mum, of course, thought she was doing the girl a favor and wanted to keep her out of trouble. She was unaware what would happen to her.

We didn't see Zahra for almost a week. Mum was suspicious about her disappearance and was concerned about her. She finally asked her stepmother if she was ok. Her stepmother, in tears, said, "No, she is not, Zahra is dying." Mum rushed to their room to find her burned and bruised. One day, when nobody was at home, the three brothers and her father, who sometimes were in Isfahan and sometimes in Ahvaz, had cornered her, and asked her about the mystery man she was seeing. Although the Arabs lived in Iran, they still conducted much of their lives according to their own culture and traditions. The brothers had no idea she was talking to a non-Arab man. She defended herself by saying he was going to marry her. That was enough to condemn her to death.

The brothers, afraid of killing her because they lived in our home, had made every effort to make sure she died on her own. They broke her arms and burned her body by heating metal on the primus stove and marking her lips, and body. They attacked her in every possible way and then left town and went back to Ahvaz. Her wounds had become infected and by the time mum found her she was lucky to be alive. Mum who had no idea this had happened to Zahra, went straight to her stepmother and told her to tell her brothers that if she died they would all be responsible. Mum only wanted her to stop seeing the guy and had no idea of the consequences her warning would have on Zahra's life.

About a month later, I saw Zahra coming out of their room. She still looked terrible. The incident had broken her sprit. We didn't see much of her anymore until later that summer when we heard a cry. Mum thought she was being beaten again and ran to the yard toward their room. Zahra came running out with her clothes on fire.

At first we thought the brothers had tried to burn her. Mum put the fire out and called an ambulance. By the time the ambulance arrived, she had suffered third degree burns. It was horrifying to watch; all the skin had to be removed. The paramedics, laid her on her back in the middle of the yard and, much to her anguish, pulled off the burned skin as if they were peeling a banana. She was screaming in pain. They put medication on her skin and then transferred her to hospital. She was in a special burn unit for the first 24 hours until she was out of immediate danger. Uncle Azam, who had attended burn patients, paid a visit every night and took care of her burns. Mum tried to find out if her older brothers were responsible but everyone, including Zahra, said she was trying to pass by the burning primus stove when her jersey skirt suddenly caught on fire.

The police were never notified. There wasn't much point in contacting them because, in most cases, they won't open a file if there isn't enough evidence. I believe that Zahra had been threatened and was so frightened for her life that even if she had been set on fire she would never say a word. We lived this way for nearly a year until mum finally realized it could not continue. Zahra's recovery was slow and after nine months they left our home in the spring of the following year.

There were many other incidents, such as the married Arab brothers who came to our home looking for new wives. Mum realized she couldn't change the nature of the beasts and finally had it with all the people in our home. By now, most of them had found jobs. She gave them notice and, as gently as possible, encouraged our freeloading boarders to leave. Eventually everyone moved out, either through government grants or by finding part-time jobs and government housing.

Because of all the people living in our house, I had to keep my curtain closed all the time and I was covered head to toe any time I managed to get out of the room. I was only allowed to use the washroom if the boys of the families living with us were inside their rooms. This rule applies to all women in strict religious families. They are not supposed to be seen by men outside the family. When there are boys in the yard, it is a girl's responsibility to stay inside and unseen, even if she sees them only as friends. The Islamic regime has made people believe there is no friendship between men and women. Everything is presumed to be about sex.

Mum was a modern girl at one time but, as she grew older, the mullah's preaching altered her common sense. In her youth, she even kept a dog as a pet. Now, she was lecturing me that touching a dog is prohibited in Islam. I understand the rules of Islam and many of them have scientific merit. Indeed, people touching a dog, or other pets, may transfer bacteria to themselves or an infant but being a hypocrite is not what Islam wants to teach us.

In the time of Ali, a woman took her son to him and asked him tell her son not too eat too many dates because he had pimples on his face. Ali asked the woman to come back tomorrow. She took her son back the next day, and Imam Ali gave him a lecture and taught him moderation. The woman, who thought Ali could have saved her some time by giving him the same lesson yesterday, rudely asked the Imam, who was the Khalifeh or governor, why couldn't he say the same thing yesterday. Imam said that yesterday he was eating dates himself and could not tell her son not to do something while he was doing it himself. Islam teaches: 'Do as I do, not, as I say.'

Zahra and her family were the first of the families to leave. We never heard of her again but her older brother stayed in touch with us for a while. Mum said he was interested in marrying me. I was only 12 years old at the time. He was in his late 30s. Mum told him that, first of all, I was too young. She would never marry me off at such a young age. Second, she would never give her daughter to a man who brutally punished his own sister. Soon after that, he married a woman a few years younger than him and invited all of us to the wedding. Mum didn't take me. A couple of years later, that woman divorced him and he then married his 12 year old cousin. By then he was in his early 40s. Years after they left our home mum saw Zahra again. She still carried the scars on her face and arms, but was in a much better sprit. She had been married off to an Arab man who had lost his wife and she had fulfilled the role of mum for the man's six children.

As one family moved out, another family moved in. I was angry with mum for letting others come and go; we needed some rest. She was trying to help but a family from Khoram-Shahr, one was mum's old neighbor and my father's friend, was doing everything to take advantage of us. They had known my mum for a long time and seemingly assumed we owed them something and now they were looking for barter. I noticed mum talking to these people often—and she would stop any time I entered the room. After they finally moved out, my mum told me that they asked her permission for their son to marry me. I was barely a teenager. Their son was in his twenties. This truly frightened me. I was afraid and had plans to run away if my mother decided to bring the same ordeal on me that her parents had inflicted on her. Fortunately I didn't have to.

†HE DIFFICVL† †EEIIAGE YEARS

As I entered my teens, I became an intensely unhappy person. In my second year of middle school, I was in extremely poor health and had a very hard time studying. I was feeling increasingly alone and depressed. I was tired of being sick and malnourished all the time and of being punished for others' pleasure. And, like teenagers everywhere, was tired of being treated like a kid. At the same time, there was no one to whom I could talk about my problems. Sometimes, I was sure I could see ghosts and dead spirits walking around and I heard frightening sounds from the closet in the room where I studied. My grades were sliding down the chart. I hated the school I had to attend. The girls in this part of town were very rude and vulgar and I didn't act or talk like they did. The school was full of bullies and gangs of girls. Just about everyone took my politeness and shyness for granted and mocked me. They were a tough crowd and it was hard for me to survive among them. I didn't share their values or secrets. I was constantly ridiculed at school, even by one of my teachers. It is hell to be a teenager, particularly in that hostile environment.

During the coffee break at school one day while I was talking to one of my friends, a girl pushed me down the stairs from behind. I was quite petite, weighing barely 80 pounds. I was thrown into the schoolyard and landed on my face sideways on my temple. I was unconscious for a few moments. I didn't hear anything and was unable to get up. No one called an ambulance. When thousands of men were being killed on the battlefield, no one really cared about a girl, particularly one as unpopular as I.

A friend of mine came and yelled my name and I finally regained consciousness. Because I was sick most of the time, I had to wear a heavy load of clothing. The first thing I heard was one the teachers saying, "She wears so much clothing she can't even control herself." This teacher hated me so much that one cold, snowy December day, she kept me outside for the entire two hour class because I had forgotten to bring my book to school. It was apparent to me that she had some deep-seated hatred toward me that I had no way of understanding.

None of the teachers rushed to help me nor I was aided or taken to a doctor to see if there was any possible injury. The girl who pushed me was never reprimanded. I had a headache and was sent home early in the afternoon, I told mum about the incident and only then learned the reason the teacher had it in for me.

When Uncle Asgar divorced his wife, whom he later remarried, mum had asked the teacher's younger sister to marry him. The teacher had told my mum that since she was the oldest, she would have to marry first. She was offended when mum refused and said, "I am interested in your sister not in you."

Now, having me in her class, I guess it was payback time. She took her revenge out on me in any possible way she could. On my final exam day, she said to me, If it was up to me, you would never have graduated. I was puzzled by mum's easy-going reaction. I would have expected more from a teacher than to carry a grudge into the next innocent generation. But, literate or illiterate, some people never seem to understand that scaring and bullying is unfair revenge against someone that had no part in the past situation. I had no idea why she was so angry at me and I was astonished that mum knew all about this and yet, when from time to time I told her about this teacher, she never seemed to be concerned. I could have died that day.

After that incident, I was bedridden for a few days and mum made an effort to report her to the school principal but she didn't make any effort to move me from this school.

Perhaps the real reason for her not pursuing a showdown was because she herself was very depressed and my father seemed to enjoy her pain more than ever. She and my father didn't talk to each other for more than a year. No one cared about the effect of that poisonous environment. I would much rather have seen them divorce than living together where they were continually at each other throats. She was lonely and cried most of the time. Mum and I were constantly arguing about prayers and just about everything else. I was immensely depressed myself and, unlike in my younger years, we had drifted apart. I didn't seem to be able to bring myself down to make her happy any more.

My mother, Siavash, when he was at home, and I shared one of our larger rooms of about 360 ft^2 as our living and common bedroom. The three of us shared one room because we couldn't afford to heat individual rooms. Manoocheher used one of the upper rooms, which was accessed by the staircase to the roof. I never understood why he was trying to be so isolated. Mum said that he was a man and a man needs his space. She tried to provide a comfortable living arrangement for him but didn't seem to be aware that I needed my own room and comfort as well. We fought for hours when I said I want my own room. I wasn't happy to sleep in the same room with her and Siavash but mum was unswayed.

My father occupied a smaller room of about 160 ft^2 next to the room we all slept in. My parents shared a house but never shared a room together whether they had a relationship or not. Sometimes they didn't speak to each other for nearly a year. When we were sleeping in the room next to my father's room, I could hear him counting money.

Much business in Iran, as elsewhere in third world countries, operates off the books on a cash basis. Every night, my father came home with bags full of money. As soon as the rest of the family turned out the lights and went to bed, he would retire to his room to count it. I never knew how rich my father was until one night, around 1. a.m., I interrupted him as he counted his money. He brusquely demanded to know what I wanted. I asked him for a few dollars to buy school supplies. He replied, as usual, that he did not have any money to give me; that the money I saw belonged to other people and he had to give it back to them. Puzzled, I questioned him why people gave him money to count instead of just taking it to a bank. He angrily threw me from the room. Disappointed, I retreated to my bed, a mattress barely two inches thick laid directly on the floor. But, I was still confused. All I knew was, I could see a pile of cash on the table in front of him, a suitcase packed full of counted money and an open potato sack filled with more money, perhaps $200,000. In addition to the money I could see, his friends and family, not aware that he did not share his wealth with us, would inadvertently mention or ask our opinion of my father's new car or his fabulous new house and garden, things we knew nothing about. We could see that he always had money for anything he desired to buy for himself, travel and gifts for his own relatives but none for our family.

My father used to buy pomegranate by boxes, brought them home when we were away and buried them in the dirt in the garden, supposedly to keep them fresh longer. I would never have wanted to touch the fruit he buried in the dirt in which humans were buried but his point was: he would rather bury his money than spend it on us.

My mother and Siavash finally caught on to his money counting routine. Siavash went to my father's room one night and asked for some money for the family. They got into an argument and my father threw a hammer at him. Luckily, Siavash ducked behind a door. This was the second time Siavash had to dodge an object thrown by my father in anger. The last time, it was a less lethal china vase that missed by an inch.

On another occasion, my father promised me some money if I would help him find a $100,000 check he had misplaced in his room. When I found the check, after an hour search, he reneged on his promise. I told him that I needed money for school. He yelled at me to get out of his room and go ask my mother. Sadly, she really did not have any money.

It is not completely accurate to say we had no money. My father hoarded huge sums of untaxed cash in his room and safe. We just did not have authority to use any of it and would not consider taking it, even though we needed it for food and life's basic necessities.

A Narrow Escape

One day I came home to find mum had cleaned my father's room which he had not allowed her to touch for months. We didn't have any modern conveniences, such as a vacuum cleaner or drier. We had an antique washer, older than me, that had come off a ship but after many years of use had stopped working. Our refrigerator was also a ship salvage and the stove my father purchased was leaking natural gas.

Looking back, comparing my life in Iran with my peers in North America, I find it puzzling that people consider many of the inconveniences of the third world to be exotic. We may have lived an exotic life but it wasn't by choice.

Mum had to sweep the floor the old fashion way, with an 'exotic' date leaf broom. Then she washed my father's originally white bedding, that had turned nearly black, with bleach in a small tub by hand as many as times as necessary to clean it. In cold and heat, winter and summer, mum cleaned rooms and bedding but never received a word of thanks from my father. That day, when my father entered his room, instead of thanking her, he sneered that she probably wanted money and started laughing; inciting another heated verbal argument.

Mum decided that she and I would change our sleeping room. Near dusk, she burned some tree limbs we had in the garden and when they became red enough, she transferred them to the room above the basement, which was located on the south side of our home. I welcomed the idea of sleeping separately. For my parents, who had to live under the same roof, this was as far away from each other as they could get. Of course, it didn't bother my father; after all they had been on non-speaking terms for nearly a year.

That night, in the early hours of the morning, mum woke me, saying she could not breathe, felt nauseous and had a headache. I got up to get her some water and an orange only to discover my body was out of control. I hit the wall and nearly fell to the ground. I didn't know what to make of it but then I noticed the fire was smoking. We were lucky; if mum had not awakened and we had not got out the room, we would have suffocated by carbon monoxide and the medics could have gathered our bodies the next morning. My father seemed almost sad on hearing we survived. After all, if mum had died, he was the guardian of the boys and the authority figure. Years later, he expressed to my cousins that he dreamed of having picked our pieces among the ruins of our home after the bombing.

The morning after that near fatal accident, I woke up to see Manoocheher kissing my face and rubbing my neck while mum and Siavash were talking. I didn't take it for anything; mum was watching and I thought it was all right. Later many terrible things happened in that room. It got to where I didn't want to step foot in this room, or the other hideout to which he took me, to visit past events.

While we still slept in the same room for another week or two, mum was much more cautious and warmed it up with the heater. A few nights later mum woke me up again, asking me why I had hit her. I had no idea what she was talking about but I know I must have hit her hard because a few nights later I was hitting my pillow when I woke up.

Years later, a psychologist and psychiatrist suggested to me that I was releasing pent up anger. I couldn't stand my father and his cruel behavior. I couldn't stand watching him enjoy our suffering. I hated him so much I would have strangled him with my own hands if I were strong enough. I wished a million times that he would die. I could feel that he hated me, just as much. He broke promises he made to me over and over again, just to see me cry. Watching his devilish smile when I shed tears is a picture that will never go away. I truly believe he enjoyed his sadistic, psychopathic behavior. He promised my brothers that he would pay for them to go to university but would tell me that I was just a girl and wasn't supposed to continue my education. I know the slap was probably the lava floating on the volcano of rage I was experiencing. Unfortunately, instead of receiving treatment then, all the signs were ignored.

Another day, I heard my father's nieces laughing. I asked them what was so funny. They said, Don't you know that your father has promised our mum you will be our next sister in law? Their younger brother, was nearly a midget, 4 feet tall and retarded to the extent he had to be told what to do, what to eat and where to go. I told them, My father can go to hell for all I care. Don't count on me being your next sister in law. Thanks to your auntie and uncles there has never been a single day of happiness for my mother in her marriage to your uncle. I am not planning to sacrifice my life for the same reward. I guess he heard of my reaction.

Mum was furious when she heard what he had promised and they had another big argument. Not only because of me; he was also planning to marry Siavash and Manoocheher to two much older nieces. My father kept telling them, If you marry them I will do everything for you. The boys might have listened had it not been for my mum's advice. I never saw a shred of righteousness in my father. I knew if I listened to him, he would deliver me to the wolves and will leave me there to get to his next business deal.

SACRED RULES BROKEN

I remember vividly the day Manoocheher, started molesting me. Like most girls in Iran, I was never properly taught about sex, a taboo subject that good girls don't talk about. I am sure my mother wanted me to remain innocent as long as possible. I didn't know what a menstrual period was until I had one when I was nearly 13 years old. Alarmed, knowing I needed feminine attention, I went to mum and asked her what was happening to me. At first, she questioned me if I had done anything to myself to cause my menstrual period to start so early. Mum didn't want me to look feminine because she was afraid my attention would be divided. The first time I decided to have long nails, even though I was in my early twenties, we fought for days before I finally had to tell her to back off.

I was brought up immensely naïve. So much so, that for years I even justified my molester's actions and let myself believe he had no malicious intent and it was just his immaturity that caused him to fall into temptation. He, on the other hand, knew exactly what he was doing. He violated the trust between us and I fell into his incestuous trap. While a part of me knew that he was violating a trust and doing something horribly, horribly wrong, another part wasn't sure. He didn't give me any choice in the matter but deep down I rationalized the acceptance of his absurd explanation that, since we were related; whatever he did was all right.

He was twenty-one at the time. I was a few weeks shy of my thirteenth birthday. Although I was entering puberty, I had no clue what went on between a man and a woman sexually. However, most of my peers, friends and girls from school, had at least a rudimentary education about sex. Unlike my family, their nightly family discussions included talk about who had just married and cracked jokes about what happened in the bedroom. Even if their family didn't talk about it, girls learned about sex from older sisters, cousins and girlfriends who had recently married.

Mum kept telling me she was not anything like her mother but in reality she was an authoritative figure and everything was conducted her way. Maybe she was more lenient than her mother but she was not exactly a Venus, Goddess of Love, toward me. I was not a bad girl but I was fed up with her controls. I was not allowed to leave home alone to go out with my friends. I was not to talk to them unless she knew what I was talking about. I was not allowed to talk to girls about anything controversial. Mum kept a watchful eye on me when I had a friend over for a study session before leaving us alone. She even listened to my phone calls and joined our conversations. I was not allowed to wear anything she didn't approve and God forbid that I should talk to a boy. For me, sex was unknown territory, even though on one occasion I had seen my parents having sex while mum lay next to me. I simply turned away. I was taught not to ask about the subject and never questioned why. We barely had money to live; sex wasn't the important issue in our family and was never a subject of my curiosity.

Mum would have threatened to behead me if she caught me talking to friends about sex. She was not the only one thinking that way. I thought I would be joining the league of women when I became an adult and naively assumed she would be interested when it was time for me to blossom. I am sure my mother thought she was protecting me by keeping me in the dark about what is natural and should be treated as a human development but her obsession to keep me innocent had the opposite result.

Shortly before he started molesting me, Manoocheher came home seriously ill with pneumonia. My father had recently made him a boss in his mining business. The pay was very good and Manoocheher jumped at the offer, even though the job was in remote villages and he might not be able to make it home for weeks. Mum was furious with my father for sending her beloved son to the hinterlands and asked why he didn't chaperon his workers himself. Manoocheher found the job harder than he expected and with no real work knowledge could not handle the mountain of difficulties. Panicked by stress and the harsh environment, he got on the next bus to Isfahan. He arrived home in the early hours one morning in rain and snow. We had a heavy bolt on our exit door and no one could get into the house unless someone on the inside opened it. Mum woke up and opened the door for a very sick boy. Alarmed by his condition and fearing for his life, she took him to a doctor who gave him a note saying he had to rest for a week.

He was angry with our father for leaving him in the middle of nowhere and stopped working. Father had glaucoma and was legally blind. He couldn't drive by himself and had a very hard time managing his business. Manoocheher knew how to pressure him and said he would not work unless he received higher pay. Meanwhile, mum was attending him like a good mother, making barbecue lamb for him every day to help get his strength back. He stayed at home for several months becoming obviously bored. Although sibling rivalry existed between me and the boys, I never thought one of them might hurt me and then justify their actions with unimaginable excuses. He became quite friendly with me and I genuinely welcomed his attention. Nothing alerted me that I should think of him as anything but one of my siblings.

The day my molestation started it was very hot. Mum had gone out to visit a friend and join other women in a prayer session for a few hours. Mum and I had a terrible relationship in those days. She was always angry with me and I didn't ask where she was going. I didn't care and was glad that she would be leaving me alone for a couple of hours. Like any teenager, I was going through tough times.

After she left, Manoocheher and I were in the yard. Our washing machine was not working and we all had to wash our clothes by hand. He was washing his clothes as we talked when suddenly I saw a change in his behavior and in his eyes and face. He started smiling at me and reached out his hand and grabbed my shoulder, hugging me. It was unlike him but I was a sucker for affection. It was unusual for my family to show such affection. We only hugged each other when one of us left on a trip or returned from one. As children, the boys and I had wrestled so the physical contact did not alarm me.

This show of affection momentarily pleased me until he started to touch my breasts. I jumped back and asked what he was doing. He replied, "I am your brother, it's ok. Remember, I washed you when you were little so I have seen you already." I was confused. I didn't know how to respond. I got quiet. I guess he thought I was consenting because he proceeded to put his hand in my pants and touch my genitals. When he saw that I was uncomfortable he took his hand away but he didn't stop rubbing my small breasts. He said that if I ever had a boyfriend, I should let him, my related blood sibling; make me pregnant, instead of my boyfriend.

He kissed me on my lips. That was the first time in my life a man kissed me in that way. It was a sexual kiss, a French kiss. I hated it. He sucked my tongue and rolled his tongue in my mouth. He sat me on his lap like a little kid on a predator's lap and kissed me again and again. Then he laid me down and took my clothes off, slowly. I was numb. I lay like a baby whose diaper he was going to change. I was scared, shaking, shivering and pleading with him, "No, please not, mum is going to kill me." I am still haunted by that devilish smile and it still saddens and infuriates me when I look back, remembering. He touched me all over. My body was warm but I couldn't stop shivering. Manoocheher knew I was very upset but he also knew I wouldn't dare say anything to my mother. I feared that I was the one who would be severely punished or even killed; as does happen in Iran. I still had chilling memories of the time mum punished me when my uncle accused me of doing something sexual when I was an innocent nine year old and did not even know why I was being punished.

Manoocheher continued to molest me at every opportunity. For the first few days he did not take his own clothes off. Then, one afternoon we were sitting outside. I was wearing only a green tee shirt and a pair of pants. This must have been a turn-on for him because he suddenly pulled his pants down and, to my shock, showed me his penis. I panicked and ran away. He ran after me, caught me and took my clothes off while I tried to fight him. He forced me to kneel down and, as if I was his whore, kept saying, "I want to give it to you." He knew how vulnerable I was but he also knew he dared not break my hymen because if I got pregnant or he was caught he could get the death penalty. Whether out of fear or consideration, he resorted to anal rape. When he was done with me, he threw my clothes at me, telling me, "Go wash yourself."

From this point on, he treated me not as his sister but as his whore. If I asked him to do something for me, he would say that he would do it the next time I gave myself to him. Every time mum went out, I would beg her to take me with her but she would say, "Manoocheher is at home; don't fight until I come back." He would smile knowingly and say, "No mum, we don't fight." For a year, he molested me again and again. Each time he wanted something more, graphic, depraved and erotic. He would make me kneel and perform oral sex on him for what seemed like hours. He did unspeakable, sexual positions to me, over and over again.

My self-esteem hit bottom; the feeling of being dirty and used goods filled every vein in my body. I didn't know how to stop him and put an end to his degrading behavior toward me. Finally, I got the courage to tell him that I was going to tell mum. He mocked me and laughed, "Like mum is going to believe you? Anyway, I'll deny it." I knew he was right. Years later, when I finally confronted him, he did just that.

Mum loved him so dearly that she closed her eyes on me. While she expressed her love toward her two boys, I only existed. As years passed, the beautiful mother I had adored disappeared and the new woman was nothing like her. She wouldn't have believed me and could have killed me in an 'honor killing' with little danger of being convicted, even though I was the victim. I tried to test the water to find out what would happen to me if I told her. While Mum was at her prayer mat one afternoon, I cautiously told her we had been given an assignment about women who fall into a trap and do bad stuff. I asked what would happen to her and what the family reaction would be.

Mum, who had become almost fanatically religious, said that if she is guilty they should kill her with stones or put her in a large sack and throw her into a pit with a wild bulldog. I had heard of this punishment being carried out by obsessive families in the province of Isfahan. She continued that if she was not guilty, she should be married off as soon as possible. This wasn't quite the answer I was looking for. My father, who adored Manoocheher even more than my mother, wouldn't care about me either. After all, he too had raped his own sister, resulting in her death.

Emotionally, I was a wreck. Physically, I couldn't take the burden anymore and became severely sick. The constant pain was more than I could swallow. On one occasion I became suddenly and violently ill. The symptoms were similar to what we now know as HIV. Even though AIDS is world wide, Iran never educated anyone about this devastating disease. I didn't know what AIDS was but Manoocheher, who was sexually active, could have passed AIDS on to me. We didn't have money for mum to take me to a doctor so I lay on my thin mats to either get better or die.

Frankly, at the time, death would have been the preferred choice in comparison with what I was going through. My father, who had stopped paying even for the groceries, arrived home. On seeing me sick, he asked what the matter was. I told him I was sick. He didn't ask why I was sick; he just dismissed me with, "It is because of all the junk food you eat."

While he was spending thousands of dollars on family reunion parties, he would not give mum money for food. My eyesight weakened and I was severely malnourished; at age 12, I weighed barely 100 pounds. We didn't have food to put on our table. His words were like swords going through my body. Burning tears fell from my eyes. As I was praying to God to take my soul away and free me from this painful life, I passed out. My father had already destroyed the last shred of love I had ever tried to feel for him. This just squeezed the tube.

Later that night I woke up to find Khosro, who had been forgiven by mum for getting married, and his wife by my bedside for the first time in many years. They had come to visit mum and found me sick. My sister-in-law is a nurse. When she saw me, she tried not to show emotion but the anguish and worry in her eyes was apparent. She knew my illness was serious when the ice she put on my forehead melted in a matter of minutes. She said I had to be taken to emergency right away. Mum took it lightly and I refused to go. I had no desire to survive. In a few days, I miraculously recovered without ever knowing what my sickness had been.

Little by little, I was turning against God. I stopped doing my daily prayers and mum and I got into intense arguments as to why I didn't pray when she ordered me to. Not being able to talk about my ordeals, I fell into a long, dark depression. I avoided mum and stopped talking to her. She continually talked about how wonderful Manoocheher was. I resented her for loving this predator.

I was powerless to end the ordeal to which this pedophile subjected me at every opportunity. He was too smart to get caught, too strong for me to physically resist and I was afraid I would be blamed if I told my parents. Mercifully, the molestation stopped when my father decided to leave, apparently for good this time, and asked Manoocheher, his favorite son, to leave with him. Siavash was unhappy that Manoocheher did not want to stay with us and persuaded mum to ask him to come back.

By this time, my father was very rich again. He easily outbid mum, offering Manoocheher a large amount of money to keep working for him. Money aside, Manoocheher had another incentive to get away from mum. They had a recurring argument about the military. She wanted him to join, as his brother Siavash did, and learn to be a man. He refused, telling Mum she was crazy and just wanted to get him killed in the war. My father had been paying Manoocheher over $800 per week to be his flunky and gofer, an extraordinary amount in 1983 Iran for a boy with little education and no skills. In addition, he had a completely free ride living at home. When faced with the choice of going with his rich father or staying with his penniless mother, he took the money and ran. My mother was heart broken at his departure. I secretly rejoiced and thanked God for delivering me from evil.

After they departed, mum tried to send my father's furniture and Manoocheher's belongings to them. Among Manoocheher's private collection of photos of women, mum found a number of birth control packages. Some were opened; some were still sealed. Apparently, Manoocheher had brought girls to his room on a regular basis. I can only speculate the reason he had a need or desire to have sex with me. Perhaps he had a bet with his friends or simply couldn't resist the temptation of violating a taboo. Perhaps he saw himself as Adam, trying to reach for the apple that he shouldn't touch. Whatever his reasons, he left me with a great anger and sorrow and lifelong scars.

Not only him; my father also left me scarred by ignoring me and letting me down. At that age, I didn't need another doll but I did need my father. He deliberately caused me pain and the wounds he left, although old, are still raw. They may not visible to the naked eye because I have mastered masking my emotions for years. If I could open up my heart, it would be pockmarked like the surface of the moon with the stab wounds he inflicted on it.

I had it with both Manoocheher and my father. In those years, I fantasized about taking them into the woods, tying them to a huge tree in a remote, deserted area, gagging their mouths so no one could hear their screams, injuring them enough to bleed but not die and then leave them alone for the avenging bulldogs to finish off. For that is what they did to me; consumed my soul one cell at the time. But, this was a fantasy that I no longer wish to carry in my heart and mind. Today, I believe there is a great God up there watching everything. I am certain they will pay a heavy price. The dear Lord will take my revenge.

The last time I saw Manoocheher in Iran was a year later, in 1984. A couple of months after mum and I returned from Mecca, my father was sending him to Pakistan to dodge the draft and I happened to come home from school as he was preparing to leave the country. He was determined to avoid the military. To his credentials as child rapist, arsonist, thief and all-around nogoodnik, he added draft dodger. In his first try to make it out of Iran, he was nearly killed near the Pakistan border. He finally made it across the border wearing women's clothes. My father spent $300,000 supporting his lifestyle in a five star Lahore hotel for two years. He, like my father, started boasting about his parents and how rich his father was and his mother owned a multi-million dollar house.

He hosted parties and even saved one of his friends who had been deported back to Pakistan from Germany. He gave him $3,000 and helped the spoiled boy of a *real* rich family that didn't need his generosity, to make it to the United States. We, on the other hand, were never sure if we could buy groceries for the following week. My father had turned Manoocheher into an exact copy of himself; ruthless, heartless and greedy.

CROSSING THE LINE

The long nightmare of molestation by Manoocheher was over but I felt damaged or like a dirty napkin. My head was spinning. I didn't know how to digest the pain. If I had a choice of living elsewhere I certainly would have but I was stuck. The hardest part was keeping the secret. I couldn't blame mum for loving a son but it made me sick seeing her showing so much love and affection for this monster. The fact that mum and Siavash loved Manoocheher bothered me but the hardest part was I had to pretend that I loved him too. And, pretend that I was still an innocent little girl, which I wasn't any more. I cried for hours nearly every day and all mum would say was, "What the hell is wrong with you?" I always replied, "Nothing." Of course, that was a lie.

I grew up watching my uncles and grandpa smoking opium, now and then. Although opium is highly addictive, it is the drug of choice among most of the Persian people. I liked the smell of the opium when I was young but I never had any desire for drugs. When my brain was working straight, I knew drugs were not the answer to my problems and would only add to the pile. Yet, I was so drowned that I would grab anything to make the pain to go away. I had a thirst for being understood. I wanted God to tell me that he hears my pleas and would turn this life around. I expected him to be there for me because I knew He silently watches everything. To make my confession to God; I was embarrassed to talk about it but I did something I dared not talk about until this book.

I was never in the closet and never came out of one either, however, I had a fleeting teenage brush with lesbianism. I had a classmate who was incredibly stunning. She was very beautiful and mature for her age; medium height, very slender, olive skin, long black hair down her back with an incredible flexible body. Like a gymnast, she could bend over backwards and touch the ground with her hands.

Aside from her beauty, I envied the distinctive, burgundy, ballet type leather shoes she wore. I wanted some like them so badly I even asked mum for some, knowing I would get probably get a resounding lecture, which is exactly what happened. The other thing that I think made us kindred souls was remarks she made that caused me to suspect that her brother was also molesting her.

She said she used to work in the circus. As far as I know there was never an operating circus in Iran, particularly at the time of the revolution. I didn't believe her for a minute about the circus. What I believed was her stunning features. Slowly but surely, I found myself becoming sexually attracted to her. Even now, it is puzzling how a naïve kid like me suddenly found herself, in the middle of mathematics class, fondling her friend's breasts. I don't recall everything that led up to it but I remember we had an urge to touch each other and talked about going to the washroom. I had never had any attraction toward women. I grew up around women in large public, Roman style bathrooms where all the women were naked and never had a lustful twinge. Although growing up a tomboy, I never felt I had been born in a wrong body. I knew this feeling was wrong and because it was wrong, I had an urge to do it.

In my naïve mind, according to my philosophy, I wanted to challenge God. I was mad at God and blaming Him for delivering me into this family. I wanted Him to see how it feels to be walked over. When I was still being molested, I asked God to take my miserable life away. I asked Him what I had done to deserve this. When he didn't reply, I decided that I would turn my back on Him, just as He had done to me. I felt I was becoming evil but it didn't make me feel any better. I decided there would be no turning back and no boundaries to what I would try.

I was a fool to think God wasn't watching but I didn't care. I was rebelling, hoping He got the message. I knew He wouldn't approve of what I was contemplating and neither would my mother but I felt revenge in doing so. I was foolishly stubborn and stopped doing the daily Muslim formal prayers, although, in my heart, I always knew He existed. I was determined to get even with Him and even told Him I would deny Him if He did not respond.

After our spontaneous experimental touching in math class, we decided to take the fun to the next level. We had to be careful since, in Iran, although women were free of suspicion in public washrooms; they were never supposed to be in the washroom together. There is no such a thing as being openly gay or lesbian in Iran. Anyone caught performing a homosexual act in the presence of two men or four women witnesses is instantly sentenced to death. Whether a slow death or quick death is prescribed depends on the severity of the act.

There are severe punishments that are carried forward for some unfortunates. Before and after the revolution, the government that ruled Iran always had someone watching on others. That is the way it goes in older civilizations and countries. Minding other people's business is a way of life and they earn a little money here and there by reporting someone for something they find indecent or immoral. It doesn't bother them in the least that by doing so, this person may receive a death sentence. Despite the draconian penalties, covert homosexuality persists in Iran, just as it does in every corner of the earth.

Public homosexuality seems to be a product of the new millennium but I am positive homosexuality existed, in or out of the closet, in every culture. Medieval aristocrats with unfettered access to virgin girls still desired to have a virgin boy at their side. For centuries, in the male dominated Roman Empire, men flaunted other males, as their teachers, friend and lovers. The principal reason for having a wife was to produce an heir to continue their lineage. Underground taboo relationships will always fascinate deviates.

Over two centuries ago, the Gajar dynasty opened the doors to the mullah's influence and forced women to wear garb similar to the burqa imposed on Afghani women. In the late 1800s, Naseredin Shah's, the third king of the dynasty, constant companion was a man called Malichaq. Although the king had a harem of hundreds of women there is historical evidence that Malichaq was more like a mate than a friend or companion. Though every informed Persian knows this story, the event still goes unspoken.

In the year 1992, the current regime reported that nearly 8,000 male students in the mullah's schools were caught having sex. I have not heard of Iran reporting the new numbers but the news from Iran indicates there has been a boost in overt homosexuality in the last few years.

It is not merely because it is a new American phenomenon that every fashion designer or goodlooking guy seems to be gay. That is not so in Iran. In my culture, a contributing factor to homosexuality is that marriages are getting harder to come by. Men and women don't earn enough money to be able to live as a family. Not to mention, they are obligated to fulfill the expectations of their parents. Since the revolution, there has been no opportunity for men and women to associate with one anther freely. If unmarried men and women are seen together, the very least they will face is harassments from radicals.

In Iran today, about the only safe way to have sex with the opposite gender is to get married. For some it isn't financially or publicly possible. The government of Iran encourages men and women to have short-term marriages, called Sigeh, which is similar to having a girlfriend or boyfriend with a mullah's blessing of the sexual union. However, *Sigeh*, in the Persian culture, is regarded as degrading for a woman and many, for good reasons, won't accept it. If they find themselves pregnant, a man has little or no responsibility toward the baby and men are not generally kind toward someone else's offspring.

There are rumors of prostitution but not many men in the right mind want to have anything to do with a prostitute. Not only might she give him the HIV virus, an epidemic that has been kept quiet for that last twenty years; having sex with a prostitute is doubly risky to one's health as there is a death sentence for the customer. The accused may escape the death penalty by marrying the prostitute. In the Persian culture, prostitution is highly immoral whereas sex with the same gender is easy to come by and conceal.

The afternoon after fondling my friend's breast, I came home from school, excited and a little nervous about the next step. As usual, I was daydreaming and sort of studying and thinking about tomorrow's adventure. Mum was praying in the same room that was my study/living room. She suddenly stopped and read me the translation of the chapter from the Koran that said that women were sisters and that they should not touch each other sexually. If they did they will pay the consequences of their actions since it is considered a great sin in the eyes of God.

It seemed that God had accepted my challenge and was ready to deter me if I ignored his direct message. My gut was telling me it wasn't coincidence. What were the chances of mum reading to me the precise chapter condemning lesbianism just at the time I was about to experience it and start exploring a taboo subject?

I was silent for a few minutes. There is no word to describe how I felt. My shoulders got heavy and I could feel the pain in my body. I know God does not routinely go around passing direct messages to people but I know He must have heard me pretty loudly to warn me that way. I had so many problems that, now that I was heard, I had no intention of getting on the wrong foot with God. I got up, went to another room and promised myself this experience would not ever happen again. The next day, when I went to school, I told my friend that we would not do what we had discussed and she agreed. She was still my friend but the thought of having touched her bothered me a great deal for the rest of the year.

One summer day, when I was home alone, I cut the tip of each finger and wrote a coded gibberish letter with my own blood, swearing that I would never again do such a thing or look at my female friends in any way other than as sisters. I was emulating my grandfather who, after gambling away his inheritance, punished himself by burning his forearms as he took a vow never to gamble again. He never gambled again.

I was equally determined not to backslide. I have kept my promise to God since that day. Years later, mum found that letter. She was very curious about it. I told her I had cut my finger and was trying to stop the bleeding. She looked at it carefully and said, "There seemed to be an awful lot of blood for a cut finger." I did not share details with her and she reluctantly let it go.

Before all this happened, when I dreamed of romantic love, I always envisioned myself in a Cinderella story. I was dressed in a beautiful gown, coming down the stairs of my prince's house. He would ask me to dance with him. I never saw myself with another woman. Although, I have been attracted to other women in my life as role models, my only reason for being attracted to them has been their personality and intelligence, not their bodies. I am not ashamed to confess that, sure, sometimes fantasies cross my mind but I have not slipped since I made my promise. I look at other women as sisters and nothing more. Now, I have a different view about women's beauty, I admire beauty in any form and shape, particularly in women. I believe God likes beauty just as much as we do and that is why He has created this amazing universe. Simply because I adore the Mona Lisa painting doesn't mean I want her in my bed. There is a fine line between pure admiration and sexual attraction. If I crossed that line, I would be the first to know.

Witnessing Death on the Street

After Manoocheher was finally out of my life and had no way to touch me again, the shock effect of molestation and the overwhelming guilt finally hit me. I started to mourn for myself, for the loss of my innocence and self esteem. I was emotionally unresponsive and would stare at a corner for hours without blinking. When school was over, I did not go out for days. When mum wanted me to come along with her, I refused and like a sick cat, crawled into a corner under a blanket and wept. I was free, in a way, but I couldn't tell a soul about what had happened to me. I could not tell mum, and had no way to see a counselor. Everything about girls had to be consulted with the parents and even if I did attempt to see a doctor, I would have ended up facing mum. I feared what she would to do me if she found out and I had no way to protect myself against her anger and rage.

I knew how much she loved Manoocheher. She saved him from a deadly disease. Even though she could have caught meningitis. When he caught his arm, mum went the distance to get quality surgeons to do an emergency operation on him. I was the cretin she wouldn't believe. I had experienced her anger and physical attacks. For that reason, I didn't dare to share my feelings with her as I did in my childhood. We had both evolved over the years. I was looking for answers while mum thought she had them all and I should be satisfied with hers. We argued unmercifully.

In those days, mum was kind but was like an old Vietnam veteran, with a sensitive temper. When she was herself, her method of survival was to stand up for your rights head on. She didn't waste any time on little people. She was too busy working to get the shops attached to the house back into her name. when she wasn't feeling like herself, it was sad to see her. She looked like an injured lioness, crawling on her prayer mat, crying tears of regret, anger and pain on her poor face.

My father had tricked her into giving the shops to the boy. Now, in order to sell the house and get us out, she had to have them in her name. It wasn't an easy task because Manoocheher was a draft dodger hiding in Pakistan. In order for him to return mum's shop back to her name, he would have to return to Iran and he wasn't going to come back; not even if all of us died.

I felt powerless, as if I was disappearing; evaporating like a drop of water and no one saw or heard my pleas for help. I felt worthless and began to entertain the idea of killing myself. Jumping in front of a bus isn't the ideal suicide method but was one I considered until one drizzly, foggy morning in late October. I woke up early and as I prepared for school I had a feeling that something horrible was going to happen that day.

School started at seven thirty a.m., and I had to leave our home around seven. Just as I stepped out the door, I heard a car hitting something or someone. When I got closer, I saw a bus near a man's body lying on the pavement. A few people had stopped and, according to Iran's tradition, threw money at the accident scene to help the family with the funeral. Nobody had called an ambulance and apparently the bus driver had fled the scene. The smell of blood made me nauseous and as I got closer I had a chance to see what would happen to me if I killed myself in this fashion.

I knew the man lying dead in the street. He was one of the local merchants who had a shop near the school. He most likely was on the way to work. The fog must have brought visibility to zero and he probably slid when he tried to turn left from the right side of the street. The bus driver did not see him; he fell off his old bike and his head hit the front wheel.

I had never seen human remains this close up. It was shocking and saddening, especially since I stopped at the man's store a couple of times on my way to school. His body lay lifeless on the asphalt with his brain scattered all over. His scalp had broken wide open like an oyster. The impact must have been strong because part of his skull had been thrown around like pieces of a coconut shell. Due to the cold weather, his brain was still a light pink. People were not the only observers. Street cats were watching and gently rubbing their tongue over their muzzles. Crows, some flying around and some sitting on the nearest tree croaking, were waiting to pick up the particles of cheese cake they might think it was. It didn't matter to them if it was human brain or cheese; it was food. There was a pungent odor of blood and flesh radiating many yards from the body. Covering my mouth with my scarf, I ran toward my school feeling nauseated. Fortunately, not too many at school had witnessed the tragic accident. There was no counseling or shrine set up by the teachers to help those who had seen the gruesome event.

When I came home I told mum and Siavash, who was home for a few days on vacation from military duty, what I saw. Siavash seemed calm. It didn't matter to him but I had expected a more empathetic reaction from her, she didn't seem to understand or to be concerned about the impact witnessing this significant accident could have on my mental health or life. Without judging I genuinely respected mum for taking part in what she strongly believed, but deep down I wasn't happy that she was going to the distance for strangers while my needs were ignored.

In retrospect, now I know the diagnosis wasn't that great for her either. She must have suffered from depression and posttraumatic disorder from watching all the bodies of soldiers killed in the war being carried toward the graveyard on the shoulders of their loved ones. Muslims are suppose to take part in carrying the coffins of martyrs on their shoulders. It is considered a great blessing and war casualties were recognized as martyrs.

TRUE RELIGION VERSUS
PHONY RELIGION

Life continued as usual, at least on the surface. Inside my heart and mind nothing was usual. I was walking on the edge while Siavash, now nearly half through his military service, was busy day-dreaming about the day he could get out of Iran. Mum was busy doing her due diligence to be able to sell the house and make his dream come true. Little by little, she slipped away into even darker depression.

I will never forget one late November morning when I woke early to find mum missing. I thought she must have gone out shopping but morning turned to afternoon; I came home and she was still missing. My suspicions turned to worry until Siavash told me mum had been sitting in the storage closet on the way to the roof since morning. I was worried and asked him what she was doing up there. He said he did not know but she did not look good. I ran to the stairs to the roof and asked her what she was doing. She said she wanted to die and threatened that if I came any closer, she would go on the roof and jump. I tried to reason with her and calm her down. I told her that I loved her and missed her and expected her to fight, just as she had always taught me to. Around eleven p.m., she finally came down. She was still crying. We didn't talk much and the next day I stayed at school, thinking it might be better for her not to see me. She cooked one of my favorite rice dishes and brought it to school. She said, she knew I would be hungry.

On regular days, to alleviate her pain, mum took long prayers. Prayer is essentially a form of meditation and it helps the spirit of the person to deal with difficult times. At the time, I was too young to understand why mum's prayers took so many hours each time. The more depressed she became, the longer her prayers became. Sometimes, she spent the whole day praying, which caused many of our arguments. I know now that depression doesn't go away with meditation and prayers alone. I have never doubted the power of prayer but mum was in desperate need of therapy to get back on the track of life and take me along with her. Mum, although an intelligent woman and a kind mother when she was herself, was blinded by extreme religious convictions and sometimes forgot her priorities. She continually asked for forgiveness for everything, including being alive.

She thought salvation required continuously praying to God and the more she prayed the wider the gap between us became. I have never looked at God as an angry God and I loved Him dearly in my own way. I have never had anything against any religion. I believe God has given us prayer as the ultimate closeness and mediation for our sake and if we do it, it will bring us closer to Him. I also believe God expects us to be the key maker of our own happiness and it is wonderful and refreshing to know He values humanity as equally important as prayers. He sent the Angel Gabriel to Prophet Mohammad with the message that empty prayers have no value. I don't believe that prayers are the answer to complex human problems. I hated to see mum being manipulated by the preachers and forgetting about me.

In a recent conversation with my mother about religion, she mentioned that she had purchased a book about Moses, written by a mullah who guaranteed that if one does the prayers, he or she ultimately will have the same power as Moses, who crossed the Red Sea. I asked, with all due respect to Islam and other religions, if these secrets really worked for the man who wrote the book, why wasn't he using them instead of printing and selling them on the rare chance that the prayers come true and someone becomes another Moses. Isn't God supposed to give that power and permission? If he wants anyone to have the power of Moses, he will grant it without special prayers and chants, Moses didn't do any of them and he was chosen. That is where the fine line is drawn between being religious and being used to advance a theory. I am not bad mouthing my mother. I love her to death. I love religion but being religious does not mean being blindsided and manipulated.

There is a blunt proverb in the Persian language for people who fall into the traps of people such as Musab al-Zarqawi, Bin Laden, et al. It says, 'If the doctor who claims he can cure your bald head knew how to cure baldness, he would have done it for himself before he went bald.'

I strongly believe in religion but religion can change people. Religion is the path to salvation but Islam, like other religions has been used for personal agendas. It is not the religion that is wrong; it is the preachers who sabotage the word of God. Mum, like most religious women was naïve and the regime's mullahs took advantage of her good heart and flooded her brain and the brains of her like minded sisters with irrational lies and preaching, orchestrated to blindfold the female force. Women out number men in Iran; what better way to control the majority than through religion? Unfortunately, for the rest of the nation, so many religious women are fooled by the charms of the Iranian mullahs that they don't care to know what is true and what is not; they just accept what they hear. When it comes to God and Heaven, mothers have blindly sacrificed their children, presumably to please God. The regime knew just how to get them to do that.

There is another Persian proverb directed at those overly religious or ambivalent about the truth. We say, 'The cat has becomes pious,' usually referring to someone who has lived a sinful or less-than-righteous life who suddenly realizes his days are numbered, becomes religious out of the blue and will do anything to receive a passport to heaven.

To understand the proverb, you should know that the real Persian cat, unlike the meek, decorative animal we see in North America is a notorious thief. Often depicted in Persian poetry and stories as a deceptive animal, they steal people's dinner from the balcony of a five story building and escape at nearly 30 miles per hour. Although they live inside the homes of people, no one feeds them, they come and go as they wish and have a reputation as a miniature version of wild cats.

The truth is, God has never authorized behavior such as we see different places in the world. Those who kill innocent people and call themselves Muslim and even pray fervently are not true Muslims. Throughout history, evil people distort God's word for their own selfish motives. When Prophet Mohammad, himself an Arab, heard individuals plotting something he didn't approve he made it very clear that, although of Arab descent, these people were not following him.

Back in Iran people joked about the mullah who never practiced what he preached. The mullah told his audience that if the baby peed on the Persian carpet, it should be burned, no matter how valuable the carpet. After the sermon, the mullah returned home to find his wife had burned his most prized Persian carpet because there was a baby induced spot in the center. He asked her why she had burned their valuable carpet. His wife replied, "I just did what you instructed in your sermon." He moaned, "Oh woman, smarten up, that was for the other people, not for us."

Iran has slipped into a coma of ignorance ever since the Safavids forced religion on Iran. Most Iranians, in particular the older generation consider themselves religious people and the true followers of Islam.

Killing in Islam's Name

I have inherited my outspokenness from the brave Kurdish heritage of my mother. I believe a person should speak up when he has something to say and can do so without suffering fatal repercussions. Siavash was not so inclined. He was never a brave individual and with the exception of secretly reading a few books that were not on the regime's approved literature list, he had never done anything overtly to offend the government of Iran. Nevertheless, he found himself in the hot seat in a military court.

Mum had finagled a relatively safe posting for Siavash but he still wound up in danger of his life. He was accused of reading books about communism, a pertinent subject for the time and place. In a logical world, there is nothing wrong with reading an opposition book, unless you are in a country such as Iran where it is a capital offense. Like any other country after a revolution, Iran had many supporters that turned against it overnight. Their opposition was not without merit. The regime had banned any unauthorized books about the socialism and communism movement. They even banned books of ancient Persian history that told wonderful stories of ancient kings because the government censors interpreted some of the material in the history books to be critical of the contemporary policies of the revolutionary regime.

A mullah named Tabrizy was in charge of the courts for the military and for citizens accused of reading subversive literature or having connections to any opposition group in Tabriz. He is indubitably one of the most callous and inhumane men who ever lived. He hanged two of his own sons to prove how devoted he was to the regime. Incredibly, he made their mother stand up publicly and watch the sentencing and execution, which was televised all over Iran. I watched his sons hanged and cried for them. The mullah and their mother, however, were as impassive as stone and shed not a tear as their son's bodies shivered and twitched as the rope tightened around their necks. Tabrizy performed this unthinkable act, sacrificing his own sons, to show how cold bloodedly dedicated to the regime he was.

His example and message affected many, including Siavash who had been interrogated several times in his court. Before his case was resolved, my mother again called on the genial general who had arranged Siavash's enlistment and relatively safe posting. The general referred her to another general. Mum pulled out all the stops. In full Islamic mother regalia, she called on the second general and successfully appealed to him, as a single mother who needed her son nearer to her home, to arrange a transfer for Siavash to a post near Isfahan. Thanks to the inadequate records and primitive computer system of the Iranian military, Siavash and his case fell through the cracks and did not resurface.

Against this backdrop, my relationship with my mother was at an all time most poisonous level, heading downhill to disaster. When she did not see me in the room or I was out of her sight, she would come and sit down beside me. Invariably, she became angry at my silence and started swearing at me. Eventually, I became completely numb to her temperaments. My mother saw me as her enemy. When she asked me a question, I would just stare unconsciously into her eyes. She would become infuriated at my silence. I wasn't acting. I couldn't remember what she'd asked me a minute before. She would slap me and say, "Answer damn it, or I'll beat you more." Perhaps she thought I was trying to torment her but I simply couldn't answer. She would swear at me telling me to get away from her before she killed me. My depression and anxiety level was so high I was completely numb. It didn't occur to her or her boys that I might be suffering from the same problem she did when she was young.

It was hard to believe that she was the mother I had loved so much. That mother seemed gone. She had become toward me exactly what her mother had been toward her when she was my age. I hated it. I earnestly prayed to God to take my life so my mother would be sorry and feel the same emptiness inside that I felt. "Please dear God, don't be angry with my mother. If she is not happy with me, it is my fault that I came into this world. Please end my life so she will feel my absence in her life and know how much I loved her when I was here." But as I prayed and heard no answers, I slowly turned against Him as well. If He could let me live this way, I had no use for Him. Although I had nearly lost my faith in God and didn't pray to Him, I knew he existed. I had nothing against God personally but since everyone took advantage of me, I lumped God into the same crowd. I was wishing for a miracle; dreaming that any day now, someone would knock on my door saying that I was their lost child and rescue me. Of course, it was all a fantasy. Yet, every night when mum was praying, I sat outside on a bench in the yard, looking at the stars, hoping that God would acknowledge me, even as he ignored my plea for deliverance from my wretched life. Nevertheless, I stopped pretending that I prayed to Him and finally told mum to get off my back. She was furious. She could only talk about her boys and how wonderful they were and how much she loved them. When I asked her how she felt about me, she just laughed. I felt she was too strict with me, as her mother had been with her. When she saw me trying to copy the behavior of other girls, it made her angry. It was during this difficult time that I began writing poetry instead of talking. Through my poems, I could communicate with her and say to her what I couldn't say otherwise. I could tell her about my anger, my fear and my loneliness. Reading these poems to her provided a temporary respite from the near-constant hostility between us. I always loved my mother, even though she did not treat me well. We had non-stop fights when she found out I hade been thinking of committing suicide. At the time, when she burst in rage I was fourteen years old.

PILGRIMAGE TO MECCA

For as long as I can recall, one of mum's wishes was to make a journey to Mecca. This pilgrimage is a tenet of the Muslim faith. Every Muslim is expected to make the trip during his lifetime. They trip must be arranged well in advance. Before father abandoned us the last time, to convince mum that he really was a good husband, he had registered them both for a trip to the holy site. They were on the waiting list four years before securing their reservation.

They were supposed to go to Mecca the following summer but now that my father was again out of the house and out of our life, he refused to go with my mother. The feeling was mutual. It was impossible for them to go together. They would have killed each other before landing in Mecca.

There was another reason mum was not willing to go to Mecca with my father. There is a strict rule that *Tavaffs*, the mandatory Arabic Muslim prayers recited as the pilgrim rotates around the Ka'ba, must be pronounced correctly. If a man and woman traveling together do their prayers wrong on the day of Hajj, they cannot talk to each other again until the errant one performs the ceremonies the right way or sends someone to do so on his behalf. My father didn't care about the rules and regulations and wasn't up to the challenge.

If my father ever prayed, I suspect it was that the person signing his business contract did not read the fine print.

There are a series of rules in Islam, some stricter than others, but there is always a way to find a balance. If one considers Islam as a vast ocean, when it is impossible for someone to meet a requirement, it can be considered as small as a needle hole. When it is possible to teach Islam the way it should be, we should go as far as we can. When it isn't possible to meet every requirement, Islam can be managed by covering its necessary basic rules.

As God has said, "My desire is for humans to be able to follow the religion easily. By not making it too hard on them, people will be able to follow." An example of this word of God is: when a non-Muslim converts to Islam, he or she is not punished for not knowing the rules of Islam or not knowing how to pray. The convert only needs to say that there is one God, Prophet Mohammad was sent by God and Ali is the Imam. Even if he doesn't say that Ali is the Imam, he still instantly becomes Muslim. This is called a conversion of convenience. The requirements are different for those born and raised as Muslims. Mum was afraid my father would cause her endless arguments and waste all her efforts. However, if she traveled with anyone other than her husband, the rules did not apply and it did not matter if someone else did the Hajj incorrectly.

Mum was leaning toward having Siavash accompany her but my father refused to give the reservation to him and proposed to sell it. Siavash took their reservations to the register's office dedicated to Mecca. The man in the office looked at Siavash with surprise and asked, "You want to sell it?" Siavash replied that is what his father wanted. The man asked him, "Do you realize this is almost like a winner's ticket for the lottery?" When he heard that, Siavash changed his mind and came home and told mum what the man said. My father, however, had made up his mind there was no way he would attend the ceremonies with mum. He put and ad in the newspaper offering to sell his opportunity to go to Mecca. We didn't have the money, so the situation fell into a dormant phase. My father had no luck finding a buyer.

At this point, I was neither a Muslim, nor an atheist. I did believe God existed but we didn't have a relationship. In my childish imagination, God was the God of every one else and I was on my own, busy with my own problems.

By coincidence, one day as I was walking through the large room where we kept the TV set, I saw an image of Mecca on the screen. Mum called to me and said, "This is the place where I am going for a month. See how splendid it looks." It was true, it was indeed splendid but, as I had lost all of my faith in God, I asked her with an attitude, "What are you going to bring me as a gift when you go to Mecca?" She replied, "I'll bring you a doll."

I snapped at her, "I am fourteen years old. It has been years since I stopped playing with dolls? I gave my only doll away to another child when I was ten years old." I wanted to tell her that, thanks to your son, I am not as innocent as you think I am. There is not one shred of innocence left in me. I bit my tongue and instead said, "If your God, that you are going to so much trouble to visit in Mecca, is truly who claims to be, He will manage for me to come with you and see his house for myself." Her mouth was wide open in shock and she didn't respond. We went our separate ways but I knew she would soon get back to me.

Throughout that year, the more stressed I became, the more I crumbled through school and had a hard time passing my exams. The exams were not my only worries. I had a hard time doing pretty much anything and had no sense of self-worth. One day, when Mum got angry with me for something that I did not feel was my fault, I swallowed ten 5 mg Valium. Nothing happened. I even failed at suicide.

On another occasion I had a very open conversation about suicide with one of my classmates at school. She was so concerned that, not knowing it might be a deadly mistake, she found my phone number in the telephone book and called my mother. When I came home from school my mother, who had pent up her anger all day, opened the door. I could tell she was even more upset with me than usual but I had no idea what I had done this time. Her eyes normally changed when she was fuming. When I asked her what the problem was, she didn't reply, only telling me to eat my dinner. As usual, I picked at my food and ate very little.

She eyed me with anger the entire time I was eating. Suddenly she burst out, "You think I don't know what you are up to and that you don't eat so you can die? Your friend told me that you're trying to kill yourself." I kept my cool, shrugged my shoulders and said, "Well, if I die, you for one will be happy. You won't have to worry about me anymore."

This made her furious. "I'll kill you myself," she screamed. She picked up a small sledgehammer and threatened to hit me with it. I yelled at her, "Go ahead, I had enough with you. Bring it down, smash my head and you will be spending your days in prison, crying for what you have done." She said that she did not care. I knew she must be in shock and wasn't herself. Or, maybe she was. She was about to bring the hammer down on my head when Siavash jumped in and stopped her. I ran away and she ran after me, waving the hammer and shouting, "I have to kill you."

Mum threatened me repeatedly, "One of these days, I am going to hammer you." I was scared of her. I would have been relieved to live in a foster home had such places existed. I half-joked with her that I would leave if she kept mistreating me. She said to me, "Go ahead and become a prostitute. If you step out of my house, I don't have anything to do with you as long as I live. I consider you dead." Depression, anxiety and life pressures from every angle had made her into a monster. I don't blame her now but at the time I could not understand why she was hurting me so much.

The constant arguments had an enormous impact on how I conducted myself. I felt I was the worst thing that had ever happened to our family. I was physically fragile and sick nearly every day. Inside, I had my own demons to face. Outside I had to face the sarcasm of my peers and teachers who had a good laugh at my dorky looks and poor grades. On top of that, the constant arguments because I had stopped reciting my daily Arabic prayers continued. It advanced to pretty much everything had become an issue. It seemed to me that mum punished me for just breathing. When I was sick, she would tell me, "I'll wait until you get better, then I'll punish you." This was hardly an incentive to get well. I wasn't so sure there was a reason for me to live any more The trip to Mecca changed our mental health and improved the relationship between us. My options were; Go with mum or stay home with grandma. I didn't want to stay home and have my grandmother baby-sit me. In my opinion, she needed someone to baby-sit her. She was very demanding and I didn't think I could stand her domineering for a month. I think mum saw this as an opportunity to bring me closer to God and hoped it would be a chance for us to have a healthy relationship.

I started looking forward to the trip but there were obstacles and little time to overcome them. As usual, the biggest problem was money.

Although my father was once again a millionaire, he refused to pay a penny, not for food and certainly not for my trip. After he left us, he continued to pay for groceries for a couple of months. When he was sure he was not coming back, he stopped paying for groceries.

Ignoring reality, my mother persuaded me to call my father to ask him for money. She said maybe he would change his mind and do something good for once in his life. She wanted me to give him another chance, so I did.

He had just taken an expensive trip to western Iran, visiting my mum's family, explaining his split with my mother and lying that she had asked him to leave. On this trip, my father bought a German shepherd, reportedly paying $750 for the dog; then and now, a lot of money for a dog in Iran or anywhere else for that matter. He said that he didn't have any money to give to me. I asked him how could he not have any money if he'd just spent that much for a dog. I was asking for $500, less than the price of his dog, for a pilgrimage to Mecca. He responded, I don't have any money for you and I like my dog more than I like you. I couldn't help bursting into tears. The receiver fell out of my hand. Since that day, I have never had any desire to meet him face to face.

He was not only cruel to me and my mother but cruel to animals as well. He stopped feeding the dog, starved him and beat him daily until he ran away. The dog was later found dead in a remote area of the town of Najaf-Abad.

By this time, we had only a few Persian rugs left, having sold the rest to keep a roof over our heads. Mum loved those rugs but she was determined to take me on this trip. Reluctantly, she decided to sell the last few rugs. All we had left was an old, faded, threadbare carpet in the living room, covering an even more pitiful pileless carpet, with which we tried to cover the moldy floor we lived on for many years. I wasn't happy to go along at such a price but mum had made up her mind; like it or not I had to go with her.

There were other obstacles. I had to pass a medical examination. In an ideal world, I wouldn't have passed. It was a formality required by Saudi Arabia and pretty much everyone with money to make the trip passed. My health was not good; I was dizzy all the time and had fainted in crowds more than once while waiting for mum to finish a conversation with friends. I passed the exam. I didn't tell the doctors anything that I thought would jeopardize my trip to Mecca and they didn't discover anything. Whether it was God's will or a coincidence; it was a positive reason to see the house of God.

Eventually everything fell into place. The only remaining detail was to prepare the special pilgrim's garb we would wear when we made the seven rotations around the Ka'ba, the holiest shrine in Islam.

The Ka'ba is a cube shaped building built before Islam by the Prophet Abraham to worship God. Centuries later, it was turned into a temple for worshiping idols. When God chose the Prophet Mohammad the Ka'ba became the house of God, the most sacred site for Muslims around the world and the destination for the Hajji or pilgrims. People who can afford the trip and even many who cannot, come from all corners of the world, to Hajj.

Motivated by the austere life of the Prophet, women wear a simple outfit made of white cotton fabric for the holiest of pilgrimages; circling the Ka'ba. Men wear two seamless white sheets. Mum wanted to make me a chador. I told her I wouldn't wear it. I wanted to wear whatever I was comfortable with. I told her that I believed that God should exist in my heart, not in what I wear. This wasn't an easy concept for her to accept. We argued repeatedly. Sometimes she would swear at me and wish me dead. Often she would say, "Because you are coming with me on this holy trip, I can't punish you now but I swear to God, I will punish you when we come back." This created mixed emotions for me and I seriously began to regret my decision to go with her.

During the final stage of preparation it is the custom for Hajji, a person going to Mecca as a pilgrim, to call and, if possible, go to see family members and loved ones to ask their forgiveness, their blessings and to offer to pray for them. Mum persuaded me to call my father's family to ask for their blessings and forgiveness. This was extremely difficult and, in some cases, impossible to do. I called my aunt several times but she pretended she didn't know me before hanging up on me. In retrospect, she might have had Alzheimer's disease but since we had such a poor relationship I suspect she was just being her usual charming self.

Things were hardly easier on my mother's side. We hadn't seen most of them in years and they were actually angry with her because she wouldn't live with my abusive father. They thought of her as a disgrace to the family and wanted to have nothing to do with her.

At last, it was time to go. I had never flown in an airplane but it turned out that I loved it. We obviously could not fly over Iraq and we could not fly the most direct route, over the Persian Gulf. The Iraq air patrols had given Iran an ultimatum that they would shoot us down. Our flight had to take the long way around, three-and-a-half hours over Turkey, Syria, and Jordan before we entered Saudi Arabia. We arrived in Jeddah, one of the largest international airports in the Middle East, at 2:00 p.m. It was hot, over 40° C (104° F) and quite humid. Most of the people on our journey were sweating profusely. Sweat poured from our faces. I was a native of a hot climate and the heat didn't bother me at all. When we entered the airport, I found myself comfortable and somehow at home.

There were two places we had to go during our 36 days in Saudi Arabia, Mecca and Medina Utopia, the place where the prophet Mohammad lived for the last few years of his life. According to his last testament, he was buried in his own home. We were scheduled to go to Mecca first. After a suffocating, ten-hour bus ride with faulty air conditioning and no food or water, we arrived at the house that had been rented for us. It was an old tumbledown place that the leader of our group had rented for almost nothing. To our dismay, we belatedly discovered that he was a member of my father's family. I had a hard time understanding why we would travel with people who either ignored or bullied us. Mum said one of her good friends had introduced him to the group leader and she didn't know he was a distant relative of my father.

It wasn't entirely the old man's fault. He had no idea about the family connection, either. His intentions were honorable but the other distant relatives in our group took advantage of us as often as they could. In the crowd of one hundred and fifty people, we were always the last to eat and last to get on the bus. A few times, we didn't even receive our lunch, which often was delivered to our rooms. The answer we got was, "Sorry, the food is all gone." My mother and I were purposely placed in the same room with two women from my father's family who found countless ways to bother us. It was a complete humiliation and even this holy journey didn't stop the leader and the other members of my father's family from teasing us

Although I was quite hungry at times, the food that was prepared in the group kitchen was almost inedible. The leader had bought the cheapest ingredients and the rice the chef was cooking was full of rat droppings. Although the chef washed it, the smell was disgusting and he used so much spice to disguise the smell that it was almost impossible to swallow. I couldn't eat most of the food and was so malnourished that on the second week of our trip I had to see a doctor. We had an offer to relocate to another group but mum refused; she said people would start talking. I wasn't pleased but couldn't blame her either. She wasn't the only woman brought up to worry about other's opinion. Ninety percent of women that grow up in family system such as mine think the same way, regardless of religion or culture.

Most people who make this pilgrimage are wealthy, in their forties or fifties and are asking God to forgive them for a life badly spent. We also had a lot of younger men and women in our group who were coming to serve God. I, however, was one of the very few teen-agers. I believe in my heart that God sent me to this journey because he wanted to heal me. He wanted to say, "I heard your cries."

We made our first visit to the mosque. I could hardly believe my eyes and I could not understand the sensation that flooded my body. There is a saying in Islam that only those who have been truly invited by God feel that sensation in their heart. I felt the presence of angels. I felt the spirits of the people who had been in that place thousands of years before me. I would sit down beside my mother and just look into the crowd. As I was searching, I felt the presence of the Angels. I was a completely new soul. I regretted the awful things I had said and done and asked for forgiveness. I am not certain whether it was from being happy or sad but I could not stop the flow of my tears when, for the first time, I made the ritual procession seven times around the Ka'ba, as Mohammad and his followers were told to do by God.

I felt honored for being invited to His place. There is, in the word of God, a proclamation by the Angel Gabriel, 'Whoever is invited to do this ceremony and is truly seeking peace, will feel it inside themselves. Not all Hajjis are invited by God.' I truly believe that God wanted me to go to Mecca since I wasn't even a Muslim in my heart when the opportunity arose. Apparently, He took an interest in me and accepted my challenge when I told Him that I needed to see a sign of His existence. I wanted to know that He was out there and hearing me. I never thought God had any interest in my existence. I guess He proved me wrong and I was glad. With pride, I bowed down and prayed at the same spot where Abraham and Mohammad prayed. All the tension in my heart, the nastiness of my thoughts, and the loneliness was washed away. I felt as if I was reborn and never felt greater. After that journey, I became a much lighter hearted person and had more patience and forgiveness.

I had finally relented on the chador standoff. Wearing all white, drinking the same water that Ishmael had found, I looked into the crowd. They were so completely at peace. As God says, there is no evil in this holy mosque. During the seven rotations, men and women press against each other but no lustful feelings are allowed. If someone feels anything sexual, he or she must sacrifice a goat or a sheep. During the month of the pilgrimage, men and women have no physical contact with each other. According to the laws of Islam, if they have sex, they can be divorced immediately.

During the approximately seven hours of the Hajj ceremonies, I felt totally different. After this, we walked along the same path that Abraham traveled with his son to sacrifice him. We threw stones at the devil with the same ferocity as Abraham and sacrificed a lamb or a goat or whatever we could afford. By the end of three days, all feelings of anger had been washed away from me. I rejoiced in my spiritual rebirth, experienced indescribable feelings and was at total peace. Emotionally, I was a much happier person and for the first time in many years I counted my blessings and prayed, not because I was forced to, but I wanted to.

During our trip to Mecca, the pleasant and healing moments I experienced made it memorable but not everything was pleasant and certainly not all of it was holy. When we were in the holy mosque, I spotted men, who for no reason, would sit right in front of me and keep staring at me. It is a great sin to feel any sexual attraction in the mosque. Not that I had any; I didn't want to initiate any such feelings in others. I turned my face around.

While mum and I were praying beside the Ka'ba, I was puzzled and outraged by the actions of the Saudi police, called *al Shurtah*, who wore the same traditional red hatband and head cover as the Saudi officials. When people kissed the Ka'ba, the police hit them hard with a folded headband that had a heavy knot in the end. Some of them had a whisk like whip made of horse's tail with which they hit people and kept saying, "Get lost, get lost." in Arabic. An Iranian man screamed, "I came all the way from Iran to worship. Who the hell are you to tell me to get lost?" The Saudi police immediately arrested him and took him out of the mosque. This was their way of saying this is our House and you are not welcome if you don't obey our rules. Times change but behavior is still the same. The Prophet was born among Arabs, as I described. He, himself, was sick of their mistreatment. I was shocked to see the barbaric police behavior in the house of God and asked mum to take me home.

During our first few days, we traveled by taxi, which turned out to be an expensive alternative. We decided to use the bus system like most other Hajjis, which meant we had to get to a station and compete with thousands of others who wanted to get on the bus. During the time of Hajj, due to the heavy population and traffic, we decided to visit the mosque during the night and come back to rest after the morning prayers at dawn. This change of plan didn't help much because the rest of the Hajjis, were using the same strategy.

Early one morning, while we were squished toward the bus, I told mum that I could not stand anymore. The next second, she was pouring water on my face. Mum had asked for oranges and water from some Pakistani men who were having a small breakfast on the side of the road. They were very kind and as soon as they noticed I had passed out, they even offered me some chocolate that helped raise my blood sugar. We waited for the next bus and people allowed me to go ahead. While the driver's assistant was asking for people's ticket, he slid his hand on my chest and started squeezing my breast and groping me. I screamed to mum that he was touching me. She screamed at him. He shrugged and moved on as though nothing had happened

After I rested for a while, mum decided to go shopping and asked some other women she had met to come along with us. Mum was very good at negotiating and with broken Arabic and a few word of English, she assumed the role of buyer for our female friends. While we were walking around the market near the Holy Mosque, I noticed the Arab men, who were dealing with mum, gazing at me. At first I thought I was mistaken but when I turned around and looked back, they were still staring. I wasn't pretty or voluptuous or flirting. I could not understand what they saw in me.

Little by little, it became obvious that the Arab men were interested in something. I just couldn't understand what more I could offer than the array of women swarming all over Mecca. Many wealthy Saudi men had a car full of beautiful women dressed like Barbie dolls with heavy duty make up, covering their faces with sheer chiffon silk. Everywhere we went, I saw the stare, the eyes and the chauvinistic attitude of Saudi men toward women. It was sickening. In conversations mum had with some women that could speak a few word of Farsi, they told her that they did not like the men's behavior but had no other way.

During the period we were in Mecca, everywhere we went seemed prosperous, I bought a chocolate box, that, even after moving to Canada, I haven't seen anything like it. Nearly everything, including dairy products, comes from Europe.

Mum and I heard there was a garden, built by Ali, and decided to visit it. It was in a part of town populated by Shiah, a minority in Saudi Arabia. I had never seen anyone that poor. Even measured against our modest life, we seemed to be wealthy compared with those people. They lived, dirt poor.

I questioned my mother, how it was possible that these people, who live just a few miles from the house of God that earns this country billions of dollars, are so poor. There are many princes in Saudi and, apparently, the wealth does not trickle down. While over five thousand princes receive huge allowances, spend their summers in Rio de Janeiro and Monte Carlo, shopping for designer items, boat riding or staying on their private yachts, these people receive nothing from public wealth.

journey to Medina

Saying good-bye to Mecca, we continued our pilgrimage to Medina. Here, we had a better place to stay, less than 20 minutes walking distance from the huge mosque complex, which encompasses our Prophet Mohammad's burial chamber and shrine. Here, there were fewer al-Shurtah than in Mecca and they were somewhat kinder. During our visit to the burial chamber, within the mosque, I noticed that a dozen or more police had surrounded the small ancient house, the actual home and burial shrine of the Prophet, and didn't allow people to kiss the shrine. According to Sunni rules, observed in Saudi Arabia, it is sin for Muslims to kiss the shrine of the Prophet, or kiss the Ka'ba. In Shiah, however, it is a sign of servitude and spirituality. Whatever the Saudis' reason, I didn't want to be hit by the whisk or told to get lost and obeyed their rules. While going around the shrine of the Prophet, I was pushed over by the crowd. I was lucky one of the policemen was kind enough to grab me before I went face down and was trampled.

In Medina we spent our days walking down the same path the Prophet Mohammad and his followers walked thousands of years ago. Again, I noticed the policemen, who dressed more formally in uniform with a red hatband on their head, instead of traditional Arabic clothes that some wore. While we were sitting, I noticed the policemen approaching women; usually Egyptian women were the ones targeted the most. These light hearted women, devoted to their prayers, wanted to reserve the place where they had sat all morning for prayer time. If they did not move when asked, the police put their hand beneath their armpits, next to their breasts and pulled them aside. These men were molesting women in a holy place. Every time the police approached me, I gave them a dirty look and jumped back and ran. Looking at their faces lusting after the pilgrims and playing their sick, twisted game, repulsed me. They were standing in the holiest Muslim site, yet had no shame and no respect for the women or the Prophet.

Almost miraculously and very gratifying was the way things were improving between my mother and me. One day, we met an Egyptian lady in Prophet Mohammad Mosque. I had brought a stainless steel tumbler from Iran with me, perhaps to have a piece of home around. The lady saw it, and asked me in Arabic if she could have it. I shook my head side to side, as a sign of no, and smiled. She was having fun with me. She offered me money. I shook my head no again. She offered me one hundred dollars. The glass was hardly worth more than a dollar. I told her she could have it if she wanted it that badly. She said she could not take it without paying me. After all, we were all here to worship and purify ourselves; she didn't want to take advantage of me. She offered me a valuable ring worth perhaps $500 in exchange for the tumbler. I said that I didn't want to sell it anymore but wished I had brought the whole set; I could have paid for my trip. We all laughed.

I was innocently joking with the lady while facing the Prophets shrine. I suppose our laughter upset some of the radicals in the crowds. Some of the other Iranian Hajjis, who were defenders of the government, approached scolded me, "You're ruining Iran's reputation." I replied that I was not ruining anyone's reputation. I was just joking around, following the Prophet's admonition to be happy and innocently having a good time. I added that if I was ruining Iran's reputation, it must be a very fragile reputation, indeed. They were frustrated by my quick repartee. My mother stepped in and said, "The Prophet Mohammad has said that whoever has kind manners and smiles, is his true follower." That was true. Contrary to the radicals' concept of the Prophet as a bitter, angry man, he was quite light hearted and always smiled. The Egyptian lady recognized that our conversation was serious and, in Arabic, told the women to get lost. Mum told them, "If you can't laugh, that's your problem." It was very reassuring to have mum defend me. I felt for the first time in a long time that we were on the same side.

One night, not long after that, two women from the Iranian government came to our hotel to talk to our group. They were trying to enlist us in a demonstration against the United States. Fortunately, as it turned out, no one in our group paid them much attention or had any interest in joining their cause.

A couple of days later the fanatics sent by the government of Iran, had organized and were getting ready to hold an anti-United States protest in front of the Baghi, a very famous graveyard in Medina; the burial place for many of the Prophet Mohammad's children and grandchildren. Saudi Arabia had announced that anti-US activity would not be tolerated. The fanatics thought the Saudis were bluffing.

When Mum and I went to the mosque in the early morning to pay our respects, there were squadrons of soldiers all over, armed from head to toe and ready to go to war. Mum and I said a fast prayer and hurried back to our apartment. Soon after we left the area, a different kind of hell broke loose. From our balcony we could hear and see the shooting. Iranians were the main targets.

Dozens of Iranians, including innocent men and women, were killed. Several hundred women, who had gathered for this protest, were running in the streets. In the frenzy and confusion, many of them were murdered, raped or mutilated by Saudi Arab men. Some women never made it home and some who did had been attacked so savagely that wounds on their breasts became infected and their breasts had to be removed.

It was a terrible tragedy for both countries. In the aftermath, the Iranian government, which had encouraged the protest, suppressed the story. It was, after all, largely about women, and no one really cared about women in Iran anyway. After that incident, the relationship between the two countries soured. For several years, the Saudi government set a quota and Iran could send only a limited number of people to Mecca. The year of my pilgrimage, there were more than 250,000 Iranian visitors. The following year there were only 60,000. The quota of pilgrims has since increased, as they are a major source of income for Saudi Arabia.

Our last few days in Saudi Arabia were very tense. Although we had nothing to do with the protest, we were shunned and chided. Many times, after the protest, Arab men insulted us and called us names. It was heartbreaking that people who walked the same ground that Mohammad walked could be so cruel. But, politics divides people despite a religious bond. I was moved by this experience, and even today any time I think of going back to Mecca, I am reminded of the protestors and the killing of innocent people. I still hear their screams for help, I see their tears and I feel their pain.

Black Freedom

The title of this chapter refers to the color of the chador the women of Iran wore while protesting; chanting slogans against the United States. It also refers to the absence of freedom in a society governed by medieval mullahs who wear the Holy Prophets clothes, presenting themselves to the public as pure, while in private they have no shame; committing inhuman actions against their rivals.

I believe the future of a nation depends on being a politically free, informed country whose citizens can criticize the government free of fear. Ideally, it is a liberal, democratic government that responds appropriately and diplomatically, defending its position without jailing protestors and torturing opponents. What I just described would be Utopia for many nations. In reality, it seems like a far-fetched dream that will never come true for most third world countries, including Iran, where every government that has come to power, whether wearing a crown or a turban, was looking out for the insiders, not the nation's best interest. Unfortunately, Iran does not have the luxury of freedom of speech that westerners take for granted. Therefore, much of the abuse Iranians endure never makes it to the world media.

A nation cannot be successful if the government revolves around a bunch of phony mullahs who elect themselves and use the nation's money for their agenda. It has been scripted in my language, 'Once a thief, always a thief.' It makes no difference who the government of Iran selects as president; Khatami, Rafsanjani or another of their ilk, it is always the same. No matter how you dress up a monkey, it is still a monkey. The selected candidate cannot betray his co-conspirators because it is a house of cards. If one falls, all fall. To avoid collapse, no matter how much they may hate each other, they will protect one another.

When we returned home from Mecca, Siavash, Khosro, his wife and their baby girl, were at the airport to welcome us. Although Manoocheher was still in Iran, he didn't come to greet his mother. My father told everyone that I went to Mecca in his place and that he fully supported me. His only contribution was to stay at home. He received the last penny of the money he had paid for the Mecca registration before signing the paper to my name.

Upon our return, I discovered that not everything in my world had changed for the better and that God doesn't interfere with our daily lives as I assumed, prior to my trip. Mum accompanied me to the Ministry of Education to set up an appointment for a mathematics exam that I missed while I was on pilgrimage. We went to the office of the vice president who had wished me luck and promised me there would be no problem taking the exams upon my return, along with soldiers returning from the war who had a similar situation. With a long face, he told me he had bad news. He apologized and said he couldn't let me take the exam and there was no alternative. I pleaded that he was the minister, there had to be a way to salvage an entire year of school. I think he didn't want to tell his peers he had given me wrong information. He took no responsibility for his mistakes, the usual case in Iran's government. From top to bottom, nobody takes responsibility for his mistakes.

My emotional and mental health was not his concern. I wasn't important enough for him to make a few calls and fix his mistake. I was just a girl. He made no effort to help me and his cold apology meant nothing. It could not give me back one year of my life that I had wasted in the course.

I had to repeat the school year. I couldn't stop feeling like a failure. Once again, I hit bottom. I was angry with my mother because she made me go on pilgrimage with her and when I needed her support she did not try to intervene. Instead, she berated me for my awful grades, suggesting I do better next year.

I isolated myself. Mum could not talk to me or bring me out of my shell. Nothing could make me happy. In desperation, she transferred me to one of the best schools in the city. It was hard for her to cover the cost of my new school and tuition but she did her best. I had to wear a gray suit at the new school. I had hated the color gray ever since my grandfather died in the hospital wearing gray pajamas. It was a depressing color for me. She bought a beautiful light gray material and sewed a chic suit, on which I received many compliments. She was trying but her efforts were a bit late; it took me a while to forgive her.

I was pleased with the suit but I still had to wear it to classes with kids academically a year behind me. This was heavy on my heart but I had a small consolation. Since I started school a year early, the other kids were actually my age. Before the failure fiasco, I was an extroverted kid, at least at school, and a critical thinker. During that year, I became extremely quiet; to the point that teachers had to hush everyone to hear my voice in the classroom. My efforts were focused on my studies.

My reserved attitude somehow offended twin sisters in my class who entertained themselves by taunting and mocking me. It seemed they disliked me; just because. Perhaps they thought I was dumb. Whatever the reason, they put chalk on my desk at every opportunity and mocked me when I cleaned it. I confronted the ringleader and gave her an ultimatum to stop putting chalk on my desk or else. She laughed and smirked, "What are you going to do? and laughed again." I told her, "You will see." and left the class. Later, I returned to class and caught her putting chalk on my desk again while her sister laughingly encouraged her to put more chalk on the dork's desk! I told her to clean it up; she refused. I warned her but she only laughed harder. She was six feet tall and stronger than me but I was not intimidated. I had vowed to stand up for myself and now it was time to prove I meant what I said. Suddenly my voice changed, my eyes burned in anger and I lashed out, slapping her forcefully. Her nose started bleeding and the bully burst into tears like a child.

I rushed to the principal's office, told the whole story and took responsibility for my actions. My tormentor brought her parents to school. I heard that her nosebleed worsened and her family planned to take the matter to the police. Fortunately, I had supporting witnesses for all the previous incidents, when she repeatedly ignored my pleas, and the finale, when I slapped her. My classmates were ready to come forward and testify. The only other person I had to explain to was mum.

When I got home, I told her about the incident. At first, she argued with me but when I related the entire scenario, she asked me why I had taken the abuse for so long. I replied that I was a big girl now and could defend myself. Besides, she could not be there all the time. Mum too, had been a victim of bullying and knew the girl deserved the slap. She looked me in the eye and said she was proud of me for standing up for myself, even though she still thought I should have consulted her first. She asked if I needed her support. I told her I would let her know if I needed her to come to the police with me. I never heard from the girl's family. They probably had not known their polite, refined daughter was a closet bully and realized they had no case against me. The twins became the quietest students in the class. And never bothered anyone else as long as I was around.

I don't believe in use of force or punishment for anyone, except as a last resort. I have had my own share. Although I will sound like a hypocrite, sometimes, the only way to communicate with someone is to speak his or her own language. What I did was harsh, but I had to stand up for me because I know no one else would have and the girl would have continued abusing me. That isolated incident was the only time I ever hurt anyone physically.

Violence against children is a common practice among many families in Iran. Even teachers used to administer severe punishment. Although the government has banned punishment by teachers, I have seen many students with body injuries and bruised eyes and skin. Although any bodily injury or harsh punishment is against the rules of Islam, mullahs praise families who take pride in bringing up their children by punishing them violently or invading their privacy.

It was a wretched year but I survived my third year of middle school for the second time. By year's end I had made some friends, had a 3.09 grade point averages and graduated with honors. This meant I could register at any high school I wanted.

At long last, I was entering high school. I was mentally more mature than most others my age and there were important issues in life that I wanted to explore and understand. I was moving forward; maybe at a snail's pace but moving at last. I was eligible to attend any high school but mum wanted me to be close to home for a couple of reasons. First, we could not afford transportation and second, she could check on me regularly. I wasn't happy about the school she chose. It was one of the most notorious schools in Isfahan and was in an area that was constantly bombed as the war got closer to the heart of the country. On the other hand, I knew I would feel tremendous guilt and never forgive myself for surviving if my family died in a bomb attack while I was in a safe school across town.

HiGH SCHOOL FROM HELL

B y the time, I was adult enough to have a choice; my freedom to choose was taken away from me.

I had enough problems at home and decided to not bring any more from school. When I registered at high school, I didn't expect it be the hardest four years of my life. High school years, globally, are supposed to be the precious years. In retrospect, mine were more like a short life sentence in hell. In the time of the Shah, this school, only a block from our home, had acquired a bad reputation for a gang of girls so violent that not many teachers were willing to teach there. When the revolution ended, the municipal government promised the people of Isfahan it would reform this school.

There were indications that they tried. From the outside it looked more like a prison than a place for education. There were bars on the windows, cameras covering the halls, barbed wire fences and squads of government watchdogs known as *Islamic Irshad*. There were undercover spies among the students, trained to pass on any information that could be used against anyone opposing the government and to watch for gang activity. Theoretically, the gangs had been disbanded but the school was still full of belligerent girls.

A month before classes started, I had nightmares about going to this school. Mum advised me to stay away from trouble. The school environment itself was trouble. I was not looking for trouble but I soon found myself dwelling on how to stay out of it.

My precious memories of high school are similar to the Harry Potter Wizard School. Unfortunately, I was not a wizard, did not have a magic problem-solving wand and did not have a wizard to watch and protect me. I looked like a dork and had no self-esteem. My most vivid memories are the miserable winter days when bombs were falling all around us and students still had to attend school.

I quickly discovered that the middle school curriculum to which I was accustomed was much simpler and easier than that of the high school, which was a combination of high school and pre-university. We don't have college in our educational system.

In primary school years, my studies were relatively easy; so much so, that I never studied any course twice. Because of my dyslexia, in my younger years the oral courses registered without putting too much effort into memorizing them. Those courses included biology, literature, poetry, art, religion, history and geography. My grade point average was B+.

In middle school, my studies suffered, my grades went down and took a further drastic downturn with one incident. During one exam, due to shortage of space in the classroom, the entire class was held in the schoolyard. I was forced to sit on my crossed ankles on the wet ground for two hours. I started to go numb. I told the teacher but she did not allow me to get up until I finished my exam. By the time I left to come home, I had not only messed up the exam badly but also had developed a permanent stigma and nervousness. To this day, every time I have any exam, the nervousness and physical pain in my legs comes back.

The course load in high school changed abruptly. Instead of five or seven courses per semester, I had to study nine to twelve books. School starts in late September and finishes in late June. There are three semesters in each year and all courses are mandatory. The first year, my courses included two hours of Arabic, and two hours of religion studies. Later, religion was eliminated and replaced by four hours of Arabic language. We also had two hours of English in the first two years, increasing to four hours in the third and fourth years.

The first year of high school requires a major life decision for all students. Every student has to choose between math, science or literature divisions. Students who wanted to pursue engineering would chose the math category, those who wanted to go to medical school would follow science and those interested in art, psychology or teaching would choose literature.

For me, as a science student, my major courses were eight hours of Biology four hours of Chemistry, four hours of Mathematics, two hours Algebra, two hours of Trigonometry, two hours of Geometry, two hours of English, two hours of Arabic, two hours Science lab, four hours of Physics, four hours of Persian literature, two hours Sports and two hours mandatory Religion, totaling forty hours per week.

I went to school Saturday through Friday afternoon. Classes started at 8:00 a.m. but we had to be in rows and listen to morning prayers at 7.30 a.m. We had to be present in the school until 4:00 p.m. but most times we were in class until 5:00 p.m. and many times we stayed in school until 9:00 p.m. for extra studies. Many of the teachers who really tried to help students, told us we would find many of these courses useless in our future studies but we still had to read them. Some of the research was twenty years old. New discoveries, although discussed in our classes, were not tested and noted in our books.

I didn't do well in math but did very well in oral courses. I wasn't a stupid student but was a very tired and malnourished one. Despite all my problems, I worked very hard all those years and, I believe, made a favorable impression on some of my classmates and teachers.

During my first year of high school, one of my best friends, Mariam, or Mary, lost her mother. I tried to cheer her up and she and I grew close. One day, I started fidgeting in biology class and threw my eraser at her. When she threw it back at me, it ended up in front of our teacher. My biology marks were A+ and the teacher liked me very much, so she assumed Mary must be the culprit. When she started to reprimand her, I stood up and defended her, telling my teacher it was my fault. She didn't believe me and said I shouldn't interfere but I insisted. We were both reprimanded but were pardoned when I explained and apologized to my teacher.

This incident, apparently, echoed throughout the school. I received letters from girls I did not know and, from a mystery girl, notes bordering on love letters. I understood the content of the letter but had no curiosity about the source or any inclination to respond. I read them to my mother, who did not know about my aborted lesbian flirtation in middle school, and we had fun with them. During high school, I received many love letters and poetry from females. If I had been gay or bisexual, the all girl school was the way to go.

There were scary funny moments in our biology lab. We had a skeleton in the lab that seemed awfully lonely. Coming from my background that lived with spirits and ghosts, I had no fear of joking with my lonely friend. Whenever we entered the lab, I grabbed his arms and asked him to dance with me. When classmates were busy, I put his hands on their shoulder. Some got hysterical and others had a great laugh. A few months after my initial dating sessions with my skeletal friend, his head was misplaced. At times when we had a lab assignment, I placed my head on his body. I got quite a reputation as the comedian at school.

During those four years, my teachers seemed to like me for standing up for my friends and on a couple of occasions they even praised me. On one occasion in fourth term, I had forgotten to read my biology lecture or bring my notebook. When the teacher called my name, other students started asking her questions and continued until it was time to go home. I dodged that bullet and never had to answer. The teacher knew they had helped me out. She just shook her head and was delightfully surprised. These were the scarce happy memories I have from high school. Most other happenings during this time were quite unpleasant and some even affected my future.

The school I was attending was its own little war zone. A student committed suicide by throwing herself out of a third-floor window into the schoolyard.

The first day of school, a teacher gave me a prize because I was the only one to correctly answer a question she asked. We never saw her again and were told she had been exposed as a leftist and executed like many other dissidents. The discipline was unbearable. Every morning, before we entered the school, we were searched. Not for guns, knives or drugs, but for makeup and perfume, to see if our eyebrows had been plucked or if our nails had been buffed. If we were manicured or wearing gold jewelry, we were in big trouble. The principal, a government watchdog, trained some of the students to serve as watchpups for her.

Officials at school were angry with me because I was deliberately late for the first prayer every day. When I did attend, I didn't recite the prayers aloud. The headmaster was standing right beside me as I was opening and closing my mouth. She said to me, "I don't hear you saying anything." I said," I have a sore throat, I can't yell." She replied, "You have a sore throat every day."

The truth was, deep down, I didn't agree with forced religion. Islam is a religion of freedom and brotherhood. The government has hi-jacked Islam. It has come to be unfairly perceived as a religion of terrorists and dictators. I didn't believe all the nonsense we were being brainwashed with. Every morning we prayed for Khomeini and cheered his name. We prayed for the government and shouted slogans like, "Down with America, Down with Israel, Down with England, Down with the West." I absolutely hated it and wondered how an entire nation came to be controlled by such ignorant people acting on behalf of equally ignorant and venal mullahs.

We had a two-hour break from noon to two in the afternoon. Prayers are mandatory for devout Muslims but they should not be forced on anyone. As the Koran says, 'There is no force in religion.' But, every afternoon, we were called to prayers and to another round of chanting and anti-West slogans. I either left to go home or, when I was around, hid. The head master would come after me and question me why I didn't pray. I said to her that she could not make me pray. I pray on my own. She was quite bitter and didn't want me to become an example or role model for other students.

This wasn't the only ordeal many of us endured. As hard as my life was, I had one advantage over most of my high school classmates. I didn't have to worry that I would be married off by the next spring. Nearly every day when I went to school I heard one of them crying that she became engaged last night and her wedding would be in early summer. Another day, I would hear someone else saying her suitor was waiting for her to finish her final exams.

We were only fifteen years old but parents didn't think it was a crime to give away their teenage daughters. Mullahs were falsely teaching that, according to the rules of Islam, Muslim parents should marry off their daughters before she had her first menstrual period.

Mum and I had many differences but when I was twelve years old, she sat me down and said to me that, no matter what; I would never be forced to marry anyone. I would be allowed to choose my own husband. I am proud to say she really meant it and proved to me that she did not want to cause me the same misery most parents, including hers, gave their daughters.

WHEN MULLAHS BECOME POLITICIANS

I believe that a politician could be a good Mullah, Priest or Rabbi. I also believe that any of the religious men make a terrible politician. In regard to the debate, some Iranian mullahs have said that Prophet Mohammad or Jesus or Moses were political; why can't we be as well? My answer to them is: First and foremost, you are not Jesus, Mohammad, or Moses and have no connection to the holy men, chosen carefully by God himself. Just wearing the same outfit doesn't mean someone is qualified to compare himself with any of those holey men. Secondly, Jesus, Mohammad, Moses or other holy men of God didn't necessarily win a popularity contest and didn't intend to. They did not pocket people's money and did not mix with politics unless necessary.

They were ordered by God himself to guide people. Apart from the holy men, who received their orders and guidance directly from God, a successful politician is required to lie, deceive and be ruthless. They are required to make decisions that often go against the guidance of any religion and we are all aware of their obligations, even though much of it has nothing to do with the laws they have set for the rest of us. We don't always agree with their decisions but we don't condemn it because we know it is politics and often necessary. As a general rule, honest politicians seldom succeed. If they do survive for a short time, it will entail heartache and day and night effort. Politics is dirty. For men of God who claim they are pure, playing with politics is trying to have it both ways.

Back in Iran, there is an interesting folk story that pokes fun at the propaganda we hear about the mullahs being honorable politicians. A poor man had a rooster that was dear to his heart. A noble and religious man stole the rooster. The poor man asked the thief if he had seen his rooster. The noble thief swore on his father's grave that he had not. Suddenly, the rooster poked his tail out from the man's coat. The poor man stared at him and replied, "I am not sure, whether I should honor your word and believe you, your father's grave or my rooster's tail?"

Third, if being a politician was such a trial for the holy men, why did they suffer so much? When people, who were pure, were trying to help, they often found themselves being accused and ostracized by those professing to follow God. Imam Ali used to cry because he was given such an enormous responsibility and wanted to do it right. When he was in power, a Jewish woman came to him and complained, "One of the governors that you have chosen, ordered me to taken off my gold ankle bracelet." Ali apologized to the woman, sent a letter to the man, and replaced him with someone else.

Today, after the revolution, as Khomeini, and his regime claim to be followers of Prophet Mohammad, hundreds of thousands of people have lost their lives, spent years in jail and lost their properties. There is a statement from Mahdy that when he comes to fight the devil, his enemy is not the devil himself but Muslims who claim to follow him, even as they wait with guns to kill him. I will take a chance and swear on my honor that Muslims, such as Khomeini, Bin Laden, Musab al-Zarqawi, Iran's government and so many other Muslims who kill to satisfy their own hate, are on the list of enemies of Islam. In recent years, after 9/11, Islam has received such a bad, undeserved reputation. Everywhere I look, someone kills, kidnaps and tortures people, even children, and it is done in the name of Islam. That is not what true Islam is about.

Iran's clock must have turned backward. Some of the misfits running the country, who were initially looked on as brutal fundamentalists, are now considered modern and moderate mullahs. If, at the very least, the so-called mullah experts had studied law, I would have more tolerance for their rules and regulations. These people don't seem to understand, it takes people with at least minimal competence, to run a country successfully.

As I grew older, I observed that conditions, dictated by zealots, had grown progressively worse for the women of Iran since the revolution. I became increasingly aware of the discrimination toward oppressed women. In my first year of high school, I began my research to know more about Islam; studying the rules of Islam and the Muslim Holy book. I concluded that practically none of the regime's policies were according to the rules of Islam.

The male-dominated government fired virtually all women from their jobs for fear there would be sexual tension in the workplace. They then rehired some of them at lower rank and wages. Desperate women who had to feed families went along with the insult. In the early stages of revolution, a mullah name Taheri was a low rank mullah who did prayers for the deceased in the graveyard to earn money. After the revolution he was quickly promoted to Hojat-al Islam and then to Ayatollah Taheri. I have no doubt that his meteoric ascension was due to the loyalty he showed toward Khomeini. He was behind the speeches and mass calls encouraging young men to join the troops used as sacrificial lambs to walk over Iraqi mine fields on the front lines. Still, he managed to appear in the country's most important paper now and then, portraying himself as one of the more moderate mullahs.

He was the Friday Prayer Speaker for the city of Isfahan. I clearly recall his proclamation that women should not be seen in public. He said that women are like 'fields of cotton,' men are the 'fire' that will consume them and the two cannot be in the same place at the same time. His ignorant ranting created hostility and pressure toward women. Female students couldn't have male teachers. Doctors and nurses couldn't attend to the opposite gender. Many other insane rules were concocted to comply with his primitive analogy.

In the mullah's warped view, everything about the female body, even if covered, is sensuous. The government discourages male doctors from performing surgery on a female if a female colleague can do the same job. If they absolutely must operate on a woman, the mullahs advise the doctor to perform the surgery looking in a mirror. They even managed to find sin in the buttons of the long, ugly rain coats that women must wear, rain or shine, during the hot summers.

Even though they were fifty-five percent of the population, during the war many jobs were permanently closed to women. In the aftermath of the revolution there was high unemployment among men. There was no place in the military for women. The regime's solution was to fire all the women and replace them with men. To keep women occupied and quiet they were encouraged to work behind the front lines as unpaid volunteers. We had no women pilots or engineers in most of the mechanical or logistical fields and although there was no shortage of talented, educated women, most occupations were predominantly, or exclusively, reserved for men. Sadly, little by little, society has come to accept these restrictions. The new generation, born and raised in this environment, doesn't know that, not so long ago, Iran was a different country in the way it treated women.

I was such a naïve person to think I would ever be free of the hassles of my youth under a government whose parliament is occupied by men who only know about women through their zippers. Or, that I would be an independent woman who could do anything she wanted. Ignorant men think only of a woman's sexuality and of her as a vessel for sin.

For our family, however, there was, a glimmer of hope on the horizon. Mum was working hard to regain title to the four shops attached to our house so she could sell it. The house was falling apart. We were concerned about the risk to our lives but we couldn't afford to rent another place. Our problems were more important than our differences. I was studying hard and trying to look at the bright side of my relationship with my mother.

Meanwhile, Manoocheher was in Pakistan, living in a five-star hotel in Lahore. He phoned mum every couple of weeks. Khosro visited us once a month, mostly to try to get money. My relationship with him had soured over the way he treated my mother. I lit into Khosro, telling him that if he didn't want to be civil, he wasn't obligated to pretend to be nice. I told him we knew he wasn't coming to visit us but to encourage mum to sell her house and give him money. He left in anger and didn't come back for two years.

Although there was still tension between mum and I, she was trying to be calm. The older I got, the more understanding I became as to why she behaved as she did. I saw her not only as my mother, but as a victim. She was a single mother who had no income. Siavash, who had just finished his military mandate, couldn't find a job. Even when mum found him one, he didn't care about money or the job. He wanted a high paying job, something that was nearly impossible for average people. Most good paying jobs are in government or family business. We had no government ties and his father didn't care if he lived or died. Also, he didn't mind him being penniless because my father knew if he earned money, my mother would be able to hang on to her property a bit longer. Mum was really looking for a buyer but nobody was interested.

On top of our personal problems, mum had to face the scrutiny of the neighbors. She was pulled to the limit. I knew her time out for prayers was her escape window. Mum was bent beneath so much responsibility and genuinely tried hard to make life the best she could for all of us. Considering she was emotionally pulled in different directions, I applauded her for not giving up on life. Time and again, I saw her sobbing. I realized I wasn't the easiest child in the world to cope with and even though she seemed harsh on me, mum saved my life many times over. She was always there with me when I ended up in emergency numerous times a year and held my hand when she could.

She was afraid for our safety. As the war progressed, red alerts became more frequent to the point we had three to four per night. The war was getting closer. Nearly every night, we had to jump out of bed and spend hours in the yard in mid-December weather. One December night, mum woke me up for a red alert. We moved out into the yard because we were afraid the ruined roof might collapse on us. We sat waiting for the bombs under the beautiful, clear, star filled sky. That night, the bombs never came. I fell asleep watching the sky. Half an hour later, mum woke me to go back inside. Groggily, I fell flat on my face, right on the sharp edge of the water pump on our small pool. I almost broke my sphenoid bone, in the interior of my eye, and could have been blinded. Luckily, the next day I only had a purple spot around my right eye.

I had to grow up fast. There were tough times ahead. I decided it was time for me to put a stop to my mum's threats. The next time she threatened to beat me and brought her hand down I grabbed her arm and told her, "Mum, you couldn't kill me when you said you would but I am not kidding you when I say stop bringing your hand down on me. I have grown up and I will break your forearm. Please don't make me do it." Mum never slapped me again and with the exception of a couple of mishaps, her terrorizing manner ended then and there. She had not realized her behavior toward me was cruel and cutting. I know this because she apologized in a recent heart to heart conversation

Hopeless War—Idiotic Strategies

In March 1982, Iran launched an attack called 'Undeniable Victory.' In one week Iran drove a wedge through the Iraqi army, destroying a large part of three divisions and isolating north and south pockets of Iraqi forces.

In May 1982, Iran recaptured the city of Khoram-Shahr, which had been occupied for more than two years, after a bloody, house-to-house fight that cost Iraq more than 6,000 defenders. Once called 'The Bride of the Persian Gulf,' when recaptured it was a devastated, flattened city. Virtually every woman, man, child and house pet unable to flee the city had been killed.

By May 1982, Iranian victories had pressured Iraq to the point that Sadam Hussein announced Iraqi forces would leave Iran's territory. Fighting continued, however.

During the year 1983, the war became relatively dormant. Apart from hundreds of men crossing the border one day and coming back the next in coffins covered with blood, nothing much was new to our soldiers. Life at home went on.

In April 1984, Sadam proposed to meet with Khomeini face to face to neutralize the situation, discuss the peace process and negotiate a settlement. Khomeini rejected him.

In 1984, the war between Iran and Iraq intensified to the point our lives were endangered daily. Iraq was bombing our large cities and bombs fell on our neighborhood within 40 yards of our home. Iraqi soldiers celebrated the capture of the border cities, killing men and raping women; not even having mercy on children. It was a miracle we were able to cheat death. Our home was not strong enough to withstand the earthshaking tremors radiating from the bombs. We expected our roof to collapse at any minute. We said our last words to one another every night before going to sleep. I could not sleep. I watched mum until she fell asleep, to make sure she was safe.

Our mullahs could only come up with stupid strategies and promises that Imam Mahdy, the last son of Prophet Mohammad's family, absent for 1,400 years, would save us. They even claimed that he had appeared in the front lines. The mullahs of Iran had no shame in lying and betraying people. Soldiers, as young as thirteen, were going to war. Told Mahdy would save them, they were sent to march through the minefields so that the rest of the army could pass through. To encourage the young soldiers to be brave, some mullahs even dressed up and rode onto the battlefields on white horses, telling the soldiers that they were Imam Mahdy or Ali come to lead the soldiers of God. They apparently thought they could win a modern war with antiquated arms and prayer, opposing Sadam

Hussein's latest Western and US military hardware and lethal gas. In a war pitting promises of virgins in paradise versus tanks and planes, the smart money is on the tanks and planes.

Sepah Pasdaran, picked up these young, brainwashed kids from schools without their parents' consent. They wrapped a bandana around their forehead and gave them a few days of primitive military training, which they would never get the chance to use. At night, they had to listen to brainwashing chants that the mullah's made them repeat, emotionally preparing them for the night of battle and suicide by walking through minefields. To make them ready to die, Pasdars gave them a pittance of money and a key that they were told was the key to heaven. These kids believed that when they died in the Iraqi ditches they would go straight to heaven into the welcoming arms of seventy-two virgins. Apparently, none paused to reflect that this was the epitome of conspicuous consumption and that even the most macho among them would be seriously overmatched in the promised paradise.

Iraq not only had the latest equipment but also never followed the rules of war. Iranians were the enemies and must be destroyed by any means. Iraqi prisoners reported that captured Iranians were shot and buried in mass graves. The Iraqi dictator followed no rules of conduct. He hid high-voltage power lines in water filled ditches covered by machine gun and automatic rifle fire. The only way to advance or reach the other side was to cross the ditches. Iranian soldiers were allowed to enter the ditches; then the electricity was turned on, killing thousands of them. The survivors who were able to step over their dead buddies faced the machine guns.

One of my cousins was trapped in the ditches, near Halabjah. Luckily, he looked very much like an Arab. An Iraqi soldier, who thought he was one of them, saved his life. Nearly all of the 10,000 young men in his unit were killed instantly. Their intestines and brains were hung on the walls of the ditches for animals to clean up. Later, the Iraqis removed the bodies and buried them in mass unmarked graves that United States soldiers discovered in Iraq in 2003, after Sadam was deposed.

The more intense the war became, the more brutal Sadam behaved. He used mustard gas, outlawed since World War I. Many of the injured soldiers were blinded or burned by the chemical gases Sadam used against them.

People in the western world didn't believe Sadam would use chemicals until the whole world saw the indescribable massacre of the Kurds in Halabja. Even in recent years, many European countries, such as France and Germany, resisted the United States entering Iraq, arguing that the weapons of mass destruction had been destroyed. The people of Iran joked about their optimism. The joke was: When a journalist asked Mr. Blair, "Why are you so sure Sadam has the weapons?" He replied, "Because we kept the receipts."

During the war, so many bodies were brought back every day and there were so many funerals held around the country that we lost count. A half million Iranians were killed on the battlefield and one and a half million refugees were displaced. I am certain the casualties of the war exceeded a half million; that is 171 bodies per day for eight years. It was as if we were cursed by a higher power. Hundreds of bodies arrived in coffins, so many that the government kept some of the bodies and parceled them out during the slower time of the year. They were afraid the mourners might turn against them and mass funerals would become a protest.

Sadam Hussein continually bombed our cities, softening Iran up for further invasion into the heart of the country. Our air force did not have planes and equipment equal to the battle. When the revolution began, Ayatollah Khomeini's principal advisors were Talegani and Montazeri.

Montazeri remained close to Khomeini for many years. He was the genius who cancelled the deal for fifty F-16s that the Shah had already purchased from the United States. For years, people mocked him, because he called the F-16s 'salvage pieces.' Indeed, if had we had those pieces, we would have been better able to salvage some dignity and challenge a country equipped with the latest combat aircraft.

Montazeri was expected to succeed Khomeini as leader until a insignificant TV incident occurred. A reporter asked a lady in Tehran who her mentor was. She jokingly said, "It couldn't be Fatimeh, because she died 1,400 years ago." Then, she just said, "I don't know."

It is incomprehensible that any sane person could take offense to such an inane interview and answer. Nevertheless, Khomeini, who was watching, ordered the arrest of the interviewer, the cameraman, the program producer and the lady interviewed. Had it not been for the intervention of Montazeri and Khomeini's daughter, cautioning him that indiscriminately killing people in the name of God would backfire, they all would have been hanged.

After this incident, Montazeri wrote a letter to Khomeini, warning him that slaughtering people for minor offenses could result in a public backlash. Montazeri was placed under house arrest, where he remained until recently when pressure from the public forced his release. The few times he tried to come out of his house he was threatened with death. The government realized that his continued incarceration could incite a revolution akin to the one that brought it to power. A very old and fragile Montazeri finally was released from house arrest in the summer of 2003 due to the protests of his followers. He is the only living-legend voice still alive and is very much against the current regime; the same regime he wasted most of his life to bring to power.

Sadam, who had spies among the Iranian Arabs, knew the Iranian military was no match for his. He intended to force the government of Iran to accept his demands. Life was interrupted constantly and the foreseeable future was grim. Our young people were being sacrificed needlessly and the war was a financial disaster. During the eight years of war, there were ten major Karbala campaigns but it was impossible for soldiers armed with little more than hope and a prayer to defeat an army with the latest weapons of war.

Coupon Strategy

As years passed, daily life got harder. Inflation was mind-boggling. The price of food and every life necessity increased tremendously, seemingly by the minute. Our lives were managed much like the old Soviet Union and other socialist countries. The government issued coupons for everything we needed but it could not control the corruption. Coupons were part of the mullah's strategy/legacy, as well. As people in government got richer, the poor got poorer. The rich got even richer than in the time of the Shah. The coupons gave the government several advantages. They tested our threshold of abuse, increased control of people based on their need for food, influenced votes for the government and were a check on who had performed military service.

In order to claim our coupons, we had to show our birth certificates. This enabled the government to find out how many people lived in each house and how many young men in a family were over the age of sixteen. The coupon strategy had other benefits for the mullahs. Many mullahs lived a lavish lifestyle by preying on the poor. These corrupt mullahs used their money and intermediaries in the bazaar to buy up most of the food and daily necessities. They kept the goods stored away, bringing them to the market when prices had gone up exorbitantly. Items that I bought as a child turned up on the market years later, after the Shah had left Iran. The mullahs sent profits from the hoarded goods to countries that helped foment terrorist activities or to buy goodwill for themselves. Syria worshipped Iran because they received free trade. In return, Syria helped Iran buy weapons from the black market, even purchasing some United States made weapons. Syria wasn't the only country to receive bribes. Food produced in our country was exported to other countries to improve relations and to feed people there while Iranian women and children starved.

Birth certificates, required to receive coupons, were stamped at each election. They wanted to know who voted and who didn't. The government of Iran invited the press from all over the world to observe elections, the intent being to demonstrate to the world, particularly the United Nations, that there is liberty in Iran and that people line up by the thousands to vote for the next president. Unlike North America, where the candidates travel around the country looking for votes, people of Iran come to the candidates. Not on their own of course; they are bussed by paid followers and workers for each candidate to come and see the man. A big voter turnout is always assured. People who work in governmental buildings and jobs are watched closely and have to vote to keep their jobs.

Iran is essentially a Soviet-style state with Communism replaced by Islam. Iranian people had never lived such a difficult life, having to stand in long lines for butter, oil, bread, and other necessities of everyday life. As people became more disgruntled, the government strategy seemed to be to keep them lined up for small things to occupy their minds.

As Ali, the first Imam of Shiah said, "Poverty comes in by the same door that ethics, humanity, and virtue go out." My version of the same quote would be 'Freedom, and humanity exit through the same door that dictatorship, repression, and poverty enter.'

Currently the Islamic version of a revolving dictatorship rules Iran. It doesn't matter whether the dictator is a priest or a mullah, what his rank or what he wears. A civilized country does not harbor and subsidize terrorists. As the world, is learning, these mindless fanatics can turn on their benefactors, contrary to common sense and humanity. A country shouldn't have to spend millions on propaganda to try to convince the rest of the world that it is a free society. One thing the mullah's seem to have forgotten; freedom doesn't need advertising, actions speak louder. If people are free, they will be the first to become unpaid patriots and advocates. If Iranians were free, they would not need to seek refuge in other countries.

As I mentioned earlier, the election of Iran's presidents is a farce. A ballot is unnecessary for Iran's governmental elections. Why waste the paper? We already know the president will be whoever Khomeini decides, regardless of how illiterate that person might be or how ignorant in matters of politics and economy; once a thief, always a thief. We must not forget that Mr. Khatami is a mullah and whoever is the next president also must remain loyal to the regime; he has to follow the rules and can't turn on his own kind. During the 25 years I lived in Iran, all Presidents were pre-selected, even in the case of Dr. Bani-Sadr. As Khomeini himself said, it is not important what people think. His words were against the people. If he didn't like or approve of something, he vetoed it.

Based on his personal agenda and backed by phony religious reasons, Khomeini declared food produced in Western countries taboo for Iranians, even though it was prepared according to Islamic law. In desperation, to avoid widespread starvation, his successor approved the consumption of shark meat. Although a delicacy around the world, shark or any fish without scales, is and has always been taboo for Shiah

The primitive initiation into governing a country was a big step for a man who barely knew how to speak Farsi. Mismanagement led to chaos and the best bet was to use the old Soviet Union coupon system, adopted when food shortages left some families starving while those with money were able to buy groceries only at inflated prices. Iran is by no means short of food if properly managed. In fact, most of its produce is exported to earn more income. It always puzzled me, why would Iran export organic food and then import other country's non-organic food? In recent years, exporting organic products has become a career market. There is a big demand for organic food in other parts of the world. Iranian farmers still practice the same farming methods as their great-grand fathers. They do not mass-produce but what is harvested is as fine as it gets.

The reason the regime gave for prohibiting western food was a bunch of baloney. They simply prohibited ordinary businesses from importing western food. This was a recipe for disaster for people who already couldn't afford food. And, it was a golden opportunity for profiteers to store needed food in their warehouses to sell later at inflated prices. The money from the transactions often went into the pockets of many high players from government. The governing mullahs reserved this lucrative practice for themselves; using religion to justify the subterfuge. Ever since this regime has come to power, average income people can't afford to buy protein on a regular basis. Most poor families have meat only once or twice per month, usually the distasteful camel meat that is cheaper than beef and lamb, the preferred meat in Iran. The rest of the time they eat rice, potatoes, other vegetables and diary products. The coupons not only gave the regime an advantage it kept people occupied, waiting in line for hours, chatting away. Officially, forty percent of Iranians live below the poverty level. Some diplomats even suggested the number was sixty percent.

A current joke circulating in the Iranian community is a dialogue between Khomeini and a Shahid or martyr.

"Tell me about Paradise," Khomeini said to the Shahid.

"Well," replied the Shahid, "There's always wonderful weather in Paradise, there are lots of trees and the water is very pure."

"What else?" asked Khomeini.

The Shahid answered, "All the foods, including the finest meats and lots of fruit, are available whenever you want them. No line-ups. People have to work only one job and there are many ways to engage in pleasure. There is no tension and everyone is happy."

Khomeini asked, "How would you characterize Paradise?"

"Well," the Shahid replied, "it is very much like the time of the Shah."

Another benefit of coupons to the government was that in the battle to silence dissidents, it provided a venue to spy on people lined up for food. The government provided people with coupons and with it came long lines and bored-to-death people chit chatting. An example of this was a conversation among people in our neighborhood. Several men and women were standing in line for chicken. One of the women got a chicken with only one wing. She looked at the people and said, "A hand is missing from my chicken." One of the men made a joke and said, "Well there's nothing strange about that, Khomeini doesn't have a right hand either and he is the president." Khomeini lost his right hand in a bomb explosion while he was president. Everyone laughed but later the Sepah Pasdaran picked up the man and took him to jail for a week where he was so badly beaten that when he was released he was barely recognizable.

Arrest of a critic of the regime almost automatically meant a sentence of either life in prison with no chance of parole or death. I knew innocent people opposed to the government who were falsely accused and stood trial for alleged crimes, usually drug trafficking. The evidence brought to court and reviewed by the judges was all orchestrated. Almost inevitably, the judge, himself a mullah, found the defendant guilty and sentenced him to death.

Since the protest in 1999, the government has created such fear that no one dares to speak out against the mullahs because they imprison people unjustly on a whim. They make false accusations about anyone who stands up to them or whom they perceive as a threat to the government. Trials are often held without a lawyer for the defendant. Even if the accused has counsel it doesn't guarantee that the lawyer will be of much help. The client's lawyer has no power to dispute the charges or defend his client. The men who created the rules think of themselves as invincible. In Iran, rules are not made to be challenged; they are made to be followed, right or wrong.

If the lawyer is vigilant enough to find a loophole, he/she frequently fears for his/her own life.

When the Islamic regime came to power, it complained to the international media about Evin prison and how its followers had been imprisoned and tortured in the dark cells. Congratulations and a big round of applause for the mullahs! They have achieved the same recognition in Iranian history as the Shah for torturing and killing their opposition. There is one difference; the Shah was man enough to admit it while the Mullah's do it and deny it.

Eight Long Years

L iving in the midst of a very long war is a nightmare that I hope you never experience. Eight years may not sound long if it passes by with happy memories but every day of the war years was an eternity and a struggle. Year after year, it took a toll on our life and we saddled up for an even harder ride. I never had the privileges of most other kids and was forced to mature too fast. The struggle for me wasn't just the lack of money; it was everything. It was cultural, social and political pressure, religious obligation, the government and turmoil within my dysfunctional family. The hardest part was: it all came at once.

Looking back now, comparing my life with the TV reality shows, mine certainly would pass for an unscripted one. Except, I didn't receive the glamorous makeover and clothes, there was no tribe and no money to win; just pure hardship, not only for me but also for all of us. Even with all the harshness I experienced, my life was icing on the cake in comparison with the life of many other women.

I watched my life going to waste and had no way to control my destiny. Day after day, month after month, year after year I expected to wake up one day and find it had all been a nightmare. Unfortunately, it was not a dream. I would much rather this story was fiction and a made up character. Alas, the story is my actual life.

As the years passed only a shadow of our lives remained. There was not a single day of happiness in those years. I don't recall ever celebrating my birthday. Despite all the happy drivel I heard from my family about what a blessing I was for the family, ironically, no one remembered my birthday.

I don't know if I did something in a past life that required retribution by living through this terrible karma; or was it all a test? I questioned it. Whatever it was, I am not sure how I made it but I am glad it is over.

During the years of war, our worries were not just work or food. Khomeini kept referring to war as a blessing. It may have been a blessing for the mullahs, who found more work in mortuaries and graveyards, but the only thing the nation got out of war was bombs and death. Iraqi planes disrupted school nearly every day. We were supposed to leave our classrooms and go to a safe place but our school had no shelter. To supposedly protect us, the government placed sections of large diameter cement pipe in the schoolyard and adjacent streets. These made excellent targets for Iraqi planes and a number of people seeking shelter in them were killed. Our principal told us to gather in the school parking lot and pray. While we presented a convenient strafing target for Iraqi warplanes, it offered scant protection from thousand pound bombs.

We were told to crouch, head down, in a fetal position in the open garage under the big pillars of the floors above. I peeked as an Iraqi plane flew over so low that I could see the flag painted on its underside and the trail of white smoke as the bombs fell. It was an awesome close up display of the power of their squadrons and a demonstration that they could get close to our cities without any opposition. I asked our principal how we were supposed to be safe in an open parking lot. She inanely replied, "It is because of the red alert." I said that we had just been buzzed by an Iraqi plane and asked why Iran did not sue for peace in a war that we could not win. She answered, "We pray that everything will be ok." I said that I didn't think prayer was working or we would have seen results by now.

I told her, "I don't want to die here, I would rather be with my family." Angrily, she said, "Fine, if you want to leave, you can leave now." The principal was one of the government watchdogs and obviously was not pleased to have me question her, especially in front of other students. I could see fury in her eyes and in her face, as if she was clenching her teeth. It was my life, not hers. How could she make me die out there in the open? Sadly, in Iran, people's lives are the government's to control.

Day and night, Iraqi pilots bombed Iranian cities, including Isfahan; recognized by the UN as one of the seven most important historic cities in the world. The Iraqi dictator, who did not care about the lives of children, cared even less about Persian history; all of Iran's historical cities were under siege. The bombing was very close to our home and we had to leave our house at night and go to the underground garage of a large hotel about fifteen minutes away. In the time of the Shah, it was called Hotel Shah Abass but, when the Islamic regime came to power, its name was changed to Hotel Abassy. Shah Abass Safavids was one the few Shahs in Iran's history whose name the mullahs allowed people to mention, not only because he opened the door of his palace to them but he also built the Shrine of Imam Reza. To honor Imam Reza, he walked from Tehran to Mashhad but even he wasn't immune from the prejudice against him.

The garage was a safe place but we couldn't live there permanently and had to go back and forth between home and the shelter. The hotel, built at a cost of over $100 million of public funds for the Shah's frequent visits in the early 1970s, is perhaps the most secure and prestigious hotel in Iran. Inside the hotel there are rare artifacts, exquisite art and vases of hand-carved stone. Huge hand-painted murals by famous artists adorned the ceilings and walls. Pure 24 Karat gold has been used instead of golden paint in the paintings embedded on the walls. Exquisite Persian carpets hung from the walls and covered unique, marble floor designs. Walls and ceilings are decorated with small mirrors and covered with gold. Rare mosaics and mirrors on the exterior walls of this beautiful hotel create a magnificent Persian aura. Built for a king, it mirrored the effect of power and was designed to show the marriage of modernism and ancient architecture.

Next to the hotel is one of Isfahan's oldest mosques. It too is a mix of ancient and modern eras. From the outside it looks like a simple modern place but inside is similar to Trump's penthouse, extravagant with luxury and style. It once served a king; it now serves a scruffy collection of oppressive and medieval minded mullahs.

The multi-level underground parking garage was not quite so opulent as the hotel but it sheltered and saved the lives of tens of thousands of people during the eight year Iran-Iraq war. As we huddled there, we all agreed; the hotel was a symbol of decadent waste but the parking garage was worth every penny of the $100 million. Initially, people reacted to the booms caused by children playing with exploding balloons, which sounded like bombs too close for comfort. Eventually we became jaded, reassured that if we heard a bomb blast, it meant we had survived it; you never hear the bomb or the bullet that kills you. We were told the shelter could withstand the explosion of an atomic bomb; we prayed it would not be put to that test. Sadam had a radio broadcast aimed at Iran on which he kept saying Iraq has a weapon it hasn't used yet. The rockets were a new kind of bomb and could have been used to deliver an atomic bomb if Israel had not destroyed Iraq's atomic facilities. There is little doubt that Iran would have been the target of an atomic bomb.

Khomeini ordered schools to remain open. In one of his speeches, Khomeini said, "Our students have no fear of being killed and I want them to keep going to school." He should have spoken for himself. He was not the one huddled in the school parking lot.

The government forced teachers to attend but students stayed away until schools were finally forced to close for lack of student to teach. We decided to take a bus and get as far away as possible from Isfahan. The nearest town that was fairly quiet and safe was Ardestan, located at the edge of the desert. Iraqis had never hit the town because there was nothing major there. With a population of 2,000, everyone worked inside their homes on beautiful Persian carpets and industries related to manufacturing carpet-making tools. People were very kind and there were a couple of old mosques that probably had not seen a tourist since Marco Polo. Even the lodging rates seemed to be retired and taking a nap in the afternoon sun. There was nothing to do. We stayed for a couple nights before becoming bored nearly to death. We returned home and looked for a safer place in a more populated area. Unfortunately, rent in other potential refuges was extremely high. We were forced to go back to the hotel parking lot.

From time to time, when there was less bombing, we continued our normal, miserable life. By this time our beloved home looked more and more like the ruins of a ghost city. Our neighbors didn't like us because our home, although large, was shabby. There is a proverb in the Farsi language referring to when people envy someone. It says, 'From the outside it kills others, whereas from the inside it kills me.' We shivered from the weather in winter and from fear of being killed day and night year round. Sadam, who was in a much stronger position, used Iranians as guinea pigs and tried out his latest weapons on us.

For ten years, after our Mashhad odyssey, we didn't go on any vacations and only bought what we needed to make it through a day.

If I wanted to hang out with my friends, they had to come to our home. Even when my best friends came over, I was still embarrassed for them to see where I lived. Because of our rundown house, most of the girls at school didn't want to come to our home. Especially after the first time they saw the inside of the house. Even in my senior year in high school, mum still didn't want me to go to anyone's house. Her rules were just as strict as in previous years.

In my little world, my closest friends were the pet chickens and roosters, which from time to time ended up in the pressure cooker. I had an eternal love for them. I admired their beauty, their colorful orange eyes that looked like a painting and a window to their innocent souls. After I fed them, I used to sit down among them and raise my arms toward them. I kept our pets as wild as I possibly could. I didn't have the habit of petting them and during those years found the birds much smarter than most people think they are. My pets came forward on their own and allowed me to rub my index figure against their small faces. The trust and comfort I received from them was something I didn't feel toward the people.

Back in adults' world, our property was in a commercial area. It was potentially quite valuable and many of the neighbors were envious of that. Nevertheless, it was almost impossible to find a buyer. Because of the economy and the war, no one was eager to spend a fortune on something that they might lose in an instant in the next air raid. People knew of my father's reputation and gossiped that we had millions of dollars in the bank. They thought we had kept this particular property as an eyesore to lower the value of their property, which we would then snap up. I wish. This fairy tale scenario caused the neighbors to become increasingly hostile toward us.

People threw rats and mice into our garden, jumped over our walls, left death threats and threw garbage into our garden—anything to be a nuisance. At night we had to be very alert, even when we were sleeping, and get up at the sound of a mouse. Soldiers who have been in the front line of wars know the feeling. Any time one of us stepped out of our home, the neighbors found a way to swear, mock or laugh at us. We could not afford to repair the house and they wanted to force us to sell it. They had found a buyer to offer a considerably lower amount than the true value. The new owner would fix it up and improve local real estate values.

One rainy night, someone climbed onto our roof and drilled a big hole in it. We followed the footprints. They led to a neighbor to whom we had been kind, giving him the leftover building materials from the time my father came back and promised us he would repair the house.

Throwing rats in our garden was sort of a Coals-to-Newcastle gesture since we already had plenty of indigenous rodents. But, I will admit, I was wrong when I thought I had seen everything. I had never seen rats this large before. One night, when we were all sleeping in our family/dining/ bedroom, I smelled something very unpleasant. It was like a sewer smell. I got up and turned on the light. A rat the size of a two-year-old cat was right there in front of me, his round eyes looking at me. I guess the rat and I were equally surprised. We both froze for a moment before it turned and ran. I grabbed a shoe, chased it and killed the poor thing.

We thought that was the end of it but we were wrong. A few nights later, we noticed rat droppings in the kitchen. We thought if we left some poison around the kitchen and house they would eat it and die or leave. And, perhaps they did but not before leaving a profusion of footprints all over the kitchen. The next afternoon I went into the kitchen to get some food that was left on the stove from lunch. At first, I did not recognize the litter of small burnt matches for what they were. I picked up one with my bare hand and looked at it. An instant later, while taking some food out of the same pot, I realized they were rat droppings and were everywhere; on the stove, on the lid of the pot, on the washed plates, spoons, forks, on the bread and everywhere else.

I ran to mum and screamed for her to come with me. When she saw the filth, she was furiously frantic but, for once, did not blame me. It was an exceptionally cold winter day; clouds covered the sky and we were expecting a heavy snowfall. The water outside was near freezing. She took all the dishes, pots and pants out into the yard and washed them in a fountain while hysterically crying out loud and yelling, swearing at God.

Mum was religious so I knew she must have been beside herself. I had never seen her that way. Her eyes didn't have the regular fire and her face was as pale as a ghost. She was yelling at Him saying, "Where are you. If you are there why don't you care about us... have you forgotten about us?" When she finally started begging Him, her cries must have been heard in the entire neighborhood. I tried to calm her down, but it didn't work. I understood her anger but was a little squeamish about her lambasting God. I knew she would repent later and, sure enough, before she went to sleep she was on her prayer mat begging Him to forgive her.

The rats had not completely abdicated. The next night, while I was in the kitchen drinking some water, I saw another rat on patrol. I closed the door and started looking for it. I found it. It was it coming toward me but I stood my ground, not realizing it had no other escape route. Suddenly, it started climbing on me. I could feel its sharp claws on my skin and it smelled horrible. This kind of rat lives in sewers and can infect human beings with the worst kinds of diseases. I forcefully threw it to the floor and stomped it with extreme prejudice. Unfortunately, we didn't have warm water to take a shower. All I could do was change my clothes and wash my hands and face. Whether by stomping or starvation, we finally won the Rat War without catching anything fatally yucky.

During a hard winter, the underground plumbing froze and burst. Our home was built on a graveyard and lime was used to speed the body deterioration. The mixture of water and lime will destroy the insects. The remaining lime in the earth and hot water flowing through iron pipes creates a catalyst that causes corrosion and holes in the pipes and eventually the minor cracks burst. It was freezing and we couldn't use our bathroom. Even if we had the money to replace the entire 60 feet of pipe, it would be morally touchy because we would have to dig up bones of people who were buried six feet under. Between our archeological and financial problems we could not immediately replace the plumbing. From that year on, we had no choice but to go to public bathrooms, which I detested.

Like many old civilizations, Persia once was part of an empire that had similarities with the ancient Romans, Greeks and others. Even in countries like modern Turkey and Greece there are still similarities with Iran. Unlike some European and Japanese spas, Persian men and women do not share the same bath at the same time. The baths are either managed for women and men at different hours or the male and female have their own separate spaces with separate entrances. The baths are still, more or less, used for the same purpose. People not only cleanse themselves from days or weeks of grime but relax, socialize and find out the latest news and gossip of the country, city or district.

Large public spas and bathrooms are still a part of the Persian culture. The modern spas have been inspired by thousand of years of public baths. The modern European spas with massages and lavish facilities have many things in common with their more traditional cousin in Iran. The baths have a common heated floor and benches in all corners, a hot water pool and fountain and individual showers. In each bath there are masseuse available for anyone who wants a body or back rub. It is quite relaxing and the masseuse give deep back rubs that help release muscle tension. The massages are all done in the public area with no dosage of sexuality added to the tab. The masseuses do often act as dating agents for potential suitor's families and keep an eye out for voluptuous available women for their client's sons.

More importantly, it is a prime matchmaking venue. Men go with their sons and women with their daughters. Even though everyone is naked, it is taboo to look at anyone sexually. It does, however, afford an unrivaled forum for comparison-shopping by parents with a surplus, or shortage, of one gender or another who are on the lookout for potential brides or husbands for their sons and daughters. I not only didn't like being naked in front of other females, I wasn't that happy with my pubescent figure. Unlike in North America, being thin is not praised but being plump and voluptuous is considered highly attractive and an indicator of future healthy child bearing.

Despite the fact that we had plenty of unwanted vermin in our home, we kept it comparatively clean. Public baths, however, were never sanitized and the public health agency did not bother to inspect. People brought diseases, particularly skin infections, to the baths and spread them around. Looking at their skin made me edgy. As icky as it was to see them, I knew they perhaps didn't have the money to take care of themselves or see a doctor. Health care is a private entity and not everyone can afford it. I couldn't confront the poor people in an ostentatious way because any deliberate hurtful comment is considered a sin in Islam. Still, I was always afraid I might be infected with their diseases.

In fact, in 1985 there was an epidemic in Isfahan of infectious Aleppo Boil. It is a devastating disease similar to a burn scar. Many of the girls at school were infected through a bite of a mosquito that had sucked an infected person's blood. Usually, it is a long process, for the bite to show up but by then it is too late. The process may take a year to complete. It goes away by itself but leaves a burn mark behind. I was not immune but was lucky that I only had it on my left elbow. Many of my friends had marks on their faces.

There was no proper sewage system in the public baths. Wastewater was running around the large main room. The place smelled as bad as our recent nemesis, the rats and, to complete the horror picture, it was infested with sewage cockroaches and other water insects.

Plumbing, or the lack of it, was not our only problem. When I came home from school I wanted to study but we only had one warm room. Of the seven rooms in the house, we could only afford to heat two, at most. I needed to study but Siavash wanted to watch TV or listen to Voice of America or Voice of Israel, in order to hear news from the outside world without the government slant. Mum had to take a little heater back and forth from one warm room to the other. Iran is one of the largest oil producers in OPEC but we had a shortage of oil due to constant bombardment of our refinery facilities during the war.

Nearly every night when I was studying, we either had a red alert or the electricity shut down. Because Iran's electrical system was also bombed constantly, we had a serious power shortage as much as ten hours a day. I needed to study for exams but we had only one gas lamp and it was not nearly bright enough to study under.

Abe Lincoln, doing his sums on the back of a shovel by firelight, had nothing on me. And, he didn't have to worry about being killed by Iraqi warplanes while doing his homework. It was a nerve-racking experience, studying under inadequate lighting while waiting for the next bomb to drop.

Although we had hard times and hardly any money, for some reason I never thought of our family as poor; dysfunctional, yes, but not poor. My father was wealthy but he never spent any money on us. Our house was worth a fortune but it was neither marketable nor edible. Ali, the first

Imam of the Shiah faith, has said, "From the same door that poverty walks in, faith walks out." It means a hungry stomach has a hard time believing the promises of God. He was right, if I had not been baptized with holy water in Mecca, renewing my faith in God, I could easily have turned to a destructive and tragic life.

Living conditions as spartan as those of a religious zealot were not as unsettling as were the ghosts. The fact that we were living in a graveyard probably influenced my young imagination but the eerie things I saw and heard were very real to me then and remain so today. When I was studying alone at night, I would hear voices coming from the kitchen or from the closet in the same room. Many nights I heard a yawning noise, as if someone was lying next to me. I was sure it wasn't any of us, but, just because I could not see him, did not mean he did not see me.

At first, I thought I was hallucinating, I even thought I had developed schizophrenia but strange things kept happening. I don't know what use ghosts have for money but during the night money would disappear from a locked closet within a locked room. I am certain no one in our family of three took it. I would hear women laughing and children playing. During the day, I would hear someone at the door but when I checked, there was no one there. I came back and sat down at my desk. I could hear women's voices talking to each other and whispering. I heard someone walking in the kitchen. One day when I was leaving my study room that was connected to the kitchen, I saw a floating light pass over my feet and go out into the yard.

I did not mention any of this to my family until, one night after locking all the doors, we went to bed. All three of us shared one large room; not only because we couldn't afford to heat three rooms but, if an Iraqi bomb had our address, the prospect of dying alone somehow seemed more frightening than the family plan. We said good night to each other when, suddenly, we heard a slamming door noise, as if someone was trying to exit the living room door entrance to our kitchen, where I usually studied. For a minute of two there was a heavy silence. Nobody moved. Mum broke the silence, asking Siavash, "Are you asleep?" He said, "No" She said, "Did you hear that?" In a quavering voice he answered, "Yes." Mum said, "Then why don't you get up and look for the noise?" He said he had locked the door. It couldn't be anyone. My mum repeated, "Then why don't you get up and look around?" My brave brother said, "Well, you guys get up, I'll follow." We got up and looked through the entire house. All of the doors were locked. We accepted the local legend that the house was haunted.

This incident happened right after Siavash started saying he was the man of the house and telling me I should obey him. I guess the ghost was testing his manhood. He was afraid of a ghost! He never repeated again that he was the man of the house. Ghosts were not the only scary issues we had to face. In retrospect, the ghosts may have scared me but they couldn't kill me. On a scale of one to ten they only ranked about a five in comparison to our health concerns that were a nine. Sadam and his bombs took the grand number ten.

During the war years, the government did very little about public health. Fighting a war and lavish mourning ceremonies for every mullah's death left little time and money to care for people. There are 180 days of holidays in Iran's calendar; most of them are mourning days. The rat and cockroach infestation was not a problem for the mullahs since they had their own special bakers, chefs and kitchens but no one else was immune. The city sewers were not cleaned for many years. The storage bins for flour were not clean and rat proof. Greedy bakers, discovering one little rat matchstick, were not about to throw away hundreds of pounds of flour so the disgusting bread made it to our table. Mum once brought fresh baked bread from the local baker that smelled as if a rat was cooked in it. I refused to eat the disgusting bread but many citizens had no choice. A few days later, someone discovered a baked rat in a loaf of bread. The local health center forced this bakery to close for a clean up. Mum changed bakeries, trying to find a cleaner one, but the new one was no better than the last. We found baked cockroaches, cockroach eggs and ants inside the bread. Iranians are not willing insect or rat eaters but the health centers are easily bribed and turned their faces the other way, ignoring health hazards.

During those years many disgusting incidents happened around Isfahan, including a restaurant that served donkey meat, crow and infected mutton. During the years of revolution protein prices skyrocketed; a greedy restaurant owner, who wanted to give free food during Ramadan, used donkey as the source of protein and then hunted the crows that came to finish off the slaughtered donkey's remains behind his restaurant; passing the crow off as chicken. The story echoed through out the country. Thankfully I never ate at this restaurant, but Khosro said he had.

In the year 1985, I don't remember how, or whether, I celebrated my fifteenth birthday. Usually, mum bought strawberries and ice cream and cooked me something that I really enjoyed. However, as living conditions got harsher, I just wanted to ignore my birthday so it wouldn't put more pressure on mum.

As I started my second year in high school the war advanced closer to the large cities. It seemed we were bombed daily. The interminable repeated year finally was over. Summer was pretty uneventful, except for dodging bombs and sleeping on the concrete floors of the parking garage nearly every night. When there were no bombs, there wasn't much excitement in our lives. We didn't have many friends and had no relationship with my father or mum's family. During the summer I rarely left the house. Mum wouldn't let me just go for a walk by myself or with friends. Once or twice, I nagged mum to take me to the nearby park. In a way, I was looking forward to winter and school to be able to get out of the house, although winter was the notorious time for the Iraqi dictator to bomb schools.

In his speeches, Khomeini kept referring to war as a blessing and a chance for prosperity. The only dubious benefit of the war was that it reduced the unemployment rate among men from 14.4 percent to near zero. War does keep people busy. We didn't have time to digest and comprehend all the horror we were experiencing in the name of God or reason with ourselves why we should experience all this misery. One positive thing about war for the government was that, in time, with any comfort, the people could have turned into an angry crowd. Before we understood what had we done to ourselves it was already too late, the mullahs had secured themselves. Perhaps that was the blessing he meant; except that it was a blessing for the mullahs, not for the nation. On the national front, both Sadam and Khomeini were stubborn and ready to pour out our nations blood. The fighting was more intense in the winter. Sadam Hussein knew that children were in school and people were more vulnerable than in summertime and stepped up his attacks accordingly. He deliberately killed innocent women and children in cold blood. He leveled a city of half a million, without reason, even killing the surviving cats and dogs.

Sadam himself proudly designed and had a monument built in Iraq that, sadly, still exists. Two swords crossed over military helmets authentic to those worn by Iranian soldiers killed in battle and buried in mass graves. He held victory celebrations at this gate every time he bombarded our cities.

Ironically, after the war the Iranian government resumed a good relationship with him, even selling his oil in defiance of the UN cease-fire restrictions after the Gulf War. The Iranian government ignored that Sadam killed half a million brave young men, injured half a million more, caused more than one and half million to leave their homes and left Iran with billions of dollars in damages. Iran's leaders shook hands with a man who didn't hesitate to drop bombs on pre-schools, public bathrooms, and civilian areas of towns. Only an equally evil, malevolent soul mate would sell out his people to help such a monster.

In October, about a week after school started, Iraqi pilots bombed some schools, killing hundreds of children. Iraq claimed they hit a military target but there were none nearby. Conditions were getting worse. Iranians endured for eight long years the same rigors and fears that people in war-torn countries experienced during WWI and WWII. Every night, before we went to bed, we said good-bye to each other. There was a very real possibility we might not see tomorrow.

One afternoon when we were all at home, our pet chickens were in the yard, pecking at food. Suddenly, the roosters started to run around in a panic. We saw no sign of danger but the chickens knew something was wrong. A few minutes later, an Iraqi plane flew directly overhead, leaving a trail of white smoke. Then came the red alert. Our chickens were terrified and began flying into doors and walls, killing themselves. Many of them had internal bleeding because their eggs broke inside of them. My mum's right hand shook uncontrollably due to the relentless fear. We couldn't take care of ourselves anymore and we were torturing these creatures by keeping them alive. It was a hard decision but we concluded it was best to slaughter them and move somewhere safer. Mum had developed a problem similar to seizures of Parkinson disease in her right hand. Sadam bombed Isfahan nearly every day. Houses all around us had been flattened and most of the city had seen some damage. It was a miracle that our old house was still on its feet

Refugees in Bandar-Abbas

After slaughtering our beloved pets, we didn't have any reason to stay in Isfahan. To save our lives, we decided to make a run for Bandar-Abbas, an international port in the south of Iran on the Strait of Hormoz opposite Oman, about as far as we could get from the war. It was a long hard trip of about 700 miles but flying was so dangerous that we elected to travel by bus. Not that we could afford to travel by air; even if we could, it was even more dangerous than by ground. Sadam had threatened to shoot down any planes, civilian or military. Thousands of people were fleeing Isfahan and there were constant red alerts as our buses drove out of the city. I carried only my books and a bit of clothing, as did Mum and Siavash. We were going to a city where we had never been and had no one to meet or support us. After an 18-hour bus ride, we arrived at 8:00 a.m., in the morning. A fresh warm breeze off the sea was the first thing I noticed. It reminded me of Abadan, my birthplace.

Now that we had arrived in Bandar-Abbas, we had to find a place to stay. Bandar-Abbas was very much like any small southern Iranian town. I noticed an absence of highrises and hotels and, despite all the money and goods that came into this city; there was little sign of progress or prosperity. After considerable searching, we found a dirty little room in a small inn. Siavash, like my father, had no style or taste at all in his choice of lodgings. It reminded me of my father's choice of rooms on the trip to Mashhad. The room had not been cleaned after the last occupants, perhaps not for months. It was dirty and the distinct smell of urine mixed with cigarette smoke was still in the unwashed bed sheets. Mum was disgusted and although we had paid for the whole day, we only spent an hour there. She didn't even let us use the bathroom. I agreed with her about the inadequacy of the room.

She set out to find something better where we could stay for a while. We went to the office of the Crescent Moon, the Islamic version of Red Cross. There, we received a ticket that would allow us to stay in a tent in a nearby park for as long as Isfahan was under bombardment.

Before we even had breakfast, the arrangement for the tent was made. I couldn't believe that we were going to live in a tent. Camping out and having fun is one thing; being forced to live in a tent is not nearly as glamorous or exciting as it sounds. I was apprehensive about living in a tent because Bandar-Abbas is located in the same tropical belt as Abadan and in the wintertime much of the province receives heavy rain.

We had to get to the park where the tent was set up. Mum was trying to be strong and brave but the 'taxi' we hired was a Toyota pickup whose enterprising owner was transporting people to the park in the back of his truck for money. Mum, who had never been in one of the trucks, got in with much difficulty and then sat in the bottom of the truck bed and cried when she saw another truck carrying animals in the back. The depth of our misery was sinking in.

Arriving at the park, I changed my mind about the tent when I saw where we were going to camp. I saw it as an opportunity to explore. The park, located about ten miles from Bandar-Abbas, was formerly the national park dedicated to Norooz, the Persian cultural celebration in the time of the Shah. Now, it was used for emergency and disaster situations, for which the war certainly qualified. The Crescent Moon had given us documents that allowed us to receive some pots and cooking utensils. "Courtesy of the government," said the Pasdar at the gate. It made me angry when he said that. The government had taken our dignity and freedom and was donating some food. Mum began crying again, "Look what we have done to ourselves." I felt sad and could sympathize with her. It was true; our lives had drastically changed since Khomeini had come to the power. But, what could we do? I told her we are alive, and that is something. I admit, it was easier said than felt.

Mum, who had been crying since we got into the truck, was near to mourning the loss of the life we had left behind. We didn't know when, or if, we would be able to go back. Leaving her home and everything behind with one suitcase in her hand and the clothing she had on, she felt lost and while still crying replied to the Pasdar, "What are you talking about? You are sitting here, safe on your ass, and tell us this is courtesy of the government while you don't have the slightest clue what we had to go through." Mum's pride was bleeding. She had it with everything and if the Pasdar, who saw mum was angry, had said one more word, she probably would have throttled the man. However, he shut his mouth and didn't reply.

After a couple of hours of rest we felt much better. I think people often achieve extraordinary feats under incredibly difficult circumstances. I tried to look at the bright side of this trip. After all, it could be worse.

We were in a small paradise with robins and nightingales singing love songs during the spring breeding season. The fragrance of flowers permeated the air. Might as well enjoy it, I thought. The garden was carpeted with flowers and there were a few mysterious lotus trees at the far corners of the garden. Lotus trees are admired in Persian poetry because of the mystic legend that spirits gather among its branches. Butterflies were flying from one flower to the next. Life wasn't that bad, after all. There was a public washroom and the government gave us some household items. Just as I was about to think we had found a perfect spot, we were warned that our paradise had other residents that we must be careful of.

This delightful little Garden of Eden had an array of rare poisonous snakes, notorious poisonous black scorpions and their not so friendly rivals, bird-eating tarantulas, and black widow spider were among the most vicious creatures in Iran, permanent residents of the park and our 'new neighbors.' We were safe from Iraqi bombings; now we only had to worry about lethal bedmates. To avoid our creepy crawly friends we were taught that if we placed stones under the carpet, about a foot apart along each edge, our many-legged co-habitants would go under the carpet and not bother us. I saw many of them crawling under the pad and could even feel them crawling around underneath but the trick worked and we lived in rustic comfort for 25 days.

Bandar has a hurricane season similar to the southern part of the United States. The cool, calm sea can change during the rainy season. Mum knew this because she lived in Abadan for many years and the two cities are on the same geographic weather belt. Two weeks before the rainy season, on the twenty-fifth day of our residence in the park, mum found an empty new school building in the heart of the city and decided to squat in it. Construction wasn't finished yet but it was in good enough condition to live in. Mum didn't mean to keep it forever, only to force the local municipal to help us to find a place to stay. It was nearly impossible to find a clean home in the city of Bandar. The municipality called upon the police to evict us but they didn't want to fight with refugees from Isfahan and we stayed on.

Our family and several of the other park resident families each got a room of about 80 ft^2. There was no washroom and we had to use the toilet facilities in the school across the street. Summer heat had not started yet, but already was at its peak for our tolerance. Summer heat in Bandar-Abbas can reach 50° C-60° C (120° F-140° F.) Like an episode of *Survivor*, we left pots of water in the sun and by late afternoon it was warm enough for bathing. This place was crawling with insects too. Our guest on the first night was an uninvited black tarantula that crawled in to say, 'hi.' He didn't receive a warm welcome. Forget animal rights, we needed someone to watch our rights. In the classroom we lived in, there was a distinctive smell of death coming out of holes the giant ants had made in the floor. The school had no doors and there were many drug users and sellers coming and going. I often wondered if the smell could be coming from the decayed body of a victim. The ants marched non-stop into the hole that the smell was coming from.

Two of the families that moved to the school with us went back to the tents. I couldn't blame them. Soon after the hurricane season started, running out of options, they decided to move back to their very dangerous hometowns. We never heard from them or what happened to them and prayed they were ok. While living in the school we became friends with a family from Kermanshah. She was as excited as if she had found her childhood friends.

For a while the volatility between mum and I had disappeared but I knew the minute she had nothing else to worry about, I would be feeling the punch. Mum's behavior was becoming more and more obsessive and on a couple of occasion she harassed me right in front of our new friends. The family included the parents, three beautiful girls and one older boy. The lady, who genuinely liked me, said to my mother that she would give her daughter to Siavash if I would marry her son. I was sixteen; he was seventeen.

I suspect that mum, who had always said I should choose my own life partner, could have been persuaded if I had not made it clear to her that she had no right to decide who I married. She was offended by my attitude but got over it and understood. During the three and half months we stayed in Bandar-Abbas there was one short break in the war. We took advantage of the temporary peace and went home to Isfahan. While there, we had to go to Najaf-Abad, my father's birthplace, for my mother's divorce. Before we escaped to the south, Siavash and I had asked her to divorce our father. Every time mum needed to attend court for her shops, she had to ask for his consent and he wasn't giving it.

Divorce Court

The day of mum's divorce hearing we went to the courthouse. It was in a building that belonged to my father's nephew. At previously scheduled sessions, the judge was absent and court recessed to a later date. Finally, we had our court date with him. Mum, Siavash and I entered the empty room. Then my father arrived, looking happy with a smile on his face, confident and eager to tear us apart. I saw him in the hallway where he, his nephew and the mullah judge all got into a 'good ole boy' conversation. My father offered to help the judge in a land transaction.

The courtroom was a small room, about 600 ft² with eight plain industrial chairs and a desk at the upper part of the room. When the judge entered the room we all stood up. He forgot to tell us to sit down, so after a while we took our seats.

The desk he was sitting behind was a large, open front metal desk without a modesty panel. He did not know, or did not care, about this minor missing detail. He sat down and glanced at the file. Apparently, due to caseload, judges don't study anything prior to the trial. Pointing at Siavash and me, he asked my father who we were. My father said that we were his children and our mother had turned us against him. The judge then took the time to read the file. While busy reading, he was picking his nose with his right index finger, pulling stuff out and looking at it. Mum and I looked at each other, shaking our heads. I exhaled and thought, "Dear Lord, what has this nation done, what have we done, to deserve such ignorant, low rank mullahs taking a ride on our back?"

Whether he saw our reaction or not, he continued reading and picking his nose. Suddenly, his left hand slid underneath his robe and he started a rubbing motion against his crotch. I can only guess what he was doing. I wasn't really interested in the details but I couldn't stop laughing. According to psychologists, uncontrollable laughter is sometime from anger. I had to cover my mouth to keep from laughing out loud. Mum, sitting next to me, frowned and whispered, "Why are you laughing?" I told her to just follow the hand movement. When she saw what he was doing, she burst into laughter and covered her face. Then Siavash was clued in. My father, who was sitting across the room, noticed us laughing. He wasn't sure if his zipper was down or what and kept signaling what is it? Siavash gave him a signal and when he saw what the judge was doing, his face got red with suppressed laughter. Our giggles finally got so loud the judge raised his head and saw us all of us red-faced and smiling. He must have thought a miracle had happened; a family came in anger and leaves happy.

It may be unfair to pick on the judge personally. His behavior was the result of ignorance and lack of proper social and professional training. Overall, virtually none of the mullahs who took judges positions in Iran's justice system had any formal training as a lawyer or studied in law schools.

On a more serious note, the judge didn't quite vote in my mother's favor. My father, to hurt my mother, was petitioning for my custody, since I was still a minor. He boasted that he would hire a maid to do my chores, buy me the best house in the town and give me an education. The judge was falling for his lies until I spoke up and asked my father, "Before you get me a maid, would you mind buying me a pair of winter shoes?" He said he didn't have any money, with no explanation of how he was going to afford all the wonderful things he had promised. I told the judge that if he forced me to live with my father, I would never forgive him and if mum was forced to throw me to this man who had abused and neglected us all our lives, I would crawl up the wall and through a window to get into her home. I pointed out that while my father was boasting about all he would do for me, he was not even willing to provide me with a pair of shoe. I told the judge that this is not a life or death matter, I can live with one pair of shoes per year. It is an example of what he really is and should prove to the court he doesn't mean what he says. The judge said he understood and told my father he is a loser. He allowed me to stay with my mum and awarded me the equivalent of US $4,000 as past support.

Later, my father refused to deposit the checks in the bank for me. I had to take him to court and ask for a piece of land that he had verbally given, in the courtroom, to Siavash and me. He had changed his mind but finally he relented and turned the land to Siavash's name only on a non-registered piece of paper. Later Siavash generously sold the land, took all the money for himself and headed for the USA.

If he had been able to control his greed and just buy me a pair of shoes, I would have most likely been forced to live with him but, thanks to his greed, mum got her divorce. I never received anything from sale of the land and it was five years before my father paid me the money in exchange for some equipment he needed.

Return to Bandar-Abbas

After seven long days in Isfahan, we took another bus ride to Bandar, arriving after an eighteen hour jouncing and happy that we made it. Three days after our trip, peace negotiations broke down and the bombing intensified, even more than previously. When we made our first trip, we thought it was only for a week or two. Now, after a month, I was excited at the prospect of going back to school. However, no school would accept me after being away for a month. We tried to tell them it was due to the war but they were skeptical. The war hadn't touched these people the way it had touched us. We had been having six red alerts a day. Bandar-Abbas on the other hand had only one red alert in six years of war. The reason was, although an ideal target strategically, Bandar-Abbas was located at the far end of Iran and Iraqi warplanes would have to refuel at one of the Arabic ports to make the round trip. If any Arab country had allowed this, it would have been tantamount to declaring war against Iran and they were not prepared to do that. Iran was not strong militarily but our soldiers were fierce fighters.

After days of our going back and forth to the Ministry of Education, Mr. Jafari, principal of the school next door, intervened and through his contacts I was able to enroll late.

Students in the south of Iran were a lot more laid back. They wore makeup and the girl's scarves barely covered their hair. They did not have to wear black or dark blue clothing and the socks that were mandatory in Isfahan. They could wear jewelry, perfume and the latest fashions. Girls plucked their eyebrows, manicured and polished their nails and their relationship with the boys was never questioned. Everyone wore any color they liked and even the school principal and teachers were the same way. I wondered, how could this be in the same country?

Catching up in my studies in Bandar-Abbas was difficult since school in the south of Iran starts in early September and is finished by the end of May. In Isfahan, school starts in early October and finishes in late June. I was nearly two months behind. The teachers couldn't seem to grasp that I had missed a lot of school. They still wanted to test me on the material they had already covered. I told the principal I would rather go back and do my exams in Isfahan. He said, OK. The school rules were so relaxed I had a hard time believing this district was supervised by the same government.

About the end of March, our friends decided to leave Bandar-Abbas. The war wasn't any quieter but they simply couldn't take the heat any more. We had a tough time as well but we stayed until the late spring when, with no air-conditioner or refrigerator, we too surrendered to the heat.

Everyone thought the war was over. Most of the refugees with whom we had shared the school and park flooded north. We were tempted but waited another month before we packed our small bags and departed Bandar-Abbas, saying goodbye to the kind man and his family who had helped us. When we got home the city was vibrant again. It seemed the war was over but we soon learned it was just another peace breakthrough. We never knew the reason but the ceasefire only lasted a week or two.

Coming back home was difficult. I had not realized the true value of my pets and the psychological effect they had on me. These innocent creatures were a blessing and had grown close to my heart. I felt a terrible sadness when we returned home to an empty house. Stepping down into the back yard, I felt like I was getting out of a Nazi detention camp alive but with an enormous heaviness and emptiness in my heart and on my shoulder because my best friends didn't make it. For years, not having anyone to talk to, my pets were my only companions and true friends. They had accepted me without judging me. Their unconditional love had given me the strength to face the toughest days of my life. Like a worried Mother Goose, I had watched the baby chicks hatching out of their eggs, taken care of them and watched them take their first step and first bite of food. I used to get up early because they were calling my name. Mum used to say to me, "Your babies are asking for you," and I had hoped to come home and feed them every day before and after school. They had given me the much-needed love I was lacking in my life. Now they were gone. Losing them made me bitter, I was angry with both dictators for continuing to fight for their own personal agendas and make us pay. We decided not to keep any more pets; we did not know if we ourselves could survive.

Immediately upon our return, I went back to school to arrange to resume my classes. The principal, that I always had trouble with, spotted me wearing a white winter coat, pulled me aside and demanded to know why I was in white. I told her I had just arrived from the south. She said she didn't care where I had been or how I had been allowed to dress, when I was in her school, I would dress according to her rules, "Understand?" To annoy her I said, "Yes, Sir." The fundamentalists of Iran don't like 'Sir' or 'Madam.' They perceive it as a western gesture left over from the Shah's time. It is considered to be swearing at them.

Within a few days of our return, Sadam took advantage of peoples returning to the cities and the war became even worse than before we went south. Due to the summer heat, going back to Bandar-Abbas wasn't an option any more.

Again, we shuttled between the hotel parking garage and home. Sadam had a pattern of stopping the bombing every few weeks. Now and then we got a break and one night when we thought it would be safe for the next few days we stayed at home. My mum, Siavash and I slept in the same room so we would have to heat only one room. In early April,

Isfahan's temperature was still cold and we left the heater on. Sometime before dawn, I woke up. I saw a halo effect of purple everywhere. Groggy at first, I thought there must be something wrong with the little heater; perhaps something had caught on fire.

Momentarily puzzled, I looked out into the yard. The entire house, and yard were purple. I looked up and saw the sky was cloudy. Suddenly I hear a loud noise, as if a jet was flying above our home. I realized it was the clouds that had reflected the fire coming out of some sort of bomb. I yelled at Siavash to wake up. I screamed, 'bomb,' waking mum, who jumped up saying, "What happened?" I put my hands on her ears and both of us crawled to a fetal position, just as an Iraqi rocket exploded overhead. Fortunately, the forty-foot rocket blew up in the air and no one on the ground was killed. We saw the wreckage on TV. It would have done tremendous damage to the entire city if it had touched down.

This began to happen nearly every day. We were not able to sleep in our own home because it was in the main target zone of the Iraqi pilots. We saw many of our neighbors and all their belongings buried in their homes. Once again, we packed our suitcases. Like a cat carrying her kitten, each of us carried our most precious possessions and spent many, many more nights along with much of the rest of the city in the underground hotel parking lot that once hosted the Shah's cars.

FEAR OF THE NEW WEAPONS

During the war, Sadam continually broadcast on Farsi radio, sending propaganda messages to us. In 1989, he kept boasting that he had new weapons. Just as he intended, we wondered what it could it be and how it could be worse than what we had already experienced. On several occasions during the war, both countries announced they would stop bombing for a few days and we returned to our home. These occasional ceasefires gave people shortlived confidence in Sadam and gave him an opportunity to mass murder more people. When we returned home, mum left to buy some fish without telling me. Siavash was standing outside the door talking to one of his friends. I was inside studying biology for my final exam for the high school diploma.

Suddenly, I heard a loud noise. Our French window, which was locked at the top and bottom, start shaking. It was a strange scene as if a ghost was pushing on the door. Shaking violently, the door broke and flew wide open. The room moved from side to side as it would in an earth quake. A small tornado roared into view, the debris-laden wind turning in the air making a horrendous, deafening noise so loud it hurt my ears. I covered my ears; afraid my eardrums would burst if it continued. Walls moved. Trees were uprooted. The extremely loud noise was the sonic barrier being broken. It sounded like a continuous thunder and lightning clap that was getting closer and closer to the ground. Thankfully, the rocket didn't make it to the ground. It was coming toward us like a meteor shower that burned in the atmosphere and broke apart.

We had suffered through relentless bombing but nothing like this. This was a new kind of bomb. I had never been afraid of dying but I didn't want to suffocate gradually under demolished walls. I shouted from fear and ran toward the door, looking for mum in the yard.

She wasn't there. When I couldn't find her my heart dropped. I ran to the front door and met Siavash who was asking where mum was. We packed to go to a shelter and wait for mum. Mum finally came home. She had thought it was safe, certainly having no premonition of a tornado, and had gone to buy some groceries. As soon as she arrived we ran to the shelter. The same night, more bombing and rockets shook Isfahan. Everyone in the shelter, rich and poor, gathered around radios hoping for good news and wondering what was next.

The bomb shelters saved our lives from time to time but our existence was too much like that of World War II detention camp prisoners in cramped, overcrowded prisons, counting the days, waiting for the war to end so we could go home. We existed from minute to minute, not knowing how long we could stand to live like this. No one could predict what Sadam would do. He would announce that he wouldn't bomb for forty-eight hours. As soon as people returned to their homes to salvage what was left from the bombing, he started a new round of bombing.

I considered his way of fighting cowardly, senseless and cold-hearted. He killed women and children and then announced to the world that he had hit a military target. I saw the burned public bathroom where innocent women and children were buried. I saw houses on fire. I saw neighbor children, running around laughing one minute; their bodies lined up in rows down the street the next. Some bodies were never recovered from those bombings. One large, two family house had completely disappeared; only arches and a gigantic hole remained. A few days later, the government sent workers from city hall with bulldozers to cover the hole and level the site.

Khomeini "Drinks the Poison"

By March 1988, the war had taken a different turn. It wasn't as intensive as in previous years. It was obvious both countries, especially Iran, were running out of resources to continue. During the eight-year war, Baghdad had helped the Mojahedin and the Democrats from Iranian Kurdistan stand up to the Iranian government. Iran used the same tactics toward the Shiah majority in Iraq and the Iraqi Kurds.

The Iraqi dictator was fighting Iran in the south and Iraqi and Iranian Kurds in the north. He was determined to crush the Kurds and consolidate his power. Sadam killed most of the Shiah protestors in southern Iraq. The Kurds of northern Iraq, with support from their brother Kurds in Iran, had fought bravely and nearly brought Sadam to his knees. To stop them, Sadam, who had used chemical weapons against Iran, resorted to using mustard gas against his own Kurds.

Halabja, a city of 45,000 on the Iran/Iraq border was devastated; five thousand were killed instantly at the scene by poisonous gas. Thousands more died later of effects of the gas. A classmate of mine was a Kurd from Halabja. She lost many of her family members and searched for the rest of her family for two weeks before giving up and traveling to Kurdistan Iran.

The images on TV that were broadcasted live from Halabja spoke a thousand words and were horrifying to watch; evidence of unimaginable brutality and cruelty. It was a mass murder that dwarfed the individual deaths to which we were almost becoming inured. We were haunted by images of a dead baby in her mother's arm, still sucking her dead mother's breast, old people sitting on the street corners died right there, bloated livestock in grotesque death. Family members gathering and throwing dirt on their head as a sign of loss; women and children in a pool of their own blood were hard to watch.

These were such difficult years that I completely forgot my own pain. My heart ached for our people. I no longer cried for myself but for others. In my mind, the only sound I could hear was the laughter of the children at play and their screams as bombs took their lives away. Hot tears still slide down my face when I remember looking at the pictures of the babies. I cried for the babies, who lost their mothers and could never have her back. I cried for the children who would never see their next birthday; their small legs, arms, hands and feet severed, their skin burned or separated from muscle, dried blood streaming down their small bodies, some with eyes and mouth left open, as if they were frozen in time. They were the future of our country.

Just when I thought Sadam was incapable of anything worse, he proved me wrong. He demonstrated, by the gas attack, how easy it was for him to kill vast numbers of people. This was his new weapon that he was warning us about. Although the whole world knew he ordered the massacre and his pilots carried it out, he denied it.

It was a wake up call for the world. Everyone noticed that, as we say in the Persian language, the snake in their sleeve that Western countries had been feeding the latest army equipment had turned into a monster. Khomeini, who never visited the front lines and had no idea what Sadam was capable of doing, was informed by the army generals that there is no way Iran could defend itself against a similar attack on our cities.

Sadam had long announced on his radio broadcasts that he had a different kind of weapon. Now we knew that he was referring to the chemical bombs. Every night there was a gathering in local mosques or schools. Pasdars told people in case of a chemical attack to stay under water. People panicked because we didn't have water on most days. Most were trying to purchase gas masks. There was a visible tension and anger toward the regime. People questioned the regime's loyalty, asking what price it was willing for us to pay in order for them to continue the fight with Iraq. Everyone was in favor of ending the war before Sadam lost his mind and patience and attacked us with his chemical bombs.

If it was possible to make matters worse, the mullahs managed. The sanctimonious idiots running our country ordered that in the case of public bathrooms destroyed by bombs, they were to be bulldozed flat and no effort made to recover the bodies because they were nude. Khomeini and his mullahs declared that it would be a sin for a male rescue worker to look at the corpse of a dead female. One wonders, were these warped minds ascribing their own perversions to others in assuming men would lust after a dead woman? Even in death, women were treated as second class.

In 1988, Khomeini ordered students to stay in school during the bombings but saner heads disobeyed his orders. For the first time, students didn't show up. In previous years, our absence was counted but this time around teachers were telling us not to come back until it is safe. Fear of getting killed was very real and, orders or not, schools closed and exams were cancelled. Even though there was no official date set for exams, I kept up with my studies.

I could empathize with Ann Frank, the Jewish teenager who wrote her memoirs while hiding in an attic in the midst of World War II. I was in a parking garage in Isfahan. Studying was an exit to shift my focus from war and the constant mental battle to do something productive. In the parking garage my choices were limited. I could sit and wait for Sadam to drop the next bomb or I could learn something. This last leg of war proved to be hardest. There were days we didn't see the sun; with as many as twenty red alerts per day, we couldn't get out. For the last couple of months before the war ended life came to a stop, nobody went to work, nobody went to school, nothing productive took place, the economy was paralyzed.

Iran wasn't prepared to have an underground war factory and people had enough. We lived in that shelter day and night until Ramadan started. Since Iran and Iraq are both Muslim countries, we didn't fight during the holy month of Ramadan. During this break, exams were held. But, my family, along with many others, still slept in the shelter. The school term was almost over and because of the constant bombing we hadn't read most of the chapters. Nevertheless, we were told that we had to be ready for exams over the entire book. I was glad I had studied the whole book in whatever time I found between shuttling from home to the bomb shelter.

By late May 1988, I had finished nine exams for my fourth year of high school. In Iran, when a student passes all other fourth year exams with good marks, she or he is granted an extra passing mark for one course. I knew I was weak in English but, under the rules, I wouldn't have to worry about my poor English.

The reason I didn't study for English was because I was insulted by my teacher's previous comments about me. Not too long before the exams, my English teacher had told my mother, "Your daughter doesn't have the intelligence to learn any languages." I figured I would prove her wrong on my on terms and spent the study period writing poetry instead of reading the material for the following day's exam because I knew I would get a free mark and the likelihood of needing English was remote.

As I expected, I passed all my courses with good marks and got a freebie in English. About two years later, when I was in university, I met her as I was crossing the bridge between the two sides of the Ziandeh River. She stopped and asked what I was doing. I briefly explained that I was accepted to study French in university and also had gone as far as grade twelve English. I was delighted by her shocked look. My guess is; she was expecting me to tell her that I was engaged or doing something she thought my intelligence was capable of handling. I did not intend to boast. I just wanted to teach her a lesson to never judge a book by its appearance. Most of my learning issues were exacerbated by the constant stress and challenges I was facing. Despite all the problems I had made it on my own.

On July 3, 1988, The *USS Vincennes* mistakenly shot down an Iranian Air Bus flying over the Persian Gulf enroute to the United Arab Emirates. The tragic mistake resulted in over 290 deaths, including 66 children.

In August 1988, Rafsanjani was elected president and at the same time the war took a strange turn. Recent research has revealed that the CIA was sharing intelligence information with the Iraqi dictator, giving Iraq satellite imaging of the location of Iran's forces. From this new finding, it is indicated that if Iraq had not been helped by the US, Iran could have won the war.

From the year 1986, Iran was progressing by starting a series of counterattacks against Iraq, capturing thousands of Iraqi soldiers and causing many other causalities. It was unbelievable for many Iranian that Iraq would so easily give up the cities it had occupied for more than seven years. It almost seemed that Sadam had voluntarily pulled his army out of Iran. Apparently, the Iranian people were not the only ones who thought so. To everyone's amazement twenty-one days after I finished my exams and got my high school diploma, the war was over.

July 3, 1988, Iran was finally forced to accept the peace process. Khomeini made an astonishing announcement. He said he 'drank the poison' referring to accepting the ending of the war. After eight years of war-enhanced hell, it was suddenly all over. The guns finally fell silent on August 20, 1988. It was quiet and we could breathe easily. But, the price we paid was extremely high. Our cities had been devastated, our lives put on hold and our dreams shattered. Most expensive of all, a huge number of our future generations had been buried.

Iranian people have marked nearly two decades of peace on their calendars but there still has not been an official peace treaty between the two countries. Both sides lost innocent souls for no reason except the selfishness of two stubborn men, ideologically different but with many similarities in the way they exploited their two countries and treated the people as commoners. This war brought nothing for Iranians except misery and wasted lives and resources, billions of dollars in damages, half a million corpses, and another half million injured. One and a half million refugees fled their homes seeking safety.

PRISONERS OF WAR

More than fifty thousand prisoners of war returned. A few even returned from the 1970 six-day war between the Shah and Sadam. They resembled people who had been lost in the Amazon or had come back to earth from an alien planet with no families to return to. Four hundred thousand, mostly young, men were injured, paralyzed, or wounded in heart, mind and body. I heard a mother say, "The way he is now, I wish my son were dead. My beautiful educated son with a PhD, can't even use the bathroom, he has to be diapered. I wish he hadn't come back from war." This soldier had become a paraplegic and could not talk or control his urination or bowel movements. Like many, she was burdened with an invalid while government that chose to fight, didn't consider how elders would take care of the permanently disabled survivors. There are no health or rehabilitation centers to take care of war-wounded soldiers. Parents who spent their youth, and energy bringing up their children, supposedly their life's fruit, now, in their old age have to take care of them again.

During the war, I thought life was tough for us, I had no idea what it was like to be in Sadam's prison and waiting for the war to be over. A cousin from my father's side was one of the prisoners of war who came back after eight years. At eighteen, he was very young and good-looking; resembling a young Michael Jackson. In fact, with his dark skin and curly hair, everyone thought he was an African-American. When he returned he was twenty-six, no longer young and good-looking and his hair had turned gray.

On his return, he was reluctant to talk about what happened to him in the Iraqi prison camp. He said he still had nightmares every night and wanted to forget the experience. And, even though he was back in Iran, he still felt unsafe. But, what he did tell was sickening.

I was as shocked as anyone on seeing the recent pictures of prisoner abuse in Baghdad's Abu Ghraib prison. What the Iraqis did to Iranian prisoners was far worse, particularly in the minds of many because both were Muslims. Iraqis and others who protested the relatively benign abuse by a few ignorant soldiers, who 'tortured' Iraqis in Abu Ghraib prison, either never heard or did not care to listen to the stories of what their own soldiers did to Iranian prisoners. These days, everyone who reads the newspapers and watches TV professes to be shocked by the action of the American soldiers who abused the power vested in them and took advantage of the Iraqi prisoners. Iraqi prisoners protested that the Americans called them names. I am just wondering, where were these people when the abuse of Iranian prisoners was happening inside Iraq? Were the lives of Iranian soldiers and their dignity worth any less to human rights?

My cousin said prisoners were held in a large compound of thick walled mud buildings surrounded by a high wire fence. The cells were windowless, dirt-floored rooms with about 200 men in each 40 ft^2 room. The Iraqis gave the prisoners ten spoons full of rice every day, so little that no one got enough food. The prisoners decided to fast every other day, therefore, a few of the prisoners would have more food on alternate days. The most disgusting thing was that the food was brought in the same bucket they had to use as a toilet. The Iraqis would presumably wash it and throw food in it. The prisoners were treated like pigs, permitted outside for an hour every three or four days and allowed to shower once a week.

One soldier, who the Iraqis suspected was an Iranian spy, was carried to the washroom where they poured boiling water on his body, splashed salt on him and beat him to death with steel cables as he protested his innocence and pleaded for his life. His blood and skin was left on the walls as a reminder to the other prisoners. True stories such as this were common.

As bad as his condition seemed, he was lucky to receive a UN visit to his prison camp now and then. Many of the prisoners who came home were listed as casualty, unlisted, or absentee, which usually meant they are dead and their bodies are either burned beyond recognition or killed on the border and buried in mass graves. It was the shock of their parent's life to see their loved ones coming home after years of being absentee. Some came home to their parent's house and there was no one still living to welcome them. The burden of these families was so heavy that during the war years Iran must have had one of the world's highest rate of heart attack. On every corner, there was a shrine giving us the bad news of someone's sudden death due to heart attack.

I may be repeating myself but it is important that people not forget. The behavior of the Iraqi soldiers was Nazi-like and the same soldiers are still serving Iraq under different leaders. They still kidnap, kill and torture, this time, in the name of Sunni or Shiah. In Persian, we have a proverb: 'It is the same donkey but its packsaddle is different.' Sadam Hussein is gone but now his parasites are the new leaders and behind the insurgents, many of them the same soldiers who killed children, tortured men, raped women and demolished cities in the occupation of Iran. And yet, the Iranian government was willing to turn its back on these atrocities for political reasons. Just two years after ending the war with Iran, Sadam Hussein targeted Kuwait and asked Iran to help him. If it had not been for the objections of the Iranian people, the insane mullahs would have run to his aid.

KHOMEINI'S DEATH

Just before his death, Khomeini pulled one more stunt from the sleeve of his robe that stunned the world with his cold heartedness. In February 1989, British author, Salman Rushdie, published a book of fiction, The Satanic Verses, apparently based on Khomeini's character. The regime called it an offense against God and Islam. Having absolutely no sense of humor, Khomeini, who saw himself as the Messiah and felt that he had the divine right to order death for people, was angered to the point that he put a death bounty of $25,000,000 on Rushdie. The author remained in hiding for many years in fear of his life until the sentence was recently lifted.

As months passed, we noticed remarkable changes in his outlook as he became frailer but there was no explanation of his state of mind or health. Rumors about his illness surfaced and we heard that his doctors were using a variety of treatments from chemo to growth hormone and bone marrow, to fight his illnesses. A couple of months before his death, there was an astonishing announcement by the government asking people to pray for his speedy recovery.

There is a secret chant in the Muslim religion that, if performed, the sick, will either die or be cured, depending on his or her past life. My mother performed this chant for me when I was infected with a particular viral infection that seemed permanent. I had a fever every day for two months and became a skeleton with skin covering my bones. The night she finished the chant, she left me and I had a dream that I was about to take off from my body when a series of saints came and stopped me.

The chant is one of the dearest sura in the Koran and most Muslims are aware of its power. Nevertheless, the person who does the chant must have a genuine reason in order to receive the miracle. I have never actively taken part in anyone's death but I knew if Khomeini survived, he would take more lives. I wished him dead with all my heart and was prepared to do anything to stop him. I did the chant, and prayed to God to give me the miracle. Soon after I finished the chant, Khomeini died on June 3, 1989, shortly after peace was restored. He had been bedridden for thirteen days, suffering from prostate cancer. It may be just a coincidence but the Shah also died of prostate cancer.

Although I wished for his death, it was not for personal reasons. The day he died was a solemn day. There is no happiness in someone's departure. I cried, not for him but for half a million people who died because of him. Under his dictatorship, between the years 1978-1989, tens of thousands of his opposition were hung or shot not including the stoning deaths of hundreds of women and men accused of real or perceived moral transgressions.

I interviewed the renowned documentary producer, Masoud Raof, who won national and international prizes for his documentary 'A Tree that Remembers.' Raof, a Leftist, was a prisoner in Iran for five years. He told me he has learned from inside contacts that the regime published the number of prisoners executed at between 100,000 to 130,000. Iran has changed but not for the better.

Khomeini was a determined man, a private and strict mullah. People did not really know who he was. The only thing the general public knew about him was the accepted story that he stood up to Reza Shah, father of the Shah, and wanted a different Iran.

He had no compulsion to share his feelings and concerns with the people. The reason no one knew anything about him was because he didn't volunteer any information and everyone was afraid to ask. Not having had power all his life, he must have been overwhelmed by the attention. He had become an instant icon who looked upon us, the people who planted him in the driver's seat, as commoners.

Who Was the Real Khomeini?

When he died, his last testament was published. For the first time he talked about his Hindi Brother and directed that some money be given to him. Apparently, Khomeini had forgotten to tell people who he really was.

When Khomeini returned to Iran, he said he was born to a villager father and never had any money. I am not certain what money he was talking about because his finances and the rest of the government members were never published.

Khomeini was born Ruhollah Khomeini Hendi on May 17, 1900. The last part added to his last name, indicates that his father was from India. He was born in the town of Khomain located in the south of Markazi Province, 323 km from Tehran and 160 km from the city of Qom. In 1930, he changed his name to Ruhollah Mosvi Al-Khomeini. It was years after his death before radio Iran announced his last testimonies referring to his brother.

Perhaps it is ironic but many who have paid attention to the flag and the logo of the Islamic Republic of Iran noticed that it is remarkably similar to the Sikh religion logo. The government of Iran has explained that the logo is indeed the name of Allah in Arabic. Nevertheless, the logo similarities, the Hindi brother, his whereabouts for all those years and why Khomeini never divulged anything about his background leave a nagging question in the minds of the cynical.

When I was discussing the research about Khomeini with a friend, he asked me if I had any prejudices about Indians? I answered, "Of course not." For all I care Khomeini could have come from Mars. He was a despicable ogre, whatever planet he came from. What I do have issues with, is that he didn't share with the people. He led them to believe he was an Iranian. People died for him and deserved to know the truth. In my view, certain character and financial records of a politician who is paid by people's tax money should be public record. The public who pays has the right to know who the individual eagerly occupying the seat is. In the beginning, people didn't know what they got themselves into before lofting him onto the revolutionary platform.

The answer as to why he didn't reveal his true identity perhaps is, he didn't see any reason to reveal his full name or where he had been to the commoners. To him, our lives and values had no meaning. The perception is that Khomeini saw himself as a saint. I heard him say that he had come to finish Prophet Mohammad's job. That is why, when people mention his name, they say peace upon him three times, whereas, Muslims around the world say it only once for Prophet Mohammad.

Neither Reza Shah nor his late son, the Shah, had any affection for Khomeini. Reza Shah and his son both killed many of their opposition. It almost seemed that God had saved Khomeini. That was not quite so.

Years ago, when Khomeini was arrested for the first time by Reza Shah, he was not an Ayatollah but a Hojat-al Islam. An Ayatollah is the purest form of Islamic achievement. For the lack of a better analogy, it is nearly equal to a Pope, except there is only one Pope. It is the highest level of virtue and knowledge that normally can only be achieved by years and years of studying and research. If an Ayatollah is equal to a Pope, a Hojat-al Islam is equal to a bishop. Ayatollah is the *fagih*; a person who can issue the order of Jihad and not even the Shah could harm a person of that rank. He would have immunity and therefore could be only jailed or sent abroad.

Khomeini was simply a Hojat-al Islam and he was in trouble. He was granted the rank of Ayatollah by five sympathetic Ayatollahs. This exception to protocol in promoting a person to such a high rank was done to save his life.

Khomeini took full advantage of his new rank. He immediately began issuing orders that were contrary to common sense, the laws of Islam and all political and human standards of any person with a shred of decency.

While living in Iran, I met a woman doctor in the post office while mum was sending some gifts to Manoocheher in Canada. The doctor said that when she was studying in India, Khomeini was a poor young man, dressed as a mendicant, singing poetry for money in the street. I had a hard time believing her until after Khomeini died and his poetry was suddenly published. We never knew he was an accomplished poet. Perhaps his softer side did not exactly fit the ruthless image he wanted to project. There is no record of Khomeini's whereabouts until he miraculously showed up in Qom in his early twenties and studied religion.

In the view of Khomeini and his followers who, sadly, are still in power, people's lives didn't mean anything. He also didn't see any reason to end the war. If he had not been forced by everyone around him to agree to a truce, he was willing to subject Iran to the disaster of the Iraqi chemical weapons.

For forty days, there was mandatory national mourning. All business, schools and television was suspended. The nation was paralyzed. His burial ceremony was more of a circus de soleil. His burial chamber is located in Behesht Zahra. Eighty kilograms of pure 24K gold was used to cover the dome built over his grave. I have heard from people who have visited his grave that the mosque built for him is covered with a one-of-a-kind, hand-made, silk Persian carpet and free food is always provided to the visitors or, as the regime calls them, pilgrims. I have never seen a need or had any desire to waste my time visiting his grave. I know he is in trouble in his after life. I had my own opinions about his life, regardless of how the regime tries to portray him. In his testimony, he named as his successor his son, Ahmad Khomeini, who died mysteriously about a month after his father's death and was buried next to him. Khamani, in order to be eligible to replace Khomeini, with the help of Rafsanjani and Majless, promoted himself from Hojat-al Islam to Ayatollah and announced himself as the new leader.

Life Changing Dream

By age 18, I had seen so many deaths and my heart had become so hard I couldn't cry. After the war was over, I couldn't have cried if I tried. I had endured so much pain that if someone stabbed me with a knife, there wouldn't have been any tears. Feeling unloved and betrayed by the men close to me, I had grown a special hatred toward men in my heart. I did not think I would ever get over the resentment or fall in love. Then one night, I had a dream.

I saw myself in my school uniform waiting to meet Abo-Al Fasel, a holy man, who had been dead over a thousand years. He died for the sake of helping others and is the symbol for kindness and virtue in Shiah Islam. In my dream, I, together with many others, was waiting in a cemetery for his holiness to appear. For a long time, Abo-Al Fasel didn't come. I was impatient to leave. I left the graveyard, still searching for him at the exit door. Suddenly he came riding on a white horse, just as we had been told he would do. As he came near me, I greeted him and he looked at me with compassion and said, "Be kind to others; love other people."

The dream had a profound impact on me, coming at precisely the time I needed to hear this message. It would change my life.

Mum's Surgery

Although mum and I always had our differences, I loved her dearly and could not bear to see her hurt. As I got older, I began to understand her fears and flaws and came to realize that she was not an enemy but a friend; one who had suffered enormously and remained in an abusive marriage because of her children, me in particular. In my early twenties, I was old enough to understand life is not always easy. Mum told me that she didn't divorce my dad early on because she feared that one day I would be questioning her about my dad and wondering if she had tried to make it work so I could have a father and a normal life. I appreciated her sacrifices and told her I would have never been so naïve and insensitive. I told her I knew his true character years before she thought I could make my own judgment.

In 1988, mum was fifty-five years old, her heart and back broken by the load she was carrying on her shoulders. She was no longer young and looked older than her age but was still having her period every month. At first we thought it was a sign of her being healthy but then we realized that she was hiding that the bleeding was copiously non-stop. This worried me. She wouldn't visit a doctor because she didn't want to confirm that she was sick. I was furious with her for being so obstinate.

One of my best high school friends had gone through the tragic experience, at age seventeen, of losing her mother. I did not want to repeat her tragedy and begged mum to see a gynecologist. When she finally relented, my fears were confirmed. The doctors told her that she needed surgery immediately to remove her womb. Fibrioids occur in as many of 80 percent of women. From the number of women who underwent surgery and the number of women who died, it appears that the main cause of these women's problem could have been the constant stress during the eight years of war. One of our next-door neighbors, a woman in her sixties, was one of the casualties of this illness.

Despite my pleadings, mum postponed her surgery. We needed money and needed it fast for her operation but didn't have anyone to ask for help. As is the custom in Iran, she had gathered some household items for my dowry in case I got married. I told her I wouldn't get married and I didn't want these items if she were dead. I begged her to sell them all so we could use the money for the operation.

A month before Iran and Iraq agreed on a permanent cease-fire, there was a short ceasefire. We had learned from experience that after each short pause, the two countries restarted the war with a vengeance. Mum had to sell everything we owned quickly in case there was a bigger storm on the way. She sold all of her crystal, valuable china, the color TV my father had bought the last time he came back to us, even our stereo and the carpets we brought from Mecca. Mum was in tears because of what she had to do but I could not have cared less about the material possessions. I value a human life more than objects. Besides, I did not think I could ever love a man after all I had gone through and I didn't think anyone should marry, if not solely for love.

A few weeks after the war ended, mum decided to have the surgery. We spoke just prior to her surgery. She was weak, having lost quite a bit of blood, and her face was pale. I was in tears for fear of losing her. I told her to have courage and hope and that she had to survive for my sake because I would miss our arguments. We forgave each other all our old transgressions and let the bitterness be washed away by the flood of tears running down our cheeks.

Her surgeon had initially told me it would take an hour maximum for the entire surgery but it must have been more complicated than he anticipated. It took over seven hours. The surgeons had removed mum's womb and ovaries because they could have been cancerous; fortunately the tumor proved benign. All the time she was in the operating room. I nervously walked around the hospital corridors. On two occasions, I almost walked into the surgery room to find out what happened to her. Unlike in North America, the patient's family can't attend the surgery. When I finally saw the doctor at the end of the corridor, I ran toward him and asked him what he had done to my mum. He laughed and said she is ok and about an hour later she was brought out of the surgical unit and transferred to her room.

I recently learned from an ABC broadcast that there is a viable alternative to the surgery that most women undergo, from which, sadly, many do not come out alive. The non-surgical option, called Uterine Fibroids, has been widely available in North America. The procedure was not available in Iran at the time and I am certain, even if it were, her surgeon would not have recommended it. Unfortunately, most women don't know an alternate option exists because the unnecessary surgery on millions of women means billions of dollars for the doctors. A Canadian friend of mine could have benefited from the non-surgical alterative without losing her life due to the agonizing surgery.

After mum's surgery, she was very weak and needed a blood transfusion. Siavash and Khosro each gave two liters of blood but, as much as I insisted, mum's surgeon did not give her any blood. My mother lost so much blood it was a miracle she survived. I later learned that the surgeon had been instructed to get blood from patients' family members to be sent to the depleted blood bank. Like any dictatorship, the government of Iran doesn't request people to donate blood to the empty blood bank; it demands it. If they don't voluntarily donate, the government simply takes the blood.

Mum had a private room in a private hospital. It wasn't luxurious. In fact, the building was an old home that had been turned into a hospital in early 1940 and had served as a hospital for World War II. But, it was clean and unlike the rest of the hospitals I had seen, there weren't blood spots and dirt all over the corridor walls and patients laying on the top of each other in the waiting rooms. A few months before mum's surgery, Siavash had his tonsils removed in a public hospital. He said the surgical room was plastered with bloodstains and hair. From the looks of the room, he wondered if the surgical knife was even sterilized. After surgery, he started bleeding and if it weren't for mum would not have gotten the care he needed to deal with the infection. Luckily, in mum's case, things in this hospital were different for the better.

During the five days of my mum's hospitalization, I was with her twenty-two hours a day. At the end of five days when she was feeling better, I asked her surgeon to dismiss her. He wanted to keep her another five days but we couldn't take it anymore. The hospital didn't have a shower and the custom of that hospital was, the relative that stays with the patient had to be up by four a.m. every morning. I simply couldn't sleep on the chair nor could I eat the super spicy food. Unlike anything I had ever seen in hospitals, the food was so spicy it was hard for me, as a healthy person, to digest it, not too mention for poor mum who couldn't drink water or go to bathroom on a regular basis

I counted off five long days till mum came home. The night she arrived she started bleeding again but her doctor assured us that this was normal. That was the good news. The really bad news was that I was now the family cook. Cooking wasn't one of my skills and in fact posed a challenge for me, especially when I had to cook dishes I had never made before. My culinary skills were limited to boiling rice and omelets. Mum's doctor gave me a special menu of dishes she should eat. I knew what the ingredients were but didn't know how to combine them into an edible concoction. As if the shame of looking in my mum's eyes and apologizing for the horrible food wasn't enough, Siavash's endless criticism really agitated me. He would tell me what he wanted to eat but when it didn't turn out like mum's, ridiculed me. His criticism was a constant aggravation. Mum would shout at him to stop but he didn't and seemed to enjoy being obnoxious.

By the time mum was able to walk again, in about three months, I had become nearly anorexic. She and all my friends were voicing their concerns. I took six months from off studying and took care of her until she was back on her feet and able to function. After this hiatus, I needed to take some classes to prepare for university and I needed to study English. Mum approved but Siavash complained that we could not afford for me to continue my education He wasn't working except for part time jobs found through mum's networking. He hid behind her and pretended to be the responsible brother. Mum told him, "You are living off me, living under my roof and you will not tell your sister what to do."

THE POTATO BUSINESS VENTURE

A few months later, after mum felt better, there was a serious shortage of rice in Iran. Rafsanjani announced that people should use alterative foods, such as potato. Although people of Iran, use many other vegetables in their diet, rice is considered the main course. Potatoes are a side dish or delicacy.

After his recommendation, many of the Bazaar members bought most of the potato crop and suddenly there was also a shortage of potatoes in the market. I could not believe that potato prices went through the roof, jumping form five cents per kilo to two dollars.

We had sold our last few possessions to find money for mum's surgery and had a bit of money left over. Mum proposed that we gamble it in a business venture. We knew where to buy potato crops. In fact, where we went, there was no shortage of potatoes. On the contrary, farmers were looking for buyers willing to pay cash for their ready to go produce.

We made a day trip to the city of Fraidan, nearly five hours away, known for its rich and delicious dairy products. We purchased 1.5 tons of potatoes, rented a pickup truck and made it home by nightfall. Mum used the exit door of our house as a temporary kiosk. Although it was quasi-legal, since we lived in a commercial zone we got away with it. Mum was the seller and Siavash was her helper. I helped by putting the potatoes into smaller sacks. We sold nearly two thirds of the load in the first three days.

Rafsanjani, who I guess felt responsible for the sudden potato inflation, announced that the government would be selling lower priced potatoes at certain locations. This was another way of making money. He and his peers are notorious for creating the demand to sell their own products.

After his announcement, our sales slowed down but we were able to sell the load and make enough money to support us for the next three months, ease the harshness of our lives and enable me to use some of the money for the university preparation courses.

Entering University

To get into a public university, I had to pass the Concours exam that is modeled after the French school system; requiring an entry test for all colleges, even for undergraduate level. This exam is similar to the L-SAT or M-CAT in North America. I took classes to review my four years of high school. I bought additional books and studied very hard, twelve to fifteen hours a day, for a year. I progressed rapidly and my language skills improved from no English to reading and writing English at a twelfth grade level in the English Institute and preliminary speaking in a non-native English environment. I was enlivened and had hope and pride that this would be the year I entered university. Of course, I was naïve to think people could enter university in Iran just because they knew the subject. I soon learned my lesson. Such wishful thinking seemed to be the right way; not so in the real world.

As long as I can remember, I had a dream to become a doctor. I had always been a little doctor at home. When anyone asked me what I wanted to be when I grew up, I said, "A doctor." That is why I chose science and biology in high school. Otherwise, studying biology four to eight hours per days for eight or nine consecutive classes would have been a huge waste. When I was only six years old, I used to inject the leftover tranquilizers from my mum's prescription into my doll. I knew how to sterilize a wound at an early age. I did research about my own diagnosis prior to seeing a doctor. Many times, I found the answers and the drug I needed and took the research with me to visit a specialist. Two of my diagnoses about my bipolar and IBS was the result of my own research. Often I heard the doctors tell me, "I only heard of this research a few days ago." I am not sure if I was born to be a doctor or if it was mum's dream that became my dream somewhere around age seven or eight. Regardless of who started the dreaming first, I wanted it badly enough to pursue it as my future profession.

The number of high school graduates greatly exceeds the available college seats for students. Only about one in six is admitted to university. The overall population is relatively young in comparison with industrial countries; a high percentage of Iran's resident are under twenty-five years old. It seems the government thinks birth control is a new world invention and opposes it. Families are having more and more children and stretching resources, especially educational resources, to the limit. New investment in education needs to be made immediately or the country will face a generation of illiterate people. Many have no money to send their children to private high schools and public schools are running two or three shifts

233

per day. An overwhelming number of students, many extraordinarily talented want to attend university, no matter how difficult the entry.

Every year millions of high school graduates compete for a limited number of seats at the universities. The competition is fierce. Everyone fights to get his or her child into university. Only a small percentage are able to fulfill their dreams; some by miracle and some with the help of whom they know. The results of the Concours determined where a person would go to university.

The year I graduated, 1.5 million students wanted to enter university. About 150,000 thousand were fighting for the 1500 seats available for medical school in the public universities. That was for all facets of the medical field, including general practitioners. My marks were not as impressive as some others during the early years and my high school teachers said I could never learn English but I had gone through many reviews and I knew the material well. After years of psychology, I know myself extremely well and I know when I can pass the tests. I used myself as a mentor for my research and I was confident that marks are not the most important part of my studies. I had proven that on one of my exams. After spending the whole night taking care of my mother, I went for my math exam and got an A.

My objective was to be like the geniuses that found their own way in life and didn't follow the behavior cliché of others. It is well known that Albert Einstein wasn't a good student but impressed everyone with his intelligence. I am not an Einstein but I understood the subject. I never claimed to know something unless I was dead sure. Despite the limited seats and extreme competition, I was confident that I would have no problem passing my exams.

Also, I was fortunate that mum wanted me to further my studies. Many parents, who didn't really care about the education of their girls, pulled students out of university after they had gone through hell to get accepted. One example was a friend who was accepted at medical school, receiving her registry the night of her wedding. Her husband, a mechanic, knew that if she became a doctor, she would have opportunities to attract a man with a different profession. He told her that he did not want her to continue her education but if she wished to, he had no ill wishes for her; they could stop the wedding process and each go their own way. Her parents overruled her desire and she was sent to her husband with tears in her eyes.

On a more positive note, my relationship with mum had become a lot more relaxed, boosting my confidence. She was trying to sell the house and other facets of life were also looking up. The war was over. I no longer had to study by candlelight and I could stay up and study until any hour of the morning. By this time, there was enough oil production that we could buy as much as we needed without standing in interminable lines.

After the war, Iran, a large oil and gas producer, allowed people to pay relatively cheap prices, compared to other countries, for the refined oil they needed. That winter, for the first time since the revolution we had enough heat. Life was easier and my hopes were high.

In spite of this, I had one lingering concern; my run-ins with my high school principal and head master. The government of Iran didn't want anyone in the universities who kicked over the traces. They ask high school principals to comment about each student who took the Concours exam. I heard alarming stories about students who had a chance to go to medical school but had received a letter saying the school wouldn't admit them because they didn't think they were qualified. I was afraid that would happen to me but I hoped that since a year and a half had passed, the principal of my high school would not remember me.

I was kidding myself during the high school years that my teachers would not remember me. I suppose now it was payback time. As we say in Persian, my face had become the face of the cow with a white birthmark on her forehead. My headmaster never forgot who I was because of all the trouble I caused and all the heated discussions I had with her, arguing that she was wrong about religion and making her admit that the rules that we had to obey had nothing to do with Islam. I pointed out to her that although prayers are mandatory for all Muslims, no one could force anyone else to pray. I tried to reason with her, bringing a sura of the Koran. This didn't set well with her or with the mullahs who were making rules to fit their policies.

Also, I had seldom showed up for mandatory morning prayers. I had never voted and never attended any protests against any country. I didn't believe the foreign policy of Iran would work and I didn't want to be part of their idiotic ideas. I stayed away from any activities that either supported or openly opposed the government. I didn't like the power that the government held over students. I had numerous discussions about Islam in my classes and expressed my opinion that Islam is not a religion that forces ideas but is a brotherhood, a kind loving religion and should be practiced that way. I could express my reasons using the words of God and the holy people in my religion. I began learning about Islam at the age of seven and the Bible at nine. I knew Islam and other religions as well. My diversity of knowledge was not a plus in the government's mind. Knowledge is a dangerous thing among a bunch of illiterate people who want to take advantage of naïve people. She wasn't going to let me get away.

I had to get a good report from the high school principal before I could get into any university. For the last month of my high school senior year, the principal gave me a discipline mark of 11 out of 20, which was an injustice and totally ridiculous. I asked her why she did that, and she told me frankly, "You never showed up for morning prayers and you ignored the political chants against the US and other countries, that was three marks. You never showed up for Muslim prayers, that was another three marks. You always argued with me about your opinion, that was another three marks." I was so angry that I could have strangled her. I told her she couldn't do that to me. She answered, "Oh yes I can. Watch me." I went home and told my mother. Mum was furious. We went back to the principal and mum told her that if she didn't change this mark, she would pursue the matter to the Ministry of Education and the court. Finally, the principal changed my mark from 11 to 15, almost certainly still too low.

While the Shah ruled, the mullahs trying to overthrow him professed to be advocates for the poor, fighting injustice and corruption. In fact, they simply ousted him to become an even more brutal, exploitive, dictatorial regime. Growing up, I observed that the people of Iran regretted their action. The poor got poorer and the rich got richer beyond their wildest dreams. The corruption and politics didn't stop at the business level; it affected every facet of our lives, including administering of university tests. In high school, I had a friend whose father was an influential mullah. She and a couple of other friends and I were discussing the Concours. She told us her father had told her just to go to the exam; she didn't have to worry about the result. He had already registered her in Alzahra University, one of the most modern universities.

The government established the university after coming to power and it mostly hosts offspring of mullahs and government officials who decide to continue their education inside Iran. It was sort of an Islamic private elite club, or the Eaton School for the royal and rich government members' kids. They had to let some other people in to protect their own image. There are also students whose parents are top officials of adversary groups supported by Iran, who are not quite welcome in other countries. They come to Iran, not only to finish their education but also to stay on to work as diplomats. Iran is a refuge for many who, by their conduct elsewhere, have worn out their welcome in other countries.

It was widely known that questions and answers were being sold before the exams. I had trouble believing this was true, even though I heard it from my own uncle. He admitted he had bought the exam for his brother-in law, who couldn't get into medicine because his high school major was literature and he had never had any pre-med courses. He was barely out of high school but was able to immediately start studying radiology. My uncle also sent his daughter to a public university to become a teacher. We all knew she couldn't get into school without her father's help and he wasn't hiding it either.

In spite of this, I was studying like a robot. I got up at 7:00 a.m. every day, had my breakfast, and by 8:00 a.m., I was at my desk, studying hard. At 1:00 in the afternoon, I had a small lunch at my desk. Then I would study till 7:00 p.m. have dinner and by 8:00 p.m., I continued until 1:00 or

2:00 a.m., in the morning. I had 11 books for each year to review, 44 books in total, and had only one year in which to do this task. I didn't take time off for three months. If my eyes got tired, I closed them but continued reviewing and repeating what I had read.

I dedicated myself to the studying so much that, as shocking as it sounds, I didn't take a shower for three weeks at a time. I decided I would take a shower when I had finished studying; rationalizing that I would then be as clean as if I had showered every day. Since I had no social life, the family could just stay out of olfactory offending range.

Finally the exam date arrived. In two days I would change my destiny by going to university. I was hoping to open up some of the closed doors I had ahead of me. I decided to rest for twenty-four hours before my exam. I told Mum that I needed to take a bath. We went to a public bathroom, as we still did not have a functional bath at home, perhaps a factor in my decision to marinate in my own juices for so long. On the way home, I felt dizzy. We were only two minutes away from our house, but I told mum I needed a few minutes rest. She said I could rest when we got home. I don't remember what happened next. When I woke up mum was shouting and crying, tears falling on my face. I asked her what happened. She said that we were crossing the street and I suddenly collapsed, right in front of a car. When I looked, there was a car next to me, about two inches away. That afternoon, I was feeling better but to make sure mum took me to a neurologist. His diagnosis was that there was no brain damage. In his opinion, I was simply too tired and the incident should have no effect on tomorrow's exams.

The next day was the Concours. Thousands of students gathered. I had three hours to finish the 300 questions. I finished in an hour and twenty minutes. I was confident I had passed the exam. When mum asked me how I did, I told her I thought I'd be going to university soon. We had to wait for more than a month to know the results, which would be published in the newspapers.

But when the results came out, my name was not in the paper. I was sure it couldn't be right and that there had to be a mistake. A few nights later, there was an announcement on the radio that there had indeed been mistakes and new names would be published. When the revised results were published, my name was not there either.

It was a great blow to me. It could not be true. I was devastated. Mum was very worried about me. To comfort me she offered her sympathy and said you will make it 'next year.' I told her there won't be any next year; I would not be able to go through the same ordeal again. My second option was the private university. In the Persian language it is called Azad University. Azad means 'free' but Azad University is not a free school. The students who enter the school privately fund it. By law they should have a vote in its future but, unlike its name, it is neither free nor does freedom exist in this university.

Government leaders, who saw it as a way of earning money, organized the private university. Rafsanjani, along with a handful of government officials, was on the board of directors and advisors. When it started, since it was private, there were no entrance exams. However, its credentials were not valid, even though it was highly regarded as a private school. Later, because of criticism by many radicals, it started to require entrance exams. Since it now had the same regulations as the public universities, its credentials were slowly accepted by most public universities in Iran and around the world.

I did not know then but later found out that my father was sending Khosro to Azad University to continue his studies in the English language. In my family some things never changed. Khosro and Manoocheher were the ones my father favored. Khosro was only attending school to stop my mum's constant sarcasm and to make his father proud so he could suck money out of him. In return, my father could boast about his son. Not motivated to do it on his own, he never passed the second semester and withdrew from the university. I, on the other hand, wanted to go to school for an education. I could register to study medicine in Azad University if my father would help me, as he did Khosro. But, my father refused to help me. The five-year medical curriculum cost 800,000 Toman in Iran's currency, which at that time, 1990, was about US $18,000. My dream of being a doctor died because I simply didn't have the funds.

I was severely depressed again and tearful much of the time. I knew the reported results were not right and that I was being manipulated and punished by the government watchdogs for my youthful arrogance. My friends in high school had warned me I was being watched but I was naïve. Boy, was I wrong! My arguments with authorities about the way students were forced to dress and pray had a disastrous fatal result on my application to university. The injustice and pain I endured didn't make me slow down. On the contrary, it made me bitter and even more determined to speak my mind against the dictatorship government.

Mum wanted to appeal but I disagreed because it was a long process and we could ultimately have wasted another year and still gotten the same answer. I still remembered missing my math exam and the futility of seeking redress from the educational authorities. Mum told me she would send me to Azad University if I could choose something other than medicine.

I considered international law but all the lawyers I talked to told me a bachelor of art is the first step and French language is necessary. Following their advice, I chose French literature. When I told mum, she said, "But you don't know one word of French." That was true, I didn't. I said that I liked to challenge myself and see what I was capable of.

I had only a few days to decide if I was to go to the private university. Mum had to figure out how we could afford it. Asking my father was out of the question and we had no one else to ask. As we say in Persian, there was no point singing poetry to a deaf ear. When it came to me, he had more than one pair of deaf ears.

Siavash considered a private university for me an extravagant expense and waste and was against it. It was amazing that my father could give money to Siavash who hated him nearly as much as I did but couldn't give me money for my education. When Siavash came back from his military service, although my father wasn't living with us, he fulfilled his promise by giving him nearly a thousand dollars.

My father didn't mind throwing money around for his sons, even though they simply misused it, but when it came to me, he sure knew how to put me off and push my buttons.

Siavash packed his bags to make his first try for Europe. He soon returned to mum, tired and lonely, saying he was worried about us. I knew he didn't have the guts to live on his own and used mum as his shell. His constant arguments about my education left a residue on my spirit and caused our relationship to break for good.

Just as I was ready to move on with my life, another calamity struck. One morning I woke up and couldn't stand on my feet. I had no control over my body. Mum took me to a doctor who could find no sign of illness. From my years of self-diagnosis, I told mum that it could be my ears. I visited an ear, nose and throat specialist. His diagnosis was that I had severe muscle spasms in my ears. He said there was inflammation around my middle ear and around the tympanum membrane. The inflammation and stress caused the labyrinth fluid to move too much and I was losing control. I couldn't walk straight without an aiding hand. I later found out it was caused by a bacteria that changed my balance system. Since then, I have not been able to ride a bike. Not that I ever had one, but as a child I rode my friend's bike.

Overnight, I went from a healthy person to one with a disability. I couldn't walk without assistance. Only time could heal me but in desperation for lack of possibilities and suggestions, the specialist recommended that I stop studying. He said it made my condition, worse. Not studying? I rolled my eyes. What else you are supposed to do when you have a big exam coming up? I had an exam in less than three weeks and I had to be ready.

By coincidence, Mr. Jafary, the kind man who helped me to register for high school in Bandar-Abbas came to visit us. He stayed with us for four days. I enjoyed his visit and was inspired by his encouraging, positive words so much that when he left I was much better. I had only one week to go but mum wouldn't let me study anymore. She said she would burn my books if she saw me studying. This struck me as unusual attitude for someone who had wanted me to study while bombs were falling all around us.

Mum kept an eye on me; I mean literally. But, she was no match for me. I had her fooled when I was only five years old. While she was praying, I opened my books, peeking at the material. As soon as she finished her prayers, I closed one eye and left one open, pretending to be sleep. She looked at me, sometime even checked on my breathing and I watched her till she went back to her prayers. Keeping one eye half-open, my studies were more like a comedy routine than studying.

Finally the day of the exams arrived. I went for my exam and came out very happy. The tests were in English, even though I was going to major in French. I knew I had passed it the minute that I walked out. I was going to go to university. But, I didn't say much this time. One week later, the names were posted in the newspaper. Early that morning, I had a dream that I picked up a newspaper and my name was listed at number 36.

At 7:00 a.m., one of my friends knocked at our door and wanted to go get the newspaper to see the result. I told her I already knew. She thought I was either joking or dreaming. I went with her, picked up the newspaper and there was my name, number 36.

Having failed one time, I didn't want to miss this opportunity. I went home and phoned Azad University at 8 a.m. sharp. I told the registrar's office I would like to register now. The registrar did not have the results yet. They asked me when I was accepted. Excitedly, I replied, "Just now."

The number of students taking the private university exam was 350,000. The number of available seats was estimated at thirty thousand. There were thirty-five thousand writing the same exam I did. My test showed I placed number eleven among all participants of the French major exam.

Classes started in early October. The first day of class, all the instructors spoke French. I had absolutely no clue what they were talking about. I came home and asked my mother if I could change my mind about majoring in French. She replied, "Sorry lady, it doesn't work like that. This is what you chose and you have to face the challenge. Didn't you say you liked a challenge?"

Mum could be so cruel at times. But, she was absolutely right, just this once, I had put my foot in my mouth. After all the trouble I had gone through to get in, I couldn't give up that easily. There was nothing more for me on the horizon. The next best thing, besides working hard, was to find some guy to marry me. Between the two choices, I would have much rather work hard and to make mum proud of me than marry someone I didn't even know.

My Father and I Meet Again

Once again, we were out of money. The only thing we had that we could sell was the telephone line we were using. In Iran, unlike in Europe and North America, people can buy and sell telephone lines. It has become a sort of investment for some people and a good source of revenue for the government and private investors. Mum told me to try my father one last time to see if he would help me now that I was in university. The last time I had seen him was nearly five years ago when they were in divorce court. Desperate for money, I reluctantly went to see him. I knew he never changed. The words of his last insult toward me; that I didn't mean anything to him and his dog was more valuable than I was, were still burning in my ears,

Happy and healthy, he was cooking food for himself and listening to Voice of America on the radio. He seemed content and it appeared that he had a pretty comfortable life but, as usual, he complained about my mother, claiming she stole his money. He invited me to share his stew. I refused to eat with him. I had no desire to share his food. He had such bitterness toward me; I had seen him trying to destroy people. I had no reason to trust him and sometimes I was even afraid of him.

When I was a child, I remember he had a fascination with Adolph Hitler even calling him a mentor. He had a long green raincoat and shaved his mustache similar to Hitler. He used to give us speeches about how wonderful Hitler was. As soon as he was starting his admiration speech, we scattered away telling him, "Whatever." After a few years, he understood, we did not share his admiration for Adolph. His behavior was menacing and very similar to his beloved mentor. He was pleased with himself when, for no reason, he killed innocent wild animals on our trips from Abadan to Isfahan and from Isfahan to Mashhad. On both trips, I observed him kill jackals and other wild animals. He enjoyed cruelty to animals and torturing and killing his dogs. He had no reason to feel any remorse for me. Although he was capable of feeling sad for himself and whoever else he chose to, he showed no morals to anyone.

I told him he could make a difference in my life if for once he chose to help me. I asked him to at least give me the money he legally owed me from the divorce settlement with my mother. He had never paid child support. His factories were working and he had plenty of money but, as usual, he told me he didn't have any money. I protested that obviously he did, just not any for me.

When he left our home years ago, he left some valuable equipment he had purchased during his trip to the USA at our house by mistake. I told him I would give them to him in return for the money he owed me. He said, "You will give them to me when you have no choice." He added to the insult, "You are just like your mother." I told him, "No, I am not, if she was like me she wouldn't have stayed with you and saved your ass. You brag about yourself but if it wasn't for her saving you, you would have died in prison where you belong." Before leaving his house, I told him he would hear from me in court if he would not help me out. He chuckled and said, "Yes, take me to court." as if he knew what was going to happen. I told him, "At least my mother had the dignity of caring for a human she brought to this world. You don't have a shred of human dignity in your body. I am not proud to be known as part of you." and I walked out of his home.

I did what I had to do to get some money out of him for our family and for my education. I went to court. The judge was another mullah. My father hates mullahs and always disrespected them, whether they were good people or not. But, on that day of our court, he turned on his charm. He made me look like a fool, who was eager to cut her father's penniless throat to get money out of him. The mullah told me, "The way you behave; if you were my daughter I wouldn't give you any money either." I told him he had no idea what this man is doing. I told him about the months of starvation he put all of us through. The judge said, "I can't see such a good man doing such a thing." I told the mullah judge, "You must be kidding me or blind. He is playing with you and pulling your leg. He hates mullahs." He judge said he forgave my insults but didn't offer to help me.

So much for expecting the judiciary system to work for women. I didn't pursue the appeal. Appeal to whom, I thought? A year later he finally needed the equipment and agreed to give me the money he had promised five years before. Since the barter of his equipment for my money, we have not met again.

FALLING IN LOVE

After the way all the men in my family had treated me, I had no interest in meeting a man, much less falling for one. I thought love is for the Smiths. I never believed I could fall in love. I chuckled at the idea of falling in love at first sight, but, despite all the odds, it happened to me. I never said anything to anyone about my feelings but being in love was the most delightful, and colorful event of my youthful years.

After only two weeks in school, I took my first test. I got a -12 on a scale of 0 to 20. My French was beyond bad. I was disappointed in myself but wasn't going to let myself fail. For the first time, I approached my French instructor, Dr. A. to discuss my situation and see what I should do to learn French. I was twenty. He was twenty-six and enrolled in a PhD program.

If Dr. A. had been in Europe, with his good looks and height, he could have been a Calvin Klein runway model. Besides his looks, his intelligence, poise, impeccable dress and cosmopolitan manner made him quite a celebrity at the school. He was very popular with the girls. But he also was an extraordinary teacher and a remarkable human being. On the campus he carried himself with dignity. His classes were joyful and despite the half hour commute from his home he was always punctual. I was most impressed with his kindness toward me and his dedication toward his students. He was a friend when I needed him most, as I am sure he was to all his students.

Although he learned French in Iran, he spoke it without an accent. He spoke several languages fluently but was modest about his talents. I didn't know it at first but later learned he was a Kurd from the same region as my mum.

When we looked into each other's eyes, I felt something that I had never felt for anyone in my life. It wasn't just because of his good looks. Throughout high school, I met many handsome teachers and male student friends but nothing ever crossed my mind or heart. I analyzed at it as a sort of taboo love. During my school years, I had heard stories about students falling in love with their teachers. I never imagined it could happen to me. That someone who could barely cry was actually able to feel emotions was surprising to me. I didn't know what to make of what I had experienced in my heart. I couldn't rationalize it. I didn't know the right word to describe it. I decided to suppress it. I wasn't pleased with myself for falling for my teacher and, in my mind, I was sure he didn't want that to happen either. Also, I didn't want to acknowledge it because there was no way for me to pursue it, even if there was a possibility. He was not only successful but coming from a prominent family could have caused some tensions. My family was dysfunctional and by no measure was I successful. I didn't want someone to have pity on me and love me because I had never been loved.

By then, I had my own reasons to have reservations about a possible relationship. I felt life had been unkind and unfair to me. I had accepted that my fate, apparently, was to be punished by Mother Destiny for things that were not my fault. I decided to make my own destiny and leave reliance on Destiny to those who had more faith in it. I didn't want to join the crowd of women, including my own mother, about whom I had heard millions of stories. I didn't want to join the young brides who were teased because of their family's behavior or lack of material stature in life. I had seen my mum's agony and didn't want to walk in her shoes. Therefore, I chose to repress my feelings and put a stop to the crush I had on him. Despite all the rationalization, it was a sweet thought which brought a smile to my face, thinking he perhaps had the same feeling about me as I did about him.

Feelings aside, the day I spoke to him, he gave me advice on how to focus on my French. He recommended that I stop taking English classes so I would not confuse the two languages. He advised me to get a tutor and read and listen to French as much as possible to train my ears to hearing French pronunciation and to make it easier to learn the language subconsciously. And, he suggested that instead of thinking about something in Persian; translate and think about it in French, even though I might make mistakes. I took his advice. I found a tutor, worked extremely hard, studied religiously for three months and in a short time my French improved dramatically. In less than three months I could make short sentences in conversational French. He started to tease other students and tell them to be more like me. Some students who had lived in France for years did not like the way Dr. A. praised me in class and got quite jealous. I didn't like the gossip I heard. Even the boys in our class were jealous of me.

I finally went to see him and asked him to please stop talking about me in class because some classmates didn't take it well and I wasn't looking for trouble. He promised he would try not to talk about me but sometimes he forgot. He constantly compared other students with me and told them they could learn from my example. He wasn't trying to cause any trouble, simply to motivate the students but, unfortunately, it backfired for me.

The jealousy was because most of the girls found him attractive and available and were trying to get his attention. I heard many of the girls would tell him how much they loved him and he would say, "Thank you." His standard answers were politically correct but I never saw myself approaching him and hearing that. I wasn't sure what to say to him or what he would say to me, I wasn't even sure what people tell each other when they feel that way. I decided not to tell him anything at all. One day, he had an open discussion about marriage in class. Everyone answered his questions except me. He finally asked me what I thought of marriage, I blushed and said nothing. He asked me, "Don't you feel anything." I said, "No." I didn't want to be an emotionally closed person but I had my own reasons and had no intentions of explaining them in front of the rest of the students.

He seemed displeased with my tomboyish attitude and that, before it started, was the end of any communication about a possible relationship. He saw me as a protégée, and did his best for me and listened to me when I needed to talk. He treated me, not just as another student but also as a friend. Unlike some bachelorettes, I was not there to find a bachelor. Being in love wasn't a priority in my New Year resolutions.

My first semester marks were average but by the end of the year I could speak French fluently. While at school, I made a lot of new friends. Even Dr. A. teased me about my popularity. It was a great feeling to be popular after many years of being an outcast.

While I was enjoying my independence, short-term fame and popularity, I could not stop talking about political issues, human rights, and women rights. I had never belonged to any opposition group and did not care for them. In my short life span I had observed that every one who claimed to have the nation's best interest at heart had pretty much lied to reach the crown and those who promised Utopia only meant to take us further into the depths of hell.

In the last few hundred years of Persian history, there have been two extraordinary Prime Ministers; Amir Kabir in Gajar dynasty and Dr. Mossadegh in Pahlavi Dynasty. Both of these two remarkable men were put to death one way or another. If they had the chance to continue their leadership, Iran most likely would have been one of the most modern countries in the world.

Since their deaths, Iran has not seen a genuine strongman who truly carried out what he intended. One man salvages the previous one's treasure. Everyone sees an opportunity to line his own pocket and takes what belongs to the nation, either in the name of the throne or in the name of God.

Hope is an element of all human ambition. It enables us to go beyond our limits to achieve extraordinary accomplishments. As much as I cared, there was no hope of harvesting the crops of our freedom. One way or another, we were being played. I was so angry about all the different claims and promises of the opposition that the thought of joining any of them never crossed my mind. To take abuse for one or another was simply not my agenda. The factor that mattered most to me was humanity and pure freedom, freedom of speech, thought, writing, and every array of freedom on the spectrum. In my mind, none of the so-called activists ever fulfilled their empty promises. I figured when one scoundrel goes another one replaces him; either way my vote would never count. Why should I pour out my blood or sacrifice my life for someone else's victory. I wanted to educate people to recognize who is the hunter and who is the hunted so they can make a wiser choice the next time they choose a new government. All the sacrifices our nation had made were because everyone was a follower. Nobody asked how the promisors would achieve their promises before they sign their contract. This is where people start jumping in front of the tanks, killing themselves without knowing why.

In the university, I tried to scratch other student's conscience by constructive criticism to help them question what was going on around them. I bent the university rules and made my own; for everyone's sake, not solely mine. The university, about half an hour distance from the admission office, was just a few days old when we moved in. With a lot of hard working faculty members, caring teachers and university officials, it was a great atmosphere to study—until we were cursed with a government watchdog. The same method of control that I had experienced in high school came to the university. We were ordered to wear 'proper' clothing—only dark colors. We were ordered not to bother our young teachers. Like second rank citizens, girls were ordered not to sit in the front of the class.

When I came to class and saw the boys sitting in the front it made me furious. I told the girls that if we sat in front, they couldn't move us. My plan worked. Ours was the only class to successfully adopt this plan. Both girls and boys sat in the same row or the boys sat behind the girls.

A few days after classes started, university officials made an unofficial visit to our class. The President of the University asked his assistant why girls were sitting in the front. His assistant started mumbling. I spoke up and told him that I couldn't hear very well and I couldn't see the board behind the boys so I needed to sit in the front and didn't want to sit alone. The officials were not happy but they didn't want this issue to spark a protest. They worried that if one university started a protest the rest might follow and everything might get out of hand.

Abduction by the Pasdar

For once, I was having the time of my life but my inner intuition was on alert. I sensed that an unpredictable event was about to happen but couldn't imagine what it would be. I began having nightmares and had a gut feeling that I was being watched. But, I didn't stop my political discussions. Frankly, I did not care anymore what was going to happen. I could only be careful but could not stop future events. There is a Persian proverb, 'When the water passes my head, it doesn't matter, one foot or ten.' It means I am drowned. I didn't really care about the details. I had it with the regime. I foolishly thought, "Bring it on."

Mum used to send Siavash to escort me to the admission office. He looked very sloppy and my classmates kept teasing me. I told him to either change his clothes or stop escorting me. He said he didn't care about me and after that I was on my own.

On an afternoon in October 1990, I was on my way to the university for a 2:00 p.m. class. Traffic was unusually heavy. I had been on the street trying to catch a cab for nearly an hour. Somebody would hop into the next cab before I had a chance. A private car drove up and the driver started asking people their destination and offering them rides. Four people, including me, got into a light gray sedan. On the way to university, the other three people got out of the car, I was about to get out when the driver offered to give me a ride to the admissions office where I was to take the university bus.

I was running very late and innocently welcomed the offer but I didn't expect him to take the back roads. Suddenly, he made a U-turn at a nearby square and went down a street away from the admissions office. I got extremely nervous when I heard him talking to the man in front that, until now, I had thought was another passenger. Hearing their conversation, I realized they were friends. I asked the driver why he was going the wrong direction. He said he wanted to avoid the traffic. I became very uneasy about the situation but tried not to show it because it would give him an even greater advantage.

By this time, the driver and his friend started talking about porno videos and women they had been having sex with. I realized this was a trap and nervously asked him why we were still on the wrong route. I told him, "I want to get out of the car now." The driver shouted at me to sit down and shut up. I looked at his speedometer; he accelerated from 55 kilometer to 80 kilometer per hour. I was terrified and realized he had kidnapped me. I was never afraid of death but was terrified by the thought of being tortured or raped. I yelled at him to stop the car but he went faster and faster. In those ten seconds, the only thought that came to my mind was to pray.

I noticed several people standing at a remote bus station and made a snap decision to throw myself out of the car. At the very least, someone would witness what happened to me. I was carrying a large bag. Before the driver or his friend had a chance to stop me, I opened the car door, threw the bag on the ground with my right hand and jumped on top of it. It was like a scene from a Hollywood action movie; except this was no trick and I did not have a stunt double.

God must have held me onto that bag. I was dragged on the street for about 15 meters before the car came to stop. I shouted, "Help, help, this man is abducting me!" People ran after the car. My left hand, knee and ankle were severely injured and bleeding as I was dragged. Seeing people chasing after him, the driver finally stopped, got out of his car and shouted at me, "I'm taking you to the Committee." Meaning the station of the Sepah Pasdaran, the mullahs' private army. Terrified, I told him: "I am not going anywhere with you." People surrounded me and everyone was asking questions. I was in shock but kept saying, "I am late for my classes."

The kidnap driver jumped in his car and left the scene. Someone got his license plate number. Another jumped on a motorcycle and followed him to his destination. A very nice gentleman gave me a ride but left me three blocks past my destination and I had to walk back. As I walked, I was crying so loudly that people must have thought I had gone crazy and gave me a wide berth. My left leg was torn apart at the knee and my ankle was scraped deeply. Both wounds were bleeding heavily and I was covered in blood and dirt.

When I finally arrived at the admissions office, no one offered any help. I was in tears and my face and clothes were a mess. I told them what had happened and asked if this is the way you protect women. It was no surprise that no one answered. Instead of taking me to a hospital, one of the university employees took me home in a university car, asked me to clean up and he would take me back to the university. The only thing that mattered to me was that I was late for class. I kept repeating, "I am late for my class. I am late for my class."

Luckily, when I got home mum had gone out. Siavash asked me what happened. I knew it wasn't really important to him, so I told him I had fallen from the school bus. I couldn't tell him the truth because he would speculate why I got into a strange car. I knew mum well and needed to tell her myself but telling wasn't going to be easy. I was terrified of her reaction and needed to buy some time and get over my nervous breakdown. My leg injury was quite deep and later got infected. But, momentarily, I put myself together, cleaned and sterilized my wound as best I knew how and went back to school.

I was an hour late for a two-hour class; the first time I was ever late. When I arrived, everyone looked at me. I was as pale as a ghost. A few minutes later, we had a break and Dr. A. asked me if I wanted to talk to him. I said, "About what?" He said, "Well, I think you need to talk." I told him the truth and told him I couldn't tell my family. He said he would tell them if I wanted him to. I told him, "No" and asked him to keep the story to himself for the moment. He said he would and assured me he would do whatever he could to help me.

I told only my best friends what had happened to me. I had to keep it quiet for several reasons. First, my mum was going to be quite mad and I didn't want her to blame me. Second, being kidnapped in Iran is very much like being raped, or even worse, in the North American culture; not a popular subject to talk about and the girl is always regarded as a whore. I was afraid people would look at me differently and I did not want that. Third, everyone would think that I had influenced Dr. A. to help me, which was not true.

He talked to the university officials and tried his best to help me. A few days later, I heard the kidnapper was caught. I was momentarily happy but my happiness didn't last very long. I was told that I had to take my mother with me to the prison to identify the man who kidnapped me. Which, by the way, was another trap.

Three days had passed and I was in severe pain but the physical pain wasn't as great as the mental anguish of facing my family and telling them. I had kept the story straight that I was on the bus, the driver had to brake suddenly, the door opened and I fell off the bus. Mum had a hard time believing it but there was no way I could tell her what really happened. I was afraid of her judgment. And, I was right to be.

I dreaded telling her the truth. I knew she was going to be furious that I lied to her in the first place. She already had issues with me because I asked Siavash to stop escorting me. Having no choice, I sucked it up and told her what really happened. As expected, she got very upset and told me that I wasn't a good girl and how stupid I had been to get in that car. It was very hard to hear her words and swallow the pain she caused me. The pain was almost as bad as being beaten up again. At first she didn't want to go to the prison with me but finally she relented. She also took me to a doctor. After a careful examination, he put me on a high dosage of penicillin, as my leg was infected all over and I could have had serious problems. The doctor told me if I had waited any longer to see him it might have been necessary to amputate my leg.

Mother and Child in Prison

The day that I was to identify my kidnapper, two university officials picked mum and me up at our home at 8:00 a.m. and took us to the prison. The prison was located in the southern part of the city in one of the best and most prestigious neighborhoods. It was next door to million dollar mansions; homes for the richest people in the city before being occupied by Sepah after the revolution.

One confiscated house had been turned into a detention center. On the outside walls, Khomeini's famous quotes were painted. Concertina wire and barbed wire topped the walls and armed men guarded the entrances. Women and men had different entrances. I suppose the visit was pre-arranged because I wasn't questioned at the women's entrance. Mum and I went through a small courtyard and entered an L-shaped room with a long hallway located at the right side of the entrance. The window of this room was covered with little handprints. I correctly assumed they were from children. Outside, it was a nice, sunny, late October day but as we entered, I noticed that this place didn't seem to get much sun. The room faced the north and there was a fountain and pump in the courtyard. The courtyard had been washed, a strange thing for October. In the summertime, we wash our yard to create a fresh breeze and cool off the house but not in October. The smell of urine was overpowering in the room. Mum covered her face and nose with her chador.

I heard a woman moaning and a baby crying, apparently from a cell in the dark hallway. Prisoners were banging on the iron bars with something that sounded like a metal tumbler. Other women were shouting, "We have been here more than twelve hours. My baby needs to go to washroom," one of the women yelled. Finally, the prison guards allowed the woman to go to the bathroom. I saw her and her infant baby stepping down to the yard to wash her baby and realized that was the source of the smell and the reason for the freshly washed courtyard.

Poor people don't have the money to buy diapers for their babies. Mothers wrap their infants in cloth and wash them from time to time. I watched a group of six women and two children leave the prison. They looked bedraggled, as if they had been here for a few days. I assumed they had all been detained here temporarily, which can be counted as hours or days. There are no rules as to how long the Pasdars or police can keep someone. Girls, as young as seventeen, covered head to toe in black chadors, worked there as prison guards. They seemed to be having a good time, joking and laughing. Being a prison guard is not considered a good job for women in Iran but the regime faithful do such jobs with pride. They call it 'God's Work,' meaning they are doing it for the sake of God.

After a very long wait, I was called and directed to a room about seven square feet that had a small window about ten inches from the ceiling. I was told I was there to identify the kidnapper but this room, supposedly an office, barely had room for one person. The walls, ceiling and floor were dark cement. There was a small desk with a chair on either side. I thought I was finally going to get some help.

Instead the Pasdar woman began interrogating me. A chador-clad woman Pasdar, a co-worker of the accused, asked me to explain exactly what happened. She took some notes on a piece of paper that I wasn't shown, and then had me write what I had just told her in my own words. She warned me that no one should know about this incident. I was not to discuss it with anyone at my university or tell anyone what I had written. She acted as though I was the one who had committed the crime. She asked me if I understood. I noticed the protection was not for me but for the person who committed the crime and for the Sepah Pasdaran's image I thought, "The guy must be one of them."

I only had a quick second to consider my options. I could answer back and yell and shout and probably be detained in this place with no lawyer for an indefinite time. Or, I could sign my testimony that said I would not discuss this incident with anyone and get out to fight another day. I signed the agreement to remain silent about my attack and left. Prior to this day, I did not know why I was abducted or why I was being treated like I was the criminal but I was beginning to have an idea.

Before the kidnapping, I had a habit of starting a conversation in French, which usually resulted in a heated argument about lack of freedom and abuse of women in particular. Now, I realized the government has ears and spies in every corner. That is how they stay in power. People will do anything for a little money or a referral for a position. I believe that my outspoken diatribes had brought on this incident. But I was not deterred; on the contrary, it made me bitterer and more determined than ever to speak out.

Six weeks passed. Immediately after I was abducted, all the school officials were sympathetic. University officials, who at first had no idea who the kidnapper was, had pursued my case with the judiciary system. I was told they were proud of me, one hundred percent behind me and would try to see that the abductor was punished. But later, when I walked by, they would turn away from me. Obviously, the Pasdar got to them.

I was getting ready for my initial court sessions when the university officials called me to the main office to tell me circumstances had changed and with the new information they were ready to drop the case. They said I could pursue the case on my own if I wanted to have closure but they could no longer be involved. Of course, nothing more was expected from the university officials who worked directly for the government.

Now, I had no choice but to go to court by myself and face this man again. If I didn't want to pursue the complaint, it was up to me. I had to ask my family to accompany me to the court. I asked Siavash if he would come with me. He shook his head no and said it was my own problem and he wanted nothing to do with it. Mum was unhappy but agreed to come along. I did not want to see the abductor again but had no choice and decided to go to court. After three months, I finally got a court date.

The courthouse was located near the University of Isfahan in a wealthy neighborhood. This was another house appropriated by the revolution. The owner of this house, however, wasn't as lucky as the detention center's previous owner. He had sent his family abroad but he was the first man to be convicted and sentenced in his own home and hung from a tree in his own courtyard. It was one of a series of houses this man had built in one long lane, all similar in construction; three stories high, one pool in the yard and four car underground garage. The interior and exterior walls were covered with cut white marble and rooms on the second and third floor overlooked the pool. The trial was in one of the smaller rooms that looked more like a guest room or nursery than a courtroom; it was approximately 60 ft^2. My case wasn't important enough to be represented by a prosecutor. I was on my own, accompanied by mum. The judge was a fortyish mullah. When I saw him, I thought to myself, oh dear God help me. There was another man in the room who appeared to be the judge's assistant. He was writing something in a large book. A desk and four chairs were all the furnishing in the room.

I told the mullah that this man had caused me a lot of pain and anguish and asked if it would be possible for him to question the abductor and me separately. The judge overruled my request. Since the day of the accident, every time I was in any car, and the driver accelerated, even if I was with my mother, I started having panic attacks, shivering and sweating. The kidnapper showed up with his father and stepmother. His stepmother whispered in mum's ear, "Your daughter is a whore." Mum kept repeating, "If you were a good girl, you would have never gotten into a car with this man." I was bombarded with accusations by both sides. My heart was pounding when I saw him come into the room. I did not have a lawyer to help me because I couldn't afford one. Unlike many other countries, Iran doesn't think it is necessary for anyone to be represented by a lawyer.

Amnesty International has protested many sentences handed down in Iranian courts but Iran's government continues to ignore the directives of the UN and other cause-driven associations and societies. In political cases, a person is not allowed to have a lawyer, even if he can afford one and can find a lawyer willing to represent him. In a country where fanatics make and break their own rules, law is just a three-letter word. The scale is always heavier on the government side. The government of Iran is aware that they charge the opposition under laws that can be challenged. So, they avoid that possibility by denying legal representation to anyone not on their side. The kidnapper didn't have a lawyer initially but as the case progressed he had got himself one. I was the one left empty handed.

The judge called the kidnapper into the courtroom. He was wearing his government uniform. The judge asked him where he worked. He said he was a soldier working for the Committee. This was when I realized why I was told not to say anything about this incident. This man was a Pasdar from the same group that supposedly worked for the poor and innocent people.

The Pasdars ride around the city in patrols, looking for sinners. They called their work the work of God but they were the devil's army. By day, they enforced the outrageous dictates of the mullahs, requiring women to wear long, ugly clothing and arresting women who break their rules. Women caught wearing lipstick had their faces scrubbed with acid soaked tissues, causing severe burning and scarring. If a few strands of hair slipped out of her scarf, a woman would be repeatedly slapped in public. An ankle exposed by a gust of wind warranted a trip to the police station for 50 lashes. They embarrassed young couples walking hand in hand by asking them for their marriage certificate. By night, they were partying, smoking hashish and opium, getting drunk on homemade wine and having sex with girls as young as nine to twelve years old.

The judge asked him why he had kidnapped me. His answer was; he wanted to marry me. I shook my head. I didn't even know his name. What was he talking about?

I never understood what he meant until much later. When I heard from victims of an opposition family. When their daughter was captured, she was forced into marriage and then was hanged. I still didn't understand the connection until a recent interview with Masoud Raouf who spent five years in an Iranian prison. I asked him about the story I had heard over and over, that many young women were raped inside the prison before receiving their death sentence. He told me that was true; according to the man-made Islamic rules concocted by the mullahs, virgin girls cannot be sentenced to death. For the government to kill them, they had to be women. The government Pasdars, who were also the prison guards, took the women who were supposed to die to a private room, each girl would be given to a guard, a temporary marriage between the guard and the girl was approved by a mullah, the guard raped her and at dawn of her wedding night, she would be hung. Her parents often received a cylinder shaped sugar cube that is customarily given to the family of a bride after the marriage has been consummated. Then they give her family news of her death.

My abductor was as calm as if it wasn't his fault. He was simply carrying out orders whereas I could have been beheaded for something that wasn't my fault. According to Iranian law, supposedly adopted from Islam, a woman who commits adultery is automatically beheaded. Now I knew why I had been kidnapped. The mullahs were free to find the victim of rape guilty of adultery and/or fornication. Theoretically, men would get the same punishment but, as I had no witnesses, the rapist would never have gotten close to execution. He was only carrying out his orders. I would have been the one punished.

There is no doubt in my mind that this was not a random kidnapping. Considering my background during high school, I was constantly under watch. I was denied entrance to a public university. It all started to make sense to me after my discussions. I was again under the eye of a government watchdog in the university and, this time, they decided to take me seriously. When I first reported my kidnapping to the university, they supported me until they found out that the kidnapper was a member of Sepah Pasdar. Maybe the school authorities were not initially involved but later they had a very supportive role toward the man who kidnapped me. I went from being a victim to a person under suspicion.

After a year and half deliberation, the judge issued his ruling or, more accurately, his non-ruling. He said he believed the man was guilty but he couldn't decide and sent me to a higher court. I asked a lawyer friend about the new judge. She said everyone knew him well. He was an important mullah with several wives. He also accepted bribes, which I was in no position to offer. She predicted he would throw my case out in less than an hour because he didn't believe women have any rights. She called it. That is exactly what happened. The judge, a big fat mullah with a long beard declared, "You are insane, thinking such a fine Soldier of God wanted to kidnap you."

I wanted to spit on his long beard and tell him go to hell. But that was not a realistic option. Instead, I left the court in tears. I appealed my case to the Supreme Court in Tehran. Another six months passed. The Supreme Court judge ruled that the whole thing was 'a misunderstanding.'

I was disappointed, but not surprised. I should have known from the moment he got out of the car and, instead of being shaken by people's reaction, said to me, "I am going to take you to the Committee," that he was protected by Pasdar. When I was questioned, he appeared in his uniform as if nothing had happened. The appeals all worked out to his advantage. In retrospect, I am certain he was simply taking orders. I had wasted nearly two years in the court system and it had ended with a whimper, not a bang. There was nothing else I could do, at least not in Iran.

†RAGEDY iп †HE UпiVERSi†Y

Life, for some, went on at the university but there was one tragedy that hit all of us when one of my classmates suddenly killed herself. I can't remember her name but I still remember her face and think about her from time to time. The day we started our French major she and I were sitting next to each other. We studied together for a month or two before we drifted apart. Two days before her suicide, mum and I were out buying me a coat, we saw her. She said hello and mum accidentally mispronounced, "I hope you are well" and instead said to her, "I hope you are not well." As soon as she left us I asked mum why she said that to her. Mum said, "I said what?" That was the last time I saw that girl.

She had fallen in love with a man of whom her parents didn't approve. Her parents decided to break up this relationship and arranged a marriage to someone else. The day before her wedding reception, she took her own life by overdosing on sleeping pills rather than submit to a loveless marriage.

Shortly after this tragedy, I got to know one of our instructors, an amazing person who had the ability to look straight into people's soul. He was in his early sixties and seemed to have the ability to look into someone's eyes and read their future. He treated me like an adult with the respect that I had strived for all my life and lacked at the time. He opened my eyes to the future and opportunities I would have overstepped. He helped me to find my vision and calling in life. He looked at me and said, "Always look on the horizon, never look in front of your shoes and when you see something in life, look for answers beyond the moment."

He resembled the wise old man, minus the long beard, of Persian poetry with the lantern of knowledge in his hand, sitting on the corner of a far away road of destiny, giving me, the last person who wasn't looking for hope, small tidbits of advices.

He told me to look up and try to understand and see things for what they truly are and not what they appear to be. He made me think deeper, question and revaluate my priorities. He impacted my life and made me a more aware person.

He told my friends and me things about ourselves we had not considered important. He said he had a premonition, before our classmate died. I recall his words that she was as fragile as crystal. I hesitantly questioned that because I didn't want to believe it. At the end of private sessions, he gave each of us one bit of advice. Turning toward me, he said, "You be careful, you are walking on the edge as well." He was right about me. I was.

We also had many discussions about Persian literature. He told us about the government changing the history books and about the book burnings at the University of Shiraz, where he formerly taught. When the Islamic Republic overthrew the Shah, they were determined to change everything, including history. They simply changed the numbers or burned the original books so no one could disagree with their version of the facts.

The professor had been able to save three sets of the most precious history books of all times, left from the ancient times of our kings. He told us that much of the history we were being taught was not true. We were shocked at how much we had lost since the Shah's time. People who used to say, "Down with the Shah," realized they had made a horrible mistake by bringing the mullahs to power, now say, "Down with us." meaning they regretted what they did to the Shah. They thought the new regime would be a good thing; it turned to be the biggest catastrophe in our history. This regime has exploited and corrupted our beliefs to our own misfortune. The majority of the Iranian people are aware of their mistakes. They need help to save themselves.

Despite my troubles that year, I finished my classes with high marks, a 3.6 average. At the end of the year, I promised Dr. A. in front of everyone in class that I would read ten short books in French and translate them into Persian. He told me that if I did that he would publish them. I kept my promise. After he read the translation, he said they were not good enough to publish. But, he wanted to send me on a trip to France, on behalf of the French Embassy, for a couple of months to practice my French. It was his way of showing his appreciation toward me as a hard working student. Unfortunately, that never happened.

SALE OF OUR HAUNTED HOUSE

At the beginning of my second year of university, our lives took a turn for the better. Years ago, when my father returned after abandoning us, he convinced mum that if she wanted to receive any money from him, she had to show him that this house belonged to all of us although, actually, he was only concerned about the boys. So, mum gave her sons two of the four shops attached to our home.

According to rules implemented during the war, every man, age eighteen to forty, had to serve his country and have proof of his military service in order for the government to allow him to buy or sell property. Manoocheher did not qualify and was no longer living in Iran. After the war, individuals who escaped the draft were considered treasonous and the government was on the lookout to find them and confiscate anything they owned. I am not sure how mum was able to get around this rule but it must have been a miracle. She was finally able to transfer the two shops from Siavash and Manoocheher into her own name with a power of attorney she had from prior years. A bank was interested in our house and a definite deal was on the horizon but, at the moment, we had very little money and nothing left to sell.

People with no money have few alternatives, none of them great. If they cannot borrow from family members, sometimes children are put to work, although it is against human rights. All else failing, good people sometimes resort to inappropriate behavior ranging from theft to prostitution. Or, if they have a nubile young girl in the family, she may be 'given', meaning sold, to a rich, usually much older man.

Not that mum wanted such a life for me or ever said she would give me away to save her boys; in the back of my mind, I knew that if anything happened to my mother, the boys would have no moral problem giving me away or leaving me on the streets. I was always vigilant and had a plan of action in case I ever needed it. Fortunately, I did not have to resort to any of the alternatives I had in mind; some that, I am sure, would have left more questions than answers. In the end, I would have slit my wrists rather than letting myself be bartered for money.

In the Shah's time, Ms. Stareh Farman Farman, an educated princess and noblewoman, started the social services system in Iran. She established a welfare system in Iran and was encouraged and supported by the Shah. Had she been permitted to continue her work, Iran would have a welfare system in place with food banks for the destitute. Life would have been much easier for the poor. Unfortunately, when she was forced to flee the country, the system died. Her work ended with the birth of Islamic radicalism and revolution. Iran now has no social service system in place.

In desperate times, I have had dreams that ultimately proved to be true. In my dream, someone asked me why I was so worried about the future. I told him about our financial situation. He said that as soon as we had only 200,000 Toman (($500) left, someone would offer to buy the house. I woke mum up and told her about my dream. She was all in favor of my dream coming true but was understandably skeptical.

In another dream, I saw a rope, vertically suspended from over the back door of our house. I could not see what it was connected to but a voice spoke to me, saying the rope went to heaven and that I should make a wish and pull it hard. I grabbed it, pulled hard and shouted, "God we need help."

Immediately, in my dream, I saw the real estate agent, who in real life sold the house, walking through the seldom-used back door. I woke up mum to tell her I was convinced we would sell our house soon. She was happy to hear that but understandably skeptical. Siavash made fun of me that I was always having these dreams. He called them cinematographic dreams, meaning they were a creation of my imagination. Months later, on the brink of financial insolvency, the dream came true. Just as our money had dwindled to $500, the bank made an offer and signed the contract. By every measure, the sale of the haunted house was a miracle. After seventeen years, the albatross was finally removed from our neck.

A few days after my dreams, something rather amusing occurred. We had a chicken stew dinner. In Persian culture, the chicken wishbone is used for betting. Mum, who was a good better, asked Siavash if he cared to break the wishbone with her. He declined but I said I would. She asked, "What you bet?" I said, "If I lose, I give you whatever money I have put aside," which wasn't more than ten dollars. "If I win, you have buy me a diamond ring." Mum laughed and said, "You are one fair individual. Ok, I will, but what make you think I will lose. I knew I would win but didn't want to break her heart. I said I was sure she would win.

The rules are: as soon as two parties broke the wishbone, they would say, "I still remember," meaning I still remember the bet. Afterward, each time the two would offer something the other that was received by hand, the opponent would say, "You forgot about me." It is all done in a loving way; there is no animosity attached when one loses but people often carry this bet for years and they try to beat each other. After a couple of months, one afternoon, mum asked me to give her some water. I ran for the kitchen and, as soon as she received it, there was a smile from ear to ear on my face and I said the magic words. Of course she couldn't buy me the diamond ring but when she sold the house, she bought it.

LEAVİNG İSFAHAN

After finally selling her home, mum wanted to spend some money on me. I guess she was enjoying her emergence from poverty and wanted to show me her kinder side. The next day she took me shopping and bought me two new jackets, both angoras with mink and fox fur around the shoulders. She got me new designer glasses from Christian Lacroix and a beautiful raincoat. On the way home, my mother said, "Don't tell Siavash how much I spent on you today, I'm afraid he might get jealous." Sure enough, when we got home, he certainly wasn't happy and expressed his opinion, just as my father did the night mum bought me the lamb coat.

Mum wanted to rent a house but Siavash insisted we should rent a room in a hotel for a few nights. We rented a room in the Hotel Kosar, which, prior to the revolution, had belonged to a very wealthy family and was named the Hotel Koorosh, after an ancient Persian king. The hotel was among their assets seized by the revolutionary government. We moved to the hotel, intending to stay only a few days, but ended up staying three and a half months which far exceeded my tolerance for hotel food. Sometimes, the innovation of the chef left me with an uncomfortable image in mind. By blood, I am a hunter, meaning everyone from my great ancestors to my father took pleasure in hunting; not as a necessity but as pleasure. However, when it comes to eating animals, I don't want to see them in a way that portrays their suffering.

I don't enjoy their pain and certainly don't like to eat anything that still has the head, feet, tail or anything attached that reminds me this food was a living creature. That is probably why I am having a hard time developing a taste for lobster while everyone else seems to indulge in it as their luxury delicacy meal.

One night, when I ordered my dinner, I ordered quail. It was my first time to have that food. When the dish was served, it was presented on a iron rod, with head and feet still attached. Looking at the crucified bird with open eyes, it was much too horrific to eat. I had my first anxiety attack that night and ended up in emergency.

The hotel itself was an old, but clean, five-star hotel and we were treated well but it seemed crazy to live in a hotel room in the city in which I grew up. Siavash didn't want to live in Iran anymore and was pushing mum to make quick decisions. I was appalled by her snap decisions. We were spending too much money. She ignored my suggestion, listening to Siavash, who wanted a way out for himself. Mum kept sending money to Manoocheher, creating a great deal of stress for me and I ended up in emergency a couple of times.

Two doctors working in this hotel had a crush on me. Siavash was pleased that someone was interested in his tomboyish looking sister and thought I should consider marriage. I was in my early twenties, a spinster by Iranian standards, but I wasn't ready for a marriage of convenience. I was reluctant to have a relationship since I had so many bad memories of men in my life. The only person for whom I could make an exception was my off-limits professor. He never made a personal approach to me and I decided to put his memories to rest. I told Siavash that I could make my own decisions and that he should mind his own business. He obviously wasn't pleased but for the moment kept his mouth shut about my future and decisions.

Life did not go well for very long. Mum and Siavash decided that I should get out of Isfahan and study in Tehran. At first, I actually welcomed this opportunity but transferring to a university in Tehran proved to be extremely difficult without contacts. I hated that mum and Siavash had again made a decision about my life and made it even more difficult.

He, of course, never worried about the consequences; he just made the decisions. I was the one that had to handle it and find out whom to bribe to make it happen. It is no secret that in Iran today, everyone has to know someone to get the right job. In every post and every office, government employees are paying off someone or getting paid off. Government employees have a hard time living on their salaries and, if they are in a position to do favors, they augment their pay by receiving kickbacks.

THE LARGE TEHRAN

My mother and Siavash having decided I should attend university in Tehran, we flew there to attempt to enroll me in Azad University. Flying over the smoky, dirty city, it looks like a large ashtray. I couldn't see the edges of the city through the cloud of haze and smoke.

The traffic is horrendous; everyone drives in everybody else's lane. It took us two hours to cross Tehran from Mehr-Abad airport located in the south of the city to the heart of downtown where we could find a hotel. Tehran is a gigantic, architecturally undistinguished city, a mixture of old and new. The city is stretched to the limit and the population overwhelms the city. Refugees from the villages bring the population to an uncountable, unthinkable number. It is, 'The Large Tehran,' as the Shah used to call it.

It is the nature of the larger city to swallow the past. Much of the heritage and tradition of old Teheran has been swallowed by the huge unattractive city. The old parts of the city are vanishing inside the newer buildings. In the time of Reza Shah, the city was distinct from the countryside of Karaj and Niavaran. Now it has become one metropolitan area and part of Tehran. The famous gathering corners and rendezvous squares of the capital, Shoush, Tajrish and Laleh Square, romanticized in old songs as coffee café rendezvous places for boys and girls, are all gone with the departure of Shah, changed into over-crowded, standing-room-only assembly places for daily workers looking for jobs, small merchants selling their produce and dealers in black market US dollars.

The word Tehran can be found in books dating back to the 10th century. In the distant past it was a village containing numerous gardens. Its importance began to increase in the Safavid period. The original city of Tehran, situated on a sandy plateau in North-central Iran on the southern slope of the Alborz Mountains, covered an area of 1,500 km². Damavand, an active volcano south of the Albourz Mountains, rising 5,678 meters above sea level is the largest mountain of that range.

The spelling of Teheran has more commonly become Tehran. The name comes from Old Persian, meaning warm place. It has warm summers and cold winters, often with snow. Rainfall is not as great as it once was, with less than 200 mm expected annually. Atmospheric pollution causes much of the rain to be acidic. The Jajroud and Karaj rivers run parallel to the city. Tehran is the latest and largest capital city in the 5,000-year history of Persia, as Iran was called before the 1935 name change.

The old part of the city, possibly founded as early as the 4th century, is a few kilometers to the northwest of ancient Rey, an important city that was destroyed by Mongols in the thirteenth century. By the early

13th century it was a small village. Modern Tehran is a comparatively young city, the origins of which date back about 700 years.

Teheran was founded by refugees from Rey but grew slowly in the following centuries. In the 16th century, Teheran became the residence of Safavid rulers. During the reign of the Safavid shah, Tahmasp, (1524-1576) a wall and four watchtowers were built around the city. By the early 17th century, Tehran had about 3,000 houses.

In 1722, Afghan invaders attacked and occupied Tehran. The city suffered tremendously under their occupation until Nadir Shah Afshar freed it in 1729 and established it as the capital of Persia. It remained an insignificant small town until 1788 when Agha Mohammad Khan, founder of the Qajar dynasty, chose it for his capital, inaugurating the modern history of Tehran. At this time, the population was estimated to be 15,000. Under the Qajar dynasty (1786-1925), Tehran grew in population and size and new administrative buildings, palaces, mosques, and garrisons were constructed. It became the country's largest city and the largest in the Middle East after Cairo.

In 1925, after the fall of the Qajar dynasty, Reza Pahlavi started an expansion of the country's capital that included the lands of many princes and princesses of the Qajar's dynasty. The shape and organization of the city was strongly modified during his reign from 1925-1979.

Tehran was a perfect picture of a large country town in the early 1900s. A small country paradise has become an over populated, busy city. The economic base of the city is food processing, textiles, cement, bricks, sugar, chinaware, pottery, electrical equipment, pharmaceuticals and auto assembly plants. Teheran is also the administration centre of the country's oil industry. About half of the manufactured goods of Iran are produced in Teheran.

The population in 1976 was about 4.5 million. In the 1980s, economic depression in the villages caused mass migration to the city, increasing the population, officially, to 7.5 million but, in fact, to as many as 10 million or more inhabitants. Tehran suffers from extreme air pollution, most of it originating from the heavy traffic and use of oil by industry. Some measures have been taken to alleviate this problem, such as encouraging buses and taxis to use compressed natural gas instead of petroleum. A three-rail underground rail system also helps reduce the heavy surface traffic.

The major landmarks of Teheran include all the Shah's confiscated palaces, Golestan Palace, Saad-Abad Palace and Marmar Palace. Some the Shah's major houses have been turned into museums. Other landmarks are Sepah-Salar Mosque, Baharstan Palace, formerly used as Parliament and the palaces of Shams ol-Emareh.

Teheran is connected by road to all major cities in Iran but distances are often vast. The railway reaches most parts of the country. There is one international airport and 2 smaller airports. There are about 40 institutions for higher education. The Iran University of Science and Technology was founded in 1928, the University of Teheran in 1932.

The landmark of Shah-Yad tower, known as the gateway to Iran, is the last reminder of the Shah. This magnificent structure, dedicated in 1971, was intended to remind coming generations of the achievements of modern Iran under the Pahlavi Dynasty. Magically, it escaped destruction by the Islamic regime, unlike the rest of the Shah's monuments. This tower not only represents the city of Tehran; it is the most photographed landmark of Iran, equal to the Statue of Liberty in New York harbor.

Shah-Yad, loosely translated originally as 'Remembrance of the Shah' is now translated as 'Freedom square.' The complex, located in Tehran's Azadi Square, covers an area of five acres. The monument is 45 meter high, 63 meters wide and the height of the main central arch is 21 meters. Designed by Iranian architect Hussein Amana, it is constructed of 8,000 blocks of white marble imported from Isfahan. Azadi tower forms the main part of the museum. Its architecture is a combination of Islamic and Sassanid style. The audio-video hall of the complex, is designed based on Iran's geographical map, displays the regional characteristics of Iran's culture, life style, religion and historical monuments. A mechanical conveyer allows the visitors to visit the hall in total comfort. Some art galleries and halls have been allocated to temporary fairs and exhibitions. The Diorama hall with twelve chambers displays agriculture, handicrafts, modern industry, etc. A cinema, library and sideline services complement the activities of the complex.

The city has changed dramatically since the departure of the Shah but despite the inflation and harsh life of this massive city, residents of the Tehran have managed to stay warm, friendly and, in most cases, genuine. I didn't have a negative impression of the people. Although city employees were characters and quite a handful, in my judgment they are a separate entity and are not to be counted as genuine Iranians.

Impossible Task

Moving to a new city and enrolling in a presumably private university is not a simple matter in Iran. The government tries very hard to keep people under control. They know if people in Tehran start a movement, there is nothing to stop other cities and villages from following. It is like a small wave at sea growing into a tsunami and a deadly hurricane. The mullah's know this first hand because they used the power of crowds against the Shah.

Everyone knows if this city revolts, it will start a tidal wave that will wash away the mullahs like the foam on the wave. It will destroy the harvest of the mullah's seeds that they have diligently sown for the last two and half decades. If Tehran rises, no one can control it. When it comes to the capital, the government is always on alert. Twenty-four-seven, they are in control. In order to manage it, the government doesn't want more people moving to the city. To attend university in Tehran, one must be a resident of the city. I wasn't, of course, and did not know anyone who was.

People returning from visiting Iran, talk about how much it has changed since Khatami came to power. The changes they are referring to are so minuscule they are almost laughable. For example, on one day women are permitted to wear lipstick in public or people are allowed to play chess and music in public. The next day it is taboo again. The regime controls every facet of every individual's life in Iran. An apparently lenient policy will back off overnight. I am not impressed by the changes I have heard about over the last ten years. Personally, it takes more than showing off a few strands of my hair, to feel the freedom.

After resting over night, the next morning we went directly to the downtown admissions office of Azad University. I was surprised at the severity of the repression in Tehran. It was even worse than in Isfahan where it had been almost intolerable.

At the university, gathering of more than four students was prohibited. Students could not stand and talk or laugh without a Fatimeh Commando demanding to know what they were laughing about. The dress code for girls was even more severe than in Isfahan. Men and women had to use separate entrances to the university.

There was a small office manned by two female government watchdogs, swathed from head to toe in black chadors. At the women's entrance, all girls were inspected and searched for make up, long nails and jewelry. One girl was caught wearing makeup. Another was wearing jewelry that she had forgotten to remove after the party she had attended. She was refused entry to the university, her name was recorded and the incident went into the girl's permanent record. I can testify from experience that, in Iran, permanent means permanent.

Compared to the West, the situation of men and women is laughable, or more accurately, lamentable. There is no freedom for either of the genders, period. Both have it tough and their options are limited but men in Iran do have an easier road than women. Comparing the female dress code to the male dress code sounds childish but it is an important issue to the mullahs. Females are not allowed to wear shorts, skirts or short sleeves, show any hair or do any activity that won't allow them to wear the bulky raincoat and scarf, in rain and shine.

Even the female athlete competing in rifle shooting in the 2004 Olympic games, in Athens, was required to wear this same suffocating clothing in the 100° F heat. Males, on the other hand, have none of the above restriction but are not allowed to wear sleeveless shirts. There are other moral issues; women are not allowed to look into a man's eyes whereas men verbalize or insult women to get their attention. The double standard is archaic and infuriating. Only female students are required to have a clear record in order to get a job after graduation, assuming there are any job openings at all! This means the student, while studying at the university, must have a good relationship with university authorities.

If the university has a record on her, there is little chance of a future career, since jobs are limited and there are too many in the work force looking for the same position. Iran has a constant shortage of nurses and medical personal but my sister-in-law, a nurse, had a very difficult time getting a permanent position with a hospital due to her record. She had been seen in a car with an unrelated boy, her future husband. They were forced to marry to avoid jail, lashes and fines. I never gave these women an excuse to say anything to me. I simply avoided wearing makeup or perfume or anything, for that matter, that made me look feminine. In my opinion, there were more important issues to fight for. I watched these women as they brought young girls, sixteen to nineteen old, to tears. My blood was boiling because of the humiliation they cause women but I was in no position to show my anger.

When I got inside the downtown university admission building, I discovered it didn't have an elevator. I had to walk up four flights of stairs to reach the office I needed. The building seemed very much like a prison, which I learned it had, in fact, once been. The offices were very small, about two square meters. There was a small window near the ceiling and one on the door. There were no windows facing outside. It was a horrible, depressing place. Even after climbing the stairs, I was happy to be told to go to the north admissions office, as the university was located in a northern suburb of Tehran.

As we left this office, I noticed a tent across the street. This was not an upscale neighborhood, but it was commercially viable and valuable. Seeing people living in tents next to a dumpster jogged my curiosity. We asked why these people were living there. One of the shop owners explained that the family had once owned a lot of property but the government confiscated nearly all. The head of the family lost all his money and was pushed to bankruptcy. To protest their fate, they were living in a tent on their remaining property.

Early the following morning, mum, Siavash and I went to the north admission office where there was another hassle. The government watchdogs searched me again but they did not let anyone accompany me to the office. I wanted mum to be with me to support me but they said only students were allowed in and if I couldn't handle it myself then I would have to leave.

After a long delay, the guards at the gate were finally satisfied that I was not armed and dangerous or packing any cosmetics and I really did need to speak to an admissions officer. They let me inside. I sighed when I passed through the search gate. Honest to God, I think it would have been an easier task to answer God's question and get through Heaven's Gate than to get through this one.

The inside of this building was the complete opposite of the other admission office. It had a serene energy and once past the newly constructed one story gate building, looked old but opulent. It was a nasty rainy February day when we left the hotel; surprisingly it had turned into a beautiful sunny morning.

As I entered the yard, I looked around curiously and was astounded by what I saw. The gate wasn't a fair representation at all. The long pathway to the offices was covered with hand made bricks, washed with the morning rain. Gardeners planted the fragrant ringlet, the national flower for Persian New Year toward the end of February. The whole interior was painted bright white with incredible plaster moldings topping large pillars. I stood on a covered marbled stoa, viewing the rose garden and the pool. The morning sun must have streamed onto the large, white pillars on the colonnade. Rooms overlooking the garden all had glass mirrored French windows; the fragrance of fresh flowers and the commotion of sparrows in the swimming pool was quite pleasant and soothing.

Walking toward the offices, I could tell from the architecture that it certainly wasn't built for the purpose for which it was being used. A universal rule for government buildings is that they are very simple, usually similar and space practical. They are not built to look opulent. I correctly assumed the previously owner was another casualty of the revolution; his private mansion confiscated and occupied by the government. In its time there must have been a lot of parties held around the garden and pool. This place was a small heaven compared to the last place I had visited. It must have been tough for all those employees to work there! Like many of them, if I didn't have anything to do, I would not mind sitting by the pool, relaxing, sipping tea and getting paid.

Age 1 - Sitting in my baby chair in our courtyard in Abadan surrounded by chickens, which I learned early were both friends and *lunch*. This was the period when mum was working on my father's bankruptcy and the boys were my caretakers.

Age 5 - Standing on the fountain in the courtyard of the Jewish family, with whom we lived in Isfahan, wearing my favorite blue suit that mum made me for my fourth birthday.

Age 6 - Ready for school in Isfahan. We had just moved to the *haunted* house. I woke mum from her morning post-prayer nap to take this picture, saying I wanted it to show my children that I had attended school.

Age 5 - My formal kindergarten picture; the age at which I faked blindness to punish the boys.

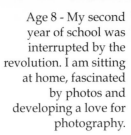

Age 8 - My second year of school was interrupted by the revolution. I am sitting at home, fascinated by photos and developing a love for photography.

Age 8 - Reading headlines of the 1978 revolution.

Age 10 - Doing my Arabic prayers.

Age 9 - City of Mashhad. Behind me is the Holy Shrine of Imam Reza, the Eight Imam of Shiah.

Age 9 - Behind mum and me is the old, un-airconditioned Mercedes Benz, the roof loaded with 300 pounds of bedding, in which our family of nine made the dreadful trip to Mashhad.

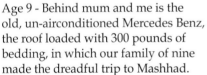

Age 13 - October 1983, a time of sickness,
molestation and heated arguments between
my parents. I was relieved that my molester
had just left Iran for Pakistan to dodge the draft.

My 16th birthday. We had just returned from
Bandar-Abass where we temporarily fled to
escape the Iran/Iraq war. Behind me is the
large walk-in closet in which I was violated
and the ghosts of our haunted house lived.

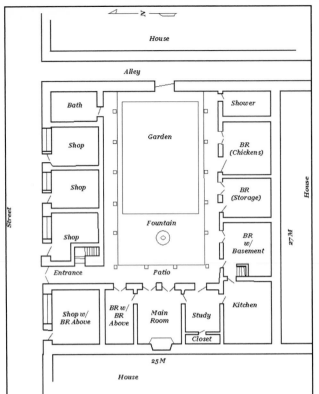

Floor plan of the haunted house.

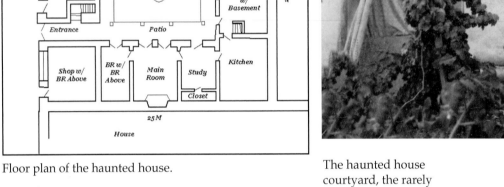

The haunted house courtyard, the rarely used back door.

Age 19 - A second trip to Mashhad after mum's surgery. Behind me is a marble statue of Hakim Abol Qasem Ferdowsi, a famous Persian poet of 1000 years ago. In my baggy clothing I look heavier than the statue.

Age 18 - Photo taken in 1989 on the last day of my senior year of high school, one month before the Iran/Iraq war ended.

Age 22 - My second year in university, 1992. We had finally sold the haunted house.

Age 24 - Visit to Abadan in1994 to obtain my birth certificate. Many years after the war, Abadan was a far different city than the beautiful images in my childhood mind.

Isfahan. Behind me is the ancient, famous hand-built bridge of Khajoo, over the Ziandeh river. A bridge is a symbol of the Muslim belief that there is a bridge between Heaven and Hell, which only the qualified can cross. Metaphorically speaking, I am standing on the Hell side.

Nagshe'-Jahan Square - The location
of Isfahan's famous Bazaar.

"Forty Pillars" - The entrance veranda of Chehel-Sotun, a 17th century Safavids Dynasty palace in
Isfahan; part of Shah Abass' quarters, it was used mainly as a guest house. Forty is a lucky number
in Persian culture. The name derives from the reflection of 18 pillars in the pools creating an
impression of almost 40 pillars.

Courtyard of Hotel Shah-Abass. The back of the hotel
leads to the famous Mosque and religious Madressheh.

The restaurant of Hotel Shah-Abass. We spent many nights in the
underground parking garage of this hotel during Iraqi bombing raids.

The Hotel Shah-Abass. The opulent interior is made
of marble with 24 karat gold used as yellow paint.

The second floor of the hotel.

Khoram-Abad - the Wild Wild West city of Iran;
my grandmother's birth city.

An 18th century tomb in the city of Mashhad.

Tag-e Bostan - Archeological site near Kermanshah, dating back to 224-651 B.C.E. The carving is of Shahpur III, who succeeded Ardishier II in the Sassanid Dynasty.

September 1995 - The Louvre in Paris; the stop on my escape to Holland and Canada.

March 2000, gaining my citizenship was the highlight of my life, one of my most memorable days.

December 1996 - Photo with Santa taken at the time when I revealed my molestation to mum, during her visit to Canada, she became so seriously ill that I appealed and prayed to all faiths for her recovery.

In the garden of the new apartment, when I applied for the "flight attendant job" that was nothing but a scam.

The perm photo; a "bad hairstyle day," during my transitional period. Friends teased me, calling me 'Cosmo Kramer' from the Seinfeld show.

Photo after I cut my hair when Lady Diana died. Friends teased me that I look like her. *I teased them back and told them that I couldn't help but notice the resemblance.*

Oct 2000, I traveled to the United States and was discriminated against by a border officer who called me a "Muslim Terrorist."

January 2001, at the village of Steveston, the place I walked for hours trying to find it shortly after I arrived in Vancouver.

September 2001, on board the cruise ship to Alaska; behind me are the glaciers.

September 10, 2001. Picture taken in Vancouver International Airport where I had a premonition of 9/11.

Summer of 2002, I finally made
it to the resort of Whistler in the
Coastal Mountains.

September 2004

After being shoveled from one office to the next, I was finally referred to a man who immediately turned down my request for transfer to Tehran. I was frustrated. I told him he was insensitive. He shrugged his shoulders and said it was not his problem and there was no way he would allow me to study in Tehran. I told him that if I were related to a government mullah or had a letter from one, he would not give me this answer. He said I was right but without a letter of recommendation, he could not do anything for me.

Even if he could, he had no incentive to help me. I had no money for a bribe and even if I did, I did not want to buy my way in. However, registering in the university without a contact seemed an impossible task.

A few minutes later, I came out with my head down. What a waste, I thought. After all this traveling, the Ministry of Education wouldn't let me transfer. My mum could read the answer in my face. She was trying to sympathize. I simply wanted her to stop talking and not try to come up with solutions for me. I was hurt because everyone else was trying to dictate what I should and shouldn't say or do with my future.

Meeting President Khatami

We decided there was no point in staying in Tehran any longer and returned to our hotel, the Hotel Laleh, formerly a Sheraton Hotel. As I crossed the lobby, heading for the elevators, swearing loudly at the regime, mum hushed me. I recognized Mr. Khatami, who later became the President of Iran. At that time, he was a Minister of Irshad Islamic in the Assembly of Iran.

Siavash went to pay our hotel bill. Mum and I got into the elevator to go to our room and pack our luggage. I pressed the button for the fifth floor. The elevator went up but the doors did not open and the elevator returned to the lobby. I pressed the button again. The same thing happened again. We went up and down five times.

All this time, mum was urging me to ask Mr. Khatami for help with my university transfer. I balked but finally agreed to speak to him. I told my mother, with an attitude, that if he ignored me, "It would be her fault." She said that was fine with her.

I went ahead, slipping quickly past his surprised armed security guards. Mr. Khatami was talking to someone else, his back towards me. Tapping on his shoulder, I said, "Excuse me Mr. Khatami, could I get a few moments of your time?" The security guards surrounded me. I glared at them and they hesitated. They probably read the anger and frustration in my face and eyes. Foolishly, I was almost wishing someone would interfere with me so I could pour out my anger. No one said a word.

Mr. Khatami turned his face toward me, surprised but smiling, and asked, "How many moments are we talking about?" He was negotiating and being funny at the same time. It is a rarity in Iran for angry looking, highly placed officials to smile. I certainly didn't expect the humor from him. I smiled back and told him perhaps no more than one or two minutes. Asked what the problem was, I briefly explained to him the situation with my transfer.

He asked me to write a note with my request. I borrowed a sheet of stationery from the dumbfounded hotel manager and wrote a brief letter, explaining what I wanted. Then Mr. Khatami wrote a note next to mine, asking the Minister of Education to help me as a favor to him. The next day, I took the letter to the same office I'd been in the day before. This time, they agreed to look at my case but told me I would have to return in two weeks.

On the way back to Isfahan, I looked at Mr. Khatami's note, thinking about the way he handled my problem. I was happy that I met him; he seemed poised and personable. I almost certainly would have been arrested if it had been someone else instead of him. Although I tapped on his shoulder, he was not afraid or uncomfortable. He seemed genuinely concern about my situation. I would never know whether he really was or not but he managed to portray himself that way. That is his secret for staying popular with people, although he hasn't done anything different than his predecessors. But, in people's eyes he is a kinder and better person than the rest of the Iranian government.

He always manages to get on the bus and take a ride with people, or get on the metro with the rest of the crowd. Although his security is not far away, he carries himself as an accessible caring man while no one is allowed to approach other officials who travel in bullet proof Mercedes Benz with armed security guards. Something about him reminded me of the exiled former president of Iran, Mr. Bani-Sadr, who is currently living in France. Both shared down to earth attitudes in dealing with the public. Unlike Khatami, Dr. Bani-Sadr tried hard to save Iran. As a result, he was honored by being named number one on the government blacklist.

After arriving home in Isfahan to wait on the university to consider my application, we had an opportunity to join a group on a trip to Mashhad for a week. On the plane, which was chartered from Russia by Iran Air, the Russian pilot encountered something similar to turbulence. He did not make an announcement but fear was quite apparent on the faces of the flight attendants. In the midst of our rough flight, the engines stopped and the plane suddenly started to fall. It didn't nose dive, the plane just had no engines. Passengers started to scream. I was sitting next to mum. She started to yell and pray to God, loudly. Although it was not a really appropriate time for joking, I tried to keep her calm and joked with her by saying, "Don't worry, we are all going to heaven. Didn't you want to go to heaven?" She screamed at me, "Shut up! No, I don't want to go to heaven." A few seconds, that seemed like minutes, later, the motors restarted and we made it to Mashhad without any harm.

Tragically, two days later, the next group was not so lucky. On the same flight, with the same airplane, which obviously had mechanical flaws, 250 people died in a crash over the Albourz Mountains.

When we returned to Tehran, I went back to the same officer and gave him my papers. He shrugged and said to come back in two weeks.

Two weeks later, we flew back to Tehran, only to be told my transfer papers had been lost. The person who was supposed to sign my papers didn't know where my file was. I told him that I would not leave the building until he found my file. If he didn't find it, I demanded to talk to his supervisor. This was uncharacteristic behavior for twenty-year-old women who came to his office. He said, ok, he would look for it. While I was waiting and watching him in his office, men were coming and going and each said something nasty about me. The person responsible for my work was whispering, mocking me, "Look at her face. She's going to cry now. She is such a mummy's girl."

Harassment toward women is very common in Iran. Most men abuse women as much as they desire. Behind all the jumbo mumbo that that the government of Iran broadcasts daily, portraying itself as the savior of humanity, there is no real validation of their claim. Men believe they are superior and behave any way they like. There are no regulations defining correct behavior and harassment toward women. No laws prevent harassment; not that they would be observed.

Men abuse women in every possible way; groping them on the streets, using foul language in speaking directly to their faces or loudly talking about women in the offices. I was insulted countless times by men in the offices, in the university or just crossing the street.

One day, when wearing open toed shoes, I was not aware my toe had torn a hole in the socks we had to wear, even in 120° F summer heat. A man on a motorcycle saw my naked toe, crossed the street and taunted me, telling me how beautiful my toe was.

Men learn their obnoxious behavior from their fathers, brothers and friends. Just about every man in the society finds it amusing to degrade women to get attention. Ironically, many women fall for the old tricks. Only a baboon monkey at his sexual peak would behave as crudely as most chauvinistic Iranian men. I was clinching my teeth and fuming inside but, realizing how badly I needed the paper signed, I swallowed my anger and did not react to his snide remarks. I waited four hours before he signed my papers, which were miraculously found beneath the top file on his desk. When I came out, mum asked me what took so long. I wanted to vent to her but I held my tongue.

Two months after our initial try, I was finally able to register in Azad University. The university, located in Zafaranieh, a quiet, wealthy, northern suburb of the city, was only a few miles from Niavarn where the Shah's palaces and residences are now large, empty museums, robbed by the revolutionaries.

The campus was another confiscated building. It appeared to me the government had confiscated more buildings than it had constructed. It was located in one of the top neighborhoods, which made it almost impossible to find an affordable place to live. We talked to numerous real estate agents who said they didn't have anything with less than a two-year lease. My transfer wasn't permanent. It was a temporary transfer for one year or a maximum of two semesters. If I was to stay in Tehran, mum and I needed to prove that we lived in Tehran permanently.

I decided we should take one step at a time and, if worse comes to worse, I would sign a lease for two years. At first mum didn't want to live with me. She had decided to go to see her mother but changed her mind when, miraculously, we found two bedrooms in the home of a friendly family close to the campus. We moved to Tehran just before March 15, 1991, the Persian New Year.

Although our rooms were located in a rich neighborhood, the house was an old, un-air conditioned relic without a sewage system. There have never been enough rentals to meet demand in Tehran. We knew we were about to move into an uncomfortable environment but had no other choice. The rooms were very small but it didn't matter because we didn't have any furniture anyway. In fact, we had to buy a refrigerator for fresh water. Unlike North America and Europe, neither privately owned homes nor rentals include appliances. The only feature normally included is a mosaic floor or, if lucky, a plain old carpet. The rooms did come furnished with lots of uninvited, multi-legged guests, mosquitoes, water cockroaches and spiders larger than a man's hand. It was a lot like our old home. Armies of the huge spiders lurked in the shady corners and the cockroaches had probably been living there longer than the owner. The kind owner did not find the insect colony a nuisance but instead considered it part of the charm of the house and didn't bother them at all.

Shortly after we moved to Tehran, Siavash said he'd had enough of life in Iran and stepped up his effort to leave the country. Mum desperate to hang on to him a little longer asked him to stay until March 28, the end of the New Year's celebrations but he left for Malaysia a few days before the end of March. Mum was very sad and cried all day long. When we returned from escorting Siavash to the airport, mum started throwing pillows and swearing at me; blaming me for Siavash's leaving. I tried to calm her down but the more I tried, the more hysterical she became. It took her weeks to adjust to his absence. But, as they say, time heals. In a couple of months she was fine and we became closer than ever.

Before I transferred my studies to Tehran, I heard stories about the city's prestigious universities and thought it would be a pleasant change to study in the capital city. I wanted to access new information coming from the outside world and get closer to the publishing houses and book shows. It was exciting but it didn't take me long to get disappointed.

Just as in the downtown admissions office, gatherings of more than two students were prohibited. Chatting was not allowed during the breaks. I noticed there were no boys in the classes but I saw boys on the street, traveling in and out of the back door of the same building. Boys had separate areas where girls were not allowed to go and they weren't allowed to come to our area. When I finally got to the classes, I noticed that the university itself was a two-story building with a wall in between. I expected I would have more freedom here than in Isfahan. Unfortunately, that was a wishful thinking. This was the prototype of what is expected to become mandatory in all university classes in Iran starting in 2005. The government is currently reviewing for a vote in the Iranian Senate.

I was not looking for trouble but I was immediately ridiculed by one of the teachers. I was quite familiar with bullying but her behavior was rather childish for a PhD university teacher. Her own unfortunate looks and ultra diminutive stature undoubtedly contributed to the bitterness she showed toward every one. She continually criticized, harassed and called me names in class. Though embarrassed, I never answered her back but I didn't appreciate the way she walked over me either. Reportedly, she was from a well off family that paid large bribes to the government and in return she was given free rein to vulgarize everyone, perhaps to salve her own ego, or lack of it. I did not know how to react.

I went home and phoned a professor I'd become friendly with in recent classes I had taken with her. She was a classmate of Dr. A. and was looking out for me, tutoring me from time to time and mentoring me to understand the new environment. She told me that Tehran was a country of its own and recommended I just grin and bear it. The woman had a history of abusive behavior, was notorious for her obnoxious cruel comments and, unfortunately, there was nothing I could do about her. She either likes you or hates you and you had better stay away from her as much as possible because she can destroy you. I thought to myself, "Oh Good Lord, everywhere I go, trouble seems to follow me." She further explained this woman is connected to top rank government officials and untouchable.

She shared with me a story that tore me apart. She told me that the year before, this teacher had failed all the students in her class to show how much power she had. My friend warned me that no matter how good I was, if she didn't like me she would fail me. Judging from the names she called me, it was obvious she didn't like me much at all. I studied very hard and got great marks in all other subjects but my friend's prediction came true. This teacher flunked me. In Iran, there is no appeal for this sort of injustice

After finishing the semester, I had the option of staying for one more semester or going back to Isfahan. Living in Teheran wasn't quite as exciting or easy as I originally thought it would be. By early summer, our two small rooms were intolerably hot and humid. We could barely breathe. Mum seemed to be quite depressed. Her health was declining rapidly; perhaps it was part of her depression and perhaps was because Tehran is one of the most polluted cities in the world. She had developed breathing and heart problems that made me quite wary. Her doctor recommended we go to the countryside. My choices were to stay in Tehran and risk her health or to take a leave of absence from school and take her to the country. I chose her health over my immediate future. I thought it might be best for both of us if we had a change of climate, relaxed and traveled. I never believed much in coincidence but before we left Tehran, something unique happened that I have always remembered.

We didn't have a phone in our rooms so I went to a phone booth to call my uncles in Khoram-Abad. When I dropped the Iranian coin in the phone, a red United States penny dropped into the change holder. I had never seen one before. I took it as a lucky sign and, for some reason I knew I would be leaving Iran soon. I just didn't know exactly when, why or how.

†HE WİLD WİLD WESŦ OF İRᗩΠ

My grandparents had retired to Khoram-Abad, my grandmother's birthplace in western Iran. It was certainly more countryside than I had ever known. We decided to move there for one year. The capital of Loerestan province, it was a small town of a few thousand prior to the revolution. It is located in the heart the Zagross Mountains, the second largest mountain range in the country, at an altitude of approximately 1,200 meters above sea level. The city is spread around in the valleys, surrounded by mountains that enfold her like a baby in its mother's arms. From an airplane it is similar to a large phoenix nest. The natural obstacles make it a nearly impossible city to capture. During the eight years war, Khoram-Abad was bombarded constantly but was never captured by the enemy.

Altitude, weather, natural beauty, hot and cold springs; the ancient history had made this little town a getaway paradise for many people escaping from the south's summer heat. Tourists used to flood the city and archeologist from around the world came to walk on cobblestone roads from thousands of years B.C. In the time of the Shah, treasure hunters used to walk around the old city searching for small treasures. Artifacts, animal motifs, and crosses, presumably made in the seventh and eight century B.C., by local metal workers of the Scythian, Cimmerian and Median Nomads cultures, were found.

Falk-Ol-Afalk, in English it means empyrean or heavenly, the tallest building, sits above the city on top of an egg shaped rock. It was built in the Sassanids era and was originally used as a fire temple, to worship God. The Zoroastrian priesthood was immensely powerful during the Sassanid period. Zoroaster, himself was one of the 124,000 prophets. His holy book is called Avesta. His name and book are mentioned in Koran. Zoroastrianism, the religion of most people during the seventh century B.C., became the state religion during the Sassanid era and there are many monuments in Iran built for worshipping God in the form of fire, particularly in the west of the country.

This religion is one of the three accepted minorities in Iran, the other two being Christians and Jews. Temple fire worship ceremonies are still practiced by many in the cities of Yazd, Kerman and Tehran.

In later years, after Arabs defeated the Sassanids, the castle served as a military headquarters. The dank, dark cells and dungeons were still used 1,000 years later by Reza Shah. My great uncle's family spent many months in these cells. His son, Mohammad Reza Shah ended the use of the castle as a prison in the early 1970s. In 1977, it was converted to an archeology museum. On one side, the museum, constructed about 1000 A.D., is accessible by the original 120 narrow seven-inch steps carved into the stone. It can be reached on the backside by a new road.

Khoram-Abad has been occupied but has never been completely destroyed by any of the occupiers. Its people are not only farmers; they proved, in the past, to also be fierce fighters and warriors. People of Loerestan province are direct descendents of Kurds and their language is a dialect of the ancient Kurdish language. Lures are generally good natured, kindhearted, extremely hospitable and generous people with loud, low-pitched voices and extreme curiosity about strangers. The people of Khoram-Abad, although they seem more religious after the revolution, still follow many of their own tribal rules that have nothing to do with Islam. And, even though they are devoted Muslims, they are quite light hearted and joke around about heaven and hell.

One of the jokes I heard in Khoram-Abad was about a man baptized into Islam who wanted to know more about the religion. He asked the mullah about heaven and hell. The mullah told him there is a bridge between the two for Muslims; all good people cross over the bridge to get to heaven and all the bad people fall into the Hell on their way across. The man asked the mullah to describe the bridge. The mullah told him; it is miles long, sharp as a sword, narrow as a hair and hot as an oven. The newly converted man was aghast. He said to the mullah, "What bridge are you talking about? The road ahead is closed."

Many women still wear traditional clothing, which is identical to that of Kurdish people. At first glance, its residents are mostly local villagers who dress in their local custom and speak an old dialect. Traditionally, people used the town as their winter quarters and returned to their country homes in summer. Lack of jobs and nation wide security has forced the villagers to search for sanctuary in the city where they stay as boarders all year round. With no shortage of guns and mild winters, the job hunters assume it is their inherent right to hunt and their conscience is not troubled if they destroy the wild life. With four season weather, green, serene, mountain ranges, beautiful woods, plenty of wild medicinal plants, natural beauty, mysterious caves and abundant wildlife, including cougar, brown and black bears, and other endangered specifies, this city was a definite must see tourist destination during the reign of the Shah. However, since the revolution, there is no protection for anyone, and certainly none for wild animals. It has become a large city with over half a million population but it is still just an over-populated small town; under constructed with no highways, major roads or tall buildings, never mind a high rise.

As I mentioned, my maternal grandmother was born in Khoram-Abad and moved her children back to this city after my grandfather retired. Although, she had moved to Kermanshah in the early years of her life and later to Abadan, she never lost the affection for her birthplace or her love for the ancient times. She was an authentic museum piece in many ways. She dressed in traditional clothing, spoke in her traditional dialect and constantly fantasized about the 'good old times.' Until the late 1950s she enjoyed riding on horses and in buggies in Khoram-Abad. To her, the miracles of the modern world were nothing but nuisances. She even lost her eyesight because she would not see an optometrist. She liked to slow roast lamb over an open fire, churn butter in a goat skin bag, milk cows and wash dishes in the river, even though she had never lived on a farm and always had others to do her chores. She never lost her love for the primitive life that closely resembled the life of early setters to America in the seventeenth century; a tough life we can't imagine living. She was a throwback to the cave women and loved every minute of her life. Like many women of her rank and mentality, she strived for the simple life. Unfortunate decisions she made for my mother directly affected my mother's entire life and indirectly influenced my life as well. If my mother had been allowed to go on with her life and continue her education she might have married a man who would have been a better father for her children; someone who could be there for us or at least be there for her.

Khoram-Abad was indeed a suitable town for grandma. Since the old times not much had changed with the exception of the traffic. The city still looks very old. People who can afford it build their houses of steel and brick but most buildings, are still made of native stone and the roofs are made from trees provided by the nearby forests. Major roads are asphalt but back alleys are still earthen. The locals have discovered many caves around the city containing amazing archeological footprints. Archeologically, Khoram-Abad has the potential for more discoveries in the future. Small artifacts from different areas are evidence that ancient history has touched the city but, to an outsider, this part of the country is still raw, with more untouched areas and resources than the rest of Iran combined. Its history is definitely different than that of Kermanshahan or Isfahan provinces. It lacks sophistication; it is primitive and quite ancient, dating back nearly 3000 B.C. to the Sumerian culture.

As a child, I visited the city in the summertime. Walking around with my grandmother, everyone knew who I was. It was a habit of my grandma to talk to people. Unfortunately, she never knew how much is too much. She revealed family secrets and gossiped to neighbors and just about everyone who said, "Hi," to her. Strangers were trying to be kind and kissing me to show affection. I was tolerant of their behavior most of the time but in some cases it was unpleasant when I was smooched too many times, and smelled their saliva on my face and hair.

In public, grandma seemed very kind, but inside she would compare me with my cousins and kept telling me, "You are not pretty enough." She had not changed an ounce from her younger days when she would shower my cousins with gifts while I never received anything from her. I didn't see the need to be nasty or complain but it made a lasting impression in my childish mind.

When mum and I visited my grandparents, before my grandpa died, I was nine years old. One afternoon when we were in the yard, she asked me what would I like her to buy me. I said nothing. She asked me if I liked the antique ruby earrings she was wearing. I replied that they seemed very nice and I did like them very much. She said that if I wanted them, I could have them. I was extremely shy and always polite with my extended family. I replied, "Yes, but I would rather you keep them for now. When you no longer use them, then you can give them to me." Happy, she replied, "Of course, I will." We didn't meet again until a few years later. When she came to see us, I didn't see the earrings in her ears. She said, "Sorry, I know you liked the earrings, but I gave them to your cousin." When I asked her why, she said, "Well, I love her so much, you can understand, can't you?" I nodded my head and in a nine year olds attempt at sarcasm said, "I guess so" I could see that she did not like my mother very much. Apparently, that altered her feelings toward me, as the not so beloved child of her not so beloved daughter.

Back in Tehran, when mum developed some serious health problems, her doctor told us she needed to rest in a country environment. Coming back years later to this town, mum and I naively thought Khoram-Abad would be a tranquil place for us to rest. A month before we left Tehran we telephoned my uncles, asking them to find us an apartment or a house. They were quite warm and welcoming on the phone and said they definitely would. We thought we were all set but when we arrived in Khoram-Abad in a pouring midnight rain, nobody seemed to expect us.

The only hotel we could find wasn't quite up to Motel 4 quality, even by Iran's standards. The city that I had not seem for years, now looked like an Amish community. People still used horses, ponies, and donkeys in many places and carried pistols and rifles in their hands. Our reception by the family was puzzling. From the lukewarm welcome we received on our arrival night, I wasn't so sure I could stay here for another week, not to mention a year.

No one seemed to be expecting us, which was surprising because we had phoned several times in advance. We had no place to live. The next morning, mum and I went to an agency and finally found a place. We rented the second floor of a newly built home. As we settled in, my uncles began trying to run our lives, insisting that we tell them where we were during the day and whom we met. I had had enough of everyone telling me what to do with my life. I told them to back off. Uncle Asgar said I should be wearing a chador; he said it shamed the family that I dressed like someone who just came from Paris. He must have meant the Paris of the early 1900s because the fashion of today's Paris is not a long, baggy raincoat like the one I had to wear. He was sticking his nose in my business and I wasn't going to let that happen. My response, although impolite, was the truth. I asked him, "Aren't you the same guy whose wife wore such a short mini-skirt that everyone could see her underwear? Now, how dare you tell me to wear a chador? I don't tell you how to manage your life and I don't appreciate your telling me what to do, how to live and how to dress. Why don't you mind your own business and we will get along just fine."

Although, I had always admired Uncle Asgar's wife's independence, she was a wild woman before her brother was killed in the war. She wore the shortest dresses I had ever seen anyone wear in those years in Iran and was a sorceress at manipulating my uncle. She only had a high school diploma and I didn't think she was qualified to be a teacher without the training and experience in that field. One of the regime's favors to people who lost family members was to give them a job, knowing that these people would not oppose anything they were told to do. Now, my uncle's wife, who had always worried more about her makeup than her salvation, went to public prayers every day, was a school teacher and expected to lecture me about right and wrong.

There is no standard in Iran for the education system. It does not matter if the students learn the latest material or not. Most of the books were still being printed with the same material since the Shah left Iran. In Iran, research is merely a joke. Most of the technology widely used worldwide has not made it to Iran yet. Although Iran, has no shortage of cash, brains or manpower we are considered a Third World country because of the lack of proper leadership. It is not essential that our children be raised to be knowledgeable but it is important for the government to rule at any price.

My other uncle, Azam, also criticized me because I would not let them order my mother around. Mum and I were getting along well. My uncle seemed awed by our new relative affluence and his obvious jealously made my mum's family bitter toward me and eroded our family connection. They thought I controlled my mother. Sure, I defended her many times but I didn't have any desire to nor did I control her or her actions.

Despite all the family conflict, I started learning to play the dulcimer, a Persian music instrument and also practiced the art of Persian calligraphy in my leisure time. Mum and I traveled all over Iran that year. It gave me unprecedented opportunity to work on my research about women and the way they are treated in different parts of Iranian cultures.

When I had time, I read books and relaxed. This seemed to be too much for people who weren't used to seeing us happy. My comfort zone seemed to be an annoying bug to my uncle's ears. I kept hearing gossip. I really didn't want to be disrespectful but he constantly bothered me. Uncle Azam told me I was wasting my life. I told him that I took care of the things that I believed to be important. Most of all, he was the source of family gossip. He seemed determined to ruin everyone's relationships and, as it says in the Persian language, using every opportunity for 'fishing in the muddy water.' In response to his criticism, I suggested he mind his own business and quit wasting his own life, If told him that if I were him, I wouldn't waste my time and money smoking opium and hanging with his pigeon breeding buddies.

Although raising pigeons may be regarded as a form of poultry commerce and a respected business venture in Western cultures; in Persian culture, it is regarded as reckless, vain, and frivolous, particularly for a family man. Even being a gang member is considered more respected than raising pigeons. So much so that none of the community eligible bachelors would ask to marry a daughter of a pigeon wrangler.

Our relatives resented our new affluence and frequent travels. Actually, the research and gathering data was secondary to the real reason. Our traveling was mostly for dental and medical care. We discovered that both were abysmal in Khoram-Abad. The dental offices we visited were universally filthy with blood spatters on the walls and floor. On one occasion, I had to stop the dentist, who extracted one of mum's molars, from using a bent used needle and force him to use a new one. These alleged dentists practiced wholesale extraction of teeth, even for kids, without telling them they could have fillings instead. We later heard that the dentists sell the healthy teeth to people who pay top money for dentures made of real teeth. I am not a hundred percent sure if it is possible to do that, but, if true, it is a disgusting idea.

On our trip back to Isfahan, we stayed in the hotel Kosar for seven days when mum had to undergo surgery to remove a tumor from her upper gum. It wasn't easy to watch but I didn't let her down and held her hand through out the surgery. I asked her surgeon to take the tumor out without breaking it. I feared the untested tumor could spread. The young surgeon made a comment that he had never seen a woman that could watch orthodontic surgery without passing out. I replied that I was not your average woman. In my early life's dreams, if I could have become a doctor, heart surgery was where my passion would have landed me. He told me, if I could continue, I would make a good surgeon. I smiled, and said, "Yes, if I could…"

Siavash made it to Holland after staying in South Asia for almost a year. Mum and I organized a charity dinner to celebrate his successful arrival in Holland. Mum asked the landlord to help with the dinner but he only invited ten people. I was irritated that mum let a stranger decide our guest list for us. For years, after the revolution, inflation drove the price of food so high that many families could not afford to eat properly. Most villagers had lost their farms and moved to cities, dreaming of a better life. They were having a hard time providing for their families and many were starving. I knew people who didn't have any protein in their diet more than once a year. Since our fortunes had improved, we wanted to share something with the less fortunate.

The basic idea of a charity dinner was to raise money and food for the poor. No poor people received anything from our charity dinner. Our wealthy property owner kept most of the lamb in his refrigerator for the rest of the winter. I bought a beautiful bouquet of white roses to honor the holy man who told me in a dream years ago to be kind to others. Mum allowed the greedy landlord to give that to his boss. Mum and I noticed that our landlord, a man about 55 years old, who already had a young second wife with three small children, had developed a crush on me. I looked at him like a father, nothing more.

BOYS WILL BE BOYS

Mum's personal reason for this charity dinner was to pray for Siavash, who, after knocking around Malaysia, had gone to Holland as a way stop in his efforts to get to Canada. He had spent all the money that mum had given him. Foolishly, he had sent $12,000 to Manoocheher who had been living in Canada for eleven years, telling him it was for his passage from Holland to Canada. Manoocheher didn't care. He spent the money on himself.

In 1994, I had the equivalent of US $15,000 in my account; the half-portion mum gave me from the sale of our house. The two boys, Siavash and Manoocheher received nearly US $30,000 each per Iranian law. Mum had money from the sale of our house but needed to be careful with how she used it. My money was for me to start a life, buy a dowry or to buy a modest car.

Siavash had been able to stay in Malaysia through frequent renewal of his temporary visa by briefly traveling to Thailand. Eventually, he was caught by immigration officials and ordered deported to Iran. Placed on a plane to Iran, he got off the plane before takeoff and disappeared. He needed the money that mum extorted out of me to buy false documents to get out of Malaysia. After I relented and sent him the money, with the help of friends, he landed in Holland, only to discover his suitcase full of clothing had been sent to Iran. He also discovered that the passport that Manoocheher presumably paid a ton of money for was worthless. He was arrested and detained by the Holland authorities.

Mum asked me to help recover his suitcase. We traveled to Tehran's Mehr-Abad airport twice to meet with the man in charge of unclaimed property. Despite my diligence and planning to get Siavash's suitcase back, the man refused my request. The contents of his suitcase, just as other properties stolen from the passengers, were shared among the employees of the Customs unit. The man told me if Siavash wants his suitcase back, he must come back to Iran.

After my unsuccessful attempt to help Siavash one more time, mum repeatedly asked me to send some money to Siavash but I repeatedly refused. Then, she ordered me to send him money. I tried to reason with her that I had no incentive to help him and would never see that money again. I didn't want and couldn't afford to lose my money. I surely didn't want to spend it on someone who had never stuck his neck out for me.

Mum surely knew how to make life miserable. We argued day and night and she cursed me obscenely. One day our argument got so heated that she put a knife to my throat and threatened that if I did not help him, she would kill me. From my years of experience I believed her. I helplessly gave in and agreed to help Siavash to get mum off my back. I reluctantly paid $3,500 to a black market document dealer to buy Siavash a passport under a false identity to allow him to travel from Holland to Canada. I checked the dealer's background as much as possible and concluded that he was smart about what he was doing and honest in dealing with his clients in a shady business. I agreed to take this risk not for her son's sake but for my relationship with her. I made Siavash agree that the money was a loan so he could get a passport and he would repay me. Deep down I knew this was just an empty promise.

Siavash had never been convicted of doing anything against Iran. He had no basis to apply for refugee status in Holland and could not remain there. His only 'crime' was to read leftist books that he ended up burning, swearing not to touch them again. There are thousands of people like him and Manoocheher, making up stories for immigration authorities of different countries while the real opposition either gets killed or never receive the status they deserve. For every person who lies to Immigration, there are hundreds of genuine applicants that might be deported.

A few years back, an Iranian funny guy told me a joke about fraudulent applications for refuge status. He said the Canadian immigration officer was talking to a man who said he was from Iran. The officer tells him, "Ok, that is good enough, tell me the rest of the story from the part where you jumped down from the walls of Evin prison." Apparently, all the guys coming from Iran escaped from the same prison, by jumping down from the walls. The applications of the liars are so colorful that they make the genuine applications almost boring. There have been a few cases of deportation from Canada to Iran. The deported individuals ended up in prison and, in a few cases, even received death sentences.

A Very Different Abadan

While we were living in Khoram-Abad, mum and I took a trip to Abadan for the first time in 20 years. The last time I was in Abadan, I was only four years old but I still remembered leaving the city. I was wearing a pair of blue jeans sewn by mum. I had my head out of the window of the Jeep my father was driving. Fresh warm sea air was blowing my hair. It left me with a beautiful image in my mind and made me wonder, when I would see this city again. I was anxious to see the actual sights to match the beautiful images in my mind. The reality was a city no longer beautiful or prosperous. With great expectations, we flew into Abadan International airport, which was not much more than a tower beside an asphalt road in a devastated, deserted area.

After all those years of anticipation, I was finally back again. As we came down the airplane stairs and stepped on its soil my heart was pounding and I was sweating but not because the weather was warm. To my surprise, beautiful flowers were everywhere but it was sad to see the physical condition of this city, which at the time of Marco Polo was called the Jewel of the Persian Gulf. Sadly, now it was anything but a jewel.

We got a cab and asked for a good hotel. The cab driver took us to a five-star hotel. Mum had many colorful memories of this hotel and had heard stories of how beautiful it was. Seeing it, my jaw dropped. I asked, "Is this the hotel?" It may have been a five star hotel in the 1970s but twenty years later, it was anything but opulent. By North American standards, it was more like a Motel 5 in the middle of a blighted area.

The streets, which mum described as boulevards now looked like sand road back alleys. The next day we went for a ride around the city. Although the war had been over for five years, signs of war remained everywhere. Every shell-pocked wall had a story to tell from the prolonged battle when Iraq tried to capture the city. The exaggerated reports I had heard of progress in rebuilding the city were nothing but empty propaganda by the Iranian government.

The city sewage system had been inoperative since the beginning of the war. The smell of wastewater was overpowering and the sewage water flowing through the city streets in open drains was an incubator of deadly diseases in the hot climate. Malaria and diarrhea, while not necessarily deadly, were rampant.

What was deadly were the large and very hungry sewage rats who fed on dead bodies during the war. Now, they swarmed the city looking for food. In a tragic incident, a two-year-old boy, left alone in a closed room by his mother to punish him, was killed and eaten by rats in the short time before she checked on him after he became silent. People started driving needle-sharp three-inch spikes through their doors in an attempt to keep the rats from clawing and gnawing through them after dark.

The main reason for our trip was not a walk down memory lane but to change my birth certificate. The regime ordered that all birth certificates be replaced by the year 1994. Printed in the Shah's time, the old certificates had a watermark of our pre-revolutionary national flag. The watermark, which included a lion and a sunset, was inherited from the time of the Sassanids, a reminder of the ancient kings of the Persian civilization which had passed from one generation to the next until the current regime. The government of Iran, free from war, had a great urgency to change the old birth certificates. The regime was determined to erase every last sign of the kingdom from our history.

The new birth certificate had to be acquired in the city in which a person was born. Mum and I went to the city hall. The end of the line was in another street and we didn't even know if we were going to be in the right place when we got to the head of the line. After we had been in line for hours, a Pasdar came out and announced, "We are done for today, no more documents, come back next week." We tried to approach him and tell him that we could not be here next week. Two young men in their early twenties protested and got into a fight with the Pasdar who pulled his gun and said he would show them what he could do. In seconds the crowd turned on the Pasdar, defending the two young men. The Pasdars wisely decided to let the protestors go. I had my camera handy and took a picture of the protestors.

Undercover Pasdar Cabbie

Two days later, a driver that we presumed to be a cabbie was driving us around town in a cab. Looking out the window of the car, mum and I saw the burned refinery where my grandfather, before his retirement, had been Chief of Security. Once it was one of the largest and most modern refineries in the world. Now, it was a shell; a mummy being given oxygen in an attempt to revive it. The government of Iran doesn't want to accept that this refinery, one of the Shah's most prized possessions, realistically had vanished along with the Shah's legacy.

It was a piece of junk and not worth repairing. After many years, they keep spending money on the wreckage of this ship that will never sail the ocean again. Visiting the city after many years, I asked the driver to slow down as we passed the old refinery so I could take a picture. Instead, he drove faster. I asked him again. He ignored me again. I thought he was deaf and couldn't hear me. I noticed that he accelerated to 100 km per hour. The speed limit was 50 kilometer per hour. If I had been alone, I would have thought I was being abducted again but mum was sitting next to me. We looked at each other. I asked him if he heard what I had said and I rolled down the window.

He suddenly pulled out his badge and said, "I am a Pasdar, and if you don't pull up your window I will arrest you as a criminal and a spy." I was flabbergasted. He was getting paid for driving us and was threatening me for trying to take a picture of a distant smoking, hulking, jumble of towers and pipe from a speeding car. I could not think of what possible value such a photo would be if I were a spy; not even if I were James Bond.

Later, mum and I got a chance to take pictures of this burning refinery but only from afar and away from the suspicious eyes of government watchdogs. It is hard to believe the stories of paranoia until an incident occurs such as the recent death of Ms. Kazemi, an Iranian born Canadian citizen from Montreal who died after being beaten by guards for trying to take pictures of Evin, the infamous Iranian prison. Although invited by government of Iran for a photo shoot, she wasn't allowed to take pictures of the most notorious prison in Iran. If I had been alone, I could have been arrested and executed. It is no justice to get killed for a photo. Even though that picture might a say thousand words, it is still not worth getting killed for.

THE PIRATE PRESIDENT

A rriving back in Khoram-Abad after our Abadan junket, there were other problems. The clean little city that had looked like a paradise in the mind of a child was now anything but a paradise. The former Utopia had become the Wild, Wild West and was filled with scary, gun-toting men roaming the streets. We could hear shooting at night.

Shortly before mum and I left Khoram-Abad, a man passed us on the street and made a crude remark toward me. In older cultures, such as Persian and some other nations, men use snide remarks to get women's attention. If they are ignored they harass her even more to show their buddies that they are capable of scoring women, much like Western girls and boys are pressured to have sex by a certain age in order to prove popular at school. I am not flattered by aggression and was quite displeased by his remarks. This nasty cultural habit reminds me of a gorilla's aggression in mating season. Responding in any manner makes these idiots feel like a winner so I ignored him. Romeo must have wanted attention badly; in his frustration he kicked me hard in my lower back. This was sign enough for me to go back to Isfahan.

By March 1994, loneliness was pent up in me. I had left my friends behind and now was treated like a child by my mum's family. I couldn't live among them or in such a violent environment anymore. It was unsafe even in broad daylight. Considering mum was still in recovery stage, I tried to break the news to her as gently as possible; I told her I would leave in a few days and she could come with me if she wished. To my relief, she agreed to move back to Isfahan.

On the day we decided to move, a surprise visit from President Rafsanjani brought chaos to Khoram-Abad. Rafsanjani is a prime example of the proverb, 'Nothing breeds wealth like wealth, or success like success.' The day he arrived, his helicopter landed on one of the largest ancient gold caches ever found in Iran. Guards stumbled onto a chain buried in the earth at the place his helicopter landed. They pulled the chain, which turned out to be fastened to a large lid. Forcing open the lid they discovered a shaft that led to a huge underground chamber complex connected through a series of hallways. The chamber contained scores of huge clay vases, five feet high and four feet in diameter with walls ten inches thick. The vases were filled with gold and jewels.

If I am making it sound like a big deal, it is because it was a big deal. This treasure was counted as one of a kind and the largest national treasures ever discovered in Persian history, dating back thousands of years. When I heard about the discovery from the locals, I thought it sounded like the treasure hunting of the Pirates of the Sea and was too good to be true until, in a later year, I revisited Khoram-Abad, and visited Falk-Ol-Aflak museum. There were twenty empty vases, big enough for three people to sit in, on display in the museum.

Rafsanjani's nickname in Iran is Shark. He is called that for two reasons. First, he has little or no facial hair. Second, and more important, he always takes any bite he wants with no remorse or shame. But, I think we should rename him Pirate, instead of Shark, because he has made himself a very wealthy man by stealing poor people's money. When he became Khomeini's follower, he was a penniless mullah. He was so poor that his white turban had turned yellow and he didn't have a spare one to replace it while it was being cleaned. Now he is constantly seen in the latest Mercedes Benz wearing one-of-a-kind hand made silk turban and garb. He is, by all accounts, one of the wealthiest men in Iran. If he is really a servant, as he calls himself, how much salary does this so-called servant receive per year, that he can afford, homes around the world?

It is not publicly known exactly how many treasure vases were discovered. Newscasts on the scene reported dozens of the vases were found at the site

Nobody, except those who stole it, knows what happened to the contents of the vases. What is known, is that none of it was spent on the people of the city or the nation. Remarkably, this was the second time Rafsanjani hit the jackpot. The first time, in 1991, it was announced that fifty tons of gold had been captured on the border between Iran and Pakistan. The next day, Rafsanjani, in a speech to the nation reported, "It was a mistake. It wasn't gold it was copper." Gold or copper, Iranian people didn't receive a penny of the money. For a long time, people made fun of him, joking, "He is the president who overnight changes gold to bronze."

He probably has a good explanation for this treasure vanishing, as well. We are still waiting to hear it. Presumably, there is no exception to the law that such treasures belong to the nation. However, there may be some fine print loop holes in the law that come into play when you are the President and your best buddy is Ayatollah Khamenei, successor to head the regime of Ayatollah Khomeini, the country's most notorious dictator who is above the law.

Nations may forget temporarily but history will turn a page when it is time to do so. As they say, 'still waters run deep.'

Return to Isfahan

With help from new friends we had met in Khoram-Abad, amid the chaos caused by Rafsanjani's visit, we finally made it back to Isfahan safely. We rented a beautiful apartment in an uptown neighborhood. We made new friends and some of our old friends from all over the country, who had missed us just as we missed them, came to visit. In early March 1994, Siavash phoned us from Vancouver, Canada. He had finally made it.

Summer swept by quickly. I was finally able to relax. Back in Khoram-Abad, I had been so stressed out that I lost most of my hair. My dermatologist recommended that I relax and do something for fun. Despite my fear of water, I decided to take swimming lessons. I had always been afraid to try to swim. I didn't know it wasn't the water I should fear but the cockroaches. Swimming pools were infested with hundreds of cockroaches swimming tranquilly among the people. I was terrified that I would pick up skin or viral infections. When I approached the manager at the pool, and showed him the cockroaches, he said, "It is ok, they are harmless, these poor creatures need to live too."

As we were getting settled in our home, my grandma passed away. All her life, she had strived for my uncle's affection. Unfortunately, her affection was not reciprocated and she died alone. Assuming mum was doing well for herself, my uncle sold the house that my grandfather wanted to give her. She never received a penny from her father's estate.

In October 1994, after being away from my studies for more than six months, it was time for me to go back to school. I was excited to see my friends and my kind teachers, especially Dr. A. Unfortunately the Fatimeh commandos were waiting for me as well. I had no desire to meet them but there was no way out. Ever since high school, as if I were going to war, to keep me safe I prayed to all the Muslims saints every day before going to school. Just as Christians wear a cross on their neck, I carried a small volume of the Holy Koran with me to keep me safe.

It didn't take long for me to have my first confrontation with the government watchdogs. The day I arrived back at school, the woman that we called Fatty Commando told me that I had to wear a veil. I was surprised by her aggressive attitude but was determined not to show any sign of weakness. She used to be nice to me because I was about the only girl who didn't try to wear makeup at school. Now she had raised the bar and made up new standards that I wasn't prepared to obey.

I was wearing a scarf with a clip in front. Without my permission, she grabbed the front of my clipped, tucked in scarf and pulled it out of my uniform and told me, "The clip isn't allowed, it has to go," I reminded her that I wore the same clip before going to Tehran. She was a clear example of what we called *Badenjan Dor-e Ghabchine* in Persian; a flatterer who changes direction with one group or another, depending on which way the winds were blowing.

She said she didn't recall that and insisted that according to the new rules I had to wear a veil. I jogged her memory again and I reminded her that these are your rules, not Islam's. Keeping cool, calm and collected I told her, as nicely as possibly, "Go to Hell."

My friends warned me to be careful because things were even tougher at the university than they were when I left. I could tell the difference. Clearly, there were more government watchdogs and Pasdar trying to keep the students under control. It was getting harder to keep them from enforcing their own rules in the name of Islam. The regimes strategy is to brain control a generation that has grown up taking orders and fearing the government. Like a poisonous weed, this government is shaping future generation as it roots become longer and deeper.

After the revolution ousted the Shah, the new government of Iran started a branch called Islamic Guidance, headed by Mr. Khatami before he became President. Islamic Guidance had nothing to do with real Islam. It was what the government wanted to preach and was used as an information source center and undercover spy agency. When I was in university, prior to my leaving for Tehran, the building was still under construction and did not have such an office.

After our argument, the watchdog woman told me I had to go see the head of the guidance office for the first time. I was not sure what was going to happen but, as always, I braced myself for the worst.

All of my friends were worried about me; the anguish was clearly visible in their faces as they wished me good luck. The head spy, a man, would not look at me because the Islamic Republic of Iran prohibits men and women from having eye contact because, even in a professional world, eye contact is considered a sin and is taboo. I understand the notion of Islam and I realize eyes can do many things but I had never looked at anyone in a seductive way. I looked at him, forcing him to look away. Not caring what he thought, I stood my ground.

He said to me, "I hear you don't wear a *magnaeh* or veil." I firmly replied that was correct. He asked me why. I asked him if I was correct in my understanding that the reason for wearing a veil was not for color or fashion but to cover my hair in order for me to be a good Muslim woman. He said I was correct. I asked him to look at what I was wearing and asked if he could see any uncovered hair. He said that he couldn't. Whether he liked it or not I continued to watch him and saw him glance at me with his peripheral vision. I asked him why I had to change to something else if I was already following the rules. I said he was forcing us to accept things that are not part of Islam. I said that the ridiculous government rules made me sick to my stomach when forced on us while calling them Islamic laws. I said that he knew, as well as I did, there are no such rules in Islam.

"You are right, it is not part of Islam," he said, "We do not force you. If I said you had to wear a chador to school that would be forced. This is nothing. Yet." I did not immediately grasp this play on semantics but I told him he could be sure I would never wear a chador in order to go to the university. He said, "We'll see," I replied, "Yes, we will." But, he conceded that I was allowed to wear the scarf and clip.

The watchdog woman followed me downstairs. Again, my friends were worried; it was clear from their eyes and faces that they were terrified for me. They asked me how it went. I told them, as good as it could be. They told me I was brave. I didn't think I was particularly brave. I was simply right, and not willing to let someone so ignorant fool me with a bunch of mumbo jumbo. I well knew that, regardless of how this incident turned out, when someone chose a life style they choose the consequences that come along with it. I chose to be outspoken and I knew my troubles had only begun.

In the starting semester, I picked Journalism as one of my courses and loved it the most. The government censored all study materials except foreign language Western newspapers, with the exception of English, which was widely used. All locally published newspapers were censored and many were closed when the regime came to power. We read French newspapers, the uncensored Le Monde, and, since only a fraction of the people could read French, the government didn't bother to stop their circulation. Knowing French gave me an advantage over the majority and I was able to read what was going on around the world.

Dr. A. told us to read an article about a subject of our choice and then we would discuss it in the class. Usually, I was the one who chose a subject for the class and most of the time I chose political issues about Iran's policy, women right and human rights. We spoke in French and had heated arguments. I was very outspoken during these arguments and my controversial comments caused the Islamic Irshad in our university to go nuts when they heard it from their connections. I knew they were listening; I simply didn't care anymore. I believe everyone reaps what he sows and I wasn't going to hide behind a mask in fear of being killed. In my judgment, fear is the twin brother of death. I did not consider myself an intrepid soul, merely true to my beliefs and true Islam. Much of true Islam that Prophet Mohammad introduced is based on our hearts and actions and judgment toward other people. Unfortunately, the Iranian government broadcasts and proclaims its version of Islam and that is what the people of Iran, both Sunni and Shiah, are being led to believe is true Islam.

The act of the government of Iran and other radicals around the globe is similar to the puppet acts of nineteenth century clowns who manipulate wooden dolls from above by cleverly attached strings. The dolls act out the play but the real players are the unseen clowns. At the end of the season, the broken dolls end up in the fireplace but their act earned the clown a permanent place in that epoch's entertainment society. Brainwashed people who follow the radicals are no more than wooden dolls. The clowns who survive are the radicals pulling the strings.

On another occasion, I was sitting alone, taking a break, when the annoying Fatimeh commando approached me. As we argued, students arrived in class and stared at us. I was wearing a silver-colored, silk raincoat. Fatimeh Commando, who followed me everywhere, came to our class after the teacher left. She told the boys not to sit in class when girls were around and told me to change my raincoat. I asked why. She said it had a sexy button on it. Surprised, I scratched my head, rounded my eyes and was left with mouth agape thinking, someone must have a real sick imagination to find a button a sex object. Then, looking me up and down, she said I wasn't allowed to wear white socks either.

Her disgusting behavior, illiterate judgment and lack of common sense, irritated me. I had it with her. Deep inside, I was burning in anger but I didn't want to burst into flames or to irritate her more. I asked her in a calm vice, "And why is that?" She said, "Because I said so." With the same tone and attitude, I replied, "Don't get ahead of yourself. Frankly, I could not care less about what you think." I told her she could tell me to jump off a cliff for all I cared, I was not going to follow her idiotic orders, simply because she said so. I also told her she had no right to tell me what to wear as long as I wore it modestly, without breaking Islamic laws or rules of the university. I reminded her that a few days ago, the president of the university had said we could wear colorful clothing as long as it wasn't too flashy. She said she doesn't get her orders from the president, and doesn't care what he said. I told her maybe she should tell him that in person.

I told her she was a spy and, in my eyes, a spy, especially against her own people, was a worthless person. At this, she started raising her voice and shouting. I shouted back. Finally, she said, "I'll show you," and stalked off.

Dr. A. came to class. He told me I seemed distracted. I replied that I was deeply disturbed and puzzled. The message is loud and clear; resistance to the new rules is an act of defiance not for the benefit of any group. My friends looked at me. One of them said, "Ghazal, you will lose your head over this. Just do as they say." I said I would try not to get killed but I would rather die than stay quiet and obey a senseless dictatorship in the name of God or any other names. When someone lives under the rulings of a monster no one can predict when or why he is going to kill his next victim. I did not know I had uttered words that I might have to soon eat.

From that day on, every day when I went to the university, I knew there was potential for more trouble. I was trying to avoid conflict with the authorities and finish my education but it seemed to me trouble was written all over my forehead. Everywhere I went, everything I did was a trigger for the next round of arguments the authorities had set up.

Taking five courses in each semester required lots of reading and attending lots of classes. I had to carry many books back and forth. A few days later, I got myself a briefcase. The watchdog woman saw me and ordered me not to carry a briefcase in the university. As much as she hated me for irritating her and creating a fuss in the university, I hated her just as much for constantly harassing me. It wasn't about me carrying the briefcase or wearing the coat; it was a personal fight. I knew her threshold and I was not going to let it go. As long as I challenged her and had Islam on my side, she didn't have any solid evidence against me. Besides, my fuss had caused the students to follow my pattern and that was exactly what I wanted.

So, I asked her why. Again, she parroted, "Because I said so." I pointed out that boys carried briefcases. She said, "They are boys and you are a girl." I asked what the difference was. She inanely repeated, "They are men, they are allowed to carry a briefcase and you are not, you are a woman." I asked what carrying a briefcase had to do with being a man or a woman. She said she didn't know. She had her instructions and was just telling me I couldn't carry a briefcase to school.

I was trying to make her understand that what she was ordering had no grounds but, like many of her peers, she too had come under the spell of the government. These people just follow orders as if they had no mind of their own to ask questions. They had become robots, or worse, mummies whose brains are in a coma while their bodies have come to life with the help of a great evil who has taken over their soul. I admit I enjoyed seeing her frustrated and laughed at her expense and frustration, just as she did at mine.

I ignored her for the next few days. Then, I was again ordered to see a Pasdar supervisor. This time it was a woman. She asked me why I didn't stop carrying a briefcase to school. I said, "Why should I?" She told me I had to follow the rules. I then asked why the rules weren't the same for boys and girls. If I couldn't bring my briefcase to school that should apply to boys as well. She told me they could bring theirs because the law didn't say they couldn't. I asked specifically which law that was. I asked her where it was written that I was obligated to follow such strict rules. I told her I came to school to study, the same as the boys did. I was taking abuse every day, I got better marks than most of the boys in my class but they received preferential treatment. They had the freedom to do anything they liked and I couldn't even carry my briefcase to school. I asked how women could be forced to be less than men when they could actually be a great deal smarter then men. She told me that if I wasn't happy I should start a revolution. I asked her if she was telling me to do that. She repeated that if I was so unhappy, I should go out into the street and start a revolution. I didn't answer her. I wasn't that stupid, I knew the conversation was a trap and very likely recorded and videotaped for the next round of interrogation. I left without her permission and shut the door behind me.

Dr. A. asked me why I was late for my class. Except for the time I was kidnapped, I was never late before. I explained in front of all the students what had happened to me. I told them that if one of these days I didn't show up for class, the chances are I am either in prison or dead. I knew I was flirting with serious trouble. He shook his head. I finally had enough conflict and stopped carrying my briefcase to school. I was running out of rope to climb and out of patience with the whole university Irshad Islamic, Pasdaran, security and authorities who, as long as they got paid, didn't care about the student's mental health. They did nothing to stop these people from verbally assaulting students and mentally torturing me and other students like me.

At the end of October the weather turned cold, I started wearing my leather jacket. It was a modest brown leather jacket. I saw a lot of students wearing colorful leather jackets. I wrongly assumed it was acceptable for me as well. I was singled out for another round of non-stop contention with the entire pack of watchdogs in the university. It seemed that everything I did was a threat to the fundamentalist government of Iran. Wearing a boring, brown leather jacket seemed to ignite and destroy their image, therefore, the entire university cadre of authorities did everything in their power to stop me from motivating other people to be like me.

My God, I thought, these people must have studied Islam in a mental institution instead of religious schools and universities.

Again, I was told to change my jacket to something else. I knew the answers but to frustrate the Fatimeh commando I asked her why. The watchdog woman gave me her usual litany, "Because I said so." And, here we go again. I told her she didn't remember that I didn't care what she said so she shouldn't give me that same old answer. I told her unless she could show me it was a legal or moral infraction, I wouldn't change it.

A few days later, I was again sent to the second floor to talk to Brother Hussein, the spy supervisor. Again, he asked me why I didn't listen to her when she talked to me. I told him she was making up her own rules that didn't make any sense. I said that if he was talking about Islam, I was fully aware of the rules. He said that I was right about Islamic laws but the university had the right to make its own rules. I told him he was abusing his power. He said I was absolutely right but that he was free to do that. I asked him if he had forgotten that this is a private university and student's tuition pays his salary. He said I was wrong; the government pays his salary.

I asked him to order this woman to stop harassing me and to stop using foul and offensive language against me in front of my friends or the next time she swore at me, I would punch her in the face. Rather surprisingly, he made her apologize to me. I left the room without getting dismissed from his office. A couple of days later, she approached me with charming language and asked me how I was doing. Wary of her motive for her change of attitude, I turned away and ignored her. She followed me. I told her we'd better stay away from each other or one of us might be badly hurt and walked away from her.

A few days later, mum was going to donate her old wool jacket to a beggar. I told her not to give it away because I might be the beggar that needed it soon. I went to school wearing the old faded black jacket. The Fatimeh Commando approached me and complimented me on the jacket. I told her that my mum had been about to give it to a beggar but I asked her not to because we had to dress like beggars in order to study in university. I said she must be proud of herself for creating such a good image for the university by making me dress like a beggar. She left in a hurry to report my comments to her supervisor.

I started my second semester of the third year. Before leaving for Tehran I had already taken three semester in Isfahan and took one in Tehran. I tried to forget about the last four months of hell in my life. My university ordeal seemed like forty years, instead of four. More than anything, I wanted to finish my education and stay in Iran to help people. I was thinking of staying with my mum if I could survive the daily fights. I tried to become invisible at school. I went in by the back gate of the university and when I saw the watchdog woman I tried to avoid eye contact. My mind was focused on how I could avoid her and stop her from harassing me. Every time she saw me, she did her usual up and down gaze at me which made me fume. It was annoying and uncomfortable but I was determined to focus on more important, meaningful issues.

Dr. A. was not my instructor in the second semester but I still had the pleasure of talking to him. Even he, a talented university professor, was bothered many times by this annoying woman. One of my friends told me Dr. A. had been taken aside by the watchdog woman and told not to stay after class and not to talk to the girls. I asked how an instructor was supposed to help students if he could only be in class at certain times. I was irritated and felt very sorry about the way he was treated. He was one of the best professors in the university. After this, girls could not talk to Dr. A. I granted myself an exemption from this decree. The watchdog woman knew she couldn't prevent me from talking to the professor.

Despite all the attention I got from Dr. A., there was never a shred of flirtatious behavior from either of us in our conversations. They were strictly study related and we both carried ourselves well enough to not leave any doubts that I was only in university to study and he was there to teach and nothing more.

Not long after the last incident, I noticed the watchdog woman was gone for nearly two months. My friends told me that one of the female students tripped her, causing her to break her leg. Sadly, this student was expelled from the university. But at least we were free of her for a few months.

I was happy that the second semester was almost over without too much trouble. I was comfortable with my studies when the whole picture of my life suddenly changed. I knew that Dr. A. would be leaving our university very soon. He had only two more weeks to go before he left, perhaps for France. I asked him if I could take a picture of him in his classroom with other students. He said that was fine; everyone else did it, so he couldn't see why not.

DEADLY PHOTOGRAPHS

That frightening Friday morning in April, 1995, when I attended his 10:00 a.m. class, I realized, as I listened to him, this was the last time that I would hear him or see him. I could feel my heart jumping out of my chest and I wanted to cry, not because he was leaving but my intuition felt trouble on the way. About ten minutes before class ended, I asked him if it was a good time to take a picture. The watchdog woman kept peeking in the class while I was getting ready to take pictures. I was careful to let her disappear before I took my shot. She had me confused with someone else. I took a shot of him sitting behind his desk and two more with him sitting among his students. I thanked him and left the class in a rush as I had a feeling I was treading on thin ice. I jumped on the first available bus from school and was soon home.

Not long after I reached home, our landlord's wife asked me to pick up the phone. It was a university official, the spy lady who told me to start a revolution, on the phone. She told me to be at school in less than half an hour and to bring my camera with me. I said that I was having lunch and I wasn't going back because I didn't have any classes. She pointed out that I didn't have classes on this day either but I came to take pictures. I asked her when taking a picture had become illegal. She said it was not but I had to get permission first. I countered, "Everyone else can take pictures wherever they want but when it is my turn, I need to get permission for everything?" I don't think she had expected me to argue with her. She finally said she was telling me for the last time that if I didn't come back to school they'd make me pay and I would be permanently prevented from leaving the country. I told her I'd get there when I could, probably that afternoon and hung up.

Mum came home and I told her what happened. She got angry with me and told me I was strong-headed and would end up dead. I said if that is supposed to happen, it will. I live my life; you live yours. I would rather be dead than live with my head in the sand and endlessly say, "Yes" to these people. I told her I was going to go to the university. When she accepted that I had made up my mind, she said, "God Speed and be brave." It was easier for her to say than for me to do. I wasn't quite sure what I was going to confront. Anyone who claims he has no fear is a liar. I was afraid but there wasn't any way that I could change the situation now and I had to face it. The authorities had questioned me before but not to this extent.

As I reached the door, mum changed her mind, saying she wouldn't let me go by myself. Mum carried my camera and we got a cab to the university. I was glad she was coming. Since she was wearing a chador, at least the authorities couldn't accuse me of being a foreigner or a spy. Mum knew more about Islam than all of the school authorities combined.

On the way I analyzed my options and tried to guess what my alleged transgression was. I figured they had nothing on me. I took a picture. I thought, So what? They can't hang me for taking a picture of my friends and my teacher but I knew that was not how they see things. If the facts were that simple our country certainly should have been managed differently. I had been told to bring my camera with me. I took it but asked mum to carry it under her chador. I had no choice but to trust her judgment and generally speaking I knew she reads people well. Our plan was if she felt it is all right or advisable to produce the camera, we would, otherwise we would not bring it out.

We asked the driver to wait for us in case we needed to leave quickly. I expected a pack of watchdogs to surround me and take me to their office. To my surprise, I couldn't even find one. I saw my friends from a distance. They were surprised to see me and approached me hesitantly, all shaky and pale, and asked what I was doing there. They said a squadron of Pasdar was looking for me everywhere. I tried to keep my sense of humor. I said I didn't see any Pasdar around. My friends said, "Ghazal, it is not funny. Don't joke about this." They told me that, after I left, the watchdog woman and the rest of Islamic Irshad gang came to the class and asked for the camera. The students told her they didn't know what she was talking about until twenty Pasdar came into the classroom, closed the door and demanded to know where I was. The students told them that they didn't know whom they were talking about. They told the students not to play games with them and asked Dr. A. my name. They threatened not to let any of us take our final exams. They took him to their office and talked to him for more than an hour.

It must have been scary for the students to feel like powerless hostages. I told them, "Welcome to my reality world." The truth was, the reaction that they saw only once, I had been going through for the last five months. This was just another chapter of my day-to-day life of run-ins with the watchdogs and authorities.

As I waited in the hallway with my mother, my friends and all the students and professors came out of their classes and surrounded me. Everyone admired and supported me. I was very happy to know that this small incident created a unity and brought support from everyone who recognized the government repression for what it was. As a Persian proverb says, 'You may be able to break one stick, two, or three but you can't break a bundle all at once.' All this time, I was trying to show the students—if we stick together, no one could break us apart. But, they can take us on one at a time, if we don't support one another.

I told them I didn't see anyone looking for me but here I am. I was told an emergency meeting had been called. I said I'd wait a while longer.

Mum and I waited for about half an hour. I introduced mum to Dr. A. and apologized to him for all the trouble and inconvenience he had gone through for me. He seemed delightfully surprised to find out that my mother was also an ethnic Kurd.

Finally, the watchdog woman showed up. I told her if no one was going to talk to me, I was leaving. Five minutes later she returned and said the supervisor was waiting for us. I was behaving more like the famous Persian cat; when they are cornered, they fight back fiercely.

The Fatimeh commando escorted us to the familiar second floor office to which I had been summoned every couple of weeks. As soon as the head spy saw my mother wearing a chador, he hesitated and his tone of voice changed. I could tell he had prepared his presentation ahead of time but now wasn't so sure he could argue it the same way. Very slowly he said they wanted the negatives. I said they were being developed and I'd turn them over in a week. I definitely didn't want to turn the negatives over to him. It is a national law that negatives belong to the photographer who takes the picture. It is his or her copyright, similar to other copyrighting laws and remains so for 25 years after his or her death. In Iran, I probably couldn't make that argument stick because the national regulations are not applied under a dictatorship but that didn't mean that I didn't believe in it.

Two weeks passed. I got word that the supervisor of the university committee guards, Head Spy Brother Hussein, wanted to see me but I ignored his messages. Finally he wrote me a threatening letter, signed and dated, and gave it to the admissions office. It was handed to me during class. It was quite obvious they had been monitoring my schedule and wanted to let me know that they know when I am in or out. The letter ordered me to see the head spy supervisor right away. I knew the man who gave me the letter. He was a kind man who had the best interest of the students in his heart. When I got out of the class, I approached him and asked who had given him the letter. He said Brother Hussein. I asked him if he knew what it said. He said that he had no idea. I asked him to read it. I wanted to make sure I had a witness in case I disappeared after going to the second floor again. He read it and shook his head. I asked him what he thought. He sadly shook his head and said, "My dear, these people are dangerous. They can make you disappear like other women who protested the rules and paid with their lives. You are playing with fire. My advice to you is to be careful." At this juncture, I was not exactly sure what that meant. I thanked him and left.

I didn't go to the office that day. Instead, I went home and talked to mum and almost said my good-byes to her. Mum told me to be brave. I chuckled, thinking, "It is easy for you to say." She added, they couldn't do anything to me as I'd done nothing wrong. I thought, I wish that was true. Being audacious under the circumstances was getting hard to do. The government of Iran doesn't need any reason or proof to punish anyone.

My only indiscretion was defending my lawful rights. I was belatedly realizing that from the government point of view, I could be seen as anti-regime and that was all they needed to hang me.

A couple of days later, I finally went to see the head spy supervisor, preparing myself for prison. He asked me why I didn't come when I was supposed to. I said I was busy with school. He asked me where my camera was. I told him that I was sorry but mum and I had an argument, that she got very angry and broke my camera. He asked me if I expected him to believe that. I said he could believe it or not, that is his choice. I told him if he didn't believe me, he could phone her at home. He said, "Fine."

I didn't let him respond or dismiss me. I simply walked out of his office. In North America it may be impolite but, in Iran, it is quite offensive and considered an insult to walk away while someone is still speaking. This behavior is only effective when the addressor is strong and to make a point to the addressee.

My behavior wasn't a bluff but a metaphor based on Persian literature. Many epic stories of Persian culture have something to do with Lion or Lioness. In fact, most Persian kings had heads of lions carved along aside their armchairs as a symbol of courage and freedom. In our literature, there are several versions of a story about Fox and Lion in which Fox tries to take over Lion's kingdom by betraying him. In the end, Lion walks away every time while Fox is still rambling. The ending, with Lion walking slowly away, with pride, portrays a brave character that doesn't give a damn in the mind of the reader. It is perceived to be speaking from a position of strength. I was trying to give them the message that I was not going down easily and I gathered from his actions that he understood that.

I didn't want to give him a chance, to question me or give him even one second to think about my answers. I knew that he could keep me from getting out of the university. In my judgment, he seemed to be smarter than his peers and I was gambling that he would not want to escalate such a small incident into a revolution. He'd already reported this incident to Khomeini and I believe he had his orders.

After I exited the meeting with the supervisor, I ran out of school as fast as I could. If he was watching me I didn't turn back to look but I wondered how much longer I could keep up this semi-fugitive life style before the next crisis or the next time I was arrested or kidnapped. On the way home, as the mini-bus was traveling though the city, I had an epiphany. I realized how lucky I had been so far. All those saints must have watched over me and my prayers seemed to have worked. Certainly someone, or my guardian angel, must have been watching over me all this time.

At Friday prayer speech, the day after I took the pictures, I watched Khomeini on the TV, mentioning an incident in our university. He condemned the incident, calling it, 'the act of a loyalist to western countries.' Also, in his speech, he said he would not tolerate anyone who is a USA advocate and will destroy with force any cancer cell, as he called it. On the Saturday after the incident, when I went to school, there was a huge placard hanging in the hallway proclaiming, "We will punish all the anti-government elements and will kill any voice defending America." The truth was, I was defending our freedom but not for the benefit of any other country.

I knew I couldn't resist a government by stroke of luck. I came up with a series of plans, A, B, C... Plan A was to relocate our home ASAP.

Leaving the Cat for Life

A map of Iran resembles the outline of a cat. When the Shah left, the Voice of America announced, "The Shah has left the Cat."

I went home and told Mum that we needed to move to a new address where no one knew who we were. I had a couple of weeks of study time and used it to find another apartment. We moved to a new apartment, and no one, not even our neighbors or my best friends, had our address or phone number. I wasn't sure I would be able to go back to the university. I stayed off the campus with no contact with anyone. I didn't want them to know where I was in case my friends were forced to confess under torture and let the authorities know where I might be.

Plan B was to leave Iran, ASAP. The plan included getting a native Iranian passport that would allow me to travel outside Iran. But, before I could do that, I had to meet with my friend in the passport office who was an expert in controlling the records. I needed some time before anyone found out who I was. I called him and told him I needed his help to get out of Iran to a safe place where I could live without constant fear of what would happen the next moment. It is quite a tiring existence when you have to watch everything you say and do.

The next morning, I went to see my friend in the passport office. He managed to arrange for my passport right away. But, we had run out of money again. I had to wait four months until mum and I could find a way to replace the money I had sent to Siavash. Due to inflation, the value of our currency had dropped drastically. Compared with US dollars, I had lost two thirds of my money. The year before I could have bought US $15,000, on the black market. Now, the same amount could only buy about US $5,000, not enough for my escape from Iran.

I wanted mum to join me in the legal leg of my journey. At first, I thought if I could just get out of Iran that would be sufficient. But the longer I thought about it, the idea of just getting out lost its appeal. On consideration, I realized that I had to think of a place that I could stay permanently and call home. I decided to take my chances on getting to Canada. Because of the money I lent to Siavash, I had to postpone my own trip. It wasn't going to happen for a while. I decided to face my fear, go back to school and at least take the final exams for the classes in which I had worked so hard.

Plan C was to get as much as support I could get from university professors and students. I had worked very hard; at the very least, I should finish the main purpose of my troubles. The university was quite crowded and I didn't think that they would do anything to me, if they spotted me.

I decided if the school security bothered me, I would start screaming and shouting and causing so much trouble that all the students and professors could not ignore my plight. This time around, we were talking about my life and I wasn't going to be as complacent as I had been in the past.

I phoned my friends and told them I was going back to school and needed their support. My friends promised to do anything they could to help me. I came in through the back entrance that did not even have a gate that closed. It was a long road in the middle of the desert. I dressed all in black to blend in with the other students. The university didn't have enough funds to finish the roof. Consequently, to my relief, there were no high tech computers and cameras to aid in surveillance of students. The authorities couldn't easily find me. Spotting one person among 7,000 wasn't as easy as it might sound if 3,800 were identically dressed females. A couple of my friends would walk ahead of me and a couple would stay with me.

During the final furtive weeks of the semester, I blended in with the other students. No watchdog spotted me and I certainly did not seek them out. Although, I attended my classes, students always huddled around me and the teachers watched out for me. It was a new experience in attending school.

When we finally got news from Canada, it wasn't good. Siavash phoned to say that he couldn't help me with my escape. Never mind that he had used my money for his own trip. I told him that I was in serious trouble. He said Manoocheher had taken all of his money. I phoned the man in Holland who arranged for Siavash's passport. I asked him how much he would charge to get me to Canada. He said he would charge US $7,000 to get me from Iran to Canada but if I could get to Europe, it would be $2,500 including my airfare. I thought that was a great deal, except that I first had to get to Europe.

Plan D was to try travel agencies. One in particular belonged to the Darius family. A member of the family was a spoiled kid who had lived in the US for years and Manoocheher had saved in Pakistan. Darius had left for Germany with a false passport, was arrested and deported to Pakistan. Manoocheher, who was living in Pakistan at the time, dodging military service, gave him a place to stay, bought him another passport and gave him US $3,000 from the money that my father was sending him; money that he should have saved for us but was giving away to his friends.

Darius went to the US and lived for many years before his mother brought him back to Iran to marry a girl his family chose for him. I felt he owed us a favor for saving his life and I was calling in the favor. His father had given him an executive job in the family owned travel agency. I asked him about arranging a tour to Europe but he ignored my request. I reminded him that he owed Manoocheher his life, if not at the very least a favor and begged him to help me. I needed to get to Europe fast and I didn't have the surety bond he was asking for. I told him that, if it would help, that my mother was coming back. I realized I was talking to deaf ears. He was incompetent and was a friend only when he was in need but, at this point, he didn't need anything. Of course Manoocheher himself, who had received plenty of money from us, said he had paid his own debts and didn't have any money. Saving my life wasn't on his short list of things to do.

Disappointed and frustrated, I explained the situation to my family doctor whom I had known since I was a child. He went to France during the summer, returning to Iran in the fall. He asked what he could do for me. I told him I needed an invitation to visit France. He told me to sit tight until he left at the end of month and get in touch with him in Paris. A month later, he charged me 500 Francs for sending an invitation for mum and me visit him in his Paris home for two months. Of course we didn't want to stay with him but we needed to get to Paris to travel to Holland.

This became plan E. I knew I had to get to Europe soon and I didn't want to waste any time. As soon as I received the invitation, mum and I were on the next flight to Tehran. We went to the French embassy. My mum got her visa but I was denied one. I decided if they were not going to help me, I would ask for asylum if I had no other alternative left.

This became Plan Z. I was not quite sure France would accept me. The country had worked so hard and long for a relationship with Iran that it was unlikely it would risk damaging their economic relationship for an Iranian citizen.

I was out of alphabet. I prayed that I would not get that far. I was confused and hopeless, wondering what's next?

For a minute, I really thought I had run out of plans and options and ended up in a dead end lane, as we say in Persian. Then, one of the embassy employees told me privately that if I could prove it would not hurt my studies to be out of Iran for a month, she would help me with a visa. Without knowing exactly how I was going to do that, I responded that of course I could. A university professor, who was getting his own visa, overheard our conversation and backed up my story. To my surprise, he said he would guarantee that traveling to France, even though I would be a month late for my classes would be a great learning experience. He said he encouraged his students to travel out of the country. In his opinion, the benefits outweighed missing a few classes. I was pleasantly astonished. I think of myself as a pretty generous person but I would be reluctant to guarantee a complete stranger. He shocked me by his confidence in me. The lady, who to her credit was very kind and considerate, took the professor's guarantee and words to the ambassador. About ten minutes later, she came back with my passport in her hand and a visa for a month. The visa allowed me to travel throughout Europe without being stopped.

I hugged her and thanked her a million times. I thanked the professor, whose name, regrettably, I didn't even ask. They both made a huge difference in my life. They reaffirmed my trust that where there is a God, there are no worries. His will reaches out a hand to you when hope seems to be fading.

I ran toward the exit. I could hear my mum on the other side of the foot thick embassy exit door. She had been waiting all afternoon, wondering if I might have asked for asylum. She was crying and banging on the gate, begging to see me. I could hear her, knocking on the door; asking God what happened to her daughter. Tears streamed down her face. When I came out, her face lit up like a child reunited with its mother. She ran to me. I wiped her tears, hugged her and told her everything was going to be all right and we should get our tickets.

The visa gave me a tight margin of 31 days preparation for my travel and was valid for 30 days traveling inside France. At the first opportunity, we reserved our tickets for September 9, 1995. Mum wanted to see Manoocheher after being apart from him for twelve years. Mum was excitedly optimistic, as happy as any mother united with her child would be. He, however, wasn't as eager to see her. On the pilgrimage to Mecca, I had tried very hard and decided to forgive Manoocheher for molesting me. I rationalized that he had been young, with raging hormones. I was a naïve child. It was all a mistake that should be forgiven and forgotten. The awful memory had faded and I resolved to try to love him as a brother.

Now, I had mixed feelings about this reunion. My female intuition was telling me I would regret it and it would not have a happy ending. Although I thought I had forgiven him, I wasn't particularly interested in seeing him. I predicted mum was going to be disappointed but didn't want to crush her. As soon as we arrived back at our hotel room, mum ran to the phone to tell him we had booked our trip. When she told him they would see each other soon, he responded in an unenthusiastic, disappointing way, "Well, that's great, but I don't have the money to go to Europe." Mum was saddened. I picked up the phone and asked him what happened to all the money we sent him. He came up with a bunch of phony reasons, and lied about how the fake passport for Siavash had cost him all his life savings. I knew he was lying because I was the one who bought Siavash's passport.

I told him that he had to find money somehow, because, whether he comes or not, mum and I were going to Europe. Mum cried after this phone call. She said he didn't want to see her after all these years of crying for him. In the midst of our poverty, she was sending him gifts. And then, she said, "What a waste." I gave mum my love but couldn't bring myself to comfort her about the gifts and money she had wasted on him. I thought to myself, that's Manoocheher, I was sure he will find a way to charm his way back into her heart again.

I packed my suitcases. Several times, mum wanted to call off her trip but I reminded her she was going to Europe because of me, not him. My intentions were for her to get of out of that depressing environment and have a bit of fun.

Finally, we were really ready to leave the country. My friend in the passport office made sure no one had my records for at least a couple of months. The day of departure, I still wasn't quite sure if I was going to make it or be called a few minutes before the flight took off. I was extremely nervous and could hear my heart beat. Even when I sat down in the airplane, I still was nervous. As we headed into the sky, I prayed to God and left myself in His hands. Finally, the airplane took off. I still wasn't really sure I had made it out, until we entered Turkey's airspace. Only then, did I breathe a sigh of relief and relax. At this point, I knew they couldn't stop the plane. I looked out the window and shed tears, saying my good-byes and God-bless my country. I prayed that some day my homeland would be free and vowed to love her forever. In my mind I bent and kissed the soil. I knew I would not soon be back, if ever.

After I left the country, one of my close friends and confidants phoned mum and told her that the watchdog woman who had made my life miserable was no longer at the university. She told mum that one of my female instructors became so angry with this woman and her rude attitude that she complained to the president of the university. All the professors supported her and didn't teach their classes for a few days. Finally, the watchdog woman was fired. No matter how little I accomplished, I am happy that I did something. I ignited a fire that wasn't there before me. The students and teachers now realized that, hand in hand, they are strong and can accomplish what they thought was impossible.

On Canada's Doorstep

Prior to our departing for Paris on the first leg of my journey, Manoocheher phoned mum from Canada and let her know that he was coming to Paris to meet her. Mum was excited and I was excited for her. She was fidgeting and couldn't sit straight at the edge of her seat. It was almost as if she was giving birth to him again. The anticipation of seeing him after twelve years had made her noticeably nervous. On September 16, 1995, after a six-hour flight, mum and I arrived at Orly airport in Paris, the city of romance, fashion and freedom.

Even the fresh air seemed fresher than in Iran. The weight of constant worry and the strain of looking over my shoulder had been lifted. It was liberating to feel free for the first time, ever. At twenty-five, I was at the peak of my youth but looked older and more stressed out than most of my peers. I had endured a hell of a life, managing only to survive and exist. I had not made any elaborate plans to celebrate the biggest day on the biggest journey of my life. Arriving at France's largest airport wrapped in a light silk fabric with a large scarf covering my head and wrapped around my neck. I was, more or less, a fashion disaster. I wasn't sure I was ready to remove the head cover permanently. I wasn't taking my temporary freedom for granted. There was a very good chance I could be sent back to Iran. I wanted to move gradually, for my own sake. My troubles in Iran were not about clothes or make up or fashion; it was about true freedom. I knew Manoocheher was probably not even aware of the troubles people like me had to face. He didn't care if the rest of the country was in hell; he was safe.

As I grew up, Manoocheher enjoyed rubbing his nose in my business and I could see that he was trying to force his opinion on me again, probably to liberate me from my outdated clothes and frame of mind. I was nearly ready to push my claws into his throat. After an hour walking around the airport, we finally spotted Manoocheher. It was a very emotional reunion. Mum was crying with happiness and Manoocheher pretended to shed tears to impress her. The first thing mum noticed and remarked on was how much older he looked. Although he was only thirty-three years old, he appeared to be in his forties. He said it was because he had worked so hard the last few years.

Knowing Manoocheher was a hardcore party boy I had a hard time swallowing his explanation. His appearance caused me to raise an eyebrow. He must have thought of himself as a rock star. He was wearing an unbuttoned silk shirt, jeans so tight they must have cut blood vessels in his legs and a cowboy style leather vest. This was his formal outfit to greet his traditional mother. He knew how to push her buttons.

We grabbed a Mercedes Benz cab. Manoocheher sat in front and mum and I sat in the back seat. Although I was fluent in the French language, Manoocheher interrupted me and tried, with minimal success, to direct the cab driver. He was showing off his *Canadian attitude* as he called it. Despite the fractured English exchange between him and the cab driver, we managed to find a very small room with three beds and a bathroom.

After a long days flight, we were famished and told him we wanted to go out to eat. Instead, he insisted mum get some rest and went out to bring us dinner. He brought back some sort of food; cheese, bread, cucumbers and fruit, claiming there was no *Hellal* meat available in the neighborhood. Hellal or kosher meat is what Muslims eat. Knowing France has the largest Muslim population in Europe, I was astonished at how many lies he had already told mum. I asked him what about fish; there wasn't any fish either? He could tell I wasn't buying his excuses and lamely offered, "No, I wasn't looking for fish. I didn't think mum liked fish." Mum and I looked at each other. I said, "Right." Living near the ocean in the southern part of the country, seafood was two-thirds of our family diet. Although we were always short of cash, mum never neglected our nourishment or let us go to bed hungry.

We had brought money for our trip but were conserving it because I was going to need it. Manoocheher owed me a lot of money but, in his mind, my money was his. He was also determined to suck mum's last penny and wasn't willing to spend any of his money on her. The first night passed uneventfully. We talked, shared a few laughs and slept late the next day.

On our first day in Paris, on the way to the Eiffel Tower, Manoocheher looked at me and said, "Why don't you take off your scarf and your baggy clothes? You're not in Iran anymore. And what is up with being so simplistic? Wear some lipstick." His comments were irritating. He needed a makeover of his own but it didn't take him long to start criticizing my appearance. I wasn't really happy about my looks but still I was insulted by his comments. He had no idea of the life I had lived and was not curious about it. I swallowed my pride and said, "I am not in my comfort zone yet. I will when I feel like it." I added, "Watch what you say to me. I didn't come on your orders and I won't need you to tell me what to do." His long face clearly showed his frustration. He wasn't pleased to have the little sister he walked all over, grown up and disobeying his orders.

Unable to force his opinions on me, he resorted to the old fashioned way he knew best, manipulation. All the way to the Eiffel tower, he stung me with his poisonous words. I was running out of patience but reminded myself he had an advantage over me. In front of the tower, I noticed him paying attention to children, running around with stranger's kids. I had never seen him this way and questioned his motives. When mum worriedly asked him why his new interest in children, he responded that he had a friend with kids age five and seven and they were adorable.

I immediately suspected he must have a child of his own. He had always claimed he had never been married or fathered a child. Mum was thrilled to hear him say he was still a bachelor and would like to have a family someday soon. I knew from personal experience he was an incestuous pedophile. I did not care if he was married, single or gay; all I cared about was that he was not a child molester. The truth was, he was lying to keep using mum. I instinctively knew he already had a family. I just didn't know what the circumstances were.

On the way to Champs Elysées, mum and I were joking with each other. Suddenly, Manoocheher found an excuse to interrupt us and harass and use foul language toward me. We had not associated for years and I was puzzled why he was degrading me. I was surprised that mum ignored both the attack and his foul language. When I asked her why she is not saying anything, mum looked at Manoocheher and said, "You see, she is always like this." Surprised by her answer, I looked at her, and said, "Like what?" She simply chuckled.

The more time we spent together, the stronger my gut feeling became that he was still a selfish, despicable, manipulating fraud.

It was only the second night in Paris. I wasn't enjoying the company and I already wanted to leave. On the first night, Manoocheher and I went out for a short walk, trying to bridge the lifelong gap. Every night, after that, he went out drinking, among other things. I told mum it was not a good idea to look into his pockets but mum did what mother's do best and ignored my advice. She discovered he had already spent over a thousand dollars, half the money he had with him the first night. He looked drunk every day and was extremely tired and restless. His eyes were red and despite getting enough sleep, he was fatigued most of the time. I could only guess what he was doing at night.

I can't say for certain he was using drugs. Whatever it was kept him occupied. He had lived in Pakistan for many years where drugs are openly bought and sold on the street, not in grams but in kilograms. I assumed if someone can live in a permissive environment and not become a drug addict, it would be foolish to move to Canada, where drugs are regulated and expensive, and take up the habit. If he was, in fact, a drug addict, Canada was the wrong place to live; he should have stayed in Pakistan.

My guess was he was meeting someone. As it turned out, I was right. After I arrived in Canada, I found out Manoocheher had arrived in Paris a week before we did. When he met us at the airport he looked very tired and pretended that he had gone to a great deal of effort to meet us on time. It was a bald faced lie. The fact was, on the flight to Paris he met a girl and traveled with her to Holland. Judging from the note she mailed him, they were romantically involved. They had only returned to Paris the day we arrived and he had to juggle between the train station and the airport. He met her every night we were in Paris. He was spending money on a girl he barely knew. More and more, I realized how untrustworthy he was. The five days that we were in Paris, he didn't spend any money on hot food for us. Not knowing mum had already looked in his pockets, he pretended he had no cash left. Mum paid for the last two days of our hotel bill.

During this time, he sold a couple of fake passports that he had brought from Canada. He insisted that I should travel with one but I rejected his generosity. I told him that if he was such an expert on fake passports, he wouldn't have been deported every time from the three destinations he tried before landing in Canada. I knew he wanted me to get caught and had no intention of being genuine. I knew him well enough not to trust him. Although I was trying to forgive him, I had not forgotten what he did to me.

After a daylong tour of the Louvre, I'd had enough of being around Manoocheher. I wanted to go to Holland as soon as possible. Mum paid for the train tickets and I had no problem with French Immigration since I had a visa for a month. Traveling through Europe by train was beautiful and the scenery was postcard perfect. Unfortunately, I had to travel with someone that I increasingly detested by the minute. Sitting across from him, I watched mum. She was busy admiring Manoocheher, closing her eyes and mind to the clues she was observing, I was getting bad vibes. The more I concentrated on him, the more I could see the evil in his soul and eyes.

Still, I kept telling myself, "I am wrong, I shouldn't be judging him." My tolerance was running lower and my frustration higher by the day. He was eroding my fragile trust. Little clues were surfacing and I was extremely nervous and on alert around him. I had to force myself to keep my mouth shut in such a free environment. Back in Iran, even though suffocating under the pressure of the mullahs, I was surrounded by intelligent people having stimulating conversations. Here, I had to put up with his arrogance, chauvinism and shallow personality, constant negative sarcasm and comments about my appearance. His awful jokes, lack of respect for women and womanizing attitude sickened me. He was going to great effort to turn mum against me and, I admit, he was quite successful. After all I had done for mum, I expected her loyalty but she had lost herself in his blather. I was surprised by her change of heart and overwhelmed by feelings of being lost. Fear of an unknown future forced me to swallow my pride until I felt secure enough to speak up.

After years of litigation, mum had finally been able to unload our big, old, white elephant of a house. As a residence, it was a dump but it was a valuable commercial site and she sold it for a reasonably good price, considering there were few potential buyers. Although not at all wealthy, she was, at least, once again out of poverty. Manoocheher was charming mum to get money out of her. She'd already bought him a large 18 Karat gold bracelet and he was hinting about a gold and diamond ring and another bracelet. I thought it was shameful to waste money on a person like him for things he did not need. I would much rather she spent her money on the poor. Every time mum and I were talking, he'd interrupt our conversation and turn it into an argument. I could see that he was doing it on purpose but Mum seemed oblivious.

After a four-hour train ride we arrived in Amsterdam, got a cab and asked the driver to take us to a hotel. He took us to a moderately priced hotel, about $60 a night for the three of us. After five days in Paris, we finally had our first warm breakfast, no thanks to Manoocheher. Now that we were in Holland, I wanted to contact, at the first opportunity, the person who would get me a passport and papers for Canada.

This wasn't quite like getting a passport through an embassy. This would be a genuine passport from another country but it wasn't precisely legal. Nevertheless, this was the only way I was going to get to Canada. Unfortunately, the person that I was to pay for supplying this passport was out of the country, or so we were told. We would have to wait for a couple of days or maybe a couple of weeks. I had heard this was the way he operated to determine if the person was willing to wait for a while or was desperate to escape, in which case the price went up. Meanwhile, Holland was hosting a European Seminar. All the hotels were reserved and we had to keep moving from one hotel to another. Every day, Manoocheher tried to convince me to remain in Holland and save the cost of the black-market passport and airfare.

He encouraged this, even though he knew I faced deportation to Iran and probable death if caught. At that time, the relationship between Iran and Holland was improving. One of the conditions that Iran had proposed for a better relationship with European countries was deportation back to Iran of its opponents. In the week that we were in Holland, 160 people were sent back to Iran. No one knows what happened to these people.

At a human rights seminar in Canada, the UN Human Rights Commission representative, Mr. Capiturn, who investigated the fate of the refugees sent back to Iran, said to me, "We only can get so much information. We can't find all the facts." He said it was not clear what happened to thousands of people who were rejected by European countries. Due to his findings and reports to the UN, Iran stopped him from going back for more research about the human rights cases. Manoocheher himself had been in my shoes a few years back and knew the danger, yet was insisting I stay in Holland and ask for refugee status. We had heated arguments day and night. I told him I wouldn't last a week in Holland. I'd made it here alive and I intended to get to a country where I could be safe. He used every trick in his bag to deter me but didn't succeed. I had made up my mind.

We were on the tenth day of the trip and had only eaten one hot meal. Forget the Adkins diet; he had put us on a starvation diet. Every day, we ate cheese and cucumbers. I don't know what Manoocheher ate when he was by himself but that's all he bought for us. I don't recall a time that my mother was so desperate for food that she actually mentioned it. One day, when Mum and I were alone, she told me, "For years and years I cooked for these children without complaining. Now that I am his guest, look how he treats me." I don't know why I felt guilty; this was the worthless son she had wished for so long to see. Finally, mum suggested we go to a restaurant and she'd pay. We found only one Persian cuisine restaurant in Amsterdam. At the restaurant, I suggested mum order a couple of dishes she had mentioned she was craving. Manoocheher, who didn't miss any opportunity to belittle me, jumped into our conversation and said to me, "Mind your own business, if she wants to choose she can use her tongue to choose for herself." I was so mad at him I had an almost uncontrollable impulse to grab the teapot from the table and throw hot water in his face but I instantly realized it was not the time or place for reaction. I didn't want to stay at the restaurant any longer. Mum said if I left she wouldn't eat. He laughingly said, "Oh, I was joking." Whatever it was, I was sick and tired of his chauvinistic attitude.

The next day, Manoocheher took mum and me for a walk. He lost track of what street we were on and we found ourselves on the famous street in Amsterdam where prostitutes sit in the windows waiting for customers. Mum and I were both uncomfortable standing outside on the sidewalk. Passersby gave us quizzical looks, as mum and I both were modestly dressed, mum told him to ask direction to our address. He rushed into a brothel to ask one of the madams.

It took him a good fifteen or twenty minutes to get directions. When he emerged from the brothel, he was smiling, happy and glowing. Mum asked him what took so long. He chuckled, "They were friendly but didn't speak English very well." His womanizing and lack of decency insulted me. Mum didn't say much, just smiled. I knew what took him so long and it had nothing to do with fluency in English. Most Hollanders are more fluent in English than most citizens of Quebec Province in Canada are.

As I remember my conversation with one of the cab drivers on the way to the hotel, he said, "No matter where you are, what color your skin is, what language you speak or what religion you have, your problems are always the same as everyone else's."

We finally got back to the hotel room. Manoocheher left for the night, returning in the early hours of the morning. Mum asked me where I thought he might be. I told her that I thought he might be 'lost' again.

In the wee hours of the morning, after he came back and fell asleep, mum counted his money and sure enough, some of his cash was missing again. Like most mothers, she was concerned but terrified he might reject her. It was obvious to me that he had an addiction, but it was not to drugs. That is why anytime he couldn't find someone else he was looking to have his own sister. I wasn't going to let that happen again but mum loved him deeply enough to close her eyes and not question his motives.

Every day, Manoocheher and I exchanged the usual insults. His problem with me was I would not obey him. He thought of me as the same kid he once mortified. On the fifteenth day of our trip he said that he was returning to Canada and wanted me to stay in Holland. I told him he could go wherever he wanted any time he wished but it wasn't up to him to tell me what to do. I'd come this far by myself and would make it the rest of the way. He said I was nothing without him. I told him we'd see. He tried to convince mum that I should go back to Iran. He lectured her for ten hours a day about how dangerous Canada could be for a young woman.

I told him he didn't have the slightest clue of what danger was because he always ran away from it. When he was obligated to fight for his country at war, he hid in Pakistan. He ran from our abandoned family to his rich father's home while we didn't know how we were going to survive. I told him I was not going back into the hell I had come out of. Influenced by him, mum kept saying, "Why couldn't you be just like other girls and wear a chador and why do you always have to voice your opinions?" I told her I had made up my mind and nothing would change it. If she chose to pray for me that was fine; otherwise, we'd say good-bye because I wasn't going to take orders from her or anyone else. We spoke very little from that point on.

A few days later, on a quiet Friday morning, mum was taking a shower and I was sitting on the sofa watching TV. Manoocheher walked in the door, all happy, smiling his devilish smile that always brought back the memories. I noticed his eyes changed. He looked at me and said we should resume the relationship that we'd had when I was a child. At first I wondered what he was talking about. Then the memories I had tried so hard to forget came flooding back. I was frozen. He repeated it again. I was shocked and my jaw dropped I knew what he was asking. I just couldn't answer. I couldn't believe what my ears were hearing. He was asking me, his sister, for sexual favors. I had tried to make myself believe that he'd made a mistake as a youth and what he'd done to me wasn't intended to hurt me. But, in an instant, his words re-ignited in my heart the deep-seated hatred I felt for him.

For so long, I had begged God to make the memories go away but the feelings were coming back to life like a dead mummy scratching his coffin. Everything that had happened years ago flash-backed to my brain. My veins overflowed with raging anger. I felt as if I was drowning and water was running into my lungs. Hate and disgust overwhelmed me. I would have felt less pain if I had been struck by lighting.

I jumped up from my seat, on fire, and raised my voice. If he had continued to say one more word, I would probably have tried to kill him right then and there. I told him, "That will only happen again over my dead body. And yours." I lost it and screamed at him to go to hell. I told him that this time I was going to tell mum what a fine son he was. Mum heard us and came out, water dripping from her hair. She asked what was going on, what I wanted to tell her.

Manoocheher smiled his devilish smile again and said it was nothing, we were just joking. Then he left and hid for the next three days. Despite the fact I did not trust Manoocheher, I couldn't open my mouth to tell mum anything. Although I loved mum, I didn't trust her because I had seen her in action when her sons were concerned. When it came to my life versus Siavash's future, she forced me at knifepoint to help him. I could not predict if she would force me to go back to Iran with her and perhaps even try to marry me off. She had my money, my documents and in a collaborated plan with Manoocheher, I didn't know what would happen. After all he was a boy, very much loved and knew how to charm mum.

When he finally returned, he took mum shopping and told me to get ready for my trip. The man who was supposed to get the passport had returned and prepared an Italian passport for me. I said I wasn't going to travel with an Italian passport. I didn't know one of word of the Italian language and if I were asked to speak it, I'd be doomed. Manoocheher used his usual foul language toward me, I said it was my life, my money, my trip and I would choose the way I wanted to risk it. I told him to tell this guy I would only travel on a French Algerian passport. Otherwise, I was not going to go anywhere and would give his family in Iran a call to tell them about his broken promises. Two days later my passport was ready.

Finally, my persistence paid off. The man preparing my passport told Manoocheher he was coming to see me, with the type of passport I wanted. He brought along his girlfriend, who spoke French fluently, to determine if I could speak French. He also asked me to dress the way I planned to for my trip. I don't know why he wanted to test me. It wasn't part of his usual routine but whatever his reason, I had no problem with testing my ability to pull it off. A few days earlier, I visualized myself entering the airport. I mentally prepared myself for my trip and in order to achieve the best result, I decided to look modern yet simple. In 1995, long skirts and boots were popular in Europe. With gelled hair and very little make-up, I looked like an authentic Algerian woman. When we met, his girlfriend and I started speaking French. He was satisfied that I wouldn't have any problem and bought an airline ticket to Canada for me.

I was to leave on October 17, 1995, from Amsterdam to London and from there to Canada. I spent hours praying to God and begging him to help me. I was about to go on the journey of my life. I wasn't going to do it without God's help. Manoocheher kept mocking me. He was walking around swearing at me, asking why I was wasting time praying instead of memorizing my passport name and information. As if the pressure of going on a journey without proper document wasn't risky enough, I also had to put up with his abuse. I had enough of his harassments and at any moment I could have lost my temper and opened my mouth. Mum did not say anything in my defense. I kept telling myself I don't want to drop the crystal ball before I was sure I was safe. I kept my cool and mediated before the journey. I calmly told him, "It is my life, my trip, I do it my way, back off." It didn't keep him quiet but for the remaining hours I ignored him.

It was a restless night before my trip. Mum gave me $400. For days, he had rambled to her ears that carrying money could cost me my life. She willingly gave him $2,400, the rest of my money, to carry, presumably for me. When we got to Canada, he was to buy me a car or something else I would need. I told him that I liked to ski and wanted to get ski equipment. He agreed. Of course, I never saw that money again; nor have I been able to afford ski equipment.

I had to get up at 4:00 a.m. to catch my 6:00 a.m. flight. I was so incredibly nervous that I forgot to hug my mother or say goodbye. I only remembered it weeks later in Canada. Manoocheher and Ahmad, the passport broker, took me to the airport. Ahmad gave me £3 and told me to make sure I called my family at each stop and let them know where I was. I was to call Siavash in Canada to let him where I was and he was to call mum.

On the way to the airport, due to a nerve-racking trip and high stress level I had a panic attack and seizure, I couldn't stop my jaws from trembling. Ahmad asked me if I was ok. He said we could postpone my trip if I was not feeling well. I asked him to give me a minute. I prayed to God for support and to watch over me. I told Him I don't have any hopes to return to Holland nor can I go back to the hell I came out of. I begged Him to help me. In a matter of seconds, the panic attack stopped. My seizure stopped and I felt the presence of angels around me. I became calm and confident. All the fear disappeared. As I got out of his car, Ahmad grabbed a cart for my suitcase. As we entered the airport he told me not to worry, if I got caught, he'd be in London a few hours later. I thanked him and told him I wouldn't get caught. Rather surprised by my conviction, he smiled and wished me good luck. I stepped into the crowd. He called to me again, telling me to be careful. I said, "Thanks but can you let me go now?" He smiled and said good-bye to me. I have not seen the man since that early morning in Amsterdam.

At 6:00 a.m. on October 17, 1995, my journey to Canada started. I was in line for the flight from Amsterdam to England behind a couple from the United States. The gentleman looked at me and I smiled. His wife and I started talking. A few minutes later, he asked me where I was from. I told him I was French/Algerian. My passport name was Julia. He smiled and said, "I've never met any French people who could speak such good English." My English wasn't good at all; he was just being kind. I smiled. We walked to the immigration counter. They were ahead of me and we were talking as I went through the immigration and metal detectors. The kind couple waited for me on the other side. I was so confident that I didn't even realize I was on the other side until I'd gone through.

On the plane, I was seated next to two Dutch men on the short flight to England. I had a very pleasant one-hour trip from Amsterdam to Heathrow. My flight landed at 7:00 a.m., England time. My flight to Canada was on Canadian Airlines at 11:00 a.m.

While I was in Heathrow, I called Siavash in Canada and told him that I had made it safely to England. I decided, fake passport or not, I am who it says on my passport for the next twelve hours and must remain calm. Just before passing through immigration, I could feel someone watching me. A dark-featured man, traveling alone and with no carry-on luggage, approached me. Speaking in French, he started asking me questions. My internal survival alarm went off. He was apparently trying to attach himself to me, presumably to create the impression that we were traveling together. I quickly rejected the flattering notion that he was attracted to my genuine Algerian appearance and was just trying to pick me up.

As I was rejecting him, random ideas came to my mind; perhaps this was a classic tactic of a drug dealer. True, I had never flown by myself but in Iran I had heard of other people's experiences that I didn't need to relive myself. The other alternative for his behavior could have been he was a person such as me, traveling with phony documents, trying to blend into the flow of people passing through immigration. The last possibility that crossed my mind was that he was an undercover immigration or customs official who mingled with passengers, looking for people like me. Speaking French, I told him I wasn't interested in his company. To my relief, he withdrew.

I then spotted a seventyish looking English couple and asked them if it was ok to walk with them, explaining that it was my first time in such a large airport. I had been warned that I shouldn't ask the police for directions, as it would increase my chance of getting caught. The couple agreed; apparently we were on the same flight. They knew their way very well but, to my regret, both seemed to be marathon runners. In my entire life, I had never seen any senior citizens walking that fast. Before I could catch them, I lost them.

I discovered I was in the wrong terminal and had to walk to another. I did not have a clue where it was. London Heathrow was certainly the largest airport I had ever seen in my life. I knew the reason most people who were caught here with phony documents was not because their documents were badly made; it was because they panicked. I was getting agitated. When I saw a police officer, despite being told I should not talk to the police, I showed him my ticket. Speaking French and broken English, I asked him for directions. He looked at my ticket but didn't check my passport and was kind enough to show me the way. I made it safely to the ticket counter where I met the English couple again. I guess they thought I was kidding when I said I didn't know the way. The lady approached me and harshly commented that, apparently, I knew my way around Heathrow well enough and had wasted their time. Unfortunately, I couldn't speak English well enough to defend myself. I apologized to them with broken English and left them behind.

I made a last call to Canada and told Siavash that I was one step away from getting on board. Then I spotted the ominous mystery man again, watching me from across the waiting room. I noticed a woman who seemed very kind. I sat down beside her. She spoke a bit of French and we started talking. I learned she was a Canadian, living in London, and had a house in West Vancouver. The rest of the hour was a blur until I got on board. Before boarding the plane, I prayed one more time and begged God to help me through everything, as he had all along this journey.

I had been scared earlier but the real terror was yet to come. Before landing in Vancouver, we made a couple of stops. The woman I was seated next to got off in Toronto and I sat by myself for the rest of the trip. I listened to Mozart and looked out of the window. Although I hadn't slept the night before, I preferred to look out at the clouds, and I thanked God for the freedom I was about to taste. It was a serene scene, Mozart and flying through the clouds went well together. For once, during this trip, I was at peace with myself. On the plane, there was a movie that I had seen in Iran three years earlier. I didn't know the star of the movie until years later when she became famous. The story was about a gymnast who became blind due to an accident. The last time I saw this movie, I felt my life was similar to hers and as she managed to survive I knew I would too. I was surprised that the very same movie was showing on the way to Canada. I took it as a sign of good luck. I felt as though God was telling me, "I am watching over you." I know God has mysterious ways for communicating with us and although maybe I was too naive to think he was trying to tell me that he was watching me by showing me familiar signs. In that moment the thought was comforting and it was what I needed the most.

DARK PARADÍSE

My life in Canada, although not a bed of roses, has been the most delightful part of my life. I am empowered and able to make my own decisions. I no longer live by anyone else's rules or decisions or pay consequences for anybody else's actions. Fear is no longer in the vocabulary of my daily prayers. I no longer am forced to take unreasonable orders or accept unjust punishment. I used to see walls and dark clouds before me, now I see light and sunrise.

Nine years ago, it was much different. I entered a culture so very different from mine that it was as though I had left my earthly life for a trip into orbit, drifted off course and landed on an unknown planet. The culture shock, the loneliness, and not being able to communicate were more than I had expected. I had to learn the ways of a new culture. With the high stress level caused by fear and the way I had traveled, I developed temporarily amnesia. For nearly three months, I couldn't remember a word of English. Like an infant, I had to begin a new life, starting with learning the Canadian version of the English language that I thought I knew. So much so, that on my first Christmas, I sat down alone and sobbed for hours.

As I build a new life in a new country, I am becoming more open than I used to be. Or perhaps I have become more North Americanized. I never thought of Canada as a Utopia. Somewhere in my unconscious I knew life would not be without struggles; I just never visualized so much struggle.

For most who have a support system, transferring from one culture to another is a fairly smooth transition. I was not so fortunate. The daily passage of our life immediately got very ugly between the boys of my family, who preceded me to Canada, and me. As years pass, I have concluded I cannot change them and they are not willing to accept me as an independent woman. I had to divorce myself from them and our relationship is a chapter from my past. Mum is distressed by our estrangement but she knows I love her and, in the end, my decisions are mine, not hers.

ΠEW WORLD REFUGEE

When the plane landed in Calgary, Canada, many people got off. Finally I was on the last leg of my journey of destiny to Vancouver. I went into the lavatory and tore up my French Algerian passport as I was instructed to do by the passport dealer. From this point on, I had no travel documents with me. I begged God, "Dear God, I am in your hands. Save me."

My flight landed in Vancouver at 2:30 p.m. My heart was jumping out of my chest. I was told to immediately ask for refugee status. I was also told that the only way Canadian authorities would allow me to stay in Canada was to land on Canadian soil without any passport. I was warned that not even the fake passport is to be discovered because if I had any papers, they would have no obligation toward me and not even human right groups could help me. If they had found anything at all, Canadian Immigration could have deported me on the next flight out of the country. All I had was my airline ticket from Amsterdam to London to Vancouver. Both of the boys in my family had gone through variations of the process in different countries and been deported many times.

Later, as I discussed this theory with immigration lawyers, I learned this was a useful tactic of the passport traffickers, which made it more difficult for them to be traced or detected. It had nothing to do with Canadian immigration, had no legal merit and wasn't done to protect naïve people like me but to manipulate the trust we vested in them to protect themselves.

Without question, this was the most important flight of my life and the outcome could have been a disaster. I prayed to revered Imams and all the saints for their aid and help. At this point, God was the one that had control over my future. I could only be truthful and honest; Canadian immigration would make their own pragmatic decision about me. Some of the officers were rude and were a giant pain in the bottom to deal with. They treated me worse than a dog.

Now, without documents, I was at the mercy of Canadian immigration. My life; my future, was in their hands. When the plane landed in Vancouver International Airport, I felt lost and more frightened than I'd ever been. This was the biggest hurdle of my journey and no amount of prayer or practice had made me ready or able to predict what to say or not to say.

Immediately upon my arrival in the terminal, I had to apply for refugee status. I was exhausted, I don't remember exactly what I said, but I do remember the person greeting the passengers got angry with me because, with my poor English, I had innocently used the word 'must,' instead of 'need' in requesting to see an immigration official. The gentleman at the gate who greeted the passengers was an old man, perhaps a volunteer. For what he interpreted as arrogant behavior on my part, he went on to punish me by insulting me and yelling at me that I 'must' sit down and I 'must' shut up and I 'must' do as he said. Although I was apologetic, he continued to yell at me, ignoring my pleas and apologies in broken English. I was trying to tell him how sorry I was if I had insulted him. I repeatedly said, "Sorry." As they say, first impressions are everything. I certainly had not made a good one so far.

After the barrage of insults, I was handed to two officers to search my luggage. They made comments that I understood but I wasn't able to reply. After that I was put in a cell with a lock on the glass door, a lavatory that doubled as a fountain and a surveillance camera and mirror. There was a narrow hospital bed in the cube shaped room of approximately 100 ft^2. Alongside my room there were other rooms. I wasn't crying but it certainly felt like it. I sat on the bed and waited. After an hour or two, I felt better and started looking around. I was looking at the room across the hall. A man was searching someone's luggage. I noticed he had put all the contents of the suitcase on the bed; then he found a man's toiletry bag. As I watched him, he found a shaver, used it on his face and gently slid it into his coat pocket. He didn't seem to know I was watching him. A few minutes later, he took the razor out of his pocket, and put it back. I shook my head and turned around. I was thinking about the comment that the taxi driver in Holland made, that no matter where you go, our problems are the same.

I escaped from Iran and mistreatment by authorities and the way they took advantage of our people, only to watch a Canadian officer do the same. Whether it was an isolated situation or not, at the moment, it didn't matter.

Finally, an immigration officer came to see me. I was taken for a background check, to see who I was and where I came from. The officer asked me to follow him to have my mug shot taken. I was asked to take off the hand made boots I had purchased in Iran. He was nice to me but it was quite obvious that he was trying to get information from me, asking me where I got my boots. I said I got them in Iran. He said they looked very nice, they could have been purchased in France; did you get them in France? Where was your flight from? I said no, they were from Iran, not France. I kept quiet. I had been told anything I said would be used against me.

I couldn't speak English very well and the immigration officers couldn't speak French. They said they could not help me unless I spoke English. I asked them to bring someone who could speak Farsi. I waited four hours before a translator arrived. It only *seemed* like days.

The immigration officer, a woman, asked me where I got on the plane. I told her I flew from Amsterdam to London and then to Canada. She didn't believe me and kept calling me 'liar.' She treated me like a criminal or even less, a dog. She kept calling me a liar and said I would be detained until I told her the truth. The woman was translating but I could understand the meaning of the word liar. I told her, "Look, I know most of the people who come over here lie to you but I'm not one of them." I added, "I know you have the right and choice to believe me or not. Regardless of what you think of me, I am telling the truth. Why don't you just check my ticket? You'll see that I am telling the truth." She repeated her order to wait. Meanwhile, I was about to pass out. By this time, I'd been without sleep for more than 24 hours. I was offered food and drink but I had experienced so many horrifying events that I was afraid to take it for fear it was mixed with a drug. I assumed the justice system in Canada was based on facts and no one could be accused unless the facts were beyond reasonable doubt. I later learned that theory applies only to criminal charges and not to all facets of the law. The way I was treated, I would not have touched the food if I were dying of hunger. I did not trust anything or anyone anymore, especially someone who kept calling me a liar when she didn't even have the slightest idea who I was. I had no reason to trust the Canadian Immigration.

Finally, after eight hours of interrogation, she called me back and said to the translator, "Oh, we are so stupid; she was telling the truth, she came from London." I wanted to tell her that I couldn't agree with her more about the level of her self-assessed intelligence. After keeping me there for eight hours, she finally decided to check my ticket as I had repeatedly requested, then admitted I had been telling the truth. She wanted to continue the interrogation, but I was frazzled. I asked her to call Siavash. I told her I would come back the next day but if I didn't get some sleep, I would faint at any moment. I told her if she wanted, I could ask him to leave his credit card as a guarantee that I'd come back. I guess she finally realized I was not going to flee anywhere. She told me to come back on November 20, 1995. I came out of detainment worried that Siavash might have been waiting for me all this time. He said he'd been waiting for four hours. I had told him I might have to stay in immigration for a few hours but neither of us anticipated it would take so long.

While Siavash was driving me to the residence he shared with Manoocheher, I naively told him about offering to leave his credit card with the immigration officer. He agitatedly interrupted saying he would not leave his credit card for me if they put me on a plane back to Iran or sent me to a refugee camp. I should not have been shocked at how little I was worth to him. He had not been too proud to beg when he needed my money to save his life. This is the way he thanked me. He not only claimed he didn't have any recollection of the money I sent him; he said it was Manoocheher who saved his life and mine. As he was talking to me, admiring Manoocheher, I was so dumbfounded I couldn't hear what he was talking about.

I had a flashback of the past, starting in Iran when he left on a two-year odyssey through Malaysia, Thailand, and Southeast Asia. Iranian passports were not useable worldwide. In the course of his roaming, he used and trafficked in fake passports and travel documents. His first attempt to get to Canada was unsuccessful. He sneaked off the Iran bound flight on which he was being deported but his suitcase was delivered to Iranian police. I went to quite a bit of trouble to get his belongings back. Eventually, with the aid of phony documents, he landed in Holland where he was imprisoned as an illegal immigrant for two months. Released from prison before he could be deported, he took sanctuary in a Dutch Reformed church. Iran wanted him back for passport violations. Holland wanted him out of the country but did not dare to arrest him inside the church. Homeless and broke, he hid in the church for six months, trying to raise funds to buy his way to Canada. How quickly he forgot.

Minutes, or maybe seconds, later, I came back to reality to find myself in his car, still listening to his lies. I had tears in my eyes and was choked with anger at how little he respected me or valued what I had done for him. I nodded my head, and sighed. So much for saving his life. I wanted to shout so many things to him but, again, as we say in Persian, I realized the futility of "singing poetry to a deaf ear." There was no point in arguing; I had seen this behavior before. It is virtually a national policy for the boys to stick up for each other. My attitude has always been that when one does something for someone else, there should be no expectation in return. I did what I did for the grace of God who saved me. I remembered the story about Jesus who brought many people back to life and none ever thanked him.

After three years of being apart, he let me know in the first ten minutes my value and my limits. He was trying to make sure I knew my limits before dreaming of his support. He didn't have to try hard because I had no expectations of him.

When we arrived at Siavash's home in Richmond, on the outskirts of greater Vancouver, I was surprised and disappointed at how few possessions they had. After living in Canada more than a year and a half, Siavash had nothing except a TV set and his bedding, a thin mattress that was folded and placed on the floor, next to the wall. Manoocheher's room was empty as well, except for his bed and some clothes in his closet. There were two old, worn-out sofas with holes and grungy spots, next to the door on the north side of the large empty living room. On the south side of the room, there was an old, round dining table with a couple of odd chairs. When I left Iran, mum and I, although not wealthy, had a comfortable life style with room-to-room Persian carpets; hand made silk rugs and beautiful furniture, I even had my own leopard skin and other collectable items. I asked Siavash if that was all Manoocheher had after twelve years of living in Canada and squeezing mum for more than fifteen thousand dollars. What had he done with the money mum sent him? He said they didn't even have all this stuff until a couple of months ago when they learned I was coming to Canada. I guess this was supposed to make me feel special.

Changing the subject from their lifestyle, I told Siavash I wanted to pursue my education. He again jumped the gun and said, "I am not going to pay for your education. If you want to study, you have to pay for it yourself." I told him I didn't ask him to pay for me. I shouldn't have been surprised by the answers he gave me. I could tell he was prepared for the conversation. Although Manoocheher was two years younger, he was always the leading brother, while Siavash trusted and followed him religiously, Manoochehr didn't give a damn about him; he only used him. I could tell the conversation was planned in advance. My sixth sense was telling me that Manoochehr was behind the planning and Siavash carried it forward. In my entire life, he was never there for me; not when I needed him to come to court with me in Iran or Canada. He always said he was not responsible for me. On the contrary, he never hesitated to ask me for help when he needed it. It was a strange role reversal; the older family member relying on the younger. It never crossed his mind that, family or not, when someone does something for someone, the attitude is gratitude. I let the grouch go because arguing was simply a waste of time.

The next day I called mum. Even though our relationship was frequently volatile, it was delightful to talk to her again. She and Manoocheher had gone back to France and stayed in Paris for four more days before she returned to Iran. Meanwhile, I was using Manoocheher's bed. I mistakenly took it as a gesture of hospitality and generosity. He'd said I could use it until he returned to Canada but then I would have to buy my own. Foolishly, I didn't see any problem. I thought he would return my money. But things didn't turn out that way.

When Manoocheher arrived back in Canada, an older woman with a two-year old child picked him up. I suspected it must be his I watched him from the window as he ran toward them and picked up the baby. When he came back from meeting his so-called 'friend,' who was, in fact, his first wife, he harshly ordered me not to leave the house without him or Siavash. He didn't want anyone to know that I was in Canada for the next few months. I asked what the problem was. I thought it would be something to do with my refugee case. He said he had business enemies who were trying to hurt him and he didn't want them to know he had been to Europe to meet me. I reminded him that he had gone to Europe to see his own mother after a twelve-year absence and that I came to Canada on my own.

Still, he insisted that I should stay at home and out of sight. Siavash said Manoocheher had done the same thing to him when he arrived and I'd better listen to him. I thought Siavash was a coward, listening to this guy's nonsense but, since I was living with them, I reluctantly accepted and obeyed. If I had a choice or knew that I had other options, I would have taken it.

In Holland, Manoocheher had told me that I could have my $2,400 back when I got to Vancouver. When I asked for my money so I could buy my bedding, he laughed and replied, "What money?" He said I owed him for all his expenses of going to Europe. He said mum gave him that money. Then he demanded that I give him the $400 that mum had given me in Amsterdam, saying that money was his too. He put out his hand and asked where his money was. It wasn't much money, just all I had. On the very first day that he returned to Canada, he was trying to run my life. I told him I would talk to mum about it and she would confirm whose money it was. When I talked to her, she said she would tell him to give me back my money. I guess she forgot to mention that to him.

Over the period of the next few months, I became an unpaid servant to the boys. Every day, they left me at home, telling me to cook and clean. I wasn't allowed to talk to anyone, particularly anyone from the Iranian community. I couldn't go for a walk by myself. I wasn't allowed to answer the phone or even have a key to the apartment. This was an unbearable experience. I was dying on the inside and very nearly on the outside. I was frustrated, and did not know where to turn or how to ask for help. I wasn't speaking English. In fact, I was suffering from a temporary amnesia that blocked me from using any word of any language I had been able to speak prior to my trip. I had became depressed due to the degrading situation I was in, I felt as if I had exited from one prison to enter another.

Siavash took me out a couple of times but it was nearly a month after my arrival. I had to go back to the airport for my second hearing. After the hearing, I was allowed to stay in Canada on a temporary basis until my refugee case was heard. I was required to report my new address to Immigration every time I moved and I had to apply for a renewal of the status every six months until all options for my case were exhausted.

A few days later, Manoocheher and Siavash took me to North Vancouver, the area where most Iranians have settled on the foothills of the Coastal Mountains. I heard people say it resembles the foothills of Damavand, the northern part of Tehran.

This outing, supposedly, was to celebrate my arrival. And, as it turned out, my new status in a related restaurant swindle. The boys and I were sitting in a local café-style Persian restaurant when Manoocheher told me, "From this week on, we will find work for you in a restaurant and then we will put you on welfare. You have to work and pay my money back."

His plan also included bringing Khosro to join this League of Boy Scouts. Khosro, who had never stepped out of Iran, relying on the false promises of Manoocheher, had shown an interest in entering Canada illegally and applying for refugee status. I asked him what Khosro was suppose to do in Canada. It was not likely he would find a job with a diploma from an Iranian high school. Manoocheher replied," It is none of your business. We will open a business." I sarcastically replied, " Like the one you own now, the cab driving business?" I added that Khosro has a wife and five girls to take care of and asked him if he was not concerned that Khosro could not leave his family behind on your false promises?

He kept insisting that he would find me a job in a restaurant. I told him I had never worked in a restaurant in my life and did not intend to. My stomach is very sensitive; even when I cook for myself I get queasy from the food smell. And, if that were not enough, I reminded him that in my temporary status, it was illegal for me to work and I could be deported if I did. He said, "The way you act, one day I'll see you standing on the street, working as a prostitute." I told him if that day came, I'd call him up and this time he would have to pay. He started vulgarizing me while Siavash was sitting at the same table, on the middle seat between Manoocheher and me.

During the conversation, Siavash said nothing to stop him from saying horrible things to me. I said to Siavash, "You see what he says to me, but you keep quiet." He said, "He is my brother. Whatever you two say to each other is not my business." Most brothers in Iran think fighting with a brother over a sister is not a good idea. The men are of the same blood and should stick together. The woman is going to marry a stranger and be out of the family circle. It is a barbaric attitude. Siavash didn't say a word. Later he would not even admit hearing this exchange.

I felt like an indentured slave, working for her master to pay back the price of her freedom. The difference was, these two were family and he owed me money. I didn't know the language. I even had to use a translator in my meetings with Immigration. If I had anyplace to go, I wouldn't have hesitated for one second. If I were younger, perhaps I could go to a foster home. I didn't know anyplace else to live. I was stuck with the abusive boys. This period of controlling was too similar to my teenage years.

A few days later, Manoocheher took me to the welfare office. I was ashamed to receive such money when I had money myself. Unfortunately, Manoocheher didn't give my money back. I was granted $500 per month but I had to pick up the check in person. There were several logistical problems. The welfare office was several miles from our apartment and I couldn't get there by myself. Even though I just had arrived, I was told by the boys that I had to pay for my own expenses, including food, bedding and transit.

Manoocheher knew that I was not going to turn the money over to him, so he would not take me. I was not allowed to leave the apartment alone. I wasn't able to go by myself. Due to the stress I was under, I became quite disoriented. I didn't know how to use the bus system and I didn't have $1.50 bus fare had I known how. Siavash kept himself busy and unavailable. I did not pick up the check for the second month. Consequently, the third month, I had to reapply. I finally was taken to a bank and exchanged the money I had brought with me to Canada, I bought my bedding and a towel.

Manoocheher, who understood I was not going to be his mistress, would not take me. It never occurred to me to tell the social services why I wasn't able to pick up last month's check. I didn't think it was part of their job description to know anything about my family. I was living an infuriating nightmare under the same roof with the person who had hurt me so much. I asked mum to come to Canada as soon as it was possible for her to obtain a visa. I wanted her to see how things were with her own eyes. I wanted her to come and see this animal she loved so much. Despite what she had seen, she still expressed her love for him over the telephone.

Manoocheher sent her an invitation. He was, after all, waiting for the diamond ring and another 18K gold bracelet she had promised him on the train traveling from France to Holland. We discussed getting a new place before mum arrived for a visit but nothing was decided.

One night in late November, all three of us were watching TV. I asked Siavash to change the channel back to something that we'd been watching. Manoocheher, who was drinking beer said, "We brought this servant from Holland, and now she is telling us what to do." Both of them started laughing. I was angry; if I'd had a gun I would gladly have shot them both. Manoocheher deserved to die for all he had done to me. I sincerely believe I would have had no trouble killing him. He was driving me to the edge of insanity. I reasoned that if I killed him I could plead insanity but I was sane enough not to play God. I have too much respect and love for Him to allow myself to play God.

I knew if I did something like that I could not face Him. Only the grace of God helped me control my anger and kept me from stabbing him. Manoocheher was an animal, dirtier than a pig but if I harmed him, he would be perceived as an innocent man and I would be the guilty, ungrateful one. Living under the same roof with him was prolonged torture. When he smiled at me, I knew why he was smiling and I knew why he was trying to get me under his control. Mum, on the other hand, who didn't know until later what he had done to me, kept lecturing me that I had to be a good sister. That night, I told him he was drinking so much he was losing his mind and his behavior was getting more disgusting day by day. From that night on, no matter what the consequences, I didn't let anyone drink at home.

A few days later, mum called to say she had obtained her visa and was eager to come for a short visit. Upon hearing that mum was coming to visit, Manoocheher said he wanted to talk to me. He brought up his marriage to the older woman, who had three grown children of her own. She told me she was forty-eight when I met her. She had a son about my age, two daughters about seventeen and fourteen and the baby girl. He said he wanted me to be a kind auntie to his child. I pointed out that when he slept around, he didn't ask me, but when he had a problem, he wanted me to protect him. I asked him how he could ask that of me after insulting me, treating me with no respect and even forcing me to go on welfare when I had brought money of my own, which he took, then denied it was mine. To add injury to insult, he took great pleasure in tormenting me for even more money. He kept insisting that I had to accept the welfare money and pay him back what he claimed I owed him.

He had not married the mother of his child until after the child was born. They met several years earlier in Montréal where Manoocheher lived for five years before moving to Vancouver. He was living in her home and had seduced her into starting a relationship. She divorced her husband, who was waiting in Iran to immigrate to Canada as soon as she received landed immigrant status. When Manoochehr relocated to Vancouver, he helped her join him and they picked up where they left off. Shortly after that, the little baby girl came along. As soon as I met them, I knew he wanted to sleep with the woman's daughter, his stepdaughter. I learned through family gossip that he admitted to mum and my father that he married her because he wanted her twelve-year-old daughter. Meanwhile, he was sleeping around with a few other women. Siavash, two years older than Manoocheher, couldn't care less. I asked Siavash how he could watch Manoocheher doing this to himself and other people and do nothing. He said it was Manoocheher's life and if he thought it was all right, he did not care what he did.

In late January 1996, four months after my arrival, the ban on my going out was lifted and Siavash insisted that I should start going for walks. He finally relented because I had to rely on him for my every move and he wasn't all too happy about it. He had driven me around a few times since my arrival and I wanted to go to Steveston, a beautiful, historical beach community about eight miles southwest of our home. Manoocheher and Siavash were working from 4:00 p.m. to 4:00 a.m. They would get home from work in the early morning and sleep most of the day.

One sunny morning, around 9:00 a.m., I started walking toward the water, I thought. I walked for hours and hours until my feet started to go numb. Exhausted, I asked a gentleman riding a bike how far I was from the water. He said, "Water?" In my best, broken English, I said, "Yes, in Steveston." He said, "You are going the wrong way! It will take you another seven hours walking to get there!" I turned around in defeat. Miraculously, I lost my way again and ended up on the dike at the end of Number Three Road, still miles from where I started. By this time, it was 3:00 p.m. I thought, the boys were surely up by now and perhaps were worried about me since it was quite unlike me not to be at home cooking and cleaning at this time of the day.

I got a quarter, found a pay phone and called home. Manoocheher and Siavash picked up the phone at the same time. I said "Hello." Someone on the other end with a sleepy voice said, "HELLO!" It was Manoocheher. I said, "I am sorry I am not home, I just wanted to let you know I am lost." He yelled, "WHO CARES! You ruined my sleep! You are lost, you are lost!"

I felt dizzy. My face was flushed and my heart was pounding so incredibly hard that I could hardly breathe. I had an indescribable feeling of defeat and abandonment. I realized Siavash insisted that I get acquainted with the city and be on my own so I would not have any reason to bother him. At first I welcomed the idea but with overwhelming stress, depression and other health problems, I had developed social phobia. As soon as I left the apartment, I became nervous and frightened, perspired and felt almost nauseous in the crowd. After the phone call, I sat down at the side of the road and held my head in my hands. I had to relearn everything and learn it fast so I could have a life of my own. It took me another 3 hours to walk home. It was very late by the time I staggered in the door. I thought, I would rather live in a foster home than have such a family. On my walk, I had plenty of time to think about my new ordeal. By the time I got home, I had forgotten my phobia. It was the push that I needed.

The next morning, I summoned up the courage to board the bus to Vancouver. I got off in the bustling downtown, found Dave Street and registered myself at immigration services in the ESL, English as a Second Language, course for new immigrants. Although Siavash had arrived a year and half before me, his English wasn't any better than mine. He saw a social opportunity in ESL and came along with me. He immediately took a liking to one of my Iranian classmates and wanted to marry her. Ever since I can remember, he has insinuated himself between me and my friends and I detested him for it. The first time I met her, I invited her to ride in Siavash's car. He harshly told me that I wasn't to invite others without his permission. However, after taking a liking to her, he insisted on giving her rides even though she seemed uncomfortable accepting his offer.

The egotistical behavior of most Iranian men is deplorable and Siavash is no exception. Even so, she and I became good friends.

Little by little, he asked her to come home with him. I said to him, "If you think you can ask her to marry you, you better dream on that. She is only 18 years old, and you are 35. Is there something wrong with you?" I later learned from Manoocheher's ex-wife, that the boys were planning a wedding in their mind. Siavash's persistence in seeing this girl eventually destroyed my friendship with her, as it did my friendship with other girls. I had had enough of him. I tried to find a job and another place to live. I wanted to become independent. This didn't sit well with the boys and their Iranian mentality. They did everything they could to keep me under their control.

I started leaving home at 7:00 a.m. to walk to the library, which wasn't that far, to teach myself how to type with a computer keyboard. Back in Iran I had taken typing lessons and practiced on a Farsi typewriter but I had never touched a computer keyboard before. The first time I asked for a computer, I had no real concept of what a computer was. A librarian asked me, "Would you like Mac or PC?" I replied, "What is the difference?" I still laugh at my own reply but it truly is very sad to know how far Iran was behind in technology in 1995; almost 99 percent of students had never used a computer.

I wanted to learn more about the Canadian culture and found it fascinating. Most Canadians I met during the preliminary stages of my life in Canada were kind and gave me the love I didn't have at home. They sincerely and genuinely opened their arms and showed me the humanity and the safe home I was looking for. I embraced the idea of being in Canada and being welcomed as part of the Canadian family.

I was at home less and less, which didn't matter to the boys, of course. The only thing that mattered was if I had cleaned and cooked prior to leaving. I signed up at a health club. It took me about forty minutes to walk there but I used any excuse I could find to get out of the house. I wanted to melt into the Canadian culture. To learn more about North America, in general, I signed up for any potential venture, organization or activity I came across that might help me understand the new culture. I left my name and number all over town as either a volunteer or as a person who needed work. Some days I received as many as twenty-five calls.

One day, around 9:00 a.m., the phone rang and Siavash and Manoocheher both ran out their rooms yelling at me, "Who is calling you at this time of the day? Who are these guys?" I said "This time of the day? This is working hours and I am looking for a job so I can get out of here." They were both half-naked and it was as if they had pre-planned their argument. They replied, "You can't use this phone any more. We need our sleep. We work hard." I said, "What are you talking about? I pay a portion of the rent on this house, I pay for the phone and you cannot tell me not to use it. Don't put the phone in your room if you don't want to wake up. When you have a phone call, I have to come and call you. You won't even pick up your own phone!" I walked away. They yelled at me, "Don't walk away from us when we are talking to you." I said to them, "That was a century ago. You are not my father and you don't act like responsible family members." I left home to hunt for a job.

Mum phoned in early March of 1996 and gave me the good news that she was set to come to Canada for Persian New Year, March 15, 1996. We needed to find a new place. In addition, we had to do something about the awful looking sofas they had. Manoocheher's actions were quite calculating. In collaboration with Siavash, he took me to an apartment he had located on the edge of the city, so far away that even with a car it would have taken half an hour to reach it. It was impossible for me to walk that distance. Even walking from the nearest bus stop, a kilometer away, was dangerous. It would have been a great way to keep me under his control.

He said I was to pay rent from the money I got from welfare but he didn't ask me if I liked the two bedroom apartment. When I asked him where I was to sleep, he said I had to sleep on the floor in the living room. I asked him why I should pay and then sleep on the floor. He parroted his mantra that I owed him money.

I told him I didn't want to move to the place he found. It was in a neglected rural area and would have been impossible for me to manage without a car. I told him I'd find a place. With much searching, I found a new centrally located condo townhouse with four bedrooms and three bathrooms. I bargained the rent down from $1,300 to $1,150 per month. From the little money the government gave me, I agreed to pay $300, plus one third of utilities, so they would not think I was in their debt for the rest of eternity. Each of them would pay $425 a month. When we were ready to move in, the boys wanted me to live in the basement. I told them that I was not moving in at all unless I had the master bedroom to share with mum. They reluctantly agreed but resented it and inevitably made my life even more difficult. Manoocheher brought a sewing machine home and for seven days and nights we labored to recover the sofas. He could have bought new sofas for the cost of the fabric. I couldn't understand the logic in this; he had to do everything the hard way.

The boys knew I didn't appreciate seeing them nearly naked, even though we were siblings. I found it immoral and showing lack of respect for me to run around the way they did. To aggravate me, Manoocheher walked around with only a towel around him or very short shorts or jockey shorts. I detested him. Soon, Siavash copied him. Every time Manoocheher looked at me, I could see his eyes changing. I was at the end of my rope. To keep myself busy, I started interacting with more and more people. I started ice-skating. I had very little money to spare on lessons and I bought the cheapest skates possible. Every time I went ice-skating; I made more friends, so the bruises were worth it. I fell so many times it became funny. Every time I fell, a horde of men ran to my rescue.

After one great fall, a lady looked at me and asked if I was alone on the ice. I said, "Yes." She asked, "Then who are all of these gentleman running to you?" I laughed and said, "I don't know, perhaps they thought I broke something." I hurt myself quite badly. I ended up in emergency twice, yet I still loved going back on the ice. The doctor who was treating me said, "I say you are crazy but, if it makes you happy, I say go for it." Skating helped me keep my spirits alive and high.

I had noticed most Iranians are not emotionally open to other cultures. In my family, I was the only one who wanted to communicate and participate outside the Iranian community. I already knew about my language and culture and I enjoyed knowing about other cultures. I never shared my story with anyone, certainly not until later years, but the moments I had with people I met outside my home were the happiest moments of my life and the people were closer to me than they ever thought they could be. In my own lonely word I compared myself with an orphan child. I wasn't a child anymore but the orphan part was still there.

At the end of April I became comfortable communicating in English. My ESL teacher couldn't shut me up in order for the rest of class to catch up. It was an awesome feeling, seeing myself, walking around, skating, curling, talking, having new friends and communicating with them in English only a short time after arriving in the country with virtually no language. I could proudly say that I understood nearly everything I heard. Not everyone was happy. The jealousy of the boys was obvious from their poisonous words and actions but I was proud of me.

My First Job

My immediate and most urgent challenge, after learning the language, was to get a job and earn money. Back in Iran I never worked. I was not lazy but in the Iranian culture, with the exception of Isfahan, the family prohibits young women, particularly students, from working, even in summer or part time jobs. Mum wanted me to finish my studies and go to post-graduate school.

Despite all the odds, I found a job as a tourist guide for visitors from other countries. Mum was furious with me. It was a chance to make pretty good money but mum and Siavash stopped me. They said they didn't want me to become a shame to the family. I asked mum what shame could it be if I worked? She said you are hanging out with men you don't know. I explained to her that I would be on a bus full of tourists. I am only to show them the city and help them with their shopping, which doesn't include me. But she forced me to turn down the job. She said I would become a loose girl, hanging out with foreign men and people would think of me as a girl with no ethics; a whore is what she meant. I told her, I would rather have a life and survive than live for others and suffer and I said to her that this is what your parents did to you and now you are doing it to me.

I was sick of her ethics. I felt it was more of a control issue. I knew I needed to get my Masters or PhD to get a job at the level mum would like me to work. Also those jobs were scarce and nearly impossible to find, particularly with no contacts. Mum's desire for my future was quite honorable but not practical. In the time of the Shah, someone with a BA would have a better chance in finding a job than today's PhD graduate. Under the current regime, more and more students find themselves living off their parents and even when they are married they sometimes have to stay at their parents home because they can't afford a life of their own.

Back in Iran, I had seen a lot of money in the hands of my father, and the last few years in my mum's. I knew a lot of things about most profitable trades such as Import/Export of Persian rugs, marble and other things my family did business in. But, my experiences were not Canadian and were, therefore, useless. As a newcomer this wasn't just my problem, everyone else faced the same challenge. For me, however, it was a lot harder because I didn't have the support system that most other people had. Also, I was still a refugee; my temporary status closed many avenues to me.

For the first time in my entire life, I had to earn my own money. My first position was as a receptionist in the Recreation office at a local college. This office job was 13 hours per week at $ 7.00 per hour. I was asked to type memos. English, at the time, was my third language. I made a typo, spelling the word Wednesday as 'Wensday' in a memo that was posted on a bulletin board. It caused a lot of laughter in the office, not all good-natured.

On top of the teasing that I had to grin and bear, the college, which charged students twice as much for everything, proclaimed they didn't have money to pay us. We were asked to work an extra 13 hours as volunteers. I refused. If it was a matter of need, I was as needy as anyone. I wasn't too disappointed that I only lasted a month in that office. It was my first job and the most boring job I have ever had.

While working in the college office, I found out that I could take martial arts at the school. Manoocheher was always a threat to me and although he never dared to touch me again, I locked my door when I was alone and he was around. To empower myself, I registered to study Kung Fu. I wasn't sure if I was ever going to use it but Manoocheher was once again looking at me in an overtly sexual way. Our rooms were next to each other and I was frankly afraid he might rape me if I could not defend myself.

After a while I switched from Kung-Fu to Jujitsu, which is a more aggressive style of martial arts.

The Starvation Period

On March 15, 1996, mum arrived in Canada for a short visit. Although it was nearly a Mission Impossible, in a futile attempt to look western and winsome, I dressed up in my most stylish outfit I had. At the airport, the first thing she noticed was my drastic weight loss. Unlike conventional Western culture, women in Persia are considered fabulous in every size, including plump; in fact, particularly in plump. She said, "Dear God, what happened to you?" I had lost so much weight that my clothes swallowed me. While growing up, I was quite petite and in my early twenties I was substantially leaner than most my peers. I had the genes for weight gain and my mother, being who she was, thought I was too skinny; as if I was to become a sacrifice to the Gods and wasn't good enough for them if I was too thin. When we traveled to Khoram-Abad, she put me on a diet of butter oil, saturated fat of boiled butter. Along with other fattening ingredients and lack of exercise, I quickly ballooned to a size 12. Six months after I arrived in Canada, I was barely a size 6. Stress and starvation were the secrets of my rapid weight loss.

The night mum arrived, while turning on a corner light, I caught my foot on the sofa and broke my little toe. Manoocheher took my toe in his hand and tried to fix it. I was in pain while he applied his questionable knowledge of physiology, trying to force my toe back into place. I could hear bones scratching one another. I told him to stop touching my toe and take me to the hospital.

On the way to the hospital, he told me that he was going to tell mum about his child. I suggested he should let her get some rest first. I reminded him that she had just arrived that afternoon after traveling through European airports the last few days. Manoocheher said it was none of my business. He left me at the hospital with my broken toe and rushed home to break mum's heart but not until after she had given him the diamond ring and a second gold bracelet he had been expecting since meeting her in France. He broke the news to her that he was already married and she did not need to get ready for his wedding that he had promised her earlier in France. She thought someday she would be part of his life and wanted to become a grandma. She had expected him to marry someone his own age, have a family, lead a healthy, honest life and allow her to be part of his happiness.

After a painful three-hour wait I received the medical care I needed. I had no other way to get home and reluctantly called Manoocheher to pick me up. Mum was still in shock and crying when we got home. It broke my heart to see her in tears on the very night she arrived. She said, "Now

I understand why you lost so much weight." I resisted the urge to tell her that Manoocheher's marriage and child were the least of my worries and had nothing to do with my weight loss. I didn't want to aggravate the situation by opening old wounds and spoil the time we had together. I just told her, "It doesn't matter; the only matter is that you are here and we need to celebrate this moment." It was not permanent but I was able to calm her down momentarily.

A week later, Manoocheher brought his wife to our home, supposedly to meet mum. He really didn't care for this woman. He grudgingly called her his wife in introducing her to mum but, in reality, he looked upon her as his mistress. They had legally married after their baby girl was born but marriage didn't stop him from being unfaithful to her. I thought she must have gone mad to divorce the father of her children to marry a younger man who has no respect for any woman, including his own mother.

For the first few days things went fairly smoothly. Then the gossip started. From what I have learned about human psychology, Manoocheher acted like a 'metro bisexual.' He dressed like a man and looked like a man but gossiped like a woman. I am not certain about his sexuality toward men. From what I observed, he had a high sex drive and was quite an explorer. Even though he didn't publicly admit he had any desire for men, his behavior, including the way he dressed, suggested otherwise. The tight jeans, button down silk shirts, bracelets and lots of gold around his neck; it doesn't take a genius to figure out that he wanted to impress someone. I regret that Persian women never question the way some men behave because the men who have same sex activity, are often the ones who pass the AIDS virus to their wives or girlfriends.

Manoocheher took mum shopping and she told me I was all he talked about. Sometimes, when I was about to leave the house, I could hear him, saying, "She will become a prostitute. She would rather be a whore than work at a job." I shook my head with tears in my eyes while heading out to hunt a job. Finally, mum had enough and told him, "Why can't you see her kinder side and how much she has done for all of us?"

Every day after that conversation, Manoocheher created a scene to bother her and bring her to tears. He tried to force her to accept his wife as her daughter-in-law or to leave Canada. I was angry with him but couldn't say much because my immigrant status was still temporary. He knew this and abused mum and me sadistically. Mum was devastated by his behavior. Although he had demonstrated this kind of behavior all his life, she insisted she had never seen him this way before. I was sorry for her and knew how vulnerable she must have felt, particularly after coming all the way from the other side of the world. It must have been extremely hard on her to realize and impossible to admit that her beloved child was a monster.

In March 1997, mum spent Norooz, the Persian New Year with us. Manoocheher had his friends over. Not only had he taken my money and left me penniless; he boasted to his friends that he was paying for my education. In fact, mum had observed my situation and had given me money for tuition and bought me a warm coat.

I didn't want to accept her money because I knew she would need it when she returned to Iran. For the last twenty-four years, Iran's economy has been volatile and I suspected she was giving me most of her life's savings. But she insisted that until I found a job I had to have some money. Five months later, mum had enough. When she came, she had great hopes for all of us but she couldn't take the insults and stand to watch my suffering and abuse any more and asked me to book her ticket. She had gambled her life to come all this way and perhaps would have stayed if our lives had been tranquil. I was very sorry but couldn't help her or myself.

She left in August, 1996, with a broken heart. The day she left was one of the hardest days of my life. I felt a great heaviness in my entire body. I missed her terribly. After this ordeal, mum has never shown any desire to return to Canada to live permanently. She would like to visit but, thanks to the Canadian Immigration, this has not been possible to arrange again.

After the college reception job fiasco, it was clear me to me that to get a good job, I needed English language proficiency and computer skills. With the help of mum, sending me some money from Iran, I enrolled in an eight-month computer course, starting in September and finishing the following April, at a school nearby. Mum's help made it possible for me to stop receiving money from the government and continue my education. Even so, this period wasn't without hardship.

Meanwhile, Manoocheher and Siavash had become even more united and were best of friends. They were not just brothers; Siavash adored Manoocheher and found everything about him likable. Shortly after mum left, we started having heated arguments. I had put up with their attitudes for mum's sake but there was no longer a reason to take their abuse and tolerate their unseemly behavior.

Manoocheher, on the other hand, used Siavash when he needed him like he did everyone else. Siavash was blind to his faults and thought of his brother as his backbone. So much so, that to please him, Siavash was ready to throw me to the lions. Manoocheher found a taxi driver position for Siavash and found another cab driver, one of his single buddies, for me to marry. I told him I had not left my country and traveled half way around the world to marry a cab driver stranger in Canada. If I had not stood up to them strongly and told them to butt out of my personal life; they would have married me off the same way my mother was forced into her marriages.

They saw me not as family but as a rival and a threat. They both dreaded my strength and confidence. Instead of being pleased, they always tried to bring me down. They have never given me a compliment but always take any opportunity to insult me. For the first few months, although I was working hard on my vocabulary, I didn't always use the right word or pronounce it correctly. On one occasion, when I was out with both of the boys, I used the wrong pronunciation in speaking to a lady. When we came out of the store, Manoocheher started laughing at me. I asked him what was so funny. He said I pronounced the word wrong. I asked him why he didn't correct me. He answered that he wanted me to fall on my face. I said that is not very nice of him; he should help me if he could but if he didn't want to help me he should butt out.

Months after I entered Canada, I was still wearing a scarf over my hair. On our way out one day, Manoocheher asked me to take off my scarf. I told him I was not ready to take it off on his say-so. A few weeks later, I was introduced to an Iranian volunteer who helped me with learning about the new culture and I decided to unveil myself for my sake. My decision was drawn from my desire to move forward and integrate into Canadian society, not to send anyone a message or imply hatred or question about Islam.

When Manoocheher noticed me, he stood at the door, questioning my ethics and asking how I could justify not wearing a headscarf when I was still praying. His gall, questioning my ethics and morals while he spent most nights with a different woman, appalled me. We repeated our eternal ritual of me telling him to mind his own business and him stepping up his aggression and arguments. I later learned that most Iranian women residing in Canada had, or still have, the same issues with their brothers and husbands. Men who rationalize their right to explore the darker side of the new culture and have extramarital sexual encounters become quite resentful and over-protective toward female family members. They resent and try to prevent their wives and sisters from having any meaningful dialogue with anyone out of the circle of their trusted friends. Some things about cultural habits never change.

In fact, it is not the culture that should change but the people that should vote for the changes. Cultures and cultural mishaps don't appear by themselves. The culture is similar to a totem poll. It never hears anything and never moves, yet people worship it and swear by it; as though the totem pole walks around hearing every word they say, even though they witnessed the birth of their totem poll at the artist workshop when he made it from scratch. In this case, people are the artists who created cultures.

Despite the fact the two knew I had very little money for food, they bought everything they liked, in large quantities, at the wholesalers and expected me to pay a share. I was also ordered to pay a share of electricity, telephone and TV. I told them that I didn't mind paying for the room but I couldn't afford to share the type of food they brought home.

I was instructed that I was obligated to pay one third of everything. And, to pay for the phone call to mum that I felt I had to make every month which cost about $35 for a thirty-minute call. For some reason we had extremely high electric bills, over $400 every other month, of which they expected me to pay one third. Siavash constantly harassed me about the electricity. They ordered me to not use the electricity if I didn't pay. If my room heater were on, he would turn it off or order me to do so. I stopped cooking because I couldn't take any more lectures and orders. I was running out of patience. I was told that if I wasn't going to cook and clean and pay one third of the electricity, I couldn't use it. One afternoon, I came home and found Manoocheher cooking a large pot of a Persian meal. My father and all three boys of the family were quite the cooks. On the way to my bedroom, he yelled at me, "You are not to touch this food. Do you hear me? You don't pay; you don't eat. If you don't do housework and don't work and don't give my money back, you have no right to touch this food."

I shook my head and I wondered what on earth mum was thinking. Even after mum came to visit us in Canada, saw his actions first hand and lived with him for six months, she still advised me to stay with the boys and be a good sister to them. Walking upstairs I had a flash back to when she told me that no matter how hard it was, it was still better to be with them than go somewhere else and be bothered by men who might want to take advantage of me and rape me. She still did not understood how evil Manoocheher was. In her mind they were family. As the Persians say, 'Even if the family breaks each other's bones, they won't eat each other's flesh.' Meaning, they stick up for each other, no matter how little they like one another.

After my share of the rent and necessities, electricity and a phone call to Iran, I only had about $60 left for the rest of the month. I spent $45 on bread, a few chicken legs for protein and some cheese. Mum had brought us some almonds and chestnuts, which I had for my lunch and dinner every day for the next three months. Financially, that period of my life was probably the harshest I can remember.

It was good to prove to myself how strong I was and learn that I was on this earth for a purpose and not just to eat a meal. I hated Manoocheher more than ever for forcing me into such deprivation. Sometimes in the middle of the night, I had the urge to go downstairs, pick up a kitchen knife, break into his room, stab him to death and then go to police and confess everything. My logic was altered and my humanity was tested many times. I prayed to God to calm me down. It was the most desperate period of my life. He simply did not want to accept or didn't have the intelligence to understand that his poisonous words hurt my pride and dignity so badly that I might snap out and kill him in retaliation for his negative comments and constant hostility toward me.

There is a proverb in my language that says, 'Words are like poisonous arrows; when they leave the bow they don't come back.' Everyone has to be careful of where they shoot their arrows. These days, there is a lot less physical abuse, at least in North America, than there used to be. Physical abuse can be brought to justice; however, we can't do much about verbal abuse.

There is an ancient story in my language that illustrates the effect of verbal abuse in a metaphoric way. The story says: A farmer cared for an injured lioness that repaid him by hunting and providing the poor man and his family with meat. She noticed he doesn't touch her and stays away from her while talking to her. One day, the lioness asked the man what it was about her he disliked. Puzzled, he said nothing. She could tell he was hiding or denying something. She insisted and said, "Either you tell me what it is about me you don't like or I am going to tear you apart and have you as my lunch." Shaking, he said, " Your mouth smells gross." Hearing that, her anger subsided. She got quiet. Then she asked him to hit her on the head with his axe. He said no, he would not do it. She insisted and told him she is going to kill him if he doesn't. In the end he did. He brought down his ax and broke the lioness head. Roaring in pain, she disappeared into the woods. A year or two passed; he never heard of her. Sure of her being dead, he went into the woods. While traveling and whistling, he saw something watching him. The lioness approached and said, "Hey, my old friend, long time no see. You didn't think I survived, did you?" He said, "No, I didn't." She said, "You said you loved me but you didn't even come to see if I needed help." Shaking, the farmer admitted that he didn't think she had survived the axe and was worried that if she did, she would be mad at him. She came near him and showed him the cut and said. "You see the cut is the only mark on my body from what you did but my heart wound is still fresh as what you said about me."

The wound caused by a small word is bigger than we think and may never heal.

Manoocheher could see the hate in my eyes but when I said I didn't appreciate seeing him naked around the house, he mocked me even more. He either didn't take me seriously or actually enjoyed seeing me hurting. Contrary to his prediction, I did not become a prostitute to feed myself. I would have starved first and almost did. Certainly, I was close to starvation and if this routine continued it could have a devastating, irreversible health effect.

Although, it shouldn't have surprised me, perhaps what bothered me the most was Siavash's uncaring attitude. He was about the only family member I thought I had but he didn't seem to be bothered by events at all. He never questioned the way things were in our home or why I wasn't eating anything. He sat at the table across from my chair and ate his food while I ate my bread and cheese. When I didn't come to the table and ate whatever I had in my room, he never commented. A stranger would have been more concerned.

Since those days, I have looked more deeply into his intentions. In addition to his non-caring, he has never been honorable. The only reason he wanted to have anything to do with me was because I always managed to find my way out, no matter how troubled I was. He knew if I was around, he could ask me to help him and I would not say no. To him and his ignorant peers, this behavior is normal. Family traditions must be respected and obeyed because that is what is expected. He, a cruel, despicable person, repeatedly told me I had to respect him. In my opinion, there is nothing normal about this behavior. Watching any human being suffer, not just a family member, without offering help is cold and brutal. Any compassionate person would have gone out of his or her way to help a neighbor or a stranger so deeply in trouble, not to mention a member of the family living under the same roof.

For me, the revenge and animosity was never about the food. I don't believe in living to eat but I do believe in eating to stay alive. Food is a fuel not the essence or the means of my livelihood and humanity. I am here on earth to make a difference, not to grow to another size or to go through extreme effort and make it my life achievement to shed pounds or shrink to a smaller size. I don't believe the size of the human body and the food we consume controls our humanity but the purpose we have and the goals we set for ourselves does.

As I said before, I believe where there is a God, there are no worries. Two of my teachers, helped me to receive bursaries, for which I am forever grateful.

When mum left, I registered not only in computer science but in English and French also at the local college at which I had worked, to complete the studies I had left behind in Iran. At the same time, I was taking a couple of English classes. I still had refugee status and could not apply for financial aid or scholarship. However, with the dedicated help of my instructors, I did very well in English and French that year and I received a $1500 prize for being one of the best students in my class. Combined with that was $1000 mum sent when she relocated her home.

I never told anyone, including my mother, that the funds I received saved my life. Infuriatingly, Manoocheher kept repeating his lie to his friends that he was funding my school.

In the end, I didn't suffer long-term effects of the starvation diet that could have had irreversible health hazards.

PHYSICAL SCARS—PSYCHOLOGICAL SCARS

I have proved, at least to myself, and promised that no matter what I experienced, I would never let it get in my way. But, I am not a super woman, just a human, as fragile and fallible as everyone else. Sometimes, I thought I had over estimated my ability but, no matter what, I didn't tell anyone about my experiences until I nearly paid the price with my life. Like the American cliché that 'what happens in Vegas stays in Vegas;' I thought 'what goes on in the family must stay in the family.' Or, in my version, whatever happened in the past belongs to the past. The price I paid, proved otherwise. The painful past and memories found a way of resurfacing and haunting me; some times in my dreams and other times in the midst of arguments with Siavash.

The physical scarring from the starvation period wasn't visible. I hid my pain behind my smile and didn't let a soul know I had not tasted hot food for months. However, the emotional trauma and psychological impact of that experience was overwhelming.

Not too long after the starvation period, I started feeling very weak. The overwhelming pain and weakness I experienced was as if my body had been shredded apart; every fiber of my being was stretched and I was losing weight. Afraid of being raped at home, I had trouble sleeping. My physician was an Iranian doctor. Since I had not developed a vast English vocabulary, in order to explain myself thoroughly, I chose to communicate with someone in my native language. He was a Bahai, a good and honorable man, but I could not bring myself to tell him the whole story. He prescribed an array of medicine but all his efforts seemed to fail. He performed a series of tests and declared that biologically everything was normal.

Despite the clean bill of health, I was still having trouble functioning in everyday life. My concentration had sunk to the bottom and I couldn't remember most of the chapters of the books I read. I had subsidized the much-needed nourishment with chocolate to gain energy. I was eating nearly a half-pound of chocolate a day. Recent studies suggest dark chocolate is good for the blood flow of the arteries. I am not sure it was correct in my case. I was loosing about five pounds a week and was dizzy and sweating profusely. So profusely that one day when I entered the bank, the lady cashier who saw me sweating as if I had just stepped out of a shower, was reluctant to cash my own check and didn't want to give me money from my own account. Puzzled, I returned to her the next day and asked her what was the cause of her hesitation the day before. She replied, "You were sweating like someone who wanted to rob the bank." Till then I had dismissed the idea that there could be something wrong. I called up my doctor he asked me to revisit him.

He shocked me by telling me I might be dying and he couldn't help me if I didn't tell him what was going on in my life. After fifteen years of keeping my molestation a secret, I finally opened up for the first time and told him about it. He was the first person to know. I explained to him about Manoocheher's current sexual inclination toward me. He was quite sympathetic, shook his head and told me, "If you like, I can have him arrested, it doesn't matter when it happened, you are still suffering and I can witness in court." I told him no, not because I didn't think he deserved it, but because of my family's reputation.

Unfortunately, many Iranians are quick to judge. I feared people's opinion and didn't want them to draw conclusions about me. During his years in Vancouver, Manoocheher had managed to charm much of the Iranian community. Many knew him, or at least thought they knew him, he had created an honorable and reliable friendly face and reputation for himself. I was simply a newcomer, a woman that people didn't know; it was easier for them to judge me than to accept the bitter truth.

The doctor said I should go and see a counselor and introduced me to a Persian psychiatrist. I cried for the entire three-hour session in his office. While I was talking to him, the psychiatrist told me, "Inside, you are like a messy house. You have to get into this house and do the cleaning up. No one else can do it for you." He sent me home with no further counseling. Part of me was sure that he was right; another wasn't so sure and didn't have the confidence or know how to fix the problem. Before he dismissed me, he suggested getting my own place and leaving the boys behind.

I was desperate to do exactly that but with the tight budget that I still had to manage, it was nearly impossible to find a suitable place. Miraculously, I managed to find a midsize room in an apartment that I could share with a man who said he traveled and wasn't there much. It was close to where we were living and the rent was about the same as I was paying. I agreed to rent the room and went home and told Siavash. I thought he would be happy that I wanted to be out and perhaps we could coordinate some sort of relationship. Instead, when I told him, he started yelling at me. He told me he wouldn't let me move there because I would become the family shame in Vancouver. It was obvious he thought the man would probably try to sleep with me. He said if I wanted to live with a man as a roommate, I'd have to leave the province.

Not knowing what to do next, I went back to my doctor and told him about what happened. He suggested that I tell my mum and Siavash about my problems with Manoocheher and get it out of my system once for all. Also, he said I should confront Manoocheher with what he had done to me and then try to let it go. I had tried to forget and forgive but it wasn't working. He tried to persuade me to resume a sexual relationship with him. I refused but every time I came out of my room, he would stare at me like a man ogling a woman in a bar. I could see his eyes changing. More than ever, I was disgusted with him.

Over time, I became increasingly frustrated and irritated and was looking for revenge. One day, Manoocheher brought home some beer. Although I go out with friends who drink, I had not allowed alcohol in our home since the first night I saw him drunk.

I put the beer in his room and told him that if he had to drink, do it in his room, not where I was sitting. We had an intense argument over the drinking issue. As usual, Siavash either wouldn't say anything or would side with Manoocheher. I was afraid. I didn't know what would happen if he got drunk. In an attempt to stop him, either I would have killed him or he would have murdered me in cold blood and denied it. He threatened to hit me. I told him that if he brought his hand down, I would make sure he regretted it for the rest of his life; I would call the police and tell them about his life in Pakistan and his passport trading in Canada and Europe. He was afraid of police like a conman.

Confronting My Molester, Fifteen Years Late

As time passed, I gradually got used to living in Canada and things were going relatively OK outside home but I needed to work on the issues I had with the boys. As my doctor suggested, in order to bring closure to my problems and save my sanity, I needed to get the skeleton out of the closet, break my code of silence and challenge Manoocheher about what he did to me. It was mind-boggling and I didn't know where to start. I certainly didn't expect him to apologize. For a few days, to prepare myself emotionally, I was looking for an opportunity to bring up the past; to question him face to face and once and forever get it off my chest and put it behind me.

The opportunity finally presented itself. One day as Siavash and I were sitting on the couch watching TV, I asked him why he always sided with Manoocheher and constantly criticized me without even hearing my side of the story. He answered that he didn't need to because he knew the truth. I said, "Right, you know nothing, and you acknowledge nothing." He said the truth was that Manoocheher was his brother and it was because of him that both of us were in Canada. I said, "Wrong."

It was time he faced the truth and separated fact from fiction. I am not a person that boasts about what I did for others but there are times when people need to be reminded of the sacrifices someone has made for them. He started raising his voice to me, hoping to force me to become quiet, but it didn't work.

I told him that it was because of me, not Manoocheher, that he made it to Canada. Just in case he had forgotten, Manoocheher had taken all the money he and mum had sent him, which left him penniless in the hands and at the mercy of Holland authorities. I was forced to loan, or more accurately give money from my small savings to get him to Canada. One story led to the next and finally I brought up the matter of how Manoocheher treated me. I talked about Manoocheher and his problem with women and sex and how he spent our money on women he slept with.

Manoocheher heard our argument and jumped in to defend himself. His argument was I had spent all my savings on Siavash. Siavash said to me, "You were in France and he went to visit you." I said, "Wake up. That was not because of me. I was on my way to Canada. He went to Europe to visit his own mother who had not seen him in nearly twelve years. He didn't even care enough about her to show up at the airport when she was forced to return to Iran." Siavash said that Manoocheher was his brother and I should be polite and listen to him. When he said that, it was as if he poured boiling water and salt on my old wounds.

In the meantime, Manoocheher left us arguing while he went to attend to whatever business it pleased him to attend. He had many girlfriends, and often spent the night with different women.

I asked Siavash if he knew what had gone on between Manoocheher and me during the time he was in the military. He said he didn't know and asked me what happened. Sensing it might be something bitter, he quickly changed his mind, saying he was not interested to know. I said, "Whether you want to know or not, I will tell you, any way." At first, he refused to hear me. I shouted at him and got the story out of my system as quickly as I could. Finally, he got quiet and listened. He was quiet for a few moments. I said I was tired of keeping my silence. Clenching his teeth and shrugging his shoulders, Siavash told me I should move out of the house right away. I asked if that was all he had to say about it. He said Manoocheher was his brother and I was his sister. God would judge what happened between us and he would say nothing to Manoocheher. He wouldn't beat up or criticize his brother because of me.

I said if the role was reversed and you were the little sister and I was the older brother, I would have stood by you and kicked anyone's ass that took advantage of you. He said, "Well you are not me and I am not you. Go get yourself a different place and move out of here. I am not coming with you. You have to go live by yourself or with a woman, not with a man." I told him he couldn't tell me what to do when he didn't care enough to get a place we could share. He told me to leave Vancouver and move somewhere else; to another province. I told him, "If you don't care how much I am hurt, I don't care what you think. I will share a room with whomever I want." He was quick to judge, saying he would tell mum of my behavior. I told him, "Me too."

The next day, mum called from Iran. She asked how everything was. I lied and said everything was fine, but I couldn't keep from choking when I said that. She told me to try to be a good sister to the boys. When she said that, I burst into tears and started yelling at her. I told her she had no idea what I was going through. I told her she didn't know a lot of things and asked how she could tell me to be nice to a monster. She said I should tell her what was going on. I told her she could not bear to know the pain I have to live with everyday I am under the same roof with Manoocheher. She said, "Well try me." I told her it was beyond her comprehension, the truth was so harsh that it would make her sick. She insisted that I tell her.

Forced incest is unheard of among people of Kurdish ethnicity or the non-Arab people of Abadan. Their sisters are considered the world to them and the princess of the family. I finally decided to tell her everything. As soon as she grasped what I was telling her, she started crying and shouting and asking me why I hadn't told her before. I told her there were many reasons. She said she couldn't listen anymore and asked me to let her go. She called me up a couple of hours later, saying she had almost had a heart attack.

Siavash overheard our conversation and, as usual, ran his judgment on me that I was the cause of mum's pain and everyone else's. Breaking this news to her, made her very sick and I was worried to death for her life. I called her as many as fifteen times a day. She was sick and not able to come to the phone to pick up messages I left with her neighbors. My heart was jumping out of my chest. I was emotionally disturbed and pulled apart to a point that I couldn't remember when I'd eaten my last meal. I blamed myself for sharing this information with mum and making her sick. Early one morning, Vancouver time, I finally got her on the phone, I was crying loudly, begging her to hold on to her life and not to lose faith in seeing me again.

Manoocheher had heard that mum was sick and could hear me crying over the phone. He came downstairs and yelled, "You woke me up with your yelling, you idiot." When I finished my conversation, I screamed at him, "Go to Hell. I don't care if I you woke you up. Mum is dying and you're telling me I woke you up? To Hell with you and your sleep." He told me if I woke him up one more time he'd break both my legs. I shouted at him, this wasn't Iran where he could do whatever he pleased. I told him if he touched me, I'd call the police and make his life Hell. He backed down and said, "Whoa, I was just joking." I believe he finally understood that I hated him so much that I meant every word I say.

Two weeks after that phone call to mum, she was better. I felt relieved. Siavash, on his way out to work, told me there was a phone bill for $400 that I should pay for the calls I made to Iran. I told him I would pay one-third, he and his beloved brother could pay the rest, she is not just my mum, she is theirs too. Manoocheher said he wasn't paying. We got into an argument. Siavash said we'd discuss it later. I insisted we discuss it then and there. Manoocheher asked me what my problem was; if I had anything to say, I should just say it.

I said, "You are my problem." I told him I had a lot to say. I told him I felt like a dirty napkin because of him. True to his promise from years ago, he denied having ever touched me. He said, "I don't know what you're talking about. I have never touched you, never done anything except be a big brother to you." I said, "Does being a big brother involve your penis as well?" He said that I was crazy. He meant I needed psychiatric help and should check myself in a mental institution. I said, "You can add injury to insult as much as you desire. It has always been this way for you. You always think that you get everything your way by insulting and degrading me but not this time. I can describe every inch of your body. I can put you behind bars where you belong for what you did to me and for all the suffering and emotional damage that you have made me endure and by reopening my old wounds since I met you in Holland. For the looks you give me and for the things that haunt me every night. I take a lot of medication just to be able to function. Seeing you, walking around naked in front of my eyes in your tiny little shorts, sometimes with only a towel around you, taking your girlfriends to your room makes me sick. I am disgusted living under the same roof with you. You are a dirty pig." He said, "If you can put me in to jail why don't you?" I said I didn't because of the family reputation, not because I care about you. Mum had asked me not to, otherwise, you belong behind bars.

The entire time Siavash was yelling at me to stop it and shut up. I was so tired of hearing him repeat that and siding with his brother. I yelled at him to shut up. I told him he had no idea of how much pain he inflicted on my heart. Soon, they both left the house without saying anything further.

The next day, Manoocheher came downstairs from his bedroom. He told us he was going to sell his belongings and leave Canada for the United States. He said if we wanted any of his belonging to let him know so he could tell us how much he'd sell them to us for. I could hardly buy a meal, much less furniture. I shrugged my shoulders as a sign of NO. As soon as he left the house, Siavash said, "Do you see what you've done? If you hadn't said anything he wouldn't be moving out. Now, I either have to buy his furniture or buy new stuff."

Furthermore, he told me to find myself another place. Meanwhile, mum kept insisting that we stay together as a family. I was hoping that I could bring her back to Canada for one more visit to compensate her for all the bad times she had in her previous painful visit. I reluctantly yielded to her pleas to share a home with Siavash in order to have the funds and support needed to satisfy Immigration for mum's next invitation to visit.

Siavash didn't want to pay Manoocheher's asking price for his stuff, so he sold it at auction and got even less than he imagined. He rented a truck and took his bedroom suite to Oklahoma with him. It amazed me how stupid he must be or how determined to spite his family. He only paid CAD $1,500 for his bedroom suite. It cost him another CAD $1,200 to take it to Oklahoma where he could buy that bedroom set for US $1,000. He just wanted to aggravate me and show me how little money meant to him while he tormented me for the four hundred dollars he had not managed to steal from me. He was trying to prove a point but I didn't care if he burned his money.

The Day I Became an Immigrant

In early January 1997, a preliminary hearing date was set. Some people, including Siavash, had hearings at the airport. In my case, I had to go to Immigration Canada and appear before a tribunal member of the Refugee Board and in the presence of an immigration officer. If I did not receive a favorable ruling from this hearing, then I had to seek a decision in judicial courts. To exhaust other options, including defending me in front of a judge or pursuing it further with humanitarian defense, I was given a chance to have a lawyer defend me.

I understood the purpose of this hearing was to argue my side as well as the concerns of Immigration Canada, as why I should be granted legal status to reside in Canada permanently. This was the first step in a long period of possible litigation and could be continued for months, as it has in other's situation.

In retrospect, it was quite a refreshing reminder of freedom and the precise reason why I left Iran. This was a first for me, to be granted a lawyer to defend me against the questions brought upon me, by a government which treats its residents equally and with respect, allows the individual to answer back and even helps her defend herself.

The day before my hearing, I was reviewing all my papers. It was a couple of days before Manoocheher, left for the US. He hadn't talked to me this politely since the first time we met in France. Suddenly he came and sat down beside me and said, very quietly, "Just in case the judge and immigration officer ask anything about me, tell them you don't know anything about me." I told him I'd tell the truth, whatever they asked. He raised his voice and said, "You imbecile. You self centered, egoist. I'm an egotist Canadian citizen. If they want to take me to court, it will take them a long time to catch me. I can run to another country but you, you idiot, they'll send you directly to Iran where you belong."

I said to him, "No, you are all that with your phony stories and reasons that you gave immigration of Canada that you had been chased by the government of Iran. If that was so, why are you so afraid?" On his way out he mumbled, "Why did I make such a mistake as to go to Holland and help her to create so much trouble for myself?" I told him, "Because there's a God somewhere out there. You were not the one that brought me here; it was God and he'll protect me no matter what. Sooner or later the truth will come out." He left home while cursing me. I heard from Siavash that he drove toward Oklahoma that afternoon; furious and afraid he might be caught in Canada. He has not returned since; not even to visit the daughter he helped to bring into this world.

The next day, after a lot of nagging, Siavash drove me to the immigration court in downtown Vancouver where I had to be at 9:00 a.m. sharp. He left me off on the street and told me under no circumstances to mention his name. He said even if they take you directly to the airport or prison, I am not going to come and get you. I said I understood. He told me to either catch a bus to come home or, if I got through early, call him up on his cell phone to see if he was still in downtown.

My lawyer, Jeff, granted to me through legal services was one of the best lawyers in Vancouver. By the grace of God, he accepted my case. I met him in the hallway. He asked me if my family members would attend the hearing. I said no, they couldn't. I didn't or more accurately couldn't bring myself to tell him the whole truth. I couldn't tell him I didn't have any relationship with any of them. I felt I had no choice but to pretend they cared about me because it is part of my heritage and part of being devalued and not having self worth. I didn't speak about my pain with him at all.

I could tell he wasn't satisfied with the answer and even seemed a little concerned, as he had the right to be. If, during the hearing, the issue of my family members came up, as why they were not present to support me, he had no answer. In retrospect, I put him in a tough position. I wasn't honest with him as I wish I had been. When he didn't know the whole story, he couldn't defend me to the best of his ability. I could tell this made him a little uneasy. I also was nervous about the pretense. We didn't have much time and proceeded without further discussion. As most realistic lawyers do, just in case things don't go well, he warned me not to have a lot of expectations. I told him I was not sure what was he talking about. He explained sometimes these cases don't go as you expect and it may take some time before you receive a favorable result. He was trying to prepare me for the worst.

I had a good feeling and told him I was not worried. He said, "Good" and we entered the courtroom. The judge was an older woman, a very nice lady who appeared to be French. I greeted her in French. In the first half hour, my lawyer started the argument and then asked me questions. I was aided by a translator to insure my statements were correctly stated. In the midst of my answers, my translator wrongly translated what I said. I interrupted him and said that is not what I meant. The lady judge smiled and said we provide translators for people who really don't need them. My lawyer explained that I had picked up the language in Canada.

She was pleased to hear that and wanted to hear me in my own words. I told the judge what had happened in Iran that caused me to come to Canada. It didn't take long for the judge to see how much distress I was in. She granted me legal residency in Canada. After hearing the testimonies about my ordeal in Iran, the kidnapping and the physical scars on my body, she ordered a short break. It was nearly 45 minutes past the hour.

Outside, I asked Jeff, what he thought. He said it could be a good thing. We were called back in and the tribunal member spoke directly to me. She said she had heard enough and knew that I had truly suffered at the hands of the Iranian government. She welcomed me to Canada. I could not believe what I was hearing. Many people wait for months to hear the news. The judge herself delivered mine to me. I guess even my lawyer was surprised. It was the greatest news I had heard since the time I was accepted to the university back in Iran and many times, more pleasurable. She certainly made my day and made a difference in my life. I came out and called Siavash. He thought I was calling from the airport. He asked where I was. I said I am outside the court. With a great deal of surprise, he asked, "Are you done?" I said, "Yes, I am. I am an immigrant." He could not believe me. We drove home and made it to Richmond by 10:30 a.m.

My status in Canada was approved and I received an official welcome letter with instructions on how to apply for my new status as a landed immigrant. Now, I had to come up with the fees for my landed process. Siavash had money but he didn't offer and I didn't ask either. I needed CAD $1,475. It took me three and half months to save some money and borrow some more to apply for my Landed Immigrant permit.

The normal processing time after applying for landed status is four to eighteen months. Miraculously, mine was processed in two and a half months. Yet, this was nothing compared to my citizenship. I had one of the fastest citizenship grants in Canada. I received my landing paper from Ottawa before Siavash received his. He was incredulous, even jealous of me and many times asked me how I managed to expedite my immigrant process. He kept asking what chant and prayer I recited. I told him, "What can I say? I have God on my side. " But truly, I didn't do anything out of the ordinary. I might have sounded lucky. But I don't believe in luck but I did pray from my heart and I knew God loved me as much as I love him and He took care of me.

After Manoocheher left, Siavash felt betrayed by me. Of course, I had nothing to blame myself for but Siavash kept saying it was entirely my fault. He wasn't prepared to find a new apartment to share. To make my life harder, every time I found a place, he would complain that he was too tired to come and see it or had an indefinite excuse and sent me to see the place and afterward wouldn't agree on price until it was too late. He was no help but he told me if we couldn't find another place, he'd live at his friend's house and I'd have to come up with CAD $1,150 for the upcoming month's rent.

I asked him if he cared if we couldn't find a place. He said, "No, I don't. I'll find my way, and you can find yours." He was ready to put me on the streets while my dear mother was worried about my relationship with him in order for him to supposedly protect me. In July, 1997, a few days before the end of month, I found a place. It wasn't luxurious and was a lot smaller than what we had but it was nearby so we didn't have to move far. Siavash agreed on the place and the rent, about $750 a month, but he didn't go to see it for himself before we moved. I had to arrange everything by myself, including the moving. I had two suitcases but he had some furniture. I asked my friend Tania to help me with the moving. She brought their family van and helped us move until 2:00 a.m.

I asked Siavash where all his friends that he was always talking to on the phone and helping with their moves were. He said he didn't want them to know he was moving. Why wouldn't he? His explanation didn't make any sense at all. Either way, he was glad that my girlfriend had come to help. The minute we moved in, the first thing he said was that he didn't like the place. I told him he should have said something when I asked him to come and see it. I didn't particularly like the place either but it was all I could find in the three days left before the next month's rent was due.

İmmigration Canada
Rejects My Old Mother

Since April of 1997, Siavash and I made several attempts to bring our mother to Canada as a visitor. The Canadian Embassy in Iran made excuses each time. Finally, the embassy answer to my numerous letters was that my mother was rejected because I was a refugee. However, by then, my case had already been heard by Canadian immigration and I had been granted permanent residency in Canada. I wrote to my district Member of Parliament explaining my situation and to the office of the Prime Minister and Minister of Immigration.

The incompetent Member of Parliament, who had no knowledge of immigration policy, referred the case to his assistant, who drew a drastic conclusion from the whole scenario. He advised me, instead of bringing my mother on a tourist visa, I should try to bring her permanently. Mum, who knows no English and had no desire to leave her country permanently, reluctantly agreed to take part in this scam concocted by the politician. Since the boys and I had entered Canada as refugees, the Canadian Immigration office in Iran took advantage of my past status and ruled that my mother would have to come to stay and would become a burden to the tax payers. The new rules didn't consider the total income of all family members and Siavash's gross income didn't look sufficient to take care of my mother. Therefore, immigration rejected her permanent and visitation rights all together. I tried for another visitor visa. The Embassy of Canada in Iran rejected it again. This time, their excuse was that they knew for sure now that she wanted to reside in Canada because she had previously applied for permanent status.

The Office of Prime Minister

Immigration Canada's response to my mother's case threw me off but didn't deter me from going forward. I wrote dozens of letters to different politicians, including Ministry of Immigration and the previous Prime Minister of Canada. The Ministry wrote back that they have no responsibility and could not help me.

Due to my persistence, someone from the Prime Minister's office finally called me. A lady told me that she could not help me and I needed to contact the Minister of Immigration. I explained to her that I had done that and I was singing to a deaf ear.

Nothing came out of that telephone call but in the midst of all my back and forth with the Office of the Prime Minister, something rather funny occurred. The day I received the call from his office, I just had come home and left some food on high heat on the stove to warm up.

While the lady, who introduced herself as the Prime Minister's secretary assigned to talk to me, was on the phone, I smelled my food burning. I asked her if I could please put her on hold for a second. She paused and, as if she was shocked or offended, replied, "This is the Prime Minster's office we don't stay on hold for anyone, not even for the President of the United States."

I was equally shocked and replied to her, "Oh, ok, sorry about that. Go on please. It is no problem. We let the home catch on fire. I will eventually call the fire fighters before the whole building comes down."

She paused for a moment and then said," Ok, go ahead, put me on hold." A minute later, after averting the crisis, I came back. I said, "Hello." I could hear her laughing but she wasn't answering. I said, "Hello" again. She said, "You are very smart, in all the years I have worked here, I have never held the phone for anyone."

Apart from the funny situation, everything else about my mother's case has been quite heartbreaking. In 2001, I went on national TV begging the Prime Minister to help me. The local MP from the opposition group had replaced the Liberal MP who damaged my mother's case. After two and half years of investigation and assurance of my hard truth story, he decided that my mother would return to Iran and took on my file. In 2004, after many trials and a ton of paper back and forth, the new MP delivered me yet another devastating blow. His office manager told me that after three years, the new Minister also rejected my plea to personally intervene in this matter.

After a dozen attempts and many applications, everything so far has failed. August of 2004 marked the eight-year anniversary of the day when

I said goodbye to my mother in the airport. I can no longer remember her face and the pictures I receive from Iran portray someone so much older, and more fragile and desperate to see her daughter.

Amazingly, on 25th of November 2004, Ms. Judy Sgro, the same Minister of Immigration that disallowed my mother to come for her eye surgery was questioned in Parliament by the leader of the opposition why she allowed a stripper to enter the country. When I read the news and heard it on TV, I thought it must be a joke. My mother was rejected for surgery and this woman enters Canada for stripping? Is the Minister of immigration that cold hearted? Apparently, the stripper earned the attention of the Minister by volunteering on the minister's re-election campaign, leading up to the June 28 election, in her Toronto area riding .

I am just wondering, next time I call my mother, what should I tell her? So far, I have told her we will find a way to bring her to Canada for her eye surgery. Should I tell her, "Mum, you are not young or a stripper, therefore you can't come to Canada." Or, should I tell her, "Canada immigration doesn't really care about older people."

My mother's application was considered a hot case that could not be trusted to leave Canada. The circumstances of my mother's case are: she had previously come to Canada and proven her willingness to obey and respect immigration laws. She left on her own, a month before her visa expired. There is nothing in her file that suggests she would not return to Iran. Although it was well meant, I was improperly advised to apply for landed immigrant status for her. Her case was turned down because of lack of funds but Immigration took that as indication that she intended to stay in Canada permanently.

The current and previous Ministers of Immigration must have taken great pride in rejecting her while every day, hundreds of people from different countries, pretending to be tourists, come to Canada and never return to their native land. Some are honest and some are hardcore criminals. That includes the very publicly known Al Qaeda crime family located in Toronto, Canada.

LESSONS OF THE NEW LIFE

Finally, after nine months of constant search for a job, all I could find was a retail position in a jewelry company that had opened branches in a large nation-wide department store. I worked there for three years, beginning in late 1996, at a starting wage of $ 8.00 per hour with a promise of raises that never came through. I was not making much, only $475 a month. I had a pleasant professional relationship with the jewelry manager who hired me. He was an older East Indian gentleman who soon retired and returned to Fiji. His assistant, a younger man, also an East Indian, replaced him.

This man was in his early forties and married with three children. While the old manager was around, the young man had been a model of propriety, but when he became manager, he immediately became overly friendly with me. At first, I welcomed him as a friend; perhaps even as a brother I never really had. I didn't see anything wrong. I had no reservations and no experience of what to expect or what to make of his friendly face and attention. I was both grateful for and delighted by his kindness.

Before circumstances became hostile between us, he seemed to be a decent enough man. I seldom spoke about my problems but when he heard that I needed money for my immigration status he offered to lend me the money. In return, to assure him that his money was a loan, I left most of the gold I had brought from Iran with him. After a while, I was able to pay the money back and the gold was returned to me. I was no longer in any of the phases of my court hearings and I was officially a new immigrant but I still didn't know anything about the laws of Canada and had heard rumors of immigrants being deported. I am now happy to say those were merely rumors. Only immigrants who are involved with drug trafficking and other criminal behavior in Canada would be deported back to their country. My employer never informed me that this was only for criminal charges and that standing up to my manager against harassment would be a positive step.

I guess he mistakenly interpreted love messages in my upfront behavior and little by little he shared with me about his unhappy marriage and relationship with his wife. He kept comparing me with her and telling me how wonderful it would be if his wife were more like me. He started telling me how beautiful I was and he would love to be with me, etc. I told him very frankly that I was not interested in married men. In my view and my world, once someone is committed, whether married or not, their availability and attraction should be directed to his or her partner and no one else. I know Islam allows multiple marriages for a man but what I believe and works for me is: one God, one love, and one marriage or at least one at a time.

He took my comments very personal and the next time around in my evaluation, refused to increase my wages. His excuse was that I had to work harder to earn more money.

Unfortunately, many large companies have been built on the backbones of their employees. Without a union, the suffering of their vulnerable employees, including me, is never heard. If the company wanted to keep me, all they had to do was give me a raise. The wages they were paying me were not enough to pay for the roof over my head and the food on my table. I was the top selling employee of the company and earned the company more than one hundred thousand dollars in their fiscal year but no matter what I did, I couldn't get the executives to understand that I was financially burned.

Our friendship deteriorated and I no longer enjoyed hearing him admire me. He kept telling me that he liked me and complimenting my long hair, so one day I cut it short. He asked me why I did that. I told him I didn't like his attention. If he wanted to lust, he would have to hunt someplace else, I was not interested. The other managers of this store admired him but to them I was just another sales person, not greatly admired and not yet that good with my English.

It seems all wrong now, but in my short work experience in Canada, I was taught by the security forces working in that store that harassment charges can only be made if someone physically touches you or uses foul language. However, foul language is not provable unless it was frequent behavior. This man did neither. I was afraid to report this harassment to the top bosses because my manager looked and acted so innocent and poised, was so friendly with everyone and had one of those baby faces, as psychologists call them. They are the ones everyone falls in love with and believes their innocence. I thought they would believe his denial over my truth. The main reason for the managers to believe him perhaps lay in what they called his work ethic. He was greatly admired for his hard work when, in fact, I was the one doing most of what he received credit for. As the Persian people say, "No matter where you go, the sky is the same color." I never was looking for trouble but it seems that trouble never stopped searching for and finding me.

This wasn't an isolated harassment incident or the only time I was harassed or discriminated against. Many times, I had male customers who, for no reason, kept coming back and making undignified remarks toward me. I brought it to the attention of the store security and my manager but, as it turned out, having the laws written on paper doesn't necessarily guarantee they are going to be practiced. In my future experiences I found out that the laws in Canada included too many clauses that criminals easily took advantage of and some of the laws practically let the criminal go free.

Cultural Adjustment

Leaving Iran behind and entering a new life in a new culture didn't necessarily mean I would have it any easier. As time passed, I found out that finding and keeping a job in Canada was equally as hard for a native of this culture as it was for me. In a desperate attempt to get myself out of the situation with my manager, I answered a couple of ads in popular local publications.

The mishaps of the new cultures were the uncharted territory, something with which I had no previous experience or a mentor to guide me. For Persians, many of the habits of the West seem strange, I am sure the Westerners feel the same about my culture. For instance, when men greet each other in Persian culture, they kiss each other on the face. Female best friends give each other a peck on the lips. Most of the younger females walk around hand in hand, as do best guy friends. We don't look at our peers in a sexual way. Those who do look at each other in such a way are known by their private actions because everyone is interested to know about everyone else's business.

After being in Canada a few months, I invited one of my friends, who was born in Germany but raised in Canada, to dinner. After finishing her dinner, she gave me a thumbs-up. I laughed. I knew what she meant of course but to show her how different our cultures can be, I translated the sign for her, not in the most philosophical terms. I told her thumbs-up in Persian culture is equal to the middle finger in the west. She laughed and gave me another set of thumbs-up.

Although Persians tolerate the thumb from foreigners, it is a whole different ball game when a native of Iran gives another a thumbs up.

Often, one culture's practices seem strange to another culture. For Persians it is the sunbathing by the westerners that seems strange. Of course, we didn't care or try to understand that we had three hundred sunny days per year that is equal to three years of sunny days in Canada. Persians don't understand and are not big on public affection and question why westerners show public affections of any sort. The French kiss in particular is considered highly degrading and disgusting.

It doesn't mean I agree with all, or any, of them, but I knew what the mishaps meant. In Canada, I had no access to such knowledge. Like most newcomers, most of my education came from my own research in books. If I had not read it, I didn't know how it worked. I was like a blank canvas that someone could splash paint on without me knowing I had been scammed.

Back to my job hunt; in looking through the Help Wanted ads, I saw several looking for escorts. Where I came from, escort meant a woman or a man who works under cover, carrying a gun to protect someone. I answered one of the ads asking for women who can work as an escort. I innocently assumed this was the same job. My first impression was, 'Wow, this is what I would like to do!' But truthfully, my gut was telling me that this sounds too good to be true.

I dithered a while and finally phoned the number of one of the ads. To my disbelief, the woman on the phone said, yes, she was looking for women who are ready to start tomorrow; something that I never expected to hear from an employer in Canada.

I said, "Really? Great. Can you tell me about the responsibilities of the job?" She said, "There is no responsibility involved. You simply go on a date and we pay you." I said, "Maybe I dialed the wrong number or I am a little confused but why are you paying me for going on a date. Is something expected?" She said. "No, but you know, if you like, you can make extra money." I am not following you. You mean it would be physical? She said, "Oh, we can't call it that but that is your discretion." I said. "Really, am I carrying a gun?" She laughed and said," Noooooo, you don't. You are wearing a cocktail or evening dress and riding in a limo with your date." As we say in Persian, 'The quarter finally dropped.' It finally registered in my brain and I understood what she meant. We were talking about the world's oldest profession.

Like a Good Samaritan I immediately dialed the police department to tell them that I wanted to report this business that exploits innocent women. The policewoman on the other end said they could not be arrested; they have done nothing wrong. I said, "I beg your pardon, even thought she is telling me I would probably want to go further with the job?" She said, as far as the police are concerned, they are legit businesses. However, she warned me, if you stand on the street or we find you doing anything of that nature, we will arrest you. In retrospect, they almost did. When I innocently waited for one my friends at the street corner, I noticed a police car pulled over. I didn't know what he wanted but after a few minutes he finally noticed the dirty looks I gave him and he left.

I continued, "So you mean, if they pay taxes, you don't arrest them." She said, "That is the way the law allows them to work and police hands are tied in this matter." She told me that if I wanted to pursue the matter I needed to write to parliament. I was not the only person who made a wrong assumption. The proliferation of massage parlors and escort services in the local and national newspapers is evidence that the problem has grown even bigger. It is obvious these people are preying on naïve, innocent women, as young as twelve years old and using them as prostitutes. The law protects these businesses because they pay taxes. In return, they have become part of the nightlife of Canada's culture that attracts a distinct line of tourists who have no morals, deep pockets and no problem in spending the cash even though, they are ruining the flowers of the future. The saddest part about the laws in Canada is; this is just the icing on the cake and it made me angry that money is preferred over people.

My next attempt to find a job landed me on the doorstep of a company based in Montreal. This company had been operating in Canada for the last seven or eight years prior to the time I applied. Each year, it had robbed a bunch of innocent people of their money, then moved on and opened under a different name. Canada's police did very little or could do nothing to stop them. Again, I saw the ad in the national paper. This seemed pretty genuine. The company was looking for flight attendants. Nothing better than that I thought. I spoke French and that was all I was required to know.

I answered the ad and the next thing I knew I received a welcome package of many papers, among which was an invoice that I had to pay for my training. With a lot of anguish, after many phone calls to a person who said they were buying a new airline that would start operation in April of the following year, I was sucked in. The promise also included that I and the rest of the people like me would be airline shareholders. I paid the first $250. Two months later, here came another invoice and then another; in all I was out $560, a fortune for me at the time.

The sad part was, I wasn't the only one these people had scammed. April came and went and we didn't hear anything. Then it was May and June. At the end of June, with my persistence and plenty of other people like me, the company agreed to have a meeting. The executives didn't show up but sent a woman dressed as a flight attendant. Well, I wasn't content to just go to that meeting. I called up Global National TV and took a cameraman and journalist along with me and wired myself with a tape recorder to record statements of the "flight attendant," who refused to talk in front of the camera. She, obviously, was part of the team of scam artists.

I wasn't surprised to find out that there were hundreds and hundreds of people like me all across Canada but was astonished that, unlike me, most of these people were actually natives of Canada or had lived in this country for many years.

Due to my diligence, an old investigation was reopened. I was in constant contact with the police investigator in Montreal, which helped me to access private information about the spending accounts of the so-called airline executives. At the expense of people like me, they had spent thousands of dollars on expensive restaurants, expensive perfume and trips to resort getaways. It brought me to tears how naive I had been to trust so easily.

It annoyed me when I called up the investigator to see what was new and he said, "Nothing at his end, what about at your end?" He received information from me! So much that he pulled my leg, saying maybe I should apply for a job with their team.

I didn't get any money back but the Crown Council of Montréal and the police were able to take this company to the Supreme Court and put a stop to their scam. They had the audacity to send me a threatening letter stating that if I pursed the matter any further they were going to sue me. I wanted so much to reply to them saying, "Suing for what? Because you took my money and I made you stop? Go ahead." We call their threat an 'empty bluff' in the Persian language. I called up their office but the number they had provided was not in service.

After the pitiful job opportunities, that seemed laughable and sad at the time, I still had to work even though the work environment was sometimes vicious. I had a co-worker, an old woman, originally from Hong Kong, who had lived in Canada for nearly twenty years. For some reason, she didn't like me and made my life quite miserable at work. She had an advantage over me, having been with the company for more than ten years. Even though she took a year off every few years, the company seemed to be happy when she returned. I gathered it was because of her ruthless business savvy that she was considered an asset. Although we were not on commission, she tried to take everyone's sales. All my co-workers and me complained bitterly but we were told because she spoke Chinese and knew the Eastern culture well, she was an asset to the company and we shouldn't say anything to her.

It bothered me that she treated me like trash and I had to put up with her behavior. My best friends are Chinese. Tina is a like a little sister to me. It wasn't her ethnicity that I had problem with. It was her arrogant behavior. I decided to treat her in a manner that would make her understand her behavior was cruel.

I had heard about people of Hong Kong eating delicacy foods, including dogs, cats, snakes and monkey. It is not the food that I have a problem with. As I mentioned earlier, as long as the animal is not treated cruelly, I don't care that people eat barbecued rats or lion burgers. Those who eat the lion burger, hoping to inject bravery into their veins, should know there are millions of bacteria in the bodies of wild animals that can make people sick and science has no clue what they are or how to treat them. Even if they are fed in laboratories under the watchful eyes of doctors there is no assurance the meat will be bacteria free.

I have been told many times that I am brave. Wild cats are an interest of mine but I would rather see them alive and photograph them, than eat them in meat chops. Metaphorically speaking, I am too similar to a real Persian cat, which fights tooth and nail, if it must. For my bravery, I have never taken a single cell of lion blood or a bite of lion steak. I believe either someone is brave or he is not. It cannot be injected. The same for intelligence; either someone is born with it, or not. Monkey brains and tiger paws don't increase intelligence.

Back in the store, I started a conversation about 'exotic food,' hoping to get this lady's attention. As usual she tried to dominate our conversation. I politely asked her if she had ever eaten monkey brain. She said, yes, of course and, as if it was caviar, boasted that it is delicious and very expensive. I asked how it was served. She explained that the monkey is alive, its skull is opened, the monkey is placed beneath the table, people gather around and pick on the brain. I had to digest my discomfort on hearing how the animal must have been tortured. I asked why people want to eat monkey brain. She said that it makes them smart. I was flabbergasted. I said, "So, all the monkey brain you have had should have made you smart, then why aren't you?" I wasn't trying to be politically correct; in fact, I considered myself a retired patriot that wanted nothing to do with anyone and to just mind my own business. I wanted to teach her a lesson that it is not nice to be a bully. I guess it hit her like a ton of bricks because she definitely changed her behavior toward all of us.

I have always respected other people' culture and, in fact, find it fascinating but some of the traditions we try so hard to keep are nothing but superstition and that includes Persian culture as well.

As I have said many times, traditions don't appear by themselves; someone who is influential must have started them. In the case of monkey brains, it is most likely that the emperors of China were told by their imagination or doctors that it would bring them intelligence but, for God's sake, we live in the 21st century; we can leave the mumbo-jumbo behind, stop the traditions that mean nothing and make room for new ones. Although I have no problem with the use of herbal Chinese medication, the use of tiger parts by the Chinese nation has driven wild tigers to the brink of extinction with only 30 left in the wild in China.

Monkey brains may just sound like a delicacy but it is a deadly one; scientist have evidence that the AIDS virus can be transferred to humans and animals. It can cause leukemia among cats and is easily transferred to individuals who have infections in their mouth. In fact, the AIDS virus lives in monkeys and was transferred by accident from Green monkeys in Africa, either from a scientist who was working on them or to people he came in touch with. And, not to mention that the number of monkeys in the wild is in serious decline.

Persian literature has taught me, it is scripted in our poetry, that when anyone wants to hit someone else with a kebab iron, he should try to hit himself with a pin first. Here is the point and example.

As I mentioned, Persians are not immune to non-sense traditions. Back in Iran, when my father was around, he used to tell me, if I cut my finger, I should pee on it. Sure, there is ammonia in the urine, that is the reason for the smell, but, if the person has an infection in his or her urine, that could be dormant and passing through the body, putting urine on the open tissue can cause serious problems. I deduced, from speaking with this lady, that she thought that the Chinese were the most intelligent people on earth. I have no doubt there are intelligent people among the Chinese, just as in any other nation but what I was appalled by was, she never washed her hands. She said she didn't want her skin to get dry.

Ironically, years later when I was in college, using public facilities, I saw girls that, after using the bathroom, came out touching their long hair and beautiful face. I wanted so badly to tell them that simple soap and water would help put a stop to many diseases and will not require the use of any tiger paws or monkey brains later. For a culture so intelligent, regardless of what they consume, I found it strange that people like her and many more that I met later, keep traditions alive that could play a very deadly role not only in their lives and our lives but in the life of many generations to come that will not have the chance to enjoy looking at the majestic animals roaming the planet. I wish the next tradition people would pick up, is simply to wash their hands with soap and water.

THE GUCCI THIEVES

The two incidents not only made me bitter toward the scam artists but also made me more determined not to let the past be repeated. Back in early 1997, a particular style of Gucci watches was popular among Asians. It became the number one item on the wish list of thieves who robbed jewelry stores.

A few nights later, when I was alone on my shift in the store, two impeccably dressed Asian men approached me, pretending to be legitimate customers. Apparently to impress me, one of them even flashed the Armani brand name imprint on the inside pocket of his coat. My gut feeling told me the same thing as when I sent the first check to the phony airline company. I had a bad feeling about these men. I took their credit card but before processing it, I called store security and asked them to look at the men in their camera and run the visa number.

My gut was right. The man in the expensive suit was a criminal wanted in Canada for the last ten years. The credit card had been stolen ten months earlier from a Japanese businessman. In one night, the thief had spent more than $7,000 in his shopping spree on this card and had hundreds of other cards. On another occasion, I helped security and ultimately the police to catch another MasterCard fraud.

RCMP informed me that the Gucci man was a big catch. I never received any appreciation letter from Visa or MasterCard; not even from any of the managers of the store or the company where I was working. But, for my own peace of mind I continued to stay vigilant and help any way I could.

My Premonition of
Princess Diana's Death

The awaking of my feminine intuition had another challenge to meet. I had yet another prophetic dream and this time I felt completely powerless. This was not the first time I had dreamed, for no apparent reason, about people I did not know who immediately died. Since my trip to Mecca, I have had prophetic dreams; even about the prophets.

When I cut my hair, I told my manager I did it because I did not want his attention and to discourage him from hitting on me. There was a more important reason.

Two weeks before the August 31, 1997, car crash that took the lives of Princess Diana and her companion, I had a dream about her. In my dream, Lady Diana appeared to be in her early twenties; just as beautiful and just as innocent as before her wedding. We were busy speaking about something when suddenly she approached me and kissed me on the left cheek. There was a great deal of emotion attached to that kiss, as if I knew it was a goodbye kiss. All flustered, with tears in my eyes, I jumped out of my dream and ran to the telephone trying to inform someone. I am not sure what I expected to accomplish but I called the British Embassy. I even wrote to Buckingham palace to warn them. After her death, Lady Diana frequently appeared to me in my dreams, showing me many things about her afterlife that, out of respect to her, I would rather not discuss. She seemed to be very happy in her afterlife.

She even shared with me about her charities, especially about her role in clearing land mines; a process that I did not know anything about until two weeks later when I saw the man who worked with her on that charity on TV, stating that since her death the funding had stopped. I guess she was trying to communicate but unfortunately I wasn't able to help her. To her memory and as a sign of pain and mourning for losing a wonderful human being, I cut my hair, which is a part of Abadan and Kurdish tradition. They do it on their own, of course, but I visited a hairdresser.

For a long time, I prayed for her soul and finally asked her to stop coming to me in my dreams because I couldn't do anything for her. She has not appeared to me since.

Now, that I am able to reach people, I would like, just this once, to defend her. I have read many books about her and watched the documentaries about her life. I know she wasn't a saint; her affairs were well publicized. Sometimes she appeared to be a weak woman, acting like a child playing, instead of being who she was supposed to be. Frequently involved but seldom in love, she even had affairs with married men who managed to steal her trust by showing her affection. Regardless of how people perceive her, Lady Diana was a good-hearted human being that deeply cared about others. No matter how big the ordeal or how heavy the millstone she overcame. That is how we measure the humanity of generations, by ability, not inability.

I have heard from many people that she is still the icon she once was. Her celebrity has remained undiminished; perhaps owing to her mysterious death. Even though her last moment was caught on camera, nobody really knows why, or if, she was killed. One thing is clear, her death may not have been a set up but her torment was. Her phone calls were tapped, her privacy shattered; greedy photographers shadowed every step she took. They feasted on her like dirty flies attracted to a wedding cake.

Unfortunately, her mistakes were greatly publicized while her charities and good works seem to fall in the shadow of her greedy lovers and contacts that she thought had her best interest in their heart and gave them her love. From the news, the picture we see of Diana has made her a bit of a Drama Queen but, from what I know about her, shared with me by her spirit, she, like many troubled women, was lost and looking for love in all the wrong places.

Ever since her death, I have been looking for answers to her affairs. The only answer that comes back to me is, she wasn't really herself. I know, looking back at her life in this world, that she is not proud to be portrayed as a tragic queen with many lovers. I wish people would understand that any passionate human being, chained in a loveless marriage, whose husband publicly acknowledges another woman and tells her to find herself a lover, confined in the museum like walls of an old palace, subjected to outdated rules of monarchy and under constant watchful eyes and ears can possibly go mental and act out of desperation to receive public attention and pity. From my personal experience, observation and research I believe she was suffering from depression. People with depression make awful choices. I have never been in her situation but I know from my own depression that I have made mistakes in desperate times. Now, I sometimes find myself thinking, 'Good Lord, what was I thinking?'

I am certain that anyone on the cover of every magazine, as she was, is going to be negatively judged by many people. She was constantly facing the scrutiny from photographers and writers and was treated as public property, with little or no respect. People, who made money out of her image, walked over her dignity and her feelings. She wasn't treated fairly and as an icon with the respect she deserved.

Most people may take this important element quite lightly but an unbalanced serotonin level in the human brain can undermine and alter one's clear vision and cause decisions that can have a devastating effect on his or her life. People who write about her and judge her character in their tabloids, should worry about their own mistakes, not hers. I would wager that if Diana could return and tell us her story, this time with a fresh start, and remain the kindergarten teacher she once was, everyone would fall in love with her again. I have confidence that people who knew her closely, would have compared her with the Madonna because of her exterior beauty and extreme kindness that she showed, in particular to the sick. For those who miss her, I am confident she knows and she misses them as well. For those who make money out of criminalizing her, LET HER REST IN PEACE. She wasn't the only mortal human being on this earth. Everyone makes mistakes, and everyone dies.

PRICELESS SURPRISES

The premonitions continued. I had a premonition about the death of Chris Farley, the comedian, on December 18, 1997. I knew he was going to die on the day he was found dead. A third person, whose death I knew was about to happen before it did, was Stanley Kubrick, director of the movie, *Eyes Wide Shut*. I asked my doctor to give me something to stop the flash-forwards because I blamed myself for the death of people I did not know. To my surprise, he told me it is a gift, or a curse, and I have to accept it. He said their deaths had nothing to do with what I see or feel. I knew he was right but it was hard to accept because I couldn't help those people. It bothered me tremendously to know the time of their pending death and not be able to stop it. I felt guilty. I begged God to stop the flash forwards about some someone's departure because I couldn't take it any more.

Even though most of my experiences seem dark, and heavy they made me who I am. Not all the events of those days were negative and heavy on my heart; some were quite exciting and fun. I had some incredible experiences that I would not want to change for anything. During this period, one of my colleagues encouraged me to write poetry and, ultimately, I wrote hundreds of poems. Writing poetry became my coping mechanism in the blue days. More premonitions led to getting to know the fun side of the culture and were part of the excitement. Among those premonitions was the day that I met a bus driver on my way to show some of my photographs to a local Vancouver magazine.

I got on the Broadway Vancouver bus and noticed the driver's irritation. I do not have a habit of talking to the driver, or any other strangers for that matter, but something prompted me to talk to him. I asked him how long he had been working as a bus driver. He replied, "11 years, 29 days, 30 minutes and 11 seconds." I said to him, "You are not happy; why are you doing this job?" He replied, "Are you kidding me? I love it." I said, "Really? But this is not what you would prefer to do." He asked what I thought he could do with his life. I told him that I saw him as either a mechanic or a fire fighter. His mouth dropped. He said he did mechanic jobs on the side and was thinking about taking a course for it and had just applied for a fire fighter position.

I got off at my stop and told him I would see him on my way back. I was certain I would see him again. I met a friend and when I returned to the bus stop about five hours later, he showed up again. He said, "It's you again!" I asked him if he thought he was seeing a ghost. He said he phoned his wife and told her what I had told him. He said, "You are giving me goose bumps." I was not trying to do that but simply wanted to help him.

Another funny incident was when a friend of mine gave me an e-mail from a friend of hers, trying to set us up. We had never met but as we talked and exchanged questions back and forth, I told him about my intuition. He asked me what I thought he looked like. I told him it doesn't work that way but he insisted I try, so I did. I envisioned him in my mind as having short blond hair with a little bit of highlight in front, wearing off-color, faded blue jeans and a pair of yellow boots. When I told him, there was a heavy silence. I had to ask him if he was still there. He asked, "Are you looking at me?" I said, "Please don't joke." He said, "No, that is how I look and I have a pair of yellow boots." The good thing was, the picture was accurate. The bad thing was, we never talked again. Apparently, I scared the hell of him.

Unwritten Chapter

In 1998, I was 28 years old. Outside, I looked like a cosmopolitan woman who had seen it all. Inside, I was still a child at heart, absorbing cultural differences. Day in and day out I was working at my job. It gave me daily access and opportunity to communicate with people from different backgrounds, learn about them and even discover some of my own personality flaws and values. My inner soul was a flower that had been seeded in a desert climate until now and had found the opportunity to blossom. Working among other people resembled a human lab. I took advantage of every opportunity to learn about the cultural and human differences in different environments. Despite all the differences between the cultures, I was fascinated by the commonalities of humans who think they have very little in common but in fact they are linked to one another.

While I was working at the jewelry counter, I learned that Tania, a Chinese girl whom I had met through her brother when he was a classmate of mine, needed a summer job. Tania and I had become very close. I passed her resume to my manager and he hired her. One night, when the store was quiet, Tania went to the other counter just to chitchat with other employees. I had a strange uncomfortable feeling in my gut. It was as if I missed her and was angry with her for leaving me behind to talk to others. When she came back, I told her about the feeling and said to her, "I believe this is jealousy." I had never experienced that feeling before. She said, "Oh well, I always have that feeling." I smiled and rolled my eyes. This was not sexual jealousy. I was reminded of a movie I saw, Bicentennial, in which a robot had to learn human experiences. Like the robot, this little incident was a bracing experience for me and marked the first time I realized I was capable of feeling possessive or jealous and able to demand attention. Although it sounds strange to many, jealousy is not inherited in our genes; it is an experience.

During the course of my work in that store, my colleagues often asked if I was dating anyone. In truth, I had never had what I considered a real 'date.' I guess, at this time, when I thought about my French teacher back in the university in Iran, I decided that was simply a crush. I started thinking that it was time to close the window on past life memories. Moving on was quite an education. I had no knowledge of dating habits in either culture. I had no idea that going for coffee is the standard of early dating in Canada. Based on my studies of French literature, I referred to them as coffee breaks.

At work, there were plenty of young good-looking men and women. They flirted indiscriminately and were continually breaking up with one person and then going out with some else the next night. I could not justify one culture over another. It was simply not making any sense to me. While observing co-workers make-ups and break-ups, I noticed that the emphasis, in North American culture was directed toward the person's looks. Since beauty is only skin deep, without that five millimeters of skin, we would all look pretty much alike. In this society, a great deal of attachment is directed toward a person's image rather than the whole package. I found it quite hard to understand; why would someone want to go out with another person, just for the sake of physical attractiveness? Women flaunt their assets, meaning their breasts and butts, but I am curious… where do personality and brain fit into this pragmatic image? The attraction to the image persona is probably the reason for a number of divorces in the society. As a Persian proverb says, 'People shouldn't get too attached to physical beauty because a night of fever can make it disappear and not too much attached to material possessions because one bad business judgment can make all the money disappear in a day.'

I did not have any desire or experience of that sort. Every time someone that I was attracted to asked me out, my face was flushed, my outspoken personality disappeared, I had a hard time remembering words in any of the three languages I knew and I started mumbling. Sadly, I still have that problem.

Perhaps my mindset was different than that of many other women. I thought, why should I play with someone's emotions? I believed if I wanted something, I had to ask for it. I detested the 'horndog' attitude of most Iranian men; neither was I pleased by the laid back attitude of Canadian men. Also, I didn't like the prevailing 'We Go Dutch' policy where everyone pays their own share, whether they get the girl or not. Somehow, without benefit of any experience, my instincts harkened back to an earlier chauvinistic era where the man pursued and wooed the woman.

I expected if someone liked me, he should just say so. And our mutual respect and desire would be based on honesty and communication. I never knew I needed to study books before going on a date to know what to say or how to say it. I wasn't very happy when I discovered that dating is a world of its own.

During the years I have been in Canada, friends have always tried to set me up with their friends. I met a nice guy who worked as an engineer for Microsoft in the United States. On his way to Vancouver for a business deal, he stopped by for a coffee. He seemed to be very nice. I accepted his lunch invitation and we had a few phone calls between his travels back and forth to Vancouver. Before I met him for lunch. I tried to ask him some questions to know him better. He kept saying he didn't have time. I was wondering, why would he want to meet me, if he doesn't have time to answer a question or two? He said write your questions down. I wanted to teach him a lesson to never say that to a woman again. If he didn't want to meet me, he wasn't obligated, but I don't like to be treated as if I am a just an appointment.

I said that was fine. I had noticed that most woman who go out with someone, even when they are going down the aisle to the altar, they still don't know what sort of flowers or music, or even tooth paste, that person might like. Some of my questions, were silly, some very valid. I nicely and professionally typed up fifty questions, each with ten sub questions which I presented to him on our next lunch meeting. He said "What is this?" I said, "Your questionnaire." He said "What?" I said, "Do you recall that you asked me to write them down? So I did." He looked surprised and a bit sad. I asked, "What is it?" He replied, "My questionnaire for Microsoft job application was shorter than this." We met one more time after that. He still wanted to pursue me, but I didn't want to be around someone who couldn't or didn't want to make the time to communicate with me.

It was childish and immature, punishing him this way, but sometimes it is the only way to make some people understand. I have never been sure why there are a great many books on relationship but people still are divested in their relationships. Are they reading these book or not? If they are reading, and trying to practice what to say to a man or woman, why isn't it working? Every one is different, so shouldn't feelings be shared honestly and words comes from the heart; not from previous experiences or a book by an expert? Reading about relationships adds knowledge and a bounce but copying word for word from the experts is almost cheating on someone's feelings.

In my world, dating is different. I found myself having a difficult time adjusting to this new phase of my life. Perhaps my other reason for not being able to date like my peers, is because I focused on the European attitude that was much more appealing to me. Or, maybe I landed on earth from the planet Venus.

Also, I laugh at the notion of a biological clock that some women hear ticking loud and clear. My great grandfather had his last son when he was nearly 100 years old and being maternal in later years of life is common among women as well as men in my family. I have never believed that there is one person for everyone in this world. This mythical ideology there has never applied or worked for me but if there is such a thing and someone has been standing on a bus stop waiting for me to arrive, he might have gotten tired of waiting and chose to leave with the wrong gal or take a shorter route. I doubt if he is still waiting. But, if the ideology is true and if that ever happens, perhaps some day my prince will find me, I will let my readers know but till then this chapter of my life, remains open and unwritten.

İncurable Chauvinist

In September of 1997, Siavash and I decided our two-bedroom apartment was a little too hot and small to continue to live in. Through my efforts, we found a better apartment with two bedrooms and two bathrooms so we didn't have to be at each other's throat to clean up the other's mess. When we moved in, I took the master bedroom. He started yelling at me, saying that wasn't going to work. I said to him, "You didn't find the place, you did not deal with the landlord, you simply moved in. I am the one who always takes care of everything; I deserve the bigger room. If you are not happy, we don't need to share this residence. I would much rather live somewhere else, preferably alone." Larger room or not, I wanted to give him a lesson for his cold-hearted behavior.

I just thought I wouldn't have to clean his bathroom. The culture of Iran raises men to be so indolent that he still expected me to do all the cleaning. He cared less if everywhere was dirty. If he wanted to clean, he did, otherwise he didn't. This chauvinistic attitude, shared by so many Iranian men, is a cultural upbringing and has nothing to do with being Muslim or any other faith.

In fact, in real Islam, Prophet Mohammad praises a man who shares housework with his wife, as his holiness did. But, according to Iranian macho culture that has been ruining so many relationships, I could not help but notice that a man helping at home is considered shameful. The family of a man thinks it lowers their manhood by doing their part. My own mother criticized Khosro for helping his wife. When I told her about Siavash's attitude, I had a feeling she wasn't concerned because she brought the boys up this way, telling them it is against their nature to have a softer side and help at home. Of course, growing up with the boys, she made it clear that the boys would help her but not every one else, including me. Every effort I made, he found a way to reject but two rules I set never changed. One, he had to wash his own dishes. Two, he had to do his own laundry. If he didn't, I was throwing his dishes in the garbage. If he left his clothing out, it would sit there until he did his own chores. If he needed me to take the load out of the washer he had to request it. He got the picture. I am not his mother to wash his socks or fold his pajamas.

Unfortunately, too many Iranian women, Muslim women and weak women from different cultures and faiths take too much abuse and enslave themselves, just to have a man figure in their lives. Women should know, they don't need a man in order to be complete. A male and a female should be a compliment and accent to each other's lives, not taking roles as master and slave. Mental slavery for women is not cultural or religious driven. It can be formed among members of any culture, any color or any back ground and come in any format and do exactly the same as it does to the women in abusive and Muslim families.

PHANTOM PAIN

Life went on but by September 1998, after years of neglect and abuse, my body demanded attention. A long list of maladies started to appear, beginning with constant headaches similar to migraines. Although Canadian health care allowed me to visit a doctor without charging any extra cash, I didn't have the money for my prescriptions. Canadian medications look cheap compared to US prices but they were still a big burden. I was having budget problem as in the years before. To overcome the pain and avoid doctors, I took as many as seven or eight Tylenols per day.

It is a miracle I am still alive and not an addict. I realize that my wrong decisions could have driven me to a path of painkiller addiction. My health problems surfaced shortly after arriving in Canada. I was not properly diagnosed with depression and my problems were being caused, not only by my past but also by my tumultuous relationship with the boys. Now, it hit me all at once. For the physical pain, I was almost constantly chewing Tylenol. For the mental burden, I tried anything to take the pain away. I started to go to the gym more often and took St. John's Wort for my blues. It didn't help. My pain was beyond the power of this little organic pill. I knew there would be complications but I simply couldn't afford anything else.

Pain forced me to visit a doctor. After a careful examination, he told me it could be my eyes, my sinuses, my teeth, or my tonsils, since they were bleeding all the time.

I sarcastically told him "Wow, that is much clearer now." I asked him which one we were going to track down first. He said, "We will get you an appointment with a specialist for your nose and sinuses and a throat specialist, and then you go to see a dentist." I came home feeling great sorrow in my heart for me.

The following day, I visited a dentist who told me that the fillings in my teeth were 'rusted' and possibly the cause of some of my medical problems. He said sixteen of my teeth needed refilled and would cost nearly $4,000. I saw the magnified pictures of my teeth and, sure enough, the silver alloy fillings had all turned brown. Prior to exiting Iran, I had gone through a lengthy ordeal to refill my teeth. Dentist's offices are filthy. With no mandatory regulations, dentists have no obligation to sterilize anything. The day I was in the dental chair, I saw blood on the equipment that was used in my mouth. I was thankful that the dentist's equipment didn't pass the AIDS virus to me.

Because the HIV virus is mostly passed through infected individuals who have unprotected sex and there is an high incidence among homosexuals, the government of Iran reacts by denying and dismissing its existence; trying to portray Iran's environment as a pretense that there is no AIDS in Iran, which is a deadly policy playing with millions of people's lives. If they don't receive the information they need to protect themselves, they simply pass it on to others.

Although I considered myself an informed individual, back in Iran I had never heard of condoms. When I first saw a used one, I recall my mother, started cursing the individual that had left it. I asked her what it was. She said, "Nothing." Mum, like many religious individuals, thought of sex as dirty. I guess she thought explaining a condom was the duty of a medical team or a minister in Iran's government. Presumably, when the policy of government is: Sex is Taboo; they don't see a reason to inform people of diseases that might affect millions.

In October 1998, I consulted with the specialist about my constantly bleeding tonsils. At first, since I was an adult, the specialist, who was also a surgeon, didn't want to perform the operation on me. A tonsillectomy in an adult usually meant severe pain and higher than normal chances for bleeding. After losing my voice for a week, my patience was stretched to the limit. I told him that if he didn't take them out, I would get a sharp knife and do it myself. I know it sounded impossible but I figured pain is pain.

If I was trying to avoid pain, it was too late. I had no voice and this piece of meat was aching and bleeding all the time. What more could I experience? I might as well give it a shot. The specialist screamed, "No, no, don't, I will do it." I asked him what made him change his mind. He said it was extremely painful surgery for an adult but if I was willing to do it myself, he was sure his procedure was marginally less excruciating. He said there was a ten-month waiting list. I said that was fine, I would take my chances. I ended up losing my voice for nearly two weeks again and before the sixth month he had to move me to the top cancellation slot for an emergency operation.

In the meantime, my life seemed gloomier day after day. There is a famous Persian proverb describing bad luck, 'Every stone falling from the sky is landing on my head.' It certainly seemed a fair statement about my situation. Health problems and difficulties of life in an industrial country seemed to come my way faster than I could find a solution for the prior one. People with depression are often inclined to physical health problems. The source of the pain may be non-existent. In psychology and medical books it is referred to as phantom pain because, even though the individual looks healthy, the pain feels real but doesn't have medical merit. By that, I mean it could even come from a non-existing limb that has been amputated or from a pain that travels through the body. The medical miracle of technology has no answer for this sort of ailment and it is recognized as incurable or unexplainable.

My back pain didn't subside but when one pain overcame another, I had so much pain from my throat that I couldn't feel the back pain for a while. Prior to the arrival of the back pain, I exercised regularly and walked several miles every day but I still developed chronic back pain. I visited a back specialist who had more bad news for me. The specialist told me that I had muscle spasms aggravated by many causes. He thought my flat feet might cause the spasms.

His diagnoses lead to my visiting the next doctor, a podiatrist. I visited so many doctors that year that I joked about it, "I am on a date with a list of doctors." My life blueprint was simple; I went to work, visited doctors or lay on the bed and ached. I was no longer able to do the skating and exercises. I had no desire to go out, meet with friends or do anything except hurt.

I finally consulted the podiatrist who confirmed the other specialist guess and prescribed a pair of orthotics. It was a must but I simply couldn't afford $475 for orthotics, nor did my insurance at work pay for such a thing. It was considered cosmetic and they would not pay for it. It had to wait until I cashed in my vacation money the following year. On the faintly bright side, it was not all in my head as I had previously been told. I felt better knowing that at least there were genuine reasons for my back pain. Knowing it was one thing; living with the pain was another.

December of 1998 was upon us and I was sobbing from the constant pain. My manager suggested that if I couldn't work I should quit, go home and go on welfare. When I heard him say that, it was as if he placed a knife into my heart. My body went cold and numb at how insensitive he was. Although he knew that before the back pain started, I had fallen on the ice on my way to work. It didn't seem to bother him at all that the back pain could very well be a work related injury. Standing for hours aggravated it. It was a great insult to hear him suggesting welfare to me.

In my opinion, welfare wasn't for me. I was educated and experienced. I could speak three languages and had plenty of potential for growth in the business world. Although he had once helped me through a difficult time with a loan for my immigration fees, since then he had changed. His ethnic background had similar treatment toward women as my culture. According to his East Indian culture, men are superior and women should listen and obey. He expected me to shut up about my pain and work full-time until after Christmas.

Motivated by the need for money, I forced myself to work through the Christmas rush. I spent Christmas in bed with a lot of pain all over my body. Siavash, my only family, didn't even knock on my door to see if I was still alive. However, since he had paid the monthly rent, he asked me when I was going to pay my share. I managed to survive by living off my credit cards and small savings and even cashed my marginal RRSP, equivalent to the 401-K in the US. Many times, I cursed the Saints for being born into this family and many more times, I cursed myself for helping him. I took my claim to the Workers' Compensation Board; then to EI, which is the Employment Insurance for workers. Although money was deducted from my paycheck automatically by both of these, neither would accept my case and threw it out. I had to continue to work, even thought I was suffering from excruciating back pain.

Ⴖewcomers' job Ⴖightmare

By the end of 1998, the store where I had worked for more than three years was closing its doors. I started looking for a job again. I interviewed with another large North American retail chain in January 1999. The lady that interviewed me was very sweet to me. I had more than three years Canadian experience in jewelry sales. I also had a certificate from Association of Gemologists of Canada. I was quickly hired at $ 14.50 per hour. This was temporary work but could become permanent. I was elated but I knew there were others who would not be so happy with my hiring. Some had probably been in their position for years and, just as I in my previous jewelry job, still couldn't get a raise. I knew how frustrating it was for them to see a newcomer hired at a much higher salary than they were receiving.

Shortly after I started, there was a meeting with an important executive I will call Madam X, who was in charge of our training. After introducing ourselves at the first session on the first day, I guess I said something funny because everyone except Madam X laughed. I belatedly realized she probably didn't appreciate my humor. I apologized but she said there was no need to apologize; we were all free to make jokes.

The group was dismissed for lunch. I went home to find a picture required for my ID badge and was about two minutes late reporting back for training class. As I entered the room, the rest of the class had just sat down and were still getting settled. At the end of the day, Madam X called me into her office, handed me a check for one hundred dollars and said, "Your personality doesn't match with us. We don't need someone like you." I asked, "What did I do? I was two minutes late because I was looking for a picture you had asked me to bring. If it was because of my joke, I am sorry." She said, "No, thank you, your personality does not match with us." This was a personal record for me. I was fired before I even started work.

Madam X was an HR executive; meaning, she knew the laws of Canada for hiring and firing employees backwards and forwards. When I went to Canadian Human Resources to complain about her unfair judgment, I was told there is no law protecting any temporary or part time employee from being fired. I am sure she must have felt great getting rid of me. I knew her treatment of me was driven by a personal agenda. There was no way she could have explained her actions to her superiors but Employee Insurance of Canada, which supposedly protects workers, informed me that unless I was a union member or full time, there was no law to protect me. Unlike in the United States, suing someone for personal issues is never heard of. I had to swallow what she did to me, and move on.

Despite the blow, I managed to keep my head up and spirits high and found another job in a jewelry shop privately owned by a Chinese woman. During the years of living in Canada, while working full time, I have also tried to pursue my passions of which Gemology was one. For one hundred dollars tuition per course, I had taken night classes and obtained two Certified Gemologist certificates from the Institute of Gemology of Canada. The only reason, other than money, that I stopped pursuing my studies at Gemology of Canada was because I found out that the world renowned Institute of Gemology, located in California, was the only universally recognized institution and I could not afford their tuition.

For the new job I had laid all my qualifications on the table. I never claimed to be a fully licensed Gemologist but I had the passion and the eye for gems the job required. I was delighted to hear that, according to the job description, I could be hired as the assistant manager. It wasn't written policy but apparently I was expected to sell $10,000 worth of diamonds per day. I was to be paid in cash. There was no direct deposit to my bank account, no vacation pay, no insurance, and no medical. More importantly, there was no record of what we sold.

Then, for reasons I never understood, the owner told her Chinese workers that I had lied to her about my qualifications, saying I was a full gemologist. Although I had shown her all my papers and certifications and she seemed to understand them fully; she even said she had studied under the same instructor; she accused me of misrepresenting my credentials. She asked me to leave after one week, stating that I was not what she was looking for. I am sure I wasn't, because I had the effrontery to ask her how she reported to the Canadian Tax Bureau for taxes she didn't seem to charge. And, where were the records of sales? Canadian law requires that all goods must be taxed. All transactions, purchases, sales and salary were in cash and no tax was charged on anything. Her business seemed highly questionable. As an assistant to the owner, I had to know because if anything unpleasant regarding taxes happened, I could have been held partially responsible.

The mountain of difficulties I faced in Canada almost made my existence in Iran pleasant by comparison. My survival instinct and experiences seemed completely useless.

I looked everywhere for a job. I even took insurance courses. I bought into the fairy tale that you can make money selling insurance in Canada, which is totally untrue. Since the national system covers most people, almost no one pays for extra insurance. The only benefit to me was, I learned a lot of little things about insurance. I took the insurance license test three times and I can swear, I was not intended to be an insurance salesman. The supervisor, who was helping me, told me he could not understand my failing the test. He said, "You know this material as well as anyone, what is wrong?" I said, "Maybe it is not meant for me." He didn't believe that but I do. I heard that a man who took the exam with me and passed it soon quit.

After these two incidents, my self-esteem was sagging. I was unable to find another job and I had no choice but to take my health case to the Employment Insurance (EI). Since I was very sick and was going to have tonsil surgery, my case was recognized as a disability. It took EI three weeks to answer me. By then I'd been out of a job for five weeks and the law doesn't require EI to pay benefits until two weeks after a case is approved. I asked the employees of EI how I was supposed to live. They were sorry but there was nothing they could do for me. I had no money at all. I had even cashed my vacation pay. I lay on my bed in constant pain and pondered my wasted education and life. There is only so much faith can do. Poverty makes the devil look too good to refuse his offer.

I lost track of my days. In desperation, I had no choice but to seek help from welfare. They told me they could not help me immediately either because I would be paid by EI in seven days. It had been more than six weeks since I had even one cent. Just because I didn't have money, didn't mean I didn't have bills. I had been living off my credit cards for almost 60 days with no money at all. Creditors were calling me and Siavash was asking for the rent money.

I finally began receiving $675 a month. I paid $415 for rent and $50 for my share of the telephone and long distance calls to mum, leaving $210 per month for food, medicine, transportation, interest accumulated on my credit cards and all other living expenses. While the EI or welfare money seems a giant favor to the unemployed; the amount of money I was granted was so little it was barely enough to cover the basic cost of living. Meanwhile, mismanagement of an enormous amount of welfare funds, necessitating cuts, was all over the news, including a very public discovery of incompetence of a former EI minister.

Near the end of the term of Mr. Chrétien, Prime Minister of Canada, Jane Stewart, his Minister of EI, lost track of over a billion dollars. In the year 2000, when Ms. Stewart was questioned, she could not explain where the money had gone. Canadians were told on national TV that since Mr. Chrétien and Ms. Stewart's father were good friends, she continued to serve as Minister, even after admitting that she had accepted hospitality from a family with a clear business interest. This clearly conflicted with federal ethic guidelines but she interpreted it as nothing but personal hospitality. Whether it was personal or business didn't much matter to me but her losing hundreds of millions of dollars affected the lives of millions, including me, who went home without any money.

There is so much waste in the government of Canada budget that at the end of each year, instead of tax cuts, there are budget cuts. I was not born a Canadian but I am now a citizen of this country and although I might resemble a stepmother getting all bottled up over a stepchild, I love Canada as much, if not more, than my birthplace.

It is painful to watch the never-ending arguments of Members of Parliament of Canada. They waste taxpayer's money on countless hours of arguing. Sometimes, it seems they get paid to argue for the sake of argument. In May 2001, Jean Chrétien defended a 20 percent raise for the MPs. I stopped watching the debates. Every MP on the hill receives a hefty check. In 2003, each Member of Parliament, excluding the Minister, earned $69,100 base salary and a $22,800 tax-free expense allowance placing them in the top two per cent of Canadian income earners. The government doesn't have money for the other 98 percent but amazingly has plenty for its own members. In the year 2004, Members of Parliament are again voting for another salary increase that will pay them about $155,000 annually plus their allowance.

Ｔоnsіllесｔоｍу

In late April 1999, I had the long-postponed tonsillectomy surgery. I award this surgery the honor of the most painful procedure I have ever undergone. I reported for the operation at 7:00 a.m. The hospital was quite far from our house and I had to ask Siavash to give me a ride because it was hospital policy to arrive and leave with a family member. As painful as the process was, it was more bearable than his complaining about being inconvenienced.

As the surgeon made the incision, despite the anesthetic, I could still feel a part of me had literally been cut. I was in excruciating pain. As I was coming out of the anesthetic, I started moaning. I could not help crying. The nurse rushed to me and gave me more morphine and I passed out. This happened several times. Finally, around 3:00 p.m., I woke up again, crying like a baby. The nurse told me I just had to swallow the pain. I recall telling her if that if she were on this bed, she would understand my agony. She gave me another shot and said, "We simply cannot give you any more morphine. You've had seven shots in less than seven hours." She gave me twelve Demerol and a prescription and sent me home. Unbelievably, Siavash paid for the prescription and bought me some ice cream and jellies. I have no other recollection of the trip home, only that we got there and I crawled into my bed. The only thing worse than being in pain is being in pain alone. I had to get up and cook and take care of myself. Although I lived with a family member, he was useless.

One of my *then* friends was an Iranian woman that Siavash took a liking to. She came to stay with me for a few nights to help me during my recovery but quickly remembered that her uncle was in town and she had parties to attend. She left the next morning.

I say *then* friend, because after I got better she asked me to do something illegal for her. Her English was not as good as mine and she wanted me to register and take the entrance exam for her to attend college. I like to help out a friend but decided this was above and beyond what a friend would ask. Besides, my law-abiding inner self kicked in and I feared that if we got caught it would take longer than an overnight to get to her uncle's next party. On another occasion, she remarked that if I were a guy she would have welcomed the idea of being with me. I was not interested in being part of her scam or becoming her lesbian lover, so I said, "Adieu" to her, which in French, means goodbye forever.

Because of my age, fear of infection was quite real and the pain was overwhelming but my surgeon assured me I would have no trouble recovering fully. In addition to the twelve Demerol, he prescribed

50 Tylenol III, two to be taken every four hours. I didn't finish more than half of them before I stopped taking them. He was also kind enough to keep checking on me by phone everyday to make sure I was alive and healing well.

Every day, I got up, made some soup, went back to bed and moaned until the next time I felt hungry. There were many times I wished I were dead. I even thought of overdosing. I felt an enormous void inside of me. An overwhelming loneliness was pent up in me that would not been cured if I were invited to every party in town. I sometimes cried myself to sleep. I felt unwanted, uninvited and abandoned. But, as the Persian proverb says, 'You can't expect much of your host when you pay someone a unexpected visit.' I had a strong resentment toward my family; my father for creating me, my mother for not letting me die when I was younger, Manoocheher for hurting me and Siavash for not being more compassionate and caring about me. I was bitter with Siavash and was not talking to him.

A few friends came over to see me a week after my surgery and life resumed. I had gotten better on my own and my friends decided to have a party in a restaurant for my 29th birthday. This was the first and last time I have ever celebrated my birthday or anyone even remembered it at all. I blew out candles on a cake for the first time. In a party of six unrelated people, I opened for the first time, a present from someone other than my mother.

Even though I was receiving disability payments and technically was not supposed to work, I had to have money for the pile of prescriptions I was taking. No one is allowed to stay on disability more than a few months and I did not plan to. I just wanted to be able fix my teeth and pay my medical bills.

I found a job paying $12.00 per hour as an undercover security officer for a chain of supermarkets. I was proud of my previous role in helping the police catch one of the largest organized criminal groups in Canada but I never in a million years thought that I would have to do this job for living.

The job description didn't explain much about the responsibility and danger I would be facing until after I finished my training. It certainly wasn't a glamour job nor was it rewarding enough for the personal risk involved. Not to mention, no one ever says thank you to any police or security officer for saving their lives or property.

The job was spotting thieves and shoplifters, of which there were an alarming number. Some are unarmed but others are dangerous; armed with knives and guns. A gang of drug addicts even carried infected needles with which to stick anyone who tried to stop them. Some are homeless people who steal food to exchange for drug money and some are regular people saving a buck. They are young, middle aged and old. I was genuinely surprised when I found out how many 'good' people steal from stores. Just plain people walk around the store eating or hiding food in their clothes and bags.

I worked in the security job for three months. It worried me that I was technically violating disability law. I did not want to do it but I had to have money to pay my medical and dental expenses. Since the surgery, the pain had reduced but had not gone away. On the last day of my probationary period, my supervisor, who is now a police officer in a neighboring community, called me into the back office. With his friend in the room as a witness, my supervisor accused me of lying about my work eligibility status. He said he had been investigating me and learned from his sources that I had been receiving disability payments ever since he hired me. I knew who had talked to him. A man I worked with at the jewelry company had seen me at work in the grocery and had reported me to the East Indian manager who harassed me. I had rebuffed his advances so he decided to get revenge. He had phoned my supervisor, telling him I was on disability.

My supervisor said I was taking the government's money illegally and was worse than a thief. I said I was not a thief. I had brought my health problems and the costs to many government agencies; none could or would help me. If I had that kind of help, I would never have gone back to work while I was still not well. And, if I had any alternative, I would never work in such a dangerous job, even if I were well. I may have lied to earn money to take care of my health issues but I had to do it because the government would not help.

In 2004, the government of Canada used taxpayer's money in sponsoring scams for over one hundred million dollars. The Minister and MPs involved were not considered thieves when EI lost track of over one billion dollars. But, I was a thief for receiving $1,860 in three months while I worked at a job.

I told him I was not happy or proud of what I did but I had no choice. Sometimes in life, people make tough decisions because they don't have an alternative. I told him that, morally, my conscience was telling me I was wrong but I had no other alternative and nobody to help me. I pointed out that the money I received was originally deducted from my own paycheck during the time I was well enough to work.

This man, who became a police officer, was widely known among store employees to spend the night with another undercover employee who moonlighted as a stripper. We also heard that he picked up other women in bars and here he was lecturing me.

It seemed that the resemblance of my life to Les Miserable was never ending. This time, I was more like the male character that was jailed for many years for stealing a loaf of bread.

After his tirade, he gave me the choice of resigning or being fired. I chose resignation. I was shaking like a tree. I told him he had been given wrong information and was making a mistake. I was using this money to stay alive, not piling it up in my pocket. He was indifferent to my plight.

I left the security office fuming. He kept saying he was worried about my mental health, I find that hard to believe because he not only fired me that day; he also reported me to the EI supervisors. I didn't pocket any taxpayer money and never had any intention of doing so. In fact, I eventually repaid over $2,000 of disability payments and interest. I wasn't recognized as a thief by EI because; despite the fact it knew all along that I needed the money for medical attention, the authorities never made an effort to help me. On the way, home, I looked down from the high bridge, thinking how easy it would be to just jump. I finally got a grip on myself and controlled my emotions. I forced myself to think of the bright side. As we say in my language, "Every bad event happens for a reason." I consoled myself with the thought that I could have been killed had I stayed on that job.

EMERGENCE OF DEPRESSION, "STONES FALLING FROM THE SKY"

For a long time, I believed 'every stone falling from the sky landed on my head.' It meant that I had more than my fair share of struggle and turbulence in my short life. But, it is not fair to say that I didn't have a hand in bringing the depression on myself as well as receiving it from Mother Nature. The unwanted gift of genes prone to this disease, which I like to call the silent monster, was delivered to me through my family tree. I had an explanation but no valid legal excuse, except self-preservation, for the security job fiasco. This was one of the lowest points of my life and depression won.

Recently, someone asked me; "What is depression like?" We were sitting in a room with no windows, only walls and a door. I told her that the room we are sitting in is an example of depression. A depressed person lives in a room with no window to the outside world. On bad days, when he or she wants to leave the room, he shakes as if his legs were not his and have a mind of their own, his arms wants to stay, his body wants to stay but his will wants to go out. People with depression live in this room everyday. On my good days, my mind was like a freestyle swimmer, swimming competitively to compensate for lost time. When I get to the middle of the ocean, I run out of energy. I bob up and down in the water and I am terrified that I am going to die. By the end of the day I am restless and panicked. I want to be back in that room and curl up against the wall. Other swimmers pass me, swimming comfortably; they think I am crazy for working too hard. This is how the rest of the word sees the depressed person. After hearing this, the woman was in tears for me.

During the time I was severely depressed, I was like a vampire. Sunlight bothered me. I lived for the night and couldn't wait till sunset. I agonized during the day but felt less pain and was more comfortable during the night, which is common among people with depression. I felt content when I went to bed and fell asleep, whereas people without depression couldn't wait to wake up and start their day bright and early.

I am not suggesting that Canada was a prison, quite the contrary, but living in confinement, even though there is no physical barrier is what people with depression feel. They cannot see the sparkling stars, the shining sun or the moonlight. They do not hear the birds sing in the morning or feel the gentle breeze off the ocean, or anything for that matter, beyond the borders of their comfort zone. They feel no security and know no sanctuary.

No matter how wonderful the environment, the walls are the only things they can see. They feel lost and lonely and out there somewhere. It is a scary sensation that caused me to walk on the edge of a black and white path for the next four years. I felt the slightest sudden move or wrong step could tumble me into the hills of death. The shadow of depression was a dark and deep cloud of scary ghosts that tormented me every second and followed my every step. I was so tired of living that way that I kept nearly 120 sleeping pills at my bedside. I looked at them every day, and tried to imagine what it would be like if I took my life. Death was very appealing but I couldn't get over my love for God and I knew He would not forgive me for taking the life He had given me before He was ready for me. I cried for help and I cried because if I died, I had no one to cry for me after I was gone.

I didn't have much going for me but at last I decided that I had choices. It took me nearly a year to shift from being unhappy to being slightly content and knowing who I was, what I had and what I could do to change the future. This was the beginning of an even more traumatic period of my life; I wasn't yet diagnosed with depression.

Depression doesn't appear in one day. It starts slowly, like a candle but in full bloom burns like a mid-July forest fire. It may take years for someone with the heart of a lion, determination the size of an elephant and a support system as vast as all the world's armies to make that person's depression, the cancerous disease, go away. Just like cancer, the silent monster doesn't need much to trigger a return. In a sense, a depression survivor is very much like an individual who has survived cancer. I am not a cancer survivor nor am I completely free of my depression but I learned things that have helped me to overcome my depression on most days.

Depression is a manipulative disease. I learned a great deal about it by researching it. As strange as it sounds, it reflects one's personality and feeds on the best a person can offer. Again, it is in a sense very similar to cancer in that it uses the same tactic to destroy. There is nothing pretty or happy about depression. If there is a silver lining to the cloud of depression, it is that it makes my writing darker, yet more appealing, than when I am happy. I have used it to my benefit to create the writing that I am most proud of. I wrote my best poetries during these bleak times. From time to time when I feel depression free, I even enjoy reading the depressed passages because they look like the Mona Lisa's of my work. So, in a way, depression and I have found a way to work with each other. She wants a piece of me and offers me something in return.

After the job incident, the misery of my days was far from over and seemed endless. Fortunately, I had earned just about enough to restore my teeth. I was going from dentist to orthodontist, having X-rays taken by the dozen. My teeth were so sensitive it was impossible to restore them all at once. I had lost so much weight that I was at the lowest weight I have ever been in my adult life. I was becoming anemic. When I tried to eat, I became nauseated. After a year of misery, I managed to restore one side of my mouth.

For the remainder of my dental work, I visited a dentist who was reputed to be one of the best in Vancouver. He told me he would do a job I would never forget. Indeed, he has done just that. When I complained, while under the happy gas, about pain in the nerve he administered a second drug. A female dentist that later became a good friend told me that drug was a steroid. Steroids are sometimes used as an anti-inflammatory. He damaged my upper right molar nerve, which eventually damaged the tooth. Even the steroid didn't help and in a few days I had to be taken to Emergency in pain.

The doctor there diagnosed my problem as something to do with the damaged nerve. I followed up with a neurologist who confirmed the Emergency doctor's suspicions and gave me a shot in my neck to calm the nerve, which fell out of the tooth the following year. Four years later, in 2003, I could no longer stand the continual pain and had to undergo root and gum surgery to stop the pain and sensitivity.

The *Best Dentist in Vancouver's* malpractice and prescribing a wrong medication very well could have had a hand in my subsequent suicidal period. One of the recognized side effects of steroid drugs is depression. I recently read about Jane Pauley, the famous talk show host and author who was also diagnosed with bipolar and depression. During her interview, she confirmed that if she had not received steroids, her mental illness would never have surfaced Steroids essentially induce the release of a hormone hypercortisolism, which has been found in patients with depression. It is also a fact that other mental disorders might occur at the same time as manic-depressive mode or bipolar. The list includes anxiety disorders, post-traumatic stress disorder, obsessive-compulsive disorder and depression. Unfortunately, I was suffering, at the time, from at least three ailments on that list; post-traumatic stress, anxiety disorder and depression.

To keep my spirits alive, I kept looking at the bright side. I had limited choices; either I sat down and cried for my misery or kept going. As we say in a Persian proverb, 'At the end of a dark night, there is always a glorious bright day.' I hoped that proved to be true. I kept telling myself that after all the pain I had endured, I was still in charge of my own life and that meant a lot to me.

After the security job, I decided to go back to school and try to finish my studies; this time for good, despite Siavash's counter-productive sar casm. He kept repeating a hurtful comment about professional students. A person might be confused about his or her future but I am sure nobody intentionally plans to ruin his or her own life. I certainly didn't want to ruin mine and I was appalled at how he could criticize me when he never raised a finger to help me, or anyone else for that matter.

In order to have the world of cyber space at my fingertips and aid me in my research, studies and writing papers at school, I managed, in July 1999, to buy a computer on the installment plan at fifty dollars per month. My computer diploma didn't help me get a job but it helped me to learn lots of usable programs and also aided me with photography, another passion of mine. Siavash thought of a computer as a luxury, much as he thought of my glasses when I needed them. He did not contribute to the purchase of the computer but once I had it, wanted me to teach him how to use it. I told him to do what I did; register for a diploma computer course, pay the tuition, take computer classes and then buy his own. He replied that he didn't have time for all that. I told him charity was a two way street and he had been going the wrong direction for too long for me to feel generous now.

For a short time, I used the living room table as my computer desk until he complained that I was disturbing his television viewing. Although I was across the room, he said the keyboard sounds bothered him. So, I bought an *Assemble it Yourself* desk and set it up by myself, all 300 pieces.

I was trying to find a profession to pursue that I could be passionate about, where, for the first time, I could define who I was. Around that time, I happened to watch a program about survivors of WWII Nazi camps. The program revealed that nearly all of the camp survivors were depressed and needed psychiatric help, with the exception of one person who later wrote his autobiography. The documentary of the Auschwitz survivor indicated that his contentment came from understanding his environment and trying to control what he could and live with things he had no control over. He didn't have control over his freedom but he had control over whom he spoke to in the morning. He had control over combing his hair, brushing his teeth and choosing to read a book or not to read for the day. In such a confined and controlled place, if he had big expectations he wouldn't be able to meet them. He brought himself down and limited his expectations to focus on survival and small victories.

CELEBRATING CHRISTMAS
WITH MY JEWISH FRIEND

The year 1999 proved to be a difficult, agonizing year for me. I had lost many friends and found new enemies. The only bright light of that year was finding my new friend, Monica. A skilled dentist and wonderful individual, she and I met in her office. She helped me with the restoration of some of my teeth and after her professional work was done became a good friend. We had much in common and hit it off the minute we met. Her parents lived in Alberta and according to her stories, she didn't have much of a family either. Since we were both alone, I invited her for Christmas dinner. It was interesting to say the least, a Muslim and a Jew celebrating Christmas. In retrospect, it brings tears and a smile to my face. Wouldn't it be nice if the whole world could do the same, leave aside their differences aside and focus on commonalities. We seemed to have much in common and spent hours talking about different issues.

In my ideal world, where all religions get along peacefully, this is the picture I see in my mind and I use humor to describe it.

Before the Wailing Wall, in Jerusalem, a Jewish man worships God. Judging from his long woven beard, long unkempt hair and the yarmulke, resembling a small, flattened Japanese rice plate on his head, he appears to be a deeply religious man, in deep thought. He has a Torah in his hand and whispers words of God slowly.

Joining him, is an Arab man, wearing his famous Samurai robe with a white ghutra napkin folded neatly on his head, tidied up by a double tube black aghaal around his forehead. His neatly trimmed beard is not as long as the other man's. He sits next to the Jewish man. He has a Koran in his hand and reads slowly.

Joining them is a Catholic priest wearing his beautiful chasuble, the flashy, ceremonial outfit with gold filigree and embroidery that looks like part of the John Galliano Fall Couture Collection. He has a Bible in his hand. The three men sit side by side, say 'hello' to each other and call one another 'brother.'

This passage may look funny but it is not that far fetched from reality. But isn't it true that what the holy men of God, Moses, Jesus and Mohammad, the founders of three Abrahamic religions, wanted to teach us is that it is not how we worship but whom we worship? In our world, unfortunately, emphasis is so much on our differences that it has contributed to global agitation and animosity caused by people who think one's God is better than another. We cannot say that my God is better than yours because there is only one.

We are all forgetting something. We are here on earth for a purpose. Going round and round and hurting and killing others for the benefit of our doubts, is not going to take us any closer to God. God himself has said many times, in different holy books, that he values humanity over long prayers. Prayers are the candles that light our personal pat, but the good deeds are the marks for entrance to heaven and even more, for pleasing God himself.

I am not a priest, an Ayatollah or a Rabbi but I am certain that, from any religious perspective, what we see happening around the globe in the name of God, is the work of the devil. The vicious killing, in the name of Islam, Jihad or any other religion, of people who have done no harm to humanity is nothing more than wanton, brutal murder. These sick acts will remain a curse on the souls of the guilty for eternity in hell. Malicious deeds should never be confused with the word of God or the deeds that He expects us to do.

Just a reminder; it is not how we worship but who we worship that counts. And, because we are all created by the same God and came, ultimately, from the same ancestor parents, we are all brothers and sisters.

Photography

For as long as I can remember, even before I started writing in the first grade, I have had a camera in my hand and a love of photography in my heart. As a child, I avidly collected photos. Unlike most everything else in my life that I had to struggle with, photography, poetry and writing were effortless and flowed naturally. Since moving to Canada, I enjoy the art of nude photography. My photographs are poetic in Michelangelo's style to show goodness and beauty in the subject and not to be provocative or degrading. Although public nudity goes against my religion, I believe if God didn't intend to give someone a gift, He wouldn't have. If Michelangelo was not supposed to be who he was, he could not have earned the respect of generations by creating the masterpieces he did. In my mind, a picture of a beautiful woman is like a Monet painting. You admire what God has given her without disturbing or touching the beauty. My photographs are artistic, not obscene. I don't care for the undignified pictures of woman in porn magazines. One's dignity should never be transgressed for someone else's pleasure or money.

My problematic life had not allowed me to fully indulge in two life passions where I could freely express my inner soul, feel safe and have no fear. One was poetry; the other was photography. Back in Iran, my passions never blossomed because of pressure from my mother and lack of money. I was not allowed to do anything my way, unless I was given the ok by her or later by Siavash. Now, I didn't feel that I had to obtain anyone's permission.

I have always read my poetry to Siavash, hoping to get through to him. However, like father, like son, his limitation for understanding any art, lack of passion and constantly criticizing and mocking me, destroyed the bridges to my inner self; the only passion that I had allowed myself to indulge in. I could no longer write. My photography did not set well with him either. I gave up on him and cared less about his opinion. All my life, I have lived by the golden rules and I strongly believe that what goes around, comes around. I believe they are important. I didn't see myself as a wise old person, just the only one I knew well and I didn't want to have a lot of regrets later in life. One proverb I have intended to follow is to try to never do anything that I will regret tomorrow.

Siavash and I, although born from the same mother, might as well have come from different planets. Simply because he was older than me, didn't make him a wiser person. I don't believe age has anything to do with wisdom. He saw me as an incompetent and confused woman who should listen to the older boys of her family in order to have a better life.

I didn't seek his attention and had no desire to share my thoughts with him, since every time I tried he had a hard time digesting my words. He thought of me as a rambler with profane proclivities that he condemned. We never discussed my work anymore because there was nothing he understood about it.

Like too many men, he sees what he wants to see. He, my father, Manoocheher and men around the globe like them, with a limited capacity of comprehension, see a woman only as a sex object. A nude woman is sending them an invitation to have sex with her. If she sleeps with them, she is a bad woman who they will never take home to mother. If she doesn't, she is still a bad woman trying to use her assets to initiate sex with them. Either way, in their minds, she is nothing more than a whore.

On one occasion, he happened to see some of my work, including nude photos of my female clients. He charged into my room without knocking and demanded, "Is that what you do on the Net—sending nude photos to men?" My blood flooded to my face. I told him to get out. He was a carbon copy of my father; judgmental, presumptive, abusive and authoritative. Our relationship continued to deteriorate and become even worse. Every day, he seemed to enjoy looking for any excuse to bother me. He said he would tell mum about my racy 'work.' I beat him to the punch and called my mother to explain everything to her. Although she always suppressed me and was vigilant about my wearing Islamic approved clothes, she surprisingly understood. Perhaps because she was a world apart or perhaps she understood his behavior was abusive. Either way, I was glad to hear her say that she trusted me and trusted my judgment.

Discovering My Mental Disabilities

I have always been open-minded about anyone going back to school at any age. In my view, knowledge is not limited to a certain generation or age. When I sat down in class, I felt like an older sister among younger siblings. Almost none of the university credits I had brought from Iran were accepted by the undergraduate system in Canada, with the exception of education from England. My situation is still very common among immigrants who want to continue their education in Canada. I had to resume my studies at the point I left off three years ago at the same college.

I registered in my second year of French Literature. I hit the books pretty hard, trying to focus on my studies and hoping for a better future. I had hardly spoken or written French in three years. I did well on my orals and my French teacher, Ms. Christian Richards, was impressed with how quickly I regained fluency but I was a dud at taking tests. The harder I studied, the worse I did on my quizzes. She suspected that I had dyslexia. She said she had a nephew with the same problem and was very understanding.

When I started attending school at a young age, I never studied after class. I remembered everything and even an honor student friend of mine, said to me, "I don't know how you do it. I study hard to remember but you never study and you know everything." This changed as I grew older and I started to question my learning and remembering ability.

In my teen years, I even discussed my suspicions with my family doctor. I told him about the mental disability history of my family that might be a factor. In Iran, however, it is not a good idea to even mention such a diagnosis to a female patient who has the genetic potential or exhibits signs of mental disability because she could be labeled mentally incompetent, eccentric or just plain crazy and treated brutally in society. Even her family would ostracize her. He quickly dismissed the possibility. Therefore, it came as a shock after all these years to be diagnosed with a mental disability.

I had agonized over why I couldn't do better on written exams, even though I studied hard and knew the material. I told my teacher that I would talk to a counselor at the college but I couldn't convince myself to talk to him and kept procrastinating. I wasn't sure I could bear hearing the results. I went home and said a prayer to God. I asked Him to give me the courage to follow this through. Somehow, I found it humiliating to admit I had a mental disability. As a fully functional person I was having a hard time fitting into society. Now, I was afraid I would be more ridiculed and become an outcast. My oral marks were good, I surpassed my classmates even in comparison to non-handicapped classmates who worked hard. I don't need much work because a deep dyslexic mimics sentences. My oral competence continued to be a lot more advanced than my written exams.

I had to go through the school to do the testing for dyslexia but the school would not do it for free. Dr. Dennis, a psychologist at the College, volunteered to conduct part of my tests free. Arranging for the rest of dyslexia tests took on the proportions of a major campaign. I went to a local government funded office that was supposed to help people with disabilities. I grew weary of the promises by authorities; tomorrow and tomorrow, this person was on holiday, that person was on sick leave. Six months passed. I didn't get any better at writing tests and had not been tested for dyslexia.

Dr. Denis started the English part of the tests, which didn't come out very well. Since IQ was measured based on English cognition and not on my mother language, the results were not accurate. However, when he measured my problem-solving ability, I tested 10 percent above the average. Possibly, this is because I have had so many problems in my life I have created my own survival method.

Finally the complete testing took place. I had to go through another full week of agonizing tests. Dr. Garry, who was in charge of evaluating my tests, did a battery of tests on me, both when my stomach was full and empty. I had to do Rorschach, computer, hearing, word, and drawing tests, among others. When the tests were complete, Dr. Garry called me into his office and showed me a chart. He said, "Look at this chart. Does it mean anything to you?" I said, "No. Why?" He said, "In my forty years as a clinical psychologist, I have never seen anything like this! This is your self-esteem line. People normally score between 1-5 on this line. You scored 25." He continued, "My God, you are like a machine that has no tires left, and is running on the rims. It will stop soon though. I have never seen anyone so crippled whose self-esteem is so high and who is so stubborn as to be able to learn languages with such auditory deficiency."

Then he showed me the chart that he was working on. It seems the development of my middle ear was arrested around five years old. I am not deaf, in fact I consider my normal range hearing better than average: I can hear a sound of a computer or TV working at night, while it is turned off. The entire time they asked me questions, I couldn't hear it in one ear. He said that was due to my poor auditory system. Although I can hear words, I cannot differentiate between, 'B,' 'D,' 'P,' 'T,' 'C,' 'Ch,' 'F,' and 'T,' and I cannot hear anything over 3,000 HZ for these sounds. His test also showed that I have trouble focusing on writing and hearing at the same time. Although a common practice at all levels of education for students and people who attend seminars, it is very difficult task for me to do.

For years, I had agonized over not hearing everything, every time. I had had hearing tests but not for specific sounds of the alphabet; nobody had suspected to find out what Dr. Garry did. I asked him what caused the middle ear to not grow to the right size. He said there could be many reasons, among them ear infection. My ears could have been hurt by external pressure or other biological factors. I suspect all the slaps I received to my head and face could have affected my hearing.

When I left his office, I didn't know whether to be happy or sad. I know he was trying to compliment me on my self-esteem but it wasn't as if I had a better choice in life and said to myself, "Gee, I guess between all my choices, I am going to pick high self-esteem."

The only benefit of testing perhaps was to finally get confirmation that some of the shortcomings I had long suspected were true It was official but, now what? I certainly didn't go out celebrating. My achievement of discovering a new item on the long list of skeletons in my life's closet didn't exactly make me jump for joy.

When the government finally tested me, I thought the idea was to give me some alternatives; that was the least I was hoping. That certainly wasn't part of the government program. It hit me very hard and took me a while to digest the idea of being diagnosed with a learning disability. As a normal person I had an uphill battle. Now, Dr. Garry had pronounced me crippled and the hill got steeper. All my life, I had survived by having a second option already planned; an escape hatch. This time, I wasn't prepared. I had to figure out what to do next; school would soon be over in late April.

The Day I Hit Rock Bottom

In April 2000, after not working for a year, I needed to go back to work again to save some money for books. All the time I was off work, I had been, with the help of God and a student loan, paying only my rent, food and bare necessities. God, however, was not writing any checks and I had to find a way to support myself during the summer during the time I wasn't getting any money from student loans.

I found a job at YVR, Vancouver International airport at the duty-free customer service counter. It was a pleasant working environment but my salary was barely enough for rent, food, and transportation. I wasn't earning enough to support myself and there definitely was no allowance for parties and leisure activities. Siavash was going to nightclubs and parties nearly every night. When my friends who were at the party or the club or concert, asked him why I hadn't come along, he lied that he asked me but I didn't want to go out.

After the battery of tests, the emotional turmoil of living with a non-understanding family member and my financial difficulties made my sprit plummet. Increasingly, I began to feel that my life was not worth living. Emotionally withdrawn and bent under the heavy load of difficulties, I felt an extreme heaviness on my shoulders. I had less and less interest in continuing my life. Living was too distressing and death started looking like an easier alternative.

As long as I live, I will never forget the way my room and I looked on that day, July 17, 2000, when I thought I was going to end this ugly life. I was on the phone with a government employee, explaining my situation and begging someone to help me, I asked her if, due to my low income, there was any way I could receive temporary financial help to help me pay my rent and for the barest of life necessities. I was earning $415 a month and simply could not survive on that pittance.

When she said there was nothing the government could or would do to help me, I burst into tears and asked her to please send someone later in the afternoon to pick up my body. She said she was sorry, I said, "So am I." She kept me talking and asked for my number and address. I finally conceded that if she was going to send someone to collect my body, she needed the address. I gave her my address and apologized for unloading myself on her.

I walked into the living room and while looking around, perhaps in my mind for the last time, I thought very seriously about killing myself. It wasn't the first time I had these thoughts but it was the first time I had expressed them to this degree and I wanted it to be the last time. All I could see was my messy, endless, pointless life. I had no desire to live and no fear of death. It was the lowest day of my life. I had hit rock bottom. I had come home from work and had nothing to eat. It seemed my education and my dream to get my PhD was unreachable. My future was vanishing and all I could see was a cloud of darkness; the very same cloud, the very same reason that I had left Iran.

I summed everything up in my mind pretty quickly. As if I had hit the review button, in seconds, I saw my life and a long list of reasons for ending it flash before my eyes. My father left when I was a very young child, Khosro, the only family member who was ever kind to me, left me behind, Manoocheher hurt me, my mother harassed me non-stop, I survived a war only to have the government harass and pursue me, forcing me to flee for my life, leaving my education behind. I had endured years of illness, pain and starvation and now I didn't make enough money to have food on my table. What else could have gone wrong in my life? I could not think of a reason to live.

I was debating the best method to end my life when I heard a loud knock on the door. I didn't answer the first knock. I just wanted whomever it was to go away. A few minutes later, I heard a louder knock. I rubbed my eyes and wiped my tears and opened the door. It was a female police officer and a gentleman at the front door of my apartment. At first I thought I had done something, although I couldn't think what it could be. I asked the officer what I could do for her. She said that they had received a call about a suicide attempt at this apartment. I wanted so badly to tell her she had the wrong address but she looked me up and down and knew it had to be me. She came in but I asked her to keep her male colleague outside. She let him in but asked him to wait outside my room. She asked me why I wanted to kill myself. I wanted so much to keep it inside but I couldn't.

I told her, "Don't you see? Take a look around you. I'm a mess. I have no love from my family, no shoulder to cry on. I don't even have any food." While sobbing I told her I did not want to live this life anymore. She asked me if I had been treated for the abuse. I told her about the psychiatrist who told me I should clean up my own room and solve my own problems. She looked me in the eye and said; "You see the badge and these stripes on my uniform? I swear on my honor, I will get you the help you need." Judging my fragile self worth, she was very careful about not letting me do anything to take my life. She waited outside my room for only a few seconds until I got dressed. She took me to the local hospital and only left me after I was in good hands in the hospital.

I later sent a letter to the commanding officer of this remarkable person to thank her for her outstanding humanity and the kindness she showed me. Regrettably, I cannot mention her name but if she happens to read this book I want her to know that she is in my prayers every day. In recent months, I have tried to locate her, as the twists of my life seem to be endless. The commanding officer that wrote me back is no longer on the force. I asked for the police officer that helped me. Strangely, there is no record of her in the police records and no record of the incident. Whoever she was and wherever she is located, she is an angel and so is the lady who made that call.

At the hospital a doctor came and talked to me. He said, "You know it is a stupid idea to commit suicide." I told him there is no boundary between reality and illusion when your days are nights and your nights are full of nightmares. When hope exists only in dreams, nothing seems stupid. I know in the eyes of society, suicide, is an abnormal act, but what is normal is what we create inside out. We follow the rules we create ourselves. Then we call it normal and abnormal. I was not trying to be a philosopher but what I said was what I strongly believed and had absorbed in life.

I have studied human psychology. I am aware it is not right to say life can only have worth when something positive emerges. My goal in life has always been to become an independent person who can make a difference in this world. I don't want just another day. I am not happy to live for the next Christmas or the summer. I am not happy just to live. My existence is intertwined with what I can achieve to help other people in this life. It may look like an impossible goal for someone growing up in difficult circumstances such as mine. It may be a large shoe to fill but I do not dream small.

Everyone has goals. Some want to be rich. Some desire to have a life with a family. Large or small, dreams are different but they uniquely describe that individual. Since the time I could count my own fingers, my dream was to help humanity. It may not be normal for a child to dream so large but nothing about my life was ever normal.

I used to sit in my room and think about the proverb, 'If I put my mind to something I can achieve it.' I wondered what would happen to someone if they don't have the ability to achieve what they decided on. Sure, I have five times everyone else's self-esteem but that alone can't do much. I was an example of my wondering. I detested when I heard people saying that if I tried harder, I would 'get it.' I read my books as if I wanted to eat them. I didn't just read them, I devoured them over and over again and because of my condition, I still fell behind. Suicide is a desperate attempt for someone to hang on to his or her dignity.

Nothing about my life was normal by conventional standards. Why should be this any different than anything else? I asked the doctor to look at my medical records for the past two years. I had been diagnosed with a litany of ailments for which there seemed to be no cure. My constant battle to live was taking its toll on my body and soul. After listening to me carefully, he said, "We need to help you get well; then we can look at your life issues." He asked me to promise him I wouldn't kill myself that night. I told him I couldn't promise things that were out my hands. If I was going to, I couldn't stop it. But I promised that I would try hard to keep positive thoughts in my mind. He said, "Fair enough."

I was sent home in a taxi while Siavash sat at home watching a sitcom. When I arrived, he looked at me and asked where I had been. I told him I was in the hospital; that the police came and picked me up and took me to the emergency room. He shrugged his shoulders and left to go to work driving his cab.

The next day, I got a call from a local psychiatric clinic. It was the same doctor who'd seen me years before. I reminded him of what he had told me about cleaning up my own room. I felt that if he had been a competent doctor, he would have diagnosed my depression and started me on medication to help me right away. Instead he sent me home with a cliché. Although he had acknowledged that what Manoocheher had done was wrong, instead of helping me, he simply advised me to forget about it.

Studying psychology, I learned a good doctor should never tell the patient that he or she is on his or her own. When there is post-traumatic stress and talk about suicide, it should always be taken seriously, no matter if it is the first attempt or the first time mentioning it. In my eyes, he simply had let me down. I couldn't understand how a knowledgeable psychiatrist, a medical doctor, could give such stupid advice. I wasn't myself and at this stage I could have harmed myself. I couldn't get over the fact that he was an Iranian male and a suspicion that his judgment was driven by the cultural attitude Iranian men have toward women. I requested another doctor.

†HE BOOK OF LIVIПG IП HELL
COMES †O LIFE

From July 2000 to January 2003, I regularly had to visit a therapist for much-needed cognitive therapy once or twice a month and a psychiatrist once a month to receive medication that helped me to stabilize the neurological hormone or serotonin level. The lady therapist, Ms. Gayden Hemmans was a wonderful human being and helped me enormously through my bad days. One day when I was talking about my past, she shed tears. I asked her why was she crying. She replied that she was only human, and entitled to her feelings. I thought I had offended her I said, "I am sorry if I said something that affected you, I didn't mean to." She replied, "No it is ok, your story is very powerful. You should write it."

I always wanted to write my story, and at some point in my life, I knew I could write powerful passages. Back in Iran, when I was fourteen I wrote my first fiction story and received a letter saying the magazine wanted to publish more of my work.

All these years, I had done whatever came along to stay alive. In my heart, I had known I was supposed to be a writer since the second grade when I picked up my blank notebook and recited from memory a composition I had forgotten to bring to class. But, I was rusty. It was so long ago I could no longer remember how to write, especially because English was a foreign language to me. I was so lost and in such denial in unknown territory that I didn't know where to begin to write a sentence, much less an entire book. Looking back, my first assignment in English as a Second Language (ESL) seemed so childish. My disbelief deterred me. With anguish, I asked, "Do you really think that I can write, even though English is my second language?" With a confidence I didn't find in myself she answered, "I believe in you." I guess I took that statement and ran with it.

There is a Persian expression that "everything happens for a reason," meaning even a catastrophic event can be used as a detour for the right cause. Only God knows why things happen and how they are meant to help. I am having a hard time being thankful for becoming suicidal but, if it weren't for that drastic event, I would have never written this book. This conversation took place during our last session on November 11, 2000. Our follow up session was scheduled January 16. 2001.

That day, I came home and sat down at my computer to write my book. I started thinking about a title. As I alternately stared at the blank page and out the window, I asked myself what to call this book. Around 4:00 p.m. November 11, 2000, I typed *Living in Hell* on the title page. The first words and then pages of this book flooded into my mind.

It was as if the words rushed onto the page. I was on a high with overwhelming joy, like a blind person given the gift of vision or a thirsty person, lost in the Sahara, who is given water. It may come across an exaggeration but I felt this must be how Helen Keller felt when she made a breakthrough into the world. I kept writing until my fingers and wrist felt numb. Passages flew onto the page and in a matter of hours, I had the makings of a book. I write in what is called the unconscious writing style. The first draft is normally a stream of consciousness train of words that seem to scramble to get out onto the blank page. I had never written in this volume before and didn't know how to edit. But, as the therapist suggested, I should finish my writing first before worrying about the editing.

For the next twenty-nine days, I sometimes wrote 40 pages a day. The hardest chapter to write was about the molestation. It took me three days to write four pages.

By the time I reached the year 2000 in unfolding the twists and turns of my life, I had written nearly 400 pages. I decided the working title, Living in Hell, had been truly inspirational and it stuck. I divided the chapters into five-year periods and gave each chapter a name.

When I went to see her on January 16, 2001, I was excited and told her I had good news. She asked what the good news was. I said, "I wrote it." She replied, "Wrote what?" I said, "Don't you remember you asked me to write my story?" She hesitantly said, "Ok? and?" I said," I wrote it." She laughed and said, "You are joking, right?" I said, "No, I am not. I am serious." She was trying to be kind and find words that matched her disbelief. She said, "It takes people years to write a book. You can't write a book in a month." I smiled and insisted, "I really did. If you like, I can give you a draft." We were supposed to meet and I was to bring her a draft but, one time after another, she didn't show up for the appointments and I was assigned to another therapist. When I asked why, the receptionist and doctors kept telling me she was sick. In the five months of our sessions, I always had a feeling there was something wrong with her stomach. I hesitated to ask her anything because she said she did not like to involve patients with her personal life. I respected her privacy and never brought it up.

In 2003, I phoned the center to find out how she was doing. The receptionist paused and said, "You don't know?" I said, "Know what?" She said the lady you are calling for passed away in 2002 from stomach cancer. It was a somber day for me. I remembered her words, "I am holding a mirror for you. You can look deep into and look into your own soul." She encouraged me, not only to live but also to live for a much more valuable reason. She made me feel worthy, with or without a piece of graduation paper. She helped me with gathering my thoughts on many of my blue days. Because of her I am still alive.

In mid September 2004, I had an urge to get in touch with her family. I went to the mental health center where we met and asked the lady's secretary to help me contact her family. She quite understood and two days later called me with the number of Gayden's husband, Erick. He apparently welcomed the idea of talking to me. I was a little nervous but I called him and introduced myself. To my surprise, he knew me well and knew about some of my conversations with Gayden. He said that she had never before discussed anything about her patients with him but she did about me. She had even said that she wanted to adopt me, although I was already an adult.

On one occasion when she cried for me, trying to be funny, I jokingly asked, "Why don't you adopt me?" Her answer was, "You are too old for me." We both laughed but I guess she was privately thinking about it. She and I shared many tears, and many laughs and she always hugged me.

I asked him if I could go along with him and pay my respects to her sometime. He said I could come and help spread her ashes at the local beach. He could tell I was a little taken aback, not in a negative way but I had never attended anyone's ceremony of pouring ashes on the water. I understood that his invitation was because she and I had been close and he considered me family. It was an honor for me. My only reservation was, according to the rules of Islam, I couldn't touch her ashes. There are many conditions and logic behind the Islamic laws that were outside the limit of our short conversation but he was kind enough to understand and tell me, "That is fine."

For the past year or so, after learning she was gone, I couldn't help but regret that I didn't say goodbye to her. So, in a way, this was my chance to say to her what I wanted. On September 19, 2004. I went to Erick's house and asked him to bring me her ashes. We set up a small table with her ashes, surrounded by a bouquet of white flowers that I thought she might like and lots of candles. I asked Erick to give me a moment. I cried that I missed her, told her how much she meant to me and I prayed for her soul from the Koran.

We took her ashes to Steveston Beach, found the right spot, put her ashes in her favorite bowl and added a rose shape candle, that Erick brought with him, to the top. Setting her ashes on the water, we poured white flowers around the bowl. Like a princess, taking a ride in her carriage behind white horses, she slid away on top of the waves, dazzling in the sun. As if the road to her final resting place was paved with glittering diamonds, she drifted away toward her castle, disappearing on the horizon. At this moment, we were both choked. I whispered, "Goodbye, Gayden." I could almost feel her standing next to me. I thought, if she were here, she would say the ceremony was beautiful. Suddenly, Erick said, "It was a beautiful ceremony."

Although I still have depressed days, my depression has substantially subsided. Because of her and her efforts I am still alive and my depression is in control mode. I no longer live on the high dosage of medication or visit a psychiatrist every month. I made a conscious decision that I don't want to live in a dream world and suffer any longer. I have been able to prevail on my blue days more often than I suspected I would. Pain is unavoidable but suffering is optional.

The trick is to only allow myself to dream when there is a chance to turn the dreams into reality. The process of getting better is far from over but not as far as it once was. Every now and then, I still have nightmares in which I run from the demons that existed in my past life. In my dreams, I shout and see myself in battles with forces trying to destroy me. I wake up from my dreams sweating, with tears streaming down my face. I see myself running into dead ends and about to die when I suddenly wake up, my heart pounding, my body drenched with sweat. Although the nightmares are not fully gone, they are dramatically reduced. These days, I manage to smell the flowers and enjoy the sunrise and the moonlight. For the first time in years, I see beauty in life. I look forward to the night, not to curl up in bed and hide from the whole world but to get me to tomorrow.

Light at the End of the Tunnel

After the medication started to take effect, I felt a bit more like myself. An interesting series of event unfolded in the months following the climax of my depression. In early fall of 2000, I received a call from a friend who said her talent agency was searching for Italian looking people. She had taken the liberty of passing my name and number to the casting agent. A few days later, the agency called and asked me to appear for a half-day movie project.

I had never played in the movies but I had heard that the main factor that makes an actress authentic was to put herself into the character she played and relax; the rest should flow easily and naturally. I welcomed the idea. It sounded exciting and fun and I was interested in seeing the professional actors in action.

The following morning, I had to be on the ferry to the North Vancouver, studio where most of the *Dark Angel* TV series was shot. The film studio was not quite Paramount or Universal. In fact, when I arrived for the 5:00 a.m. casting call, I was hesitant to enter. The place, located at the edge of city beside the vacant shipping yards, looked like a large automobile graveyard. I waited fifteen minutes outside the gates until the other extras and aspiring actors arrived and then we entered. The interior wasn't any more impressive than the exterior. It looked like a perfect location for Halloween movies. I had a hard time believing any glamorous actress would show up for work in such a dirty, muddy shipping yard. The word bad is an understatement for the condition of this location. It was beyond bad by any imagination with no working bathroom or lavatory. I felt such pity for the Grammy award winner movies that had to work in this slump, as they called it in Vancouver Hollywood. Everything was port-a-potty. There was no glass in the windows and broken glass littered the floor of the bare-bones warehouse storage sheds of which part of the roof had collapsed.

The building looked remarkably authentic as an antique early 1900s building. Indeed, I learned that was exactly what it was. This place wasn't a TV set but truly a cargo port for the early settlers arriving in Vancouver. The script called for us to get on a shipwreck located at the end of the dock.

At the end of the shipyard, a large old vessel was sitting with a frightening number of holes in its body and face. At first glance, it looked like a ghost ship, long lost in the Bermuda triangle, that had been found. Short of *Pirate of the Caribbean* flags, everything else matched their ship. She certainly qualified as their shipwreck. Due to the heavy rust, there were large holes visible all over the ship and some of the decks were off-limit. The water rats inhabiting the ship and warehouse freely flaunted and did not appear to be bothered by the coming and going around their home. Seeing them brought a flashback to our haunted house in Isfahan. The boat hull was so fragile that in case she collapsed, divers and marines had to be present, to save anyone who might fall into the freezing water.

The story was called 'Almost America.' It was based on a successful popular Italian mini-series. The story was about the hardships and turbulence of Italian families in the 1950s trying to make it to Vancouver, Canada. The trip from Italy to New York to Halifax and final destination Vancouver was filmed over a period of time.

I was one of the people who the producer picked for one scene. When it finally was my turn, the day was already gone and by the time that scene was over, it was nearly midnight. I was called back for five days for the role and appeared in more that five or six scenes. On the last day, the shooting took place on the deck of the old ghost. It was near the end of October and at 2:00 a.m., Vancouver's murky waters are dark and frightening and would be difficult to survive. The breeze coming off the water toward the shore turned into a cold damp cloth wrapping around the body.

When I made it to the second deck, I could not stop shivering from the freezing wind coming toward the land. The worse part wasn't being on the deck of the ship that might sink at any time or the cold weather but I was given a skirt to wear as part of my costume. It may be feminine but I can't tolerate wearing a skirt in cold weather. I seemed to have a show of my own because when I asked the producer to let me go; he refused and gave me his jacket instead. After coming down from the upper deck, I was asked to be in yet another scene, crossing the star of the show; who, remarkably, resembled one of my cousins back in Iran. I had no previous experience working as an extra in the movies but according to people who actually earned a living from this line of work, the attention and preferential treatment that I received from the movie producers and staff was extraordinary.

I thought that was a bit of an exaggeration and didn't quite characterize the treatment as preferential. In my view, he simply felt sorry for me, because I was freezing; it was clear to me that the Italian producers liked my authenticity. I was among the last ten people chosen for the final shots. But, finally, after five days and five nights, life on the stage was over. The production wrapped up and we were sent back to our relatively humdrum normal lives.

Overall, the experience was interesting for me and I took away from it just that, a fun experience and nothing more. But, I felt sorry for so many young people that dream of being the next hotshot actor or actress and try so hard to be discovered. They all want to be the next highly paid Hollywood star and seemed to stress themselves a little too much for something that can be such a vain, superficial world. In the meantime, they undermine their true natural ability and talent that could earn them a decent living if they focused on a trade more in public demand.

Meeting My Mentor

Back in real life, another interesting event happened. Maybe it was by coincidence and perhaps it was the walk on the edge of the cliff of life and death that had given me a new pair of glasses to see clearly through the glare.

A few months before July 2000, I had an idea about patenting an invention. I did some research to find out how and where to begin.

When I don't know my way around I believe in asking questions. I did a profile search on the Internet, looking for people who had experience in inventions and patenting. As bizarre and unlikely as it sounds, I came across a screen name I felt comfortable to communicate with. When I Instant Messaged him, he seemed, at first, a little hesitant but very open minded and honest in his answers. I could not tell from the profile if the person was male or female but I knew a bit about his/her profession. I had a comfortable gut feeling and didn't feel this was a stranger; on the contrary, it was as if I had found a lost friend.

For many, the Internet is an off-limits, scary place but my perception of the Internet is that for the millions who hide behind screen names, there are just as many honest people who are happy to answer questions and help others. My impression of the people I meet on the net is, they are simply cautious; just as I am wary of them. Perhaps because of my psychology background I have had good experiences communicating through the infinite world of cyber space without being burned. In fact, I am grateful for all the people I have met. I have made many friends, even lawyers and people I subsequently worked with via the Internet, simply because I used it as a positive tool. It is indeed the closest vehicle to the space ships of the future that allows me to instantly be in any country at any given time.

My new online friend and I talked for a long time and at the end of our conversation exchanged phone numbers. I called him first. He is a southerner and has a certain regional charm with matching accent. For someone as new to the English language as I was, a southern accent was hard to understand. I recall that our first few phone calls were not quite as easy for me as it is now. I later confessed to him that during our first few conversations I just said, "Yes," because I wanted to be polite but hardly understood a word he was saying.

A few months after our online meeting, on his way to the Northwest to visit a daughter, he came to Vancouver to meet me. In our first meeting on the net, he told me that he was, among other things, a publisher. Since my book was a different genre from what he published, I didn't want him to get the impression that I was interested in his friendship or mentoring in order to take advantage of him. We never discussed the publication of my book. However, after he read the rough manuscript, he saw potential in the book and began to help me with editing and marketing. Our journey of becoming good friends and his mentoring me has been affirmed over the course of the last few years.

A Priest Friend
Teaches Me to Forgive

Before I met my mentor, I had a Catholic friend, who had a strong inclination to become a priest. He and I talked for several months as friends, discussing the differences in religions and my relationship with my family. He helped me understand that to get over my pain, I needed to forgive them. It was easier said than done but when I finally grasped that the motive for forgiveness is to heal myself, to allow my soul to breathe and escape the web of my demons eating away at my soul, I welcomed the idea. Forgiveness, in my case, didn't mean I would become lovey-dovey with them and invite them for supper; I was just trying to free my soul.

After one of our pivotal phone conversations, I was on the couch, watching the sun setting through the living room window. I reflected upon what he said and started to let the pain and animosity go away. I closed my eyes and repeated to myself that I forgive the members of my family who have hurt me for so long and I slowly whispered their names.

As I breathed in and out slowly, I felt as if the weight of centuries was lifted from my shoulders. I had never felt greater. When I was through meditating, I called him up and thanked him.

Many of our conversations were about religion, of course. At the time he wasn't a priest yet but was debating with himself about entering the seminary. In months to come, he invited me to visit him in beautiful New Hampshire. On this visit, my Catholic priest friend confessed to me, a Muslim woman, that the main reason that has stopped him from becoming a priest was his desire to have a family with a modest Christian girl. He kept a Bible on the toilet sink; not the standard bathroom literature. He seemed to be confused as to what is right or Godly, which irritated me. I was shocked when he said he had feelings toward beautiful women coming for confession. Thankfully, if that is the word, he said he didn't find me attractive.

Coincidently, the night I forgave my family I took a break from my writing. I happened to see the first segment of the movie *Good Will Hunting*. Those who have suffered from similar trauma can predict my reaction. It got me going when I noticed the story was familiar. I saw parallels to many of the challenges I have faced in my life. I'm neither a mathematician nor a genius but I know what I want from my life. Like Will's good friend in this movie, I would have given anything to change my circumstances.

Unlike Will, I knew all my life what I wanted to do, I only had to go round and round the circle because others made decisions on my behalf. While watching this movie, I was breaking into a sweat. I was deeply moved when the psychologist was telling Will it was not his fault. I was thinking, how many times have I heard that phrase? Everyone I've ever told about the molestation has assured me that it was not my fault. But, the statement wasn't making it any easier on me, either.

God knows that if I could change that horrifying experience, I would. It is not ok what happened. It is not ok to let that person get away without punishment. What Manoocheher has done to me, changed my life dramatically; as if he took some part of me and buried it. For so long I have felt a deep void in my heart and soul; ever since that day in Holland when he asked me to resume what he thought we had. The pain and agony of the bitter memories I had tried to lay to rest were ignited many times stronger. It haunted me and my life has not been peaceful since. I am aware it is not up to me to punish him. It is up to a higher being.

Like Will, in the movie, I have had very little trust in others. I have left people before they left me because I was afraid of losing them. I didn't want to look like a failure in life. I was afraid of who I had become. I was afraid of the loneliness that was building in me. I was afraid of ending up alone in a nursing home, sitting in a rocking chair in my room, a blanket covering my legs, looking outside through a small window. This image had always haunted me until I met my priest friend. He taught me a valuable lesson; that forgiving is allowing the memories to die and handcuffing the demands and closure for my piece of mind, not anyone else.

I'm sure millions of women and men have stories like mine and never talk about it. But, how can good come from a bad experience when no one ever has the courage to share their experiences? Maybe it was an act of God; maybe it was stroke of luck that I was encouraged to unload and share this experience with everyone. Writing about it brought me that benefit. To make others understand the enormity of molestation and to help people who have been in similar positions heal, has given this experience meaning. I can say I am ok now. The pain doesn't go away by itself and it is not ok to keep it a secret. Because now, I sincerely believe for real that what happened was not my fault.

Air Force Dream

In December 2000, I decided to join the Canadian Air Force. I wasn't trying to jump from one branch to another but there were great opportunities in the armed services that I could take advantage of. With less than 17 percent body fat, I was in relatively good shape. In order to join the Canadian Air Forces, one had to be a Canadian citizen, physically fit, able to endure the boot camp training and younger than 34.

I was just about to start my citizenship process. I asked the Air Force to give me a copy of their rules and regulation. I sent my file, along with a cover letter, to Citizenship, and asked the department to grant me citizenship as quickly as possible. I had already been in the country more than three years and the process of becoming a citizen could take up to two years after application. A few days later I received a call from Ottawa Minister of Citizenship and was sent to see a judge for my citizenship exam. In early May 2001 I received my official citizenship in a ceremony held in the Citizenship office.

I received the citizenship and took it to the Air Force. I passed my written exam but my eyesight disqualified me for the position I was applying for. I wanted to be a helicopter pilot. I asked them, "What if I had corrective eye surgery?" The answer was that the Air Force does not accept anyone who has had eye surgery and if they find out at any time during my career that I have had eye surgery, I would be dishonorably discharged and face court marshal for lying to the army.

Here was an opportunity for me to remove all my scars and I couldn't pass it. I thought long and hard and realized I wanted to have the corrective eye surgery more than anything. I was tired of looking at my face in the mirror every day and being teased about the hump on my nose and not being able to read the alarm in the morning, or anything for that matter, without my glasses. On a more metaphoric level, the glasses were a reminder of the period of malnourishment. Every day when I looked at them, it brought back painful memories.

On the other hand, I also liked the idea of flying; somehow it seemed so liberating and appealed to me. Between the two choices, I know I have to live with my eyes for the rest of my life, whereas, even if I climbed the ladder in the Air Force, it would not be too long before I reached retirement age. I just wished there could be a compromise but the army doesn't bend its rules. I decided to pass on attempting a career in the Air Force, focus on the courses I was taking at the college and have the surgeries I wanted most.

CRIMINAL ETHNICITY

In early 2001, after failing to join the air force, I obtained my Canadian passport. I decided to use the ticket my priest friend had sent me and visit him. Now a Canadian citizen, I was sure I would not have any problem traveling through the United States. My friend had booked my trip from Seattle airport. I took a bus ride to the United States/Canada boarder, a little excited and a whole lot happy. Like a first grader, I surged ahead, the first person in line to the first officer, with my Canadian Passport and my ticket in my hand and a smile from ear to ear.

The border officer apparently had something against Iranians or woke up on the wrong side of his bed. He looked at my documents over and over, and searched me over and over again. Little by little, my excitement turned to anxiety and I noticed the rest of the people on the bus were checked out while I was still in line. I asked him why he was so suspicious of me; I am just visiting a friend. He kept asking me unrelated questions. He asked how I met my friend. Is he your boy friend? How long have you known him? Do you love him? It got on my nerves. I finally had enough and said, "You can't ask me those questions; I am a Canadian." Although I was carrying my passport, half the people on the bus didn't even have one. He had an inexplicable hate toward Iranians and Muslims and said, "I can and I will keep you here for as long as I want. For all I know, you are a terrorist Iranian."

In retrospect, that sounded like what I used to hear back in Iran. I remember when I was being scrutinized in the university back in Iran, they called people like me 'American Patriots' and here I was, standing on the border of America being called a 'Muslim Terrorist.' He kept searching me for 45 minutes and finally let me go when I said I wanted to see a supervisor. I knew he was doing something wrong because the other officers seemed hesitant about his motives. Interestingly enough, after 9/11 happened and even as recently as 2004, I have been Instant Messaged through AOL by many people, some even educated and in charge of publications, who call themselves patriots and call me a Muslim Terrorist. When I asked them why they assume I am a terrorist, their reply is that all Muslims want to kill Americans. When I reasoned with them and asked if they knew that in the year 2003 alone, 21,080 violent crimes occurred in the State of Washington; nearly none by a Muslim or an Iranian, they seemed to be speechless and disappeared in the unlimited, untraceable world of cyber space.

What happened on 9/11 is not ok. It is not ok to let the terrorists get away. I understand the fanatics and terrorists are a dangerous crowd. Some are Muslim in name only, born into a faith that they barely know anything about.

I know the Iranian government better than most people and I am aware they have a hand in raising terrorists but no one should be accused of being a terrorist just because he or she has an ethnicity that has been associated with the terrorist groups. Judging individuals without merit is a dangerous territory. One must be careful walking that path. There is no benefit to unreasonably scrutinizing the innocent; only to give the terrorist more misguided excuses to use naïve people and turn them to walking bombs.

LIFE AFTER THE DISABILITY DIAGNOSES

Back in Iran, one of my biology teachers shared with her class the following quotation she had read in a store window, 'Personal wellness is an invisible crown on the head of every healthy individual; only a person with disability can see it.'

Before I was diagnosed with depression and mental disabilities, I never knew how frustrating it could be to live in another's shoes. Now that I know I am the one with a disability, I have a different perspective and appreciation for remarkable people, particularly for soldiers of war, who seem to adjust to their lives so well. Much of their struggle seems effortless, yet, only they know how to appreciate live life fully while the rest of us take most everything they struggle with for granted.

Hopefully, with the help I was getting and my multi-lingual talent, I could find a better job in the cruise ship industry. Famous cruise lines from around the world anchor in Vancouver's harbor to celebrate the beauty of this jewel of the Pacific Ocean. I sent my application to the agency that represented a cruise line office located in Miami. The position was Cruise Director and I felt it was a great opportunity. If land based, I could work and go to school at the same time. If hired to go to sea, I could take a laptop with me and continue my education from a distance.

It would have been an ideal job for me. I felt I had the personality, confidence in public speaking and the languages that would come in handy. It perhaps could have become more than a temporary position. I received my first notice of interview. I had truthfully indicated on the application that I was taking an anti-depressant. Before I even had an interview, I was turned down for being on an antidepressant.

I began to see the real world effect of my health problems on my future. Anticipating a recurrence of this problem in my job search, I abruptly stopped the medication. When I told my psychiatrist about the dilemma, he told me that the medication doesn't stop a person from working; instead, it helps him or her focus more. He joked that the cruise ship industry might benefit if all their employees used the drug. I appreciated his humor and support but I have yet to convince the cruise line. I knew they would protect themselves, even though denying me employment because I was taking an anti-depressant was against Canada's human charter. The cruise line, however, was a Norwegian company, registered offshore in International waters and was exempt from Canada law.

The cruise line made it very clear; they do not hire anyone who uses an anti-depressant. According to Canadian law, even verbally asking a potential employee if he or she is using any medication is illegal, unless the usage has a dangerous effect on the ability of the person to do the job; for instance, flying an airplane or driving a truck or train. The cruise line did not make it a secret that they abuse the law. During four years of correspondence with Human Rights, they gave the same answer over and over again; they are exempt and don't care what Canadian law and the Human Rights charter says. And yet, Canada still allows this cruise ship to stop at its port. The relaxed Canadian laws offended me. The ultimate message is that Canada really cares about people and human rights but can't do anything for them when it involves a lot of money. We have to favor the larger companies over people.

When the cruise line turned me down in October of 2000, I focused on my school again. This time, I took the advice of Dr. Garry, the clinical psychologist who had advised me to stop studying French due to my auditory difficulty. I chose to study Psychology.

Psychology wasn't as interesting or as liberating as flying; but it was another area that interested me. Not only could I learn more about me but it would also enable me to use my talents for a good cause. My philosophy was to continue something that I had passion for and psychology seemed to be the next logical step.

I applied for a student loan, which barely covered my tuition, books and rent. During the school years in Canada, I had no regular source of income except student loans and supported myself with part time and full time jobs in the summer and worked about 10-15 hours part time in winter when it was possible to do so with the load of my studies. In September 2000, another ailment was added to my endless list of health problems. For seven months, I had excessive and continuous menstrual periods that, at first, had me and my doctors concerned about cancer. It was finally stopped by a high dosage of anti-depressant, anxiety and stress medication. The stack of medical bills piled up; forcing me to again look for a job.

In December 2000, I applied for work at a large financial institution. I was hired as a part time employee and worked for nine months as a customer service representative. I learned a lot of valuable information about finances. After being discriminated against, I let the job go. I learned that racial issues are not inherent in man; it is a learned behavior. Where I come from, people don't call each other colored or white; we are all Persians. No matter the color of our skin, our race, what language we speak, what religion we follow or where in the world we live, anytime we gather under one roof we are united as part of one culture and that is Persian.

I have met managers who delight in humiliating employees and, to make it seem professional, call it training. They admit that everyone makes mistakes. Amazingly, they can recite all of yours but recall none of their own. Every conversation in the staff room seemed to be about me and my dyslexia. Constantly shifting branch assignments and logistics made the job untenable. Health problems surfaced again. I was constantly questioned; even accused of stealing money I had never touched. It was all a mistake but when their own staff found their error, they never apologized for harassing me. I realized the job wasn't for me. Once more, I was forced to resign. This time the manager was much kinder. She told me that I should come back to work but I told her I needed some time off for my health. She said they could not provide that because I was still a part time employee and asked me to send her my resignation.

I blamed myself for contributing to my own problems but it was without malice. I even thought to myself; if I had been more obedient, perhaps I would never have had to leave my native country.

All my life, I had tried to live a life style that was not really possible under a regime with barbaric rules and conditions. As strange as it sounds, I knew how to survive that difficult life. Life in Canada should have been easier and more comfortable than my life in Iran. Surprisingly, I had more stress in this lifestyle than I had back in Iran because I didn't know how to live and function on my own. In Iran, I had fewer decisions; I just had to obey directions from my family in their attempt to make me a person whose name they could mention proudly.

I felt overwhelmed and lost. When I was on my own, I wanted to do normal activities like everyone else; gossip, enjoy the afternoon sitting in a café doing nothing, watching people pass by, waste a day at the spa, have a girl's night out and shop till I drop. When I was invited to a night out with friends, I couldn't go because I could never let my guard down. Trust was becoming more and more a rarity for me and missing from my vocabulary. People who want to get to know me have to earn my trust; not only earn it but work at it till I am able to let them into my heart. All my life, every time I trusted someone, I was taken advantage of; even by my girl friends. After a couple of not so pleasant experiences, I made a resolution not to allow anyone to take advantage of me anymore. I stopped my friendships and stopped my relationship with my family. The rule is: If the person doesn't apologize and change behavior, on strike three, the friendship is over. I leave the person behind for good; he or she will never see me again. It may be harsh but I was fed up with being walked over. For once in my life, I decided to go with a rational decision instead of how my heart feels.

Adios to Family Abuse

After more than a year in treatment, I was feeling much better. I told Siavash it was time for us to say *Adios* to each other. He had exceeded his three strikes a dozen times. Since we were living in the place I had found, I felt entitled to ask him to move out. This didn't sit well with him.

By late 2001, Siavash, who was as tired of me as I was of him, decided to visit his brother, Manoocheher, and my father and stay with them. As soon as he became a Canadian citizen, he rushed to see his beloved family. All of my father's family in the United States are quite wealthy and have their own businesses. I have heard that my father is bedridden and attended by nurses. Although he hurt me severely and repeatedly, I don't wish him dead. I doubt that it ever occurs to him that he owes me an apology for bringing me into the world and then neglecting and abandoning me. On his last visit, Siavash said my father didn't even remember my name. I don't think he realizes his days are numbered and to save his soul he must somehow apologize for his behavior. Alas, he will never know if I have forgiven him because he has never asked for forgiveness.

Siavash's plan, when he left Vancouver, was that he and Manoocheher would move to California together to build a new brother-to-brother family business. Manoocheher had been doing his usual business; curb owning cars, meaning buying, repairing and selling used cars. He also bought and sold fake documents as he did in Canada and was living a simple life working as a laborer for his wealthy half-brothers.

I wished Siavash the best and told him that I was going to rent his room. He agreed. Shortly after leaving, he called me and said that he was worried about his furniture and whom I might bring into the apartment. I rented his room to a hotel manager, who was seldom there, that I had checked out. Siavash wasn't happy that I had rented the room to a man. He returned to Vancouver immediately, claiming it was to keep me safe. In reality it was because Manoocheher changed his mind and their *California Dreaming* plans.

While Siavash was in Oklahoma, Manoocheher met a Persian girl at a party honoring Siavash's visit. Two days after meeting her, he asked her to marry him. Her family had made inquiries about him and decided he was a wonderful guy that could make their daughter happy. Of course, the family didn't know he had molested his own sister and his own mother had shunned him. Siavash, like a good protective brother, collaborated in not disclosing this information to his future sister-in-law's family. Nor, did he mention to the bride-to-be that her fiancé was already married and had a wife and child in Canada.

When Siavash returned to Canada, he insisted that I ask my renter to leave. Like a fool, out of respect for my family, I did. He later said he came back to rescue me from being raped by my roommate. Siavash had wasted his time and $1,500 airfare flying to Oklahoma. He blamed me for the expense of his trip; claiming that if it were not for his concern about me, he would have been successful out there.

A couple of months after he moved back, he claimed he had left a pile of US cash, equivalent to $2,000, beneath his bed. He accused either my short-term ex-roommate or me of taking it. I told him that if he really left that much cash under a bed he knew was going to be rented, he was as big a fool as he was a liar. Then again, I suspected he would do anything to irritate me. Our relationship went from sour to poisonous. I told him I wouldn't talk to him until he apologized. He said he hadn't done anything to apologize for. I determined to get away from him for good.

As long as I can remember, Siavash always complained about his jobs and his life and pretended he was penniless. Although Siavash hated my father, his behavior has been nearly a carbon copy of him. As they say, 'The apple doesn't fall far from the tree.'

Working in the bank, I had the opportunity to confirm my suspicion of his finances. I knew it was wrong but I wanted, once and for all, to put a stop to his whining and to have an answer for his lies. Before he left for Oklahoma the first time, we opened a joined account to pay the rent. So, I didn't necessarily break any law. I had a password and looked up his account. But, unlike what he often accused me of, I didn't touch his money. I kept quiet until one day when we were having a conversation about money and whose turn it was to pay the bills. He said he didn't have any money. I let him finish, then I asked what account he was talking about because the two I saw had more than fifty grand in each account. His face flushed with blood and his mouth was wide open. He said, "You looked up my account, didn't you?" I said. "Yes indeed, I did it because I always believed you but now I know you were lying." He said, "I didn't give you permission," I told him I didn't need his permission. I added that it was time for him to stop lying about not having money, "I don't care if you have money. I know I am not going to get any of it, even if I starve. If you pretend to be penniless because you are afraid I will ask for money, don't worry. I am not going to ask for your help." As a cruel Persian proverb says, 'If you want to borrow money, borrow it from someone who is not a beggar himself.'

A couple more months passed. Siavash decided to visit Oklahoma again to start up a company of his own. This time, as he packed his bags, I told him to make sure he has not left any cash beneath his bed because he won't see a penny of it upon his return. He asked me to keep his furniture for him or buy it. I agreed to buy it if he didn't come back. Before he left, I reminded him to be careful in dealing with Manoocheher because he was the same snake who had bitten him twice before and would do it again. Siavash packed to stay in the States for good but returned almost immediately. I woke up the morning following the day he left to find him sitting in the living room.

My prediction had come true. This time, he didn't dare blame me. He was very quiet and didn't say much. I eventually asked him what happened and why he was back so soon. He said I was right about Manoocheher. He admitted that I knew Manoocheher's true character better than he did.

For a while, Siavash and I had a moderately friendly relationship because I was able to help him with his business decisions. Although, he rarely asked my opinion, he didn't hesitate to ask when he needed it. I gave him the best advice I could; the same I would have given my best friends. He never showed any appreciation. On the other hand, I have learned never to ask for his help for even the smallest thing. Invariably, he doesn't feel well or doesn't have time to help me. I just assume I was born alone.

In the Persian language, there is a proverb: 'If God closes one door, He will open a better door.' Or, as some say, 'When God closes a door, He will open a window.'

Another door opened in 2001. My mentor took his interest in my work one step further and agreed to invest in my photography business as well as helping me prepare my book for publication. This began a fantastic business partnership that has allowed me to work freely at my own pace. But truly, he has been more than just a business partner; he has become the family and mentor I never had.

Removing Past Scars

In August 2001, I decided to remove all the physical scars left behind from years of abuse. I started with laser surgery on my eyes. After wearing glasses for 18 years, I decided that was long enough. I believe that if technology can repair a malfunctioning body part or create a physical attribute that improves my comfort and confidence, I should take advantage of that technology. Anyone who has faced ridicule for his or her eyesight or physical appearance will know where I am coming from. I found a great surgeon who performed laser surgery on my eyes.

While the doctor was performing the surgery, unlike many, I was not only quiet but also delighted. He gently touched my cornea with a fine brush, which tickled me. When he was burning my cornea, I smelled a scent reminiscent of chicken barbecue. When I told him that he laughed and said, "Must be a Persian barbecue."

Next on the makeover list was surgery to reform my broken nose. The surgery was partially medical and partially cosmetic. I had breathing problems ever since bashing my nose years ago in Iran while playing basketball. My nose surgery was scheduled a few days after my eye surgery. I was supposed to inform my eye surgeon of the time conflict but my nose surgeon was leaving to work in a hospital in Saudi Arabia. It was my last opportunity. I rushed into both of the operations four days apart. I thought; it is only physical pain and I can bear a bit of pain. Bad idea.

He asked me if I needed an anesthetic. I declined at first but, fortunately, a friend talked some sense into me. I changed my mind and asked him for the anesthetic. Boy! I had no idea what I had bargained for. I asked him if there would be any pain after the surgery. He said, "Very little." Right. As long as I live, I will never take the word of another surgeon who tells me there is no pain involved in a surgery.

When I came out of surgery, I was moaning and asked the nurse where my surgeon was. She wanted to know why I needed to talk to him; thinking perhaps it was a medical emergency. I said it is private. Hesitant, she finally paged him. I was semi-conscious. Morphine doesn't seem to affect me as much as it does others. When he came to my bedside, I grabbed his tie, and pulled him toward me. I woozily told him, "You liar, this thing is killing me." In his beautiful German accent, he replied, "If I had told you the truth, you wouldn't have done it." I told him, "Damn it, it would have been my choice not yours." We both laughed; then I passed out. Even though I was in pain, I knew he realized I was joking and was only trying to be funny to get over the pain. We laughed again when I visited him in his office for the last time.

After the surgery, I waited all afternoon for Siavash to pick me up. Although he knew I was having surgery, not surprisingly, he didn't even call the hospital. Fortunately, I had the phone number of two carpools. I left messages with both. One of them was a nice guy whom I had just met a couple of weeks earlier. He and his wife were kind enough to pick me up on their way home from work. When I got home, Siavash, who had been watching TV all afternoon, had to go to work. I asked him if he would get my medicine. He said ok, but he forgot. The next day, he said he was too tired and that he would do it later. Unfortunately, later was too late. I was in an out of consciousness and couldn't get up and get my own medication. The following morning, my entire face was infected and the recovery took a lot longer than normal.

One week after my surgery, I went back to summer school. I was now taking second and third year courses in my psychology major. I had a chat with my teacher about my condition but he was as stubborn as I. He said, "If you don't come to class, you lose a mark." Not willing to lose marks, I caved in and decided to return to school.

The day I returned to school, I was wearing a pair of bulky, dark glasses for after the surgery and the bruises on my face were quite visible. On the walk to class, I received lots of double takes from pedestrians, probably wondering if I had been abused or caught in a fight. My classmates screamed when they saw me. They all thought I had been in a big fight. One of them, knowing I had martial arts training, started a story that I had kicked a few guy's behind. I laughed very hard when I heard that. When my teacher entered class, he jumped back as if he had seen a Halloween ghost. Not wanting to make a fool of himself by admitting he had forced me to come to class, he jokingly asked, "What happened to you, why aren't you in bed?" Luckily, I was in a good mood. To cover his stupidity, I said, "What you see is the price someone pays when they have been nasty to their professor." For a few days everyone had a good laugh out of my eggplant face.

A Visit to Mother Nature

After finishing my surgery, I decided to take a vacation. Following the suicidal period and surgeries, I certainly needed it but couldn't go alone. I was still taking medication that sometimes left me drowsy and did not feel safe on my own. So, I enlisted my mentor as a cruise mate. An Alaskan cruise seemed just the ticket. For someone who doesn't like to go to a resort spa but loves to swim or relax in a natural waterfall, nature can be a healer. The eight day cruise is one my most memorable experiences and, for a change, all are good memories. The beauty and serene environment was mesmerizing.

I had my first kayaking experience in the calm, shallow waters off a small island in Alaska that was a nesting ground for bald eagles. Just offshore, seals rested on a rock. Humpback whales seemed very comfortable swimming nearby. These magnificent giants made the trip memorable. It was my first experience for nearly everything. I felt such a rush of adrenalin in my body, nearly as much as the day I landed in Canada. The marine life closest to the humpbacks I had ever seen were the White sharks of the Persian Gulf, which were not nearly as peaceful and friendly or as majestic to photograph.

It is hard to believe that this beautiful paradise is only usable five months a year between May through September. Handmade artifacts by the native residents and artists were a must. The rush of tourists to the diamond and fur stores was heaven for shopaholics and a Disneyland for the never satisfied women. Every shop was full of tourists of different nationalities. The memories included lots of laughs and good food. Tourists seemed to get a shock seeing me with bruises beneath my eyes. My mentor had come with a mantra, "I swear, I didn't hit her." It was the trip of a lifetime, while it lasted.

Premonitions of 9/11

My mentor companion's flight back to the US was set for noon September 10, 2001 on American Airlines. I took him to the airport to catch his flight. Approaching the Vancouver terminal, I was inexplicably nervous. Once in the terminal, I checked the monitors, hoping his flight was cancelled. I suddenly had a premonition. I saw fire and blood on the monitors and had an ominous feeling in my gut. When he took a picture of me, I prayed to God that it wouldn't be the last time I saw him. I couldn't tell him what I had just seen but asked him if he wanted to delay his flight a few days; he insisted that he had to leave.

I was on the edge of my seat the entire day. I kept checking the news and called his cell phone, which, of course, was not turned on while on the plane, a dozen times to see if he had made it home safely. At 3 a.m. Vancouver time on the morning on September 11, 2001, I received an e-mail from him that his flight had been delayed and he had just made it home, eight hours behind schedule. Finally, I was able to breathe easier and went to bed.

I didn't make a big deal out of what I had seen. I convinced myself that maybe the images were side effects of the prescription drugs I was taking, as they had increased my nightmares. I was awakened around 10 a.m. when a friend phoned and asked if I had heard the news. I said, "What news?" He said two planes, one American and one United, had crashed into the Twin Towers in New York. I not only felt sad but was uncomfortable with myself. This was the second major premonition in my life. I had known something was going to happen to an American Airline flight but I didn't know whom I should tell about what I had sensed. There is nothing more overwhelming than knowing something is going to happen and not having the power to stop it. Perhaps I was the only one in the world who sensed this pending disaster but couldn't help the thousands of people who were burned in the towers and killed in the air. I never spoke of this experience with anyone till very recently.

War on a Different Front

In October, 2001, shortly after that somber September day, US forces entered Afghanistan to liberate the Afghans from Taliban oppression and as the first major encounter in the world war against terrorism. Mercifully, the war was short and relatively bloodless but it made a huge difference in the lives of millions of women. After twenty years of Taliban subjugation, women were able to come out of their homes and enter the real world, some for the first time in their life. Although Osama Bin Laden, the man behind the 9/11 massacre, has managed to elude capture, thousands of Al-Qaeda members were killed or captured and the nation is in the throes of establishing a liberated democracy.

In recent months in Vancouver, I met a man who has personally met and admires Osama Bin Laden. This man didn't believe Bin Laden was capable of the crime. He believed this was an American CIA cover story. I was not surprised he thought that way. So many people have been brain washed by false, fundamentalist Islamic claptrap that it will take generations to undo what he has done.

As a famous poetry and proverb in the Persian language says, 'When an eccentric throws a stone in the well and closes the well, it will take hundreds of wise men to undo what he has done.'

On a personal front, I had it up to my neck with Siavash's arrogance. I politely asked him to leave my place. He had an endless litany of excuses. His share of the rent was so small it didn't bother him. He chose to live with me, not because he was fond of me but because it was economically to his advantage. He wanted to stay one way or another. Whether I wanted him to stay or not was irrelevant. I gave him a month's notice and asked for the keys to my apartment. He said it was his apartment. Since the first time he left for Oklahoma, I was the one who signed the checks for the rent. He had transferred all the utility bills into my name to make a smooth transition.

It finally got to a point that I threatened him that I would call the police if he did not leave my place in 24 hours. He left his furniture at my place for six months, trying to make me bring him back. I gave him one final ultimatum that if he did not take his furniture out of my place, I would give it to charity. I was the sister who had never seen anything but abuse from my family and had been used as a stepladder. It was ingrained in me to respect him as a family member but enough was enough. I simply couldn't take it any more.

More Mental Discoveries

In the summer of 2002, I was referred to another psychiatrist; this time at the University of British Columbia.

At this time, I was taking mostly third and fourth year psychology courses. After doing research papers about dyslexia and bipolar disorder, I deduced that I had all the symptoms of bipolar disorder although I had never been diagnosed as such by a doctor. My research suggested that the charming little girl that mum thought was too talkative was actually in the manic mode of bipolar disorder. I recall that I couldn't stop talking and was exceedingly charming. That pissed my mother off. She thought I was a spoiled showoff.

The goal setting and excessive energy was also part of my manic depression, bipolar. I could not focus on the same task for more than a few minutes and was extremely energetic. Also, my life goal-setting was directly influenced by the bipolar disorder. In retrospect, the five times more than usual self esteem wasn't exactly an exaggeration but I had a hard time justifying it. In doing my research, I concluded that my excessive determination was also part of the climax of the disorder. Doctors had missed it or dismissed it for good. If I had been diagnosed with bipolar disorder in childhood, my life might have taken a different turn.

I also researched dyslexia. Unlike many people with dyslexia, I am able to read and write, although I repeatedly write some words incorrectly most of the time. But, with the help of spell check, I am able to function about as normally as most everyone else does in a second or third language. Curious, I dug deeper and discovered that the neurons of a deep dyslexic brain work differently. A simple translation; I am wired differently.

Just about everything depends on whether one is right brained or left brained. Right-brained people receive information in the left lobe, which is where the activity lies for most people interested in art, music and literature. Left brained people receive the information in the right lobe where the ability to solve math and physic problems lies. Also, that is where the final draft of data, the so-called long-term memory, is stored.

The extent of short-term memory, where we receive information till we store it long term, is only ten to fifteen seconds. This means, if we don't store the information in long-term memory, we have no recollection of it later.

My brain receives the information in the right globe and then transfers the data to the left side of brain. I lose five seconds each time and that is why I can only remember fifty percent of what I have read. I don't have the same trouble with material I absorb through imagery. In fact, the best way for me to remember is to have an image of the data I am trying to recall.

The research is more complicated and there is much more to it than the explanation above and many other factors about neurons are involved but, in simple terms, this is what is called deep dyslexia.

The only good thing about being deep dyslexic is that I have the ability to mimic just about every word or sentence. I can recall, many years later, anything that has been stored in my long-term memory. In fact, my long-term memory is almost photographic. I can recognize someone that I have met from the cologne an individual used three months before or from their voice or color of their shirt.

An example of this occurred when I was back in Iran. When mum, Siavash and I went to Teheran to enroll me in university, we took a cab from the airport to downtown. Three and half months later, when we were flying back and forth between Khoram-Abad and Tehran, I recognized the same cab driver from the cologne he wore. To satisfy my curiosity, I asked him if he had used that scent before, he said he had used it a few months back. I recalled the entire first trip we had with him, even our conversation.

It is bittersweet but interesting that when one's normal ability is distorted by some kind of malfunction, other senses seem to become stronger.

After a long delay I met the new psychiatrist at UBC. On the day of my appointment, I brought him my research and asked him if he cared to look at it. He agreed and after reviewing it, concluded that I was right. In addition to dyslexia, he also said I was bipolar. In his opinion, my bipolar was mild. He asked me to take part in an upcoming research study, which I agreed to do. During the four months of our visits, he explained to me the excessive energy I felt was because of the manic mode of bipolar. To control that, he gave me a medication that also changed my previous depression medication to a fairly new research drug that had enormous side effects and a skin rash.

Accused of Plagiarism

In September 2002, I started a new semester. Due to my laundry list of disabilities, the school agreed to allow me to enroll full time while taking only two courses. My choice of classes was Brain and Behavior and Conception. A few days into the new semester, as part of the research study, my psychiatrist decided to try a new drug. He warned me that the side effects of the drug would be lack of short-term memory, vocabulary difficulty and even auditory and pronunciation difficulties.

I didn't want to be on the drug, but had little choice if I was to continue to receive treatment. After using the drug for only a few days, I could see the impact on my writing. I told both of my instructors, who were PhDs, one an expert on the brain, the other on human psychology and conception, about my disabilities. The woman, who was the instructor for the Brain and Behavior course, immediately dismissed me and told me to bring her an official letter from the college counselor; otherwise she had no responsibility toward me. I had no trouble with her being to the point and at the next session I provided her with the letter. She said she understood my problems but I don't think she really did or cared to understand.

A few days after we started the class, we had our first test. With the exception of three people who had prior courses with her, the rest of the class got failing marks.

The questions were not multiple choice but written. Although, I understood the questions very well and I had explained my problem to her in the class, she said she couldn't understand a word of my writing. I approached her after class, trying to explain what happened. She said she did not want to hear my excuses and told me that just because I had a disability, it didn't mean she was going to give me a free mark. I told her, I did not expect a free mark and assured her that I worked twice as hard as anyone else, especially since my English vocabulary was limited in comparison to most of the other students.

A week or two passed. She realized that everyone had issues with the exam and said she would give the class another opportunity. She asked us to be prepared for a test, including a ten-page essay about the research on light and how eyes distinguish the difference in color. I had studied that theory in the first semester of a psychology course. I borrowed two more books on the subject from the library. I spent eighty hours and went through fourteen drafts of my paper to make sure I would receive the twenty-five percent mark for this paper and recover from the previous failing mark. I was ready for my test. A strange thing happened during the course of preparing and typing my essay; I had a flash back and felt this paper was going to cause a great deal of pain. There were tears in my eyes and I knew something was not quite right. I quickly dismissed the ominous feelings.

I took the test and on the following Monday went to her class to see what happened. I asked her if I could meet with her about my final paper, something I never do. I trusted her and showed her the first draft of my term paper, which was in a considerably less mature stage and less professional than the twentieth draft. She looked at me and asked if I had any help with my writing. I said, "No. Why?" She said we needed to talk. I asked her if I had passed the exam or failed. She said she didn't mark it. I was beginning to get worried and said, "So?" She said, " I looked at your paper and I looked at the questions in the exam; I am certain the paper is not your writing." I asked," Why do you say that?" She said. " It is so good, I can't even write like that. It is not yours." Adding injury to insult, she added, "I reported you to the Dean of Faculty and he agreed with me that someone else has written it for you." I tried to explain to her, that I write at night, slowly and I write well on my own. She insisted that there was no way my writing was my own.

My face flushed with anger and disappointment. I lost it and told her I would sue her for her accusation. I went downstairs and phoned the Dean of the Faculty of Psychology. At first he didn't want to pick up the phone. I told his assistant that he will regret it if he doesn't answer my call. She told him how fragile I was. He, of course, wasn't worried about me but if something happened to me, he would face a lot of aggravation and paper work. He immediately sent someone to meet with me and calm me down.

In my life, I have been unfairly accused of many things but my joyous feeling has been in my writing. Writing a passage is a passport to tranquility and a way out of the harsh reality of my life. It calms me down and allows me to evaluate myself as an individual. Pride in my writing was something I couldn't allow to be taken away from me. It is part of who I am. A great writer is like a master painter. He does not copy other people's work. He spends hours in deep thought, uses his imagination and dwells on words to perfect each phrase to create a masterpiece. When someone accuses a writer of plagiarism because "his work is so good, it is not his" he might as well kill him because the accusation is as sharp as a knife.

When I went home that day, I felt a great deal of pain in my spine and lower body. The stress had caused extreme nerve reactions. Any time I sat down, my feet and legs fell numb, then started to throb and ache so much it became unbearable. I had to see my doctor, my psychiatrists and a chiropractor. Their best opinion was that the pain was caused by extreme stress.

Following her accusation, I got a letter from the Dean's office confirming his conclusion and proudly expressing his satisfaction that a cheater like me got caught. I stopped going to her class and went to see the counselor. I told her I wanted to appeal. I was told that when the dean pronounced on something, the chances of reversing his decision were very low. I told the counselor I would take my chances.

On a better note, my Conception class with Dr. Farhad Dastur was a great joy. His teaching wasn't just for a course or based on one book or one class. His intentions were to teach students something that would stay with them for the rest of their lives. It was he who planted the seeds of a better understanding and the notion of concepts in my mind. Based on his teachings, I learned normal is what we perceive, not what is actually out there.

Of all the teachers that I ever knew, I expected this lady to understand me better. Perhaps it was this expectation that caused me the physical pain. She was a trained neuropsychologist, a PhD in the field of psychology and an expert in brain and human anatomy.

I learned it is not the certificate that makes an individual a selfless teacher. It is his or her intuition, intelligence and, most of all, intentions that separate the excellent teacher from a mediocre one or a placebo. A good teacher is like a heavenly rain that helps to germinate the seeds of knowledge in the uncharted theories of the student's psyche. A bad teacher is like an acidic rain from hell that destroys any potential for further growth and will drown curiosity in the lagoons of ignorance. The gap between the two teachers is deeper than the Grand Canyon and wider than the Pacific and Atlantic Oceans combined.

After finishing one course with a 4.0 average, I had to fight for my pride and to remove from my record the failing zero mark the other teacher had given me. The day I went to the appeal hearing, I requested that the woman who accused me not be present at the conference. It was a sad day, particularly because I had to sit down with a bunch of teachers that had taught psychology for years but had not the slightest clue of what deep dyslexia is. When I entered the conference room, the Dean of Faculty greeted me at the door and said, "I am glad to see you." I told him, "Don't be. This is war. Today we are going head to head and I am not here to lose." Before I started, I told the committee that due to stress related muscle spasm, I was not able to sit for long periods of time and asked them to understand that if I walked out the door it meant I needed to stretch my legs to get rid of the physical pain I was experiencing.

The Dean sat down next to me. I heard the accusation and burst into tears. I passed them the drafts of my paper, my book, and my poetries and virtually everything I had written over the years. I asked them if the Dean of Faculty had the right to condemn me before hearing my side of the story. They started telling me that they could not decide by my writings. I showed the printout for the side effects of the prescription drugs I was using and explained how it impacted my writing. They began chatting with each other quietly. I broke the room's silence and told them that if they did not find my evidence enough to prove I was wrongly accused,

I will sue the teacher, the Dean of Faculty and the school President; I will pursue it for as long as it takes, even to the supreme court, and I will make sure the media calls your offices for an explanation.

I wasn't looking for sympathy, only to get my injured dignity healed. They asked me to leave them for a few minutes and then called me back. After four hours of looking up and down my writing and comparing the notes, their final decision was that I didn't plagiarize. They admitted I was right; my essay was my own work. With no apology and no return of my wasted tuition, they took the failing mark off my record.

I called the Vice President of the school, asked him for an explanation and wrangled an appointment to meet with him. He looked and acted like an insurance fraud Vice President captured on an undercover camera. He kept saying, "Don't call my office." I told him I wanted answers and until I got some, he would get calls. I told him the teacher has to be reprimanded so she won't repeat what she did to me. He refused, saying she was one of the best teachers and did a good job. Despite the fact, I had humiliated the Dean of Faculty and the rest of the committee he would not concede that the teacher should have asked me for an explanation before passing judgment and contended she did not owe me an apology.

After that hearing, I decided enough is enough. If I went up the ladder of Psychology courses, she was one of the teachers with whom I would have to take additional courses. I couldn't go through that agony again. I decided to put my education on hold for the time being and focus on what is most important to me. Maybe someday I will resume school where I left off. After all, I was going back to school to learn and for my own peace of mind, not just to obtain a piece of paper. I decided to do my own research and learn what I needed my own way.

During the last couple of years, I have kept in touch with Dr. Farhad Dastur, as well as my French teacher, Ms. Christian Richards and Ms. Ronda Porter, my English teacher. All three teachers impacted my life and lit my path with the light of knowledge. They cleared my mind and empowered me to take the next step in pursuing my dreams. As Saadi, the great Persian poet said, "A man is not alive because he is on this earth; he is alive in the heart of people who always remember him, because of the marks he left behind, even though he is dead for centuries." I will always remember these teachers who have helped me, regardless of the passage of time. Their unique way of teaching is what makes them remarkable.

A Difficult Year

In politics, 2002 marked another year in honoring the students killed in the massive 1999 protest in Iran. Thousands of students were arrested and are still paying a price for voicing their opinion. Some are still in jail for a crime that we consider part of our charter of rights. The continuation of Iranian protests is a signal from the people; voicing their opinion and hoping the mullahs hear their pleas. In 2002, the people of Iran began hearing about Shirin Ebadi, a woman lawyer who ended up in solitary confinement in Evin prison for defending her client. She became world-renowned and was honored with the Nobel Peace Prize for her humanitarian efforts.

On a personal front my problems were stress and depression. Hundreds of milligrams of medication were altering my body and mind. I was fatigued all the time. Sometimes, I couldn't sleep for two days and other times my energy was so low I couldn't get out of bed. I made many wrong decisions, including allowing my mother to persuade me to let Siavash back into my life again and helping an Iranian woman who gave me a lot of heartache.

My relationship with my mother was souring because I had thrown her beloved son out of my home. She kept telling me that if I wanted her to come visit I should let him come back. Physically, I didn't feel well and although I went to the gym and took horseback riding lessons, I felt overwhelmed. My medication left me physically fatigued and numb and my focus was at an all time low.

After months of her sobbing, she finally got to me, I couldn't stand to hear any more of her cries, I told her that if he was going to come back and live with me, he had to behave respectfully toward me. He promised he would. I don't know why I believed that. We decided to work out a plan that he would share the responsibility around the home.

He had to give notice to his landlord, so, for a month I had an extra room. A month before he moved back in, I met an Iranian woman who needed help and a place to stay for a month. I treated her like a sister and did my best to comfort her. I let her into my life, fed her and helped her any way I could. Through other friend's effort, she had found a man in Holland that was interested in her. They had hours long phone calls. In the end, she left me with a hundred dollar phone bill.

She had never met the man with whom she appeared to be in love; only exchanged photos over my computer. They seemed to be in love and I was ecstatic for her. I finally had to ask her to move out because Siavash was moving back. She had not found another room yet so I gave her a few more days. When Siavash moved back, he was friendlier with her than I expected. He even told her she could stay with us as long as she wanted.

The man in Holland was sending her flowers via special order. I told her to be honest with him and not pretend to be someone else. She was in her forties and he was at least five years younger. She seemed forgetful about her age and her first marriage. Before they met in person, his ardor cooled and his plans changed. Regretfully, she thought I had something to do with his change of heart. She told common friends that I had phoned the guy and told him not to marry her, which was not true. I would have been delighted to see her happy. In the year 2002, just about everything seemed to go wrong. Everywhere I turned, it seemed someone held a grouch against me. Even when I helped somebody, it turned out to be a disaster. Thankfully, time passes quickly.

War with Iraq

I am not a war enthusiast. For eight years, I lived and grew up surrounded by the Iran/Iraq War. As 2003 approached, there was one question on everybody's mind. When will the United States attack Iraq? War should never be the first choice but sometimes it is the only choice and in the case of the Iraqi dictator, war became unavoidable.

Many years of trials and diplomacy had failed. Despite pressure and sanctions from the UN, money, estimated at over twenty billion dollars, received from the sale of Iraq's oil and allocated for prescription drugs and food, was used to sustain Sadam Hussein's lavish life style, build marble palaces and purchase weapons and ammunition. If Satan had a son, it must have been Sadam Hussein. He ignored international sanctions, was obligated to no one, followed no laws or rules of common decency and brutally suppressed his citizens by rape, torture and murder.

For those who don't know what the sound of war is like, I offer a corollary. Imagine living in a land of giant dinosaurs. The sound of the falling bombs was similar to the perceived voice effects of ancient dinosaurs. The impact of the bombs hitting the ground was like the footsteps of these giants getting closer and closer. Every bomb from the sky was as if the earth moved beneath their footsteps. The sound of their hungry roars was the air defense missiles going off. Although they seldom hit anything in the sky, the missiles left a chilling audio print on my memory. The air defense missiles zoomed into the sky like shooting stars, exploding like a never-ending Fourth of July fireworks display. I have yet to enjoy a firework exhibition since. Children loved the aerial fireworks but enthusiasm waned when reality hit. Many were casualties of their innocent curiosity when the shells of the missiles fell from the sky and hit their small bodies. With every roar, with every firework we could hear our hearts palpitating faster and faster.

Fear of the unknown, dreading the next strike and wondering if this would be the one in which we would die was a sickening feeling, eating into everyone's soul.

Having attested to the horror of war, I am convinced that forcefully liberating Iraq from Sadam and his parasites is the only way to bring freedom to that region. We don't want future generations anywhere in the world to have to fear anyone like him. Tragically, the price of freedom for everyone jeopardizes the lives of the cream of civilization, frequently far from their homeland. It was ever so.

If the people of Iraq ever read this book, they will most likely think of me as someone who sat in the comfort of her safe home and banged out a book. Fine. The least they can do is read this book; then they can criticize me, curse me or praise me. They are free to say what they like. That is the beauty of freedom; something they never had before. Only those who suffered at the hands of the Iraqi monster know what a truly evil person he was.

Millions like me don't care if the coalition didn't find huge stocks of chemical weapons. They didn't need to find the 'weapons of mass destruction.' I have already seen him using them against Iranian soldiers and will never forget the devastating images of his slaughter of Kurds in the Northern provinces of Iraq. He was a threat to his own people and humankind. I am simply glad our world has one less ogre to worry about.

Surprisingly, Sadam wasn't captured in his spider hole until after his sons and grandson was killed. Contrary to his public boasts when speaking to a crowd while brandishing a shotgun in his right hand and puffing on a Cuban cigar, courtesy of his good friend Castro, with his left, that he would fight to his last drop of blood and kill until he was killed; he didn't even shoot the gun he had next to him.

The people of Iraq, although fed up with Sadam Hussein and his inhumanity, have not unanimously embraced Americans for their sacrifice and efforts to free them. On the contrary, many see the United States as occupiers and a greater threat. This animosity comes from being unaccustomed to freedom. People who have never experienced freedom emerge to hear their idol's speech. Listening to a mullah such as Musab al-Zarqawi, and Muqtada Al-Sadr, who sees himself as a younger version of Khomeini, has created the mess from which Iraq must find a way out. The Iraqis need to hold themselves responsible and stop blaming everything on everyone else. If there is no change in the Iraqi people's thinking they will be brain washed more and more, killed over and over again and will see their country heading for disaster even deeper than it is now.

Too many Iraqi's have been led to think and too many of the rest of the world seem to agree, that it is the United States troops job to protect the hospitals, the museums, the schools, the university, every household item and everything in between from being looted and robbed by other Iraqis. The duty of the US troops was to liberate them from a dictator and give them a chance to develop a free nation.

If every individual had taken responsibility for his own actions, Iraq would not have to contend with the disaster it is facing now. And, it will get worse if Iraqis listen to people who are benefiting from insurgency. In this book, I have said repeatedly, "No one can help a cancer patient who doesn't believe in therapy." Unless people want to change, no one else can make that effort on their behalf, although, the US troops are not marching away, leaving the nation on the brink of a civil war and reoccupation by insurgents, who would restore a murderous regime. Having said that, it is the responsibility of every Iraqi citizen to care for their own local government and be proud that they now have the right to vote. It is much easier and more civilized to denounce one's government through democracy than by civil war. As a Persian proverb says, 'We don't open a knot with teeth, while we can do that with fingers.' If they don't like the current government, they should vote for someone who they consider their best representative. Beheading and murdering civilian contractors and peace advocates is not exactly going to create a peaceful image of the Iraqi nation in the minds of the rest of the world. The Iraqi nation used to hold the key to the oldest civilization on earth. They should know, that is the image that the world wants to see them, not the current one.

I have been asked this question many times over, "Don't the people of Iran or Iraq have anything else to do except go to the mosque and protest?" I know the answer because I lived in that region most of my life. It is quite complex to answer fully someone who has not lived there. Where I come from, productivity is a word seldom heard. People trust the elderly and rely on their experience. The elderly trust the mullah and rely on his expertise. The mullah, who is supposed to be knowledgeable in all matters, takes advantage of the people if he happens to be like Bin Laden.

Of course, not all mullahs are the same. There are scholars among them. I know at least one but most of them pretty much preach the same message. Just to illustrate how ignorant some can be, I present this example. A few months ago, I was speaking to someone in Iran and mentioned I was having difficulty concentrating during prayers due to pre-occupation and stress. That person said that in a similar situation, the mullah suggested to him that he stop praying. I asked what his problem was and he said he kept saying his prayers over and over again. It is a rule of Islam that after three repetitions, a person must stop but he didn't because he couldn't.

From what I heard, I suspected the man was suffering from a compulsive disorder, which is when a person does one task over and over again, whether it is washing their hands, their clothes or praying. When I heard the mullah's suggestion, I was shocked to realize how little knowledge they have. Instead of advising the man to visit a doctor, he gave him wrong advice. In many cases, they advise prayers and potions instead of real medicine.

This may be an isolated case but most mullahs don't really have any knowledge except what they have read in religious books, some of them written hundreds of years ago. So, in a way, people are walking backwards. Until the majority of society learns that mullahs can help them with religious issues but don't know squat about political, social, medical and other matters, we cannot separate religion from state and will have the same problem for years.

Also, the not so religious, moderate Iraqi people are shown on CNN, sitting in cafés sipping tea. Instead of watching CNN and discussing world affairs, they could create support groups to help their own people stop the insurgents and looters. I know, as well as the Iraqi people, our societies are very tight knit. By that, I mean every one knows everyone; if someone has a gun or is looting, everyone knows who he is.

If people decide to rebuild their country, they can do it and they shouldn't wait for the Americans or any other country to do it for them because it will take them twice as long. Yet, they choose to do nothing because they are victims of groupthink, which is ultimately a fruit of the poisonous tree of dictatorship. Dictatorship destroys people's intuition, ingenuity, and responsibility. Everyone seems to think it is someone else's job to help. Contrary to the assumption of the people of third world countries, the progress in western countries is not because of the governments; it is because of the people.

People demand progress. They choose leaders they believe can deliver on their promises. If they don't, they get fired. Living in Canada for the last nine years, I understand nothing is free and nobody does anything just to be nice, every one helps everyone, because they feel it is a responsibility. I wish, from the bottom of my heart, that people of the volatile countries would heed my words. They can demand better and change the government of their countries, their destiny and the future of their children.

The people of Iraq need to stop falling for the message of insurgents and stop helping them. In September, 2004, Iraqi terrorists freed an abducted Canadian journalist. He said he saw Iraqi police helping the insurgents, even waving them through check points while he and two other handcuffed captives were relocated from one imprisonment location to the next. Since then, thousands of Iraqis have been fired from the force. The Al Zarquawi group has ambushed many of them who truly wanted to serve their country.

American contractors building bridges, roads, schools and restoring electricity, caught between the factions, are beheaded without plausible merit or objective. The deranged terrorists who, without mercy or reason, kill foreigners who have come to Iraq for humanitarian reasons chant the same justification, "For the Grace of God." Which God are they referring to? The God we have come to know doesn't approve of murder as an Act of God. I believe the changes in Iraq have to start with changes in people's morals, values, humanity and knowledge. I am not claiming to be an Ayatollah but common sense tells me it doesn't take an Ayatollah to see the problem and seek a definite and immediate solution for the murders in Iraq.

I believe that if the leaders of both Sunni and Shiah would publicly declare that people such as Al Zarquawi are pursuing their own agenda, shun them from the Muslim community and condemn people who follow them; the terrorists, who are using Islam for their own revenge, would be denied the support and supplies needed to wage their war of terror, They live and breathe by tricking naïve people into their trap. According to rules of Islam, murder is not justified, certainly not for the sovereignty. Anyone who chooses to take such measures should be condemned. In real Islam, he is not considered a Muslim but a murderer.

Terrorists, who can no longer use Islam as an excuse, would have no support from the people who think that they will, by their actions, land in heaven and terrorism would be stopped. It is every Muslim's duty to recognize the evil. Al Zarquawi, Bin Laden and their like have used and tried to ruin Islam. It is the duty of every Shiah and Sunni to stop them.

When Imam Mahdy, the Messiah of Islam comes, some Muslims will fight against him because what they have been taught is not true Islam. Among those who will pick up weapons to fight against him are those Muslims who pretended they were his followers before he appeared. They have been mislead by the devil himself who, contrary to Hollywood stories, does not appear in the form of a gigantic beast with two horns on his head and fire pouring from his mouth but in the form of individuals, who have sold their souls to him. Al Zarquawi, who proudly takes responsibility for many of the recent murders and Bin Laden, who has washed his hands with people's blood, are men who have been manipulated by Evil himself and will do anything to manipulate people. What they portray as the Gates of Heaven and their fairy tales of the afterlife are a lure into a burning chamber in the depths of hell. Muslims need to recognize the faces of evil in their soul and stop following them.

The world debates whether the Iraqi war was justified. I strongly believe that war was the only solution to removing Sadam. Some may disagree with me but everyone is entitled to their opinion. Why don't we ask the people who were tortured under Sadam how it feels to be able to sleep at night without shivering that his guards might come and take him? Why don't we ask the Kurds, who lost thousands, how it feels to live without a constant threat? For us, and by that I mean people who live in the west, it may be easier to believe that Sadam could be reformed. Because we live in a safe and free world, we don't realize know different it is for the people who have to face fear on a daily basis. American's don't claim to be saints. The people of the United States generally realize now their government made a mistake in backing Sadam in the 1980s. The United States had just been through the hostage crisis in Iran. Lingering doubts about the side chosen in the Iran/Iraq war and Iraq's invasion of Kuwait in the 1990s undoubtedly influenced Americans to support President Bush in taking Sadam down.

To answer those who say we could have done it with diplomatic negotiations; he was not just one person. Sadam was a monster, breeding more of his own kind. It is not even important whether or not he destroyed all his chemical bombs. A man like Sadam should never be trusted and should not have been allowed to sit in power for so long. His actions were predictable, only, in that they would be barbarous and brutal. It will take generations for the people of Iraq to trust Americans. As for the rest of the world, they will some day realize this was the right thing to do. This war was not for revenge but for freedom.

Politician's Words
Versus People's Lives

The year 2003 was both a joyful and a bittersweet year for Iranian women. For the first time an Iranian woman won the Nobel Peace Prize. Equally notable, for the first time, the battle was over a woman who had lost her life, expressing her rights. The Iranian born, Canadian citizen photographer was killed and buried in Iran because of the lenient policies of Canadian politicians. For a government like Iran, politicians shouldn't show what Vice President Chaney referred to as 'the softer side.'

I, along with virtually everyone else in Canada, expected Canada's government to go into a rage and pull their Ambassador out, at least until her body was delivered to her family in Canada but they disappointed us. It has been Canadian policy for the last ten years to show a tougher side with Iran but as soon as the media stops covering the event, everything seems to go back the way it was.

For the past few years, Canada has been deporting some Iranian refugees. According to International Human Rights, the fate of these returnees is unknown. At the same time, Canada has been lifting sanctions; allowing Iran to send their student followers to universities across Canada. I have personally met many of the 'students' supported by the government of Iran who are fundamentalists. They can come to Canada and stay as long as they want, whereas many of the opposition have been deported. The Canadian policy toward Iran has certainly been more relaxed in the last few years than in the preceding decades.

I think I speak for a majority of Canadians in being proud to be part of the Canadian family. We also think some politicians are wasting taxpayer's money, sitting on benches in Parliament, arguing their own personal issues toward the US government. They take the threat of Iranian fundamentalists too lightly. In the view of many of us, that is why Canada has become the gateway for the terrorists.

Canadian politics has been under scrutiny since 9/11 but, inexplicably, most Canadian politicians seem to blame the United States as the aggressor in the war with Iraq. Although Canada didn't participate in the war we saw a devastating effect close to home. One Canadian hostage, working for a humanitarian group, was kidnapped and nearly killed. Canadian hostages have been lucky so far but citizens of other countries have not been so fortunate.

France refused to contribute coalition troops but as recently as August 2004, two French journalists were taken hostage in an attempt to change French policy forbidding Muslim students to attend school wearing a headband. I find the policy a complete nuisance, particularly for a country that always harps on freedom of speech and individual rights. That was one of France's excuses for not joining its allies in the war. To allow the politicians to make arbitrary rules affecting millions of its residents is folly. People should be free to wear what they like as long as it does not offend or harm anyone. In any case, this excuse in France nearly cost the life of two individuals who had nothing to do with this law. The fundamentalists are not just one country's problem. It is a world-wide epidemic.

The Spanish train station bomb in March, 2004, killed 191 people. In September, 2004, the confirmation of a universal problem hit our hearts hard when Chechen Islamic separatists staged a hostage calamity at a school in southern Russia that ended with the death of 323 people, including 156 children. This is the third terrorist incident in Russia in recent months.

Who is to listen to politicians who seem to have cotton in their ears? In 2003, Carolyn Parrish, Canadian Member of Parliaments, outside the House of Commons, said, "Damn Americans . I hate those bastards." In August, 2004, in rejecting the policy of the US missile defense, she insulted US politicians, calling them a 'Coalition of idiots.' The people of the US may choose a Democrat or a Republican as their next President but whomever they choose is a reflection of their personality and we need to respect their choice as their neighbor and friend. When the Prime Minister was asked about her comments, he said, "There is no place for this kind of language." When the Member of Parliament was asked to react to the Prime Minister comment, she said she doesn't have to answer to anyone, meaning the Prime Minister. As a Canadian, I expect politicians to work for the people, not to try to feed their own personal agendas toward anyone or any country.

Calling the United States government names is putting a strain on Canada/US relationship. I think the majority of Canadians agree with me that, frankly, we have enough Idiots in our own parliament; we don't need to insult any other country's politicians.

When the Prime Minister can't keep his MPs mouths under control, we have a problem. She finally took a boot, when she stomped on a George Bush doll and insulted the Prime Minister personally by calling the machinations of the Prime Minister's Office disgusting and saying, "We're moving far too close to the Americans." The leader of the conservatives said she wasn't fired from the Liberal Party because of her attitude toward the US, or for undermining Canada's reputation, she was fired because she insulted the Prime Minister personally.

In July 2004, Canada had an election. There was a particular MP that worked on my mother's immigration case, among others, and ruined most of them. I read many stories about him, including that he pocketed more than one hundred thousand dollars sitting on the 2010 Winter Olympic committee, for which he did practically nothing. During the election, many journalists asked about the money but he refused to answer how he received the money or what it was for.

I wrote a letter to the Prime Minister's office, suggesting that this MP is just looking for a retirement package and has done absolutely nothing for the community. The office of the Prime Minister replied that they have had more letters on this matter and will look into it.

While siding with the election party president, this MP was re-elected to do the same job he performed so poorly. In the previous election, people had disregarded him and proved they didn't want him to be their MP.

Earthquake in the City of Bam

Iran started the year 2004 faced with a massive recovery from a deadly earthquake in the city of Bam. The powerful earthquake, in December 2003, registered more than 7.0 magnitude on the Richter scale and destroyed the two thousand year old city by shock after shock, taking more than 43,000 lives.

Although I have never visited the city of Bam, I had heard and read extensively about its history. Located 200 kilometers south of the city of Kerman, it is the remainder of the ancient city of Arg-e-Bam, which occupied six square kilometers and was protected by 38 towers. The best estimates are that 8,000 to 13,000 people resided in the ancient city that was constructed entirely of locally available material, mud, straw and trunks of palm trees. The Arg was one of the remaining temples of Zoroastics.

The history of Bam was found among the ancient records and books of the Sassanids period between 224-637 A.D. Historians debated the dates. Some believe it could date back before the 12th century but from the records it was clear that Bam was reconstructed in the Safavids period 1502-1722.

It was sad to see so many people lose their lives but, for the first time, Americans joined hands with the Iranian people. I watched a woman reporter without a headscarf reporting from Iran. That was a 'revelation' that has never happened before. This earthquake assistance achieved more in terms of bringing the two nations closer than the last twenty years of diplomacy.

Miracle Drugs Can Do No Wrong?

On a more personal note, as 2003 came to a close, my body reached a critical point in reacting to the prescription drugs I was using. I had a reverse effect to the drugs that were supposed to help me. Instead, I found myself uncontrollably shaking and unable to walk or even speak, as if I had a seizure. My psychiatrist had a hard time explaining it. The drug was supposed to control the seizure, not cause one.

I decided to stop my medications all together, although I was advised not to. When I stopped the medication, the impact on my body was immense. Only a person who has kicked an addiction can understand the withdrawal I experienced. If I had fallen from a twenty-foot height onto a rock, it would have probably been less painful. I had extreme pain in my legs and muscles. It was as if I had been thrown into a meat shredder. My whole muscle mass was aching and I was nauseous for three months. Siavash who had moderately altered his behavior went back to his comfort zone and did what he knew best, being negative and sarcastic.

In a conversation with my mother, she asked me why I was so unhappy about sharing an apartment with Siavash. I told her that he did not care if I was alive or dead. She gave me the usual 'we are family' speech but called a couple of nights later and told me to do whatever I think is best for me. She had asked him why he behaved so cold toward me. He answered her, "Why would I care about her. She will always manage to find her way. She always dresses well and eats expensive, delicacy food."

I cook my own food to save money but I am selective about what I eat. My living strategy is simple; to live as if it is my last day, enjoy it fully and say all the things I want to say. I don't want to have regrets. I want to let the people I care about know it before I inhale my last breath. I don't believe in 'I hope…' 'I wish…' 'I would have' phrases. I say what I have in mind and act the way I know I will be happy with my conscience. I am not a saint; nor am I a devil. I am only human and fallible and have done things I am not proud of.

Like many people I set resolutions for 2004, among them to bring my mother to Canada for a visit; to give her a chance to enjoy her trip and also to aid her with much needed surgery on her eyes.

A Pivotal Year

The year 2004 has become an important year of my life. Although I am yet to achieve all the resolution I set on the New Years Eve. I have accomplished many other things. Among them, I have set myself free. All the years that I put up with Siavash's attitude and abuse was because he was the only family I had in Canada and I thought with his help I could help our mother. She was my incentive to put up with his treatment. When the 2003 taxes were due, I found out he had declared his income so low that he didn't have to pay much tax. Consequently, his financial records didn't qualify him to invite our mother.

My whole world shattered. I asked him to move out. He had excuses, as usual. I gave him until January. He kept saying, "No, I will move in February, when my work is finished." He meant he does whatever he desires.

One day in early January, Siavash and I had a conversation which, little by little, evolved around the past. I told him about all the things that happened years ago. He said he didn't remember. I reminded him of all the times he slapped me as a child and now I have hearing problems. He said every child receives slaps from older siblings. It didn't bother him in the least that he may have caused the auditory damage. I told him an apology would have been good. He said he saw no reason to apologize.

This conversation took place as he was sitting on the leather couch I had purchased, watching the television set I paid for and eating my food. He said I was not a good person. He called me ruthless and shameless. I digested my anger thinking he doesn't mean what he says. I then asked him why he would say that. He said it was because I had not allowed him to leave his belongings with me while he was traveling. He continued to insult me, calling me a bastard and railing about what an awful person I was. I watched him with anguish. When he finished, I asked him, "Are you done?" He said, "Yes." I told him to pack his bags, he was moving out right now, tonight.

He laughed. He thought I was joking. I said, "I am not joking. You are sitting on my couch, eating my food and burning my electricity and telling me I am not a good person. Well, let me prove to you how good I was and how bad I can be." It was pouring rain and the weatherman had predicted snow for the next couple of days. I asked him if he remembered how many times I walked three miles home in snow or rain, day and night while he sat at home or in his warm car. I ordered him to get up and get out. He got very sarcastic and mocked me.

I said, "I am calling the cops." He laughingly said, "Go ahead; make my day." I called the cops but they said they would not interfere; it is not serious enough. I told the female dispatcher, "If you don't pick him up now, you can pick him up in an hour in a body bag. Will that be a serious enough matter for you to come?" The lady thought I had gone mad. She asked, "Do you realize this is a recorded conversation?" I said, "Yes, I am aware of that. This man has abused me enough. I am not going to take it any more. For his sake and for the law's sake, come and pick him up." She repeated that the police could not do that. I replied, "Fine, call in an hour. I will have his body ready." I wasn't joking. I had it up to my neck. If he wasn't going to walk out, he could be carried out. Family or not, I wanted him out; dead or alive.

I knew they would call back, which they did in one minute as two police cars pulled into the driveway. Before I went down to meet the police, I told Siavash I did not want to ever see him again.

I went downstairs and explained everything to the cops about the mental torment and anguish he caused me. I told them that if they wanted to take me to jail, I had no trouble with that. It was either my life or his. They questioned me for a few minutes and asked me who pays the rent. I told them that I pay most of it. They asked me who pays the other bills. I told them that I pay all of them. They asked me if I had a contract. I took them inside and showed them the apartment contract in my name. The cops noticed my disturbed state. They asked me how old Siavash was. I told them he is 44.

They remarked, "He needs to get a life of his own." After looking at the contract carefully, they told him, "Sir, you need to leave." He argued that I was crazy. I told them that if I am crazy, that is fine but I don't want him near me I don't want to be around a family member that has no respect or appreciation. I am not married to him nor am I his mother. He is a middle-aged man still acting like a teenager. I told them, I don't want to see him and if he comes to pick up his furniture, there should be a cop present or he can send his friends to pick up his belongings.

Two nights later, my mother called from Iran, she was crying, telling me how her son slept the night in the snow in the cab of his truck and badgering me about the well being of her beloved son.

I told her, "Mum, I love you with all my heart but if you are calling to talk about him, take this phone call as goodbye. I am not willing to hear any more about him. As for him sleeping in his truck in the snow, half the hotel rooms in the city of Vancouver are empty. Tell him to find himself a motel room. I don't own a free Motel 6." Ever since that conversation, mum and I have managed to communicate ok.

PUBLISHING WORLD

After September 11, 2001, I wanted to publish my book more than ever. My focus was to find a publisher. I found that is not as easy as I had thought it would be and I learned more about the publishing business than I was really interested to know. I was told this book would create a controversy for any publishing house and a danger of being targeted or ostracized like Salman Rushdie. I had a hard time finding agents who would take a risk. Even publicists were wary of getting on board with me. It became clear to me that although the United States is the most powerful country in the world, the people feel quite vulnerable. It made me realize that perhaps this book would be more powerful than I had visualized and help people understand the cultures by which they feel threatened but really know nothing about.

Before my mentor, who thought he was retired from publishing, decided to publish my book, I mailed nearly 175 letters to agents trying to find someone to represent me. About ten percent replied favorably. Of those, only three were major agencies. I sent my manuscript to those that showed interest and waited almost a year for replies.

In the meantime, I found one agent that I wanted to work with. The initial reply was a generic 'Thank you but I am not interested' letter from his staff. There is an old salesman adage, 'The sale doesn't begin until they say no.' I phoned the agents office after hours when the assistants were gone and sure enough, the boss was working late and picked up the phone. He was a tough New Yorker with no apparent sense of humor. When I later met him, I discovered that behind that giant, serious man there was a fragile person, just like the rest of us. He was putting on a mask to look strong; and succeeding.

I never told him that his employees had already said, "No." I described my book to him. He seemed interested and asked me to send it in. I sent my manuscript directly to him. Three months later, we signed a contract and he became my agent; for a while, at least. After ten submissions to publishing houses, he told me that he wanted to get one more round of editing on this book.

Through him, I met my editor, Lou, who reworked the book. The serendipity in this effort was that through Lou, it all started to come together. During the following year, I met many of the people who became friends and part of my network. After another round of submittals, I felt my agent's initial interest was gradually being eroded by the lack of enthusiasm from publishers who really didn't care if this book would make a difference in anyone's life.

The large publishing houses were more interested in the money they could make out of books about pop singers that were more saleable; stories about celebrities who donate their large breast implants to a museum and replace them with more appropriate smaller ones; or, the sad story of another who left her husband for her boyfriend. And, the married actor who discovered he is gay and his mission is to find God in his rap music. I was offended by their decision to turn me down while publishing such books until it dawned on me that it is not really about me but about the green. The mission is not about what the public learns but what the public pays.

Just like the gossip columns and tabloids, so much of the printed material on the shelves of bookstores is trash for the mind and nothing more than reams of wasted paper. Unfortunately, with no state regulation of what books and newspapers should be printed, a handful of greedy publishers take advantage of the younger generation to earn their way. They will take any measure, even if that means giving our future generations inappropriate material, dissolving the message of human value and education. Printing harmful material is a serious hidden issue and a price we cannot afford to pay. Because of this epidemic, books that would make a difference in someone's life have been left behind.

A year and half later, in early 2003, I decided it was time for me to take drastic measures and get real with the publishing and pursue the publishers myself. It was the right time for the agent and I to end our contract and we did so with business integrity and no animosity.

That didn't mean I gave up on my book. I decided to put it aside for six months and then re-read and re-write it. I persuaded my friend and mentor to get back into harness and publish the book. Although he considered himself retired as a publisher, when he read some of the changes I intended to make to Living in Hell, he was encouraged enough to work on it. Perhaps the real reason was he also cared about me more than anyone else in my life has and he knew how much this book meant to me. By September 2003, I had finished re-editing Living in Hell and added the current changes. In early March 2004, I had appended everything and called it *finis*. As if the twist of *Living in Hell* wasn't enough, I had to have one last twist. I closed my computer and my file on the book and went to bed for the night.

For several days following the completion of my masterpiece, I had to take care of some business. When I reopened my computer, I discovered to my horror that all my saved files had disappeared. Apparently a virus had crashed my computer and I lost seven months work. I nearly pulled out all my hair. For the next fifteen days, I restored as much saved material as I could but I still had lost nearly 300 pages. I sat down and re-wrote all the missing stories from memory. I was able to add them to the closing draft and, I console myself that the new version is an improvement compared to the lost one. I finally finished on September 17, 2004, which, coincidently, was the ninth anniversary of the date that I set sail from Iran for the New World.

†HE "AXIS OF EVIL,"
ПUCLEAR †HREA†S

The new nuclear threats, the 'axis of evil,' as President Bush named them, have been in the spotlight since October 2003. Iran and North Korea couldn't be more different on the world spectrum of nations, yet they have had much in common since last year. North Korea announced the beginning of work on its old atomic reactors to produce electricity. Iran announced that it is enriching Uranium for peaceful purposes.

Neither of these countries needs to enrich Uranium for peaceful purposes as they claim, nor can they afford the process. While millions are starving in North Korea, their dictator is developing nuclear energy full steam ahead. Iran has no need for uranium, except to build an atomic bomb. Iran's petroleum reserves are estimated to be a fifty year supply of oil and 500 years for natural gas. Iran also has ideal geographic and climatic conditions for electricity generating windmills. Wind exploitation studies started in the time of the Shah and some towers were constructed but after the Shah was deposed the project was never finished. The people of Iran are not quite starving but they are getting there, due to inflation, while Iran's mullahs seem to have billions of dollars to waste.

If either of these two countries achieves atomic bomb capability and power, the rest of the world could not rest. Iran is the harvesting nest for the next generation of terrorists armed with atomic bombs. North Korea has said it already has the bomb and will test it. I am not sure what destiny has for the poor people of North Korea. I pray that the people of Iran can hang on tight for a little longer; hopefully a hero and relief are on the way.

As recent as November, 2004, Iran came under national scrutiny. Thankfully, Iran has recently announced it will leave its nuclear program in a dormant stage and for now, at least, comply with the IAEA regular visits to the its nuclear facilities without set appointments that would allow the Iranian government to be prepared for inspection.

KHOMEINI'S ODYSSEY
1978-2008

As I mentioned in an earlier part of the book, when mum and I visited my grandfather for the last time, during the short period of time he had left, he wanted to give something to my mother. Unfortunately, my grandmother didn't let her have anything but among his possessions was a book that he had purchased in his youth when he started to read and write. The name of the book was Shah Nematolah Vali Prophecies. My uncle Asgar, my mother, grandpa and I were sitting on the patio. He asked my mother to read it for him. I jumped in and asked if I could read it. By coincidence, I opened the page describing the Shah and his destiny. I kept reading, while they listened. As a child, the great poets and prophecies mesmerized me. The prophecy was written by this great poet mystic who had an amazing insight about the history of Iran. He was also a direct descendent of Ali.

Shah Nematolah Vali was born in the province of Shiraz nearly seven hundred years ago in the year 731 Hijra by the Muslim calendar. Today's calendar is 1425. His poetry prophecy goes back to the time of the Sassanids in 224 A.D. Every historical event he mentioned and predicted has occurred and with the same details he wrote in his book.

In his book, the poet identified Khomeini as a distant member of Hussein's family, a descendent of Prophet Mohammad, as evidence by the black turban that Khomeini wore.

The poet wrote about Khomeini's time in detail. He wrote about a long war, lack of security and hunger and difficulty all across Iran. He concluded the regime would stay in power for 30 years. I recall that when I read that passage, I calculated my age to find out how old I would be when that happened. I was eight at the time; the year Khomeini's regime would lose power was predicted as 2008.

The regime knows about this book, as well as other Persian literature advocates. This book gave them the exact month and year of the end of the Shah's reign. While coming to power, the regime used the book to diminish the Shah's self esteem and to manipulate people's confidence in him and fan their suspicion into a flame. The regime also had such fear of this book that it was one of the first books burned in the post-revolutionary cleansing process. New editions were altered to prophecy that the regime would stay in power until the end of eternity, portraying Khomeini and his successors as the Messiah.

The poet also predicted that after this regime, a king named Reza would come to power. In his time, there would be problems and a harsh life but he didn't refer to war as he did during this regime. During Reza's time, the poet predicted there will also be difficulties and his Kingdom would last 15 years.

After Reza, there would be another mullah in power. The poet did not mention his name but said he is a descendent from Hassan, the first Son of Ali. And, he is the genuine ambassador of Mahdi, the Messiah of Muslims. He predicted that in his time, people would find peace and prosperity all over Iran. After this mullah, the poet predicted something else, which is in line with the Bible but not suitable to mention in this book.

Conclusion

As an Iranian woman, I was brought up to take the pain and keep quiet because that is how society would accept me. I am sick and tired of this game. I do not care how others judge me for telling the truth. I can no longer take the pain or bear to watch others in pain while I mask my emotions with a smile or stay passive. I cannot meekly obey anymore and I will break down any walls that keep me from telling the true story of women in Iran who have been suffering too long.

For a long time, I avoided looking in a mirror. I detested that God had created me as a woman. Being a woman in Iran meant being weak and second class and I detested that idea. I convinced myself that God granted my mother's wish to have a baby girl or maybe the last wish of my dead uncle. During the war, I justified my creation as perhaps God spared my life by making me a woman so I would not have to fight in a terrifying war. But, deep down, I wasn't sure of any of the explanations and motives.

I finally got the courage to stare at myself in the mirror and question me. I realized God created me as a woman, not because I was the leftover of Adam's rib and not because I was powerless and ought to be saved but because God loves beauty and loves creatures who can share love with others. I know now, that God loved me to create me as a woman. Women can give love by becoming a wife, a mother, a grandmother, a teacher and a leader to the generations to come.

It has taken me a long time but I am now aware that I was wrong to feel ashamed of whom I was. No one should ever feel the pain and sorrow that someone else forces upon him or her. Like many women, my mother did what she thought was best, trying to protect me in her own way. I have forgiven her for the abuse she unknowingly put me through. She didn't know any better and although she hurt me, from time to time, by praising her son, this is how she was brought up and she subconsciously followed the example set by her mother. Also, it is part of the Persian male dominated culture that unliberated women accept and follow.

Nearly nine years have passed since the day I stepped on the soil of Canada. Now, unlike the day that I arrived, I know where to go, who to talk to and how to speak. I am no longer penniless and alone. I have tackled, with mixed results, several professions. I like to think I have become wise enough to recognize that I don't need others to validate me. I need my self worth and my inner peace. I am successful and I have made a commitment to use my research and experiences to write and conduct seminars across the country; to speak to people in order to aid them in their dark days. I know that if I keep concentrating on my horrible past,

I jeopardize my future. Someone else ruined my past; only I can ruin my future. My life story is more a drama than a fairy tale. My childhood was robbed from me. My teen years and youth never existed. I fought all the evils but they are still here. I simply deal with them differently. I hope no one else has to repeat my experiences and I hope they can use my life and book as a reference. I realize, today, that events happened to me for a reason. Perhaps, if it weren't like this, I would not be who I am today. I understand, now, that my pain was unavoidable but the suffering that I put myself through was optional.

At last, I am free. But there are millions of other women like me that have not been able to free themselves. I have come to realize that the worst demons are not the exterior ones but the one within I have proved to my siblings that I am neither a revolving door nor a stepladder. To find my own place in this world, I must love and respect me before I could be there for anyone else. This is not just a personal lesson. It can be used on a much larger stage. As a Persian proverb says, 'No one will scratch my back, except my own thumb.' I believe if all of Iran stood united, there would be a change. Otherwise, it will take another four years before someone comes to the rescue. My heart goes out to my fellow countrymen. I mourn each unsuccessful attempt to get rid of the current regime. Countries that close their eyes to the injustice mystify me; especially those that have endured similar sufferings and repression from dictators throughout history. Yet, they choose to do business with Iranian dictators who have no shame in brutally suffocating every breath of freedom and brand every hero a traitor.

It doesn't take much to fulfill our duties as countrymen, brothers, neighbors, humans or even strangers. If only we understand and respect each other's boundaries. If we are not capable of loving, we don't need to love one another but we do need to respect one another, whether it is color, culture, religion or something else that makes an individual and is close to the heart of the person we are dealing with. If we follow our mind, instead of our heart, ultimately it will allow us all to live in a more tranquil world. Unfortunately, that is not how it is. We can write pages of history, not with blood and bullets but with honor, respect and freedom. It sounds pretty simple and straightforward. Yet, everywhere we look, we see bloodshed in the name of country, race and too often, inexplicably, in the name of God. We need to remember that whoever suffers is part of us. We are all traveling the same road.

I cannot be Noah and save women from drowning in the ocean of their abusive lives. I cannot walk through fire like Abraham or part the Red Sea like Moses. I cannot be Messiah and revive the glory of the empire of women in Persia. I cannot be Mohammad and create a new religion that forces men to respect women and protects individuals from false reassurances. But, I can be a voice for those who cannot freely express their frustration toward the inequality and barbaric rules and abuse. We can join our voices and hand in hand grow on the repressive government like weeds on a wall and tear apart the walls of ignorance. Like a river, we will find a way to the sea of freedom. We can create equality and look forward to a better world as free individuals.

No matter where we come from, regardless of our nationality, language, religion, and culture—we are all brothers and sisters. Help others to help you, and help us to build a better, peaceful world.

"So long and God bless."

Afterword

*"The only thing necessary for the triumph
of evil is for good people to do nothing."*

Edmond Burke

Under any dictatorship many people, good people I might add, choose to remain silent and passive because they wrongly assume that is the best solution. Unhappy and unsatisfied, they do not speak up, thinking someone else will. Many fall victim, waiting on a hero to appear to save them, not realizing the hero they are waiting for is one of their own. He too remains silent because he is waiting for someone else. Sadly, no hero emerges.

I strongly resent the idea of needing a hero to save me. As I mentioned earlier, I believe there is a hero in everyone one of us. What we need is to believe in ourselves.

In the 21st century, our minds are still set on humiliation, taking lives and retaining power. In Afghanistan, Al Qaeda paralyzed justice and subjugated women rendering them invisible and powerless with no rights. Terrorists killed thousands of innocent souls on 9/11 and created a negative image of Islam in the eyes of the world. In Iraq, Sadam Hussein killed millions of his countrymen in order to stay in power for more than three decades.

To the world's betterment and relief, Sadam is, at last, deposed. We all saw his capture; hiding like a rat at the bottom of an earthen spider hole, a stark contrast to his marble palaces a few miles away. He no longer rules Iraq but his shadow still darkens the land, delaying freedom and threatening the new government. The continued malaise, warring factions with an agenda and resistance by remnants of the regime prolong reaping the fruits of liberation. It is a horrendous task but the civilized world must cooperate and persevere until the mass of the Iraqi citizens understand and appreciate the meaning of freedom.

I believe, we can't fight a problem if we don't recognize its existence. The world must change this violent attitude before it carries into future generations. I believe no one can cure a person that doesn't recognize that he is sick. The majority of the population in Iraq do not appreciate the meaning and advantages of freedom because they have never had it.

For Westerners to understand how terrorism starts they need to look deeper than a person with a gun in his hand; and to get personal with the terrorist culture.

From an early age, I recognized the significance and potential end result of political actions. I lived most of my life in a turbulent, war-torn country. I believe my political/religious studies have made me a fairly astute political observer.

To help the reader understand current issues that have an enormous impact on our daily lives, this Afterword provides a glimpse into the mystique of a culture that seems, somehow, to have become a greenhouse for cultivating terrorists. It is for curious minded individuals who seek honest answers to their questions about the controversial issues that affect our lives. The questions and answers will provide an insider's reaction and rebuttal to the never-ending post 9/11 rumors that we hear as facts about Islam.

ALLAH OR GOD, IS HE THE SAME?

God or Allah is a name for the Lord. If you are referring to the God of Abraham, creator of heaven and earth, we are on the same page. The Lord has many names. He is called differently in different languages. In French it is Le Dieu, in English it is God, in Arabic it is Allah, in Farsi it is Khoda. Names shouldn't separate us. There can only be one God, Allah, or Le Dieu.

The two sects of Islam, Shiah and Sunni, are divided by their respective concept of Imams but the orders of God are still common to both sects and must be followed as they have been for thousands of years.

WHAT IS SHIAH? WHAT IS SUNNI?

Before relating the historical events that define the schism between Shiah and Sunni, I want to assure my Muslim readers that I do not intend to offend anyone. I have no desire to intensify the volatile relationship between Shiah and Sunni. In fact, to do that purposely is a sin that I do not intend to commit. I am Shiah but I would rather pray behind a sincere Sunni religious leader who has the interest of humankind in his heart than a devious Shiah Sheikh who is willing to destroy and slaughter anyone who doesn't share his beliefs. I am not here to judge anyone's beliefs or morals. I am simply describing the events without personal opinion. God does not need my defense. He is fully capable of taking care of Himself.

The foundation and origin of Shiah and Sunni are the same. Both are Muslims, read the same holy book of Koran, believe in the same God or Allah, pray in the same direction and are forbidden the same foods and pleasures. Their differences, relatively minor compared to the differences in Islam and other religions, revolve around who has authority to rule Islam.

Two events have caused a schism among Muslims since the Prophet's departure; the origin of the argument goes back nearly 1,400 years.

The first major difference between Shiah and Sunni is: Shiah believe the legitimate leader of Islam must be a direct descendant of Prophet Mohammad whereas Sunni believe a Khalifeh may be selected from tribal leaders.

On the Prophet Mohammad's last Hajj, he told the people this was his last year and he would soon die. He picked Ali up by his belt and said, "Whoever believes in me, would believe in Ali after me."

When Prophet died, 11 A.H./632 C.E., his close companions, Abu Bakr, Umar and Uthman protested naming Ali as Imam. Instead, they chose as Khalifeh Prophet's father-in-law, AbuBakr, who was succeeded by Umar and he in turn by Uthman, who did not honor the rules of Islam. Disappointed by the dissolute third *Khalifeh*, Uthman, the people killed him, took his bloody shirt to Ali's house and asked him to guide them. In 35 A.H./656 C.E., twenty-four years after the death of Prophet Mohammad, Ali was chosen as leader. Sunni respected him as the Forth Khalifeh but Shiah considered him the first Imam. Ali was assassinated in Kufa Mosque on the 19th of Ramadan, year 40 A.H./661 C.E. While reciting morning prayers, he was hit on the head by a poisonous sword. He died three days later on the 21st. As a saint, Ali knew he was going to be killed but even he wasn't allowed to postpone his own death. On the morning of his assassination, he saw his slayer sleeping. Ali woke the man and told him "Get up and do your prayers and do whatever you are here to do." Ayesheh, one of the Prophet Mohammad wives, recruited this man. She was a daughter of Abu Baker, who forced the prophet to marry her when she was very young. The Prophet was not willing to marry the young girl but was forced to by the Arab Sheikhs who threatened him. In those times, a marriage between tribes was usually a contract for peace. His marriage to this young girl caused quite a bit of heartache for him and controversy among historians throughout history.

Ayesheh wanted to be queen. After Ali was chosen leader, she declared war on him, leading to the historic battle of Jamal. Ali had to order Jihad for the protection of his followers but told them to only defend in the event she attacked. Imam Ali, the first Imam of Shiah, ordered the last legal holy war. It was invoked to stop *Khavarej*, a self proclaimed dominant group of Arabs, from ostracizing and killing innocent people who had accepted Ali as their leader. She lost the battle but didn't contain her anger and hate toward Ali. Next, Ayasheh seduced a man and told him if he killed Ali she would marry him. Ebne Moljam was part of a group of *Khavarej*, which translates as 'the outsiders.' To compare this group and current Muslims, Bin Laden is an outsider because he makes his own rules and follows not true Islam but his perception of Islam. So it was with this group, at the time. They were the fanatics who followed nobody and made up rules as they went along. So much so, they would beat one of their own if he picked a date off the ground that had fallen from a tree but had no hesitation to kill a family passing by; a man, his pregnant wife, his infant and their unborn baby whose only sin was that, in answer to their question, he said he thought Ali was innocent of the frauds of which he was accused.

After a long period of animosity, Shiah and Sunni alike revered Ali but after his death the selection of his successor was contentious. Shiah considered Ali's son Hassan to be the second Imam. Sunni appointed Muawiya, governor and ruler of the time, as *Khalifeh*. To avoid bloodshed Hassan abdicated, signing a peace treat to guarantee his family's safety.

When Hassan also was killed in 49 A.H./669 C.E. his younger brother, Hossain, became leader of Prophet's household and, for Shiah, the third Imam. Muawiya broke with tradition and nominated his son, Yazid, to succeed him as Khalifeh, thereby establishing the first Islamic monarchy, the Umayyad. The succession of Yazid, instead of Prophet's progeny, offended pious Muslims because Yazid was a drunkard who flouted the laws of Islam.

The second major event that caused even more differences between the two sects, occurred when, as opposition to Yazid, son of Muawiya grew, a call went out to Hossain to come to Kufa and assume leadership. Interrupting his Hajj, he set out from Mecca with an army of fifty men, along with a larger number of women and children, perhaps as many as 200. Yazid heard of the plan and intercepted Hossain's party with an army of 1,000 men, diverting it to the plain of Karbala. The following day he confronted an army of 10,000, who had orders to kill him unless he signed a pledge of allegiance to Yazid. Hossain refused to honor the corrupt Yazid, choosing to fight and die for his principles.

The defining event for the separation of Shiah and Sunni was the battle at Karbala in the month of Moharam, 680 A.D. The night before the battle, he spoke to his followers and told them they could return to their hometowns if they so chose because he and his family were going to be killed. Under cover of night, nearly everyone left him. The next morning, Hossain and seventy-one other males, including his six-month-old baby boy, Asgar, faced Yazid's troops in the desert. They fought bravely but their water supply was soon exhausted and all were killed.

A cousin of Hossain, Abo-Al-Fasel, or based on Persian pronunciation, Ob-Al-Fasel, which in Arabic means 'generous father,' tried to bring water from the nearby Euphrates River, which was controlled by Yazid's troops. He lost both arms and then was beheaded as he tried to carry the water sack in his teeth. Due to his heroic sacrifice, he is known as the 'Giving Father.' He is greatly honored among Shiah and has a special place in the hearts of Persians.

Hossian and his family were beheaded because he refused to accept the decadent behavior he witnessed. He protested slavery and the selling and degradation of women. When he was killed, his body was buried in Karbala, where it is today. His head was sent along with the women but was later returned and buried alongside his body. Most of his children were killed on the way to their home and are buried in different locations from Karbala to Syria. Yazid's fighters set fire to the family's tent where a nephew lay sick and was nearly burned to death. His sister, Zainab, saved his life, picked up the fight and started the crusade to spread the word of the Ashora incident at Karbala. On the way to Damascus, Yazid removed the scarves from the heads of the women of Prophet Mohammad's family, baring their hair to insult them. Because of their fair skin and light hair, they were introduced as foreigners. As they passed through the streets, women of the Arab fighters gathered around Zainab and gave her and the children, bread, cheese and dates, the traditional food for mourners on observation days. Arab men, who had fought them, threw stones at her. At each stop, Zainab spoke to those who gathered around her. By the time she reached Damascus, people had learned what happened at Karbala. They turned on Yazid and revenged Zainab and her family.

Since Hossain's death, Shiah have observed two days of mourning annually in his remembrance. The month of Moharam, the first month of the Arabic calendar, formerly a month of celebration, is now a period of mourning for Shiah and called Ashora.

This unjust war divided the two sectors of Islam. Subsequently, Sunni have recognized as Imam individuals who are not direct descendants of Prophet Mohammad but are chosen by the Sheikh or religious leaders. Shiah follow only those they consider true Imams, individuals who are direct descendants of Prophet Mohammad, chosen by God and in contact with God through the Angel Gabriel

An Imam must be a spiritual leader, which means he has the ability to interpret the message of God and mysteries of the Koran as the Twelver did. An Imam, although able to sin, must stay sinless, free of human error and choose God over all earthly pleasures. Only Ali and his descendents lived such a life. In true Shiah, the role of Imam is completely separate from politics, although, when ordered by God, he could qualify as a political leader.

The last Imam, also known as Mahdy or the Messiah of Muslims, is equally respected among all Muslims. Although, the Ashora incident has divided Shiah from Sunni Muslims for nearly 1,400 years, Muslims from different countries and backgrounds that I have come to know, are united in the Shiah belief about Mahdy; in his existence, his temporary absence and that he is the savoir.

Sainthood in Islam

What is sainthood in Islam? Who is a saint? How can we tell if someone is a saint? I mean no disrespect toward any religion that believes sainthood is a title that one individual can award to another but according to Islam, in particular Shiah; sainthood is a gift from God Himself.

Saints are sinless but, unlike angels, they are capable of committing a sin if they so choose. Saints are capable of performing miracles and communicate with God though the Angel Gabriel. Moses was the only prophet able to communicate with God directly.

An example of this ideology comes from the Holy Koran. God calls upon believers and tells them that if someone claims to be a saint, you must ask him to perform a miracle.

A prayer is not a miracle. One test of a miracle is if the claimant can immediately solve a proverb that would not otherwise be scientifically possible.

A miracle is an act that everyone agrees would be impossible to achieve under normal circumstances. Such an act is a guarantee of individual sainthood. To prove his sainthood, God permitted a prophet to perform a miracle. Saints have performed a variety of miracles. For Noah, it was his ark and saving his followers and animals from the rising water. For Abraham, it was the fire that turned into a garden when he was thrown into it. For Moses it was his cane turning into a gigantic snake upon meeting Pharaoh and his parting the Red Sea, which closed in on his pursuers after he and his followers crossed safely.

In recent years, scientists have offered natural geologic explanations for the Red Sea incident but the Koran has written that it was indeed a miracle. Jesus brought the dead back to life forty days after their departure, restored vision to the blind and performed other healing miracles on the sick.

Mohammad performed other miracles but his defining miracle was the gift of the Koran. Although illiterate, he read the chapters from his heart. Readers of Arabic marvel at the poetic language of the Koran which even scholars are unable to duplicate. Also, in one of his trips, a Sunni Muslim, who later became one of his followers, stopped the Prophet on his way to Mecca under a full moon and ordered him to perform a miracle or he would be beheaded. The Prophet smiled at his ignorance and asked the man what miracle he wanted. His captor said, "I want you to cut the moon in half and lay each half horizontally, side by side." The Prophet prayed, pointed his finger at the moon and cut it into two pieces like a watermelon, side by side. People located on the same geographic belt that observed the miracle recorded this historical event in Arabic and other Middle East languages.

The Koran says that since man appeared on earth, 124,000 Prophets have come and gone. Adam was the first prophet and Mohammad the last. Some brought new religions; others delivered the same message as their predecessors down through the generations. All left us with guidance to follow.

A candidate for sainthood in current times could be a man or woman who could give us a definite, comprehensible solution to universal problems, such as a cure for AIDS or cancer or answer our persistent questions, such as whether there is other intelligent life in the universe. For a saint there is no time limit, no language difficulty or distance limitation. A saint can understand anyone from any culture that speaks any language. Eligible saints in Shiah Islam are recognized as Noah, Abraham, Moses, Jesus, Mohammad, the Twelvers of Shiah, and the Fatimeh, sole surviving daughter of Prophet Mohammad.

Another example of a saint is the tenth Imam of Shiah when he wrote, in the Roman language, to a Roman princess, inviting her to Samara and asking her to marry his son. He amazed his court with his fluency in a language he had not studied. The Roman princess accepted the invitation and became the mother of the twelfth Imam of Shiah.

WHAT IS TERRORISM? HOW DOES IT START?

To understand what the benefit is, we need to understand what terrorism does to people. Terrorism is not about the massacres or the long parallel lines of coffins draped with American flags. Instant death is painless for the one taking the journey. It is not painless for the survivors and that is the terrorist's intent.

Terrorism is about causing pain and fear among the survivors and those who hear their story. Killing one person or one thousand people in six billion is not going to significantly reduce the number of humans on earth. Even so, 9/11 had the desired crippling fear that has disrupted lives worldwide; causing multitudes to avoid flying or vacationing and others to work at home, fearing both the commute and a vulnerable work place.

Terrorism is about a minority exercising power over a majority. It is a form of modern mental slavery causing fear that can paralyze an economy. As Persians say, "Fear is the twin brother of death." Fear of death can immobilize as effectively as a chain. Those who can't face their fear become a slave of terrorism and that is precisely what the terrorist wants to achieve.

Terrorists cause fear for a reason; he becomes the master of his victim. After a terrorist attack, the terrorist owns people's peace of mind and sense of security. Terrorists call the shots and count on the inability of their targets to predict the next move. They wrap an invisible chain around people's collar and can move them in any direction they desire. Terrorists come and go but the fundamentals of terrorism stay the same. Today it is Bin Laden, tomorrow someone else. Terrorism will not go away in a month, a year or ten years unless all nations cooperate to isolate and exhaust them into impotence and futility.

Terrorism is akin to race hate acts of the skinheads and the KKK. It is a learned behavior, much like that of humans who enslaved other humans for their own pleasure and economic benefit. Slavery has been abolished in most cultures but discrimination and harassment continue. Not so long ago, parents taught their children that black people were created to be the servants of white people because they believed that was what the Bible taught. Obviously this is not what the Bible taught but was the perception of people who taught the Bible to others.

Terrorism is nothing new. Looking back at history, terrorism, on a smaller scale, has been carried out by leaders of many different religions. Virtually all have in common one or both of two agendas; establishing and maintaining control over a populace or imposing or destroying a religion. Hundreds of years ago, European nations persecuted minorities and Jews. For four hundred years, from the eleventh to the fourteenth century, the Catholic Church launched eight Crusades against Jews to liberate the Holy Land. Today, it is Muslim extremists following the same path in reverse.

Terrorism is almost always an act of defiance, sometimes with a personal agenda. Terrorists do not see their killing as terrorism. They regard themselves as patriots and soldiers of God defending their values. They justify killing as their duty and expect no retribution for their sins. The difference between a psychopath and a terrorist is, terrorists work in large groups. But, they try to justify their heinous actions in pretty much the same way.

On first consideration, the act of one person enslaving another to do the house chores and that of another killing a white man enjoying his vacation would seem quite different. However, both are the end result of the same misguided conviction.

In the first instance, one class of individuals through indoctrination, intimidation and force is imposing its will on another class. The empowered class enslaves the underclass, whether by chains on their hands and feet or a chain on their mind. In the second instance, it is an act or vengeance for transgressions against their ancestors and is intended, through threat, abuse and violence, to force a majority to bow to the will of the minority and accept and obey the dictates of a man who calls himself, not a terrorist, but a Soldier of God.

IS TERRORISM PART OF ISLAM?

No, terrorism is not part of Islam. Regrettably, too many have been led to believe that terrorism has something to do with the Muslim religion. That, undoubtedly, is the principal reason there is animosity between the West and some Muslim countries. The truth is, religion has nothing to do with the terrorist's goals. It has been purposely and maliciously used to benefit those who portray it otherwise for their own agenda. Terrorism is not restricted to Muslims. Timothy McVey, the man executed for bringing down a government building in Oklahoma in 1995 was an American Christian and, in his own mind, a patriot. Similarly, in Muslim countries, some parents teach their children that Westerners are part human, part devil and must, therefore, be destroyed because it has been so decreed by self-proclaimed messengers of God, come to earth in the form of humans such as Bin Laden. They believe that those who serve him are pure and it is their duty to kill every non-Muslim. Astonishingly, this message is the antithesis of the medieval message of the Inquisition in thirteenth and fourteenth century Europe. True Islam does not approve the brutal acts of depraved men who use it for their own evil agenda. The crimes inflicted on the world by these malevolent pirates do not reflect true Islam. Terrorism, although frequently closely associated with religion, is a separate entity. It is not about God or religion but about power. Those who recruit terrorists exercise power over them and they in turn over others. In their sick, twisted minds creating fear is being in power. Today, Muslim fanatics/terrorists use Islam as an excuse for their own agenda.

Terrorists, hijackers and kidnappers are modern day Pirates or Mafia Godfathers that, instead of coming from Europe, come from the heart of poor countries. Their only reason for being Muslim is to have a coverup. There is nothing new about the modern world pirates. As long as humans have been on this planet, some have always found a way to fight for personal benefit and used religion to justify it. Using Islam is the latest victim of their trick.

WHO BECOMES A FOLLOWER OF TERRORISTS?
Poor, naïve people succumb to the lure of the warped message of the terrorist; trusting that therein lays their salvation. The extremist give them false hope and empty promises of money and heaven. Khomeini took over the Iranian nation by making the same promises. The unfortunates betrayed by terrorists are among the poorest in human society.

Terrorism grows in an environment where there is a lack of knowledge. Poor people are susceptible because they can't afford advanced education. They learn their prejudices from people with malice in their hearts. The world's poor, mostly Muslim, can only continue a bare bones existence in countries run by an abusive government.

Children in a Harlem project look rich in comparison with their own kids who grow up in shacks with hills of dirt as their playground, where they sit on the bare floors of half ruined rooms called classrooms in schools that have no doors or windows, walls marked by bullets and a black board that is hardly black and barely writable. It is not a pretty picture. Children, barely fed, walk miles to be on time in this shanty school. Hoping for a better future than their parents, they are eager to learn to read and write, even though their worn and outdated books are nearly unusable. In many third world countries, education is still considered a luxury and not all parents can provide even a minimal learning opportunity for their children. An illiterate generation fosters ignorance and a citizenry more malleable and prone to blindly follow than an educated one.

Devoted Muslims are obligated to pray five times a day, fast during Ramadan and shun most pleasures of this world in order to receive the pleasures of the next. Most Muslims live in potentially the richest region on earth, unfortunately, it is also among the most volatile and poorly managed spots on earth.

Death is a very real and imminent possibility for too many of these deprived individuals. Consequently, they are overly and blindly religious. Their hearts and minds are easily manipulated by the unscrupulous. This environment is a green house for the poisonous Terrorism Plant, waiting to be seeded and cultivated.

Religious people are easier prey, more readily manipulated than the secular who place less stock in the afterlife and take their pleasure as they find it in this one. For a poor Muslim, whose life is a joyless day-to-day struggle, heaven is the relief to which he is looking forward. If he is told his key to heaven is under a stack of five American bodies, then five Americans it is. He will eagerly kill them to get that key. He has been taught that because Americans don't pray to Allah, they are imperialist infidels intent on sucking the oil and money from poor nations and deserve to die.

An example of misguided interpretation of Islam; on May 28, 2003 a Florida woman, an Islam convert, sued on religious grounds for the right to wear a veil in her driver's license photo. There is no justification in Islam for such a demand. Callow, naïve individuals concoct a mix of tradition and religion that only they understand and then try to force their interpretation on others.

WHO BENEFITS FROM TERRORISM? WHAT IS THEIR BENEFIT?

The beneficiaries of terrorism are those who draw attention and instill fear by indiscriminate killing in the name of religion or political doctrine. More accurately, it is the founders and leaders of terrorist organizations who benefit. The grunts doing the actual dirty work are like drones to a queen bee and will disappear if the architects of their evil are eliminated. Bin Laden is the brain. The foot soldiers are just the tools that point and shoot; killing without remorse because they have been convinced they are fulfilling their holy destiny. When one is captured he takes pride in his crimes and readily admits them. He rejoices in his actions, giving a thumbs-up and looking forward to his dubious reward in heaven.

WHY TERRORISM? HOW CAN WE CHANGE THE PERCEPTION OF FUTURE GENERATIONS?

We all remember our childhood and the action heroes we admired. For children in the West, action heroes range from Arnold Schwarzenegger to Batman. A child in Afghanistan doesn't play video games and real guns are popular and easily available. His heroes are Bin Laden, Khomeini and Sadam Hussein.

Iraqi children grew up with Sadam Hussein lauded as a hero despite the atrocities he and his callous sons committed. As cold hearted as this may sound; if Sadam Hussein's grandson had not been killed in action along with his father and uncle, we would have been fighting him again in our lifetime. His legacy would have been to inherit the underground support of Saddam loyalists and to try to elevate himself to renewed dictatorship.

Middle Eastern children are indoctrinated by environment to be the fighters, terrorist and dictators of tomorrow. They chant hatred against the West before they can count their own fingers. When a child grows up with a real gun in his hand and has seen death up close in his family and in his neighborhood, whether in Israel's Gaza Strip, in Afghanistan, in Iraq or in Iran, there is a great likelihood that child will become an enemy of the West. The solution is to not only change his action heroes but also to create a peaceful environment. Instead of bullets and blood, let the child grow up among friendly faces of every color from every nation and background. The US military may be able to put down one resilient generation but they cannot bear the cost forever. All nations must unite to stop the malicious teaching to the children.

WHAT IS JIHAD? HOW DOES HOLY WAR BENEFIT TERRORISTS?

Jihad is the Holy war of Muslims that has been rarely ordered. People in this era only know Jihad as an international crisis. Few people knew the Arabic word *Jihad* prior to 9/11 or, more recently, the Madrid train station bomb massacre. Even though it strikes fear in the western world, most still do not know the true meaning of the word. Heard repeatedly these days on radio and TV, it invokes an angry image of machine guns, suicide bombings and the blood of innocent people painting the streets. The images speak a thousand words of militia attacks in Baghdad; vindictive guerilla attacks around the world and soldiers arriving home in body bags. The world is justifiably terrified by the prospect of another 9/11.

It breeds fear on our thin skins and our minds struggle to understand the depravity of such an enemy. We question the nature and integrity of a religion whose devotees pray five times a day and fast, from dawn to dusk, the entire month of Ramadan. Can it be the same religion that teaches people not to kill an ant unless they absolutely must? To heal our wounds we often drive patriotism in a direction where there is a fine line between discrimination and nationalism.

In the time of Prophet Mohammad, Jihad was interpreted the same for Shiah and Sunni. However, since the division of the two sects, some Sunni Sheikhs have a different interpretation of Jihad. As an informed Shiah, I can only speak for the Shiah Muslims. But, I believe truthful Sunni Muslims, mostly moderates who seek true answers, agree with the belief of Shiah about Jihad.

There is ongoing debate among many Shiah Ayatollahs. Since the time of Imam Ali, Jihad is no longer used as an attack order but as defense tactic. Islam forbids attacking. Since Islam has not been attacked, a Shiah Ayatollah cannot issue this order. According to the rules of Shiah, the order can only be used to defend and should not be abused, manipulated or taken lightly. It is not a simple or casual instruction. In the wrong hands it can have far reaching lethal consequences.

Muslim extremist use illegal Jihad to gather followers and to bridge the gap between their personal agenda and Islam. Killing is against the basic tenet of all religions, not just Islam. Warped men declare holy wars and falsely preach that religion makes it permissible to kill. An example of the abuse is Bin Laden, who calls himself a Sheik, compares his evil soul with Prophet and has issued more than 1,500 orders of Jihad into cyber space.

Today's terrorists are not the same breed as those decades ago. They are sophisticated modern pirates who hide behind the religion, rob it of its core and its followers of their dignity. They tear humanity apart to achieve their goals. In olden times, it was all for God, now it is for money and power. Terrorist claim they are fighting Imperialism. Khomeini made the same claim but in truth he simply replaced the Shah with himself as a brutal, unprincipled dictator.

The imposition of Jihad is comparable to the use of an atomic bomb. It is the last resort and is to be used only against the enemies of Islam who would stop people from worshipping ALLAH or GOD. It is only to be used to save Islam from destruction. Only the purest of men, closest to God, who have studied religion for decades and hold the highest office of virtue and servitude to God and Islam, can issue an order for Jihad.

In a battle for the survival of Islam, even though God himself had already given him the order, Prophet Mohammad consulted with his closest confidants before issuing a Jihad. Jihad, ordered by the wrong man for personal reasons or any motive other than saving Islam and killing anyone who has not participated in an act to destroy Islam is not Jihad; but pure murder.

Jihad is not meant for the wrong reasons; a mask for murderers to hide behind, pretending they are fighting for a holy cause. People kill each other for many reasons and attempt to justify their act with various excuses. Islam is one of the excuses the murderers try to use for their inexcusable sin. Bin Laden and others who claim authority to issue Jihad are imposters not qualified for the job. They are fake mullahs with a pile of linen wrapped around their head, hiding behind lies and a long beard, poisoning innocent souls and using them for their own agendas. Men, such as Bin Laden, who slaughter innocent people to achieve their warped objectives, are not considered Muslims by rational Muslims. Such barbaric acts were condemned by Prophet Mohammad and are not allowed in Islam. Those who use people's lives and the name of God to achieve their own evil master plan are not practicing Islam.

The Koran warns, 'No matter how smart they are, no matter how they try to make up rules for Islam, God is aware of their inner motives and will not forgive them.' Our religion's leaders teach us to not judge people by the color of their skin, to not play God and to not punish others for our own sake or for what we think is right. No matter by what name your belief is called, if you care about and are good to other human beings and you do not kill, rape or steal and want the same for others that you want for yourself, that is all that matters.

There is a story in Islam that illustrates this concept. In the time of the Prophet Mohammad, there was a wealthy innkeeper named Hatam Taiie who was famous among both Shiah and Sunni. He served food on golden plates without charge to all travelers who came to Hejaz, in present day Saudi Arabia. They could stay at his inn as long as they wished. Some ingrates, who arrived tired and hungry, after resting and eating instead of thanking him, took the golden plates with them. He told his servants not to stop them.

This generous man did not believe in God. Despite his best efforts, the Prophet could not convince him to accept the God of Abraham. He denied God to the last day of his life. Because he lived in denial, most of the faithful assumed he would burn in Hell. However, when Hatam Taiie died, God sent a message to Mohammad through the Angel Gabriel that the man who had denied Him all his life would be saved. God said, "He was good to people, his generosity resembled mine, I spare his eternity from punishment, despite the fact he didn't accept me as his God."

This true story can be a lesson to us all. We can't predict what God's judgment will be. He sees everything, hears everything and doesn't need us to protect Him. We cannot pass judgment, condemn their belief or punish someone because they do not believe or worship exactly as we do. We must look beyond our differences. I have researched Islam extensively. I love Islam with all my heart. Islam is the religion of equality brotherhood and sisterhood among all human beings, especially between women and men. All religions need to understand that we all pray to the same God. It is not my God or your God or someone else's God. He is our God.

Most people in North America only know about Islam what they have heard and read in the news. It is a pity this great religion has not only been wrongly used but has also been presented in an unfair negative way.

WHO CAN ORDER JIHAD? WHO IS AN AYATOLLAH OZMA?

In Shiah, Ayatollah Ozma is a Fagih and the highest religious scholar. An Ayatollah's position is, in most respects, comparable to the Pope. Only a lawful, knowledgeable panel of Ayatollahs whose only commission is to save Islam from vanishing and whose decision is not affected by personal agenda or profit can order Jihad. He is a source of great wisdom but seeks the opinion and counsel of his peers. All the members of an Ayatollah Ozma's council must agree on the order for Jihad. It is an enormous responsibility that can change the destiny of nations. I emphasize, it is only issued to protect Islam from vanishing. It is not for severity, not for forcing anyone to embrace a religion and not for personal issues.

When he gives the order of Jihad, it becomes every Muslim's duty to leave their lives behind, pick up a weapon and fight with an army and only with an army.

WHY DO PEOPLE IN NON-MUSLIM POOR COUNTRIES BECOME ENEMIES OF THE WEST?

Media plays a great role in portraying the West as the heaven for the wealthy. Westerners are perceived as enjoying money from oil and other precious natural sources of the poor countries.

Back in Iran, 'Baywatch' was a popular show, among men, on satellite television. Iranian men looked on all American women as a bunch of half naked whores. Nevertheless, they enjoyed looking at them. When I moved to Canada, I realized this was a very low budget TV series. I intend no offense to the director, actors and actresses but they really don't know how they are perceived among other nations.

The cliché, 'What happens in Vegas, stays in Vegas.' should be applied to some of the programs that are broadcast overseas. Some may jeer the notion that people on the other side of the ocean judge a nation on what they see on TV. Believe it or not, it is true. People in those countries assume people of the West sweep money on the streets and live in utmost comfort. That is why coming to the West is the dream of many of them. We all know that movies and television do not present a realistic image of life in the West but the man in the street in Iran or Iraq does not know it. He is scrabbling to survive while believing Westerners receive their money and live a great life doing nothing.

Critics argue that, although it was not deliberate, the West bears some responsibility for terrorism, citing debatable exploitation of vulnerable countries. Defenders counter with equally cogent arguments. The solution lies with religion, politics, education and the relationship of the disappointed, disadvantaged and disillusioned nations with the West.

Exploitation is not the exclusive province of the West. It is a worldwide tragedy and a disgrace that dictators exploit national resources while the mass of the population lives in misery.

A case in point: In Equatorial Guinea, West Africa, the Kuwait of Africa, President Obiang, the dictator/president runs the country as a family business. He appoints family members to influential, lucrative posts overseeing national resources. His son has mansions in his home country and in Europe and was caught by a concealed camera spending a half million dollars on a shopping spree at Cartier in Paris. In contrast, the people of Equatorial Guinea live in shacks on less than a dollar a day. As a famous Persian proverb says, 'It didn't rain money from the sky; either he is a thief or his father was.'

The source of Equatorial Guinea's wealth is oil. It is no surprise that American oil companies are the biggest developers of the Guinea oil fields. Some would have you believe that there is something wrong with this arrangement. The US companies provide the capital and technical skills required to explore and develop Equatorial Guinea's oil reserves but they operate at the pleasure of the man in control. The alternative is to leave the oil in the ground, which benefits no one. It is not the fault of the oil companies that Equatorial Guinea's dictator plunders the oil revenue unmercifully and they cannot control it.

It has been publicized that Obiang is treated like royalty by the US oil company's president, plying him with an 18th century bottle of champagne and Persian caviar. Business savvy people understand that they are trying to find new oil reserves to benefit their stockholders and satisfy an oil hungry world. Obiang's is the palm they must grease to gain access to Equatorial Guinea's oil.

It is imperative that the United States not be completely dependent on oil from the volatile Middle East. It must develop alternative oil sources to supplement domestic shortfall. The uninformed and misinformed populations of countries that complain they are being exploited do not understand that responsibility for their misery is not on US shoulders alone. Their own dictatorial government must take the lion's share of the blame.

The United States has laws prohibiting doing business with countries where the president is also a dictator but no such prohibition is in force for Equatorial Guinea. Detractors will whine that the oil is more important to the United States than fairness. The hard truth is; if United States companies were not developing these resources, other countries would be doing so under terms even more odious to the host nation.

Having said that; if revolution ignites a fire in Africa, when the people look at who buys their oil, it is the United States that will be blamed, not the oil companies or the greedy dictator. The unfair element to US citizens is that while the oil company president vacations in a safe corner of the world on a private island protected by bodyguards; the ordinary people, the little people of America will pay the price if, on their next trip to Africa on their honeymoon or a missionary trip, they are cornered by African guerillas and rebels.

Hatred of the United States starts when the suffering people look at a small window that portrays America as bloodsuckers while African and Asian children are dying of starvation, neglect and disease. Americans are presumed to have it all. This is not true but, because the people receive little benefit from the deals that large US companies strike with their government, they blame the people of American and not the oil companies. Hate for everyone in the US and the West will simmer in their souls until it eventually erupts.

Twenty years ago, Khomeini broadcast exactly the same message of exploitation to Iran, claiming that Iran's money and resources were going to America and into the pocket of US citizens who were getting rich out of our misery.

Today, his successors are still broadcasting the same fiction throughout the world. It is shameful to admit but that is what I heard and, for a short while, believed as a child. Because I was a child of revolution and war, I can smell volatility and lies miles away.

A patriot can be someone as notorious as Cuban dictator Castro or the North Korean dictator, Kim Jung, who both know no religion at all, Sadam Hussein who raped women and prayed to God or Khomeini whose moral values were as featherweight as his fine linen turban.

WHAT IS THE SOLUTION? HOW CAN WE END TERRORISM?

The question is, how can we change people's mistaken interpretation of their religion and counter the blasphemous lies they are being fed? The good news is, if we persevere as nations united against terrorists we can deter and defeat them. The bad news is, it can't be done in one generation or by the removal of any one person.

Terrorism is a world wide epidemic. It did not come from outer space and aliens do not direct it. The criminals that commit atrocities live among us. Their legacy can only be ended if civilized nations band together. We don't need an American organization to end terrorism. We need a World Wide Anti-Terrorism Organization. One nation cannot win this war on diverse terrorists while the rest of the world whistles. Today the United States carries the burden; tomorrow it will be every country's nightmare.

We will all eventually pay a price. Terrorism is a weed growing in the mind of the innocent. It takes more than guns and troops to eradicate it. It takes knowledge and awareness.

For such a task, we need a World Intelligence Agency. We need personnel and informants from the 'hood' who have been there and understand the mind of the terrorist; who can read their mind and anticipate their actions. The best FBI profilers are, presumably, reformed criminals now working alongside the FBI. There must be a lesson there.

A man in Jakarta, convicted for bombing a hotel killing hundreds of tourists, gave a 'thumbs up' in court when he was sentenced to death and proclaimed that he was going to heaven. God never approved such barbaric cruelty. I will bet my seat in heaven that when judgment day comes, he and other evil people who use religion to justify killing innocent people will not make it through the Pearly Gates.

The bad news is not only his killing innocents; the worse news is the next generation will grow up with even less remorse and will not hesitate to commit worse crimes. For these people the cause is holy. The Ayatollah or the Sheikh has given him the thumbs up. From what I have been taught about God's justice, he doesn't operate on who prays and who doesn't. It is not my job to speculate on whether these terrorist will go to hell or to heaven but I seriously doubt that God is going to appreciate anyone assuming his role and killing others whether the cause is holy or pure evil.

Contrary to popular belief, not all Muslims are brainwashed and poor. Bin Laden, a distant prince of the Saudi crown family is a multi-millionaire and owned stock in the Twin Towers he destroyed. He purports to be the Muslim Messiah. It is easy to believe someone of the same religion and from the same cultural background. So, Bin Laden pretends that he is one with the poor, sits on the same pad in the cave and eats the same crappy food with his fingers from the same tray.

It is logical for his followers to believe him as Messiah instead of an American that they see as evil, even though the American is telling them the truth. As we say in Persian, 'Truth will eventually come out.' Just prior to the United States 2004 presidential election, Bin Laden, in his latest video, spoke directly to the American people; the same people he called evil and wanted dead. He made his first mistake by proudly accepting responsibility for 9/11. Many of his followers did not think he was behind 9/11, believing it was a CIA plan. Without defending anyone, we all know the CIA has been behind many plans around the world, including deposing the Shah of Iran, but killing thousands of US citizens for no plausible reason, wasn't part of their agenda.

Bin Laden has the advantage of culture and religion and that is why his supporters have not turned him in; not even for fifty million dollars. Consider this. An uneducated tribesman, living in a no-mans land among men who cut their watermelon with the same machete they slaughtered their sheep or camel with the night before, is not going to be comfortable at St. Moritz or on Park Avenue. Does he really need or care to have fifty million dollars? I think not. Long before he finishes counting his money his soul will be floating overhead, looking down at his beheaded body. Afghanistan, like most Islamic countries, follows the judiciary system of an eye for an eye or, in this case, a head for head.

Humanity working toward a better future

After atomic bombs were dropped on Hiroshima and Nagasaki, Japanese despised America. As always happens after such cataclysmic events, even many shortsighted Americans questioned the morality of the attack. The United States, wisely, did not offer to compensate individual Japanese. Instead, the US provided the knowledge and resources that allowed Japan to grow into a viable, prosperous country. As a result, Japan became a US ally instead of an enemy.

The success of this plan was not because of all the fancy gadgets the Japanese make now. It was because the United States and Japan made peace with each other, shared stories and shared pain. People healed because they got to know each other as humans, not as numbers of dead or foreigners with strange looking faces. Today, the people of Baghdad or Afghanistan are only pictures. Even though we put a name beside those pictures, we have not yet effectively communicated. It is hard to see them as our neighbors because they dress poorly and live in shacks shabbier than the worst hovels in the West. Children from the poorest families in the West have a better future than even the more advantaged children of Afghanistan and Iraq. We have difficulty communicating with them because they seem so strange and so angry.

Before I fled Iran, I was told that if I fell flat on my face, unconscious on the streets of Canada or the United States, no one would lift a finger to help me. In my heart and mind, I knew this couldn't be true but I had no evidence or reason to believe otherwise. When I arrived in Canada, I saw a different picture. Westerners became humans and I could communicate directly with them. I tried to understand their culture. Regardless of differences in skin, language, or religion, I saw common problems. I saw humans like myself; just as susceptible to temptation, just as tired of injustice and just as caring toward others.

It is the nature of humanity that we would have a hard time eating a pet chicken but we slaughter poultry by the millions because we didn't see them grow up. If we can turn Iraq and Afghanistan into countries such as Japan, the entire world will benefit. These countries will be elevated to a sophisticated, industrial level and we can see each other as compatible friends. If we can get to know each other personally, the fringe will be more likely to rebel against the idea of hurting the West. If we share wealth and knowledge perhaps all the casualties of war will not have been in vain.

Knowledge, sharing of wealth and a one-on-one network is the key to our peace puzzle. The third world society needs to realize Westerners are just as human as they. People are people, where ever they live and they need to know we care about them. People power can turn enemies into friends. I am a native of the region and know the people. They are as human as people of any other country. Belligerent societies, fairly treated, will see the light and reject backward ideas if they know they have a reliable friend.

They must realize that terrorism is not about religion or God. It is about man's inhumanity to man. Until we can capture their hearts and cleanse their minds from the poisonous speeches and thoughts inherited from hundreds of years of misery, we will have to sit on guard and keep watching our backs. Terrorism is like mould; it grows where there is no sunshine. It grows when people are so naïve as to believe religious leaders with a personal agenda who deliver bogus religion. The chain of ignorance forces people into invisible prisons. It's parishioners are brain washed people who act as robots and will do anything they are told they must do to take them to heaven.

As long as we try to exercise power and do not bring their life style up to a level close to the West, they will look at life in the United States and continue to think that all its wealth is derived from oil taken from their country. That is our choice; we can turn our enemies into friends or keep making more enemies.

WOMEN BEHIND A MENTAL VEIL

It is hard to believe, in this era when women in backward countries are used as little more than baby makers, that Islam abandoned slavery many centuries prior to its constitutional prohibition in the modern world. Even though this horrendous practice still thrives in Iran, Saudi Arabia, Jordan and elsewhere in the Muslim and Arab world, it is considered a great sin. By enslaving women, the mothers of generations to come will suffer for sins they didn't commit. One after another, they will walk the same path. The basic element of freedom is having the choice. Often, when that is taken away, women are not able to break the cycle.

AFGHANISTAN recently had a national election. For many of its citizens it was the first time to vote. As bright as this news is, a look at the women in line to vote is sobering. Their eyes didn't necessarily show happiness and many still wore burkahs. Although the Taliban and Al Qaeda are out of power, the brain washing they did still rules the heart of the people.

Under the Taliban, Afghani women were condemned to a burkah prison for life. It was part of the terrible life style imposed by the Taliban and is a symbol of the lingering influence of the Taliban that will continue until every burkah is burned. The Taliban claim that the burkah is required by the rules of Islam. That is a lie. The burkah is not a Hijab, or requirement, for Islamic woman and they cannot point to any rule or law in the Koran that justifies it. It is just a tool to manipulate and keep the women disciplined and under control. And, it is still working. The Taliban are gone from power but many women in Afghanistan are still hesitant, or are not allowed by the men in their lives, to come out of their burkah.

The effect of decades of indoctrination and subjugation by the absurd rules imposed by the Taliban will not be erased until a generation of women is educated. There is nothing in Islam requiring women to be secluded or prohibiting them from pursuing an education. In fact, our prophet was in favor of education and equality for women. His daughter, Fatimeh, was never obligated to cover her face or hands and was one of the first female teachers in Islam; teaching crowds of men numbering in the hundreds. What we see in fanatical societies should not be mistaken for the rules of Islam.

S AUDI ARABIA looks modern today, fourteen hundred years ago it was most likely much like Afghanistan today.

Capital punishment is still meted out as it was in the time of the Prophet. The punishment may be carried out the same way but the sins are entirely different. In the time of the Prophet, if a man accused of stealing had a compelling reason and told the Prophet that he couldn't provide for his wife and children, he wouldn't be punished. If, his Arab Sheikh master paid him so little that he had to rob to save his family, it was the Sheikh who was punished, not the poor man.

Although Saudi Arabia claims there is no crime in their country, they are still beheading critics of royalty and poor people who are forced to steal because they cannot afford life. To my amazement, in a recent PBS interview with some Saudi Arabia women. They didn't exactly embrace the idea of being liberated, to vote, drive their cars. They all said they wanted to be left alone. Some even thought the restrictions on women are justified. A woman doctor applauded the custom saying, "The restrictions are fine."

The Saudi family runs Saudi Arabia much as a family business. Every nephew and grandson is a prince and receives a large piece of the royal pie. Among those close to the royal family was notorious Saudi terrorist, Osama Bin Laden, who received public money supposedly to be used for welfare for the poor; the same unfortunates who are beheaded because they don't have enough money to live on. For those who think all Saudi residents are rich, I tell them is a false impression. The year I traveled to Saudi, I saw unbelievably dirt poor people in Medina, whose lives were as bleak as that of the Afghans.

Women in Saudi Arabia are no better off than poor people. They are veiled in public and live in harems surrounded by other women. Their duty is to serve a man, usually one with many wives. Many criticize the Prophet for polygamy and ridicule him or anyone else who has practiced it. I need to clarify the rules of polygamy and when, where and why it was practiced.

Islam and women: is there equality and respect for women in Islam?

Islam believes in freedom and equality for women. Koran was given as a miracle to the prophet Mohammad to be the guide for future generations to follow until the end of time in pursuit of the way of God. The Koran repeatedly mentions the equality of women and men. Muslims have been taught that the doors of Paradise are beneath their mother's feet. Respecting mothers is emphasized everywhere from the Koran to the words of the Prophet and Imams.

His prophecy was not to force women into polygamy. He said clearly and repeatedly that if a man chooses to have many wives, he must divide his time and wealth equally and that failure to do so is a sin. Many Muslim women have fallen for the perverted version of polygamy. It is time for them to brush up on the rules and stand up for their rights. The Prophet did not give these one-sided privileges to men; men took them on their own. It has nothing to do what prophet they follow or what religion they profess.

The Prophet himself did not lead a polygamist life until his only wife, Khadigeh, the love of his life with whom he lived faithfully for many years, died in his arms. When she died, he didn't want another wife but, as a prophet and a symbol, other tribal chiefs influenced him to marry. Many people find this part of history hard to believe. How could he be forced to marry? He was called the Rohol-Amin in Arabic, which means a man of integrity who never lied to save himself. I choose to believe a prophet's word over a historian selling books.

He was forced by the Sheiks of two of the tribes to marry a nine-year-old girl called Ayasheh. She was stunningly beautiful and already the center of controversy. The Prophet cried of many hardships she brought to his life. After his death she became the number one enemy of his son in law, Ali.

In modern times, most people think marrying a nine-year-old girl is a sick idea and I agree. However, we are speaking of more than 1400 years ago. I discuss further, in the Marriage section, the reason women in Islam were married so young.

Governments, such as Iran, attempt to spread the impression that their Islamic republic is a benevolent society. That is simply the propaganda of a regime using Islam to hurt people. Their actions speak louder, revealing it to be a close-minded, fanatical regime with a theory of male supremacy.

Like many women around the world, Iranian women go through hell on earth in their lifetime but won't talk about it. In Iran today, women are still being stoned in the name of God.

Prophet Mohammad brought a new religion and gave women rights when they were slaves and had none. He built a religion and a nation based upon love and respect.

Islam is criticized for not giving women all rights or at least making them equal to men. If Prophet had said to a man that his wife was his equal, she likely would not have survived the night. We can pass judgment on something the Prophet intended to be beneficial but was misused in the hands of his followers. Or, we can use his words the right way and leave bitterness and judgment aside to make a better world.

The outside world wonders why Islamic women cover themselves so completely. It is a custom rooted in the Koran's requirement that women dress modestly that has evolved into overkill. Men deprived of female beauty were so sexually repressed that they were conditioned to over-react to any glimpse of a woman's skin or hair. Men of the Prophets time were not as restrained as the educated male of our era. Women had to cover up to protect themselves.

I traveled to Saudi Arabia when I was fourteen. I can tell you, it hasn't progressed much in the treatment of women since the Middle Ages. I was groped by a bus driver and saw many women groped by police who were supposed to serve the Prophet and keep thieves out of his mosque. I saw men stare insolently into women's eyes. The subtly overt harassment made me angry.

WHAT IS THE LEGAL AGE IN ISLAM FOR MARRIAGE? HOW MANY WIVES CAN A MAN HAVE?

Before explaining this title, I want to draw the reader's attention to scientific studies of the reasons the human body and puberty have evolved with time. In primitive areas, puberty is coming later while in others, like North America, girls are maturing earlier than in the past. Due to the climate and the hardships women endured, the maturity age for girls was different than it is today. They married at an early age and many died by age thirty. By age fifty, they resembled a woman of ninety today. In hot climate countries, puberty may occur as early as nine to thirteen while in colder climates it can be as high as seventeen years of age.

One other factor that shouldn't be forgotten; the Arabs of Prophet Mohammad's time were not living in desert palaces. They were Bedouin and did not enjoy a Pharaoh's life style. I have observed the life of many Bedouins. Their children do not grow up like ours. Their six-year-old girl is equal to our ten year old. The last factor to remember is that marriage was not always about sex. The desert tribes were almost constantly in battles and many men died. Their wives and children had no one to provide for them. These widowed women either had to become prostitutes and beggars or part of a man's extended family with the respect of his name. This was the course followed by the Prophet. As a Muslim, I can understand why Islam originally allowed men to have more than one wife but I believe if Mohammad were alive today, he would find that rule unfair to women and rescind it. Fourteen hundreds years ago, when he allowed polygamy it was not to degrade women. Wars killed so many men that there was no one to take care of the surviving women and children. Marriage saved them from prostitution, slavery and starvation. As strange as it sounds to the rest of the world, Prophet didn't allow polygamy for the sake of men but for the sake of women.

Polygamy is part of Islam but has its conditions and strict rules. However, men who practice it only know the number of women they can marry and could not care less about its rules. Fifteen hundred years ago, the short life span due to hard labor, disease and war, gave people as reason to pass on their genes to their offspring before their own youth was over. I am not trying to justify Islam or undermine a generation but we need to consider that our ancestors were quite satisfied to marry because that was how it was. In Saudi Arabia, Persia or Greece, rules were pretty much universal.

According to the Fagih of Shiah Sector, today, officially, a girl must have reached puberty to be married legally. In addition, her parents are expected to consider her physical, psychological and emotional maturity. Undoubtedly, there are still instances of marriage of very young girls, without considering any of these factors. Thankfully, the marriage of pre-pubescent girls is a declining practice.

Plural marriages are not permitted today in all Islamic countries. However, Islamic law permits men to have five permanent marriages. There is also a proviso in the fine print for additional marriages for a specific period of time that allows an unlimited number of common law wives, mistresses or concubines. These temporary 'wives' have only to be approved by a mullah. In all cases, men are supposed to be able to meet the financial and physical needs of all his wives.

Men who cannot find suitable marriage partners often seek temporary marriages called *Sigeh* or, lawful girl friend/boy friend. Religiously, a man is bound to treat the woman with respect and cover her financial needs. Sigeh, however, imposes no legal obligation upon a man who has a sexual relationship with a woman. I should emphasize that under the mullah's law, men don't have any obligation toward any woman, married or Sigeh. Women brave enough to attempt to have an independent life have been found dead.

For a number of reasons, primarily poverty, some submissive women have found Sigeh a way of life. Sadly, most of these women find themselves in conflict with the man's wives and families and some are even killed. If they survive the brutalities of the families of the men they marry for a short time, they still find themselves shunned as legal prostitutes. Legal or illegal, these women are the true victims of poverty and social stigma and easy prey for abusive males.

WOMEN OF PROPHET'S FAMILY

Some clerics say Mohammad's daughter, Fatimeh, never appeared in public and therefore women should stay at home where they are protected. That is simply not true. She was one of the first women in Islam to teach. In her conferences, 400 men attended at one time. Fatimeh was as capable and as literate as her father and her husband, Ali. Her appearance on the battlefield with her father and husband was a sign of her equality. She was the complete opposite of the weak woman she is sometimes portrayed as in Shiah. She wasn't allowed to pick up the sword and kill but she joined her father and husband in battle and saved her father's life. She defended her husband when powerful enemies were trying to kill him. Shiah followers believe enemies searching for her husband killed her and her unborn child in her home.

After Fatimeh died, her father, Ali, brought up their young daughter, Zainab. The great-granddaughter of Prophet Mohammad, she was as brave as her mother. She stayed with her holy family in the battle at Karbala, where her brother was killed, sixty years after Mohammad's death, and saved the lives of the children.

Women of Mohammad's family were as strong and involved as their men, not only in daily chores but in affairs that concerned the followers of Islam. We hear less about them because history doesn't always tell about the sacrifices that women made. Men have ruled Islam and, although women have made unspeakable sacrifices, they don't receive their fair share of praise.

ISLAM AND LOVE BETWEEN MAN AND WOMAN

This is probably something you have never heard about Islam; a man falling in love with his future wife. Over 1400 years ago, romantic love stories were not every day occurrences among the nomadic Bedouin tribes. Prophet Mohammad was only twenty-five when he fell in love with and, defying the mockery of the prominent tribes, married Khadejeh, a forty-year-old businesswoman. He was a messenger of God and could have as many wives as he desired but he refused others until his wife died. The marriage produced several children but only one, a daughter, was born after he became Prophet and only she survived. When their daughter became eligible for marriage, Prophet Mohammad allowed her to choose her husband by interviewing hundreds of men through a sheer curtain.

Maybe the selection process would be unusual today but it was quite liberal for the time. Today, an even more primitive process is in vogue in Islamic countries where young women are not allowed any part in the selection of their husbands. Prophet Mohammad gave his daughter absolute freedom to choose her husband but today, people who pretend to follow him, force their choice upon their daughters. It has been said by Prophet that when a man marries a woman, on the night of their wedding, he should wash her feet in a small basin and then pour the water around the house and ask God for prosperity.

He is responsible for all the house chores. He can request help from his wife and, if she likes, she can help. Otherwise, he is responsible to hire help or even a nanny for his children. A woman is not obligated to do house chores or to clean up after the children. She is not obligated to cook, clean or do anything she doesn't feel like doing it. This is all documented in Islam, of course, but who is to listen... women wear many hats, partner, bill payer, mates, nannies, teacher, cook, and the list goes on and on.

Divorce in Islam

Islam gives a woman every right to divorce her husband if she is not taken care of physically, emotionally and financially or is in any other way disadvantaged. If she says three times that she divorces her husband, he is divorced. She receives not only child support but also she can take anything she brought to her husband's house as part of her dowry, whatever the husband bought her in the time she was in his house or she bought with her own money.

However, the rules of Islam doesn't apply for women in Iran who cannot easily divorce their husband, easing the way for many men to have more than one wife. If a wife tries to stop her husband from taking a new wife, he can divorce her instantly with no compensation. A woman may be able to obtain a divorce with ample, substantiated reason but she will receive no compensation.

Honor Killing among Muslim nations

Under Islamic law, unlawfully or deliberately killing another human being is taboo, period. Honor killing is completely taboo and not part of Islam. This is the origin of honor killings as practiced by the desert tribes. If the death was accidental, Islam recommends, instead of taking another life, forgiveness and that money be paid to the family of the victim. If the killing is intentional, Islam demands an eye for an eye. The murderer is to be killed in the same manner he/she killed his victim. It is never a justified punishment in Islam. Prophet Mohammad specifically forbade the act.

Nevertheless, it is a crime rooted in the pre-Islamic belief that if a girl disgraces her family, a family member must kill her to restore the family honor, ignoring the fact that the civilized world does not see any honor in murder. It was a widely practiced custom among Arab tribes before Islam. Men took pride in killing their female relatives for real or suspected transgression of tribal laws and customs. Among the Bedouin of Saudi Arabia condemned girls were usually raped and buried alive by their fathers and brothers. If an Arab man returned from war or business after a long absence to find his wife had given birth to a child, his wife and the child were in great danger of suffering an honor killing. If the baby were a girl he would order his wife to kill it. If she refused, he would bury the baby alive. If his wife interfered, she would be killed also.

The Prophet was heart broken by this barbarism. His rulings were intended to end slavery, child labor and many other horrible crimes common among the Arabs. Unfortunately, banning the practice does not stop sick-minded psychopaths who continue to justify their crimes by misinterpreting Islam.

There seems to have been a resurgence of this barbaric act in recent years. Many honor killings in Islamic countries have been reported to Amnesty International.

I n PLACES SVCH AS JORDAN, IRAN, IRAQ, AFGHANISTAN, and other backward countries around the world, the culture has come to believe that the family has a divine right to dictate marriage choice to women. Girls who dare to have a boyfriend are almost always presumed to be sexually active. Even today, many girls in Third World societies are killed by their fathers, brothers and uncles just on suspicion of having 'disgraced' the family. I have seen pictures of women in a pool of their own blood. Women in Jordan are murdered in the name of Islam by their own brothers, fathers and mothers in "honor killings." There are many things done in the name of religion that have no religious basis.

I RAN
Unfortunately, honor killing, which is culturally and religiously taboo has risen and is even used by the regime since it came to power. Every day, women in Iran are hanged or stoned. Husbands abuse and may even stab their wives but the women don't dare report it because their spouse would be out of jail in no time and they would be in even greater danger. Brothers can rape their sisters on their wedding eve with little fear of retribution. In my own family, my grandmother, saying she did not want to take the secret to her grave, confided on her deathbed to my mother, that my father raped one of his younger sisters who died two days later, hemorrhaging from internal injuries. He was not punished.

Women fear going to family members or unsympathetic parents who will try to force their daughter to stay in a violent marriage until she dies or something happens to her husband. Family criticism and violence against women are very common. Although the government publicly tries to avoid the appearance of any direct role in the violence, the truth is that the government praises the dominant role of men in society.

There was a sarcastic quotation painted on the wall of a military camp in Tabriz where Siavash served as a soldier, 'When a woman dies, a flower will grow on her grave. If all the women die, the world would be a garden of flowers.'

This ambiguous saying is supposed to express the softness and gentleness of women. The bitter truth is, it means a woman can only be redeemed through death; a good woman is a dead one. The message is; a woman who stands out and is heard, undaunted by the mullah's threats is impure.

IRANIAN WOMEN AND CULTURAL ABUSE

There is a ridiculous and infuriating difference between boys and girls in Iranian society. Boys and girls study in separate schools. Girls learn to become modest and obedient. Boys learn to take control of their family, to become macho and violent to prove themselves men. No matter how much parents tell the girls they love them, it is obvious to anyone who has lived in the culture that boys are favored. Most men force their wives to get pregnant repeatedly, even into their mid-forties, in order to have a boy, to carry the blood of their name to the next generation. This is culture preference and has no Islamic basis. Prophet's own blood and name was transferred through his daughter Fatimeh, not his sons.

Although the couple may already have half a dozen girls, parents want more sons. In America, daughters are daddy's little girls. In Iran, sons are daddy's little boys. Boys are the bloodstream and the main inheritors of the family estate. Boys receive two parts of inheritance to one for a girl. In simple words, each boy equals to two girls.

A Persian proverb is the basis of violence against women in the Iranian culture. The proverb illustrates, but does not excuse, the cruel mentality of male chauvinists who think of women as livestock. The proverb, 'You have to kill the cat by the bed.' refers to the gratuitous punishment of the bride in the bridal chamber on the wedding night. Most modern males publicly refute this as justification for senseless violence against their bride but their actions suggest otherwise. Women are brutally assaulted by their husbands every day just to confirm his power and authority. A newlywed husband, encouraged by his family, is expected to punish his bride in the first weeks of marriage to 'put her in her place.'

It is not likely you will find this practice described in books. There are many behaviors practiced in cultures around the globe about which only an insider would know. Sadly, the wives enable the continued practice of this ignorant custom. These good women will never admit physical abuse or complain to her family about what she is enduring. She knows she will get no sympathy and has little choice but to accept the assaults. Her parents wanted her out of their lives and do not want her back. She is resigned to blind obedience for life.

The effect of the punishment in the early days of marriage resembles a butterfly in a jar. It will dance for you if you shed a light on its wings. A woman will put up with abuse, as though it were a mirage in the far distance, striving for her husband's approval and attention. She will even perpetuate the nightmare by joining him in abusing her own daughters. Unfortunately, she is passing on submissiveness down through generations to come. Before the revolution, Iran was tracking the footsteps of advanced countries in marriage matters. Arranged, forced marriages were considered crimes and were being denounced for what they were; pedophilia and child molestation. They were more common in remote villages but, as people become poorer, a lot of wealthy old men are being 'given' girls as young as nine.

Many marriages in Iran are still arranged by the families. Girls have little or no voice in selecting the person they marry and most are not happy to be given to a stranger. This practice has actually proliferated since the percentage of women in the population has increased due to eight years of war that took the lives of half a million young men. There is seldom such a thing as marriage for love. If the girl is lucky, she marries her cousin, who she has at least known for years and there is always a chance they may fall in love after they are married. If she is from a rural area, she may meet a boy she likes at university or work but there is no guarantee that the family of the boy or girl will approve their marriage. Poor people sell their children because the old men are not after a dowry, normally a mandatory requirement in Persian culture. It is, in fact, a reverse dowry. The groom pays the bride's family for the body and soul of his bride, who may be younger than his own children or grandchildren. Girls who said 'No,' on the day of the wedding reception to a forced, loveless marriage to a man they did not know, have been killed in their white dresses. It is past time that people around the world know what is going on beneath the black chadors, which hide so much of Iran's pain.

Families watch their daughters carefully as they would a ripening crop before harvest. If a girl simply calls a girl friend, she may be suspected of calling a boyfriend. Married women are also subject to suspicion. Gossip is entertainment and part of the life style and for men in a hardscrabble world. Sadly, in much of the Muslim world, just a rumor can cost an innocent woman her life, particularly if she is attractive and is seen, even inadvertently, talking to eligible men.

When someone challenges men and their treatment toward women, they defend themselves by bluffing, "What mistreatment?" We provide them with food, home, children, clothing, gold jewelry, property; all the comforts of life.

In reality, a woman cannot even wear the jewelry without her husband's permission.

Iranian men put property under the name of the wife and children to avoid taxes but the wife has no authority to sell it. As for having children, all a woman can do is take orders. Only in the cities do some women take birth control pills. They are expensive and there is no coverage for drugs from the government. Some men don't let their wives use a contraceptive of any kind. A woman is a mate, a servant for man, a mother, and a baby-making machine until she dies or is past childbearing age.

Having children doesn't stop a man from abusing his wife. If a woman interferes with her husband who wants to punish the children, she will be assaulted as well.

Many men complain that after having children their wives are not attuned to their physical needs. They reason, therefore, that it is their right to take their itches elsewhere to be scratched. Whether their wife is satisfied is not an issue. The husband is immune from any punishment for his dalliances but if his wife has a lover, she has committed adultery and will be stoned to death. This double standard, in any society, is inhuman and infuriating.

Iranian women are not only under pressure from the government, which ignores or violates their rights continually, but they are also violated and tortured by their own loved ones. If a girl avoids marrying a man that her family thinks is suitable, her life in the family is finished. She will be beaten severely and almost inevitably forced to accept and give herself to a husband she does not know and does not want to be with.

Although the government publicly says that women have to be willing to marry the prospective groom, physical punishment of recalcitrant girls is praised and reinforces the notion that parents own their daughters.

Among most uneducated families in backward cultures, especially Iran, girls are like livestock. If she does not want to be given in marriage, she will be sold, just like property. Fathers, mostly, but sometimes both parents, give away or sell their daughters without their consent to a man that they have never met.

There are degrading words that parents use to humiliate their daughters and induce them to accept the life sentence to which they are being condemned. They call the daughter a 'stubborn she-mule.' My father and brothers called me that name. It is common in Iran for boys to humiliate their sisters. A boy thinks he should never have to apologize for breaking his sister's heart.

She is merely an object. If there is a good deal to be made on her, she must be sold; otherwise, she will be 'outdated.' Mothers and fathers often tease women over eighteen. If she has refused to marry someone whom her parents think is suitable; a girl will be denied life necessities, such as clothing and pocket money. She has a strict curfew and cannot talk to her friends. Her father, mother or elder brother will beat her if she breaks these rules.

Mothers become violent toward their daughters and other females who do not conform to the lifestyle that they themselves have accepted. The rebellious girl becomes unpopular and is ignored. Life becomes lonely until she bows to the will of her parents and accepts an arranged, loveless marriage that she is expected to endure until she dies.

Parents in my culture admonish their daughters with another proverb, 'I give you away wearing white 'bridal gown' and I expect you to come out of this marriage wearing white shroud.' It means that no matter how hard the marriage might be, you have to stay in it.

For those who are forced to get married right out of high school and wish to continue their education there are night schools but few husbands, even if they had a car, would allow his wife go to school alone at night. The cities are not safe at night, even for men. There is no security or public safety in Iran. When dark falls; crime rises. If anything happens to a woman while she is out, she is responsible for her own death or rape. Much like I was responsible for my kidnapping. I was lucky to come out alive.

Polygamy in Iran

As previously explained, polygamy is a part of Islam but culturally it was prohibited, whether a man was Muslim or belonged to some other religion. Polygamy was not condoned in many ethnic and Muslim cultures. Kurds, the non-Arab residents of Khuzestan considered it an insult to their daughter if the son-in-law married another woman. Although men in Iran are culturally prohibited from having more than one wife, religiously they can marry, or shall I say own, five wives at a time. Many men take full advantage of the opportunity, regardless of whether they can provide financially for their wives. During his reign, Mohammad Reza Shah banned plural marriage but permitted men who already had multiple wives to retain them. After his overthrow, the Islam revolutionary government reinstated the practice.

Since the revolution, however, it has been legal for a man to marry another woman while he is married to one or more other wives, whether the incumbent wives agree or not. He can easily divorce any of his five permanent wives when he reaches his limit. This law is documented in Iran's constitution and is commonly practiced. He can have any number of common-law wives, concubines, mistresses or lovers by simply having a mullah sanction the extramarital affair for a specific period of time.

In the minds of the mullahs who make the rules, it is acceptable for a man to destroy a family to satisfy his own desires. This is an example of the inane, prejudicial rulings coming out of the Iranian judiciary system and family courts. According to the law, as practiced in Iran, she has no right to oppose her husband's multiple marriages or affairs.

On the contrary, women are expected to welcome a new wife. A husband might resort to any means, including extreme violence, to convince a wife to accept his new wife. If, as not infrequently happens, his persuasion results in her unexpected death there is usually no investigation. The police routinely close the case on the sudden death of women. In a country ruled by mullahs executing men's laws, these events are perfectly acceptable. Women who do protest are considered troublemakers and are unpopular, even with other women.

Divorce in Iran

The Iranian government falsely propagandizes to the world that the judiciary system is based on Islamic law. It fails to mention that when it comes to people's rights, the government, not Islam, defines the rights. The officials wrap it around the Islamic laws to try to make it appear legal and acceptable.

According to the rules of Islam, women are equal to men. Seemingly at odds with this concept is the law that a woman receives only one-half share for each share a man receives in an inheritance. The original reasoning for this disparity was that women traditionally received a dowry, which she retained, she was to be fully supported by her husband and had no expenses whereas a man had the responsibility providing for his family. The exception is, if a woman has been independent and helped her family, she also should receive equal shares with the males of the family. Iran says today's judiciary system is based on the rules of the Prophet's time. However, there is a double standard; some rules are ok and some are not. A Persian joke sarcastically reveals the fallacy of people who want it both ways. The ostrich is called the Camel Bird because of the hump on its back. The joke is: A man asked the camel bird to give him a ride. She said, "Sorry, I am a bird." He said, "Ok, then fly." She said, "Sorry, I am not really a bird but a camel." The Iranian government is a camel bird.

The only time a woman is likely to be granted compensation is when her husband has multiple wives and she can prove that he does not adequately support her and her children. Even today, for most women in Iran, divorce is shameful. The family of the woman would rather see their daughter dead than divorced. My mother was finally able to divorce my father after twenty-five years of abuse and neglect. Siavash and I supported her decision but her brothers turned their faces away from my mother, telling her she was the shame of the family. I scolded them,

"Where were you when my father was torturing us? If you really cared for your sister, why didn't you help her? Now you are ashamed of her? I think you should be ashamed of yourself for ignoring her misery all these years and then calling my mother the shame of your family." My uncles despised me for pointing out reality and telling them to back off and mind their own business. I became the burr under the family saddle blanket.

Oppression in Iran

Since mullahs gained control in Iran, women are treated much as they were in medieval times. Women who once were independent and decision makers of our society now are pressured to remain silent or face threats and harsh treatment. A large number of vocal women dissidents have been imprisoned and many executed. Less daring women simply go on with their life, cocooning themselves like a larvae, not daring to speak up against their unequal status with men.

In present day Iran, the Sepah Pasdar, men and women with little or no education, are allowed to interpret and enforce civil and religious law. The system is trying to silence all critical voices. They know it is easier to kill one person than to face a crowd and kill many. The Shah paid a heavy price for his mistake in not stifling his opposition. When a journalist asked him about his opposition, he candidly commented, "If they want to leave the country, we will gladly provide them with a one way ticket."

The mullahs are not as generous as the Shah. They don't allow their opponents to become a source of rebellion against them in foreign countries. The mullahs kill their opposition in the name of God, much as the Catholic Church did during the Inquisition. At the beginning of the revolution, Germany, allowed the Kurdish Democrats, a small European resistance group, on it's soil. Many were killed in a bomb blast in a restaurant. Germany prosecuted the killers despite Iran's open resentment toward Germany for its actions.

These few people were not the only casualties engineered by the government of Iran. The famous author, Salaman Rushdie, got a little more attention that he desired. Khomeini condemned his book, Satanic Verses, and denounced him as a man who had insulted Islam and sold his soul to Satan and must be killed. The government of Iran put a price on his head and only lifted the Fatwa after Khomeini left this earthly life to meet his own justice.

Among the mullahs are people like Mr. Khatami, who, I believe, if he is not able to do anything productive, at least pretends that he is trying to do something and Mr. Montazeri, who genuinely regretted helping Khomeini. Once a confidant of Khomeini, he was imprisoned in his own home for many years after warning Khomeini that he was being too harsh toward his opposition. He was recently released from house arrest but has no standing in the government.

Khomeini and his regime earned its place among the most callous and brutal of dictators who have ruled Iran. He introduced ever more creative methods of torture that were exposed in an award-winning documentary called 'A Tree that Remembers' recently broadcast in Canada.

Mullahs like Rafsanjani and Khamenei, are the business gurus of Iran. They think of nothing except their own pockets and have strangled police officers with their own hands. Yet, they rule in the name of God and live lavishly on public funds intended for the poor. Rafsanjani claims his family wealth comes from pistachio trees. People in Iran have a joke, wondering what kind of fertilizer he uses that causes his trees to grow money instead of pistachios. If he sold his beloved pistachio garden, he would not have been able to buy half of the properties he has bought around the world and in recent years in Vancouver, Canada.

The government of Iran does not stop the killing because its perpetuation depends on it. Like the dictatorship of Chile, Iraq and others named herein, the dictatorship of Iran retains power by lethal force. The difference is, in Iran, everything is done in the name of God.

Iranian government and lies they televise about Islam

The callousness of Iran's governing mullahs in Iran is beyond imagination. Although it is a common color now in Iran, there is nothing in my religion prescribing black. We used to wear black only for mourning. Our prophet Mohammad recommended wearing white, and bright colors. From the time that the Islamic government of Iran came to power, black seems to be their favorite color.

The ubiquitous chador that we see the women of Iran wearing is portrayed as required Islamic clothing. The chador, in fact, is not a Hijab or Islamic outfit. The shorter, knee length version of chador was worn during the Qajar Dynasty; the beginning of the mullah's political influence. It became a symbol of Muslim women's dress code although it does not look and is not Islamic. In short, Chador does not represent Islam yet it does represent the Mullah's Dynasty. They are determined to establish this smothering, sweltering piece of black fabric as a national symbol and preach falsely that it is required by Islamic law to justify their abuse of power and true Islam.

If this regime had come to power before the advent of modern media, radio, TV, newspapers and books we would have witnessed the birth of a new prophecy and new prophets, Khomeini the 13th and Khamenei the 14[th,] added to Islam. This is an example of how the brainwashed close their eyes and minds to the truth and accept the propaganda. It is a bitter reminder of how a pure religion has been manipulated for personal reasons. The growth of this regime is like a cancerous tumor and is evidence of the victory of superstition over the true message of Islam.

In Iran, facts are only true if the mullahs say so. Islam, however, doesn't care whether a mullah or a regular person tells the truth, as long the message is based on true Islam.

In a discussion about Islam and how we know what to choose and when we know we are crossing the line, my teacher, speaking about Prophet Mohammad, whose testimony ironically has divided Shiah from Sunni, told this story. A follower asked the Prophet, "What we are going to do without you?" The Prophet answered, "I have left you with the Book of God, my family, and to assist and guide you, also you have your mind." Mind in this sentence means, heart, conscious and knowledge.

To answer people who asked him about the rules of Islam and how they would be applicable for generations after his departure, he replied, "Bring up your children for your own time and, if you must, send them to China for their education." Most people knew of China at the time because of commercial travelers on the Silk Road. That meant he strongly believed in education and in going to any length to get it and in helping future generations to understand the rules accordingly. He wanted to tell us that we should accept changes as time passes. Everyone can interpret the truth the way they like but he said that if you know in your heart you are doing something wrong, you shouldn't do it. These words do not sound old-fashioned or as if they come from an illiterate fanatic.

WOMEN WHO SPOKE UP

Zahra Kazemi: The photographer from Montreal, an Iranian born Canadian citizen, was invited by the government of Iran but, while photographing a demonstration, unwisely and perhaps unwittingly overstepped her bounds in photographing Evin, Iran's notorious prison whose walls are painted with the blood of generations of tortured men, women and even children. Sadly, she was spotted by government watchdogs in the wrong place at the wrong time and paid with her life for a photograph. She died in a coma as a result of a brain hemorrhage caused by blows to her head while in a Tehran detention center. She died for doing what she believed was the right thing. Her body was never sent back to Canada.

Shirin Ebadi: A lawyer, she won the Nobel Peace Prize for defending her political clients. After that, she, herself spent time in solitary confinement and is one of the lucky few to survive Evin prison. Ms. Ebadi tried to defend Kazemi for what it was probably a communication failure. To everyone's disbelief, the case was dismissed.

Emerging from the two-day court trial in Tehran, which the ambassador of Canada was not allowed to attend, she was furious, stating this is not justice. Despite all her efforts, I have heard so much undeserved criticism of her.

Most people around the globe don't realize there is continued violence against women in Iran. Many who do see the abuse choose to remain silent about women's issues in Iran. There is virtually no news about the fate of Iranian women jailed for phony drug charges or for political reasons.

Human rights groups have so many cases that abuse against women simply isn't a priority. This is partly thanks to the government and partly because people, mostly men, deny violence against women exists in Iran. After all, Iran is a country ruled by men. If it weren't for the education that the Shah introduced for women, most Iranian girls would never have seen the inside of a school in their entire lives.

The Iranian justice system does not encourage anyone, plaintiff or defendant, to be represent at trial by an attorney. If the charge is political, the accused is not permitted to have a lawyer. In civil or non-political criminal cases, the litigants or defendant may have an attorney if they can afford one. If the family can't afford a lawyer, the accused is guaranteed not to get a fair trial and may not get one, even with one. They are at the mercy of a mullah judge, picking his nose and scratching his balls, who makes, bends and breaks the rules on a whim. No one dares to stick their neck out and put their lives on the line for fear of being killed by the regime's enforcers.

A PLEA FOR UNITY

Presumably, we are not living in an ancient time when men were allowed to slap, kick and punish their daughters, sisters and wives. However, men still practice such aggression, using metaphors, culture, pride, men's rights and holy books to defend their barbarism. From Iran to Afghanistan, Pakistan and Jordan; from India to Africa and Indonesia, authorities in too many countries take genocide and abuse against women very lightly. The male-dominated countries could not care less about women. The problem is, these women are the mothers of the next generation and when these women grow up in fear, they breed fear on the skin of their infants.

Women lose their lives at the hands of the same family that puts their name on the missing lists in the newspapers. In the name of justice, the government puts many women to death for alleged but unproven adultery, drug use or helping drug dealers. Some of them are educated women facing fabricated charges because they tried to educate other women. An accusation can kill a person; a suspicious mind can put an end to a life. Modern CSI technology and DNA evidence is very much a non-heard-of investigation fairy tale.

While the governments talks about or ignores the problem, killing and rape continues, unreported and shrouded in the mystery of a traditional cult. Hampered by international relations and signed foreign policy agreements, there is nothing, or very little, the West can do to change the treatment of their population, particularly abuse of women.

If we all believe in one goal, we can end the torment and abuse that goes to the grave with innocent women who die in these countries every day.

Women should care for themselves and each other and be aware they are the next generation's mothers, sisters, and wives. God has given us powerful minds and gifts but we must control our destiny to change it.

We know we have been denied our rights. Together we can send a strong message of defiance. We can and shall overcome the ignorant customs and unjust treatment. But, we need to know that no one is going to offer it.

We, as abused women and men have to fight for our rights to attain the respect that we deserve. I don't believe in heroes anymore but I do believe in a strong generation to fill the shoes of one.

I know the poet has never been wrong but I personally don't like to wait for a savior to appear. I believe there is a hero in each and every one of us. We all hear that nothing comes from nothing. If we all sit and wait for someone else to do something, that someone else may never be born or may never come. Every one has a duty to stand up for themselves and others if they can.

From my observations, that is the goal of those who march and shout for freedom. The opposition has its own political agenda which, unfortunately, comes before their common goal to overpower the theocracy. In fact, the factions of the opposition try to out maneuver one another. Their goal is to put an end to the current government so they can control the next one or be the next person who wears the crown.

Sadly, their goals, and agendas have separated them from the country's sovereignty and care for the people. In order to restore any country's sovereignty people need to set aside their differences, their agendas and their dreams of what part of the pie they want and focus on the country. This is a common strategy and goal for any successful nation.

As a Canadian, it is tax cuts and budget surplus that matter to me now. For multitudes of North Americans, all that matters are what's on sale, what's the catch and what's the latest technology. I don't deny I am now part of this mindset. I could not and would not want to live the way that I did not too long ago.

What is missing in our lives if we find such things as 'The Survivor' TV series exciting and challenging? Is it really challenging when you live under the eyes of the world, have the medical and emergency help you might need and the Charter of Rights and Freedoms if something happens? If it were for forty years instead of forty days, would anyone have survived? That is one heck of a deal, living on a remote island with a camera recording your every move and getting a million bucks at the end. Imagine living in those conditions, without the cameras and emergency support, for years instead of days, with no prize money and no glamour or glory at the end of the game. I suspect the outcome would be different, as it is in reality in third world countries where many lives are wasted.

In the real survival challenge, poor people in most under developed countries live below the poverty line. This is also true in Iran, even though it is one of the richest countries in the world. It is time we looked closely at other cultures and feel their misery.

North American women, in general, are concerned with the way they look, the way their hair and nails are done, etc. Nothing wrong with that, unless that is all we care about. We should stop and look deep inside because we not only owe food and a safe home to our families; we also owe it to our brothers and sisters in other cultures. If their problems are only theirs, if we think we don't live on the same planet, what are we then? Aren't we less than human? Are we not just a product of our own century? We shouldn't let our differences dilute and alter our humanity and conscience.

Please, now that you know, do not let this book sit on your shelf. Tell these stories to other women. Men, you are welcome to help. After all, we are meant to compliment and complete each other, soul and body. Let us be one life, one soul. Care for us as we care for you. Help us to help you and ourselves.

God Bless.

Acknowledgements

I do not believe anyone becomes an accomplished individual by chance or luck or on his or her own. Nor, do I believe in easy miracles. God has said, over and over, "You start the job and I will help you finish it."

I don't believe in a dream that lingers on the gloomy horizon like a thick fog over a lake on an autumn morning. At some point in a successful person's life, someone took an interest in and a chance on that person. I don't believe in relying on chance but I do believe in giving somebody a boost by supporting his ideas and standing behind him. I don't care for the metaphoric explanation that if you dream you will catch it someday. I believe in hard work, dedication and God. And, I believe in meeting the right people at the right time.

The people and friends I mention in Iran are real but to protect their identity, the names are not. The names of most of my friends and associates in North America have been similarly altered but places and events that I mention that happened to me personally are all true.

In order for me to make it this far there is a long list of people who believed in me. I didn't have a loving, supportive father or a caring family but I did have a persevering, passionate mother and I have been blessed with a long line of friends and individuals who believed in me and helped me.

Living in Hell would not have been written if it were not for the sacrifices of my mother. I especially dedicate this book to her. Mum, I love you.

I am grateful to my godmother, Roma Dehr, and her partner Fred, who I call my godfather. They have been incredibly kind to me. Separated by age and two very different cultures, she is Italian and I am Persian, she has loved and guided me since we met. Roma has positively impacted not only my life but also the lives of many others. She is a remarkable woman, author, publisher and mentor. It is my great good fortune to have them both as friends and godparents.

There are teachers who just teach a course. There are others, who not only teach but also impact lives. All of these individuals are wonderful human beings who it was my pleasure and good fortune to have as teachers.

I am forever grateful to Dr. A. my university professor in Iran, wherever he may be, for the kindness he showed me when I needed a friend. He had a great and lasting impact on my life.

I am also grateful to two wonderful teachers who unknowingly saved my life; Ronda Porter, my English instructor, and Christiane Richards, my French teacher, who helped me to confront my shortcomings.

And, to another remarkable teacher, Dr. Farhad Duster, whose magical words always seemed to portend the future. He gave me support, without false hope. He helped me to move forward and closer to my dreams.

I am indebted to many friends, especially: Larry Rosen, a fellow author, for his unselfish support in introducing me to his contacts who he knew could help me.

James Dalessandro, a dear friend and wonderful human being who has shared his wealth of experience with me.

I cannot thank Ms. Loretta Napoleni, author of 'Modern Jihad,' enough for her enthusiastic support.

My sincere appreciation goes to my editor, Lou Aroncia. A good editor is a lot like a good doctor. He diagnoses the symptoms and prescribes the right medication. Lou had a vision for this book that I couldn't find for myself. He gave me much needed direction and elevated this book to a higher level.

My special gratitude to the late Ms. Gayden Hemmans for initiating the idea and encouraging me to write this book. She believed in me and opened my eyes to a whole new world. She was a dear friend and a comfort to me at a difficult time in my life.

A special thanks to Joshua Sohn, a great lawyer who has read my manuscript and given me his honest opinions but is, most of all, a good friend.

Last, but not least, to my good friend, Bill, a one-man army. If you plan to cross the Alps or just cross the street, you want him by your side. He never lets you down and will not let you let down. He is the mentor, friend, cheerleader, editor and publisher that most writers can only dream about. His work is more than editing. He helps me say in English what I am thinking in Persian. He holds the key to the grammar locker and transmits energy to the passages that I write. Life has been better for many people because of him. Knowing him has been a pleasure and a blessing in my life.

To all of these remarkable people and many more, whose names I don't mention here, who have touched my heart and life at some point, this book is my contribution to all of you.